Microsoft® Official Academic Course

Installing and Configuring Windows 10
Exam 70-698

WILEY

VP & PUBLISHER	Barry Pruett
SENIOR EXECUTIVE EDITOR	Bryan Gambrel
MICROSOFT PRODUCT MANAGER	Heidi Johnson of Microsoft Learning
MARKET SOLUTIONS ASSISTANT	Jessy Moor
TECHNICAL EDITOR	Ron Handlon
CHANNEL MARKETING MANAGER	Michele Szczesniak
CONTENT MANAGEMENT DIRECTOR	Lisa Wojcik
CONTENT MANAGER	Nichole Urban
PRODUCTION COORDINATOR	Nicole Repasky
PRODUCTION EDITOR	Umamaheswari Gnanamani
COVER DESIGNER	Tom Nery

COVER PHOTO: © shutterstock/wavebreakmedia

This book was set in Garamond by SPi Global and printed and bound by Strategic Content Imaging.
The covers were printed by Strategic Content Imaging.

ISBN: 9781119331315 (PBK)
ISBN: 9781119331346 (EVALC)

The inside back cover will contain printing identification and country of origin if omitted from this page.
In addition, if the ISBN on the back cover differs from the ISBN on this page, the one on the back cover is correct.

Preface

Welcome to the Microsoft Official Academic Course (MOAC) program for becoming a Microsoft Certified Solutions Associate for Windows 10. MOAC represents the collaboration between Microsoft Learning and John Wiley & Sons, Inc. publishing company. Microsoft and Wiley teamed up to produce a series of textbooks that deliver compelling and innovative teaching solutions to instructors and superior learning experiences for students. Infused and informed by in-depth knowledge from the creators of Windows 10, and crafted by a publisher known worldwide for the pedagogical quality of its products, these textbooks maximize skills transfer in minimum time. Students are challenged to reach their potential by using their new technical skills as highly productive members of the workforce.

Because this knowledgebase comes directly from Microsoft, architect of the Windows operating system and creator of the Microsoft Certified Solutions Associate exams, you are sure to receive the topical coverage that is most relevant to students' personal and professional success. Microsoft's direct participation not only assures you that MOAC textbook content is accurate and current; it also means that students will receive the best instruction possible to enable their success on certification exams and in the workplace.

■ The Microsoft Official Academic Course Program

The Microsoft Official Academic Course series is a complete program for instructors and institutions to prepare and deliver great courses on Microsoft software technologies. With MOAC, we recognize that because of the rapid pace of change in the technology and curriculum developed by Microsoft, there is an ongoing set of needs beyond classroom instruction tools for an instructor to be ready to teach the course. The MOAC program endeavors to provide solutions for all these needs in a systematic manner in order to ensure a successful and rewarding course experience for both instructor and student—technical and curriculum training for instructor readiness with new software releases; the software itself for student use at home for building hands-on skills, assessment, and validation of skill development; and a great set of tools for delivering instruction in the classroom and lab. All are important to the smooth delivery of an interesting course on Microsoft software, and all are provided with the MOAC program. We think about the model below as a gauge for ensuring that we completely support you in your goal of teaching a great course. As you evaluate your instructional materials options, you may wish to use the model for comparison purposes with available products.

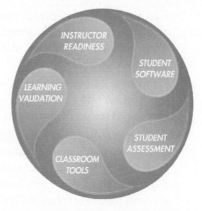

Illustrated Book Tour

■ Textbook Organization

This textbook is organized in twenty-one lessons, with each lesson corresponding to a particular exam objective for the 70-698 Installing and Configuring Windows 10 Microsoft Certified Solutions Associate (MCSA) exam. This MOAC textbook covers all the learning objectives for the 70-698 MCSA certification exam. The exam objectives are highlighted throughout the textbook.

■ Pedagogical Features

Many pedagogical features have been developed specifically for Microsoft Official Academic Course programs.

Presenting the extensive procedural information and technical concepts woven throughout the textbook raises challenges for the student and instructor alike. The Illustrated Book Tour that follows provides a guide to the rich features contributing to Microsoft Official Academic Course program's pedagogical plan. Following is a list of key features in each lesson designed to prepare students for success on the certification exams and in the workplace:

- Each lesson begins with an overview of the skills covered in the lesson. More than a standard list of learning objectives, the overview correlates skills to the certification exam objective.

- Illustrations: Screen images provide visual feedback as students work through the exercises. The images reinforce key concepts, provide visual clues about the steps, and allow students to check their progress.

- Key Terms: Important technical vocabulary is listed at the beginning of the lesson. When these terms are used later in the lesson, they appear in bold italic type and are defined.

- Engaging point-of-use reader aids, located throughout the lessons, tell students why this topic is relevant (*The Bottom Line*), provide students with helpful hints (*Take Note*), or show cross-references to where content is covered in greater detail. Reader aids also provide additional relevant or background information that adds value to the lesson.

- Certification Ready features throughout the text signal students where a specific certification objective is covered. They provide students with a chance to check their understanding of that particular exam objective and, if necessary, review the section of the lesson where it is covered.

- Knowledge Assessments provide lesson-ending activities that test students' comprehension and retention of the material taught, presented using some of the question types that they'll see on the certification exam.

- An important supplement to this textbook is the accompanying lab work. Labs are available via a Lab Manual, and also by MOAC Labs Online. MOAC Labs Online provides students with the ability to work on the actual software simply by connecting through their Internet Explorer web browser. Either way, the labs use real-world scenarios to help students learn workplace skills associated with configuring a Windows infrastructure in an enterprise environment.

■ Lesson Features

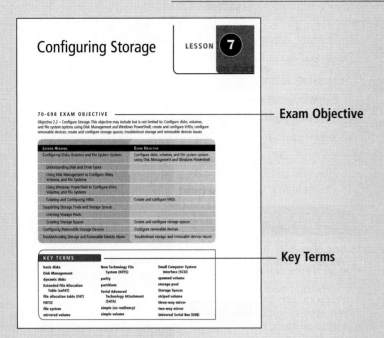

Exam Objective

Key Terms

Easy-to-Read Tables

Certification Ready Alert

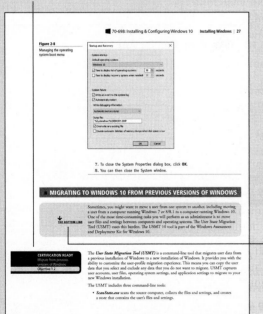

Bottom Line Reader Aid

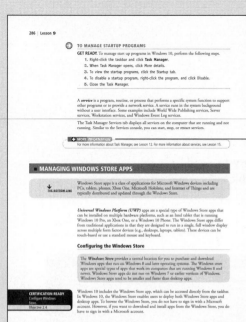

More Information Reader Aid

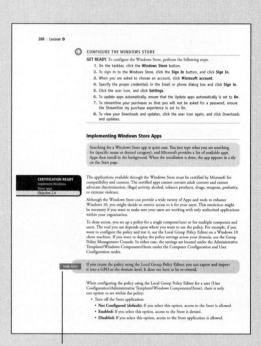

Take Note Reader Aid

Warning Reader Aid

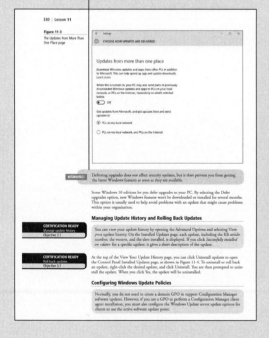

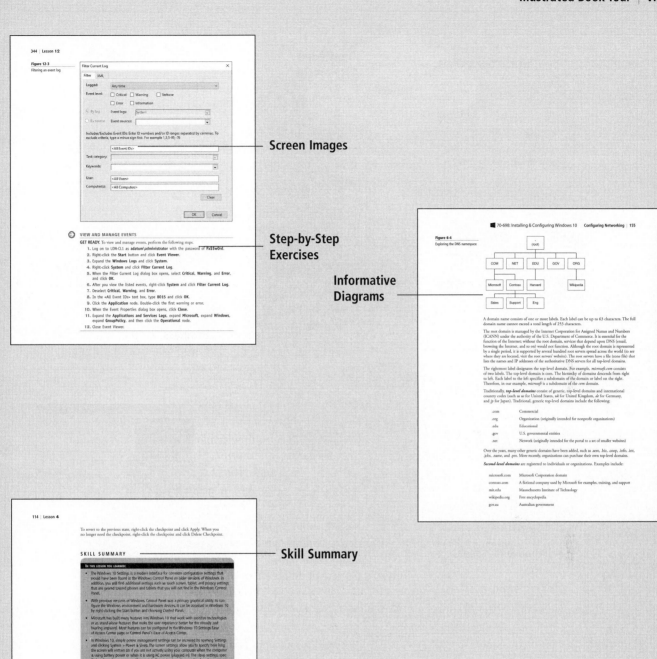

Screen Images

Step-by-Step Exercises

Informative Diagrams

Skill Summary

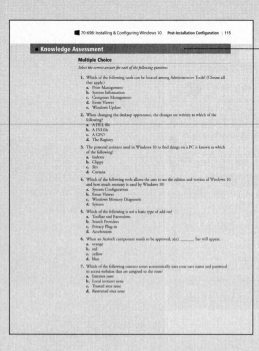

Knowledge Assessment

Business Case Scenarios

Conventions and Features Used in This Book

This book uses particular fonts, symbols, and heading conventions to highlight important information or to call your attention to special steps. For more information about the features in each lesson, refer to the Illustrated Book Tour section.

CONVENTION	MEANING
↓ **THE BOTTOM LINE**	This feature provides a brief summary of the material to be covered in the section that follows.
CERTIFICATION READY	This feature signals the point in the text where a specific certification objective is covered. It provides you with a chance to check your understanding of that particular exam objective and, if necessary, review the section of the lesson where it is covered.
TAKE NOTE* ➕ MORE INFORMATION	Reader aids appear in shaded boxes found in your text. *Take Note and More Information* provide helpful hints related to particular tasks or topics.
⚠ WARNING	*Warning* points out instances when error or misuse could cause damage to the computer or network.
A ***shared printer*** can be used by many individuals on a network.	Key terms appear in bold italic.
`cd\windows\system32\` `ServerMigrationTools`	Commands that are to be typed are shown in a special font.
Click **Install Now**.	Any button on the screen you are supposed to click on or select will appear in bold.

Instructor Support Program

The Microsoft Official Academic Course programs are accompanied by a rich array of resources that incorporate the extensive textbook visuals to form a pedagogically cohesive package. These resources provide all the materials instructors need to deploy and deliver their courses. Instructor resources available at www.wiley.com/ includes:

- **Instructor's Guide.** The Instructor's Guide contains solutions to all the textbook exercises as well as chapter summaries and lecture notes. The Instructor's Guide and Syllabi for various term lengths are available from the Instructor's Book Companion site.

- **Test Bank.** The Test Bank contains hundreds of questions organized by lesson in multiple-choice, best answer, build list, and essay formats and is available to download from the Instructor's Book Companion site. A complete answer key is provided.

- **PowerPoint Presentations.** A complete set of PowerPoint presentations is available on the Instructor's Book Companion site to enhance classroom presentations. Tailored to the text's topical coverage, these presentations are designed to convey key Windows Server 2012 concepts addressed in the text.

- **Available Textbook Figures.** All figures from the text are on the Instructor's Book Companion site. By using these visuals in class discussions, you can help focus students' attention on key elements of Windows 8 and help them understand how to use it effectively in the workplace.

- **MOAC Labs Online.** MOAC Labs Online is a cloud-based environment that enables students to conduct exercises using real Microsoft products. These are not simulations but instead are live virtual machines where faculty and students can perform any activities they would on a local virtual machine. MOAC Labs Online relieves the need for local setup, configuration, and most troubleshooting tasks. This represents an opportunity to lower costs, eliminate the hassle of lab setup, and support and improve student access and portability. MOAC Labs Online are available for students at an additional cost. Contact your Wiley rep about including MOAC Labs Online with your course offering.

- **Lab Answer Keys.** Answer keys for review questions found in the lab manuals and MOAC Labs Online are available on the Instructor's Book Companion site.

- **Lab Worksheets.** The review questions found in the lab manuals and MOAC Labs Online are gathered in Microsoft Word documents for students to use. These are available on the Instructor's Book Companion site.

Book Companion Web Site (www.wiley.com)

The students' book companion site for the MOAC series includes any resources, exercise files, and Web links that will be used in conjunction with this course and any errata.

■ Microsoft Certification

Microsoft Certification has many benefits and enables you to keep your skills relevant, applicable, and competitive. In addition, Microsoft Certification is an industry standard that is recognized worldwide—which helps open doors to potential job opportunities. After you earn your Microsoft Certification, you have access to a number of benefits, which can be found on the Microsoft Certified Professional member site.

Microsoft Learning has reinvented the Microsoft Certification Program by building cloud-related skills validation into the industry's most recognized certification program. Microsoft Certified Solutions Expert (MCSE) and Microsoft Certified Solutions Developer (MCSD) are Microsoft's flagship certifications for professionals who want to lead their IT organization's journey to the cloud. These certifications recognize IT professionals with broad and deep skill sets across Microsoft solutions. The Microsoft Certified Solutions Associate (MCSA) is the certification for aspiring IT professionals and is also the prerequisite certification necessary to earn an MCSE. These new certifications integrate cloud-related and on-premise skills validation in order to support organizations and recognize individuals who have the skills required to be productive using Microsoft technologies.

On-premise or in the cloud, Microsoft training and certification empowers technology professionals to expand their skills and gain knowledge directly from the source. Securing these essential skills will allow you to grow your career and make yourself indispensable as the industry shifts to the cloud. Cloud computing ultimately enables IT to focus on more mission-critical activities, raising the bar of required expertise for IT professionals and developers. These reinvented certifications test on a deeper set of skills that map to real-world business context. Rather than testing only on a feature of a technology, Microsoft Certifications now validate more advanced skills and a deeper understanding of the platform.

Microsoft Certified Solutions Associate (MCSA)

The Microsoft Certified Solutions Associate (MCSA) certification is for students preparing to get their first jobs in Microsoft technology. Whether in the cloud or on-premise, this certification validates the core platform skills needed in an IT environment. The MCSA certifications are a requirement to achieve Microsoft's flagship Microsoft Certified Solutions Expert (MCSE) and Microsoft Certified Solutions Developer (MCSD) certifications.

The MCSA: Windows 10 certification shows that you have the primary set of Windows operating system skills that are relevant across multiple solution areas in a business environment.

MCSA Exam 70-697, Configuring Windows Devices is the other exam needed to complete your MCSA: Windows 10 certification.

If you are a student new to IT who may not yet be ready for MCSA, the Microsoft Technology Associate (MTA) certification is an optional starting point that may be available through your school.

You can learn more about the MCSA certification at the Microsoft Certification website.

Preparing to Take an Exam

Unless you are a very experienced user, you will need to use test preparation materials to prepare to complete the test correctly and within the time allowed. The Microsoft Official Academic Course series is designed to prepare you with a strong knowledge of all exam topics, and with some additional review and practice on your own, you should feel confident in your ability to pass the appropriate exam.

After you decide which exam to take, review the list of objectives for the exam. You can easily identify tasks that are included in the objective list by locating the exam objective overview at the start of each lesson and the Certification Ready sidebars in the margin of the lessons in this book.

To register for the MCSA exam, visit the Microsoft Certifications webpage for directions on how to register with Pearson VUE, the company that delivers the MCSA exams. Keep in mind these important items about the testing procedure:

- **What to expect.** Microsoft Certification testing labs typically have multiple workstations, which may or may not be occupied by other candidates. Test center administrators strive to provide a quiet and comfortable environment for all test takers.

- **Plan to arrive early.** It is recommended that you arrive at the test center at least 30 minutes before the test is scheduled to begin.

- **Bring your identification.** To take your exam, you must bring the identification (ID) that was specified when you registered for the exam. If you are unclear about which forms of ID are required, contact the exam sponsor identified in your registration information. Although requirements vary, you typically must show two valid forms of ID, one with a photo, both with your signature.

- **Leave personal items at home.** The only item allowed into the testing area is your identification, so leave any backpacks, laptops, briefcases, and other personal items at home. If you have items that cannot be left behind (such as purses), the testing center might have small lockers available for use.

- **Nondisclosure agreement.** At the testing center, Microsoft requires that you accept the terms of a nondisclosure agreement (NDA) and complete a brief demographic survey before taking your certification exam.

Acknowledgements

We thank the MOAC faculty and instructors who have assisted us in building the Microsoft Official Academic Course courseware. These elite educators have acted as our sounding board on key pedagogical and design decisions leading to the development of the MOAC courseware for future Information Technology workers. They have provided invaluable advice in the service of quality instructional materials, and we truly appreciate their dedication to technology education.

Brian Bridson, Baker College of Flint

David Chaulk, Baker College Online

Ron Handlon, Remington College – Tampa Campus

Katherine James, Seneca College of Applied Arts & Technology

Wen Liu, ITT Educational Services

Zeshan Sattar, Pearson in Practice

Jared Spencer, Westwood College Online

David Vallerga, MTI College

Bonny Willy, Ivy Tech State College

We also thank Microsoft Learning's Heidi Johnson, Larry Kaye, Rob Linsky, Colin Lyth, Paul Pardi, Merrick Van Dongen, Liberty Munson, Keith Loeber, Natasha Chornesky, Briana Roberts, Jim Clark, Anne Hamilton, Erika Cravens, and Jim Cochran, for their encouragement and support in making the Microsoft Official Academic Course programs the finest academic materials for mastering the newest Microsoft technologies for both students and instructors.

About the Author

Patrick Regan has been a PC technician, network administrator/engineer, design architect, and security analyst for the past 23 years. He has taught computer and network classes at Sacramento local colleges (Heald Colleges and MTI Colleges) and participated in and led many projects (Heald Colleges, Intel Corporation, Miles Consulting Corporation, and Pacific Coast Companies). For his teaching accomplishments, he received the Teacher of the Year award from Heald Colleges and he has received several recognition awards from Intel. As a senior system administrator, he supports approximately 120 servers and 1,500 users spread over 5 subsidiaries and 70 sites. He has authored a number of textbooks, including books on SharePoint 2010, Windows 7, Windows 8.1, and Windows Server 2012 for John Wiley & Sons.

Brief Contents

Contents

Preparing for Installation Requirements

70-698 EXAM OBJECTIVE

Objective 1.1 – Prepare for installation requirements. This objective may include but is not limited to: Determine hardware requirements and compatibility; choose between an upgrade and a clean installation; determine appropriate editions according to device type; determine requirements for particular features, such as Hyper-V, Cortana, Miracast, Virtual Smart Cards, and Secure Boot; determine and create appropriate installation media.

Objective 1.2 – Install Windows. This objective may include but is not limited to: Install on bootable USB. * Other Objective 1.2 topics are covered in Lesson 2.

LESSON HEADING	EXAM OBJECTIVE
Preparing for a Windows 10 Installation	
Determining Hardware Requirements and Compatibility	Determine hardware requirements and compatibility
Choosing Between an Upgrade and a Clean Installation	Choose between an upgrade and a clean installation
Determining Appropriate Editions According to Device Type	Determine appropriate editions according to device type
Determining Requirements for Particular Features	Determine requirements for particular features
Determining and Creating Appropriate Installation Media	Determine and create appropriate installation media
	Install on bootable USB

KEY TERMS

AppLocker

Assigned Access 8.1

BitLocker

BranchCache

Business Store

clean installation

Client Hyper-V

Continuum

Cortana

Credential Guard

Current Branch for Business

desktop PC

device driver

Device Guard

DirectAccess

EFS

Enterprise Mode Internet Explorer (EMIE)

Group Policy management

hybrid computer

joining to a domain

laptop	User Experience control and lockdown	Windows 10 Pro
Long-Term Servicing Branch		Windows Hello
private catalog	virtual desktops	Windows Spotlight
Remote Desktop	Windows 10	Windows To Go
RemoteApp	Windows 10 Education	Windows Update for Business
smartphone	Windows 10 Enterprise	
tablet	Windows 10 Home	x64
upgrade installation	Windows 10 Media Creation Tool	x86

■ PREPARING FOR A WINDOWS 10 INSTALLATION

THE BOTTOM LINE

Windows 10 is the newest client operating system. Different from previous versions of Windows, Windows 10 is released as an "operating system as a service," which means that it will receive ongoing updates to its features and functionality. To clearly differentiate it from previous versions of Windows and make this new format clear, Microsoft chose to skip Windows 9 and name it Windows 10.

Before installing Windows, you should do a little bit of planning and ask the following questions:

1. What will the computer be used for?
2. What type of environment will the computer run in?
3. Does the computer need to be portable?

Determining what the computer will be used for will help you determine what hardware you need. For example, for a computer-aided design (CAD) system, you need a fast processor, lots of memory, and a fast video card. In addition, a CAD system would greatly benefit from a solid-state drive.

Determining the environment that the computer will be used in will help you determine if you need special equipment to keep the computer clean. If it is in a dusty environment, dust will accumulate, which can cause systems to overheat.

Today, being mobile brings its own challenges. You want a system that can give you long battery life, but sufficient power to perform the necessary tasks. In addition, it will help determine what hardware you might need that is portable. For example, does the system need external or high-quality loud speakers, or do you need a large screen to work from? In some situations, you might only need a smaller computer (small laptop or notepad) that allows you to check emails, take notes, write reports, and construct spreadsheets.

Now that you understand what the computer will be used for, you can determine its form factor, which specifies the size, configuration, and/or physical arrangement of a computing device. Some of the common form factors are:

- *Desktop PC*: The traditional PC that comes in a box that lays down (desktop) or stands upright (tower). Desktops can be inexpensive systems that can handle basic office tasks, or they can be very expensive when required to provide maximum performance, such as CAD systems or video editing. Because desktop PCs tend to be larger, they are not very portable.
- *Laptop*: A portable computer that provides mobility for traveling users or users who might work from home. Although laptops tend not to be as powerful as the desktop version, today's laptops can provide superior performance. Laptops can be enhanced with

docking stations, external keyboards, mice, and monitors. Recently, laptop sales have surpassed desktop PC sales.

- *Tablet*: A computer that is a smaller version of the laptop, with a screen that makes up the body of the computer. Tablets can be used for reading emails, doing presentations, creating reports, taking notes, and so forth.
- *Hybrid computer*: A laptop that can convert to a tablet. These devices typically have faster performance than tablets and include a keyboard for faster typing.
- *Smartphone*: A small device with a screen that can be used to read email, keep track of tasks, access calendar information, manage address books, and run a wide range of applications.

Another device worth mentioning is the gaming console, such as Xbox. Although this system is designed to run games, it might also have additional applications and features.

Determining Hardware Requirements and Compatibility

To determine what you need to install Windows 10, you also need to look at the minimum system requirements for Windows 10. You should also determine if your system is compatible with your current hardware or the hardware you are about to purchase.

CERTIFICATION READY
Determine hardware
requirements and
compatibility
Objective 1.1

The system requirements for Windows 10 are:

- **Processor:** 1 gigahertz (GHz) or faster processor
- **RAM:** 1 gigabyte (GB) for 32-bit or 2 GB for 64-bit
- **Hard disk space:** 16 GB for 32-bit OS or 20 GB for 64-bit OS
- **Graphics card:** DirectX 9 or later with WDDM 1.0 driver
- **Display:** 800 × 600

Many computers in enterprises today easily meet the minimum hardware requirements for Windows 10. Although this represents the minimum requirements, in many instances, you should consider twice, four times, or more if you want decent performance or to run more complex and demanding programs. For example, you might consider a quad-core processor with a minimum of 4 GB of memory. If you are running memory-intensive applications, such as a CAD station or video processing, you might consider 16 GB or more of memory and an expensive video card with a monitor that supports much higher resolution. Solid-state drives can also give a performance boost.

A computer is a collection of hardware devices, each of which requires a piece of software called a device driver in order to function. Windows 10 includes a large library of device drivers, but it is still sometimes necessary to obtain them yourself from vendors.

As most people know, a PC is a collection of hardware devices, all of which are connected together and installed in a single case. Disk drives, keyboards, mice, modems, and printers are all types of devices. To communicate with the operating system running on the computer, each device also requires a software element called a device driver. The *device driver* provides the operating system with information about a specific device.

For example, when you use a word-processing application to save a file to a hard disk, the application issues a generic WriteFile function call to the operating system. The application knows nothing specific about the disk drive hardware; it just issues an instruction to store a particular file there. When the operating system processes the function call, it accesses the device driver for the hard disk drive, which provides detailed information about how to communicate with the drive. If the user selects a different target location for the file, the operating system accesses the device driver for that location, whether it's a hard drive, a floppy drive, or a USB flash drive.

In most cases, the information the device driver provides is integrated into the Windows interface. For example, the Properties sheet for a printer includes generic system information, such as which port the printer is connected to and who is permitted to use it. Other tabs, and particularly the Device Settings tab, are based on hardware-specific information provided by the device driver.

➕ MORE INFORMATION

Devices and Device Manager are covered in Lesson 3.

In addition to providing information about a device, drivers also permit the operating system to modify the hardware configuration settings of the device. For example, when you configure a printer to print a document in landscape mode instead of portrait mode, the printer device driver generates the appropriate command and sends it to the hardware.

The process of installing a hardware device consists primarily of identifying the device and installing a device driver for it. This process can occur during the operating system installation or at a later time, but the steps are fundamentally the same.

A major part of the Windows 10 installation process consists of identifying the devices in the computer and installing the appropriate drivers for them. The Windows 10 installation package includes hundreds of drivers for many different devices, which is why many installations finish without any user intervention. Sometimes, however, you might have to supply device drivers yourself.

If you have an older system that contains legacy devices, you might have trouble finding the proper driver for those devices. If the driver is not built in to Windows, you might need to go the device manufacturer's website to find legacy hardware.

When seeing if your device is compatible with Windows 10, you should look for devices that have been tested and certified by the Windows Hardware Quality Lab (WHQL). You can then check the manufacturer's website or you can visit the Windows Compatibility Products List, which can be found using your favorite search engine and searching for *Windows Compatibility Products List*.

Choosing Between an Upgrade and a Clean Installation

If you buy a new computer with Windows 10, Windows 10 was preinstalled. However, if you already have a computer that is running Windows 7 or Windows 8/8.1, you might want to upgrade to Windows 10. Each method has its advantages and disadvantages.

CERTIFICATION READY
Choose between an upgrade and a clean installation
Objective 1.1

A *clean installation* of Windows is when you install Windows where there is no operating system, data, or programs stored on the hard drive, or you perform the installation of Windows while reformatting the current disks, so that you are installing Windows on an empty disk. An *upgrade installation* of Windows is when you have a system that is running Windows 7 or Windows 8/8.1, and you run the Windows installation program, replacing the Windows 7 or Windows 8/8.1 operating system with Windows 10.

A clean installation allows you to start as if the machine is new. If you decide to perform a clean installation on a machine that has Windows 7 or Windows 8/8.1 installed, you will remove any existing corrupted files, problem programs, or erroneous settings. However, if you perform a clean installation, you have to then install all programs, copy over desired data files from a backup, and reconfigure the system.

An upgrade of Windows 10 is a time-saving feature that allows you to keep your programs, files, and settings. In that way, you will be able to use the same programs and access your data quickly after the upgrade. However, if you have corrupt non-Windows files, problematic programs, or erroneous settings, you might still experience those problems after the upgrade. Sometimes, the upgrade does not go smoothly (usually caused by incompatible programs or device drivers), and it could make your system unusable after the attempted upgrade. Lastly, if you are using a legacy device, the device might not run under Windows 10. Of course, before you perform an upgrade, you should always make sure you have a current backup in case you need to roll back or recover lost programs and data.

You can upgrade from Windows 7 or Windows 8/8.1 to like versions of Windows 10. For example:

- If you have Windows 7 Starter, Windows 7 Home Basic, or Windows 7 Home Premium, Windows 8, or Windows 8.1, you can upgrade to Windows 10 Home.
- If you have Windows 7 Pro, Windows 8.1 Pro, Windows 8.1 Pro for Student, Windows 7 Professional, or Windows 7 Ultimate, you can upgrade to Windows 10 Pro.
- If you have Windows 7 Enterprise or Windows 8/8.1 Enterprise, you can upgrade to Windows 10 Enterprise.

If you want to migrate to a different edition (such as Windows 8.1 Pro to Windows 8.1 Enterprise), you must perform a clean installation.

In addition, you can only upgrade from a 32-bit version of Windows 7 or Windows 8/8.1 to a 32-bit version of Windows 10 and upgrade a 64-bit version of Windows 7 or Windows 8/8.1 to a 64-bit version of Windows 10. If you want to upgrade a 32-bit version to a 64-bit version, you must perform a clean installation.

Determining Appropriate Editions According to Device Type

Similar to previous client version operating systems, Windows 10 has multiple editions to choose from. The barest version is Windows 10 Home, which has the fewest number of features. Windows 10 Pro has more features, and Windows 10 Enterprise and Windows 10 Education have the most features. Of course, Windows 10 Home is the least expensive, whereas Windows 10 Enterprise is the most expensive.

CERTIFICATION READY
Determine appropriate editions according to device type
Objective 1.2

Windows 10 has multiple editions and versions. The desktop editions of Windows 10 include:

- *Windows 10 Home*: Designed for consumer-based personal computers and tablets.
- *Windows 10 Pro*: Designed for personal computers and tablets for small and medium-sized businesses and for advanced users. It is similar to Windows 10 Home, but has extra features to meet the needs of small businesses. It includes BitLocker, EFS, domain join, and Group Policy management.
- *Windows 10 Enterprise*: Designed for personal computers and tablets for large enterprises. It builds on Windows 10 Pro by adding advanced features designed to meet the demands of medium- and large-sized organizations. It includes AppLocker, BranchCache, and DirectAccess. Windows 10 Enterprise is only available to Volume Licensing customers.
- *Windows 10 Education*: Designed for personal computers and tablets aimed at schools (including staff, administrators, teachers, and students). Windows 10 Education has the same features as Windows 10 Enterprise. Windows 10 Education is only available through academic Volume Licensing.

Some of the features that are available in Windows 10 include:

- *AppLocker*: A feature that allows you to specify which groups or users can run, or not run, a particular application in your organization
- *Assigned Access 8.1*: A setting that lets you restrict a specific standard account to using only one Windows Store app for use as a kiosk station
- *BitLocker*: A feature that protects a system from being accessed if the system is lost or stolen by encrypting a volume

- *BranchCache*: A wide area network bandwidth optimization technology that allows the local caching of shared folders and websites so that you don't always have to access over a slower WAN link
- *Business Store*: A feature that allows administrators to find, acquire, manage, and distribute apps to Windows 10 devices
- *Client Hyper-V*: Virtualization technology that allows you to run virtual machines so that you can run older applications on older operating systems or run a different operating system on the same machine as Windows 10
- *Continuum*: A feature that allows you to turn your phone into a big-screen projector or attach a keyboard or mouse to your phone
- *Cortana*: A voice-activated personal assistant
- *Credential Guard*: A feature that stores credentials, such as NTLM hashes and Kerberos tickets, and provides them to the necessary applications. To keep them secure, the credentials are stored in a secured isolated container, which uses Hyper-V and virtualization-based security (VBS)
- *Current Branch for Business*: A feature that allows you to delay upgrades (new versions) and updates
- *Device Guard*: A feature that helps protect a system by locking a device so that it can only run trusted applications
- *DirectAccess*: An advanced VPN technology that allows remote users to securely access internal network file shares while connected to the Internet
- *EFS*: Short for Encrypting File System, a feature that provides file-level encryption transparently
- *Enterprise Mode Internet Explorer (EMIE)*: A compatibility mode that runs Internet Explorer 11 or higher that lets websites render using a modified browser configuration that's designed to emulate either Windows Internet Explorer 7 or 8, avoiding the common compatibility problems associated with Web Apps written and tested on older versions of Internet Explorer
- *Group Policy management*: An infrastructure that allows you to centrally manage computer settings and configuration
- *Joining to a domain*: A feature that allows you to join an Active Directory domain
- *Long-Term Servicing Branch*: An option for organizations that only want to receive features updates every two to three years, so that the current systems can be stable
- *Private catalog*: A feature that provides a list of applications that users within the organization can download apps from
- *RemoteApp*: A feature that enables you to run a program remotely through Remote Desktop Services, although the applications appear to be running on your local machine
- *Remote Desktop*: A program or feature that allows you to connect to a remote computer, and access the desktop and applications just like you were accessing the machine directly
- *User Experience control and lockdown*: A feature that allows you to customize and lock down the Windows 10 user interface
- *Virtual desktops*: A feature that allows you to run and switch between multiple desktops
- *Windows Update for Business*: A free service for Windows 10 Pro, Enterprise, and Education editions that can provide updates to your users based on distribution rings
- *Windows Hello*: A credential technology that provides multi-factor authentication, including a personal identification number (PIN) or biometrics (face, iris, or fingerprint)
- *Windows Spotlight*: An option that displays a new image on the lock screen each day
- *Windows To Go*: A feature that allows you to boot and run Windows from USB mass storage devices such as USB flash drives and external hard disk drives

Table 1-1 shows some of the common features available for the various editions of Windows 10.

Table 1-1

Features Based on Windows 10 Editions

FEATURE	HOME	PRO	ENTERPRISE	EDUCATION
AppLocker	No	No	Yes	Yes
Assigned Access 8.1	No	Yes	Yes	Yes
BitLocker	No	Yes	Yes	Yes
BranchCache	No	No	Yes	Yes
Business Store	No	Yes	Yes	Yes
Client Hyper-V	No	64-bit SKUs only	64-bit SKUs only	64-bit SKUs only
Continuum	Yes	Yes	Yes	Yes
Cortana*	Yes	Yes	Yes	Yes
Credential Guard	No	No	Yes	Yes
Current Branch for Business	No	Yes	Yes	Yes
Device Guard	No	No	Yes	Yes
DirectAccess	No	No	Yes	Yes
EFS	No	Yes	Yes	Yes
Enterprise Mode Internet Explorer (EMIE)	No	Yes	Yes	Yes
Group Policy management	No	Yes	Yes	Yes
Joining to a domain	No	Yes	Yes	Yes
Long-Term Servicing Branch	No	No	Yes	No
Private catalog	No	Yes	Yes	Yes
RemoteApp	Client only	Client only	Client and host	Client and host
Remote Desktop	Client only	Client and host	Client and host	Client and host
User Experience control and lockdown	No	No	Yes	Yes
Virtual desktops	Yes	Yes	Yes	Yes
Windows Update for Business	No	Yes	Yes	Yes
Windows Hello	Yes	Yes	Yes	Yes
Windows Spotlight	Yes	Yes	Yes	Yes
Windows To Go	No	No	Yes	Yes

*Cortana is only currently available on Windows 10 for the United States, United Kingdom, China, France, Italy, Germany, and Spain.

Microsoft also introduced the Windows 10 Mobile and Windows 10 Mobile Enterprise, which are designed to run on smartphones and small tablets.

Windows 10 supports two platforms:

- **IA-32:** Designed to run on systems with the 32-bit x86 processors. IA-32 can only access up to 4 GB of memory.
- **X86-64:** Designed to run on the x86-64 processors. Windows 10 Home can support up to 128 GB of memory, whereas the other desktop editions can support up to 2048 GB of memory.

Windows runs on a desktop computer that has Intel and Intel-compatible processors based on the *x86* (a 32-bit architecture) and *x64* (a 64-bit architecture) architectures. The 32-bit and 64-bit architectures determine how data is processed and how much memory can be accessed. A 64-bit architecture can process larger numbers or larger chunks, allowing for faster processing. In addition, a 32-bit processor can access up to 4 GB of memory, whereas a 64-bit processor can theoretically access up to 16 exabytes (16 billion gigabytes), although it will most likely be limited by the motherboard and software. The 32-bit versions of Windows 10 support up to 4 GB of memory. The 64-bit version of Windows 10 Home supports up to 128 GB of memory and the 64-bit versions of Windows 10 Professional and Enterprise support up to 2048 GB of memory.

To install a 32-bit version of Windows, you can use an x86 or x64 processor. To install a 64-bit bit version of Windows, you can use only a 64-bit processor. Software written for a 64-bit architecture does not work on a 32-bit architecture. Most programs designed for 32-bit versions of Windows will work on a 64-bit version of Windows by using Windows on Windows 64 (WOW64). However, some 32-bit system software, such as antivirus programs, does not operate on a 64-bit architecture. In addition, 64-bit hardware requires 64-bit drivers. Drivers designed for 32-bit versions of Windows do not run on 64-bit versions of Windows, and drivers designed for 64-bit versions of Windows do not run on 32-bit versions of Windows. If you transition from a 32-bit version architecture to a 64-bit architecture, you might not find 64-bit drivers for all your devices, particularly for older devices.

If you want to use 64-bit Windows, keep the following in mind:

- 16-bit applications (applications generally written for Windows 9x) or 32-bit kernel drivers will fail to start or function properly on a 64-bit edition of Windows 10.
- Installation of 32-bit kernel drivers will fail on the 64-bit system.
- Installation of 64-bit unsigned drivers will fail by default on the 64-bit system.

Determining Requirements for Particular Features

Windows 10 is an operating system that is designed to work with a wide range of devices and has many features and built-in programs so that you can use the computer almost immediately after installation. However, some of these features require special hardware or are features meant for special hardware.

CERTIFICATION READY
Determine requirements for particular features
Objective 1.1

Windows 10 offers a lot of additional features if you have the correct hardware that is required by those features. Some examples include:

- For speech recognition, you need a high-fidelity microphone and driver.
- For Windows Hello to use biometric facial, iris, or fingerprint recognition, you must have a specialized illuminated infrared camera or a fingerprint reader that supports the Windows Biometric Framework.
- To support Touch, you need a tablet or monitor that supports multi-touch for full functionality.

- Some applications require a graphics card that is compatible with DirectX 10 or newer versions for optimal performance.
- Secure boot requires firmware that supports Unified Extensible Firmware Interface (UEFI) and has the Microsoft Windows Certification Authority in the UEFI signature database. The secure boot process takes advantage of UEFI to prevent the launching of unknown or potentially unwanted operating system boot loaders between the system's BIOS start and the Windows 10 operating system start. Although the secure boot process is not mandatory for Windows 10, it greatly increases the integrity of the boot process.
- To use BitLocker that can encrypt your drive to protect your data if your computer or disks are stolen, you need Trusted Platform Module (TPM) or a USB flash drive. You also need to use Windows 10 Pro, Windows 10 Enterprise, or Windows 10 Education.
- BitLocker To Go is aimed at providing BitLocker encryption for USB devices. Therefore, BitLocker requires a USB flash drive.
- To run Client Hyper-V (where you can run test virtual machines or virtual machines running older operating systems), you need to have a 64-bit system with second level address translation (SLAT) capabilities and an additional 2 GB of RAM. You also need to use Windows 10 Pro, Windows 10 Enterprise, or Windows 10 Education.
- To support Miracast so that you can mirror a smartphone, tablet, or PC to a wireless monitor or TV, you need to have display adapters that support Windows Display Driver Model (WDDM) and a Wi-Fi adapter that supports Wi-Fi Direct (Wi-Fi standard that enables devices to easily connect with other wireless devices without using a wireless access point).
- Wi-Fi Direct Printing requires a Wi-Fi adapter that supports Wi-Fi Direct and a device that supports Wi-Fi Direct Printing.
- Virtual smart cards require TPM 1.2 or higher.
- Cortana is only currently available on Windows 10 for the United States, United Kingdom, China, France, Italy, Germany, Brazil, Mexico, Japan, Canada (French) and Spain. If you wish to use voice commands, you need to have a microphone.

Before moving on, you should also understand that to use some of the Windows 10 features, you need to have a Microsoft account, which is a Single Sign-On web service that allows users to log on to websites, devices, and applications using one account.

Determining and Creating Appropriate Installation Media

Traditional Windows was installed with an installation DVD that was purchased or was downloaded as an ISO file and burned to a DVD. Starting with Windows 8, you could place the Windows installation on a USB device. To perform the installation, you just connect and boot from the USB device.

CERTIFICATION READY
Determine and create appropriate installation media
Objective 1.1

For Windows 10, you can also search for and find the ***Windows 10 Media Creation Tool***, which can be used to create a copy of your Windows 10 ISO file on a USB flash drive or DVD. You can then use the USB flash drive to install Windows 10.

The high-level steps to use the Windows 10 Media Creation tool to create a bootable USB flash drive are:

CERTIFICATION READY
Install on bootable USB
Objective 1.1

1. Format a USB flash drive.
2. Copy the Windows files onto the USB flash drive.
3. Make the USB flash drive bootable.

USE THE WINDOWS 10 MEDIA CREATION TOOL TO CREATE A WINDOWS 10 INSTALLATION MEDIA ON A USB DRIVE

GET READY. To use the Windows 10 Media Creation tool to create a Windows 10 installation media on a USB drive, perform the following steps.

1. On a Windows 10 computer, double-click the **MediaCreationTool.exe** file. If you are asked to allow this app to make changes to your PC, click **Yes.**
2. When the Windows 10 Setup dialog box opens, on the License terms page, click **Accept.**
3. On the What Do You Want to Do? page, select **Create installation media for another PC** and then click **Next.**
4. On the Select Language, Architecture, and Edition page (as shown in Figure 1-1), select the appropriate language, edition, and architecture (32-bit (x86), 64-bit (x64), or both). Click **Next.**

Figure 1-1

Selecting language, architecture, and edition

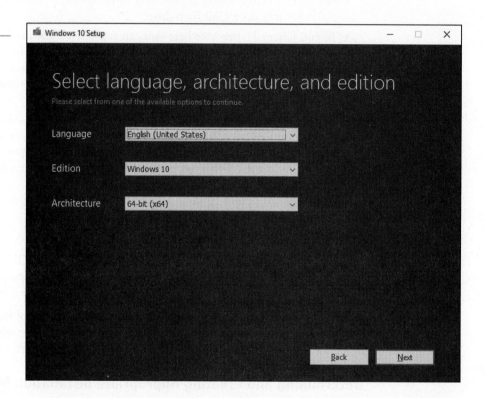

5. On the Choose Which Media to Use page, select **USB flash drive.** The USB flash drive needs to be at least 3 GB. Click **Next.**
6. On the Select a USB Flash Drive page, select your USB flash drive and then click **Next.** The Media Creation Tool downloads Windows 10 and creates the media on the USB drive.
7. On the Your USB Flash Drive Is Ready page, click Finish.

 USE THE WINDOWS 10 MEDIA CREATION TOOL TO CREATE A WINDOWS 10 INSTALLATION MEDIA ON AN ISO FILE

GET READY. To use the Windows 10 Media Creation tool to create a Windows 10 installation media on a USB drive, perform the following steps.

1. On a Windows 10 computer, double-click the **MediaCreationTool.exe** file. If you are asked to allow this app to make changes to your PC, click **Yes.**

2. When the Windows 10 Setup dialog box opens, on the License Terms page, click **Accept**.

3. On the What Do You Want to Do? page, select **Create installation media for another PC** and then click **Next**.

4. On the Select Language, Architecture, and Edition page (as shown in Figure 1-1), select the appropriate language, edition, and architecture (32-bit (x86), 64-bit (x64), or both). Click **Next**.

5. On the Choose Which Media to Use page, select **ISO file** and then click **Next**.

6. When the Select a Path dialog box opens, specify the location and file name of the ISO file, as shown in Figure 1-2. The Media Creation Tool downloads Windows 10 and creates the media on the ISO file. Click the **Save** button.

Figure 1-2

Selecting the name and location of the ISO file

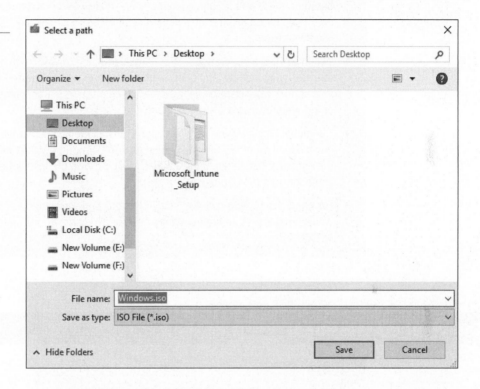

7. On the Burn the ISO file to a DVD page, click Finish.

After the ISO file has been created, the ISO file would be written to a writable DVD disk.

SKILL SUMMARY

IN THIS LESSON YOU LEARNED:

- Windows 10 is the newest client operating system. Microsoft listened to customer complaints to develop Windows 10. Different from previous versions of Windows, Windows 10 is released as an "operating system as a service," which means that it will receive ongoing updates to its features and functionality.

- To determine what you need to install Windows 10, you also need to look at the minimum system requirements for Windows 10. You should also determine if your system is compatible with your current hardware or the hardware you are about to purchase.

- The device driver provides the operating system with information about a specific device.

- If you buy a new computer with Windows 10, Windows 10 was preinstalled. However, if you already have a computer that is running Windows 7 or Windows 8/8.1, you might want to upgrade to Windows 10.

- Similar to previous client version operating systems, Windows 10 has multiple editions to choose from. The barest version is Windows 10 Home, which has the fewest number of features. Windows 10 Pro has additional features, and Windows 10 Enterprise and Windows 10 Education have the most features.

- Windows runs on a desktop computer that has Intel and Intel-compatible processors based on the x86 (a 32-bit architecture) and x64 (a 64-bit architecture) architectures. The 32-bit and 64-bit architectures determine how data is processed and how much memory can be accessed.

- Windows 10 is an operating system that is designed to work with a wide range of devices and has many features and built-in programs so that you can use the computer almost immediately after installation. However, some of these features require special hardware or are features meant for special hardware.

- Traditional Windows was installed with an installation DVD that was purchased or was downloaded as an ISO file and burned to a DVD. Starting with Windows 8, you could place the Windows installation on a USB device. To perform the installation, you just connect and boot from the USB device.

- For Windows 10, you can also search for and find the Windows 10 Media Creation tool, which can be used to create a copy of your Windows 10 ISO file on a USB flash drive or DVD.

■ Knowledge Assessment

Multiple Choice

Select the correct answer for each of the following questions.

1. Which of the following Windows 10 editions allow joining the system to a domain? (Choose all that apply.)
   a. Windows 10 Home
   b. Windows 10 Pro
   c. Windows 10 Enterprise
   d. Windows 10 Education

2. Which tool is used to download Windows 10 installation files and create a bootable USB flash drive so that it can be used to install Windows 10?
   a. Windows 10 Media Creation tool
   b. Setup.exe
   c. USB Create tool
   d. Express tool

3. The personal assistant used in Windows 10 to find things on a PC is known as which of the following?
   a. Indexer
   b. Clippy
   c. Siri
   d. Cortana

4. Which type of computer is a laptop that can convert to a tablet?
   a. Laptop
   b. Desktop PC
   c. Smartphone
   d. Hybrid computer

5. Which of the following is the minimum amount of memory needed to run the 64-bit version of Windows 10?
   a. 512 MB
   b. 1 GB
   c. 2 GB
   d. 4 GB

6. Which of the following versions of Windows 10 support Client Hyper-V? (Choose all that apply.)
   a. Windows 10 Home 64-bit
   b. Windows 10 Enterprise 64-bit
   c. Windows 10 Pro 32-bit
   d. Windows Enterprise 32-bit

7. Which of the following editions of Windows 10 support Credential Guard and Device Guard? (Choose all that apply.)
   a. Windows 10 Home
   b. Windows 10 Pro
   c. Windows 10 Enterprise
   d. Windows 10 Education

8. Which of the following is the maximum amount of memory that is recognized by the 32-bit version of Windows 10?
   a. 1 GB
   b. 2 GB
   c. 4 GB
   d. 8 GB

9. Which of the following hardware is needed to use Windows Hello?
   a. High-fidelity microphone
   b. Illuminated infrared camera or fingerprint reader
   c. Graphics card that is compatible with DirectX 10 or newer
   d. A multi-touch monitor

10. Which of the following allows administrators to find, acquire, manage, and distribute apps to Windows 10 devices?
    a. Windows Spotlight
    b. Continuum
    c. BranchCache
    d. Business Store

Best Answer

Choose the letter that corresponds to the best answer. More than one answer choice may achieve the goal. Select the BEST answer.

1. A user has a computer that is running Windows 7 and is approximately three years old. Because Windows is running a little bit slow, the user wants to install a fresh copy of Windows 10. Which kind of installation should be run?
   a. Migration
   b. Upgrade
   c. Clean
   d. Replacement

Matching and Identification

1. Specify the edition of Windows 10 to upgrade to (Home, Pro, or Enterprise).
   a) Windows 7 Pro
   b) Windows 8 Pro
   c) Windows 8.1 Enterprise
   d) Windows 7 Home Premium
   e) Windows 7 Ultimate

Build a List

1. Specify the correct order of the high-level steps necessary to use the Windows 10 Media Creation Tool to create a bootable USB flash drive. (Not all answers will be used.)
   _____ Copy the Windows files onto the USB flash drive.
   _____ Partition the USB flash drive.
   _____ Format a USB flash drive.
   _____ Make a USB flash drive bootable.

■ Business Case Scenarios

Scenario 1-1: Installing Windows 10

You are an administrator of an organization that has 150 client computers. Sixty systems are running Windows 7 Enterprise, 60 systems are running Windows 7 Professional, and 30 systems are running Windows 8.1 Professional. You also need to purchase 25 more systems, which will run Windows 10. Which edition and version of Windows 10 should be deployed and how would you deploy Windows 10?

Scenario 1-2: Upgrading to Windows 10

You have a computer that is running Windows 8.1 Professional. You want to upgrade the computer to Windows 10 Enterprise.

Installing Windows

70-698 EXAM OBJECTIVE

Objective 1.2 – Install Windows. This objective may include but is not limited to: Perform clean installations; upgrade using Windows Update; upgrade using installation media; configure native boot scenarios; migrate from previous versions of Windows; install to virtual hard disk (VHD); boot from VHD; install on bootable USB; install additional Windows features; configure Windows for additional regional and language support. * Additional coverage of install on bootable USB is included in Lesson 1.

LESSON HEADING	EXAM OBJECTIVE
Installing and Upgrading to Windows 10	
Performing a Clean Installation	Perform clean installations
Upgrading to Windows 10	Upgrade using Windows Update
	Upgrade using installation media
Using Native VHD Boot	Configure native boot scenarios
Installing and Booting Windows 10 on a VHD	Install to virtual hard disk (VHD)
	Boot from VHD
Migrating to Windows 10 from Previous Versions of Windows	Migrate from previous versions of Windows
Estimating Data Storage Requirements	
Securing Migrated Data	
Understanding the USMT Syntax	
Installing on Bootable USB with Windows To Go	Install on bootable USB
Creating and Deploying a Windows To Go Workspace Drive	
Booting into a Windows To Go Workspace	
Installing Windows 10 Additional Windows Features	Install additional Windows features
Configuring Windows 10 for Additional Regional and Language Support	Configure Windows for additional regional and language support

KEY TERMS

.NET Framework 3.5

.NET Framework 4.6

Disk Management Console
(diskmgmt.msc)

Diskpart

dynamically expanding
virtual disk

fixed-size virtual disk

hardlink folder

High Touch with Retail Media

language pack

Lite-Touch, High-Volume
Deployment

LoadState.exe

Native VHD boot

ScanState.exe

User State Migration
Tool (USMT)

VHD format

VHDX format

virtual hard disk (VHD)

Windows To Go

Windows To Go workspace

Workspace To Go Creator
(pwcreator.exe)

Zero-Touch, High-Volume
Deployment

■ INSTALLING AND UPGRADING TO WINDOWS 10

THE BOTTOM LINE

If you have a single computer on which you need to install Windows, you will most likely install Windows from a bootable DVD or bootable USB device. However, if you have multiple computers on which you need to install Windows, there are better ways to deploy Windows with minimal effort, resources, and time, while minimizing problems during and after Windows deployment.

When selecting an appropriate server deployment strategy, you can choose from three models:

- High Touch with Retail Media
- Lite-Touch, High-Volume Deployment
- Zero-Touch, High-Volume Deployment

The *High Touch with Retail Media* strategy is the basic local installation strategy used by small organizations with fewer than 100 unmanaged client computers, a simple network infrastructure, and no staff to perform complicated or large deployments. The administrator will go from computer to computer to perform the installation, using a Window installation disc (usually the retail media) or bootable USB drive. So the High Touch with Retail Media strategy is a hands-on, manual deployment in which you insert the Windows installation disc in the drive, install Windows, apply any patches, install any applications, and manually configure the computer. If you are using retail media, you also have to activate the computers online or by using a phone. If you need to install only a few computers, the strategy makes sense.

In many cases, a small company can purchase a new computer with Windows already installed. In these cases, you need to unbox the computer, connect it to the network, apply patches, install any necessary applications, and configure the computer. Other options would be to bring in a consultant or service company that can provide IT support when needed.

Of these three strategies, High Touch with Retail Media requires the most work and time. You can reduce the burden by using scripts and/or answer files. You create the answer file (unattend.xml), place it on a USB storage device, and start the computer with the Windows installation disc. During the startup process, Windows looks for the answer file on the USB devices. If the answer file is found, the Windows setup program uses it to automate or partially automate the installation.

Unfortunately, creating the script and/or answer file requires some technical experience, which might not be available to small companies. Although you can create the answer file by downloading and installing the Windows Automated Installation Kit (AIK), and running the System Image Manager (SIM), a number of non-Microsoft websites provide unattend. xml files. However, if you download one of these answer files, you need to review it, using a text editor such as Notepad, to provide the proper product key and to use your own company information.

The ***Lite-Touch, High-Volume Deployment*** is aimed at medium-sized organizations with 200 to 500 client computers and at least one site with more than 25 users. This strategy uses network infrastructure and servers to deploy Windows. The organization would also use various tools, including answer files, scripts via the Windows AIK, and the Microsoft Deployment Toolkit (MDT) to deploy Windows.

The Lite-Touch, High-Volume Deployment strategy is highly automated but requires a little interaction at the beginning of installation. However, if an organization configures a database and deploys Windows via the Windows Deployment Services role, you can reach nearly zero-touch deployment. Of course, using the Lite-Touch, High-Volume Deployment strategy requires more planning, and you need to do more work up front to install and configure the necessary components than the previous strategies.

At the very least, during a Lite Touch Installation (LTI), a user has to boot the client system, launch the Deployment Wizard, and select a task sequence to run. Other prompts might appear as well, depending on how the administrator scripted the installation.

At its simplest, the process of performing a Lite Touch Deployment consists of installing an operating system on a reference computer, customizing the reference computer to reflect the desired workstation configuration, capturing an image from the reference computer, and deploying that image to the target computers on the network.

An LTI deployment requires only relatively simple tools, such as MDT 2016 and Windows Assessment and Deployment Kit (Windows ADK) for Windows 10, which Microsoft provides free of charge. However, as the name implies, an LTI deployment does require some user interaction at the client.

The ***Zero-Touch, High-Volume Deployment*** strategy is for large organizations with more than 500 managed client computers and at least one location with more than 25 users. The Zero-Touch, High-Volume Deployment strategy is similar to the Lite-Touch, High-Volume Deployment strategy, except that it uses System Center Configuration Manager, MDT, and Windows AIK to provide a fully automated deployment that requires no user interaction. Although System Center Configuration Manager has to be licensed and requires a little bit more effort to install and configure, the up-front cost and effort is offset by automated deployment of a large number of computers and by lower support costs because configurations are consistent across all client computers. This strategy also provides streamlined maintenance because System Center Configuration Manager also handles applications, device drivers, and updates.

When you need to deploy multiple computers, you want the deployment to go smoothly. Therefore, for larger deployments, you should follow these basic steps:

1. **Plan:** Choose a strategy based on your organization's business requirements and needs.
2. **Test:** Test the deployment before you perform it (to ensure that the images and processes function properly) and before you touch the user computers. By testing, you can reduce the number of support and maintenance calls.
3. **Store images:** Select a file server on which to store the images. During the deployment process, these images will be applied to your server computers.
4. **Distribute:** Apply images across the network to the target server computers, or apply images from removable media such as a USB flash drive or a DVD.

The Zero Touch Installation (ZTI) deployment method enables administrators to perform push installations on computers, with no user interaction at all required at the client. To use this method, however, you must have System Center Configuration Manager (SCCM) installed, which is a complex and expensive product.

Performing a Clean Installation

When you perform a clean installation of Windows 10, you will use a Bootable DVD or USB flash drive to perform the installation. You don't need a previous version of Windows on the computer. However, if you do have a previous version of Windows, you can perform a clean installation that will remove all content by formatting the drive, so that the rest of the installation will be done as a fresh system.

CERTIFICATION READY
Perform clean installations
Objective 1.2

During Lesson 1, you learned how to create a bootable Windows 10 installation USB flash drive using the Windows 10 Media Creator tool. To boot from a USB flash drive, you insert the flash drive into a USB port, and turn on the computer. If the system does not boot from the USB flash drive, you might need to configure the BIOS Setup program to boot from it, and you might need to configure the boot order so that the USB flash drive booting will occur before any other boot drives.

 INSTALL WINDOWS 10 FROM WINDOWS 10 INSTALLATION USB FLASH DRIVE

GET READY. To install Windows 10 from a Windows 10 installation USB flash drive, perform the following steps.

1. Insert the Windows 10 installation USB flash drive in a USB port and then turn on the computer. Press F12 (or whatever key that allows selecting the boot device) and select the Windows 10 installation USB flash drive.
2. The computer switches to the Windows graphical interface and the Windows Setup page appears, as shown in Figure 2-1. Using the drop-down lists provided,

Figure 2-1

The Windows Setup page

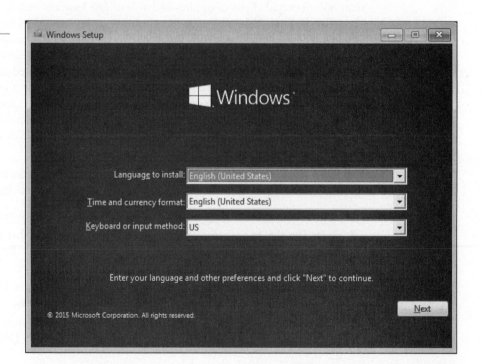

select the appropriate Language to install, the Time and currency format, and the Keyboard or input method. Then click **Next**.

3. On the Windows 10 Install Now page, click **Install now**.

4. On the License Terms page, select the **I accept the license terms** option and then click **Next**.

5. Click the **Custom: Install Windows only (advanced)** option.

6. The Where Do You Want to Install Windows? page appears, as shown in Figure 2-2. From the list provided, select the partition on which you want to install Windows 10, or select an area of unallocated disk space where the Setup program can create a new partition. Then click **Next**.

Figure 2-2

The Where Do You Want to Install Windows? page

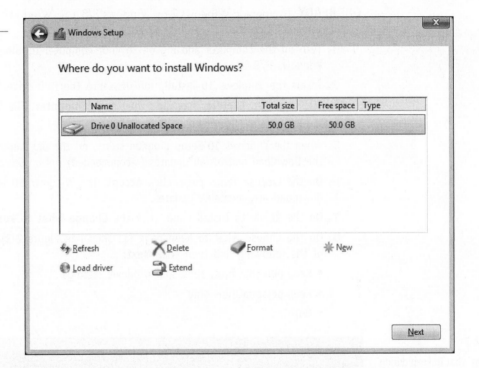

7. After several minutes, during which the Setup program installs Windows 10, the computer reboots and the Get Going Fast page appears. Click **Use Express Settings**.

8. The Choose How You'll Connect page appears. Click the **Join a domain** option. Then click **Next**.

9. On the Create an Account for This PC page, in the Who's going to use this PC text box, type **User1**.

10. In the Enter password and Re-enter password text boxes, type **Pa$$w0rd**. In the Password hint box, type **Default**. Click **Next**.

11. On the Windows desktop, on the right side, the Networks pane opens. When prompted to determine whether you want to allow your PC to be discoverable by other PCs and devices on the network, click **Yes**.

At this point, you can remove the USB flash drive from the USB port.

The instructions to upgrade using a Windows 10 installation DVD are similar to installing using a Windows 10 installation DVD.

CERTIFICATION READY
Upgrade using Windows
Update
Objective 1.2

CERTIFICATION READY
Upgrade using
installation media
Objective 1.2

Upgrading to Windows 10

If you need to upgrade from Windows 7 or Windows 8/8.1 to Windows 10, you can use a Windows 10 bootable DVD or bootable USB drive. You can also upgrade to Windows 10 by using the Windows 10 Media Creator tool.

Before you perform any upgrade, you should always make sure that you have a current backup of all programs, settings, and data files. You should also make sure that the backup is stored away from the machine you are trying to upgrade.

 UPGRADE TO WINDOWS 10 FROM WINDOWS 10 INSTALLATION DVD

GET READY. To upgrade Windows 7 or Windows 8/8.1 to Windows 10 using a Windows 10 installation DVD, perform the following steps.

1. Turn on the computer and log on to your computer running Windows 7 or Windows 8/8.1.
2. Insert the Windows 10 installation disc into the DVD drive.
3. Click the **File Explorer** icon and then click **Computer**. The Computer window opens.
4. Double-click the DVD drive.
5. When the Windows 10 Setup program starts, on the Get Important Updates page, keep the Download and install updates (recommended) option selected and then click **Next**.
6. On the License Terms page, click **Accept**. The Windows 10 Setup program will download any available updates.
7. On the Ready to Install page, click the **Change what to keep** option.
8. On the Choose What to Keep page (as shown in Figure 2-3), you can choose one of the following and then click **Next**:
   • Keep personal files, apps, and Windows settings
   • Keep personal files only
   • Nothing

Figure 2-3

Specifying what to keep during a Windows 10 upgrade

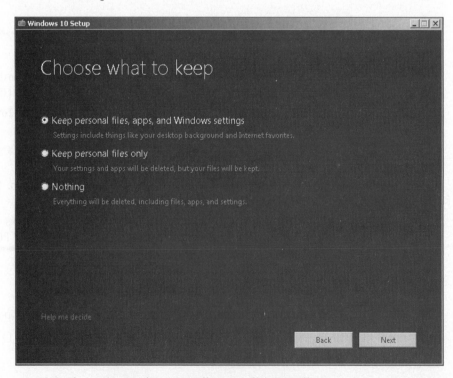

9. Back on the Ready to Install page, click **Install**.

After a few minutes, Windows will reboot and complete the upgrade.

When Windows 10 was initially released, Microsoft offered a free upgrade from Windows 7 or 8/8.1 to Windows 10 for the first year. These free upgrades are done over the Internet with Windows Update. In addition, because Windows 10 is released as an "operating system as a service," Windows 10 machines will receive ongoing updates to its features and functionality.

Using Native VHD Boot

CERTIFICATION READY
Configure native boot scenarios
Objective 1.2

Native VHD boot allows the computer to mount and boot from the operating system contained within the VHD file. If the computer supports Native VHD boot, Native VHD boot will also work without an operating system present on the host computer or a hypervisor, such as Hyper-V.

A *virtual hard disk (VHD)* is a single file on your disk that functions like a separate drive. It can host native file systems (NTFS, FAT, exFAT, and UDFS), function as a boot disk, and support standard disk and file operations. This allows virtual disks to run on a computer that doesn't have a VM or hypervisor and also simplifies the image management process.

TAKE NOTE

A virtual hard disk in Windows 10 does not require a parent operating system or a virtual machine manager in order to run. A virtual machine manager (hypervisor) is software that manages and monitors virtual machines.

UNDERSTANDING VHD FORMATS

When setting up a VHD, you have to determine the format and hard disk type. Each is designed to meet a specific goal. There are two VHD formats to choose from when creating a VHD boot file:

- *VHD format* supports virtual disks up to 2 TB in size.
- *VHDX format* supports virtual disks up to 64 TB. VHDX is more resilient to power failure but is only supported on Windows 8 or newer systems.

There are two hard disk types available:

- A *fixed-size virtual disk* is allocated to its maximum size when the VHD is created. It works well with production servers where user data protection and overall performance is critical.
- A *dynamically expanding virtual disk* will grow to its maximum size as data is written to the virtual hard disk. It should be used in testing and nonproduction environments. If you are using this disk type, consider storing your critical applications and user data outside the VHD. This reduces the overall file size and makes it easier to recover should the VHD image become corrupted.

CONFIGURING NATIVE BOOT SCENARIOS

Besides using VHDs with virtual machines, you can use VHDs with native boot in the following scenarios:

- You can attach a VHD by using the Attach vdisk command, which activates the VHD so that it appears on the host as a disk drive instead of as a .vhd or .vhdx file.

- You can mount reference VHD images on remote shares for image servicing.
- You can maintain and deploy a reference VHD to execute in physical or virtual computers.
- You can configure VHD files for native boot without requiring a full parent installation.
- You can configure a volume that has multiple VHD files that can contain different application workloads.
- You can use Windows Deployment Services (WDS) to deploy VHD images to target computers for native boot.

To use native VHD boot, you must have the following requirements and limitations:

- You must have at least two partitions: a system partition that contains the Windows 10 boot-environment files and the Boot Configuration Data (BCD) store, and a partition to store the VHD file.
- The .vhd file format is supported for native boot on a computer with a Windows 7, 8/8.1, or 10 boot environment, but you will have to update the system partition to a Windows 10 environment to use the .vhdx file format.
- The local disk partition that contains the VHD file must have enough free disk space for expanding a dynamic VHD to its maximum size.
- VHD files cannot be nested.
- Native VHD boot is not supported over Server Message Block (SMB) shares.

CREATING A VHD FILE

To create a VHD file, you can use the **_Disk Management Console (diskmgmt.msc)_** and/or the Diskpart tool. The Disk Management Console is used to partition, format, delete, shrink, assign, and change drive letters for hard disks (internal/external), optical disk drives, and flash drives. Diskpart is a command-line tool that enables you to manage objects (disks, partitions, or volumes) by using scripts or direct input at a command prompt.

In the following example, you will create a VHD boot file on Windows 10 Pro and then install Windows 10 Enterprise to create a dual-boot system to test Windows 10 performance and compatibility with your existing computer's hardware.

 CREATE A VHD BOOT FILE USING THE DISK MANAGEMENT CONSOLE

GET READY. To create a VHD boot file using the Disk Management Console, log on as an administrator to a computer running Windows 10 Pro and then perform the following steps.

1. Right-click the **Start** button and click **Disk Management**.
2. Click **Action > Create VHD**.
3. When the Create and Attach Virtual Hard Disk dialog box opens, as shown in Figure 2-4, click the **Browse** button to navigate to the folder where you want to store the VHD file.

Figure 2-4

Specifying the folder where you will store the VHD

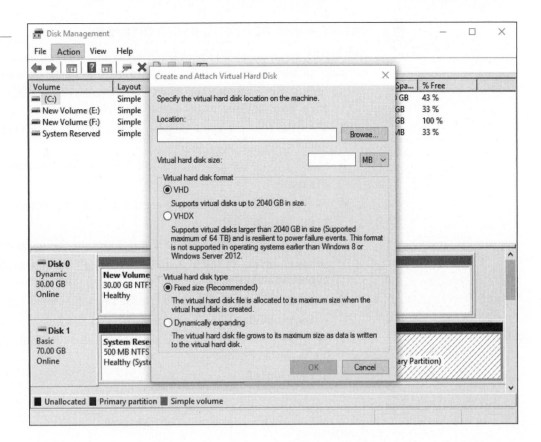

4. In the File name text box, type a name for the VHD file and then click **Save**.

5. For the Virtual hard disk size setting, type **30**, click the drop-down arrow, and then select **GB**.

6. In the Virtual hard disk type section, leave the default setting of **Fixed size (Recommended)**.

7. Click **OK**. The VHD file is created.

Installing and Booting Windows 10 on a VHD

After creating a VHD, you install an operating system by booting from a DVD or a bootable USB drive with the appropriate image.

CERTIFICATION READY
Install to virtual hard disk (VHD)
Objective 1.2

After creating the VHD, your next step is to install the Windows 10 operating system on the VHD. You can perform the installation by booting from a DVD or a bootable USB drive that contains the Windows 10 Enterprise installation files.

Windows 10 Setup will take you through the normal setup screens, prompting you for the language to install, time/currency formats, keyboard or input methods, and licensing terms. When you reach the Where Do You Want to Install Windows? page, you can open a command prompt by pressing Shift+F10.

CERTIFICATION READY
Boot from VHD
Objective 1.2

From the command line, you can use ***Diskpart*** to create and attach the VHD. Attaching the VHD ensures it appears on the host as a drive and not a static file. The following example selects and attaches to the virtual hard disk created earlier.

CREATE A VHD BOOT FILE USING DISKPART

GET READY. To create a VHD boot file using Diskpart, log on as an administrator to a computer running Windows 10 Pro and then perform the following steps.

1. Turn on the computer and insert the Windows 10 installation disc into the DVD drive. Press any key to boot from the DVD (if necessary).

2. When the Windows Setup program opens, press the **Shift+F10** key combination.

3. At the X:\Sources> prompt, execute the following command:

   diskpart

4. To show the disks available, execute the following command:

   list volume

5. To create a virtual disk on the F drive, execute the following command:

   create vdisk file="F:\windows10.vhd" maximum=30000 type=expandable

6. To select the virtual disk, type the following command:

   select vdisk file="F:\window10.vhd"

7. To attach the virtual disk to the system, execute the following command (as shown in Figure 2-5):

   attach vdisk

Figure 2-5

Attaching a virtual disk

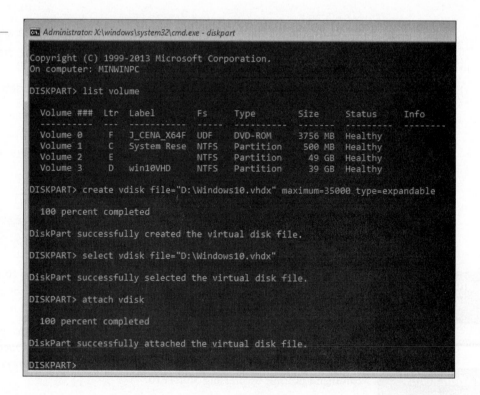

8. To exit Diskpart, execute the following command:

   Exit

9. To exit the Command Prompt window, execute the following command:

   Exit

10. Back on the Windows Setup page, specify the appropriate language, time and currency format, and keyboard or input method. Click **Next**.

11. Click the **Install now** button.

12. On the License Terms page, select the **I accept the license terms** option and click **Next**.

13. When you are prompted to select which type of installation you want, click **Custom: Install Windows only (advanced)**.

14. Select the virtual drive that you just created (as shown in Figure 2-6) and click **Next**.

Figure 2-6

Specifying on which drive to install Windows 10

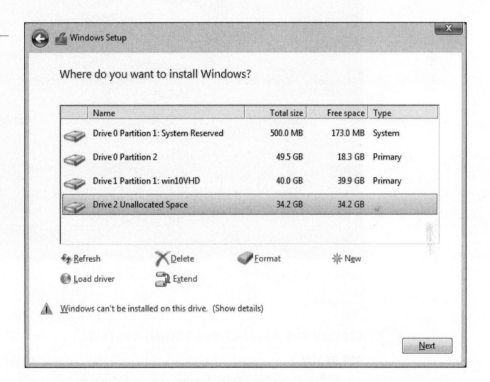

15. After several minutes, during which the Setup program installs Windows 10, the computer reboots.

On reboot, you have the option to select the instance of the operating system you want to run (see Figure 2-7). You can then select the normal Windows installation, or the Windows 10.vhdx installation.

The operating system boot menu configuration is stored in the Boot Configuration Data (BCD). You can use the System Properties dialog box to change the default operating system and how long the list of operating systems will be displayed so that you can choose which operating system to boot. For more control of the operating system menu, including changing the operating system listings, you can use the BCDEdit command.

Figure 2-7

The Windows 10 boot menu

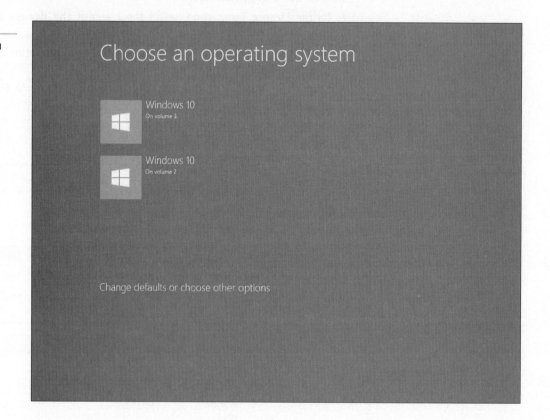

SPECIFY THE DEFAULT OPERATING SYSTEM

GET READY. To specify the default operating system, perform the following steps.

1. Right-click the **Start** button and click **System**.

2. When the System window opens, click the **Advanced system settings** link.

3. When the System Properties dialog box opens, on the Advanced tab, in the Startup and Recovery section, click the **Settings** button.

4. When the Startup and Recovery dialog box opens (as shown in Figure 2-8), you select the Default operating system that will be chosen when the Time to display list of operating systems expires.

5. You can specify the Time (such as 15 seconds) to display list of operating systems in seconds.

6. To close the Startup and Recovery dialog box, click **OK**.

Figure 2-8

Managing the operating
system boot menu

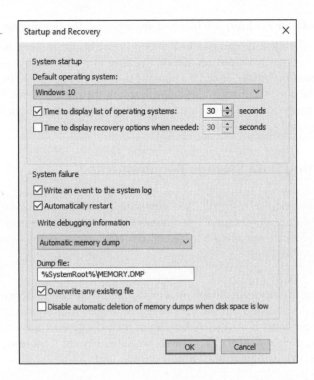

7. To close the System Properties dialog box, click **OK**.

8. You can then close the System window.

■ MIGRATING TO WINDOWS 10 FROM PREVIOUS VERSIONS OF WINDOWS

THE BOTTOM LINE

Sometimes, you might want to move a user from one system to another, including moving a user from a computer running Windows 7 or 8/8.1 to a computer running Windows 10. One of the most time-consuming tasks you will perform as an administrator is to move user files and settings between computers and operating systems. The User State Migration Tool (USMT) eases this burden. The USMT 10 tool is part of the Windows Assessment and Deployment Kit for Windows 10.

CERTIFICATION READY
Migrate from previous
versions of Windows
Objective 1.2

The *User State Migration Tool (USMT)* is a command-line tool that migrates user data from a previous installation of Windows to a new installation of Windows. It provides you with the ability to customize the user-profile migration experience. This means you can copy the user data that you select and exclude any data that you do not want to migrate. USMT captures user accounts, user files, operating system settings, and application settings to migrate to your new Windows installation.

The USMT includes three command-line tools:

- *ScanState.exe* scans the source computer, collects the files and settings, and creates a store that contains the user's files and settings.

- *LoadState.exe* loads the files and settings onto the destination computer.
- UsmtUtils.exe deletes hardlink folders in use by applications no longer removable through normal measures, checks the store file's consistency, and restores selected files. A *hardlink folder* provides a way for the New Technology File System (NTFS) to point to the same file from multiple locations on the same volume. The store file contains the user state migration data. UsmtUtils can be used to check for corrupted files or a corrupted catalog in the store file.

Estimating Data Storage Requirements

When you elect to store migrated user state data on a network, local, or removable drive, you must be aware of the amount of data you need to store. This is particularly true if you plan to store the migrated data from many computers onto a single network server.

Estimating the storage requirements for the migration can be difficult because the amount of space required depends on the data storage strategies your organization uses and the types of files they generate. If your users keep all of their documents and email data on servers, their migration stores will likely be relatively small. If they use local storage for those things, migration stores can be significantly larger.

Some of the storage estimates you can make are as follows:

- **User system settings:** Typically, 5 MB is sufficient for the user-specific registry settings. The actual size of the registry will depend on the number of applications installed on the computer.
- **USMT operations:** USMT itself requires 250 MB of space for its page file and other operations. ScanState will not create a migration store if less than 250 MB is available on the target computer.
- **Temporary space:** Both ScanState and LoadState require temporary space to run. You can determine the exact amount of temporary space required by running ScanState with the /p option.

Email, when it is stored on local disks, is frequently one of the biggest consumers of storage space in a migration store. You can try to arrive at a general estimate for the average amount of space devoted to stored local email based on the length of time users at the organization have been saving their mail and the number and nature of the attachments they might send and receive.

Document files, such as those created by Microsoft Word and Excel, are typically small—50 MB of storage can hold a great many documents like these. However, if your users often work with other types of documents, such as PowerPoint files, large images, or audio and video, the amount of space required for each user can easily run into several gigabytes.

Another issue when estimating the storage required for migration stores is whether you will compress them. Compression is enabled by default in USMT; to disable compression, you must run ScanState with the /nocompress option. A compressed migration store consists of a single image file containing all of the files to be migrated and a catalog file.

An uncompressed migration store is a directory containing a mirror image of the directory tree containing the files to be migrated. When uncompressed, you can access the files in the migration store at any time, such as to run a virus scan on them. Obviously, though, the uncompressed store occupies more storage space than the compressed one. The difference in size depends on the types of files in the store. An average document file might compress at a 2:1 ratio, whereas image files might compress at 8:1, assuming they are not already in a compressed format.

Using the ScanState tool, you can calculate the disk space requirements for a migration store without actually creating the store, using the /p command-line option. The syntax for the command is as follows:

```
ScanState.exe <StorePath> /p:<filepath>
```

The StorePath variable is the location where the store would be created. This command doesn't actually create the store, but the path is still required. The filepath variable is the location where the program should create the XML report file containing the results.

An example of the results appears as follows:

```
<?xml version="1.0" encoding="UTF-8"?>

<PreMigration>

  <storeSize>

    <size clusterSize="4096">11010592768</size>

  </storeSize>

  <temporarySpace>

    <size>58189144</size>

  </temporarySpace>

</PreMigration>
```

The <storeSize> section specifies the amount of disk space required to create the migration store, in bytes. In this example, the store would require just over 11 GB. The <temporarySpace> section specifies how much space ScanState needs to run, not including the base 250 MB specified earlier. In this case, the space required is just over 58 MB.

Securing Migrated Data

The user state information that you migrate using USMT can often contain sensitive data, and depending on where you create the migration stores, security can be an issue. It is possible to encrypt the migration stores in their compressed state by adding the /encrypt option to the ScanState command line.

You must then also add the same option to the LoadState command, so that the program can decrypt the store. The only difference is that you would use the /decrypt option instead of the /encrypt option.

When you use the /encrypt option by itself, ScanState and LoadState use the Triple Data Encryption Standard (3DES) encryption algorithm. However, you can add one of the following arguments to configure the programs to use a different standard:

- **/encrypt:AES:** Uses the Advanced Encryption Standard algorithm
- **/encrypt:AES_128:** Uses the Advanced Encryption Standard algorithm with 128-bit encryption
- **/encrypt:AES_192:** Uses the Advanced Encryption Standard algorithm with 192-bit encryption
- **/encrypt:AES_256:** Uses the Advanced Encryption Standard algorithm with 256-bit encryption

- **/encrypt:3DES:** Uses the Data Encryption Standard cipher algorithm and applies it three times to each data block; this is the default setting
- **/encrypt:3DES_112:** Uses the Data Encryption Standard cipher algorithm with 112-bit encryption and applies it three times to each data block

TAKE NOTE All of these encryption options might not be available to you, depending on your location. To determine which encryption options you can use, you can run the UsmtUtils.exe program with the /ec option.

Understanding the USMT Syntax

The ScanState.exe and LoadState.exe programs have similar syntaxes, in which you specify the location of the migration store, the scripts you want to use to specify what to migrate, which user accounts you want to migrate, and how the program should store the data.

Table 2-1 lists some of the most common command-line options for ScanState and LoadState and their functions.

USMT also includes the following modifiable .xml files. These files can be used with ScanState and LoadState to perform a targeted migration:

- MigApp.xml includes rules to migrate application settings.
- MigDocs.xml includes rules to migrate user documents from the source computer.
- MigUser.xml includes rules to migrate user profiles and user data.

When you use USMT, you should use the following three-step process:

Step 1: Plan the migration.

- Determine whether to refresh or replace your system, identify what you want to migrate (application settings, operating system settings, files, and/or folders), determine where to store it (remotely, locally in a hardlink migration store, or directly on the destination computer), and determine which files will be included in the migration.
- If necessary, modify the MigApp.xml and MigDocs.xml or create and modify a config.xml file. In general, it's best to leave the original .xml files in place and create and modify a config.xml file to keep your changes separate from the default .xml files.

Step 2: Collect the files and settings from the source computer.

- Back up the source computer and close all applications before running ScanState; otherwise, USMT might not be able to migrate all the data.
- Run ScanState to collect the files and settings using an account with administrative privileges. Specify all .xml files you want the command to use:

    ScanState \\server\migration\mystore /config:config.xml /i:migdocs.xml /:migapp.xml /v:13 /l:scan.log

- After the store is completed, run UsmtUtils with the /verify switch to ensure that the store you created was not corrupted. Replace *X* with the store location and *mystore* with the actual name of the store:

    UsmtUtils /verify x:\mystore\store.img

Table 2-1

USMT Command-Line Options

COMMAND-LINE OPTION	SCANSTATE OR LOADSTATE	DESCRIPTION
StorePath	Both	Specifies the location where the program should create or from which it should read the migration store
/o	ScanState	Overwrites any existing data in the migration store
/vsc	ScanState	Uses the Volume Shadow Copy Service to migrate files that are locked open, eliminating some errors
/hardlink	ScanState	Creates a hardlink migration store at the location specified in the StorePath variable
/encrypt: *algorithm*	ScanState	Creates an encrypted migration store, using the specified algorithm
/decrypt	LoadState	Decrypts the migration store as it restores the user state
/key: *keystring*	Both	Uses the key specified by the *keystring* variable to encrypt or decrypt the migration store
/keyfile:filename	Both	Uses the key specified in the file identified by the filename variable to encrypt or decrypt the migration store
/nocompress	ScanState	Disables the default data compression used when creating a migration store
/i: *filename*	Both	Specifies the name of an XML file that the program should use to determine what to migrate
/genconfig: filename	ScanState	Creates a Config.xml file containing all of the migratable data on the computer, but does not create the migration store
/config: *filename*	Both	Specifies the Config.xml file the program should use when creating or reading the migration store
/localonly	ScanState	Creates a migration store containing only the files on local, fixed drives
/c	Both	Causes the program to continue running, even if nonfatal errors occur
/all	Both	Migrates all user accounts on the computer
/ui: *domain\user* /ui: *computer\user*	Both	Migrates a specific user account
/ue: *domain\user* /ue: *computer\user*	Both	Excludes a specific account from migration
/uel:<*numberofdays*> /uel:<*YYYY/MM/DD*> /uel:0	Both	Migrates only the users who have logged on to the computer within a specified number of days or since a specific date or who are currently logged on to the computer

Step 3: Prepare the destination computer and restore the files and settings.

- Install the operating system on the destination computer, install any applications that were on the source computer, and then close any open applications.

- Run the LoadState command on the destination computer to migrate the files and settings. Make sure you specify the same .xml files you used when you ran ScanState during the collection process in Step 2:

  LoadState \\server\migration\mystore /config:config.xml /i:migdocs.xml /i:migapp.xml /v:13 /l:load.log

- After completing the LoadState process, you must log off and then log back on the machine to see if some of the settings changed (for example, the screen saver, the fonts, the wallpaper, and so on).

 CREATE A CUSTOM CONFIG.XML FILE AND EXCLUDE CONTENT FROM THE MY PICTURES FOLDER

GET READY. To create a custom config.xml file and exclude content from the My Pictures folder, log on as an administrator to a computer running Windows 10 Enterprise and then perform the following steps.

TAKE NOTE To complete this exercise, you must have USMT installed on your computer.

1. On LON-CL1, press the **Windows logo key + q**, and in the Run box, type **cmd** and click **OK**.

2. From the search results list, right-click **Command Prompt** and then click **Run as administrator**.

3. Change to the directory that contains the USMT tools. In a default installation, this would be found by using the **cd** command as shown:32-bit machines:

   ```
   cd "c:\Program Files (x86)\Windows Kits\10.0\Assessment and Deployment Kit\User State Migration Tool\x86"
   ```

   64-bit machines:

   ```
   cd "c:\Program Files (x86)\Windows Kits\10.0\Assessment and Deployment Kit\User State Migration Tool\amd64"
   ```

4. To create a config.xml file, type the following command:

   ```
   scanstate /i:migapp.xml /i:miguser.xml /genconfig:config.xml /v:13
   ```

   Log messages regarding the creation of the file will be sent to the scanstate.log file. Both the log file and the config.xml file will be created in the directory from where you run the ScanState command.

5. To exclude the My Pictures folder from the migration, change migrate="yes" to **migrate="no"**. (The following code is an excerpt from the config.xml file created in Step 4.)

   ```
   <?xml version="1.0" encoding="UTF-8"?>

   <Configuration>

   <Documents>

   <component displayname="My Pictures" migrate="yes" ID="http://www
   .microsoft.com/migration/1.0/migxmlext/miguser/my pictures/data"/>

   </Documents>
   ```

6. Save the file.

This file can now be used with ScanState to collect information from the source computer and with LoadState to prepare the destination computers.

■ INSTALLING ON BOOTABLE USB WITH WINDOWS TO GO

↓
THE BOTTOM LINE

Windows To Go is a feature available with Windows 10 Enterprise clients that allows you to boot a full version of Windows 10 Enterprise from an external USB drive on a host computer.

CERTIFICATION READY
Install on bootable USB
Objective 1.2

Windows To Go is a feature in Windows 10 Enterprise edition that allows you to create a *Windows To Go workspace* on an external USB drive. This enables your users to boot a full version of Windows 10 from removable media. The drive uses the same image installed on a corporate desktop and laptop; therefore, you can manage them in the same manner and use the same tools. The drive itself must be connected to a host computer running on a Windows 7 or later certified operating system to function.

Creating and Deploying a Windows To Go Workspace Drive

You can create a Windows To Go workspace drive for employees working from home, contractors on temporary assignment, and employees who travel between sites and need access to corporate resources and applications. This provides them with mobility while also allowing you to manage the devices as part of your corporate policies.

The *Workspace To Go Creator (pwcreator.exe)* is used to create Windows To Go workspaces. You can also use a USB duplicator product, but that will require you to duplicate the drive before it is booted and initialized.

To create a Windows To Go workspace, you need:

- A USB drive that supports Windows To Go (32 GB or larger)
- A computer running Windows 10 Enterprise edition
- A Windows 10 Enterprise ISO, Windows 10 Enterprise/Education installation media, or a corporate Windows image (.wim) created from Windows 10 Enterprise/Education media
- Local administrator access on the computer

To protect the drive in case it is lost or stolen, you have the option to configure BitLocker To Go during the setup of the workspace. BitLocker To Go allows you to encrypt a removable drive and restrict access with a password or a smart card.

Once your removable drive is set up, you can deploy the Windows To Go workspace centrally or by allowing individual users to create their own workspaces. Central management and deployment requires System Center Configuration Manager 2012 Service Pack 1 or higher.

 CREATE A WINDOWS TO GO WORKSPACE

GET READY. To create a Windows To Go workspace, log on as an administrator to a computer running Windows 10 Enterprise edition and then perform the following steps.

1. On LON-CL1, right-click the **Start** button and click **Control Panel.**
2. When Control Panel opens, in the Search Control Panel text box, type **Windows To Go.** From the search results, click **Windows To Go.**
3. Select the USB drive you connected earlier and then click **Next.**

4. Click the Windows image that appears or click **Add search location** to locate one. Click **Next** to continue.
5. Click **Create** to format the drive.
6. (Optional) Select the **Use BitLocker with my Windows To Go workspace** check box and then type a password. Click **Next**.

 TAKE NOTE Enabling BitLocker on the Windows To Go workspace will protect the drive if it is lost or stolen. Using this feature requires you to type a password each time you use the workspace.

7. Click **Create** to set up the Windows To Go workspace.
8. Click **Yes** to automatically boot from the USB drive when you restart the host (as shown in Figure 2-9) or click **No** if you want to change the PC's firmware settings to use the workspace.

Figure 2-9

Selecting the Windows To Go startup options

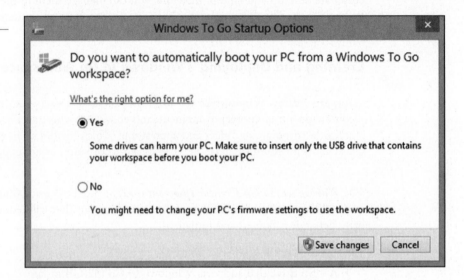

If you click Yes, your computer will automatically boot to the Windows To Go workspace every time a USB drive is detected. If you click No, you will need to change startup options in your computer's firmware. You do this by entering your firmware setup using the appropriate function key for your specific type of BIOS. This is usually the F12 key, but you might need to check the manufacturer's website to determine the appropriate key.

If you decide to modify this setting later or want to use the Windows To Go workspace drive on another computer and need to make sure it is configured appropriately, access the Windows To Go control panel using the steps in the following exercise.

 CHANGE WINDOWS TO GO STARTUP OPTIONS

GET READY. To change Windows To Go startup options, perform the following steps.

1. On LON-CL1, log on to your Windows 10 client device with administrative privileges.
2. Right-click the **Start** button and click **Control Panel**.
3. Click the **Hardware and Sound** category.

4. In the Devices and Printers category, click **Change Windows To Go startup options**.

5. Click **Yes** to automatically boot from an attached USB drive or click **No** to configure the settings manually.

Booting into a Windows To Go Workspace

To take full advantage of the Windows To Go workspace, you need to have a good understanding of what the requirements for the host computer are and the resources that can and cannot be accessed on the host.

When deciding on the host to use for a Windows To Go workspace drive, you should make sure it has been certified for use with Windows 10.

Table 2-2 lists the hardware requirements for Windows To Go workspace hosts.

Table 2-2

Hardware Requirements for Windows To Go Workspace Hosts

HARDWARE	REQUIREMENT
Firmware	Must support booting from USB.
Processor architecture	Must support the image on the Windows To Go drive.
External USB hubs	USB hubs are not supported; you must connect the drive directly to the host computer.
Processor	1 GHz or faster.
Memory	2 GB or greater.
Graphics	DirectX 9 graphics device with a WDDM 1.2 or greater driver.
USB ports	USB 2.0 or greater. Using a USB 3.0 port will result in increased performance in both drive provisioning and when the drive is used as a workspace.

In addition to the information listed Table 2-2, the Windows To Go image on the USB drive must be compatible with the processor architecture and the firmware on the host PC.

Table 2-3 lists the processor/firmware types and Windows To Go image requirements for Windows To Go workspace hosts.

Table 2-3

Windows To Go Compatibility with Host Firmware and Processor Types

HOST PC FIRMWARE	HOST PROCESSOR	WINDOWS TO GO IMAGE THAT CAN BE USED
32-bit Legacy BIOS	32-bit	32-bit image only
64-bit Legacy BIOS	64-bit	32-bit and 64-bit images
32-bit UEFI BIOS	32-bit	32-bit image only
64-bit UEFI BIOS	64-bit	64-bit image only

Once you have identified a suitable host for your Windows To Go workspace drive, insert the drive and power on the computer. If you configured a BitLocker To Go password, you must enter it before you can access the drive. The first time you boot a host from the Windows To Go workspace, it scans for hardware devices and then installs the appropriate drivers. The information it finds is cached; therefore, the next time you boot from the same computer, the process will be faster because drivers are loaded automatically. The Windows To Go workspace operates just like any other installation of Windows, but there are a few differences you need to be aware of.

Once you log on, you will notice the internal disks on the host system are offline to protect against accidental exposure of data. If you insert the USB drive into a system that is already running, you will also notice that it will not be listed in File Explorer. The Hibernate feature is disabled to prevent data corruption during roaming and the Windows Store is disabled by default. The Windows Store application is disabled because applications licensed through the store are linked to your hardware.

■ INSTALLING WINDOWS 10 ADDITIONAL WINDOWS FEATURES

THE BOTTOM LINE

Windows 10 has many optional features or built-in programs available that provide additional functionality. However, not all of the programs are available after the initial installation. Many of these features are aimed at business networks, which might not be useful for everyone. To install the additional features, you open the Windows Features dialog box and turn on the appropriate feature.

CERTIFICATION READY
Install additional
Windows features
Objective 1.2

You don't necessarily want to install every feature that is available. First, Windows 10 features take up space and some consume resources (memory and processing), which result in slower performance. In addition, adding additional features can provide security problems due to increasing your attack surface (a program or service that could potentially be used by an attacker). However, if you reduce the attack surface of the web server too much, you can eliminate necessary functionality needed by the users.

The Windows 10 features include:

- ***.NET Framework 3.5* (includes .NET 2.0 and 3.0):** Is needed to run applications written for older versions of .NET.

- ***.NET Framework 4.6* Advanced Services:** Is needed to run applications that require .NET Framework 4.6. .NET Framework 4.6 is installed by default, whereas .NET Framework 3.5 is not.

- **Active Directory Lightweight Directory Services:** Provides an LDAP (Lightweight Directory Access Protocol) server, which provides a directory for authenticating users on a network. It's a lightweight version of the full Active Directory services and will only be useful on certain business networks.

- **Embedded Shell Launcher:** Replaces the Windows 10 Explorer.exe shell with a custom shell. This feature is aimed at a traditional Windows desktop application in kiosk mode.

- **Hyper-V:** Provides a Microsoft virtualization platform that allows you to create, manage, and use virtual machines. These virtual machines can be useful for portable demonstrations, or running applications that can only be run on older operating systems.

- **Internet Explorer 11:** Provides a Microsoft legacy web browser.

- **Internet Information Services:** Provides Microsoft IIS web and FTP services.

- **Internet Information Services Hostable Web Core:** Allows applications to host a web server using IIS inside their own process.

- **Isolated User Mode:** Allows applications to run in a secure, isolated space if they're programmed to do so.

- **DirectPlay:** Was part of DirectX and is used for networking and multiplayer gaming.

- **Windows Media Player:** Allows you to play audio and video files and view images.

- **Microsoft Message Queue (MSMO) Server:** Improves communications on unreliable networks by queuing messages rather than sending them immediately.

- **Microsoft Print to PDF:** Allows you to print any document to a PDF document.

- **MultiPoint Connector:** Allows your computer to be monitored and managed by the MultiPoint Manager and Dashboard applications.

- **Print and Document Services:** Enables printing over the network, faxing, and scanning. It can also be used to add Line Printer Daemon (LPD) and Line Printer Remote (LPR) network printing protocols.

- **RAS Connection Manager Administration Kit (CMAK):** Allows you to create custom remote access profiles for VPNs.

- **Remote Differential Compression API Support:** Compares synchronized files, so that some of the entire files do not have to be sent over the network.

- **RIP Listener:** Listens for Routing Information Protocol announcements sent by routers.

- **Simple Network Management Protocol (SNMP):** Allows you to manage routers, switches, and other network devices.

- **Simple TCP/IP Services:** Includes a few optional network services, such as the "echo" service, which could be useful for network troubleshooting on some business networks.

- **SMB 1.0/CIFS File Sharing Support:** Enables file and printer sharing with older versions of Windows and other operating systems.

- **Telnet Client:** Provides a telnet command that allows you to remotely connect to the command-line interface on computers and devices running a telnet server.

- **TFTP Client:** Provides a tftp command that allows you to transfer files to computers and devices using the Trivial File Transfer Protocol.

- **Windows Identity Foundation 3.5:** Is an older .NET application that is used by identity-aware applications.

- **Windows PowerShell 2.0:** Is a more advanced scripting and command-line environment.

- **Windows Process Activation Service:** Is used with Internet Information Services web server, which is responsible for managing the activation and lifetime of the worker processes that contain applications that host Windows Communication Foundation (WCF) Services.

- **Windows Subsystem for Linux:** Enables you to use the Ubuntu Bash shell to run Linux applications.

- **Windows TIFF iFilter:** Enables the Windows indexing service to analyze TIFF files and perform optical character recognition (OCR). It's disabled by default as this is a CPU-intensive process.

- **Work Folders Client:** Allows you to synchronize folders from a corporate network to your computer.

- **XPS Services:** Enables printing to XPS documents.

- **XPS Viewer:** Allows you to view XPS documents.

INSTALL WINDOWS 10 ADDITIONAL FEATURES

GET READY. To install Windows 10 additional features, perform the following steps.

1. Right-click the **Start** button and click **Programs and Features**.

2. When the Programs and Features window opens, click **Turn Windows features on or off**.

3. When the Windows Features dialog box opens (as shown in Figure 2-10), select or deselected the desired feature.

Figure 2-10

Turning Windows 10 additional features on or off

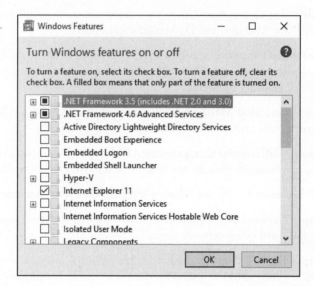

4. To install the applications, click **OK**.

CONFIGURING WINDOWS 10 FOR ADDITIONAL REGIONAL AND LANGUAGE SUPPORT

↓
THE BOTTOM LINE

Microsoft has designed its products to support a wide range of languages and regional settings. After Windows is installed, you can install additional language packs. Then, when you have different people who prefer to use different languages, they can change the language at any time. As a result, menus, dialog boxes, and other interface items will be shown in their preferred language.

CERTIFICATION READY
Configure Windows for additional regional and language support
Objective 1.2

To change the language to be used, you need to do three things:

1. Add the language to Windows.

2. Download and install the language pack.

3. Set the language as your primary language.

A *language pack* is a software component that allows the localizing of Windows so that it can support a specific language.

ADD A LANGUAGE

GET READY. To add a language to Windows 10, perform the following steps.

1. Click the **Start** button and click **Settings**.
2. When the Settings window opens, click **Time and language**.
3. Click the **Region and language** tab on the left side of the window, as shown in Figure 2-11.

Figure 2-11

Adding a language to Windows 10

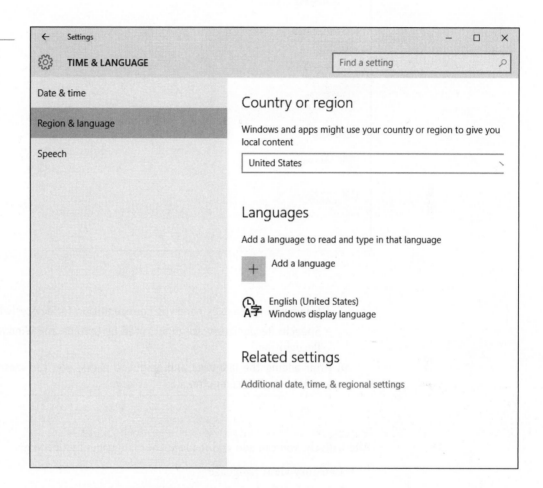

4. Click **Add a language**.
5. Browse for and click the desired language. The language is displayed under the Languages settings.
6. If the language has a Language pack available designation, click **Options**.
7. To download the language pack, when the Language Options page opens, as shown in Figure 2-12, in the Download language pack section, click the **Download** button.
8. Optionally, you can download the following by clicking the appropriate Download buttons:
   • **Basic typing:** Is used by spell checking, text prediction, word breaking, and hyphenation

Figure 2-12

Managing language options

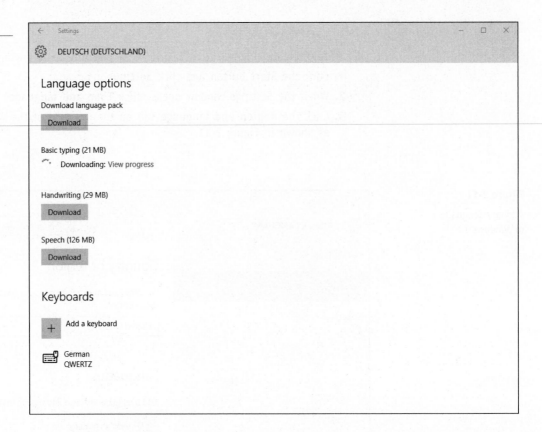

• **Handwriting:** Enables handwriting recognition for devices with pen input
• **Speech:** Recognizes voice input, used by Cortana and Windows Speech Recognition

9. After adding the language and language packs, you can close the Settings window and reboot your computer.

Alternatively, you can add and manage your languages by opening:

• **Category view:** Language
• **Icon view:** Clock, Language, and Region > Language

To specify the primary language, open the Region & Language page, select the desired language, and click Set as default. You would then sign out of Windows, and sign back in for the language to take effect.

Besides changing the default language, you can also configure the region location, and change the date or time formats. By opening the Region & Language page, you can specify a country or region. Windows and apps might use your country or region to give local content.

To change the date and time formats to match your region, you would open Settings > Time & language, and click the Date & time tab, as shown in Figure 2-13. You would then click *Change date and time formats* to specify the first day of the week, and the format of the short date, long date, short time, and long time.

Figure 2-13

Managing time settings

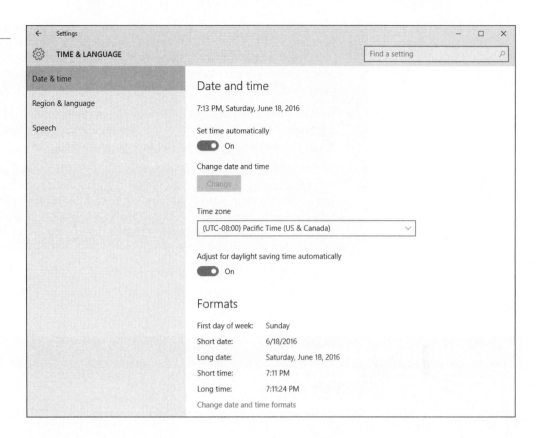

SKILL SUMMARY

IN THIS LESSON YOU LEARNED:

- If you have a single computer on which you need to install Windows, you will most likely install Windows from a bootable DVD or bootable USB device. However, if you have multiple computers on which you need to install Windows, there are better ways to deploy Windows with minimal effort, resources, and time, while minimizing problems during and after Windows deployment.

- When you perform a clean installation of Windows 10, you will use a bootable DVD or USB flash drive to perform the installation. You don't need a previous version of Windows on the computer. However, if you do have a previous version of Windows, you can perform a clean installation that will remove all content by formatting the drive, so that the rest of the installation will be done as a fresh system.

- Native VHD boot allows the computer to mount and boot from the operating system contained within the VHD file. If the computer supports Native VHD boot, Native VHD boot will also work without an operating system present on the host computer or a hypervisor, such as Hyper-V.

- A virtual hard disk (VHD) is a single file on your disk that functions like a separate drive. It can host native file systems (NTFS, FAT, exFAT, and UDFS), function as a boot disk, and support standard disk and file operations.

- To create a VHD file, you can use the Disk Management Console (diskmgmt.msc) and/or the Diskpart tool. The Disk Management Console is used to partition, format, delete, shrink, and assign and change drive letters for hard disks (internal/external), optical disk drives, and flash drives.

- The User State Migration Tool (USMT) is a command-line tool that migrates user data from a previous installation of Windows to a new installation of Windows. It provides you with the ability to customize the user-profile migration experience.

- Windows 10 has many optional features or built-in programs available that provide additional functionality. However, not all of the programs are available after the initial installation. Many of these features are aimed at business networks, which might not be useful for everyone. To install the additional features, you open the Windows Features dialog box and turn on the appropriate feature.

■ Knowledge Assessment

Multiple Choice

Select the correct answer for each of the following questions.

1. Which of the following ScanState.exe command-line options can be used to exclude a single user account from a user state migration?
   a. /ue
   b. /uel
   c. /ui
   d. /uil

2. The ScanState command has been used to collect user files and settings. Which of the following tools can be used to verify that the store is not corrupted?
   a. bcdboot
   b. LoadState
   c. UsmtUtils
   d. bcdedit

3. Which of the following is the maximum size that a VHD format supports?
   a. 1 TB
   b. 2 TB
   c. 4 TB
   d. 16 TB
   e. 64 TB

4. Which of the following allows the computer to mount and boot from the operating system contained within the VHD file?
   a. Bootable USB
   b. Language pack
   c. Hardlink folder
   d. Native VHD boot

5. Which program grabs user files from a system so that you can migrate them to another computer?
   a. ScanState
   b. LoadState
   c. GrabState
   d. HardState

6. Which package is used to localize Windows 10?
   a. .NET Framework
   b. Language pack
   c. Hardlink pack
   d. VHD pack

7. Which Windows 10 graphical program can be used to create a VHD file?
   a. Diskpart
   b. Disk Management Console
   c. USMT
   d. ScanState

8. Which of the following is the minimum USB requirement to use Windows To Go?
   a. USB 1.0
   b. USB 2.0
   c. USB 3.0
   d. USB 3.5

9. Which of the following features allows you to boot a full version of Windows 10 from an external USB drive?
   a. WindowsBootUSB
   b. WindowsUSB
   c. WBootUSB
   d. Windows To Go

10. Which of the following is used to create the Workspace To Go workspace?
    a. ToGo Spawner
    b. Workspace To Go Creator
    c. Workspace Management console
    d. Workspace Cloner

Best Answer

Choose the letter that corresponds to the best answer. More than one answer choice may achieve the goal. Select the BEST answer.

1. Which of the following is the *better* reason to use USMT to migrate user state data rather than Windows Easy Transfer?
   a. Because USMT commands can be incorporated into automated deployment scenarios
   b. Because Windows Easy Transfer only supports certain versions of Windows
   c. Because USMT uses XML-based configuration files
   d. Because Windows Easy Transfer has a graphical interface

2. Which of the following ScanState options provides the strongest encryption for a migration store?
   a. /encrypt:AES_auto
   b. /encrypt:AES_128
   c. /encrypt:AES_192
   d. /encrypt:AES_256

3. Which of the following is the *best* location option for a migration store when there is a shortage of storage space?
   a. Network
   b. Removable
   c. Local
   d. Hardlink

4. Over the next three months, an administrator wants to deploy hundreds of computers running Windows 10. Which of the following strategies should be recommended?
   a. High Touch with Retail Media
   b. High Touch with Standard Image
   c. Lite-Touch, High-Volume Deployment
   d. Zero-Touch, High-Volume Deployment

5. An IT professional for a small company that supports 50 client computers wants to deploy Windows 10 to 20 of the older computers. Which deployment strategy should be used?
   a. High Touch with Retail Media
   b. High Touch with Standard Image
   c. Lite-Touch, High-Volume Deployment
   d. Zero-Touch, High-Volume Deployment

Build a List

1. Specify the correct order of steps necessary to migrate the configuration settings of an unsupported application using USMT.
   List the application settings that need to be migrated.
   Determine which applications are not natively migrated by USMT.
   Create an XML file that specifies which resources to migrate.
   Install Process Monitor.
   Determine what changes to the registry and/or file system each setting makes.

2. Specify the correct order of the four steps that would be used to deploy multiple computers via a Zero-Touch, High-Volume Deployment.
   _____ Test
   _____ Store images
   _____ Plan
   _____ Distribute

■ Business Case Scenarios

Scenario 2-1: Migrating User State Information

Morris is responsible for planning the upgrading of Windows 7 and Windows 8.1 workstations to Windows 10. The deployment must be completed over a weekend. He will be performing a PC-Refresh scenario, installing the new operating system on the same computers and the same volume as the old one.

The workstations have a lot of data to migrate to the new operating system because the users store their email and their document files on local drives.

Morris' biggest problem is allotting the disk space needed for the migration stores. The deployment server cannot handle several gigabytes of user state data from each of 100 workstations, and the workstations have just one hard drive each, with a single volume that is nearly full. Which storage solution can Morris use to support the deployment of large numbers of computers simultaneously?

Scenario 2-2: Booting to a Corporate Windows Image

There are several people in your organization who work from their own home offices. Your manager decides that these users can use their own personal computers as long as they boot from a corporate disk image. What would you recommend that would not delete or change the users' personal systems?

LESSON 3

Configuring Devices and Device Drivers

70-698 EXAM OBJECTIVE

Objective 1.3 – Configure devices and device drivers. This objective may include but is not limited to: Install, update, disable, and roll back drivers; resolve driver issues; configure driver settings, including signed and unsigned drivers; manage driver packages; download and import driver packages; use the Deployment Image Servicing and Management (DISM) tool to add packages.

Objective 3.3 – Configure system and data recovery. This objective may include but is not limited to: Perform a driver rollback; resolve hardware and devices issues; interpret data from Device Manager. * Other Objective 3.3 topics are covered in Lesson 13.

LESSON HEADING	EXAM OBJECTIVE
Managing Devices	
Using the Devices and Printers Folder	
Interpreting Data from Device Manager	Interpret data from Device Manager
Managing Driver Packages	Manage driver packages Download and import driver packages
Installing, Updating, and Disabling Drivers	Install, update, and disable drivers
Rolling Back a Driver	Roll back drivers Perform a driver rollback
Configuring Driver Settings	Configure driver settings, including signed and unsigned drivers
Resolving Hardware Issues, Device Issues, and Driver Issues	Resolve driver issues Resolve hardware and device issues
Using the Deployment Image Servicing and Management (DISM) Tool to Add Packages	Use the Deployment Image Servicing and Management (DISM) tool to add packages
Capturing Images	
Modifying Images Using DISM	

KEY TERMS

Action Center	**disk image**	**signed driver**
Deployment Image Servicing and Management (dism.exe)	**driver package**	**System Preparation Utility (sysprep.exe)**
	driver rollback	
device driver	**driver store**	**Windows Deployment Services (WDS)**
Device Manager	**file-based disk image**	
Devices and Printers	**sector-based disk image**	**Windows Imaging Format (WIM)**

■ MANAGING DEVICES

THE BOTTOM LINE

As most users know, a computer is a collection of hardware devices, all of which are connected together and installed in a single case. Disk drives, keyboards, mice, modems, and printers are all types of devices. To communicate with the operating system running on the computer, each device also requires a software element called a ***device driver***. The device driver provides the operating system with information about a specific device.

Windows 10 includes a large library of device drivers, but sometimes it might be necessary to obtain them yourself. For example, when you use a word-processing application to save a file to a hard disk, the application issues a generic WriteFile function call to the operating system. The application knows nothing specific about the disk drive hardware; it just issues an instruction to store a particular file there. When the operating system processes the function call, it accesses the device driver for the hard disk drive, which provides detailed information about how to communicate with the drive. If the user selects a different target location for the file, the operating system accesses the device driver for that location, whether it's a hard drive, a floppy drive, or a USB flash drive.

In most cases, the information the device driver provides is integrated into the Windows interface. For example, the Properties sheet for a printer includes generic system information, such as its name, model, and features (see Figure 3-1). Other tabs can show which port the printer is connected to and who is permitted to use it. The Device Settings tab (see Figure 3-2) is based on hardware-specific information provided by the device driver.

In addition to providing information about a device, drivers also permit the operating system to modify the hardware configuration settings of the device. For example, when you configure a printer to print a document in landscape mode instead of portrait mode, the printer device driver generates the appropriate command and sends it to the hardware.

The process of installing a hardware device consists primarily of identifying the device and installing a device driver for it. This process can occur during the operating system installation or at a later time, but the steps are fundamentally the same.

Figure 3-1

The General tab of a printer's
Properties sheet

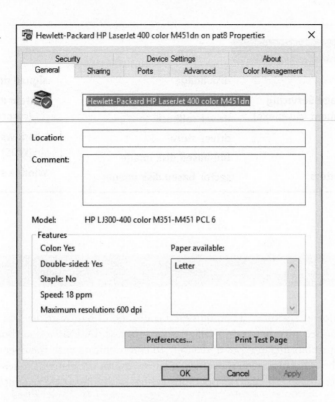

Figure 3-2

The Device Settings tab of a
printer's Properties sheet

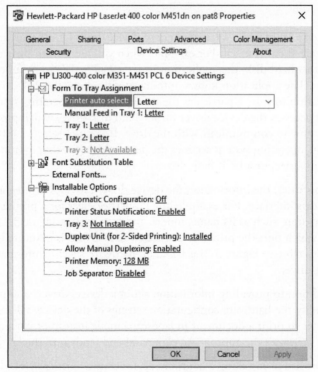

A major part of the Windows 10 installation process consists of identifying the devices in
the computer and installing the appropriate drivers for them. The Windows 10 installation
package includes hundreds of drivers for many different devices, which is why many
installations finish without any user intervention. Sometimes, however, you might have to
supply device drivers yourself.

➕ **MORE** INFORMATION

Printers and printer drivers are covered in more detail in Lesson 8.

Using the Devices and Printers Folder

Windows 10 includes the ***Devices and Printers*** folder, which quickly allows you to see all the devices connected to the computer and to configure and troubleshoot these devices. It also allows you to view information about the make, model, and manufacturer and gives you detailed information about the sync capabilities of a mobile phone or other mobile devices.

The Devices and Printers folder (see Figure 3-3) gives you a quick view of devices connected to your computer that you can connect or disconnect from your computer through a port or network connection. This includes mobile devices, such as music players and digital cameras, USB (Universal Serial Bus) devices, and network devices. It does not include items installed inside your computer, such as internal disk drives, expansion cards, or RAM. It also does not display legacy devices, such as keyboards and mice connected through a PS/2 or serial port.

Figure 3-3

Devices and Printers

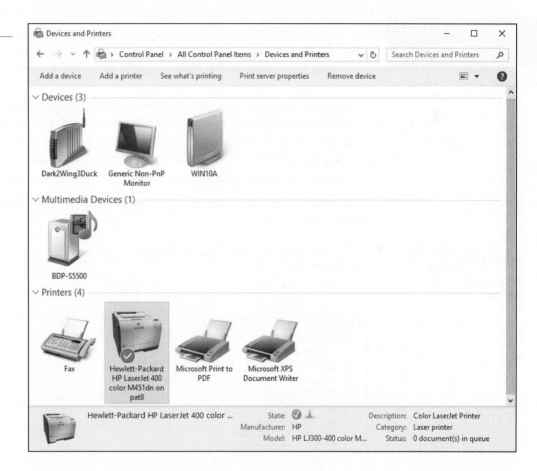

To open the Devices and Printers folder, open Control Panel and, under Hardware and Sound, click View devices and printers while in Category view or double-click Devices and Printers in Icon view.

When you right-click a device icon in the Devices and Printers folder, you can choose from a list of tasks that vary depending on the capabilities of the device. For example, you might be able to see what's printing on a network printer, view files stored on a USB flash drive, or open a program from the device manufacturer. For mobile devices that support the new Device Stage feature in Windows, you can also open advanced, device-specific features in Windows from the context menu, such as the ability to sync with a mobile phone or change ringtones.

Most PCs use USB connections for peripheral devices, and Plug and Play is an integral part of the USB standard. When you connect a printer, a camera, a scanner, or another type of device to a computer running Windows 10 using a USB port, the system usually detects it, adds it to the Devices and Printers folder, and installs the appropriate device driver for it.

You can also manually install a device by selecting Add a device, which displays the Choose a Device or a Printer to Add to This PC page.

Interpreting Data from Device Manager

The Windows 10 tool for managing devices and their drivers is called **Device Manager**. You can use Device Manager to get information about the devices installed in the computer as well as to install, update, and troubleshoot device drivers.

Although it is not immediately apparent, Device Manager is a snap-in for the MMC. This means that there are many ways you can access Device Manager, including the following:

CERTIFICATION READY
Interpret data from
Device Manager
Objective 3.3

- Open the Hardware and Sound control panel and click the Device Manager link.
- Open the Computer Management console from the Administrative Tools program group in the System and Security control panel and then click Device Manager in the scope (left) pane.
- Run the Microsoft Management Console shell application (mmc.exe), select File > Add/Remove Snap-in, and then select Device Manager from the list of snap-ins provided.
- Open the Start menu, type Device Manager or the file name of the Device Manager snap-in (Devmgmt.msc), and then execute the resulting file.
- Search for Device Manager using Cortana and then execute the resulting file.

Each procedure launches Device Manager and displays a window with an interface like that shown in Figure 3-4.

Figure 3-4

The Windows 10 Device
Manager

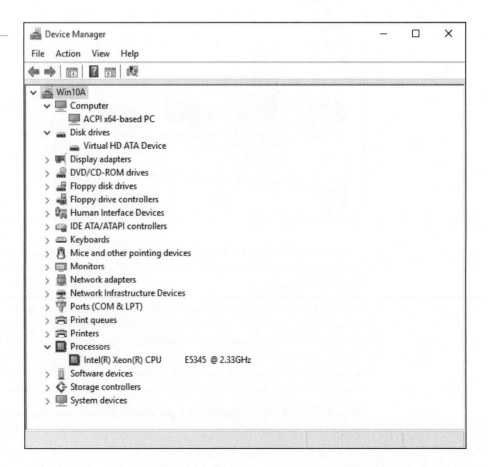

Device Manager is capable of displaying information in the following four modes:

- **Devices by type:** Displays a list of device categories, which you can expand to show the devices in each category. This is the default Device Manager view.
- **Devices by connection:** Displays a list of the interfaces that hardware devices use to communicate with the computer. Expanding a connection shows the devices using that connection.
- **Resources by type:** Displays a list of resource types, including Direct Memory Access (DMA), Input/Output (I/O), Interrupt Request (IRQ), and Memory, which you can expand to show the resources of each type and the devices that are using them.
- **Resources by connection:** Displays a list of resource types, including Direct Memory Access (DMA), Input/Output (I/O), Interrupt Request (IRQ), and Memory, which you can expand to show the connection associated with each individual resource and the device using each connection.

To examine the properties of a device, simply locate it in the tree display and double-click it to open its Properties sheet.

The tabs on the Properties sheet vary depending on the nature of the device you select, but virtually all devices have the following four tabs:

- **General:** Displays the name of the device, its type, the manufacturer, and its location in the system. The Device Status box indicates whether the device is functioning and, if not, provides troubleshooting help.
- **Driver:** Displays the device driver's provider, date, version, and digital signer. The tab also provides buttons you can use to display driver details, update, roll back (used when an upgrade of a device driver fails or causes problems with a system), or uninstall the driver, and enable or disable the device.
- **Detail:** Displays extensive information about the driver and its properties.
- **Resources:** Displays the hardware resources being used by the device and indicates whether there are any conflicts with other devices in the computer.

Managing Driver Packages

The **driver store** is the Windows 10 driver package repository, which is located in the %SystemRoot%\System32\DriverStore folder. When you connect compatible hardware, Windows 10 installs the driver from the appropriate device automatically from the driver store. Administrators and standard users can connect a device and Windows will install the appropriate device driver from the driver store without assistance from the IT help desk. Corporate administrators can preload the driver store and remove unnecessary drivers to control which devices can be used with the corporate systems.

CERTIFICATION READY
Manage driver packages
Objective 1.3

A **driver package** is a set of files that make up a driver. A driver package includes:

- The .inf file
- Any files that the .inf file references
- The catalog (.cat) file that contains the digital signature of the device driver

CERTIFICATION READY
Download and import
driver packages
Objective 1.3

The drivers may come with the device, or may be downloaded from the manufacturer's website. The process of copying a driver package to the driver store is called staging. Before the driver package is copied to the driver store, the operating system verifies that the digital signature is correct.

To view the list of installed device drivers, you can use the following command:

```
driverquery.exe
```

To list all third-party packages, execute the following command:

```
pnputil.exe -e
```

To add packages in the C:\Drivers folders, execute the following command:

`pnputil.exe -a c:\drivers\*.inf`

To add and install a driver package, execute the following command:

`pnputil.exe -i -a d:\usbcam\usbcam.inf`

To delete a package, execute the following command:

`pnputil.exe -d oem0.inf`

Installing, Updating, and Disabling Drivers

When you connect a device, Windows automatically tries to identify the device and load the appropriate driver. However, if the driver cannot be loaded, you will need to manually install the driver with Device Manager, or run a third-party program (provided on disc with the device or downloaded from the manufacturer's website) to install the driver. Device Manager can also be used to update, disable, and roll back device drivers.

CERTIFICATION READY
Install, update, and disable drivers
Objective 1.3

When you install or update a driver using Device Manager, you can point to a location on your computer where you have already saved the new driver or you can run a search of your computer and the Internet. To install or update a device driver, use the following procedure.

 INSTALL OR UPDATE A DEVICE DRIVER

GET READY. Log on to Windows 10 using an account with administrator privileges and then perform the following steps.

1. Open **Device Manager** and then locate the device that you want to update.
2. Double-click the device you want to update, so that its Properties sheet appears.
3. Click the **Driver** tab and then click the **Update Driver** button. The How Do You Want to Search for Driver Software? page appears, as shown in Figure 3-5.

Figure 3-5

The How Do You Want to Search for Driver Software? page

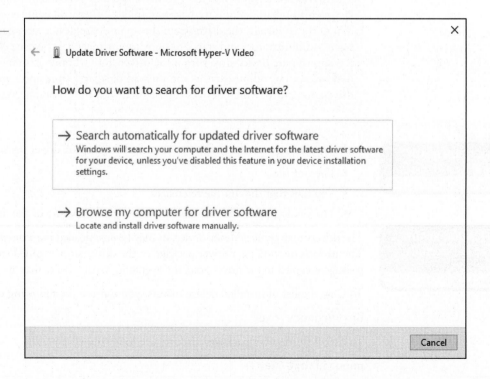

4. Click **Browse my computer for driver software** to specify a location for the driver or to select from a list of installed drivers. Click **Search automatically for updated driver software** to initiate a search for a driver.

5. Click **Next** when you locate the driver you want to install. The Windows Has Successfully Updated Your Driver Software page appears.

6. Click **Close**.

7. Close the Device Manager window.

With Device Manager, you can disable any device in the computer, using any of the following procedures:

- Select the device and choose Disable from the Action menu.
- Right-click the device and choose Disable from the context menu.
- Open the device's Properties sheet and then click the Disable button on the Driver tab.

Disabling a device does not affect the hardware in any way or uninstall the device driver; it simply renders the device inoperative until you enable it again. Obviously, you cannot disable devices that are necessary for the system to function, such as the processor, and some devices that are in use require you to restart the system before they can be disabled.

TAKE NOTE

Disabling a device releases the hardware resources it was using back to the operating system. If you restart the computer with the device disabled, Windows might reassign those hardware resources to other devices. If you reenable the device, the computer might allocate different hardware resources to it than it had originally.

Rolling Back a Driver

Driver rollback is a system recovery feature in Windows 10 that enables you to reinstall the last device driver that was functioning.

CERTIFICATION READY
Roll back drivers
Objective 1.3

CERTIFICATION READY
Perform a driver rollback
Objective 3.3

When you update a device driver in Windows 10, the operating system does not discard the old driver completely. It is not uncommon for new drivers to cause more problems than they solve, and many users find that they would prefer to go back to the old version. Windows 10 makes this possible with the Roll Back feature, which you initiate by clicking the Roll Back Driver button on the Driver tab of the device's Properties sheet. This procedure uninstalls the current driver and reinstalls the previous version, returning the device to its state before you performed the most recent driver update.

Installing a new hardware device or a new device driver is a risky undertaking. There is always the possibility of a problem that, depending on the devices involved, could be trivial or catastrophic. For a peripheral device, such as a printer, a hardware misconfiguration or faulty driver would probably just cause the new device to malfunction. However, if the device involved is a graphics adapter, a bad driver could prevent the system from functioning.

Fortunately, when you update a device driver, the previous driver package is automatically saved and information is added into the registry. This allows you to roll back one prior driver version. If the current driver is the only one that was ever installed, the Roll Back feature is not available. Roll Back is not available if you have not updated the driver in the past.

ROLL BACK A DEVICE DRIVER

GET READY. To roll back a device driver, log on with local administrative privileges and then perform the following steps.

1. Right-click the **Start** button and click **Device Manager**.
2. Expand **Network Adapters**.
3. Right-click the adapter and choose **Update Driver Software**.
4. Click **Browse my computer for driver software**.
5. Click **Let me pick from a list of device drivers on my computer**.
6. Deselect **Show compatible hardware**.
7. Select **Marvell** for the manufacturer, select **Microsoft Network Adapter Multiplexor Driver** for the network adapter, and then click **Next**.
8. When an update driver warning appears, click **Yes**. When Windows alerts you that a problem was encountered while installing the driver, click **Close**.
9. Right-click the adapter and click **Properties**.
10. Click the **Driver** tab and then click **Roll Back Driver**.
11. When prompted to roll back the driver, click **Yes**.
12. Click **Close** to exit out of the Adapter Properties dialog box and then close the Device Manager window.

Configuring Driver Settings

> Configuring driver settings has been discussed throughout this lesson, including accessing the various dialog boxes using the Devices and Printers folder and Device Manager. This includes changing the settings or resources for an individual device.

CERTIFICATION READY
Configure driver settings, including signed and unsigned drivers
Objective 1.3

Windows was designed to work with a large array of devices. Unfortunately, in the past, there were times when a device was added and a driver was loaded, and the driver caused problems with Windows. As a result, Microsoft started using signed drivers to help fight faulty drivers. Although signed drivers do not fix a faulty driver, they do make sure that the publisher of the driver is identified, the driver has not been altered, and the driver has been thoroughly tested to be reliable so that it will not cause a security problem.

A *signed driver* is a device driver that includes a digital signature, which is an electronic security mark that can indicate the publisher of the software and provide information that can show if a driver has been altered. When signed by Microsoft, a driver has been thoroughly tested to make sure that it will not cause problems with the system's reliability or security.

Drivers that are included on the Windows installation DVD or downloaded from the Microsoft update website are digitally signed if they pass the Windows Hardware Quality Lab (WHQL) compatibility tests. A driver that lacks a valid digital signature, or was altered after it was signed, cannot be installed on 64-bit versions of Windows. If you have problems with a device driver, you should only download drivers from the Microsoft update website or the manufacturer's website.

TAKE NOTE
On a 64-bit version of Windows 10, you cannot install a driver that lacks a valid digital signature or that has been altered after it was signed.

Windows 10 comes in 32-bit and 64-bit versions. All drivers must be signed for 64-bit versions of Windows 10. If you are using a newer version of Windows that is not a 64-bit version, you can use the File Signature Verification program (Sigverif.exe) to check for unsigned device drivers in the system area of a computer.

DISABLE DRIVER SIGNATURE ENFORCEMENT

GET READY. To disable driver signature enforcement, log on with local administrative privileges and then perform the following steps.

1. Click the **Start** button and click **Settings**.
2. When the Settings window opens, click **Update and security**.
3. Click the **Recovery** tab.
4. Under Advanced Startup, click **Restart now**.
5. On the Choose an Option page, click the **Troubleshoot** option.
6. On the Troubleshoot page, click **Advanced options**.
7. On the Advanced Options page, click **Startup Settings**.
8. Click **Restart**.
9. On the Startup Settings page (as shown in Figure 3-6), press **7** or **F7** to disable driver signature enforcement.

Figure 3-6

Startup Settings page

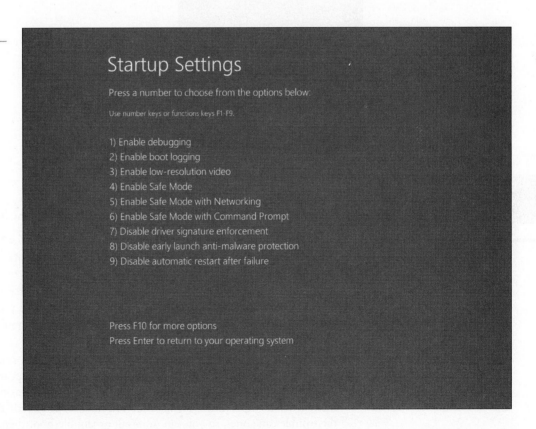

Your computer will restart and you will be able to install non-digitally signed drivers. If you restart your computer again, the driver signature enforcement will be reenabled.

CERTIFICATION READY
Resolve driver issues
Objective 1.3

Resolving Hardware Issues, Device Issues, and Driver Issues

The *Action Center* (as shown in Figure 3-7) shows important notifications related to the security and maintenance of your computer. When problems occur, you will be alerted to investigate them further.

Figure 3-7

Viewing the Action Center

CERTIFICATION READY
Resolve hardware and
device issues
Objective 3.3

To troubleshoot hardware or driver problems, consider some of the following techniques:

- Open the Properties sheet for the device and check the Device Status box on the General tab. If the device is malfunctioning, this tab informs you of its status and enables you to launch a troubleshooter.

- Open Device Manager and delete the device entirely. Then restart the system and allow Windows 10 to detect and install the device over again. This process causes Windows to reallocate hardware resources to the device, which could resolve the problem if it was caused by a hardware resource conflict.

- If the device or driver malfunction prevents the system from running properly, as in the case of a bad graphics driver that prevents an image from appearing on the screen, you can start the computer in Safe mode by pressing the F8 key as the system starts. Safe mode loads the operating system with a minimal set of generic device drivers, bypassing the troublesome ones, so you can uninstall or troubleshoot them.

Device Manager also displays all of the devices installed on your computer. When a device is experiencing problems, Device Manager uses symbols to provide information about the particular error condition.

When there is an issue with a device, you will see one of the following symbols (each symbol represents a specific type of problem):

- **Blue question mark inside white circle:** The driver installed; it might not provide full functionality.
- **Red "X":** The device is installed in the computer and is consuming resources; the protected mode driver is not loaded; the device installed improperly.
- **Black exclamation point on yellow field:** The device is in a problem state; the device might be functioning; problem code will be displayed with the device.
- **Blue "I" on white field:** Use automatic settings not selected for the device; the resource was manually selected; this does not indicate a problem or disabled state.
- **White circle with down arrow:** The device was disabled by an administrator or user.
- **Yellow warning symbol with exclamation point:** There is a problem with the device.

When you open the properties of a device that is experiencing problems, Device Manager displays a problem code that can help identify a specific problem.

Windows 10 uses built-in hardware diagnostics to detect hardware problems on your computer. When problems are identified, a message appears that lets you know about the problem. If you select the message, the Action Center appears, which provides a central location to view any problems with your hardware or software.

When there is a problem, you will see two types of messages in the notification area (the lower-right corner of your desktop):

- **Red items (white flag, red circle with white x):** These are important messages that indicate a significant problem that needs to be addressed. For example, your firewall is turned off or spyware or antivirus applications need to be updated.
- **Yellow items:** These are messages that suggest tasks that can make your computer run better—for example, updating an application or configuring Windows Update to automatically download and install updates rather than checking with you beforehand.

How you troubleshoot a device depends upon the type of problem you encounter. For example, when you notice a device with the black exclamation point in a yellow triangle, you can double-click the device to investigate the problem further. Figure 3-8 shows that the device cannot start and the specified request is not a valid operation for the target device.

Figure 3-8

Troubleshooting a device

Another item of interest when troubleshooting device problems is to look for an Other Devices folder. This folder contains devices detected by Windows but lacking a driver for the device.

■ USING THE DEPLOYMENT IMAGE SERVICING AND MANAGEMENT (DISM) TOOL TO ADD PACKAGES

↓
THE BOTTOM LINE

A *disk image* is a single file or storage device that contains the complete contents and structures of a disk. The image has the necessary information to install a copy of Windows onto another machine. Often, the images contain additional software packages, drivers, and features, which are also deployed as a single, complete package. To service a Windows image, you would use the command-line tool *Deployment Image Servicing and Management (dism.exe)*.

CERTIFICATION READY
Use the Deployment
Image Servicing and
Management (DISM) tool
to add packages
Objective 1.3

The simplest use of an image is as a reference or master computer. On the reference computer, you install Windows and any necessary drivers, you configure Windows, and then you configure additional software. In addition, you update Windows and any applications that run on the computer. When you finish, the reference computer is a pristine computer that is ready to be used by the user. Instead of giving the computer to a user, you take a snapshot of the computer by copying the drive's contents to an image file. The image can be stored and accessed from a central location so that it can be copied to other computers.

Some system image programs use sector-based images and others use file-based images. A *sector-based disk image* copies each sector to a file. One well-known example of a sector-based image is an ISO image, which is an image of a CD or DVD disk. One problem with using sector-based images is that you must take additional steps to remove the computer name and the security identifier (SID), which uniquely identifies a computer running Windows on a network. In addition, sector-based images might not work when installed to computers that run on different hardware.

A *file-based disk image* captures images based on files on the disk. The advantage of using a file-based image is that it is hardware-independent, so it can be deployed to computers that are using different hardware. It uses single-instance storage, which keeps a single copy of a file that may be referenced multiple times in a file system tree. When applying a file-based image, the applied image is nondestructive, which means that data files still exist after the image has been applied. Examples of file-based images include virtual hard disk (.vhd) and Windows Imaging Format (WIM).

A *Windows Imaging Format (WIM)* file is a file-based image format developed by Microsoft that enables a file structure (folders and files) to be stored inside a single WIM database. WIM files have the following features:

- They incorporate compression.
- They enable multiple images to be included in a single WIM file.
- They use single-instancing of files when multiple WIM files are appended.
- Because WIM image format is a file-based image, it can be used on different hardware platforms and various size disks.

WIM file format supports offline servicing, which enables you to open a WIM file in Windows and directly add or remove folders, files, drivers, and operating system components.

Capturing Images

> After configuring the reference computer, you use the sysprep command to prepare the computer for capturing and shutdown of the computer. You can then use DISM to capture the reference computer to an image file.

To manually capture the image using DISM, you need to perform the following tasks:

1. Boot the computer using Windows PE.
2. Map a drive to a network share.
3. Use Diskpart to assign a drive letter to any partitions that you need to capture that do not have any drive letters assigned. Unless you customized the system partition, you will not have to create an image of it because it will be automatically re-created.
4. Use DISM to capture the system partition (if the system partition has been customized).
5. Use DISM to capture the primary partitions and any logical partitions.

Before capturing a computer, you need to prepare the reference computer with the sysprep.exe utility. The Microsoft *System Preparation Utility (sysprep.exe)* prepares a Windows computer for cloning by removing specific computer information, such as the computer name and security identifier (SID). On Windows 10, sysprep.exe is located in the C:\Windows\System32\Sysprep folder.

The sysprep.exe command supports the following options:

- **/generalize:** Instructs sysprep to remove system-specific data (such as event logs, the computer name, and unique SIDs) from the Windows operating system installation.
- **/oobe:** Instructs Windows to present the Windows Welcome Wizard when the computer starts next time. The Windows Welcome Wizard enables you to name the computer and generate an SID and any other required unique information.
- **/shutdown:** Instructs the computer to shut down and not to restart.
- **/audit:** Instructs the Windows operating system installation to run in audit mode the next time that the computer starts.
- **/reboot:** Instructs the computer to restart. Use this option if you want to verify that the OOBE phase runs correctly.
- **/quiet:** Runs sysprep without displaying on-screen confirmation messages. If you automate sysprep, use this option with an answer file.
- **/unattend:answerfile:** Applies settings in an answer file to sysprep.

The basic command to prepare a computer for imaging is

```
sysprep /generalize /oobe /shutdown
```

To actually capture the images using the DISM command and save the .wim files to the C drive, use the following commands:

```
DISM /Capture-Image /ImageFile:c:\windows-partition.wim /
CaptureDir:C:\ /Name:"Windows partition"
```

```
DISM /Capture-Image /ImageFile:s:\system-partition.wim /CaptureDir:C:\
/Name:"System partition"
```

Note that you can also save the image directly to a network shared folder.

When you use the /Capture-Image option, you can use the following options:

- **/ConfigFile:** Specifies the location of a configuration file that lists exclusions for image capture and compress commands.
- **/Compress:** Specifies the type of compression (maximum, fast, and none) used for the initial capture operation.
- **/Bootable:** Marks a volume image as being a bootable image. This option can be used only with Windows PE images and only one volume image can be marked as bootable in a .wim file.
- **/CheckIntegrity:** Detects and tracks .wim file corruption when used with capture, unmount, export, and commit operations.
- **/Verify:** Checks for errors and file duplication.
- **/NoRpFix:** Disables the reparse point tag fix. A reparse point is a file that contains a link to another file on the file system.

When you capture the image, you need a place to store the image. Therefore, you need to share a folder so that it can be accessed over the network. After you boot the reference computer with Windows PE, you have to execute the following command:

```
Net Use G: \\Server01\Images
```

You are then prompted to enter a user name and password. Use the following two commands to copy the image files to the network share:

```
copy C:\windows-partition.wim G:\Images\
```

```
copy c:\system-partition.wim G:\Images\
```

Another tool that can be used to create an image is *Windows Deployment Services (WDS)*. WDS is a Windows server role used to deploy Windows (Windows XP and above and Windows Server 2003 and above) over the network with little or no user intervention. If the client can perform a PXE boot, you perform an installation over a network with no operating system or local boot device on it. The WDS server can store and help administrators manage the boot and operating system image files used in the network installations.

Besides deploying Windows, WDS can also capture a Windows image using the Windows DS Capture Image program. To capture an image with WDS, you need to perform the following tasks:

1. Modify an existing boot image to create a capture image.
2. Boot the reference computer with the modified boot image.
3. Run the Windows Deployment Service Capture Utility.

When you use the Windows Deployment Service Capture Utility, you can use it to capture only volumes that contain operating systems prepared with sysprep. In addition, the wizard can save an image only to a local drive letter. Although you could use a mapped network drive, it is recommended to use a local location to avoid corruption due to network problems.

Modifying Images Using DISM

If you are using the Deployment Image Servicing and Management (DISM) tool, available on the Windows Assessment and Deployment Kit (Windows ADK), you can apply an existing corporate Windows 10 image (.wim) file to a VHD file, which is used with virtual machines running on Hyper-V. DISM is a command-line tool used to service Windows images offline before they are deployed. It can also be used to install, uninstall, configure, and update Windows packages and drivers. This image can be deployed to computers on which an operating system is installed or computers without an operating system present.

DISM has the /Online or /image option. The /Online image specifies that the action is to be taken on the operating system that is currently running. The /image is used to specify an offline Windows image.

To modify an image file, you must mount the Windows image in an NTFS volume using the Mount-Wim option. For example, to mount the D:\Images\install.wim file to the C:\Offline folder, use the following command:

```
Dism /Mount-Wim /WimFile: D:\Images\install.wim /index:1 /MountDir:C:\
Offline
```

After you make changes to the image, you need to commit the changes by using the /Commit-Wim option:

```
Dism /Commit-Wim /MountDir:C:\Offline
```

When using DISM to modify an image, you must first mount the image. When done, you must then commit the changes and dismount the image. To unmount the image, use the /Unmount-Wim option. If you want to commit the changes while you unmount the image, add the /Commit option. To discard the changes, use the /Discard option. For example, to unmount the image mounted to the C:\Offline folder while saving the changes, execute the following command:

```
Dism /Unmount-Wim /MountDir:C:\offline /commit
```

To get information about an image or WIM file, use the /Get-WimInfo option. For example, to get information about the C:\offline\winstall.wim file, execute the following command:

```
Dism /Get-WimInfo /WimFile:C:\offline\install.wim /index:1
```

Microsoft updates, hotfixes, service packs, and language packs are usually downloaded from Microsoft as a Windows Update stand-alone Installer (.msu) file but sometimes can be downloaded or extracted as a cabinet (.cab) file. The .cab file can usually be extracted from the .msu file using the extract.exe command. To add the software updates hotfix, service pack, and language pack that is in a cabinet (.cab) file or as a Windows Update stand-alone Installer (.msu) file, you can add the package using the /Add-Package option. For example, to add the C:\Update\Update.cab file, execute the following command:

```
Dism /image:C:\offline /Add-Package /Packagepath:C:\Update\Update.cab
```

To remove a package, use the /Remove-Package option. For example, to remove the update.cab file, execute the following command:

```
Dism /image:C:\offline /Remove-Package /PackagePath:C:\Update\Update.
cab
```

You can use the /Add-Driver option to add third-party driver packages that include a valid INF file. For example, to add mydriver to the Windows image, execute the following command:

```
Dism /image:C:\offline /Add-Driver /Driver:C:\Drivers\mydriver.INF
```

If you point to a path and use /Recurse, all subfolders will be checked for valid drivers. For example, to add drivers from the C:\Drivers folder, execute the following command:

```
Dism /image:C:\offline /Add-Driver /driver:C:\Drivers /Recurse
```

To remove a third-party device driver, use the /Remove-Driver option to specify the name of a device driver (such as oem0.inf, oem1.inf, and so on). For example, to remove the second third-party driver (oem1.inf) that has been added to the system, execute the following command:

```
Dism /image:C:\offline /Remove-Driver /Driver:oem1.inf
```

To get a list of features that are on an image, execute the following command:

```
Dism /Image:C:\offline /Get-Features |more
```

To enable a specific feature on an image, such as TelnetClient, execute the following command:

```
Dism /image:C:\offline /Enable-Feature /FeatureName:TelnetClient
```

To disable a specific feature on an image, such as TelnetClient, execute the following command:

```
Dism /image:C:\offline /Disable-Feature /FeatureName:TelnetClient
```

If an image is too large for the intended media (such as a CD), you can split the file into multiple parts by using the /Split-Image option. When the /Split-Image option is used, multiple .swm files will be created, starting with filename.swm, filename2.swm, filename3.swm, and so on. For example, to split an image called E:\Images\BasicImage.wim to the E:\Images\SplitBasicImages.swm with a maximum file size of 600 MB, execute the following command:

```
Dism /Split-Image /ImageFile:E:\Images\BasicImage.wim /SWMFile:E:\
imaging\SplitBasicImages.swm /FileSize:600
```

To add an image to an existing .wim file, you would use the /Append-Image switch instead of the /Capture-Image command:

```
Dism /Append-Image /ImageFile:c:\windows-partition.wim /CaptureDir:C:\
/Name:"Windows partition"
```

SKILL SUMMARY

IN THIS LESSON YOU LEARNED:

- To communicate with the operating system running on the computer, each device also requires a software element called a device driver. The device driver provides the operating system with information about a specific device.

- Windows 10 includes the Devices and Printers folder, which quickly allows you to see all the devices connected to the computer and to configure and troubleshoot these devices. It also allows you to view information about the make, model, and manufacturer and gives you detailed information about the sync capabilities of a mobile phone or other mobile devices.

- The Windows 10 tool for managing devices and their drivers is called Device Manager. You can use Device Manager to get information about the devices installed in the computer as well as to install, update, and troubleshoot device drivers.

- The driver store is the Windows 10 driver package repository, which is located in the %SystemRoot%\System32\DriverStore folder. When you connect compatible hardware, Windows 10 installs the driver from the appropriate device automatically from the driver store.

- A driver package is a set of files that make up a driver. A driver package includes the .inf file, any files that the .inf file references, and the catalog (.cat) file that contains the digital signature of the device driver.

- A disk image is a single file or storage device that contains the complete contents and structures of a disk. The image has the necessary information to install a copy of Windows onto another machine.

- To service a Windows image, you would use the command-line tool Deployment Image Servicing and Management (dism.exe).

Multiple Choice

Select the correct answer for each of the following questions.

1. Which of the following can be used to roll back a faulty printer driver?
   a. Print Management Console
   b. Device Manager
   c. Activity Center
   d. Rollback.exe

2. Driver signing ensures that the driver files provided for Windows 10 are compatible, reliable, and function appropriately with the operating system. Which of the following is responsible for managing how drivers are digitally signed?
   a. Windows Hardware Quality Labs (WHQLs)
   b. Network administrators
   c. Windows Device Quality Labs (WDQLs)
   d. Windows Device Signature Labs (WDSLs)

3. Which of the following indicate how the computer will respond when a user tries to install device drivers that are not digitally signed? (Choose all that apply.)
   a. Block
   b. Ignore
   c. Warn
   d. Alert

4. When a device has been disabled, which of the following symbols appear?
   a. Blue "I" on a white field
   b. Red "X"
   c. Black exclamation point on a yellow field
   d. Blue "X"

5. When an administrator is ready to capture an image that will be used with future deployments, which of the following actions must be performed in order to remove the computer name and other specific computer information?
   a. Run the DISM command.
   b. Run Startnet.cmd.
   c. Run sysprep.
   d. Attach a vdisk.

6. Before modifying a WIM image, which of the following actions must be performed?
   a. Mount the image.
   b. Dismount all other WIM images.
   c. Commit the changes.
   d. Run sysprep.

7. When modifying the changes, which of the following options is used with the DISM command to finalize the changes?
   a. /finalize
   b. /commit
   c. /save
   d. /done

8. Which type of file is used to add a Microsoft Windows update to a WIM image using the DISM command? (Choose all that apply.)
   a. .exe
   b. .msi
   c. .cab
   d. .msu

9. Which of the following is included in a driver package? (Choose all that apply.)
   a. Any files that the .inf file references
   b. The executable file
   c. The catalog (.cat) file
   d. The .inf file

10. Which command can be used to manually add a package to the driver store?
    a. Driverquery
    b. Pnputil
    c. Slmgr.vbs
    d. sysprep

Best Answer

Choose the letter that corresponds to the best answer. More than one answer choice may achieve the goal. Select the BEST answer.

1. An administrator loads a driver for a new scanner, and now the scanner does not work. Which of the following is the *best* way to restore the old driver so that the scanner will work properly?
   a. Run the Device Manager troubleshooter.
   b. Manually install the old driver.
   c. Perform a system recovery.
   d. Roll back the driver.

2. While running Windows 10 and connecting to a shared print queue using a v4 driver, which of the following locations is the *least* likely location from which the driver will be downloaded?
   a. WSUS server
   b. Windows Update
   c. Windows 10 local driver store
   d. From the print server itself

Matching and Identification

1. Write the DISM command that is used to perform each respective function.
   1. Remove a package.
   2. Mount a WIM image.
   3. Add a driver.
   4. Commit the changes to the image.
   5. Unmount a WIM image.

Build a List

1. Specify the correct order of the steps that must be completed to roll back a device driver.
   _____ Click Roll Back Driver.
   _____ Open Device Manager.
   _____ Right-click the device and select Properties.
   _____ When prompted to roll back the driver, click Yes.
   _____ Click the Driver tab.

■ Business Case Scenarios

Scenario 3-1: Troubleshooting Print Devices

A user has contacted you because he cannot print documents to a device that is directly connected to a USB port. After talking to him, you discover that he updated the driver before leaving the office yesterday. What is the problem and how should you address it?

Scenario 3-2: Working with Images

You are an administrator for the Contoso Corporation. The previous administrator has created images that the help desk deploys on new computers. The company developers have updated the company inventory program, and the program needs to be installed on any future programs. What should you do?

4 LESSON

Performing Post-Installation Configuration

70-698 EXAM OBJECTIVE

Objective 1.4 – Perform post-installation configuration. This objective may include but is not limited to: Configure and customize start menu, desktop, taskbar, and notification settings, according to device type; configure accessibility options; configure Cortana; configure Microsoft Edge; configure Internet Explorer; configure Hyper-V; configure power settings.

Lesson Heading	Exam Objective
Configuring Windows 10	
Configuring and Customizing the Start Menu, Desktop, Taskbar, and Notification Settings	Configure and customize start menu, desktop, taskbar, and notification settings, according to device type
Using Windows 10 Settings	
Using Control Panel	
Configuring System Settings	
Changing Date and Time	
Configuring Accessibility Options	Configure accessibility options
Configuring Power Settings	Configure power settings
Configuring Cortana	Configure Cortana
Understanding the Registry	
Configuring Internet Explorer	Configure Internet Explorer
Managing Cookies and Privacy Settings	
Configuring Security Zones	
Using Dynamic Security and Protected Mode	
Configuring SmartScreen Filter and Phishing	
Managing Add-Ons	

LESSON HEADING	EXAM OBJECTIVE
Configuring Compatibility Mode	
Configuring Security Sockets Layer (SSL) and Certificates	
Managing Favorites	
Managing LAN Settings	
Configuring Microsoft Edge	Configure Microsoft Edge
Configuring Hyper-V	Configure Hyper-V
Creating and Configuring Virtual Machines	
Creating and Managing Virtual Switches	
Creating and Managing Virtual Disks	
Creating and Managing Checkpoints	

KEYTERMS

accessibility options	favorites	Pop-up Blocker
ActiveX controls	hibernate mode	power plan
ActiveX Filtering	host	proxy server
add-ons	hybrid mode	registry
Administrative Tools	Hyper-V Manager	Secure Sockets Layer (SSL)
checkpoint	Hyper-V Virtual Machine Connection	security zones
Client Hyper-V	hypervisor	sleep mode
Compatibility View	InPrivate Browsing	sleep settings
Computer Management	Internet Explorer	SmartScreen Filter
Control Panel	live tiles	Startup RAM
cookie	Microsoft Edge	taskbar
Cortana	Microsoft Management Console (MMC)	Tracking Protection
desktop		virtual disk
differencing virtual disk	Network Address Translation (NAT)	virtual machine (VM)
Dynamic Memory	phishing	virtual machine monitor (VMM)
dynamic security	pin	Windows 10 Settings
Ease of Access Center		

■ CONFIGURING WINDOWS 10

THE BOTTOM LINE

Windows 10 is a robust and flexible system that is made to work on and support a wide range of hardware. For example, Windows 10 can work on a tablet, a laptop, or a desktop computer. Windows 10 also supports mobile devices so that you can take your computer or device with you while accessing your files and programs.

Because Windows 10 contains a graphical user interface, the primary tools to configure Windows are Windows 10 Settings and Control Panel, which are also graphical tools.

Configuring and Customizing the Start Menu, Desktop, Taskbar, and Notification Settings

The *desktop* (as shown in Figure 4-1) is the main screen that you see when you first start the computer and log on to Windows. Like the top of an actual desktop, it is where you perform your work by opening and running one or more applications. It also includes the Recycle Bin, which is used to recover files that have been previously deleted.

CERTIFICATION READY
Configure and customize start menu, desktop, taskbar, and notification settings, according to device type
Objective 1.4

At the bottom of the desktop, you will find the *taskbar*, which shows you the programs that are running and allows you to navigate between those programs. On the taskbar, the Start button is shown at the lower-left corner.

When you click the Start button, you open the Windows 10 Start menu (see Figure 4-2), which is a blend of the Windows 7 Start menu and the Windows 8 Start screen.

Figure 4-1

Viewing the Windows 10 desktop

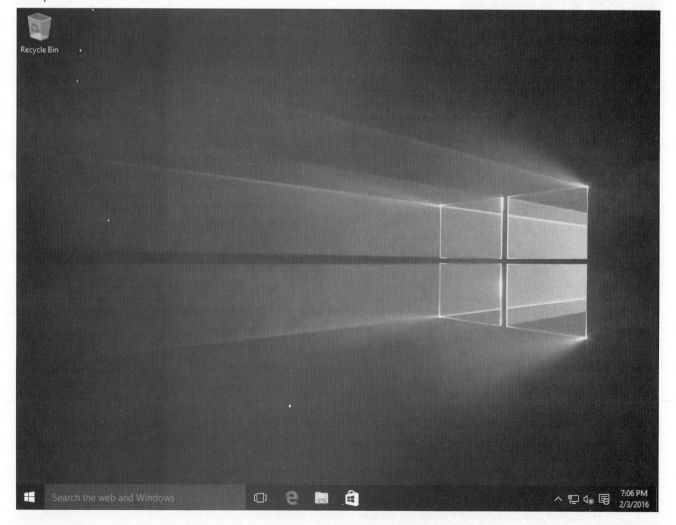

Figure 4-2

Opening the Windows 10
Start menu

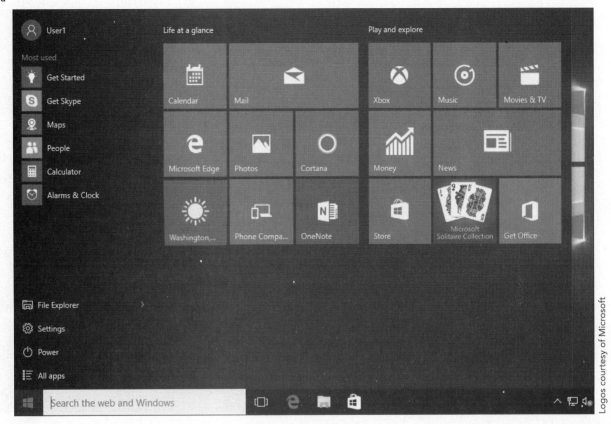

The left side of the Windows 10 Start menu shows the most used programs and provides you with access to File Explorer, Settings, Power, and All apps. When you click All programs, all installed programs are shown in alphabetical order (see Figure 4-3). When you right-click an installed application, you can choose Pin to Start or Pin to taskbar.

When you *pin* a program, the icon for that program displays on the taskbar even when the program isn't running. This provides you with quick access to your frequently used programs. Shortcuts for Task View, Microsoft Edge, File Explorer, and Store appear there by default. You can unpin programs from the taskbar as well. You'll learn about shortcuts later in this lesson.

The right side of the Windows 10 Start menu displays tiles, which are larger than the icons found on the Windows desktop. Unlike the static icons, tiles can contain dynamic content provided by the software they represent. For example, the tile for a web browser can contain a thumbnail of the currently open website, while the Messaging tile can display part of your latest incoming email. Tiles in Windows 10 that contain this type of dynamic content are called *live tiles*.

The tiles on the Start menu are configurable in a number of ways. You can move the tiles around, change their size, change their groupings, and control whether they display live content. It is also possible to remove seldom-used tiles and add new tiles for applications, files, and shortcuts on the computer.

Figure 4-3

Accessing Windows 10
All programs

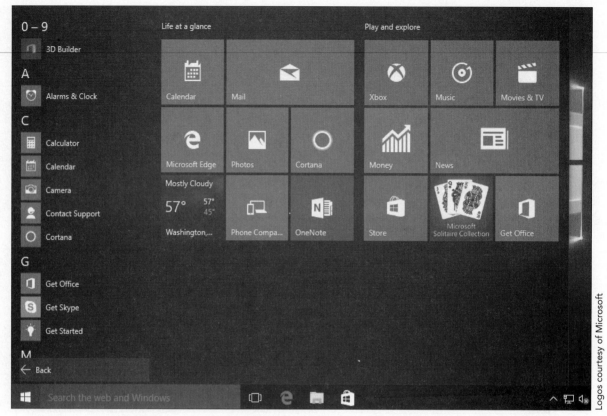

Logos courtesy of Microsoft

USING A TOUCH SCREEN

Windows 10 can be used with a pointing device (such as a mouse, trackball, or glide pad) or by using a touch screen. Operating a touch screen requires familiarity with certain finger gestures, such as the following:

- **Tap:** Press a fingertip to the screen and release it. This function is identical to that of a mouse click.
- **Double-tap:** Press a fingertip to the screen twice in quick succession on the same spot. This function is identical to that of a double-click.
- **Press and hold:** Tap a point on the screen and press down for approximately two seconds. This function is the same as that of mousing over a designated spot and hovering.
- **Slide:** Press a point on the screen and draw your finger across it without pausing. This function is the same as clicking and dragging a mouse.
- **Swipe:** Draw a finger across the screen in the indicated direction.

To customize the taskbar, right-click it and then click Properties to open the Taskbar and Start Menu Properties (as shown in Figure 4-4). The Taskbar tab allows you to specify the following settings:

- **Lock the taskbar:** Prevents the taskbar from being moved or resized.
- **Auto-hide the taskbar:** Hides the taskbar until you hover the mouse pointer over the area where it is hidden.
- **Use small taskbar buttons:** Reduces the size of the taskbar by changing the size of the icons, which in turn changes the width of the taskbar.

- **Taskbar location on screen:** Allows you to specify the location (Bottom, Left, Right, or Top). To move the taskbar, you can drag the taskbar from one edge to another.
- **Taskbar buttons:** Specifies how the application icons behave. You can choose from *Always combine, hide labels, Combine when taskbar is full*, or *Never combine*.
- **Notification area, click the Customize button:** Opens the Settings System page with Notification & actions, Apps & features, and other options (as shown in Figure 4-5).

Figure 4-4

Customizing the taskbar and Start menu

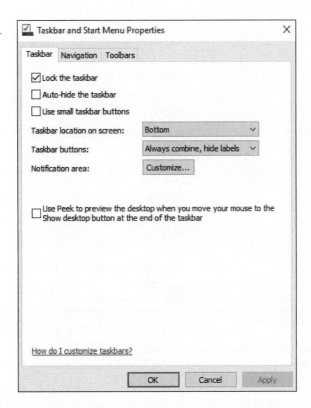

You can then configure the following:

- Turn notifications, notification banners, and sounds on or off for some or all apps.
- Choose whether to see notifications on the lock screen and when you're presenting your desktop.
- Choose the behavior for notification area icons, such as only show notifications, or Only icon and notifications.

If you click the *Select which icons appear on the taskbar* option, you can specify all icons in the notification, or you can specify which icons will show in the notification (such as Network, Volume, and Microsoft OneDrive). If you click the Settings arrow in the upper left of the page and then click the *Turn system icons on or off*, you can turn on or off various icons (such as Clock, Volume, Network, Power, Input Indicator, Location, and Action Center).

Using Windows 10 Settings

The **Windows 10 Settings** is a modern interface for common configuration settings that would have been found in the Windows Control Panel on older versions of Windows. In addition, you will find additional settings such as touch screen, tablet, and privacy settings that are geared toward phones and tablets that you will not find in Control Panel.

Figure 4-5

Customizing the notifications and actions

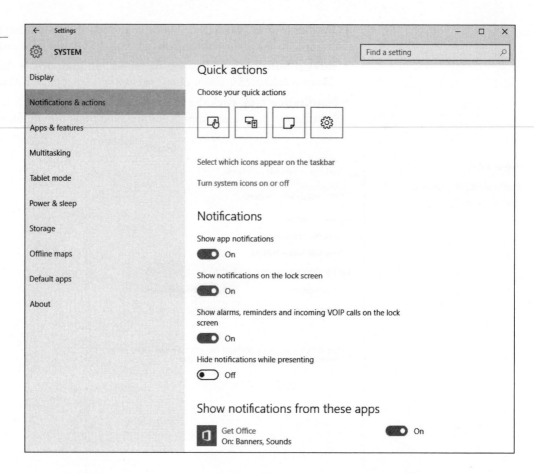

When you click the Settings arrow in the upper left of the page twice, you back up to the common Settings page (see Figure 4-6). These settings are organized as follows:

- **System:** Allows you to configure the display, notifications & actions, apps and features, multitasking, tablet mode, power & sleep options, and default apps
- **Devices:** Provides quick access to hardware devices, such as printers, which you can use with the currently selected app
- **Network & Internet:** Keeps track of Wi-Fi connections and allows you to configure VPN, dial-up connections, Ethernet connections, and proxy settings
- **Personalization:** Provides settings for the background, colors, lock screen, themes, and Start menu
- **Accounts:** Allows you to change the profile picture and add accounts
- **Time & language:** Allows you to configure Date & time, Region & language, and Speech
- **Ease of Access:** Provides settings for Narrator, Magnifier, high contrast, closed captions, keyboard, and mouse settings
- **Privacy:** Allows you to configure camera, microphone, speech, account information, contacts, calendar, messaging, and application radios control for Wi-Fi/Bluetooth connection
- **Update and security:** Allows you to configure Windows Update, activate Windows, perform backups and recoveries, and configure Windows Defender

Using Control Panel

With previous versions of Windows, *Control Panel* was a primary graphical utility to configure the Windows environment and hardware devices. It can be accessed in Windows 10 by right-clicking the Start button and choosing Control Panel. See Figure 4-7.

Figure 4-6

Accessing Windows 10 Settings

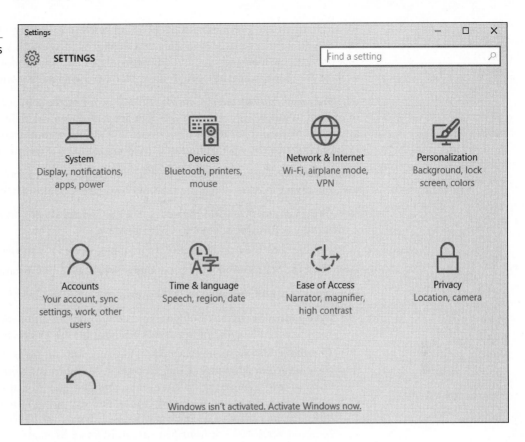

Figure 4-7

Opening Control Panel

Each category includes a top-level link, and under each top-level link are several of the most frequently performed tasks for the category.

As with current and previous versions of Windows, you can change from the default Category view to Classic view (a large icon view or a small icon view). Icon view is an alternative view that provides the look and functionality of Control Panel in Windows 2000 and earlier versions of Windows, where all options are displayed as applets or icons.

The *Microsoft Management Console (MMC)* is one of the primary administrative tools used to manage Windows and many of the network services provided by Windows. It provides a standard method to create, save, and open the various administrative tools provided by Windows. When you open Administrative Tools, most of these programs are MMC.

Administrative Tools is a folder in Control Panel that contains tools for system administrators and advanced users. There are three ways to access Administrative Tools:

- Open Control Panel and then click Start > Control Panel > System and Security > Administrative Tools while in Category view.
- Double-click the Administrative Tools applet while in Icon view.
- Click the Start button > All programs > Windows Administrative Tools.

Some common administrative tools (as shown in Figure 4-8) in this folder include:

- **Component Services:** Configures and administers Component Object Model (COM) components. Component Services is designed for use by developers and administrators.
- *Computer Management:* Manages local or remote computers by using a single, consolidated desktop tool. Using Computer Management, you can perform many tasks, such as monitoring system events, configuring hard disks, managing system performance, managing users and groups, and managing shared folders. It includes other administrative tools, including Event Viewer, Task Scheduler, Performance Monitor, Services, Disk Management, and Device Manager.
- **Defragment and Optimize Drives:** Optimizes drives by rearranging files of a specific hard drive in a contiguous order.

Figure 4-8

Opening the Windows 10 Administrative Tools

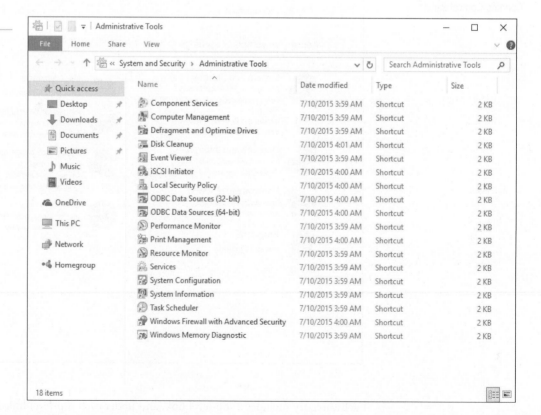

- **Disk Cleanup:** Frees up space on a hard disk by removing temporary files and unneeded Windows Update files.
- **Event Viewer:** Views information about significant events, such as programs starting or stopping or security errors that are recorded in event logs.
- **iSCSI Initiator:** Configures advanced connections between storage devices on a network.
- **Local Security Policy:** Views and edits Group Policy security settings.
- **ODBC Data Sources (32-bit and 64-bit):** Uses Open Database Connectivity (ODBC) to move data from one type of database (a data source) to another.
- **Performance Monitor:** Views advanced system information about the processor, memory, hard disk, and network performance.
- **Print Management:** Manages printers and print servers on a network and performs other administrative tasks.
- **Resource Monitor:** Displays information about the usage of hardware (CPU, memory, disk, and network) and software (file handles and modules) in real time.
- **Services:** Manages the different services that run in the background on your computer.
- **System Configuration:** Identifies problems that might be preventing Windows from running correctly.
- **System Information:** Shows details about your computer's hardware configuration, computer components, and software, including drivers.
- **Task Scheduler:** Schedules programs or other tasks to run automatically.
- **Windows Firewall with Advanced Security:** Manages the host-based firewall, including enabling/disabling Windows Firewall and creating exceptions.
- **Windows Memory Diagnostic:** Checks your computer's memory to see whether it is functioning properly.
- **Windows PowerShell:** Provides a task-based command-line shell and scripting language designed especially for system administration. Windows PowerShell tools only show if PowerShell is installed on Windows 10.

You might assume that these tools are used only to manage the local computer. However, many of them can be used to manage remote computers as well. For example, you can use the Computer Management console to connect to and manage other computers, assuming you have administrative rights to the computer.

Configuring System Settings

Some of the most important configuration settings for a user are the System settings within Control Panel. These include gathering general information about your system, changing the computer name, adding the computer to a domain, accessing Device Manager, configuring remote settings, configuring startup and recovery options, and configuring overall performance settings.

To access the System settings, you can do one of the following:

- In Control Panel, in Category view, click System and Security and then click System or click View amount of RAM and processor speed.
- In Control Panel, in Classic view, double-click the System applet.
- Right-click Computer and choose Properties.
- Right-click the Start button and choose System.

In Windows, there are often several ways to perform a task.

At the top of the screen, your Windows edition system type is shown. If Windows comes in 64-bit, it shows 64-bit Operating System in the middle of the screen. Toward the bottom of the screen, you will see the computer name and domain (if any), if Windows is activated, and the Product ID. See Figure 4-9.

Figure 4-9

Displaying System settings

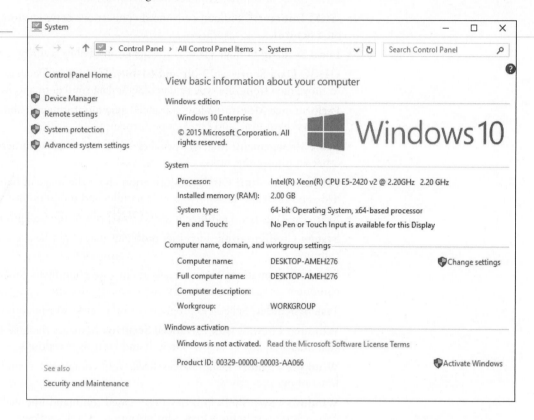

To help identify computers, you should name each computer with a meaningful name. This can be done within the System settings within Control Panel. You can also add a computer to a domain or workgroup.

Every computer must have a unique computer name assigned to a network. If two computers have the same name, one or both of the computers will have trouble communicating on the network. To change the computer name, open System from Control Panel. Then click the Change Settings option in the Computer name, domain, and workgroup settings. In the System Properties dialog box, with the Computer Name tab selected, click the Change button. See Figure 4-10. Any changes to the computer name or workgroup/domain name will require a reboot.

Changing Date and Time

One of the easiest but most essential tasks is making sure that the computer has the correct date and time, which is essential for logging purposes and for security. If a secure packet is sent with the wrong date or time, the packet might be automatically denied because the date and time is used to determine if the packet is legit.

To access the date and time settings, perform any one of the following three steps:

- In Category view in Control Panel, click Clock, Language, and Region and then click Set the time and date.
- In Icon view, double-click Date and Time.
- If the date and time show in the Notification area, double-click the date and time.

Figure 4-10

Displaying System Properties

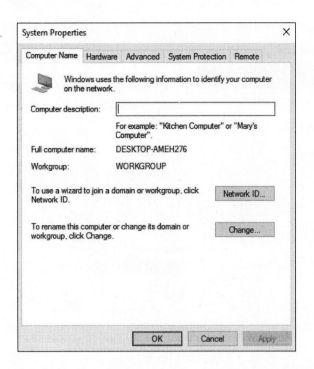

To set the clock:

1. Click the Date and Time tab and then click Change date and time.
2. Double-click the hour, minutes, or seconds and then click the arrows to increase or decrease the value.
3. Click OK.

To change the time zone, click Change time zone and then click your current time zone in the drop-down list. Then click OK.

If the computer is part of a domain, it should be synchronized with the domain controllers. If the computer is not part of a domain, you can synchronize it with an Internet time server by clicking the Internet Time tab and then selecting the check box next to Synchronize with an Internet time server. Select a time server and click OK.

Configuring Accessibility Options

Microsoft has built many features into Windows 10 that work with assistive technologies or as stand-alone features that make the user experience better for the visually and hearing impaired. Most features can be configured in the Windows 10 Settings Ease of Access Center page or the Control Panel Ease of Access Center.

CERTIFICATION READY
Configure accessibility options
Objective 1.4

The *Ease of Access Center* page (see Figure 4-11) provides many *accessibility options*, which help visually and hearing impaired users use Windows more easily and efficiently. The primary tools include Magnifier, Narrator, On-Screen Keyboard, and High Contrast.

Narrator is a text-to-speech program that reads aloud the actions you take, such as clicking and typing. This feature can also narrate certain events, such as error messages.

Figure 4-11

The Ease of Access Center page

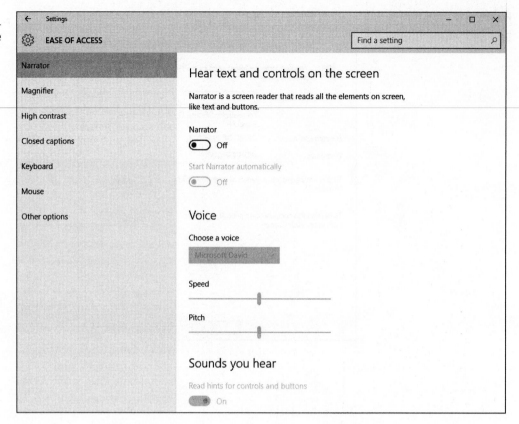

Magnifier helps visually impaired users see a selected portion of the screen or the entire screen more clearly by increasing the size of text and graphics. The Magnifier application window is quite small and provides you with access to Magnifier settings. Here, you can set a certain magnification level and choose how the magnification "lens" follows the mouse pointer and text cursor. The lens looks like a magnifying glass icon on the screen.

On-Screen Keyboard (see Figure 4-12) presents a keyboard on your screen from which you can type and enter data (rather than using a keyboard). You can use a mouse, stylus, or another pointing device to "press" keys.

Another accessibility feature is the High Contrast theme (see Figure 4-13), a color scheme that makes some text easier to read and some images easier to identify on-screen.

The bottom portion of the Ease of Access Center includes other accessibility options you can configure for visually or hearing impaired users, including:

- Using the computer without a display
- Making the computer easier to see
- Using the computer without a mouse or keyboard
- Making the mouse easier to use
- Making the keyboard easier to use
- Using text or visual alternatives for sounds
- Making it easier to focus on tasks

Figure 4-12

The On-Screen Keyboard presents a fully functional keyboard

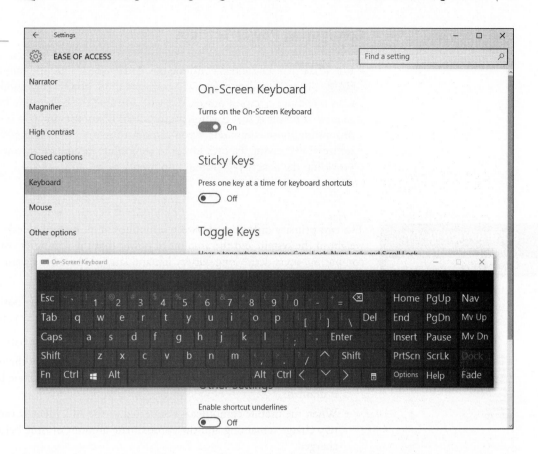

Figure 4-13

The High Contrast settings

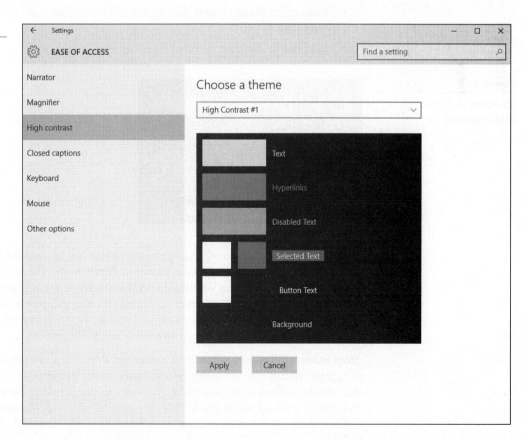

Configuring Power Settings

It is a fact that computers consume power. If you increase the number of processors, RAM, displays, or drives, you will consume more power. For mobile computers, if you consume more electrical power, you will consume the battery life faster. Another way to look at power is that if you have hundreds of computers, you can reduce the cost of running those computers if you can optimize the power usage. Windows 10 can utilize power-saving features found in computers to operate at lower power levels while providing the necessary computing power.

CERTIFICATION READY
Configure power settings
Objective 1.4

The two primary differences between a mobile computer and a desktop computer is the size/weight of the system and the amount of power that the computer consumes. For mobile computing, users desire long battery life and large corporations want to save money by reducing power consumption.

By default, the Windows 10 desktop contains a power tile in the notification area on the right side of the taskbar, as shown in Figure 4-14. With the power tile, you can:

- Determine whether the computer is currently using AC or battery power.
- When the mobile computer is running on battery, identify the percentage of the battery charge remaining and the approximate amount of time before the battery is drained.
- When the mobile computer is connected to the AC, identify the percentage of the battery charge remaining and the approximate amount of time before the battery is fully charged.
- Discover the current power plan in use and determine your ability to change to another power plan.
- Find links to the Control Panel Power options.

Figure 4-14

The Power tile in the notification area

In Windows 10, simple power management settings can be accessed by opening Settings and clicking System > Power & Sleep, as shown in Figure 4-15. The screen settings allow you to specify how long the screen will remain on if you are not actively using your computer when the computer is using battery power or when it is using AC power (plugged in). The *sleep settings* specify how long the computer will operate before going into sleep mode when the computer is using battery power or when it is using AC power.

Sleep mode is a low-power mode for computers that uses a minimum amount of power so that the system can be quickly restored back to the previous state without rebooting the computer. Sleep mode is useful if you want to stop working for a short period of time and quickly pick up where you left off. For older versions of Windows and other operating systems, sleep mode can be referred to as Stand By mode, Suspend mode, or Suspend to RAM.

Figure 4-15

Configuring Power settings

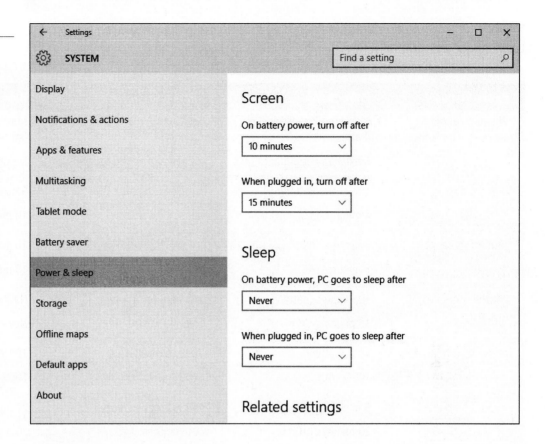

Before continuing on to the next section, you should understand the difference between sleep mode, hibernate mode, and hybrid sleep. *Hibernate mode* saves all computer operational data on the hard disk to a hibernation file (Hiberfil.sys) before turning the computer completely off. In other words, hibernate mode is a suspend to disk. When the computer is turned back on, the computer is restored to its previous state with all programs and files open and unsaved data intact. Hibernate mode will be discussed later in this lesson.

Hybrid mode is a combination of sleep mode and hibernate mode. Hybrid mode writes information to the hibernation file when the computer enters a sleep state, which allows for a fast wake time. If the system loses power completely and suddenly, you can restore operations from the hibernation file.

Power management is balancing power consumption with performance. Windows 10 includes extensive power management capabilities, including supporting the Advanced Configuration and Power Interface (ACPI), which can be configured using power plans. The power plans can be configured using the Control Panel Power Options, using Group Policy, or via the command prompt.

Power Options is the primary interactive power configuration interface that can be used to select the power plan, modify the settings for the default power plans, and create new, custom power plans.

A *power plan* is a collection of hardware and system settings that manage how a computer uses power. Windows 10 includes three default power plans:

- **Balanced (recommended):** Balances performance with power-saving features
- **Power Saver:** Saves power by reducing PC performance and screen performance so that you can maximize battery life
- **High Performance:** Maximizes screen brightness and PC performance

Table 4-1

Default Power Plan Settings

POWER SETTING	POWER SAVER	BALANCED	HIGH PERFORMANCE
Wireless adapter power-saving mode	Maximum Power Saving (battery) Maximum Performance (AC)	Medium Power Saving (battery) Maximum Performance (AC)	Maximum Performance (battery) Maximum Performance (AC)
Dim the display	1 minutes (battery) 2 minutes (AC)	2 minutes (battery) 5 minutes (AC)	5 minutes (battery) 10 minutes (AC)
Turn off the display	2 minutes (battery) 5 minutes (AC)	5 minutes (battery) 10 minutes (AC)	10 minutes (battery) 15 minutes (AC)
Put the computer to sleep	10 minutes (battery) 15 minutes (AC)	45 minutes (battery) Never (AC)	Never (battery) Never (AC)
Adjust plan brightness	40% (battery) 100% (AC)	50% (battery) 100% (AC)	100% (battery) 100% (AC)
Turn off hard disk	5 minutes (battery) 20 minutes (AC)	10 minutes (battery) 20 minutes (AC)	20 minutes (battery) 20 minutes (AC)
Minimum processor state	5% (battery) 5% (AC)	5% (battery) 5% (AC)	5% (battery) 100% (AC)
System cooling policy	Passive (battery) Passive (AC)	Passive (battery) Active (AC)	Active (battery) Active (AC)
Maximum processor state	100% (battery) 100% (AC)	70% (battery) 100% (AC)	100% (battery) 100% (AC)

Table 4-1 shows the default power plan settings.

To select one of the default power plans, you can use any of the following procedures:

- Open the Windows Mobility Center and, in the Battery Status tile, select one of the plans from the drop-down list.
- Open Control Panel and click or tap Hardware and Sound > Power Options, and select the radio button for the desired plan, as shown in Figure 4-16. To display the High performance, you must click the Show additional plans down arrow.

You can use the Control Panel Power Options to modify a power plan or to create a new power plan. To create a custom power plan, use the following procedure.

Figure 4-16

The Control Panel Power
Options

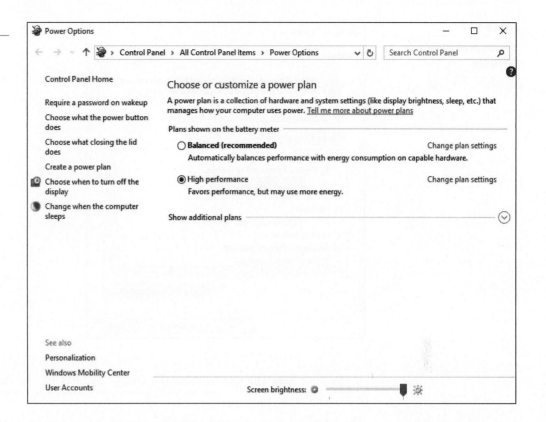

CREATE A CUSTOM POWER PLAN

GET READY. Log on to Windows 10 using an account with administrative privileges and then
perform the following steps.

1. Open **Control Panel** and then click or tap **Hardware and Sound >
   Power Options**.

2. When the Power Options page opens, click **Create a power plan**.

3. When the Create a Power Plan Wizard opens, select the radio button for the default
   power plan that will be the basis for your new plan.

4. In the Plan name text box, type a name for your power plan and then
   click **Next**.

5. On the Change Settings for the Plan page, modify the display and sleep settings
   as desired for the On battery and Plugged in power states and then click **Create**.
   The Choose or Customize a Power Plan page appears.

6. For the new plan, click the **Change plan settings** option.

   The Change Settings for the Plan page appears again.

7. When the Change Settings for the Plan page opens, click **Change advanced
   power settings**. The Advanced settings dialog box opens, as shown
   in Figure 4-17.

8. Modify any of the settings as desired and then click **OK**.

Figure 4-17

The Advanced settings
dialog box

9. Click **Save Changes** to close the Change Settings for the Plan page.

The Advanced settings give you a high degree of control for the power plans. Some of the options include:

- **Hard Disk: Turn Off Hard Disk After:** Specifies the amount of time of inactive use before a mechanical disk will stop spinning.
- **Wireless Adapter Settings: Power Savings Mode:** Allows you to control power by selecting one of the following options: Maximum Performance, Low Power Saving, Medium Power Saving, and Maximum Power Saving. If you need fast Internet connection, use the Maximum Performance or Low Power Saving. If you don't need Wi-Fi, turn your Wi-Fi antenna off when you don't need it.
- **Sleep after:** Specifies how long a machine will sleep after inactive use.
- **Allow Hybrid sleep:** Enables hybrid sleep mode.
- **Hibernate:** Specifies when a machine goes into hibernation.
- **Allow wake timers:** Allows a system to be woken up from sleep mode to perform tasks at certain times such as Windows updates.

Configuring Cortana

Cortana is a search feature and personal assistant for Windows 10. It can help you find programs and files on your computer and manage your calendar events. It can also deliver sport scores, weather, news, navigation, reminders, and more. When you search, you can either type what you are looking for, or if you have a microphone, you can speak to Cortana.

CERTIFICATION READY
Configure Cortana
Objective 1.4

When you first start Cortana, you must specify your name or nickname and specify your Microsoft account, which enables Cortana to give you suggestions, ideas, reminders, alerts, and more. You can then access the Cortana settings, as shown in Figure 4-18. You can then customize Cortana further by adding your home address and work address so that it can make decisions based on where you live and work.

Figure 4-18

Configuring Cortana

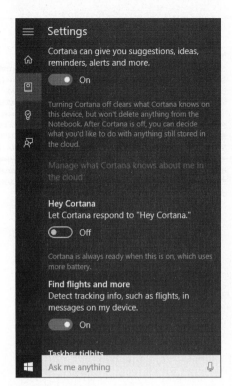

When you click Cortana, you will see four small icons:

- **Home:** Displays news and personalized items that Cortana thinks you will be interested in at the moment.
- **Cortana Notebook:** Specifies what appears in the Home view and in search results as a whole. You can also add additional accounts (Connected Accounts).
- **Reminders:** Shows reminders that Cortana has gathered.
- **Feedback:** Sends feedback to Microsoft.

■ UNDERSTANDING THE REGISTRY

THE BOTTOM LINE

The *registry* is a central, secure database in which Windows stores all hardware configuration information, software configuration information, and system security policies. Components that use the registry include the Windows kernel, device drivers, setup programs, hardware profiles, and user profiles.

Most of the time, you will not need to access the registry because programs and applications typically make all the necessary changes automatically. For example, when you change your desktop background or change the default color for Windows, you access the Display settings within Control Panel and it saves the changes to the registry.

If you do need to access the registry to make changes, you should follow the instructions from a reputable source closely because an incorrect change to your computer's registry can render your computer inoperable. However, there might be a time when you need to make a change in the registry because there is no interface or program to make the change. To view and manually change the registry, use the Registry Editor (Regedit.exe), which can be executed from the command prompt, Start Search box, or Run box. See Figure 4-19.

Figure 4-19

The Registry Editor

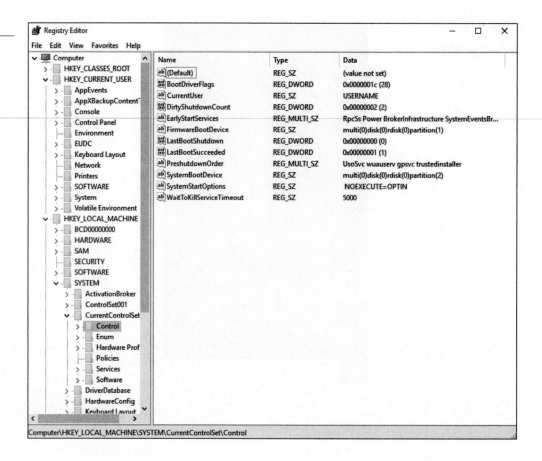

The registry is organized according to several logical sections, often referred to as hives, which are generally named by their Windows API definitions. The hives begin with HKEY and are often abbreviated to a three- or four-letter short name starting with "HK." For example, HKCU is HKEY_CURRENT_USER and HKLM is HKEY_LOCAL_MACHINE. Windows Server 2008 R2 has five Root Keys/HKEYs:

- **HKEY_CLASSES_ROOT:** Stores information about registered applications, such as the file association that tells which default program opens a file with a certain extension.
- **HKEY_CURRENT_USER:** Stores settings that are specific to the currently logged-on user. When a user logs off, the HKEY_CURRENT_USER is saved to HKEY_USERS.
- **HKEY_LOCAL_MACHINE:** Stores settings that are specific to the local computer.
- **HKEY_USERS:** Contains subkeys corresponding to the HKEY_CURRENT_USER keys for each user profile actively loaded on the machine.
- **HKEY_CURRENT_CONFIG:** Contains information gathered at run time. Information stored in this key is not permanently stored on disk, but rather regenerated at boot time.

Registry keys are similar to folders, which can contain values or subkeys. The keys within the registry follow a syntax similar to a Windows folder or file path using backslashes to separate each level. For example:

HKEY_LOCAL_MACHINE\Software\Microsoft\Windows

refers to the subkey "Windows" of the subkey "Microsoft" of the subkey "Software" of the HKEY_LOCAL_MACHINE key.

Registry values include a name and a value. There are multiple types of values. Some of the common key types are shown in Table 4-2.

Table 4-2

Common Registry Key Types

NAME	DATA TYPE	DESCRIPTION
Binary value	REG_BINARY	Raw binary data. Most hardware component information is stored as binary data and is displayed in Registry Editor in hexadecimal format.
DWORD value	REG_DWORD	Data represented by a number that is 4 bytes long (a 32-bit integer). Many parameters for device drivers and services are this type and are displayed in Registry Editor in binary, hexadecimal, or decimal format.
Expandable string value	REG_EXPAND_SZ	A variable-length data string. This data type includes variables that are resolved when a program or service uses the data.
Multi-string value	REG_MULTI_SZ	A multiple string. Values that contain lists or multiple values in a form that people can read are generally this type. Entries are separated by spaces, commas, or other marks.
String value	REG_SZ	A fixed-length text string.
QWORD value	REG_QWORD	Data represented by a number that is a 64-bit integer. This data is displayed in Registry Editor as a binary value, and it was introduced in Windows 2000.

Reg files (also known as Registration entries) are text files used for storing portions of the registry. They have a .reg file name extension. When you double-click a reg file, the registry entries are added to the registry. You can export any registry subkey by right-clicking the subkey and choosing Export. You can back up the entire registry to a reg file by right-clicking Computer at the top of Regedit and selecting Export or you can back up the system state with Windows Backup.

■ CONFIGURING INTERNET EXPLORER

THE BOTTOM LINE

Windows 10 includes two browsers, Internet Explorer and Microsoft Edge. *Internet Explorer* is the traditional Microsoft browser that offers a number of features to protect your security and privacy while you browse the web, including phishing filters, Protected Mode, Pop-up Blocker, Add-on Manager, download files or software notification, and the use of digital signatures and 128-bit secure (SSL) connections when using secure websites.

CERTIFICATION READY
Configure Internet
Explorer
Objective 1.4

Internet Explorer has changed significantly over the years. As a result, it has a lot of features and functionality. Some features can be simple features such as the Zoom feature (Tools (gear) button > Zoom). Because you use the web browser to access information from throughout the world over the Internet, your computer or private information might be at risk of being accessed by others.

Managing Cookies and Privacy Settings

Your web browser can reveal plenty of information about your personality and interests. Therefore, you need to take steps to ensure that this information cannot be read or used without your knowledge.

A **cookie** is text stored by a user's web browser. It can be used for a wide range of functions, including identifying you as a user, authenticating you as a user, and storing your site preferences and shopping cart contents. Cookies can provide a website with a lot of helpful information that can make your browsing experience easier and faster, but they also can be used by spyware programs and websites to track your online behavior. Unfortunately, some websites will not operate without cookies.

DELETE COOKIES AND TEMPORARY INTERNET FILES

GET READY. To delete cookies and temporary Internet files, perform the following steps.

1. Open **Internet Explorer**.
2. Click the **Tools** (gear) button and then click **Internet Options**.
3. On the General tab, under Browsing history, click **Delete**. The Delete Browsing History dialog box opens (see Figure 4-20).

Figure 4-20

Deleting cookies and temporary files

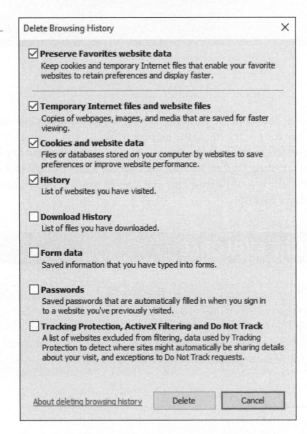

4. Ensure that the **Cookies and website data** check box and the **Temporary Internet files and website files** check box are selected. Click **Delete**.

Being aware of how your private information is used when browsing the web is important to helping prevent targeted advertising, fraud, and identity theft.

→ **CHANGE PRIVACY SETTINGS**

GET READY. To change privacy settings, perform the following steps.

1. Open **Internet Explorer**.
2. Click the **Tools** button and then click **Internet Options**.
3. Click the **Privacy** tab (see Figure 4-21).

Figure 4-21

Configuring your privacy settings

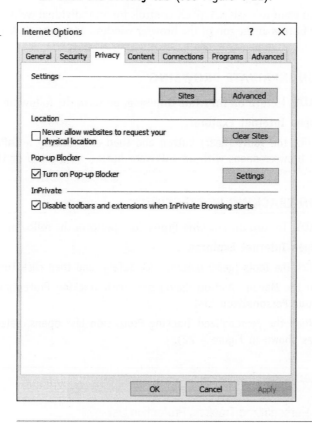

If you click the Advanced button, you can override certain settings and if you click the Edit button, you can allow or block cookies from individual websites.

To prevent Internet Explorer from storing data about your browsing session, Internet Explorer 11 includes *InPrivate Browsing*. This helps prevent anyone who might be using your computer from seeing where you visited and what you looked at on the web.

When you start InPrivate Browsing, Internet Explorer opens a new window. The protection that InPrivate Browsing provides is only in effect during the time that you use that window. You can open as many tabs as you want in that window, and they will all be protected by InPrivate Browsing. However, if you open another browser window, that window will not be protected by InPrivate Browsing unless you configure that window to also use InPrivate Browsing. To end your InPrivate Browsing session, close the browser window.

Some websites can be used to gather information about which pages you visit on the Internet. *Tracking Protection* blocks this content from websites that appear on Tracking Protection Lists. A Personalized Tracking Protection List included with Internet Explorer is generated automatically based on sites you visit. You can also download Tracking Protection Lists and then Internet Explorer will periodically check for updates to the lists.

Pop-up windows are very common. Although some pop-up windows are useful website controls, most are simply annoying advertisements—with a few attempting to load spyware or other malicious programs. To help protect your computer, Internet Explorer's *Pop-up Blocker* can suppress some or all pop-ups.

ActiveX controls are small applications that allow websites to provide content such as videos and games and to allow you to interact with content such as those used in toolbars and stock tickers. However, these applications can malfunction, deliver unwanted content, or can contain malware. *ActiveX Filtering* in Internet Explorer prevents sites from installing and using ActiveX applications. Of course, when ActiveX Filtering is on, videos, games, and other interactive content might not work.

When you want to enable ActiveX controls for an individual website, visit the website, click the Filter button at the top of the browser window, and then click Turn off ActiveX Filtering.

 TURN ON INPRIVATE BROWSING

GET READY. To turn on InPrivate Browsing, perform the following steps.

1. Open **Internet Explorer.**
2. Click the **Tools** (gear) button and then click **Safety > InPrivate Browsing.**
   A browser opens with an InPrivate button at the top of the window.

 TURN ON TRACKING PROTECTION

GET READY. To turn on Tracking Protection, perform the following steps.

1. Open **Internet Explorer.**
2. Click the **Tools** (gear) button, click **Safety,** and then click **Turn on Tracking Protection.**
3. In the Manage Add-on dialog box, with Tracking Protection selected, double-click **Your Personalized List.**
4. When the Personalized Tracking Protection List opens, select **Automatically block** (as shown in Figure 4-22).

Figure 4-22

Turning on tracking protection

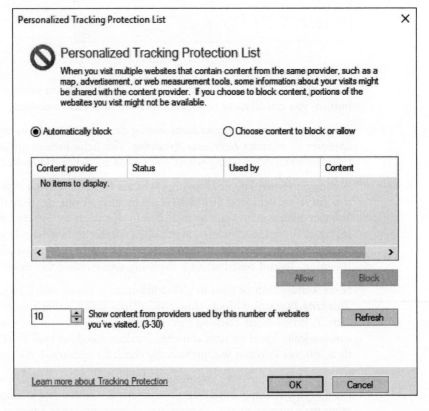

5. Click **Close.**

CONFIGURE THE POP-UP BLOCKER

GET READY. To configure the Pop-up Blocker, perform the following steps.

1. Open **Internet Explorer**.
2. Click the **Tools** (gear) button and then click **Internet Options**.
3. Click the **Privacy** tab.
4. Click the **Settings** button. The Pop-Up Blocker Settings dialog box opens.
5. To allow pop-ups from a specific website, in the Address of website to allow text box, type the URL of the site and then click **Add**.

   Repeat the process to add additional sites to the Allowed sites list.
6. Adjust the Blocking level drop-down list to one of the following settings:
   - **High:** Blocks all pop-ups
   - **Medium:** Blocks most automatic pop-ups
   - **Low:** Allows pop-ups from secure sites
7. Click **Close** to close the Pop-Up Blocker Settings dialog box.
8. Click **OK** to close the Internet Properties dialog box.

 CONFIGURE ACTIVEX FILTERING

GET READY. To configure ActiveX Filtering, perform the following steps.

1. Open **Internet Explorer**.
2. Click the **Tools** (gear) button and then click **Safety > ActiveX Filtering**.

   There should now be a check mark next to ActiveX Filtering.

Configuring Security Zones

> To help manage Internet Explorer security when visiting sites, Internet Explorer divides your network connection into *security zones* based on four content types. For each zone, a security level is assigned.

The security for each security zone is assigned based on dangers associated with that zone. For example, it is assumed that connecting to a server within your own corporation would be safer than connecting to a server on the Internet.

The four default content types are:

- **Internet zone:** Anything that is not assigned to any other zone and anything that is not on your computer or your organization's network (intranet). The default security level of the Internet zone is Medium.

- **Local intranet zone:** Computers that are part of the organization's network (intranet) that do not require a proxy server, as defined by the system administrator. These include sites specified on the Connections tab, network, paths (such as \\computername\ foldername), and local intranet sites (such as http://internal). You can add sites to this zone. The default security level for the Local intranet zone is Medium-Low, which means Internet Explorer allows all cookies from websites in this zone to be saved on your computer and read by the website that created them. Lastly, if the website requires NTLM or integrated authentication, it automatically uses your user name and password.

- **Trusted sites zone:** Trusted sites that you believe you can download or run files from without damaging your computer or you believe you can download data or that you don't consider to be a security risk. You can assign sites to this zone. The default security level for the Trusted sites zone is Low, which means Internet Explorer allows all cookies from websites in this zone to be saved on your computer and read by the website that created them.

- **Restricted sites zone:** Sites that you do not trust; downloading or running files might damage your computer. You can assign sites to this zone. The default security level for the Restricted sites zone is High, which means Internet Explorer blocks all cookies from websites in this zone.

To determine which zones the current web page falls into, look at the right side of the Internet Explorer status bar.

 MODIFY THE SECURITY LEVEL FOR A WEB CONTENT ZONE

GET READY. To modify the security level for a web content zone, perform the following steps.

1. Open **Internet Explorer**.
2. Click the **Tools** (gear) button and then click **Internet Options**.
3. In the Internet Options dialog box, click the **Security** tab.
4. Click the zone on which you want to set the security level (as shown in Figure 4-23). Drag the slider to set the security level to High, Medium, or Low. Internet Explorer describes each option to help you decide which level to choose. You are prompted to confirm any reduction in security level. You can also click the custom Level button for more detailed control.

Figure 4-23

Configuring the security content zones

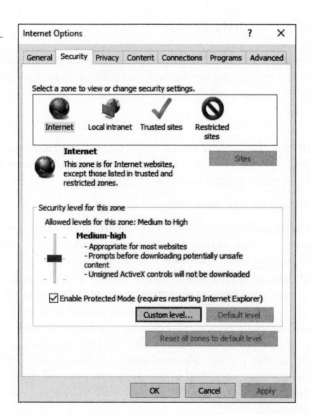

5. To customize individual settings, you click the **Custom level** button to open the Security Settings dialog box.

6. Select radio buttons for the individual settings in each security category. The radio buttons typically make it possible to enable a setting, disable it, or prompt the user before enabling it.

7. To close the Security Settings dialog box, click **OK**.

8. To close the Internet Options dialog box, click **OK**.

For each web content zone, there is a default security level. The security levels available in Internet Explorer are:

- **High:** Excludes any content that can damage your computer
- **Medium:** Warns you before running potentially damaging content
- **Low:** Does not warn you before running potentially damaging content
- **Custom:** Creates a security setting of your own design

The easiest way to modify the security settings that Internet Explorer imposes on a specific website is to manually add the site to a different security zone. The typical procedure is to add a site to the Trusted sites zone to increase its privileges, or add it to the Restricted sites zone to reduce its privileges.

 ADD A SITE TO A SECURITY ZONE

GET READY. To add a site to a security zone, perform the following steps.

1. Open **Internet Explorer**.

2. Click the **Tools** (gear) button and then click **Internet Options**.

3. Click the **Security** tab.

4. Select the zone—either **Trusted sites** or **Restricted sites**—to which you want to add a site.

5. Click **Sites**. The Trusted sites or Restricted sites dialog box opens.

6. In the Add this website to the zone text box, type the URL of the website you want to add to the zone and then click **Add**. The URL appears in the Websites list.

7. Click **Close** to close the Trusted sites or Restricted sites dialog box.

8. To close the Internet Options dialog box, click **OK**.

Using Dynamic Security and Protected Mode

Internet Explorer offers multiple security features to defend against malware and data theft, including dynamic security and protected mode. ***Dynamic security*** is a set of tools and technology that protects your computer as you browse the Internet with Internet Explorer. It includes ActiveX opt-in, Security Status Bar, Phishing Filter, Address Bar Protection, and protected mode.

The Security Status Bar keeps you notified of the website security and privacy settings by using color-coded notifications next to the address bar. Some of these features include:

- The address bar turns green to indicate websites bearing new High Assurance certificates, indicating the site owner has completed extensive identity verification checks.

- Phishing Filter notifications, certificate names, and the gold padlock icon are now also adjacent to the address bar for better visibility.
- Certificate and privacy detail information can easily be displayed with a single click on the Security Status Bar.
- The address bar is displayed to the user for every window, whether it's a pop-up or whether it's a standard window, which helps to block malicious sites from emulating trusted sites.
- To help protect you against phishing sites, Internet Explorer warns you when you're visiting potential or known fraudulent sites and blocks the site if appropriate. The opt-in filter is updated several times per hour with the latest security information from Microsoft and several industry partners.
- International Domain Name Anti-Spoofing notifies you when visually similar characters in the URL are not expressed in the same language.

If Internet Explorer is still using its original settings, you'll see the Information bar in the following circumstances:

- When a website tries to install an ActiveX control on your computer or run an ActiveX control in an unsafe manner
- When a website tries to open a pop-up window
- When a website tries to download a file to your computer
- When a website tries to run active content on your computer
- When your security settings are below recommended levels
- When you access an intranet web page, but have not turned on intranet address checking
- When you started Internet Explorer with add-ons disabled
- When you need to install an updated ActiveX control or add-on program
- When the website address can be displayed with native language letters or symbols but you don't have the language installed

To help protect your computer, Internet Explorer protected mode means that it runs as a low-integrity procedure, which means that Internet Explorer writes to only low-integrity disk locations, such as the Temporary Internet Files folder and the standard Internet Explorer storage areas, including the History, Cookies, and Favorites folders. As a result, protected mode is a feature that makes it more difficult for malicious software to be installed on your computer.

TAKE NOTE

Protected mode is not a complete defense against malware. Therefore, it is recommended to use an up-to-date antivirus package with antispyware capability and to keep your system up to date with Windows and Internet Explorer security updates and patches.

 ENABLE PROTECTED MODE

GET READY. Before protected mode can be enabled, you must ensure that UAC is enabled. To enable protected mode, perform the following steps.

1. Open **Internet Explorer**.
2. Click **Tools > Internet Options**.
3. Click the **Security** tab.
4. Click **Enable Protected Mode**.

Configuring SmartScreen Filter and Phishing

> *Phishing* is a technique based on social engineering. With phishing, users are enticed to go (usually through email or other websites) to illegitimate websites that look similar to legitimate websites in an effort to persuade users to supply personal information, such as passwords and account numbers.

To help protect against phishing, Internet Explorer 11 includes *SmartScreen Filter*, which examines traffic for evidence of phishing activity and displays a warning to the user if it finds any. It also sends the address back to the Microsoft SmartScreen service to be compared against lists of known phishing and malware sites. If SmartScreen Filter discovers that a website you're visiting is on the list of known malware or phishing sites, Internet Explorer displays a blocking web page and the address bar is shown in red. From the blocking page, you can choose to bypass the blocked website and go to your home page instead or you can continue to the blocked website, though this is not recommended. If you continue to the blocked website, the address bar continues to appear in red.

To protect your privacy, information that is submitted to the SmartScreen web service is transmitted in encrypted format over HTTPS. This information is not stored with your IP address or other personally identifiable information and will not be used to identify, contact, or provide advertising to you.

You can set up the browser by using express settings or by configuring settings individually. The express settings option enables the SmartScreen Filter, but you can disable it at any time by clicking the Safety button on the toolbar and selecting SmartScreen Filter > Turn off SmartScreen Filter (which displays the Microsoft SmartScreen Filter dialog box).

Even without SmartScreen Filter turned on, you can remain safe from phishing attempts as long as you obey the following unofficial rules of web surfing:

- Don't trust hyperlinks.
- Never supply a password or any other confidential information to a website unless you type the URL yourself and you are sure that it is correct.

Managing Add-Ons

> To make Internet Explorer more flexible, Internet Explorer allows you to add *add-ons* to your browser, such as extra toolbars, animated mouse pointers, stock tickers, and pop-up blockers. Add-ons are downloaded from the Internet and installed as an executable program.

The four basic types of add-ons supported by Internet Explorer are as follows:

- **Toolbars and Extensions:** Enable the browser to open and manipulate websites or file types that Internet Explorer does not support natively. Some applications add their own toolbars to Internet Explorer, enabling you to work with their documents within an Internet Explorer session.
- **Search Providers:** Enable the user to perform searches directly from the Internet Explorer interface using search engines on the Internet or the local network.
- **Accelerators:** Enable users to send text or other media they select in an Internet Explorer browser window to another application, such as an email client or an Internet resource (such as a blog).
- **Tracking Protection:** Enables you to import and export XML files containing InPrivate filters.

VIEW YOUR CURRENT ADD-ONS

GET READY. To view your current add-ons, perform the following steps.

1. Open **Internet Explorer**.
2. Click the **Tools** (gear) button and then click **Manage Add-ons**.
3. Under Toolbars and Extensions (see Figure 4-24), under Show, you can select one of the following views of your add-ons:
    • To display a complete list of the add-ons that reside on your computer, click **All add-ons**.
    • To display only those add-ons that were needed for the current web page or a recently viewed web page, click **Currently loaded add-ons**.
    • To display add-ons that were preapproved by Microsoft, your computer manufacturer, or a service provider, click **Run without permission**.
    • To display only 32-bit ActiveX controls, click **Downloaded controls**.

Figure 4-24

Managing add-ons

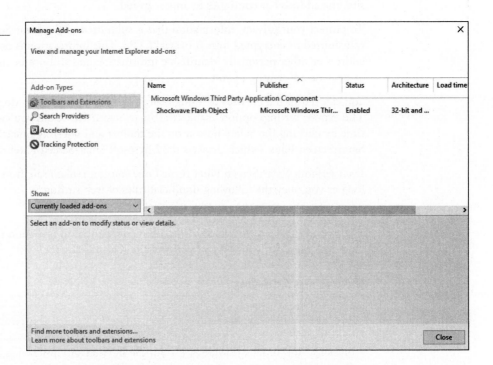

4. Click **Close**.

 DELETE ACTIVEX CONTROLS

GET READY. To delete ActiveX controls you have installed, perform the following steps.

1. Open **Internet Explorer**.
2. Click the **Tools** (gear) button and then click **Manage Add-ons**.
3. Under Show, click **Downloaded controls** to display all ActiveX controls.
4. Click the ActiveX control you want to delete and then click **More information**.
5. In the More Information dialog box, click **Remove**. If you are prompted for an administrator password or confirmation, type the password or provide confirmation.

DISABLE ADD-ONS

GET READY. To permanently disable add-ons, perform the following steps.

1. Open **Internet Explorer**.
2. Click the **Tools** (gear) button and then click **Manage Add-ons**.
3. Under Show, click **All add-ons**.
4. Click the add-on you want to disable and then click **Disable**.

Configuring Compatibility Mode

> Through the years, web pages have changed quite a bit. Unfortunately, as newer technology is implemented on websites, sometimes websites don't look like you expect them to. Images might not appear, menus might be out of place, and text could be jumbled together. In these situations, you can try to run the site in compatibility mode.

Once you turn on *Compatibility View*, Internet Explorer automatically shows that site in Compatibility View each time you visit. You can turn it off by removing it from your compatibility list.

 VIEW COMPATIBILITY VIEW

GET READY. To turn Compatibility View on or off, click the Compatibility View button, or perform the following steps.

1. Open **Internet Explorer**.
2. Click the **Tools** (gear) button, and then click **Compatibility View settings**.
3. In the Compatibility View Settings dialog box (as shown in Figure 4-25), you can perform the following tasks:
   - **Display intranet sites in Compatibility View:** To include all of your internal corporate websites, make sure the Display intranet sites in Compatibility View option is selected.

Figure 4-25

Managing Compatibility View settings

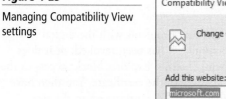

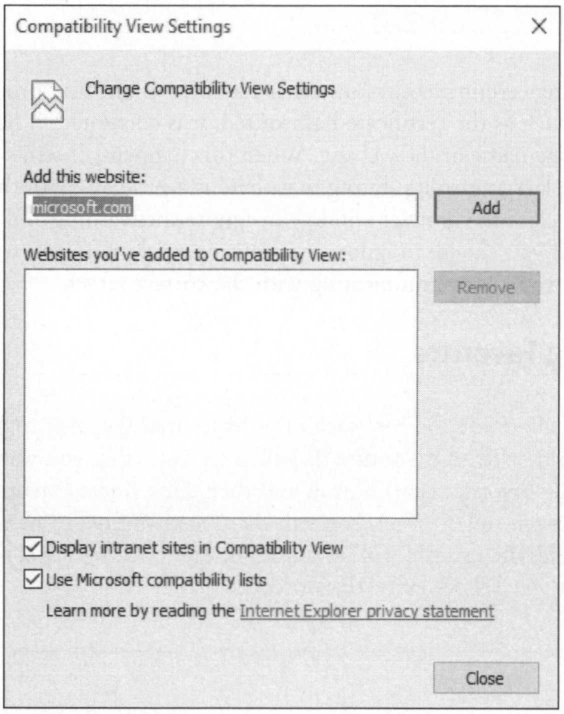

- **Use Microsoft compatibility lists:** Selecting this option automatically put sites into Compatibility View if they are on the list compiled by Microsoft.
- **Add this website:** To run a website in Compatibility View, type the website into the Add this website text box, and click the Add button.

Configuring Secure Sockets Layer (SSL) and Certificates

You might need to transmit private data over the Internet, such as credit card numbers, Social Security numbers, and so on. You should use HTTP over SSL (HTTPS) to encrypt the data sent over the Internet. By convention, URLs that require an SSL connection start with https: (instead of http:).

Secure Sockets Layer (SSL) uses a cryptographic system that uses two keys (one key to encrypt the data and another key to decrypt the data). The public key is known to everyone and a private or secret key is known only to the recipient of the message. The public key is published in a digital certificate, which also confirms the identity of the web server.

When you connect to a site that is secured using SSL, a lock appears in the address bar. Clicking the lock icon displays more information about the site (see Figure 4-26), including the identity of the certificate authority (CA) that issued the certificate. For even more information, you can click the View Certificate link to open the Certificate dialog box.

Figure 4-26

Viewing certificate information

When visiting certain websites, Internet Explorer might find problems with the digital certificate, such as the certificate has expired, it is corrupted, it has been revoked, or it does not match the name of the website. When this happens, Internet Explorer blocks access to the site and displays a warning stating that there is a problem with the certificate. You then have a chance to close the browser window or ignore the warning and continue on to the site. Of course, if you choose to ignore the warning, make sure you trust the website and you believe that you are communicating with the correct server.

Managing Favorites

Favorites allow you to keep track of websites that you visit frequently so that you can visit them quickly in the future. If you're on a site that you want to make a favorite, tap or click the Favorites (star) button and then click Add to favorites. You can also save a favorite by pressing Ctrl+D. You will then be prompted to name the favorite and identify which folder the favorite will be stored in. The favorites are stored in the user's profile folder (c:\Users\<Username>\Favorites).

Some of the popular tasks are:

- To view your favorites, click the Favorites (star) button.
- To organize your favorites, click the Favorites (star) button, click the small down arrow next to the Add to favorites button, and then click Organize favorites.
- To export the favorites to an HTML file, which can be imported into another machine, click the small down arrow next to the Add to favorites button, click Import and export, and then click Export to a file.
- To import the favorites from an HTML file, click the small down arrow next to the Add to favorites button, click Import and export, and then click Import from a file.

Managing LAN Settings

> Although Classless Inter-Domain Routing (CIDR) helped use the IPv4 addresses more efficiently, additional steps were necessary to prevent the exhaustion of IPv4 addresses. *Network Address Translation (NAT)* is used with masquerading to hide an entire address space behind a single IP address. In other words, it allows multiple computers on a network to connect to the Internet through a single IP address.

NAT enables a local area network (LAN) to use one set of IP addresses for internal traffic and a second set of addresses for external traffic. The NAT computer or device is usually a router (including routers made for home and small-office Internet connections) or a proxy server. As a result, you can:

- Provide a type of firewall by hiding internal IP addresses.
- Enable multiple internal computers to share a single external public IP address.

The private addresses are reserved addresses not allocated to any specific organization. Because these private addresses cannot be assigned to global addresses used on the Internet and are not routable on the Internet, you must use a NAT gateway or proxy server to convert between private and public addresses. The private network addresses are expressed in RFC 1918 as:

- 10.0.0.0–10.255.255.255
- 172.16.0.0–172.31.255.255
- 192.168.0.0–192.168.255.255

NAT obscures an internal network's structure by making all traffic appear to be originated from the NAT device or proxy server. A *proxy server* is a server that acts as an intermediary for clients seeking resources outside their networks. Medium and large organizations typically use a proxy server. In addition, these organizations require their clients to use the proxy server when accessing the Internet. By using the proxy server, organizations can monitor traffic and provide better security. For organizations that use proxy servers, because client traffic has to go through the proxy server to connect to the Internet, users need to use the proxy server to access Office 365, Microsoft Intune, and Microsoft Azure.

 CONFIGURE A CLIENT TO USE A PROXY SERVER

GET READY. To configure a client to use a proxy server, perform the following steps.

1. Open **Internet Explorer**.
2. Click the **Tools** (gear) button and click **Internet options**.

3. Click the **Connections** tab.

4. Click the **LAN settings** button.

5. In the Local Area Network (LAN) Settings dialog box (see Figure 4-27), deselect the **Automatically detect settings** option.

Figure 4-27

Configuring proxy settings

6. Select the **Use a proxy server for your LAN** option.

7. In the Address text box, type the host name or IP address of the proxy server. In the Port text box, type the port used by the proxy server, such as **80** or **8080**.

8. If you do not want to use proxy servers to access local resources, select the **Bypass proxy server for local addresses** option.

9. Alternatively, you can click the **Advanced** button. In the Proxy Settings dialog box, you can specify individual proxy settings for HTTP, Secure, FTP, and Socks. You can also specify exceptions that you do not want to use the proxy server for. Click **OK.**

10. Click **OK** to close the Local Area Network (LAN) Settings dialog box.

11. Click **OK** to close the Internet Options dialog box.

■ CONFIGURING MICROSOFT EDGE

THE BOTTOM LINE

Microsoft Edge is the new Microsoft lightweight web browser with a layout engine built around web standards designed to replace Internet Explorer as the default web browser. It integrates with Cortana, annotation tools, Adobe Flash Player, a PDF reader, and a reading mode. Extension support was developed and added to the Windows 10 Anniversary Update in July 2016.

At the top of the window, you will find the following buttons:

- Reading view
- Add to Favorites or Reading List
- Hub (Favorites, reading lists, history, and downloads)
- Make a web note
- Feedback
- Settings

To open Edge Settings (as shown in Figure 4-28), click the Settings (. . .) button and then click the Settings option.

Figure 4-28

Configuring Microsoft Edge

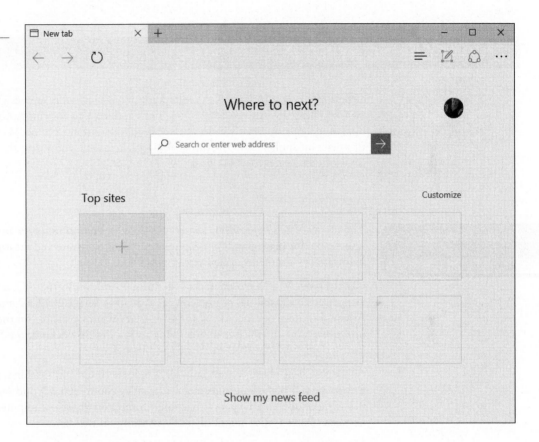

Under Settings, you can:

- Enable or disable the favorite bar.
- Set Edge to start with a New tab page, My previous tabs, or a specified web page.
- Set whether new tabs will be top sites and suggested content or a blank page.
- Set your search engine to Bing, Google, or any search engine of your choice.
- Clear browsing history and delete media licenses, pop-up exceptions, and location permissions.
- Set the Reading style to Default, Light, Medium, or Dark, along with the Reading font size.

If you click the Advanced Settings option, you can then:

- Enable or disable Flash Player.
- Opt to use caret browsing.

- Set privacy options.
- Manage saved passwords.
- Opt to save form entries.
- Choose to block pop-ups and cookies.
- Manage protected media licenses.
- Send Do Not Track requests.
- Enable or disable page prediction.
- Enable or disable SmartScreen Filter.
- Turn on or off Cortana integration.

■ CONFIGURING HYPER-V

THE BOTTOM LINE

Client Hyper-V enables you to create and manage virtual machines (VMs) using a virtual switch. These VMs can be used to test your applications for compatibility with new operating systems, allow you to run applications written for older versions of Windows, or isolate an application. The physical machine that Hyper-V and the virtual machines run on is often referred to as the ***host***.

CERTIFICATION READY
Configure Hyper-V
Objective 1.4

The Hyper-V is a ***hypervisor***, sometimes called a ***virtual machine monitor (VMM)***, and is responsible for managing the computer's physical hardware and creating multiple virtualized hardware environments, called virtual machines.

Client Hyper-V, a Microsoft replacement for Windows Virtual PC, provides the same virtualization capabilities as Hyper-V in Windows Server 2012 R2 and Windows Server 2016. Although it does not include all the advanced features available on the server version, it does utilize the same interface and underlying technology. By default, the Hyper-V feature is not installed on Windows 10 Enterprise (64-bit) machines.

Although Client Hyper-V runs only on Windows 10 (64-bit) machines running the Windows 10 Enterprise (64-bit) operating system, it enables you to run 32- and 64-bit VMs simultaneously, connect to a Hyper-V machine running on another computer, and move machines between Client Hyper-V and Hyper-V running on the server.

Using this feature, you can build a test lab that runs entirely on a single computer. For example, if you need to test an application's compatibility with several different configurations of Windows 10, you can create a VM for each configuration. After your testing is complete, you can easily remove the VMs or export them to your production network.

To run Hyper-V, you need the following:

- Windows 10 Enterprise (64-bit) version
- A 64-bit processor that incorporates second level address translation (SLAT) technology
- A minimum of 4 GB of memory (running more than one VM at a time requires more)

ENABLE THE HYPER-V FEATURE

GET READY. To enable the Hyper-V feature, log on to the computer running Windows 10 Enterprise (64-bit) with administrator privileges and perform the following steps.

1. On LON-CL1, right-click the **Start** button and click **Control Panel**.

2. In the Search Control Panel text box, type **Features**. Then from the Results list, click **Turn Windows features on and off**.

3. Click the **+** displayed next to the Hyper-V folder, as shown in Figure 4-29.

Figure 4-29

Enabling the Hyper-V feature on Windows 10 Enterprise

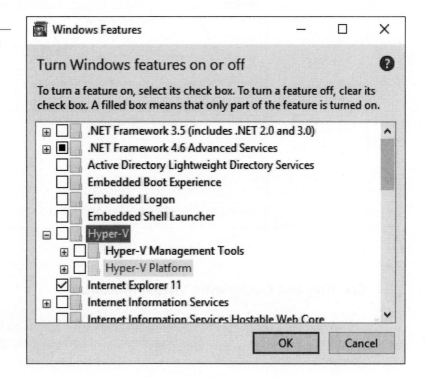

4. Select the check box next to Hyper-V and then click **OK**.

   Windows searches for the required files and then applies the changes to the computer.

5. Click **Close**.

6. Restart your computer to complete the installation.

   A restart starts the Windows hypervisor and the Virtual Machine Management service.

After installing Client Hyper-V, you see two new tiles after logging on with the administrative account:

- *Hyper-V Manager* **(see Figure 4-30):** This is the management console for creating and managing your VMs and setting up your test network.

- *Hyper-V Virtual Machine Connection:* This is used when working with a single VM that you have already created. It is very similar to the Remote Desktop Connection utility.

Figure 4-30

Opening the Hyper-V Manager console

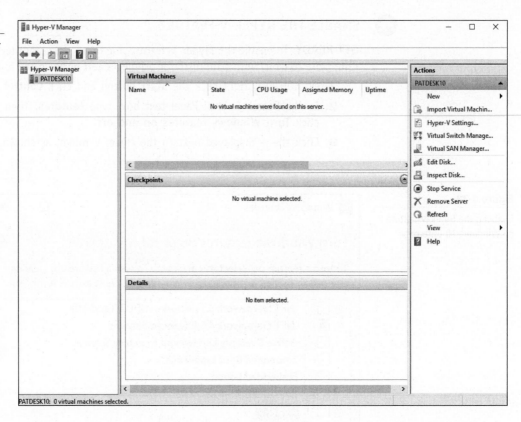

Creating and Configuring Virtual Machines

A *virtual machine (VM)* is a self-contained, isolated unit that can be easily moved from one physical computer to another, runs its own operating system, and includes its own virtual hardware configuration.

Within the Hyper-V Manager console, you can import VMs (Action > Import Virtual Machine) and create virtual hard disks (Action > New > Virtual Machine) to be used by VMs or by the host PC. You can also manage a VM's configuration by modifying the startup order of devices (for example, CD, IDE, network adapter, floppy), allocate memory, determine the number of virtual processors to use, and add hard drives/CD drives to an IDE/SCSI controller.

When you create a virtual machine, you must define the virtual machine's virtual hardware, including:

- The name of the virtual machine
- The location where the virtual machine will be stored
- The VM generation
- How much memory the virtual machine will use
- The virtual switch the virtual machine is connected to

- A virtual hard disk used by the operating system
- The operating system installation options

When you create virtual machines in Hyper-V, you have to choose one of the two virtual machine generations:

- **Generation 1:** Provides the same virtual hardware used in older versions of Hyper-V. Generation 1 VMs support 32-bit and 64-bit guest operating systems.
- **Generation 2:** Provides new functionality on a virtual machine, including PXE boot by using a standard network adapter, boot from a SCSI virtual hard disk or DVD, Secure Boot, and UEFI firmware support. Generation 2 VMs only support 64-bit guest operating systems.

Once a virtual machine has been created, you cannot change its generation.

When creating and configuring a virtual machine, you can specify how much memory is assigned to a virtual machine. The *Startup RAM* specifies the amount of memory that you want to allocate to the VM when it starts. When you are using Dynamic Memory, this value can be the minimum amount of memory needed to boot the system.

In Windows 10, Dynamic Memory is enabled by default. *Dynamic Memory* reallocates memory automatically to the VM from a shared memory pool as its demands change. If a virtualized server needs more memory, Hyper-V can increase the memory allocated to the system, and then reduce it when the traffic subsides.

 CREATE A VIRTUAL MACHINE

GET READY. To create a virtual machine in Hyper-V running on Windows 10, perform the following steps.

1. On LON-CL1, right-click the **Start** button and click **Control Panel.**
2. In the Search Control Panel text box, type **Administrative Tools.** Then from the search results, click **Administrative Tools.**
3. When the Administrative Tools opens, double-click **Hyper-V Manager.** If you are prompted to determine if you want to allow this app to make changes to your PC, click **Yes.**
4. Right-click the host and click **New > Virtual Machine.**
5. When the New Virtual Machine Wizard opens, on the Before You Begin page, click **Next.**
6. On the Specify Name and Location page (as shown in Figure 4-31), in the Name text box, type the name of the virtual machine.
7. The default location to store the VM is C:\ProgramData\Microsoft\Windows\ Hyper-V\ folder. Click **Next.**
8. On the Specify Generation page, Generation 1 is already selected. Click **Next.**
9. On the Assign Memory page, the default startup memory is 1024. In the Startup memory box, type **2048.** Click **Next.**
10. Normally, you would select a virtual switch. However, because a virtual switch is not configured yet, on the Configuring Networking page, click **Next.**
11. On the Connect Virtual Hard Disk page (as shown in Figure 4-32), change the size to **50** GB. Click **Next.**

Figure 4-31

Creating a virtual machine

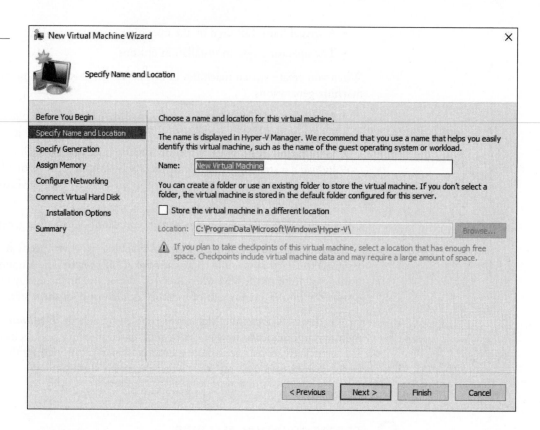

Figure 4-32

Creating a virtual hard disk

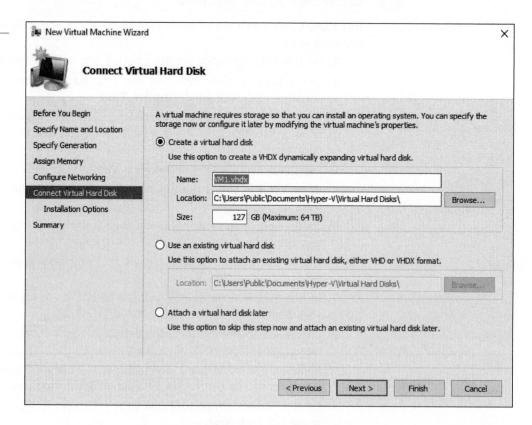

12. On the Installation Options page, select the **Install an operating system from a bootable CD/DVD-ROM** option, as shown in Figure 4-33.

Figure 4-33

Specifying Installation Options

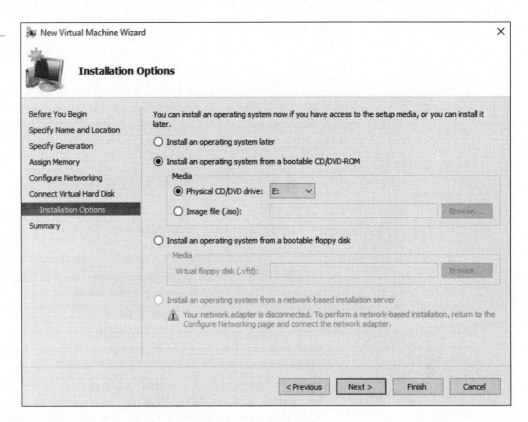

13. Select the **Image file (.iso)** option. Then click the **Browse** button. When the Open dialog box opens, browse to and double-click a Windows installation ISO file. Click **Next**.

14. On the Summary page, click **Finish**.

After the virtual machine is installed, you have to install an operating system, just as you would have to install on a physical machine. Some of the operating systems that Hyper-V supports are:

- Windows 10
- Windows 8.1
- Windows 8
- Windows 7 with SP1
- Windows 7
- Windows Vista with SP2
- Windows Server 2012 R2
- Windows Server 2012
- Windows Server 2008 R2 with SP1
- Windows Server 2008 with SP2
- Windows Small Business Server 2011
- CentOS and Red Hat Enterprise Linux
- Debian virtual machines on Hyper-V
- SUSE

- Oracle Linux
- Ubuntu
- FreeBSD

In some cases, the Hyper-V guest operating system does not function properly using the default drivers that are installed. For these operating systems, you can install guest integration services, which includes drivers for Hyper-V. It also supports operating system shutdown, time synchronization, and backup support. However, Windows 10, Windows 8/8.1, Windows Server 2012, Windows Server 2012 R2, and Windows Server 2016 already include the guest integration services.

 INSTALL GUEST INTEGRATION SERVICES

GET READY. To install guest integration services, perform the following steps.

1. On LON-CL1, in the Server Manager window, click **Tools** and then click **Hyper-V Manager**. The Hyper-V Manager console opens.
2. In the left pane, select a Hyper-V server.
3. In the Actions pane, start the virtual machine on which you want to install the guest integration services and click **Connect**. A Virtual Machine Connection window opens.
4. In the Virtual Machine Connection window, click **Action** and then click **Insert Integration Services Setup Disk**. Hyper-V mounts an image of the guest integration services disk to a virtual disk drive and displays an Autoplay window.
5. Click **Install Hyper-V Integration Services**. A message box appears, prompting you to upgrade the existing installation.
6. Click **OK**. The system installs the package and prompts you to restart the computer.
7. Click **Yes** to restart the computer.

Creating and Managing Virtual Switches

To set up a test network that includes multiple systems, you need to configure a virtual switch using the Virtual Switch Manager. This enables your VMs to communicate with each other and access your physical network for Internet access.

Hyper-V includes three types of virtual switches:

- **External:** Creates a virtual switch that binds to the physical network adapter. This enables your VMs to access your physical network.
- **Internal:** Creates a virtual switch that is used only by the VMs that run on the physical computer and between the VMs and the physical computer.
- **Private:** Creates a VM that can only be used by the VMs running on the computer.

To create a virtual switch, under the Actions pane, click Virtual Switch Manager. From the Virtual Switch Manager dialog box, select the type of switch to use and then click Create

Virtual Switch. If you select the external switch type, you need to specify the physical network adapter (on the host) to connect the switch to.

CREATE A VIRTUAL SWITCH

GET READY. To create a virtual switch in Hyper-V running on Windows 10, perform the following steps.

1. On LON-CL1, right-click the **Start** button and click **Control Panel.**

2. In the Search Control Panel text box, type **Administrative Tools.** Then from the search results, click **Administrative Tools.**

3. When the Administrative Tools opens, double-click **Hyper-V Manager.** If you are prompted to determine if you want to allow this app to make changes to your PC, click **Yes.**

4. Under Actions, click **Virtual Switch Manager.** The Virtual Switch Manager dialog box opens, as shown in Figure 4-34.

Figure 4-34

Selecting the type of virtual switch

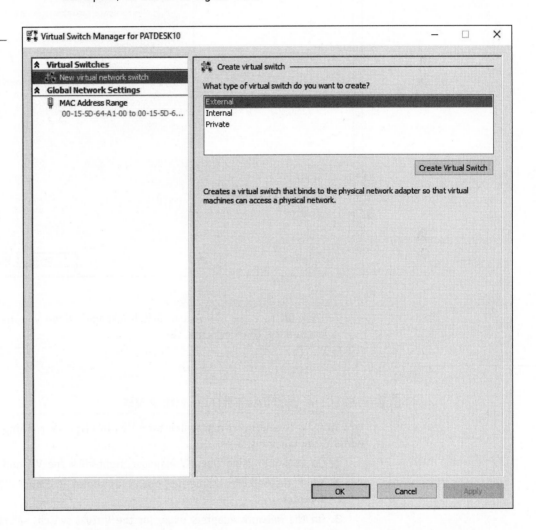

5. Select the type of switch that you want to create and click the **Create Virtual Switch** button.

6. On the New Virtual Switch page (as shown in Figure 4-35), in the Name text box, type a descriptive name for the switch.

Figure 4-35

Configuring a virtual switch

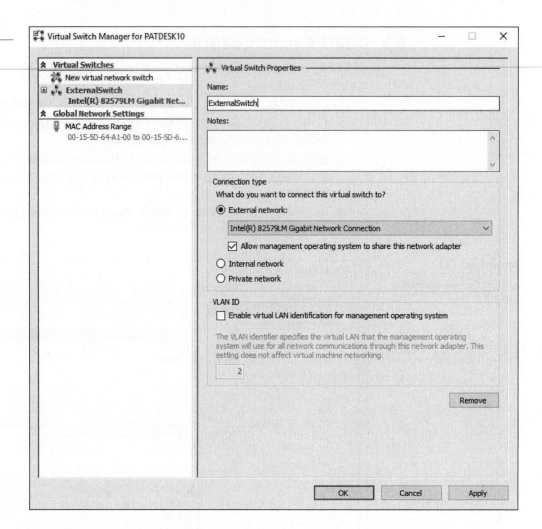

7. Click **OK** to close the Virtual Switch Manager. When you are prompted to apply networking changes, click **Yes**.

 SELECT A VIRTUAL SWITCH FOR A VM

GET READY. To select a virtual switch for a VM in Hyper-V running on Windows 10, perform the following steps.

1. On LON-CL1, using Hyper-V Manager, right-click the VM and click **Settings**.
2. When the Settings dialog box opens, as shown in Figure 4-36, click **Network Adapter**.
3. On the Network Adapters page, for the Virtual switch, select the new virtual switch.
4. Click **OK** to close the Settings dialog box.

Figure 4-36

Configuring VM Settings

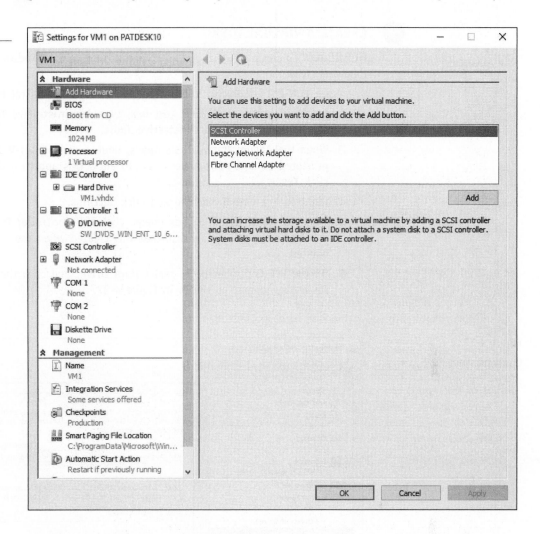

Creating and Managing Virtual Disks

A *virtual disk* is a file that represents a physical disk drive to a guest operating system running on a virtual machine. The user can install a new operating system onto the virtual disk without repartitioning the physical disk or rebooting the host machine.

The New Virtual Hard Disk Wizard provides you with a simple way to create a virtual hard disk. With the wizard, you have to specify the file format and the type of virtual disk. Besides fixed-size virtual hard disks and dynamically expanding virtual hard disks that were discussed in Lesson 2, you can also use the wizard to create a differencing virtual hard disk

A *differencing virtual disk* is a virtual disk that is associated with another virtual hard disk in a parent-child relationship. In other words, you start with a parent disk and then create a differencing disk that points to the parent disk. As changes are made, the changes are written to the differencing disk, while the parent disk remains unchanged. The differencing virtual disk expands dynamically as needed. When you use a differencing disk, you do not specify the size of the disk. Instead, the differencing disk grows up to the size of the parent disk that it is associated with.

CREATE A VIRTUAL DISK

GET READY. To create a virtual disk in Hyper-V running on Windows 10, perform the following steps.

1. On LON-CL1, right-click the **Start** button and click **Control Panel**.
2. In the Search Control Panel text box, type **Administrative Tools**. Then from the search results, click **Administrative Tools**.
3. When the Administrative Tools opens, double-click **Hyper-V Manager**. If you are prompted to determine if you want to allow this app to make changes to your PC, click **Yes**.
4. Right-click a virtual machine and click **Settings**.
5. When the Settings dialog box opens, click **IDE Controller 0**. As you can see, it already has one virtual disk that was created when the virtual machine was created.
6. On the IDE Controller page, select **Hard Drive**, and click the **Add** button. The Hard Drive page opens, as shown in Figure 4-37.

Figure 4-37

Creating a virtual disk

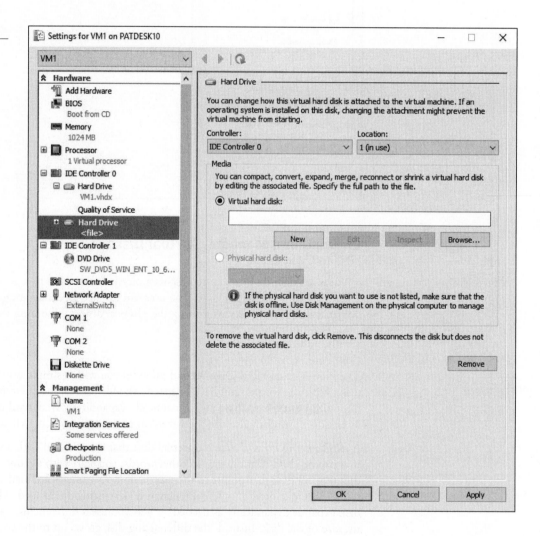

7. With the Virtual hard disk option selected, click the **New** button.
8. When the New Virtual Hard Disk Wizard opens, on the Before You Begin page, click **Next**.

9. On the Choose Disk Format page, VHDX is already selected. Click **Next.**

10. On the Choose Disk Type page, select the disk type, and click **Next.**

11. On the Specify Name and Location page, in the Name text box, specify a descriptive name for the disk. Click **Next.**

12. On the Create a New Blank Virtual Hard Disk page, specify the size of the disk, such as **10** GB. Click **Next.**

13. On the Summary page, click **Finish.**

14. Click **OK** to close the Settings dialog box.

Creating and Managing Checkpoints

In Hyper-V, a *checkpoint* is a captured image of the state, data, and hardware configuration of a VM at a particular moment in time.

When you are testing an application and want to troubleshoot compatibility issues or test a new application update before rolling it out to production machines, you can use the Hyper-V snapshot feature (right-click the machine and choose Checkpoint, as shown in Figure 4-38). By taking a checkpoint, you can return to a known state on the VM (for example, the state before you installed the application).

Figure 4-38

A checkpoint in Hyper-V Manager

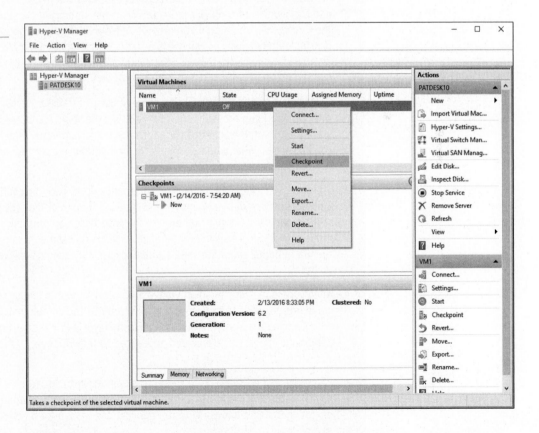

Although checkpoints are a useful tool for you when implementing a test environment in Hyper-V, this tool is not recommended for heavy use in production environments. Apart from consuming disk space, the presence of snapshots can reduce the overall performance of a VM's disk subsystem.

To revert to the previous state, right-click the checkpoint and click Apply. When you
no longer need the checkpoint, right-click the checkpoint and click Delete Checkpoint.

SKILL SUMMARY

IN THIS LESSON YOU LEARNED:

- The Windows 10 Settings is a modern interface for common configuration settings that
  would have been found in the Windows Control Panel on older versions of Windows. In
  addition, you will find additional settings such as touch screen, tablet, and privacy settings
  that are geared toward phones and tablets that you will not find in the Windows Control
  Panel.

- With previous versions of Windows, Control Panel was a primary graphical utility to configure the Windows environment and hardware devices. It can be accessed in Windows 10
  by right-clicking the Start button and choosing Control Panel.

- Microsoft has built many features into Windows 10 that work with assistive technologies
  or as stand-alone features that make the user experience better for the visually and
  hearing impaired. Most features can be configured in the Windows 10 Settings Ease
  of Access Center page or Control Panel's Ease of Access Center.

- In Windows 10, simple power management settings can be accessed by opening Settings
  and clicking System > Power & Sleep. The screen settings allow you to specify how long
  the screen will remain on if you are not actively using your computer when the computer
  is using battery power or when it is using AC power (plugged in). The sleep settings specify how long the computer will operate before going into sleep mode when the computer
  is using battery power or when it is using AC power.

- Cortana is a search feature and personal assistant for Windows 10. It can help you find
  programs and files on your computer and manage your calendar events. It can also deliver
  sport scores, weather, news, navigation, reminders, and more. When you search, you
  can either type what you are looking for, or if you have a microphone, you can speak
  to Cortana.

- Windows 10 includes two browsers, Internet Explorer and Microsoft Edge. Internet
  Explorer is the traditional browser that offers a number of features to protect your
  security and privacy while you browse the web, including phishing filters, protected
  mode, Pop-up Blocker, Add-on Manager, download files or software notification, and
  the use of digital signatures and 128-bit secure (SSL) connections when using secure
  websites.

- Microsoft Edge is the new lightweight web browser with a layout engine built around web
  standards designed to replace Internet Explorer as the default web browser. It integrates
  with Cortana, annotation tools, Adobe Flash Player, a PDF reader, and a reading mode.
  Extension support was developed and added to the Windows 10 Anniversary Update in
  July 2016.

- Client Hyper-V enables you to create and manage virtual machines (VMs) using a virtual
  switch. These VMs can be used to test your applications for compatibility with new
  operating systems, allow you to run applications written for older versions of Windows,
  or isolate an application.

Knowledge Assessment

Multiple Choice

Select the correct answer for each of the following questions.

1. Which of the following tools can be located among Administrative Tools? (Choose all that apply.)
   a. Print Management
   b. System Information
   c. Computer Management
   d. Event Viewer
   e. Windows Update

2. When changing the desktop appearance, the changes are written to which of the following?
   a. A DLL file
   b. A INI file
   c. A GPO
   d. The Registry

3. The personal assistant used in Windows 10 to find things on a PC is known as which of the following?
   a. Indexer
   b. Clippy
   c. Siri
   d. Cortana

4. Which of the following tools allows the user to see the edition and version of Windows 10 and how much memory is used by Windows 10?
   a. System Configuration
   b. Event Viewer
   c. Windows Memory Diagnostic
   d. System

5. Which of the following is *not* a basic type of add-on?
   a. Toolbar and Extensions
   b. Search Providers
   c. Privacy Plug-in
   d. Accelerators

6. When an ActiveX component needs to be approved, a(n) _____ bar will appear.
   a. orange
   b. red
   c. yellow
   d. blue

7. Which of the following content zones automatically uses your user name and password to access websites that are assigned to the zone?
   a. Internet zone
   b. Local intranet zone
   c. Trusted sites zone
   d. Restricted sites zone

8. Which of the following technologies is used to protect against phishing?
   a. InPrivate Browsing
   b. InPrivate Filtering
   c. SmartScreen
   d. SSL

9. When using SSL, the public key is found in a _____.
   a. digital certificate
   b. cookie
   c. smartfilter
   d. accelerator

10. How can a virtual switch be created for the purpose of isolating virtual machines (VMs) from the external network and the host operating system?
   a. An external virtual switch can be created.
   b. An internal virtual switch can be created.
   c. A private virtual switch can be created.
   d. VMs cannot be isolated from the external network.

Best Answer

Choose the letter that corresponds to the best answer. More than one answer choice may achieve the goal. Select the BEST answer.

1. Which of the following programs should be used to make items larger on the desktop?
   a. Settings
   b. Control Panel
   c. Device Manager
   d. System Configuration

2. An administrator needs to connect a virtual hard disk with a virtual machine (VM). Which disk format should he choose and why?
   a. VHDX because it's the only one available when creating a new disk
   b. VHD or VHDX if using an existing virtual hard disk
   c. VHD with an existing hard disk and a Type II hypervisor product
   d. Either one is possible and applicable

3. Which of the following is the key benefit for creating a virtual switch?
   a. Virtual switches enable virtual machines (VMs) to participate on the networks to which the physical adapters are connected.
   b. Virtual switches require no physical space in the rack.
   c. Virtual switches enable the Hyper-V server to participate on the networks to which the physical adapters are connected.
   d. Virtual switches have unlimited ports, freeing network administrators from connecting physical switches by uplinks or crossover circuits.

4. Which of the following network communication occurs after creating a private virtual switch?
   a. The VM on the parent partition can communicate with the physical network.
   b. VMs on both the parent and child partitions can communicate with each other.
   c. VMs on the child partitions can communicate with each other only.
   d. VMs on child partitions and the parent partition cannot communicate with each other.

5. In Windows 10, Internet Explorer runs in protected mode. Which of the following *best* describes the capabilities of Internet Explorer when running in this mode?

  a. Internet Explorer can write to the Temporary Internet files folder.

  b. Internet Explorer can write to the Temporary Internet files and the History folders.

  c. Internet Explorer can write to the Temporary Internet files, History, and Cookies folders.

  d. Internet Explorer can write to the Temporary Internet files, History, Cookies, and Favorites folder.

Matching and Identification

1. Complete the following exercise by matching the terms with their corresponding definitions.

  1. Add-ons

  2. RSS Feeds

  3. Social engineering

  4. Security zones

  5. Accelerators

  6. SmartScreen Filter

  7. WebSockets

  8. Protected mode

  9. InPrivate Mode

  10. Compatibility View

  A. Describes any attempt to penetrate the security of a system by convincing people to disclose secret information

  B. Enables browser to display older pages properly

  C. Enables clients and servers to exchange data immediately

  D. Enables surfing the Internet without leaving any record of your activities

  E. Enable users to highlight content in a browser window instead of using the search box

  F. A push technology that simplifies the process of delivering updated content to designated users

  G. Examines traffic for evidence of phishing activity

  H. Used by Internet Explorer to divide websites and assign different sets of privileges to each

  I. Provides a way to run Internet Explorer with highly reduced privileges

  J. Software components that interact with the basic functions of the web browser

Build a List

1. Specify the correct order of the steps necessary to create a virtual machine.

  a. From Server Manager's Tools menu, select Hyper-V Manager.

  b. Specify the Name and Location of the virtual machine files.

  c. Log on to the server with administrative privileges.

  d. Select a Hyper-V server and, from the Action menu, choose New Virtual Machine.

  e. Specify the Startup memory and Network Connections.

  f. Decide whether to install the new OS now or later.

■ Business Case Scenarios

Scenario 4-1: Modifying Virtual Disks

You need to modify an existing VHD file. How do you proceed?

Scenario 4-2: Resolving Application Compatibility Issues

A web-based site is needed by all users on the company's network in order to perform research on the company's competitors. After installing Windows 10, calls start coming into the help desk indicating there are compatibility problems with the site. What are some techniques that can be tried to address the problem?

Implementing Windows in an Enterprise Environment

70-698 EXAM OBJECTIVE

Objective 1.5 – Implement Windows in an Enterprise environment. This objective may include but is not limited to: Provision with the Windows Imaging and Configuration Designer (ICD) tool; implement Active Directory–based activation; implement volume activation using a Key Management Service (KMS); query and configure activation states using the command line; configure Active Directory, including Group Policies; configure and optimize user account control (UAC).

Objective 3.4 – Configure authorization and authentication. This objective may include but is not limited to: Configure UAC behavior. * Additional Objective 3.4 objectives are covered in Lesson 8 and Lesson 14.

LESSON HEADING	EXAM OBJECTIVE
Provisioning with the Windows Imaging and Configuration Designer Tool	Provision with the Windows Imaging and Configuration Designer (ICD) tool
Activating Windows	
Implementing Volume Activation using a Key Management Service (KMS)	Implement volume activation using a Key Management Service (KMS)
Implementing Active Directory–Based Activation	Implement Active Directory–based activation
Querying and Configuring Activation States Using the Command Line	Query and configure activation states using the command line
Configuring Active Directory	Configure Active Directory, including Group Policies
Understanding Active Directory Components	
Using Group Policy	
Configuring and Optimizing User Account Control (UAC)	Configure and optimize user account control (UAC) Configure UAC behavior

KEY TERMS

activation

Active Directory–Based Activation (ADBA)

Computer Configuration

directory service

domain controllers

domains

Generic Volume License Key (GVLK)

Group Policy	Lightweight Directory Access Protocol (LDAP)	Single Sign-On (SSO)
Group Policy Objects (GPOs)	multiple activation key (MAK)	slmgr.vbs
Imaging and Configuration Designer (ICD)	organizational units (OUs)	Software Licensing Manager (SLMgr) module
Kerberos	Original Equipment Manufacturer (OEM) keys	User Account Control (UAC)
Key Management Service (KMS)	provisioning packages	User Configuration
		Windows Assessment and Deployment Kit (ADK)

■ PROVISONING WITH THE WINDOWS IMAGING AND CONFIGURATION DESIGNER TOOL

THE BOTTOM LINE

With larger companies, adopting a new desktop operating system is inherently much more difficult due to wider application incompatibility, need for more user training, and greater complexity of deployment. To help with application compatibility and Windows deployment, Microsoft developed the ***Windows Assessment and Deployment Kit (ADK)*** for Windows 10. It includes multiple tools, including the Application Compatibility Toolkit (ACT), deployment tools, Imaging and Configuration Designer (ICD), User State Migration Tool (USMT), and Volume Activation Tool.

CERTIFICATION READY
Provision with the Windows Imaging and Configuration Designer (ICD) tool
Objective 1.5

The ***Imaging and Configuration Designer (ICD)*** helps you create or modify provisioning packages to update an image without deploying the image, making the changes on a new master system, and recapturing the image. ICD can also be used to create ***provisioning packages*** (*.ppkg), which are small executable programs that prepare one or more devices for corporate use. You can use it to deploy an operating system to computers, or you can use it to modify computer systems, such as connecting to a Wi-Fi network, adding certificates, connecting to an Active Directory domain, setting user rights, customizing the Start menu, upgrading editions of Windows, or enrolling a device to Mobile Device Management (MDM). It can be used to automate configuration of OEM images, or to configure Bring Your Own Devices (BYOD) devices and personal smartphones that users use on the corporate network.

INSTALL THE WINDOWS ASSESSMENT AND DEPLOYMENT KIT

GET READY. To install the Windows Assessment and Deployment Kit, perform the following steps.

1. On LON-CL1, log on as **adatum\administrator** with the password of **Pa$$w0rd**.
2. To open File Explorer, on the taskbar, click the **File Explorer** button. Then, using File Explorer, open the **\\LON-DC1\Software\Windows Kits\10\ADK** folder.
3. Double-click **adksetup.exe**.
4. When the Windows Assessment and Deployment Kit – Windows 10 Wizard opens, on the Specify Location page, click **Next**.
5. On the Windows Kits Privacy page, click **Next**.
6. On the License Agreement page, click the **Accept** button.
7. On the Select the Features You Want to Install page (as shown in Figure 5-1), deselect the applications that you do not want, and click the **Install** button.

Figure 5-1

Selecting the Windows
Assessment and Deployment
Kit features

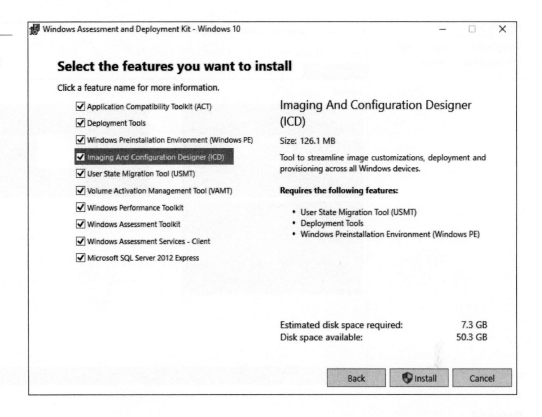

8. If you are prompted to determine if you want to allow this app to make changes to your PC, click the **Yes** button.

9. The installation will take about 5–10 minutes. When done, click **Close**.

 CREATE AND BUILD A PROVISIONING PACKAGE

GET READY. To create and build a provisioning package, perform the following steps.

1. On LON-CL1, click **Start**, and then click **All apps**. Scroll down the list, select and expand **Windows Kits**, scroll down, and then click **Windows Imaging and Configuration Designer**.

2. If you are prompted to determine if you want to allow this app to make changes to your PC, click **Yes**.

3. When the Windows Imaging and Configuration Designer (as shown in Figure 5-2) opens, click the **New provisioning package** icon.

4. When the New Project Wizard starts, on the Enter Project Details page, in the Name text box, type **Project1**. Click **Next**.

5. On the Choose Which Settings to View and Configure page, select **Common to all desktop editions** and then click **Next**.

6. On the Import a Provisioning Package page, click **Finish**.

7. When the Project1 tab opens, with the view set to All settings, under Runtime settings, navigate to and click **Policies > Camera > AllowCamera** (as shown in Figure 5-3).

8. Change the AllowCamera option from NOT CONFIGURED to **Yes**.

Figure 5-2

Using Windows Imaging and
Configuration Designer

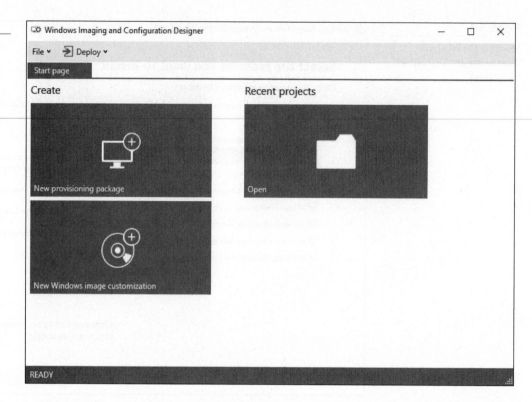

Figure 5-3

Managing ConnectivityProfiles

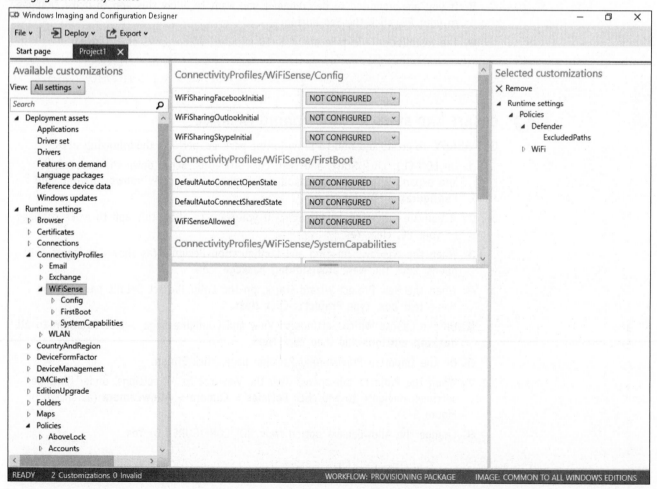

9. In the Runtime settings console tree, select and expand **Policies**, and then select **Defender**. In the subitems under the Defender node, select **Excluded paths**. In the details pane, in the Excluded paths text box, type **E:\Labfiles**.

10. Under Runtime settings, navigate to and click **Accounts > User**.

11. In the UserName text box, type **PublicUser**, and click the **Add** button.

12. Click the **UserName: PublicUser** node.

13. In the Password text box, type **Pa$$w0rd**.

14. For the UserGroup, select **Standard Users**.

15. Open the **File** menu, and click **Save**.

16. Open the **Export** menu, and click **Provisioning package**.

17. When the Build window opens, for the Owner drop-down list, change the value from OEM to **IT Admin**, and then click **Next**.

18. On the Select Security Details for the Provisioning Package page, deselect the **Encrypt package** option and click **Next**.

19. On the Select Where to Save the Provisioning Package page, in the Select where to save the provisioning package text box, type **\\LON-DC1\Software\Project01.ppkg**, and click **Next**.

20. On the Build the Provisioning Package page, click **Build**.

21. When the package is built, click **Finish**.

To see a list of all the various Windows Provisioning settings, go to the Microsoft Developer Network website and search for *Windows Provisioning settings reference*. After you have configured your settings and created a provisioning package, you can then deploy the back to a USB device or removable device.

To configure a PC, you can apply the configuration during or after deployment. To configure the device during deployment, you must use the Windows ICD command line. To apply the configuration after deployment, you just have to double-click the provisioning package, and click on Allow to let the package configure the device (as shown in Figure 5-4), including saying that the package has come from a trusted source. For mobile phones, connect the mobile device to a PC using a USB cable, and double-click the provisioning package. Similar to a PC, click to allow the package to configure your device.

Figure 5-4

Executing a provisioning package

Is this package from a source you trust?

Only add this package (Project1.ppkg) if you know who it came from.

Adding it will:

Lock down the user interface
Affect security configuration

Yes, add it   Cancel

■ ACTIVATING WINDOWS

THE BOTTOM LINE

Activation helps verify that your copy of Windows is genuine and that it has not been used on more computers than the Microsoft Software Terms allow. Windows 10 requires product activation, which validates each Windows 10 license through an online activation service at Microsoft by phone, through KMS, or through Active Directory Domain Services, in order to be fully functional. During the activation step, you install the proper license key for Windows.

You can activate Windows in two ways: manually or automatically. With manual activation, you must enter the product key and activate over the Internet to the special clearing-house website, or over the phone by using a retail product key or a **_multiple activation key (MAK)_**. To activate over the Internet, you open Settings, click Update & Security, and click Activation, as shown in Figure 5-5. When you use a MAK, you can activate multiple computers, up to a set activation limit.

Figure 5-5

Activating Windows 10

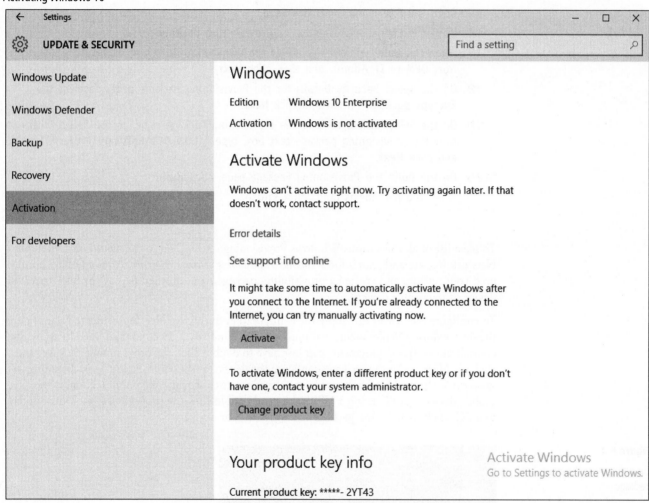

You can also use **_Original Equipment Manufacturer (OEM) keys_** with computers. Manufacturers provide OEM keys, which are typically tied to specific computers. OEM keys are usually distributed with systems running Windows 7 or higher, but can also be found on systems running Windows Server operating systems.

If you have a large number of clients and servers, consider setting up a Volume Activation Services server. When you install the Volume Activation Services server role, you can choose Key Management Service or Active Directory–Based Activation. After adding the Volume Activation Services role, you can use the Volume Activation Tools GUI to configure activation. When you use Volume Activation Services, each activated computer must contact the KMS server periodically to renew its activation status. To report on activated licenses, you can use the Volume Activation Management Tool (VAMT), which is part of the Windows Assessment and Deployment Kit (ADK).

Implementing Volume Activation Using a Key Management Service (KMS)

Key Management Service (KMS) is a service that activates Volume License versions of Windows Vista and later as well as Office 2010 and later. To activate operating systems, you need at least 25 client operating systems or 5 server operating systems. When you use Volume Activation Services, each activated computer must contact the KMS server periodically to renew its activation status. Activation lasts for 180 days and attempts to renew with the KMS host every 7 days by default. The KMS host is found by referencing an SRV record in DNS.

CERTIFICATION READY
Implement volume
activation using a Key
Management Service
(KMS)
Objective 1.5

To enable KMS functionality, you install a KMS host key on the KMS host and then activate it on the phone or by using an online web service at Microsoft. After you initialize KMS, the KMS activation infrastructure is self-maintaining. A single KMS host can support an almost unlimited number of KMS clients. Most organizations can operate with just two KMS hosts for their entire infrastructure: one main KMS host and a backup host for redundancy.

 INSTALL AND CONFIGURE A KEY MANAGEMENT SERVICE

GET READY. On a server running Windows Server 2012 R2, to install and configure a Key Management Service (KMS), perform the following steps.

1. Log on to LON-SVR1 as **Adatum\administrator** with the password of **Pa$$Word**.
2. When Server Manager opens, open the **Manage** menu, and click **Add Roles and Features**.
3. When the Add Roles and Features Wizard opens, on the Before You Begin page, click **Next**.
4. On the Installation Type page, the Role-based or feature-based installation option is selected. Click **Next**.
5. On the Server Selection page, click **Next**.
6. On the Server Roles page, select the **Volume Activation Services** option. When you are prompted to add additional features, click **Add Features**. Click **Next**.
7. On the Features page, click **Next**.
8. On the Volume Activation Services page, click **Next**.
9. On the Confirmation page, click **Install**.
10. When the Volume Activation Tool is installed, click **Close**.
11. In Server Manager, click the **Tools** menu, and click **Volume Activation Tools**.
12. When the Volume Activation Tools Wizard opens, on the Introduction page, click **Next**.
13. On the Select Volume Activation Method page, select the **Key Management Service (KMS)** option, as shown in Figure 5-6.
14. Then in the Key Management Service (KMS) text box, type **LON-SVR1**. Click **Next**.
15. On the Manage KMS Host page, in the Install your KMS host key text box, type your key. Click **Commit**.
16. On the Product Key Management page, the Activate Product option is already selected. Click **Next**.
17. On the Activate Product page, the Activate online option is already selected. Click **Commit**.

Figure 5-6

Selecting the Volume Activation Method

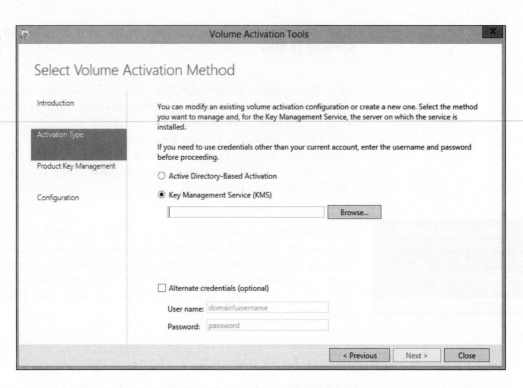

Once your KMS is configured, you can configure DNS so clients can automatically locate the KMS. If the DNS record has not been automatically created, create the following DNS record:

Service _VLMCS

Protocol _TCP.<your domain>

Port 1688

<The host that has the KMS service>

Implementing Active Directory–Based Activation

Active Directory–Based Activation (ADBA) is a new feature for Windows 8 and higher, and Windows Server 2012 and higher, which enables enterprises to activate computers when a computer is joined to the domain, as long as the computer has a *Generic Volume License Key (GVLK)* installed. No single physical computer is required to act as the activation object because it is distributed throughout the domain. To activate an ADBA forest online, you need to specify a KMS host key, and optionally specify an Active Directory–based Activation Object display name.

CERTIFICATION READY
Implement Active Directory–based activation
Objective 1.5

To use ADBA, you need to extend the domain to Windows Server 2012 or higher. You then:

1. Install the Volume Activation Services server role on a domain controller.
2. Add a KMS host key by using the Volume Activation Tools Wizard.
3. Microsoft verifies the KMS host key, and an activation object is created.

Client computers are activated by receiving the activation object from a domain controller during startup.

⊘ **INSTALL AND CONFIGURE ACTIVE DIRECTORY–BASED ACTIVATION**

GET READY. On a server running Windows Server 2012 R2, to install and configure the Active Directory–Based Activation, perform the following steps.

1. Log on to LON-SVR1 as **Adatum\administrator** with the password of **Pa$$Word**.
2. In Server Manager, click the **Tools** menu, and click **Volume Activation Tools**.
3. When the Volume Activation Tools Wizard opens, on the Introduction page, click **Next**.
4. On the Select Volume Activation Method page, select the **Active Directory–Based Activation**. Click **Next**.
5. On the Manage Activation Objects page, in the Install your KMS host key text box, type in your key and click **Next**.
6. On the Product Key Management page, the Activate Product option is already selected. Click **Next**.
7. On the Activate Product page, the Activate online option is already selected. Click **Commit**.

Querying and Configuring Activation States Using the Command Line

The Windows activation process is handled by the *Software Licensing Manager (SLMgr) module*, also known as the Windows Software Licensing Management tool. A VBScript called *slmgr.vbs* keeps track of licensing details.

Slmgr.vbs allows users to query the current installation and see details about Windows installation and its activation and licensing status. For example, to display very basic license and activation information about the current system, run the following command:

```
slmgr.vbs /dli
```

To display more detailed license information—including the activation ID, installation ID, and other details, run the following command:

```
slmgr.vbs /dlv
```

To display the expiration date of the current license, run the following command:

```
slmgr.vbs /xpr
```

You can change the product key by executing the following command:

```
slmgr.vbs /ipk #####-#####-#####-#####-#####
```

where #####-#####-#####-#####-##### is the actual product key.

To uninstall the current product key, run the following command and then restart your computer:

```
slmgr.vbs /upk
```

To force Windows to attempt an online activation, run the following command:

```
slmgr.vbs /ato
```

If you need to activate Windows offline, first run the following command:

```
Slmgr.vbs /dti
```

You then need to get a confirmation ID to activate the system over the phone by calling the Microsoft Product Activation Center and providing the installation ID you received. After obtaining an activation ID, execute the following command:

```
slmgr.vbs /atp <ACTIVATIONID>
```

Once you're done, you can use the slmgr.vbs /dli or slmgr.vbs /dlv commands to confirm you're activated.

■ CONFIGURING ACTIVE DIRECTORY

THE BOTTOM LINE

A *directory service* stores, organizes, and provides access in a directory. Directory services are used for locating, managing, administering, and organizing common items and network resources, such as volumes, folders, files, printers, users, groups, devices, telephone numbers, and other objects. One popular directory service used by many organizations is Microsoft Active Directory.

CERTIFICATION READY
Configure Active Directory, including Group Policies
Objective 1.5

Active Directory is the Microsoft directory service that does the following:

- Stores information about the identities of users, computers, and services
- Provides authentication for users and computers
- Provides authorization for users and computers to access network resources

Active Directory is a technology created by Microsoft that provides a variety of network services, including the following:

- LDAP
- Kerberos-based and Single Sign-On authentication
- DNS-based naming and other network information
- A central location for network administration and delegation of authority

The *Lightweight Directory Access Protocol (LDAP)* is an application protocol for querying and modifying data using directory services running over TCP/IP. Within the directory, the sets of objects are organized in a logical hierarchical manner so that you can easily find and manage them. The structure can reflect geographical or organizational boundaries, although it tends to use DNS names for structuring the topmost levels of the hierarchy. Deeper inside the directory, there might be entries representing people, organizational units, printers, documents, groups of people, or anything else that represents a given tree entry (or multiple entries). LDAP uses TCP port 389.

Kerberos is a computer network authentication protocol, which allows hosts to prove their identity over a nonsecure network in a secure manner. It can also provide mutual authentication so that both the user and server verify each other's identity. For security reasons, Kerberos protocol messages are protected against eavesdropping and replay attacks.

Single Sign-On (SSO) allows you to log on once and access multiple related but independent software systems without having to log on again. As you log on with Windows using Active Directory, you are assigned a token, which can then be used to sign on to other systems automatically.

Finally, Active Directory allows you to organize all of your network resources, including users, groups, printers, computers, and other objects, so that you can assign passwords, permissions, and rights to the users on your network. You can also assign who can manage a group of objects.

Understanding Active Directory Components

When you look at Active Directory, you can look at it from two sides: logical and physical. First, when you hear the term *Active Directory*, you most likely look at the logical components that make up Active Directory.

The *logical* components (which administrators create, organize, and manage) include:

- *Organizational units (OUs)*: Containers in a domain that allow you to organize and group resources for easier administration, including providing and delegating administrative rights.
- *Domains*: Administrative boundaries for users and computers that are stored in a common directory database. A single domain can span multiple physical locations or sites and can contain millions of objects.
- **Domain trees:** Collections of domains that are grouped together in hierarchical structures and that share a common root domain. A domain tree could have a single domain or many domains. A domain (known as the parent domain) could have a child domain. A child domain could have its own child domain. Because the child domain is combined with the parent domain name to form its own unique Domain Name System (DNS) name, the domains with a tree have a contiguous namespace.
- **Forests:** Collections of domain trees that share a common AD DS. A forest can contain one or more domain trees or domains, all of which share a common logical structure, global catalog, directory schema, and directory configuration, as well as automatic two-way transitive trust relationships. A forest may be a single domain tree or even simply a single domain. The first domain in the forest is called the forest root domain. If you have multiple domain trees, each domain tree would consist of a unique namespace.

An object is a distinct, named set of attributes or characteristics that represent a network resource. Common objects used within Active Directory are computers, users, groups, and printers. Attributes have values that define the specific object. For example, a user could have the first name John, the last name Smith, and the logon name as jsmith, all of which identify the user.

When working with objects, administrators use the names of the objects, such as user names. However, Active Directory objects are assigned a 128-bit unique number called a globally unique identifier (GUID), sometimes referred to as a security identifier (SID), to uniquely identify an object. For example, even if a user changes his user name, he will still be able to access all objects and have all of the rights he had previously because these are assigned to the GUID.

GUIDs also provide some security. In particular, if a user is deleted, you cannot create a new user account with the same user name and expect to have access to all of the objects and rights the previous user had access to. Thus, if you decide to fire an employee within your organization and you plan to replace that employee, you can disable the account, hire the new person, rename the user account, change the password, and reenable the account so that the new person can access all resources and have all of the rights that the previous user had.

The schema of Active Directory defines the format of each object and the attributes or fields within each object. The default schema contains definitions of commonly used objects, such as user accounts, computers, printers, and groups. For example, the schema defines that a user account has the user's first name, last name, and telephone number.

To allow Active Directory to be flexible so that it can support other applications, you can extend the schema to include additional attributes. For example, you could add a badge number or employee identification number to the user object. Indeed, when you install some applications, such as Microsoft Exchange, they extend the schema, usually by adding additional attributes or fields so that the schema can support the application.

A user account enables a user to log on to a computer and domain. As a result, it can be used to prove the identity of a user, and this identity information can then be used to determine what the user can access and what kind of authorization she has. It can also be used for auditing so that if there is a security problem in which something was accessed or deleted, the person who accessed or deleted the object can be determined.

The *physical* components that make up Active Directory include the following:

- *Domain controllers*: The servers that contain the Active Directory databases. A domain partition stores only the information about objects located in that domain. All domain controllers in a domain receive changes and replicate those changes to the domain partition stored on all other domain controllers in the domain. As a result, all domain controllers are peers in the domain and manage replication as a unit.

When a user logs on, Active Directory clients locate an Active Directory server (using the DNS SRV resource records) known as a domain controller in the same site as the computer.

Each domain has its own set of domain controllers to provide access to the domain resources, such as users and computers. For fault tolerance, a site should have two or more domain controllers. That way, if one domain controller fails, the other domain controller can still service the clients. Note that whenever an object (such as a user name or password) is modified, it is automatically replicated to the other domain controllers within a domain.

A domain controller is a Windows server that stores a replica of the account and security information for the domain and defines the domain boundaries. To make a computer running Windows Server 2012 R2 or Windows Server 2016 a domain controller, you must install Active Directory Domain Services and execute dcpromo from Server Manager.

After you have promoted a computer to a domain controller, you can use several MMC snap-in consoles to manage Active Directory. These consoles are as follows:

- **Active Directory Users and Computers:** Used to manage users, groups, computers, and organizational units (see Figure 5-7)
- **Active Directory Domains and Trusts:** Used to administer domain trusts, domain and forest functional levels, and user principal name (UPN) suffixes
- **Active Directory Sites and Services:** Used to administer replication of directory data among all sites in an Active Directory Domain Services (AD DS) forest
- **Active Directory Administrative Center:** Used to administer and publish information in the directory, including managing users, groups, computers, domains, domain controllers, and organizational units
- **Group Policy Management Console (GPMC):** Used to provide a single administrative tool for managing Group Policy across the enterprise

Although these tools are installed on domain controllers, they can also be installed on client PCs so that you can manage Active Directory without logging on to a domain controller.

Using Group Policy

Group Policy is one of the most powerful features of Active Directory; it controls the working environment for user accounts and computer accounts. Group Policy provides centralized management and configuration of operating systems, applications, and user settings in an Active Directory environment. For example, you can use Group Policy to specify how often a user must change his password, you can set the desktop background image and screen saver on a person's computer, and you can configure spell-checking so that it is required before a user can send an email.

Figure 5-7

Active Directory Users and Computers

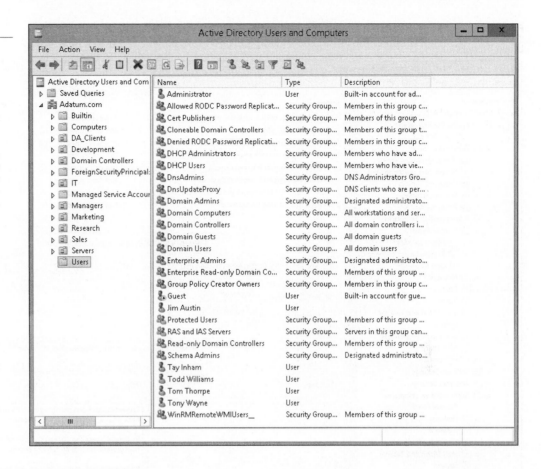

There are literally thousands of settings that can be used to restrict certain actions, make a system more secure, or standardize a working environment. A setting can control a computer registry, NTFS security, an audit and security policy, software installation, folder redirection, offline folders, or logon and logoff scripts. As each server version is released, Microsoft usually adds additional parameters. Figure 5-8 shows an example of using the Group Policy Editor to prevent a user from changing the Start menu background.

Group Policy Objects (GPOs) are collections of user and computer settings, including the following:

- **System settings:** Application settings, desktop appearance, and behavior of system services.
- **Security settings:** Local computer, domain, and network security settings, including account policies (Password Policy, Account Lockout Policy, and Kerberos Policy).
- **Software installation settings:** Management of software installation, updates, and removal.
- **Scripts settings:** Scripts for when a computer starts or shuts down and for when a user logs on and off.
- **Folder redirection settings:** Storage for users' folders on the network. For example, the Redirect to the local user profile location option moves the location of the folder to the local user profile under the Users folder.
- **Administrative Templates:** A wide range of settings that contains all registry-based policy settings.

Figure 5-8

Group Policy Editor

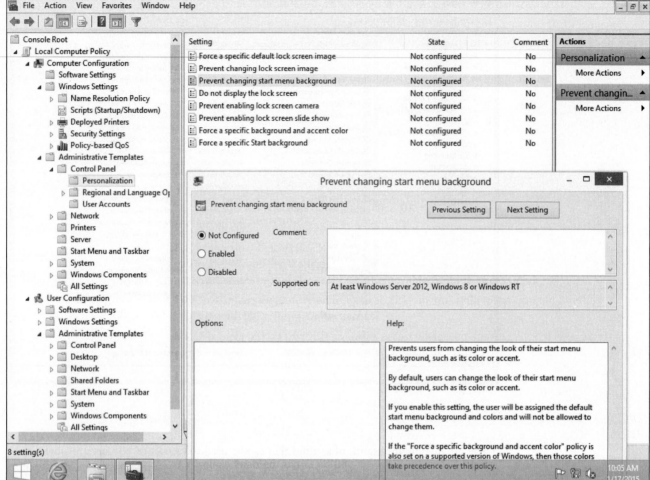

Group Policy can be set locally on a workstation or set at different levels (site, domain, or organizational unit) within Active Directory. Generally speaking, you will not find as many settings locally as you will at the site, domain, or organizational unit (OU) level. When group policies are applied, they are applied in the following order:

1. Local
2. Site
3. Domain
4. OU

If you configure a Group Policy setting at the site, domain, or OU level and that setting contradicts a setting configured at the local policy level, the local policy setting will be overridden. Generally speaking, if you have a policy setting that conflicts with a previously executed setting, the more recent executed setting remains in effect. Figure 5-9 shows the Default Domain Policy, which is linked and deployed to the contoso.com domain.

Figure 5-9

Using the Group Policy
Management Console

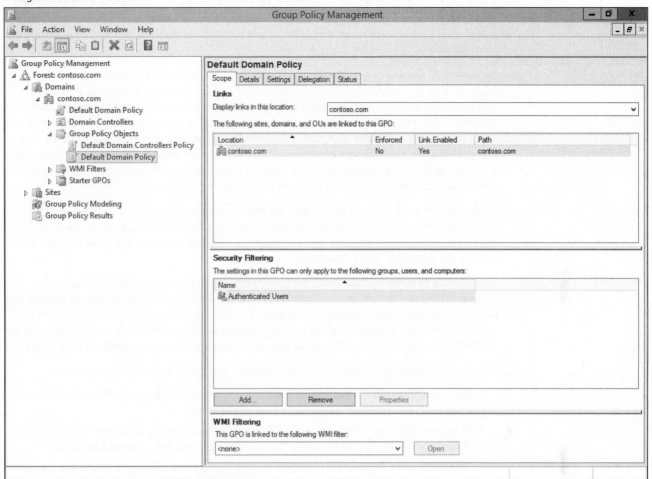

 ACCESS THE LOCAL GROUP POLICY EDITOR

GET READY. You can open the Local Group Policy Editor by using gpedit.msc at a
command line or by using the MMC. To open the Local Group Policy Editor, perform the
following steps.

1. Click the **Start** button. Then type **mmc** and press **Enter**.

2. When the Console1 window opens, open the **File** menu and click **Add/Remove Snap-in**.

3. When the Add or Remove Snap-ins dialog box opens, click **Group Policy Object Editor** and then click **Add**.

4. Local Computer is already selected, which will open the Local Group Policy Editor. Click **Finish**.

5. Back in the Add or Remove Snap-ins dialog box, click **OK**.

Most times, you need only to access the security settings that you found in the local policy. This can be done by opening the Local Security Policy from Administrative Tools.

There are thousands of settings available with group policies. In addition, as each version of Windows is released, new settings are added to allow administrators to configure new technology that has been added to Windows, to provide control that was not available previously, or to provide more granular control.

As previously discussed, group policies are organized according to computer settings (contained in the Computer Configuration node) and user settings (contained in the User Configuration node). The **Computer Configuration** node contains settings that are applied to the computer regardless of who logs on to the computer. By default, computer settings are applied when the computer is started. The **User Configuration** node contains settings that are applied when the user logs on. Group Policy settings are refreshed every 90 minutes with a random delay of 30 minutes (giving a random range between 90 minutes and 120 minutes). On domain controllers, group policies get refreshed every 5 minutes.

To manually refresh a group policy, you use the GPUpdate command. The gpupdate / force command causes the system to reapply all settings in all GPOs scoped to the user or computer because some policies' settings require a logoff or a reboot. For these settings, you can use the gpupdate /force /logoff /boot command.

Starting with Windows Server 2008, the Computer Configuration and User Configuration nodes are divided into Policies and Preferences nodes. Policies include the traditional settings that were available with earlier versions of Windows, but also have many new settings that were not available previously. Preferences allow you to configure additional Windows settings that were not available previously and they allow more control on how the settings are applied to the clients.

Computer Configuration\Policies can be organized according to the following nodes:

- **Software Settings:** Contains only one node, Software installation, which allows you to install and maintain software within your organization
- **Windows Settings:** Allows you to configure Windows settings, including Name Resolution Policy, Scripts (Startup/Shutdown), Security Settings, and Policy-Based QoS nodes
- **Administrative Templates:** Contains registry-based Group Policy settings that are used to configure the computer environment, such as Control Panel, Printers, System, and Windows components

User Configuration\Policies can be divided into the following nodes:

- **Software Settings:** Contains only one node, Software installation, which allows you to install and maintain software within your organization
- **Windows Settings:** Allows you to configure Windows settings, including Scripts (Logon/Logoff), Security Settings, Folder Redirection, and Policy-Based QoS nodes
- **Administrative Templates:** Contains registry-based Group Policy settings that are used to configure the user environment, such as Control Panel, Printers, System, and Windows components

Windows 10 includes thousands of Administrative Template policies, which contain registry-based policy settings that are used to configure the user and computer environment. For example, to configure the user's desktop image or a default screen saver, you would use an Administrative Template policy.

Administrative Templates can be located under both Computer Configuration and User Configuration. The requirements for an Administrative Template setting, such as which operating system supports the setting and the description of the feature, are displayed:

- On the Extended tab, when you click to select an Administrative Template setting
- When you double-click an Administrative Template setting

When configuring Administrative Templates, there are three states:

- **Not Configured:** The registry key is not modified or overwritten.
- **Enabled:** The registry key is modified by this setting.
- **Disabled:** The Disabled setting undoes a change made by a prior Enabled setting.

If you want to undo the group policy, removing the group policy does not necessarily remove the setting from a computer that has the setting configured with a GPO. In these cases, you need to change the policy to Disabled (or create a second policy) and apply it to the computer and/or user. After the policy is applied, the policy can be removed. The policy can also be manually removed using the registry editor:

- HKEY_CURRENT_USER\Software\Microsoft\Windows\CurrentVersion\Policies
- HKEY_LOCAL_MACHINE\Software\Microsoft\Windows\CurrentVersion\Policies

Some Administrative Templates can be used to configure a setting, such as specifying a desktop image or specifying a screen saver. Although these settings are configured with group policies, some of these settings can be changed while the computer is running. However, when the group policy is reapplied, the setting reverts back to the setting defined with the GPO. Other settings are used to lock down a computer so that users cannot modify a setting or hide the setting from the user.

 CONFIGURE THE DESKTOP BACKGROUND IMAGE WITH GROUP POLICY

GET READY. To configure the desktop background image with group policies, perform the following steps.

1. Open the **Group Policy Management Editor** for the GPO you want to configure.
2. For a domain, OU, or site GPO, navigate to **User Configuration\Policies\ Administrative Templates\Desktop\Desktop**. For a local policy, navigate to **User Configuration\Administrative Templates\Desktop\Desktop**.
3. Double-click **Desktop Wallpaper**. The Desktop Wallpaper dialog box opens.
4. Click **Enabled**.
5. In the Wallpaper Name text box, type the path and name of an image file.
6. Click **OK** to close the Desktop Wallpaper dialog box. The Desktop Wallpaper shows as Enabled.
7. Close the Group Policy Management Editor window.

■ CONFIGURING AND OPTIMIZING USER ACCOUNT CONTROL (UAC)

THE BOTTOM LINE

The *User Account Control (UAC)* is a technology used with Windows Vista, 7, 8/8.1, and 10 to enhance system security by detecting and preventing unauthorized changes to the system. Some applications might not run properly using a standard user credential if the application needs to access restricted files or registry location.

CERTIFICATION READY
Configure and optimize user account control (UAC)
Objective 1.5

When you look at accounts that run in Windows, accounts can be divided into:

- Standard accounts
- Administrator accounts

When performing normal tasks, including surfing the Internet, creating documents, reading and sending email, and running programs, it is recommended to use a standard account. If you use an administrator account and you access a malicious website or run a malicious program, the malicious code can reach further into your machine and confidential places to access your personal information.

With UAC, when a user logs on to Windows 10, the system issues a token, which indicates the user's access level. Standard users receive a standard user token and members of the Administrators group receive two tokens, a standard user token and an administrator token. Normally, both users use the standard user token. However, if you need to perform an administrative task, UAC notifies you that a change needs to be made. If you are an administrator, you click Yes to continue. If you are not an administrator, you must log on with an administrator account. If malicious code tries to access your system and make changes without your knowledge, the UAC prompts notify you, and you can stop the program from making those changes.

In Windows 10, the number of operating system applications and tasks that require elevation is fewer when compared with older versions of Windows. The default UAC setting allows a standard user to perform the following tasks without receiving a UAC prompt:

- View Windows settings.
- Pair Bluetooth devices with the computer.
- Reset the network adapter and perform other network diagnostic and repair tasks.
- Establish a local area network (LAN) connection or wireless connection.
- Modify display settings.
- Play and burn CD/DVD media.
- Change the desktop backup for the current user.
- Open Date and Time in Control Panel and change the time zone.
- Use Remote Desktop to connect to another computer.
- Change the user's own password.
- Configure battery power options.
- Configure accessibility options.
- Restore a user's backup files.
- Set up computer synchronization.

You are then prompted and require elevation to an administrator account for the following tasks:

- Install and uninstall applications.
- Install a driver for a device.
- Install Windows updates.
- Install an ActiveX control.
- Open Windows Firewall in Control Panel.
- Change a user's account type.
- Configure Remote Desktop access.
- Add or remove a user account.
- Copy or move files into the Program Files or Windows directory.
- Schedule automated tasks.
- Restore system backup files.
- Configure Automatic Updates.
- Browse to another user's directory.

In Windows 10, four UAC settings are available through Control Panel:

- **Never notify me:** UAC is off.
- **Notify me only when apps try to make changes to my computer (do not dim my desktop):** When a program makes a change, a prompt appears, and the desktop does not dim.

- **Notify me only when apps try to make changes to my computer (default):** When a program makes a change, a prompt appears, but the desktop dims. Otherwise, the user is not prompted.
- **Always notify me:** The user is always prompted when changes are made to the computer and the Desktop is dimmed.

To configure UAC through Control Panel, use the following procedure.

REVIEW UAC SETTINGS

GET READY. To review UAC settings, log on to Windows 10 using an account with administrator privileges and then perform the following steps.

1. Click the **Start** button. Type **uac** and then from the results, click **Change User Account Control settings**.

2. The User Account Control Settings dialog box opens, as shown in Figure 5-10.

Figure 5-10

Reviewing UAC settings options

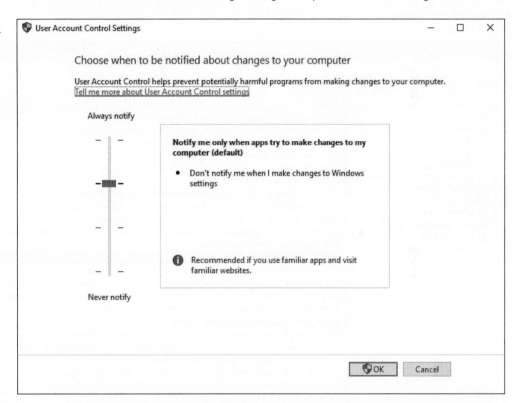

3. Read the current setting and then drag the slider up and down to each setting to review its description.
   - Always notify me
   - Notify me only when apps try to make changes to my computer (default)
   - Notify me only when apps try to make changes to my computer (do not dim my desktop)
   - Never notify me

4. In the User Account Control Settings dialog box, click **Cancel.**

Starting with Windows 8, you cannot fully disable UAC. Therefore, when you move the slider to *Never notify me*, you are not turning off UAC, you are just receiving fewer notifications and running all processes at a medium integrity level. To get better control of UAC, you can configure UAC policy via the local or Group Policy.

To configure UAC properties using Local Security Policy, use the following procedure.

 CONFIGURE A UAC POLICY USING THE LOCAL SECURITY POLICY

GET READY. To configure a UAC policy using the Local Security Policy, log on to Windows 10 using an account with administrator privileges and then perform the following steps.

1. Click the **Start** button. Type **secpol.msc** and then from the results, choose **secpol.msc**.

2. Expand **Local Policies** and then click **Security Options**.

3. Scroll down to the bottom of the policy list until you see the 10 policies with the User Account Control prefix, as shown in Figure 5-11. These policy settings are described in detail in Table 5-1.

Figure 5-11

Exploring the User Account Control policies

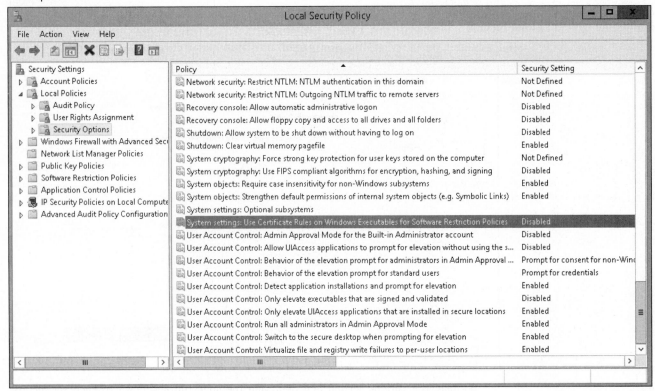

Table 5-1

UAC Local Security Policy Settings

POLICY SETTING	VALUES AND FUNCTIONS
User Account Control: Admin Approval Mode for the Built-in Administrator account	• When enabled, the built-in Administrator account uses Admin Approval Mode. By default, any operation that requires elevation of privilege prompts the user to approve the operation. • When disabled (default), the built-in Administrator account runs with full administrative privilege.

Table 5-1

(Continued)

POLICY SETTING	VALUES AND FUNCTIONS
User Account Control: Allow UIAccess applications to prompt for elevation without using the secure desktop	• When enabled, this setting causes User Interface Accessibility programs to disable the secure desktop when displaying elevation prompts used by a standard user. • When disabled, elevation prompts use the secure desktop, unless the *User Account Control: Switch to the secure desktop when prompting for elevation* policy is enabled.
User Account Control: Behavior of the elevation prompt for administrators in Admin Approval Mode	• When set to *Elevate without prompting*, administrative users are elevated to the administrative token with no consent or credentials from the human user. • When set to *Prompt for credentials on the secure desktop*, administrative users are elevated to the administrative token only after the presentation of a credential prompt on the secure desktop, to which the user must supply a valid administrative account name and password, even if she is already logged on using such an account. If valid credentials are entered, the operation continues with the user's highest available privilege. • When set to *Prompt for consent on the secure desktop*, administrative users are elevated to the administrative token only after the presentation of an elevation prompt on the secure desktop and the consent of the human user. The user is prompted to select Permit or Deny. If he selects Permit, the operation continues with the user's highest available privilege. • When set to *Prompt for credentials*, administrative users are elevated to the administrative token only after the presentation of a credential prompt to which the user must supply valid administrative account name and password. If valid credentials are entered, the operation continues with the applicable privilege. • When set to *Prompt for consent*, administrative users are elevated to the administrative token only after the presentation of an elevation prompt on the secure desktop and the consent of the human user. The user is prompted to select Permit or Deny. If she selects Permit, the operation continues with the user's highest available privilege. • When set to *Prompt for consent for non-Windows binaries (Default)*, when an operation for a non-Microsoft application requires elevation of privilege, administrative users are prompted to select either Permit or Deny. If they select Permit, the operation continues with the highest available privilege.
User Account Control: Behavior of the elevation prompt for standard users	• When set to *Prompt for credentials (default)*, standard users attempting to perform an administrative function receive a credential prompt, to which the user must supply a valid administrative account name and password. • When set to *Automatically deny elevation requests*, this setting suppresses the credential prompt and prevents standard users from being elevated to an administrative token. When an operation requires elevation of privilege, a configurable access denied error message is displayed. • When set to *Prompt for credentials on the secure desktop*, standard users attempting to perform an administrative function receive a credential prompt on the secure desktop, to which the user must supply a valid administrative account name and password.
User Account Control: Detect application installations and prompt for elevation	• When enabled, an attempt to install an application causes standard users to receive a credential prompt and administrative users to receive an elevation prompt. The user must supply authentication credentials or consent before the installation can proceed. This is the default setting. • When disabled, elevation and credential prompts are suppressed during application installations, and the installation fails. This setting is for use on enterprise desktops that use an automated installation technology, such as Microsoft System Center Configuration Manager.

(Continued)

Table 5-1

(*Continued*)

Policy Setting	Values and Functions
User Account Control: Only Elevate executables that are signed and validated	• When enabled, this setting requires successful public key infrastructure (PKI) signature verifications on all interactive applications that request administrative access. Unsigned applications will not run. • When disabled, both signed and unsigned applications run. This is the default setting.
User Account Control: Only elevate UIAccess applications that are installed in secure locations	• When enabled, Windows 10 provides access to the protected system user interface only if the executable is located in the \Program Files, \Windows\system32, and \Program Files (x86) folders on the system drive. If the executable is not located in one of these folders, access is denied, despite a positive response to the elevation prompt. This is the default setting. • When disabled, the folder location checks are omitted, so any application can be granted access to the protected system user interface upon successful completion of the elevation prompt.
User Account Control: Run all administrators in Admin Approval Mode	• When enabled, the built-in Administrator account and all other users who are members of the Administrators group can run in Admin Approval Mode. A change in the value of this policy does not take effect until the system is restarted. This is the default setting. • When disabled, the AIS service is disabled and does not automatically start. When the system starts, the Windows Security Center warns the user that operating system security is reduced and provides the ability to activate UAC.
User Account Control: Switch to the secure desktop when prompting for elevation	• When enabled, this setting causes Windows 10 to display all elevation prompts on the secure desktop, which can receive messages only from Windows processes. This is the default setting. • When disabled, this setting causes Windows 10 to display all elevation prompts on the interactive user desktop.
User Account Control: Virtualize file and registry write Failures to per-user locations	• When enabled, allows non-UAC-compliant applications to run by redirecting write requests to protected locations, such as the Program Files and Windows folders or the HKLM\Software registry key, to alternative locations in the registry and file system. This process is called *virtualization*. This is the default setting. • When disabled, virtualization is disabled, and non-UAC-compliant applications attempting to write to protected locations fail to run. This setting is recommended only when the system is running UAC-compliant applications exclusively.

4. Double-click the **User Account Control: Behavior of the elevation prompt for standard users** policy.

5. On the Local Security Setting tab, click the drop-down arrow (see Figure 5-12), choose **Automatically deny elevation requests**, and then click **OK**.

   With this setting enabled, any operation that requires elevation of privilege produces an access denied error for standard users.

6. Close the Local Security Policy.

7. Log off the computer and log on as **TCorning** with the password of **Pa$$w0rd**.

Figure 5-12

Configuring security settings

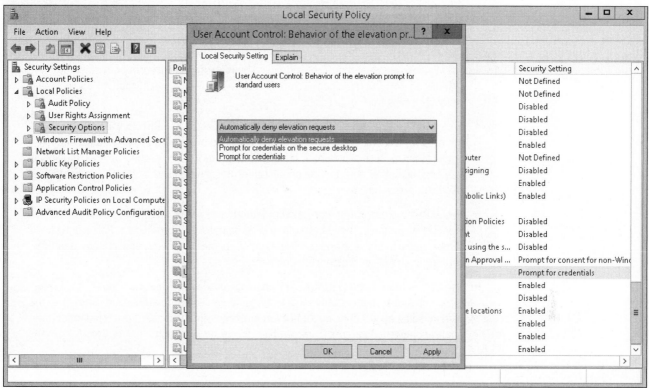

8. Right-click the **Start** button and click **Disk Management**. Because TCorning is a standard user account, she sees an error message, as shown in Figure 5-13.

Figure 5-13

Receiving access denied error message

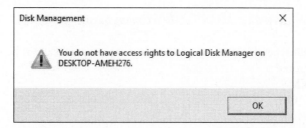

9. Click **OK** and then close the Disk Management dialog box.

If you are working on an Active Directory network, you can configure the same UAC policies for multiple computers simultaneously by creating a Group Policy Object; configuring the same policy settings; and applying it to a domain, site, or organizational unit object.

SKILL SUMMARY

IN THIS LESSON YOU LEARNED:

• The Imaging and Configuration Designer (ICD) helps you create or modify provisioning packages to update an image without deploying the image, making the changes on a new master system, and recapturing the image. ICD can also be used to create provisioning packages (*.ppkg), which are small executable programs that prepare one or more devices for corporate use.

- Activation helps verify that your copy of Windows is genuine and that it has not been used on more computers than the Microsoft Software Terms allow. Windows 10 requires product activation, which validates each Windows 10 license through an online activation service at Microsoft by phone, through KMS, or through Active Directory Domain Services in order to be fully functional.

- The Windows activation process is handled by the Software Licensing Manager (SLMgr) module, also known as Windows Software Licensing Management tool. A VBScript called slmgr.vbs keeps track of licensing details.

- A directory service stores, organizes, and provides access in a directory. Directory services are used for locating, managing, administering, and organizing common items and network resources, such as volumes, folders, files, printers, users, groups, devices, telephone numbers, and other objects. One popular directory service used by many organizations is Microsoft Active Directory.

- Group Policy is one of the most powerful features of Active Directory; it controls the working environment for user accounts and computer accounts. Group Policy provides centralized management and configuration of operating systems, applications, and user settings in an Active Directory environment.

- The User Account Control (UAC) is a technology used with Windows Vista, 7, 8/8.1, and 10 to enhance system security by detecting and preventing unauthorized changes to the system. Some applications might not run properly using a standard user credential if the application needs to access restricted files or registry locations.

■ Knowledge Assessment

Multiple Choice

Select the correct answer for each of the following questions.

1. Which type of key is tied to a single computer and cannot be moved to another computer?
   a. KMS
   b. OEM
   c. MAK
   d. Retail

2. Windows 10 displays a secure desktop under which of the following conditions? (Choose all that apply.)
   a. When the user first logs on to Windows 10
   b. When an elevation prompt is displayed
   c. When a credential prompt is displayed
   d. When a user opens Internet Explorer with SmartScreen enabled

3. Which of the following is the default configuration for User Account Control (UAC) in Windows 10?
   a. Always notify me
   b. Notify me only when apps try to make changes to my computer
   c. Notify me only when apps try to make changes to my computer (do not dim my desktop)
   d. Never notify me

4. Which of the following is the effect of setting the UAC configuration to *Never notify me* in Windows 10?
   a. It fully disables UAC.
   b. It results in less notifications but does not fully disable UAC.
   c. It allows the processes to run at a medium integrity level.
   d. No notifications will be displayed.

5. Which of the following is the default setting for Windows SmartScreen?
   a. Get admin approval before running an unrecognized app from Internet
   b. Warn before running an unrecognized app, but don't require administrator approval
   c. Don't do anything
   d. Disable Windows Smartscreen

6. When an administrator attempts to perform a task that requires administrative access, the system switches the account from the standard user token to the administrative token, which is known as which of the following?
   a. UAC Mode
   b. Credential Approval Mode
   c. Admin Approval Mode
   d. Elevated Approval Mode

7. Which command is used to attempt an online activation?
   a. slmgr.vbs /ato
   b. slmgr.vbs /xpr
   c. slmgr.vbs /dti
   d. slmgr.vbs /ipk

8. Which program is used to change the password of a user in Active Directory? (Choose two answers.)
   a. Active Directory Users and Computers
   b. Active Directory Domains and Trusts
   c. Active Directory Sites and Services
   d. Active Directory Administrative Center

9. Which of the following stores the Active Directory database?
   a. SQL server
   b. Domain controller
   c. Oracle server
   d. Jet server

10. To modify Internet Explorer settings stored in the registry, a user would look in which of the following locations in a GPO for Internet Explorer settings?
    a. Security settings
    b. Script settings
    c. Administrative Templates

Best Answer

Choose the letter that corresponds to the best answer. More than one answer choice may achieve the goal. Select the BEST answer.

1. Suppose an organization has more than 250 servers and 1,000 client computers. Which type of key should be used?
   a. KMS
   b. OEM
   c. MAK
   d. Retail

2. Which option represents the order of precedence for GPOs starting from first to last?
   a. Local Group Policy, Site GPO, Domain GPO, Organizational Unit GPO
   b. Site GPO, Domain GPO, Organizational Unit GPO, Local Group Policy.
   c. Site GPO, Domain GPO, Local Group Policy, Organizational Unit GPO
   d. Organizational Unit, Site GPO, Domain GPO, Local Group Policy

Build a List

1. Someone accidentally changed the default setting for UAC to Never notify me. To return the Windows 10 computer to the recommended default setting, specify the correct order of steps to accomplish this task.

   _____ In the User Account Control Settings dialog box, move the slider to Notify me only when apps try to make changes to my computer.

   _____ Log on to the Windows 10 computer with administrator privileges.

   _____ Click OK.

   _____ From the Windows 10 Start menu, press the Windows logo key + w, type uac, and then from the results, choose Change User Account Control settings.

2. Specify the correct order of steps to create local GPOs.

   _____ Log on to a Windows computer, using an account with administrator privileges.

   _____ Open MMC. Click File > Add/Remove Snap-in.

   _____ Select Group Policy Object Editor from the Available Snap-ins list, and then click Add.

   _____ To create the Local Group Policy GPO, click Finish. The snap-in appears in the Add or Remove Snap-ins dialog box.

   _____ Click File > Save As. A Save As combo box appears. Type a name for the console, to save it in the Administrative Tools program group.

   _____ You can now open this console to configure the settings in the GPO you created.

■ Business Case Scenarios

Scenario 5-1: Troubleshooting Access Denied Errors

One of your users was recently issued a new Windows 10 computer that was configured by a new administrator in your department. The user reports she received an access denied message while trying to view her disk properties using the Disk Management tool. The message was as follows: *You do not have access rights to Logical Disk Manager on Win10Pro.*

You remember the new administrator talking about local security policies and that he had been testing them a few days earlier. You suspect this could be the source of the problem. How would you troubleshoot this?

Scenario 5-2: Standardizing a User's Work Environment

In an organization, many computers are shared among users, and users often use different computers based on where they are working at any particular time. Therefore, you need to configure the following:

- Users must be able to access all documents that they store in the Documents and Desktop folders.
- The users should also have the TimeClock.msi file installed so that they can clock in and out.

How can you accomplish this?

Configuring Networking

70-698 EXAM OBJECTIVE

Objective 2.1 – Configure networking. This objective may include but is not limited to: Configure and support IPv4 and IPv6 network settings; configure name resolution; connect to a network; configure network locations; configure Windows Firewall; configure Windows Firewall with Advanced Security; configure network discovery; configure Wi-Fi settings; configure Wi-Fi Direct; troubleshoot network issues; configure VPN, such as app-triggered VPN, traffic filters, and lockdown VPN; configure IPsec; configure DirectAccess.

Lesson Heading	Exam Objective
Connecting to a Network	Connect to a network
Configuring IP Settings	
Exploring IPv4 and IPv6 Protocols	
Using the Default Gateway	
Understanding Name Resolution	
Configuring IP Settings and Name Resolution Settings	Configure name resolution Configure and support IPv4 and IPv6 network settings
Configuring Advanced Sharing Settings and Network Locations	Configure network locations Configure network discovery
Troubleshooting IP Network Problems	Troubleshoot network issues
Viewing IP Configuration	
Testing Network Connectivity	
Testing Name Resolution	
Viewing Port Usage	
Configuring Wireless Networks and Connections	Configure Wi-Fi settings
Understanding Wi-Fi-Technology Standards	
Utilizing Wireless Security	
Connecting to a Wireless Network	
Configuring Wi-Fi Direct	Configure Wi-Fi Direct

Lesson Heading	Exam Objective
Configuring Windows Firewall	Configure Windows Firewall
Configuring Windows Firewall with Advanced Security	Configure Windows Firewall with Advanced Security
Understanding Inbound Rules, Outbound Rules, and Connection Security Rules	
Configuring Connection Security Rules (IPsec)	Configure IPsec
Configuring VPN Connections and Authentication	Configure VPN, such as app-triggered VPN, traffic filters, and lockdown VPN
Selecting Types of VPN Protocols	
Selecting Authentication for VPN Connections	
Using Connection Manager (CM) and the Connection Manager Administration Kit (CMAK)	
Creating a VPN Connection Using the Create a VPN Connection Wizard	
Creating a VPN Connection Using Windows 10 Settings	
Configuring VPN Profiles	
Configuring DirectAccess	Configure DirectAccess
Understanding the DirectAccess Connection Process	
Running the DirectAccess Getting Started Wizard	
Running the Remote Access Setup Wizard	

KEY TERMS

802.1X

802.11a

802.11b

802.11g

802.11n

ad hoc

Authentication Header (AH)

Challenge Handshake Authentication Protocol (CHAP)

classless interdomain routing (CIDR)

Connection Manager (CM)

Connection Manager Administration Kit (CMAK)

connection security rules

default gateway

DirectAccess

Domain Name System (DNS)

domain network

domain profile

Dynamic Host Configuration Protocol (DHCP)

Encapsulating Security Payload (ESP)

enterprise mode

Extensible Authentication Protocol (EAP)

Extensible Authentication Protocol (EAP-MS-CHAPv2)

firewall

fully qualified domain names (FQDNs)

global unicast addresses

home network

host

host-based firewalls

host ID

inbound rules

infrastructure mode

Internet Key Exchange
Version 2 (IKEv2)

Internet Protocol (IP)

interval

IP security (IPsec)

ipconfig command

Layer 2 Tunneling
Protocol over IPsec
(L2TP/IPsec)

lease period

link-local addresses

Link Local Multicast Name
Resolution (LLMNR)

Microsoft CHAP version 2
(MS-CHAPv2)

name resolution

Name Resolution Policy
Table (NRPT)

name server

NetBIOS name

netstat command

Network Connectivity
Assistant (NCA)

network ID

network perimeter firewalls

nslookup.exe

outbound rules

Password Authentication
Protocol (PAP)

pathping command

Peer Name Resolution
Protocol (PNRP)

Peer Name Resolution
Protocol (PNRP) protocol

Peer Name Resolution
Protocol (PNRP) service

peer-to-peer (P2P) network

personal mode

ping command

Point-to-Point Tunneling
Protocol (PPTP)

private profile

public network

public profile

Remote Authentication
Dial-In User Service
(RADIUS) server

resolver

resource record (RR)

router

second-level domains

Secure Socket Tunneling
Protocol (SSTP)

Service Set Identifier (SSID)

stateful address configuration

stateless address configuration

subnetting

telnet

top-level domains

tracert command

Transmission Control Protocol/
Internet Protocol (TCP/IP)

transport mode

tunnel mode

unique local addresses

Virtual Private Network (VPN)

VPN Reconnect

Wi-Fi Direct

Wi-Fi Protected Access (WPA)

Wi-Fi Protected Access 2 (WPA2)

Windows Firewall

Windows Firewall with
Advanced Security (WFAS)

Windows Internet Name
Service (WINS)

Wired Equivalent Privacy (WEP)

work network

■ CONNECTING TO A NETWORK

↓
THE BOTTOM LINE

Designing network connectivity in today's networks requires you to make decisions about using IPv4/IPv6, designing a name resolution strategy, and understanding how to configure your wired and wireless network for security.

CERTIFICATION READY
Connect to a network
Objective 2.1

The most common cabling system used for wired computers is Ethernet. Most computers that use Ethernet connect with unshielded twisted-pair (UTP) cabling. Each end of the UTP cable has RJ-45 connectors. Today's workstations usually come with 100 Mb/s or 1 Gb/s connections for Ethernet, while some older machines only support 10 Mb/s. To connect a workstation to an Ethernet network, your host connects to one end of the cable and the other end connects to a switch (or for legacy networks, a hub).

If a client cannot communicate over the network, you should first check to make sure that the cable is firmly connected to the network. You should also look at the indicator lights on the network card or interface and the lights on the switch or hub to determine what the LEDs are telling you. If you have no lights on the switch or hub, make sure that the switch or hub has power and is turned on.

If the problem only affects one computer on a subnet, the problem is most likely with the computer itself, the network interface, or the cable that connects the host to the switch or hub. To help isolate a faulty cable, you can purchase a cable tester or you can swap with a known good cable. If there is a problem with the network interface card, you should verify that you have the proper drivers loaded and that the network interface is enabled.

If the problem is affecting more than one computer, you need to look for a centralized component to those computers. For example, if the switch or hub is down, the computers connected to that switch or hub will not be able to communicate.

Although wireless connections are discussed further in Lesson 10, the troubleshooting process is similar to wired networks. You must first determine if the problem is only affecting the single computer or multiple computers that are trying to access the same wireless access point. You then need to check if the wireless network has been configured properly and if the access point is turned on. Besides checking Windows to see if the network interface is enabled, you should also look for buttons or switches on laptops that can enable or disable the wireless connections. Finally, if you can connect to other hosts within the same subnet as other wireless clients but you cannot connect to wired clients or servers, you should check the network cable that connects the access point to the rest of the network.

CONFIGURING IP SETTINGS

THE BOTTOM LINE

When accessing computers on a network, you typically communicate by using their host names. If you are accessing a website, you enter a friendly name such as www.microsoft .com. Every device that connects to your network or the Internet must have an Internet Protocol (IP) address. You also need a way to associate these names to their assigned IP address.

Internet Protocol (IP) is the key protocol in the TCP/IP suite. It is responsible for adding addressing information to the packets for the sender and the receiver, as well as adding data to help route and deliver the packet. Windows 10 uses TCP/IP as its default networking protocol.

Transmission Control Protocol /Internet Protocol (TCP/IP) is a set of protocols that allows computers to exchange data within a network and between networks. These protocols (or rules) manage the content, format, timing, sequencing, and error control of the messages that are exchanged between the devices. Every device that communicates over TCP/IP must have a unique IP address. Windows 10 uses a dual-layer architecture that enables it to implement both IPv4 and IPv6 address schemes. Both share the common TCP Transport layer protocol.

Before configuring TCP/IP on your network, take time to plan the implementation. For example, how big do you expect your network to be? How will your network be designed from a physical and logical standpoint?

Exploring IPv4 and IPv6 Protocols

Microsoft, along with other industry leaders, is working hard to make IPv6 the next standard for IP addressing. In the meantime, you have a mixture of IPv4 and IPv6 devices on your network, so you need to understand how these devices are configured and how they interact with each other.

During the 1960s, several universities and research centers needed a network to share information. To address this need, a U.S. government agency called the Advanced Research Projects Agency (ARPA) developed the ARPANET, which initially used the Network Control Protocol (NCP) to handle file transfers, remote logon, and email needs. NCP, the predecessor to TCP/IP, was first used in 1972. By 1973, the protocol no longer met the needs of its users, and research was done to find a better solution. TCP/IPv4 was introduced and standardized in 1981 and is still in use today. Microsoft and other industry leaders have been working for years to roll out a newer version: IPv6.

TAKE NOTE   IPv6 is not backward compatible with IPv4. An IPv6-only device cannot talk to an IPv4 device. Your current transition strategy should be to use both in the short term.

The goal of IPv6 is to address the exhaustion of the IPv4 address space, which supports about 4 billion addresses. At the time IPv4 was created, no one considered that anything other than computers would be connected. As more computers, smartphones, tablets, and home appliances are being attached to the Internet, the IPv4 address space is quickly being exhausted.

Over the years, engineers have found ways to reduce the number of addresses needed through a process called Network Address Translation (NAT). Instead of assigning an IPv4 public address to every device on your network, you can purchase a single IPv4 address and allow all devices behind your router to share the same address. Still, as each year passes and the number of devices connected to the Internet continues to grow exponentially, IPv6 will eventually take over as the main addressing scheme. In the meantime, let's take a closer look at each of the protocols.

UNDERSTANDING IPV4

An IPv4 address is a 32-bit-long number assigned to a host on the network. These addresses are broken into four different sections called octets, which are 8 bits long. For example, the number 192.160.10.2 in binary is 11000000.10100000.00001010.00000010 (see Figure 6-1).

Figure 6-1

Converting binary to decimal

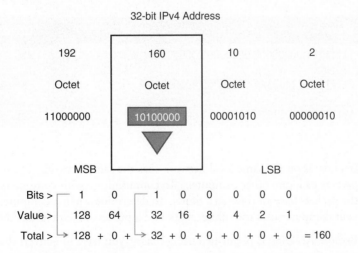

A portion of the 32 bits is associated with the network on which the computer is physically located. This portion of bits is called the **_network ID_**. The remaining bits, allocated to the host, are called the **_host ID_**. All computers on the same local network/subnet share the same network ID, but each computer within the local network/subnet has its own unique host ID.

A subnet mask, also 32 bits long, is used to determine which of the 32 bits represent the network ID and which represent the host ID (see Table 6-1). The class of IP address you are using determines the default subnet mask. IPv4 addresses are divided into classes based on the number in the first octet of the IP address. These classes were originally designed to support different organizational sizes. However, classful IP addressing is very wasteful and has mostly been discarded.

There are five classes of IP addresses (see Table 6-1).

Table 6-1

TCP/IP v4 Address Classes

CLASS	RANGE	NETWORK ID (OCTET)	HOST ID (OCTET)	NUMBER OF NETWORKS	NUMBER OF HOSTS
A	1–127*	First octet	Second, third, and fourth octets	126	16,777,214
B	128–191	First and second octets	Third and fourth octets	16,384	65,534
C	192–223	First, second, and third octets	Fourth octet	2,097,152	254
D	224–239	N/A	N/A	N/A	N/A
E	240–254	N/A	N/A	MA	N/A

*0, 127, and 255 are reserved and cannot be used for a specific host. An IP address with all 0s in the host ID describes the network, whereas 127 in the first octet is reserved for loopback testing and handling traffic to the local host. An IP address using 255s in the host ID is a broadcast transmitting to all interfaces on the specified network.

Table 6-2 shows the default subnet masks for each class along with its binary and decimal values.

Table 6-2

Default Subnet Masks for IPv4 Address Classes

CLASS	BINARY	DECIMAL
A	11111111.00000000.00000000.00000000	255.0.0.0
B	11111111.11111111.00000000.00000000	255.255.0.0
C	11111111.11111111.11111111.00000000	255.255.255.0

If a host is on the same local network (has the same network ID), it can issue broadcast packets to locate other computers. To communicate with computers on a separate network, the packets have to traverse a router. To determine when a computer is on another network, your computer uses the subnet mask and a process called logical ANDing.

Because ANDing is performed using binary, you have to convert the IP address and the subnet mask to binary form. After you complete the conversions, you match up binary 1s (between the IP address and the subnet mask). If there is a 1 in the binary address of the IP and a 1 in the binary address of the subnet mask, set the binary number in the ANDing row to binary 1. After you complete the process, add up the values, as demonstrated in Figure 6-2. When you are using it for a default subnet mask, it really isn't necessary; but when your network is subnetted, the network ID is a little harder to decipher.

Figure 6-2

Using ANDing to determine
network location

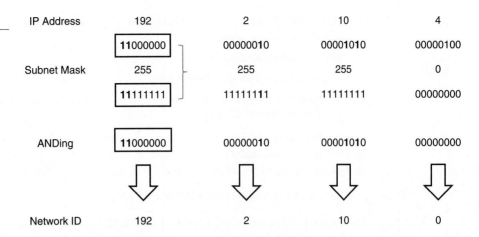

If the computer is determined to be on another network after the ANDing process is completed, the packet is sent to the default gateway configured on the computer (for example, the router's IP address). The router then uses information in its routing tables to locate and transfer your packet to the destination computer.

Subnetting is the process used to break a larger network into smaller segments. For example, a Class B IP address has more than 65,000 host addresses for a single, logical segment. Adding that many computers to a single network isn't feasible. If you break the larger network into smaller segments (for example, 254 subnetworks), each can host up to 254 hosts. You accomplish subnetting by stealing bits from the host portion of an address to create a new subnet section.

UNDERSTANDING CLASSLESS INTERDOMAIN ROUTING (CIDR)

In practical use, the IP address classes proved to be wasteful, and when the Internet first experienced a massive period of growth in the 1990s, it was feared that there might at some time be a shortage of addresses. To avoid assigning entire addresses of a particular class to networks that didn't have that many hosts, the IETF eventually published a new standard for assigning IP addresses called ***classless interdomain routing (CIDR)***.

CIDR differs from traditional addressing (now called *classful addressing*) by allowing the division between the network identifier and the host identifier to fall anywhere in an IPv4 address; it does not have to fall on one of the 8-bit boundaries. For example, a subnet mask of 255.255.240.0 translates into a binary value of 11111111 11111111 11110000 00000000, meaning that the network identifier is 20 bits long and the host identifier is 12 bits. This falls between a Class B and a Class C address, and enables ISPs to assign clients only the number of addresses they need, which conserves the IP address space.

CIDR also introduced a new syntax for IP network address references. In classful notation, an address like 172.23.0.0 was assumed to be a Class B address and used the standard 255.255.0.0 Class B subnet mask. In CIDR notation, the network address is followed by a slash and the number of bits in the network identifier. Therefore, 172.23.0.0/16 would be the CIDR equivalent of a Class B address. An address that used the 255.255.240.0 subnet mask described earlier would, therefore, look something like 172.23.0.0/20.

UNDERSTANDING IPV6 AND IPV6 ADDRESSING

IPv6 provides a number of benefits for TCP/IP-based networking connectivity, including:

As mentioned earlier, available public IPv4 addresses are running low. To overcome this problem as well as a few others, IPv6 was developed as the next-generation Internet Protocol version.

- A 128-bit address space to provide addressing for every device on the Internet with a globally unique address
- More efficient routing than IPv4
- Support for automatic configuration
- Enhanced security to protect against address and port scanning attacks and utilization of IPsec to protect IPv6 traffic

Because IPv6 uses 128 bits, the addresses are usually divided into groups of 16 bits, written as 4 hex digits. Hex digits include 0, 1, 2, 3, 4, 5, 6, 7, 8, 9, A, B, C, D, E, and F. The groups are separated by colons. Here is an example of an address:

FE80:0000:0000:0000:02C3:B2DF:FEA5:E4F1

Similar to the IPv4 addresses, IPv6 is divided into network bits and host bits. However, the first 64 bits define the network address and the second 64 bits define the host address. Therefore, for our sample address, FE80:0000:0000:0000 defines the network bits and 02C3:B2DF:FEA5:E4F1 defines the host bits. The network bits are also further divided where a block of 48 bits is used as the network prefix and the next 16 bits are used for subnetting.

To facilitate simplified automatic addressing, the IPv6 subnet size has been standardized and fixed to 64 bits, and the MAC address is used to generate the host bits within the unicast network address or link-local address when stateless autoconfiguration is used.

If a block is set to 0 and is followed by another block set to 0, it can be written as ::. Using this notation, FE80:0:AC4A:AA04:E713A:0:0:CE2B, the preceding address would be written as FE80:0:AC4A:AA04:E713A::CE2B.

TAKE NOTE

When a network card is configured in Windows 10, it automatically has both an IPv4 and IPv6 address by default. This is called a dual stack.

With IPv6, you still have unicast and multicast addressing. However, unicast addressing can be divided into:

- *Global unicast addresses*: Public addresses that are globally routable and reachable on the IPv6 portion of the Internet.
- *Link-local addresses*: Private nonroutable addresses confined to a single subnet. They are used by hosts when communicating with neighboring hosts on the same link, but can also be used to create temporary networks for conferences or meetings, or to set up a permanent, small LAN. Routers process packets destined for a link-local address, but they will not forward them to other links.
- *Unique local addresses*: Meant for private addressing, with the addition of being unique, so that joining two subnets does not cause address collisions.

You might also have an anycast address, which is an address that is assigned to multiple computers. When IPv6 addresses communication to an anycast address, only the closest host responds. You typically use this for locating services or the nearest router.

The transition from IPv4 to IPv6 is expected to take several more years. In the meantime, expect to see a mix of IPv4, IPv4/IPv6 (dual stack), and IPv6-only networks. To help with the transition from IPv4 to IPv6, several methods were developed, including 6to4, Teredo, and Intra-Site Automatic Tunnel Addressing Protocol (IPv6).

Using the Default Gateway

> A *default gateway* is a device, usually a router, which connects the local network to other networks. When you need to communicate with a host on another subnet, you forward all packets to the default gateway.

The default gateway allows a host to communicate with remote hosts. Every time a host needs to send packets to another host, it first determines if the destination host is local (same subnet) or if it is remote (where it has to go through a router to get to it). The router determines the best way to get to the remote host, and then it forwards the packets to the remote subnet.

To determine if the destination address is local or remote, the router looks at the network bits of both the sending and destination hosts. If the network bits are the same, it assumes the destination host is local and sends the packets directly to the local host. If the network bits are different, it assumes the destination host is remote and sends the packets to the default gateway.

For example, you have the following:

Sending host address: 10.10.57.3
Sending host subnet mask: 255.255.255.0
Destination host address: 10.10.89.37

By isolating the network address from the sending host, you have 10.10.57.0. By isolating the network address for the destination host address, you have 10.10.89.0. Because they are different, the packet is sent to the default gateway, and the router determines the best way to get to its final destination.

Of course, if the subnet mask is wrong, the host might misidentify a host as being local or remote. If the default gateway is wrong, packets might not be able to leave the local subnet.

Understanding Name Resolution

> Name resolution is the process of converting friendly names to IP addresses. Windows 10 uses DNS, WINS, LLMNR, and PNRP.

Name resolution is the process of associating host names to IP addresses. The Windows operating system supports four name resolution systems:

- Domain Name System (DNS)
- Windows Internet Name Service (WINS)
- Link Local Multicast Name Resolution (LLMNR)
- Peer Name Resolution Protocol (PNRP)

EXPLORING THE DOMAIN NAME SYSTEM (DNS)

With early TCP/IP networks, name resolution was done with hosts files, which were stored locally on each computer. The hosts files were simple text files with a host name and IP addresses on each line (see Figure 6-3). In Windows, the hosts file is located in the C:\Windows\System32\Drivers\etc folder. The disadvantage of using hosts files is that every time you need to add a new entry, you need to add or modify the hosts file on every computer in your organization, which is not a practical way to provide up-to-date name resolution.

Figure 6-3

Using a hosts file

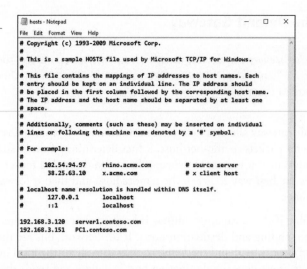

```
hosts - Notepad                                          —    □    ×
File  Edit  Format  View  Help
# Copyright (c) 1993-2009 Microsoft Corp.
#
# This is a sample HOSTS file used by Microsoft TCP/IP for Windows.
#
# This file contains the mappings of IP addresses to host names. Each
# entry should be kept on an individual line. The IP address should
# be placed in the first column followed by the corresponding host name.
# The IP address and the host name should be separated by at least one
# space.
#
# Additionally, comments (such as these) may be inserted on individual
# lines or following the machine name denoted by a '#' symbol.
#
# For example:
#
#      102.54.94.97      rhino.acme.com        # source server
#       38.25.63.10      x.acme.com            # x client host

# localhost name resolution is handled within DNS itself.
#       127.0.0.1       localhost
#       ::1             localhost

192.168.3.120    server1.contoso.com
192.168.3.151    PC1.contoso.com
```

> **TAKE NOTE**
>
> When resolving names, Windows always checks the hosts file. Although hosts files are not commonly used today, they can still be used for troubleshooting and testing.

Domain Name System (DNS) is a naming service used by the TCP/IP network, is an essential service used by the Internet, and can be integrated with other services, such as WINS, DHCP, and Active Directory. DNS servers are used to associate a computer name, such as Server01.Support.contoso.com, to an IP address.

Every time a user accesses a web page, the user must type a URL, usually a name. Before the client communicates with the web server, the client computer needs to use DNS to retrieve the IP address of the web server, similar to someone using a phone book to find a phone number. When an enterprise client needs to communicate with a corporate server, the enterprise client also uses DNS to find the IP address of the corporate service. The DNS servers are often referred to as name servers.

DNS uses *fully qualified domain names (FQDNs)* to map a host name to an IP address. An FQDN describes the exact relationship between a host and its DNS domain. For example, computer1.sales.microsoft.com represents an FQDN; the computer1 host is located in the sales domain, which is located in the Microsoft second-level domain, which is located in the .com top-level domain.

DNS is a hierarchical distributed naming system used to locate computers and services on a TCP/IP network. DNS clients send queries to a DNS server and the Domain Name System receives and resolves queries such as translating a host or domain name to an IP address. Because it is so closely tied to the Internet and TCP/IP network, it is an essential service that enables the Internet and network to function and it is required by many network services, including Active Directory.

DNS is known as a distributed naming system because the information stored with DNS is not found on only a single DNS server. Instead, the information is distributed among multiple DNS servers, all of which are linked into a hierarchical structure.

The DNS is a hierarchical system consisting of a tree of domain names/DNS namespaces. At the top of the tree is the root zone (see Figure 6-4). The tree can then be divided into zones, each served by a name (DNS) server. Each zone can contain one domain or many domains. The administrative responsibility over any zone can be delegated or divided by creating a subdomain, which can be assigned to a different name server and administrative entity.

Figure 6-4

Exploring the DNS namespace

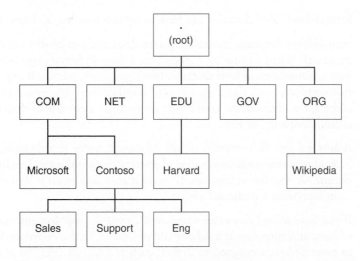

A domain name consists of one or more labels. Each label can be up to 63 characters. The full domain name cannot exceed a total length of 253 characters.

The root domain is managed by the Internet Corporation for Assigned Names and Numbers (ICANN) under the authority of the U.S. Department of Commerce. It is essential for the function of the Internet; without the root domain, services that depend upon DNS (email, browsing the Internet, and so on) would not function. Although the root domain is represented by a single period, it is supported by several hundred root servers spread across the world (to see where they are located, visit the root servers' website). The root servers have a file (zone file) that lists the names and IP addresses of the authoritative DNS servers for all top-level domains.

The rightmost label designates the top-level domain. For example, *microsoft.com* consists of two labels. The top-level domain is com. The hierarchy of domains descends from right to left. Each label to the left specifies a subdomain of the domain or label on the right. Therefore, in our example, *microsoft* is a subdomain of the *com* domain.

Traditionally, ***top-level domains*** consist of generic, top-level domains and international country codes (such as *us* for United States, *uk* for United Kingdom, *de* for Germany, and *jp* for Japan). Traditional, generic top-level domains include the following:

.com	Commercial
.org	Organization (originally intended for nonprofit organizations)
.edu	Educational
.gov	U.S. governmental entities
.net	Network (originally intended for the portal to a set of smaller websites)

Over the years, many other generic domains have been added, such as .aero, .biz, .coop, .info, .int, .jobs, .name, and .pro. More recently, organizations can purchase their own top-level domains.

Second-level domains are registered to individuals or organizations. Examples include:

microsoft.com	Microsoft Corporation domain
contoso.com	A fictional company used by Microsoft for examples, training, and support
mit.edu	Massachusetts Institute of Technology
wikipedia.org	Free encyclopedia
gov.au	Australian government

Second-level DNS domains can have many subdomains, and any domain can have hosts.

Second-level domains, also called parent domains, can be divided into subdomains (child domains). When registering a second-level domain for an organization, it is common to register multiple second-level domains (microsoft.com, microsoft.org, microsoft.net) to ensure that users can reach them regardless of whether they type .com, .net, or .org at the end of the address. An organization could then divide their second-level domains to subdomains, such as Sales, Support, or Eng.

A *host* is a specific computer or other network device in a domain. For example, *computer1 .sales.contoso.com* is the host called *computer1* in the sales subdomain of the *contoso.com* domain. A host has at least one IP address associated with it. For example, www.microsoft .com represents a particular address.

If you have *server1.corporate.contoso.com, com* is the top domain. *contoso* is a subdomain of com, and corporate is a subdomain of *contoso*. In the *corporate* domain, you find one or more addresses assigned to *server1*, such as 192.168.1.53. So as a result, when you type *server1.corporate.contoso.com* into your browser, the client sends a query to a DNS server asking what the IP address is for *server1.corporate.contoso.com*. The DNS server responds back with the 192.168.1.53 address. The client then communicates with the server with the address of 192.168.1.53.

Each node or leaf in the DNS tree is a ***resource record (RR)***, which holds information associated with the domain name. The most common resource record is the host address (A or AAAA), which lists a host name and the associated IP address.

Here are a few of the record types you will find in a zone database file:

- Start of Authority (SOA) records are the first records added to a zone. They define parameters for the zone and include the name of the primary name server.
- Name Server (NS) records list any additional name servers for the zone.
- Address (host name) (A) records associate a host name to an IP4 address.
- Address (host name) (AAAA) records associate a host name to its IPv6 address.
- Pointer (PTR) records associate an IP address to a host name.
- Mail Exchange (MX) records identify the mail host(s) for the domain.

Active Directory domains utilize DNS when implementing their hierarchy and naming structure. When you install the first domain controller on a network, you are asked to install DNS automatically. When fully integrated with DNS, all domain controllers can access the data, replicate changes throughout the domain, and register clients into their zone. A zone is a scope of names that are served by a specific DNS name server. The part of the namespace that a zone is responsible for is known as the zone of authority. A zone must contain at least one domain, called the root domain of that zone. All the information about each zone is stored in a file called the zone database file. Inside the zone database file are the resource records that DNS uses to resolve host names to IP addresses.

The DNS server that creates and modifies a locally stored zone file is called the primary name server. A secondary name server is often used and holds a copy of the zone file that it gets from the primary name server. Updates to the primary name server are automatically replicated to the secondary name server. This process, called a zone transfer, provides redundancy for name resolution if one of the servers fails.

To identify a DNS host in the namespace, you use its fully qualified domain name (FQDN). The FQDN includes the host name in addition to the domain name where it is located. For example, the server, Support, in Figure 6-4 has an FQDN of support.contoso.com.

Understanding the DNS hierarchy can help you understand how name resolution works. DNS uses two components to resolve names to IP addresses:

- **Resolver:** An application that provides address information about other network hosts for the client. During the name resolution process, if a client cannot resolve the destination's host name to an IP address, the resolver sends a query to DNS servers, including root servers, to look up the records on its behalf.

- **Name server:** A server that performs recursive and iterative queries to contact other DNS servers in an attempt to resolve a host name to an IP address if the DNS server cannot resolve it using its own records. When a computer uses a recursive query, it is putting the entire responsibility on the other computer to find the IP address. An iterative query is a call to a name server to reply with the requested data or tell it who else to talk to in order to find an answer to its request.

USING WINDOWS INTERNET NAME SERVICE

Network Basic Input/Output System (NetBIOS) is a program that allows applications on different computers to communicate with other computers within a local area network (LAN). A **NetBIOS name** is a nonhierarchical name that is used by some old Windows applications. The NetBIOS name is a 16-character string used to identify a NetBIOS resource on a network, which could be a single computer or a group of computers. NetBIOS uses the first 15 characters for a specific computer's name. The sixteenth character (known as the NetBIOS suffix) is to identify a resource or service on that computer. An example of a NetBIOS name is Server01[20h]. 20h presents File Service.

Windows Internet Name Service (WINS) is an early name resolution service that you find on some networks to help pre–Windows 2000 computers to resolve a computer name to an IP address. These older systems use NetBIOS over TCP/IP, which requires either a static LMHOSTS file or a WINS server to resolve the names. Without a WINS server, these systems rely on broadcast messages to communicate. This introduces extra traffic on the network and also prevents the computers from accessing systems on other subnets.

Since the release of Windows 2000, DNS has been the primary mechanism for name resolution. However, all Windows operating systems still include a WINS client to resolve NetBIOS names and Windows servers still include a WINS server so they can provide NetBIOS name resolution.

USING LINK LOCAL MULTICAST NAME RESOLUTION (LLMNR)

Link Local Multicast Name Resolution (LLMNR), enabled on Windows 7 and later operating systems, is a fallback name resolution technique when DNS or WINS is not available. LLMNR works only on the local subnet, so it does not resolve names for systems that are located on another network. LLMNR can be used on a small home network or an ad hoc network, or in situations in which the DNS server your client is configured to use is not available.

TAKE NOTE   LLMNR can be used to resolve both IPv4 and IPv6 addresses.

An LLMNR client tries to reach its primary and secondary DNS servers and fails over to LLMNR only if it cannot locate them. It then uses a multicast message for the name it is trying to resolve. Each computer on the local subnet that supports LLMNR checks its own host name. If it matches, it sends a unicast message along with its IP address to the computer. If it does not match, the packet is discarded.

PEER NAME RESOLUTION PROTOCOL (PNRP)

A *peer-to-peer (P2P) network* is a type of decentralized and distributed network architecture in which nodes or peers provide resources for other peers and use resources from other peers. *Peer Name Resolution Protocol (PNRP)* is a peer-to-peer protocol designed by Microsoft that is used to provide a secure, scalable, and dynamic name resolution for peer communications. One such application that uses the PNRP is Windows Remote Assistance Easy Connect.

The components that make up PNRP are:

- *Peer Name Resolution Protocol (PNRP) protocol*: Determines the interaction of the local computer with the PNRP cloud, which is a grouping of computers that can find each other. The local computer must have a default identity defined and proper permissions assigned in order to interact properly with the cloud.
- *Peer Name Resolution Protocol (PNRP) service*: Provides a secure, scalable, and dynamic name registration and name resolution protocol that relies on Internet Protocol version 6 (IPv6) and enables peer-to-peer functionality for PNRP-enabled applications.

For a Windows 10 computer to use the PNRP, the PNRP service has to be started.

Configuring IP Settings and Name Resolution Settings

Network settings can be configured either manually or automatically using DHCP. Using manual settings can introduce configuration issues that could affect communications. Using a centralized approach to IP address management requires you to have a solid understanding of DHCP.

CERTIFICATION READY
Configure name resolution
Objective 2.1

CERTIFICATION READY
Configure and support IPv4 and IPv6 network settings
Objective 2.1

Configuring TCP/IP on a Windows 10 computer can be done manually or automatically. Setting up TCP/IP manually involves configuring it to use a static IP address. This involves entering an IP address, a subnet mask, and (if you need to access computers outside of the local network segment) a default gateway address. To resolve friendly names to IP addresses, you also need to configure at least one IP address for a DNS on your network.

 DEFINE A STATIC IPV4 ADDRESS

GET READY. To define a static IP IPv4 address, perform the following steps.

1. On LON-CL1, on the taskbar, right-click the **network status** icon and then click **Open Network and Sharing Center**.
2. Click **Change adapter settings**.
3. Right-click a network adapter, such as **Ethernet**, and then select **Properties**.
4. When the Ethernet Properties dialog box opens, as shown in Figure 6-5, click **Internet Protocol Version 4 (TCP/IPv4)** and then click **Properties**.
5. Select **Use the following IP address** and then type the IPv4 address, subnet mask, and default gateway you want to use, as shown in Figure 6-6.
6. Select **Use the following DNS server addresses** and then type an IP address for a preferred DNS server and an alternate DNS server.

Figure 6-5

Configuring the properties
of an Ethernet adapter

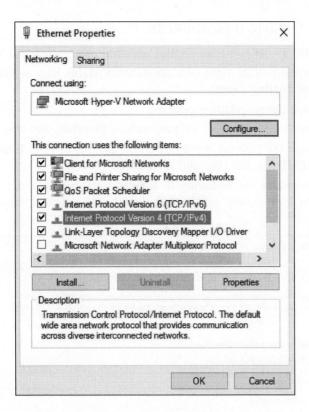

Figure 6-6

Entering a static IPv4 address

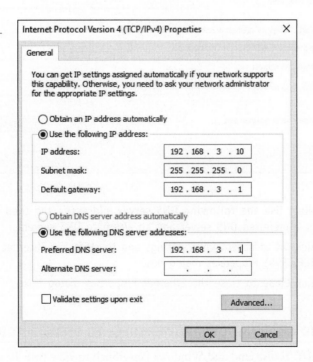

7. Click **OK** to accept your settings and to close the Internet Protocol Version 4 (TCP/IPv4) Properties dialog box.

8. Click **Close** to close the Ethernet Properties dialog box.

DEFINE A STATIC IPV6 ADDRESS

GET READY. To define a static IP IPv4 address, perform the following steps.

1. On the taskbar, right-click the **network status** icon and then click **Open Network and Sharing Center**.
2. Click **Change adapter settings**.
3. Right-click a network adapter, such as **Ethernet**, and then select **Properties**.
4. When the Ethernet Properties dialog box opens, click **Internet Protocol Version 6 (TCP/IPv6)** and then click **Properties**.
5. Select **Use the following IP address** (as shown in Figure 6-7) and then type the IPv6 address, subnet prefix length, and default gateway you want to use.

Figure 6-7

Entering a static IPv6 address

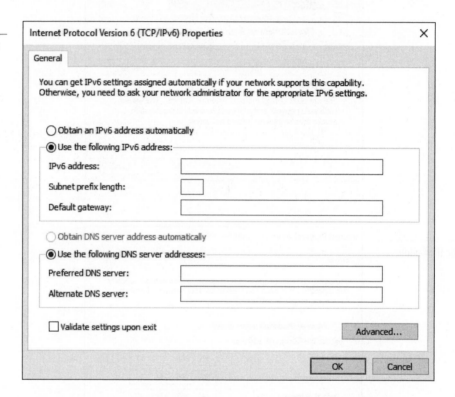

6. Select **Use the following DNS server addresses** and then type an IP address for a preferred DNS server and an alternate DNS server.
7. Click **OK** to accept your settings and to close the Internet Protocol Version 6 (TCP/IPv6) Properties dialog box.
8. Click **Close** to close the Ethernet Properties dialog box.

 USE CMD AND WINDOWS POWERSHELL TO VIEW IP ADDRESS INFORMATION

GET READY. To use cmd and Windows PowerShell to view your IP address configuration, perform the following steps.

1. On LON-CL1, right-click the **Start** button and then click **Command Prompt (Admin)**.
2. In the Administrator: Command Prompt window, type **ipconfig** and then press the **Enter** key.
3. Review your settings (as shown in Figure 6-8). You should see both an IPv4 and IPv6 address.

Figure 6-8

Reviewing the IP configuration

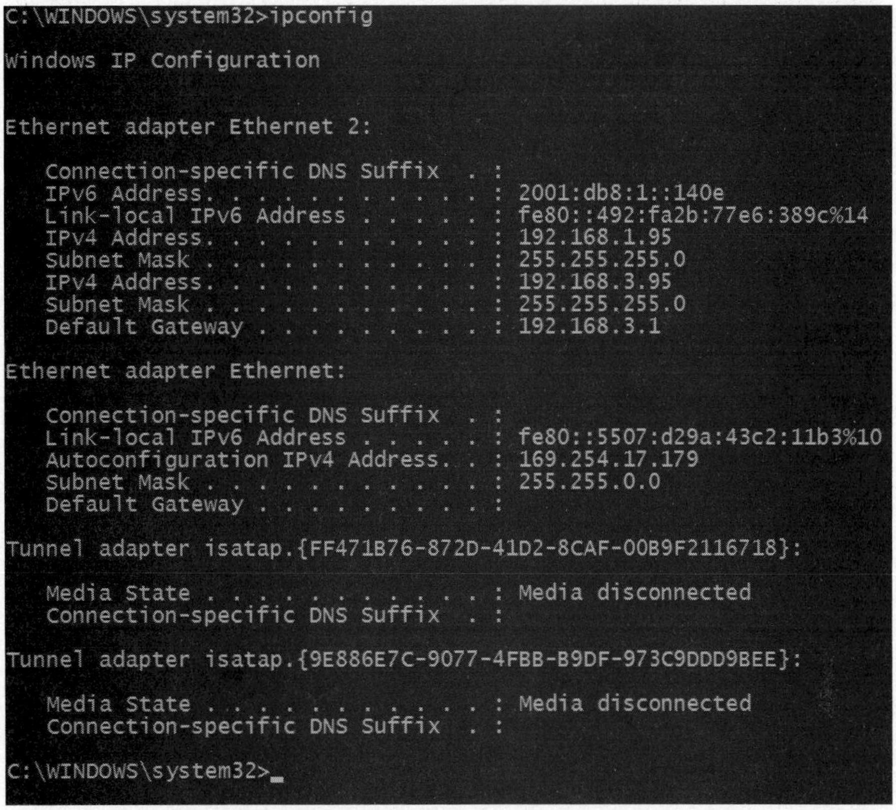

```
C:\WINDOWS\system32>ipconfig

Windows IP Configuration

Ethernet adapter Ethernet 2:

   Connection-specific DNS Suffix  . :
   IPv6 Address. . . . . . . . . . . : 2001:db8:1::140e
   Link-local IPv6 Address . . . . . : fe80::492:fa2b:77e6:389c%14
   IPv4 Address. . . . . . . . . . . : 192.168.1.95
   Subnet Mask . . . . . . . . . . . : 255.255.255.0
   IPv4 Address. . . . . . . . . . . : 192.168.3.95
   Subnet Mask . . . . . . . . . . . : 255.255.255.0
   Default Gateway . . . . . . . . . : 192.168.3.1

Ethernet adapter Ethernet:

   Connection-specific DNS Suffix  . :
   Link-local IPv6 Address . . . . . : fe80::5507:d29a:43c2:11b3%10
   Autoconfiguration IPv4 Address. . : 169.254.17.179
   Subnet Mask . . . . . . . . . . . : 255.255.0.0
   Default Gateway . . . . . . . . . :

Tunnel adapter isatap.{FF471B76-872D-41D2-8CAF-00B9F2116718}:

   Media State . . . . . . . . . . . : Media disconnected
   Connection-specific DNS Suffix  . :

Tunnel adapter isatap.{9E886E7C-9077-4FBB-B9DF-973C9DDD9BEE}:

   Media State . . . . . . . . . . . : Media disconnected
   Connection-specific DNS Suffix  . :

C:\WINDOWS\system32>_
```

4. Type **exit** and then press the **Enter** key to close the cmd shell.

5. Click the **Start** button. Then type **PowerShell**.

6. Type **Resolve-DNSName <website address>** (for example, **Resolve-DNSName www.microsoft.com**) and then press the **Enter** key.

7. Review the address records returned.

   Does the site support IPv6?

8. Type **Resolve-DNSName www.msn.com** and then press the **Enter** key.

9. Review the address records returned.

   Does the site support IPv6?

If you selected the Validate settings upon exit option after configuring IP settings, Windows 10 performs a network diagnostics test to check your settings for any problems and offers to help fix them. If you clicked the Advanced button, you could make additional configurations to your TCP/IP configuration. For example, in Windows 10, you can configure multiple gateways. When you do this, a metric is used to determine which gateway to use. Multiple gateways are used to provide fault tolerance so if one router goes down, the computer defaults to the other gateway. You can configure additional gateways and DNS settings in the Advanced TCP/IP Settings dialog box (see Figure 6-9):

- **DNS server addresses, in order of use:** You can specify multiple DNS servers to use for name resolution. The order listed determines the sequence in which your client attempts to resolve host names. If the first server does not respond to a name resolution request, the client contacts the next one in the list.

Figure 6-9

Reviewing advanced TCP/IP
setting options

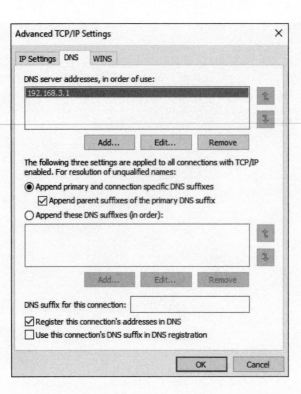

- **Append primary and connection specific DNS suffixes:** This is selected by default. If you attempt to access a computer named FileServer1, and the parent name is contoso. com, the name resolves to FileServer1.contoso.com. If the FQDN does not exist in the domain, the query fails. The parent name used (contoso.com) is configured on the System Properties/Computer Name tab.

- **Append parent suffixes of the primary DNS suffix:** This is selected by default. It works as follows: If the computer FS2 is in the eastcoast.contoso.com domain, DNS attempts to resolve the name to FS2.eastcoast.contoso.com. If this doesn't work, it tries FS2.contoso.com.

- **Append these DNS suffixes (in order):** Use this option when you want to specify DNS suffixes to use other than resolving names through your parent domain.

- **DNS suffix for this connection:** This setting overrides DNS names that are already configured for this connection. This is typically configured through the System Properties/Computer Name tab by clicking the More button.

- **Register this connection's addresses in DNS:** This option, selected by default, automatically enters the FQDN in DNS records.

- **Use this connection's DNS suffix in DNS registration:** If this option is selected, all IP addresses for this connection are registered in DNS at the parent domain.

UNDERSTANDING AUTOMATIC IP ADDRESS ASSIGNMENT

When you assign static IP addresses (IPv4 or IPv6) to your clients, you run the risk of duplicating IP addresses on your network or misconfiguring the settings, which can result in communication problems. A better approach is to dynamically assign your TCP/IP configurations from a central pool of IP addresses. This is done by using the *Dynamic Host Configuration Protocol (DHCP)* server. The DHCP server can also be configured to provide the default gateway, primary, and secondary DNS information; WINS server; and DNS domain name.

Figure 6-10 shows how DHCP communications work.

Figure 6-10

Understanding DHCP
communications

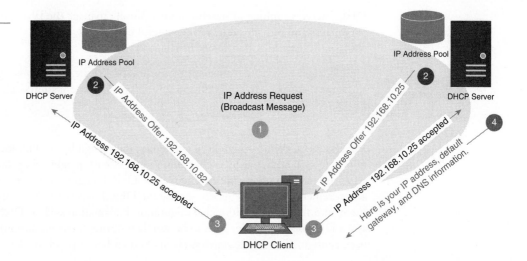

Here is a high-level overview of what happens with DHCP-enabled clients:

1. The DHCP-enabled client starts and broadcasts a request for an IP address over the network.

2. Any DHCP servers that receive the request review their pool of IP addresses (DHCP scope) and select one to offer to the client.

3. The client reviews the offers and broadcasts a message to the servers, letting them know which IP address it has accepted.

4. All DHCP servers see the message. Those whose offers are not accepted place the IP address back into their pool for a future client request. The server the client accepted acknowledges and provides additional information to complete the client configuration (default gateway, DNS information, and so on).

After a client receives an IP address and additional configuration information, it has it for a specific period of time called the ***lease period***. When the lease is 50% expired, the client tries to renew it with the DHCP server. If the client cannot renew the lease, it tries again before the lease expires. At this point, if it cannot renew the lease, it tries to contact an alternate DHCP server. If all attempts fail, and the client cannot obtain a new IP address, it autoconfigures with a Microsoft Class B subnet (169.254.0.0/255.255.0.0).

Before it chooses an IP address in this network, the client checks to make sure no other client is using the address it wants to assign. After it has an address assigned, it attempts to make contact with a DHCP server every five minutes. Once found, it is reconfigured to use an address assigned from the DHCP pool.

> **TAKE NOTE**
>
> You can use DHCP to assign IPv6 addresses through either DHCPv6 stateful mode or stateless mode. If DHCPv6 is used, you need to make sure your routers are configured to support it.

USING STATEFUL DHCP AND STATELESS DHCP

There are two ways to configure DHCP when using it for IPv6 implementations: ***stateless address configuration*** and ***stateful address configuration***.

If you are using DHCP to assign IPv6 addresses to stateful mode clients, they work similarly to the IPv4 when obtaining their IP addresses. When a client is configured to use DHCP in stateful mode, it first uses a link-local address (IPv6). After it is autoconfigured with the link-local address, it seeks out a DHCP server on the network by broadcasting a message every five minutes. When the client finally reaches a DHCP server, it configures itself with the assigned IP parameters.

DHCP servers running in stateful mode centrally manage the IPv6 addresses and configuration parameters and provide addresses to stateful clients.

Link-local addresses are equivalent to Automatic Private IP Addressing (APIPA) IPv4 addresses using the 169.254.0.0/255.255.0.0 prefix. These address always begin with FE80::/64.

Stateless mode clients work a little differently; they assign both a link-local address and additional non-link-local addresses by exchanging messages with neighboring routers. When a DHCP server is set up to serve stateless clients, the DHCP clients autoconfigure using router advertisements. These clients do not use the DHCP server to obtain an IP address, but instead use it to only obtain additional configuration information such as DNS recursive name servers and a DNS search list (domains to be searched during name resolution). If a DHCP server has been configured to service stateless clients, it does not respond to clients asking for IP addresses.

Configuring Advanced Sharing Settings and Network Locations

Windows 10 has advanced sharing settings that allow you to configure network sharing settings based on your network location. To access the advanced sharing settings, open the Network and Sharing Center, and click the Change advanced sharing settings. The advanced sharing settings are shown in Figure 6-11.

Figure 6-11

Configuring advanced sharing settings

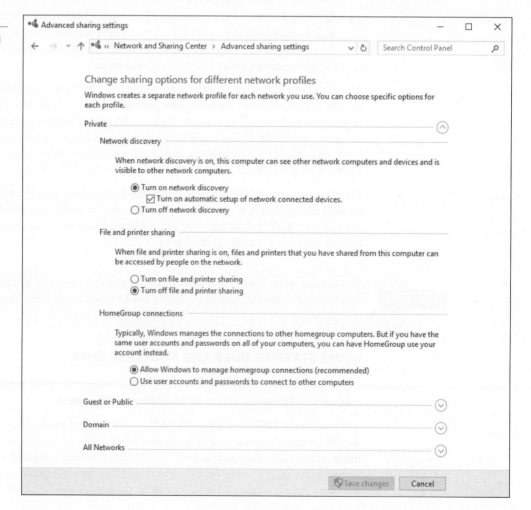

CERTIFICATION READY
Configure network
locations
Objective 2.1

CERTIFICATION READY
Configure network
discovery
Objective 2.1

Windows 10 is split into three sections: Private, Guest or Public, and All Networks. Each network profile has different defaults, which are applied when connecting to and selecting a network connection:

- **Turn on or off network discovery:** When enabled, this setting searches for other devices on the network and allows other computers and devices on the same network to find your Windows-based computer or device.
- **Turn on or off file and printer sharing:** When enabled, you can share files and printers with other computers and devices on your network.
- **Turn on or off HomeGroup Connections:** For Private connections, when enabled, you can use and manage homegroups.
- **Turn on or off public folder sharing:** When enabled, homegroup users can access files from the computer's Public folder, which is located at C:\Users\Public\.
- **Turn on or off media streaming:** When enabled, you can stream multimedia files using Windows Media Player and other programs.
- **Encryption for file sharing connections:** When enabled, people can access your shared files and folders only if you have a user account and password set on the computer.

When you first connect to a network, you must choose a network location, which will be assigned specific network sharing settings. For example, you can define your network connection as Work network or Domain network location. You could define your home network as the Home network. When you visit a client or you connect to the Internet from your local coffee shop, you would select the Public network.

There are four network locations:

- *Home network*: Choose Home network when you know and trust the people and devices on the network. Computers on a home network can belong to a homegroup and network discovery will be enabled.
- *Work network*: Choose Work network for small office or other workplace networks that are not part of your computer's domain. Network discovery will be enabled.
- *Public network*: Choose Public network when visiting public places, such as hotels, coffee shops, restaurants, and airports. You should also use this option if you're connected to the Internet without using a router, or by using a mobile broadband connection. HomeGroup is not available and network discovery is turned off, which prevents other users from seeing your computer on the public network.
- *Domain network*: Choose Domain network for domain networks, such as those at enterprise workplaces. This type of network location is controlled by your network administrator and can't be selected or changed.

When you connect to a network for the first time in Windows 10, the network location is automatically set to Public, which prevents other Windows computers and devices from detecting your system. In such situations, you might want to change the network location to Private to make your computer discoverable to other computers. If the network connection is configured for a home or private connection, and your computer is not part of a domain, you can change the network location from Settings.

 CONFIGURE A NETWORK LOCATION

GET READY. To change the network location, perform the following steps.

1. On LON-CL1, click the **Start** button and then click **Settings**.
2. When the Settings window opens, click **Network & Internet**.
3. On the Network & Internet page, click **Ethernet**.

4. On the Ethernet page, click the network connection that you want to change.

5. On the Network page, you can enable or disable the Find devices and content option, as shown in Figure 6-12.

Figure 6-12

Enabling or disabling if your PC is discoverable

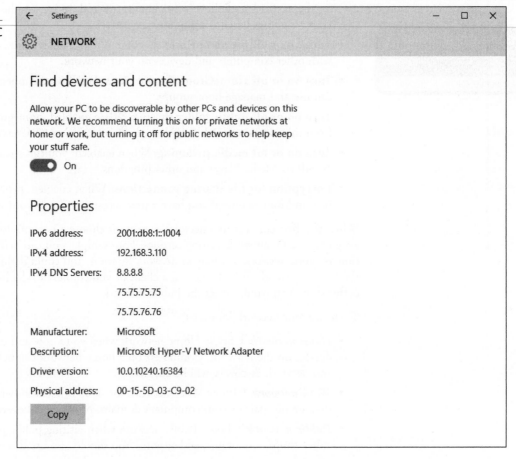

6. Close the Settings window.

■ TROUBLESHOOTING IP NETWORK PROBLEMS

THE BOTTOM LINE

Although networks can be simple or complex, there are several tools that are invaluable when troubleshooting network connectivity problems. No matter how complex the network is, you should always follow a troubleshooting methodology, which will help you quickly isolate and pinpoint the problem.

CERTIFICATION READY
Troubleshoot network issues
Objective 2.1

If you experience network connectivity problems while using Windows 10, you can use Windows Network Diagnostics to start the troubleshooting process. If there is a problem, Windows Network Diagnostics analyzes the problem and, if possible, presents a solution or a list of possible causes. To run the Windows Network Diagnostics program, right-click the Network and Sharing Center icon in the notification area and choose Troubleshoot problems. You can also right-click the adapter under Network Connections and click Diagnose.

If the problem still exists, you can also use the following command-line tools:

- ipconfig
- ping
- tracert
- pathping
- netstat
- telnet
- nslookup

In addition, you should also look at the logs shown in Event Viewer. Some error messages might be found in the System and Application logs.

Viewing IP Configuration

> When you cannot connect to a website or a server, the first thing you should check is the client IP configuration. This can be done by using Network Connections or the ipconfig command.

To view your network connections, you can open the Network Connections via Change adapter settings under the Network and Sharing Center. Right-click the desired adapter and click Status. The General tab shows if the adapter has IPv4 and IPv6 connectivity, if the adapter is enabled, how long the adapter has been running, and the speed of the adapter. It also shows you the bytes being sent and received from the adapter. If you click the Details button, you can view the network connection details, including IP addresses, subnet mask, gateway, WINS and DNS servers, and physical/MAC address.

The *ipconfig command*—one of the most useful commands when troubleshooting network problems—displays all current TCP/IP network configuration values and refreshes Dynamic Host Configuration Protocol (DHCP) settings. Used without parameters, ipconfig displays the IP address, subnet mask, and default gateway for all adapters. When you execute ipconfig /all, it displays the full TCP/IP configuration for all adapters, including host name, DNS servers, and the physical/MAC address.

If you are using DHCP servers to assign addresses, ipconfig /renew renews the DHCP configuration from the DHCP server. This parameter is available only on computers with adapters that are configured to obtain an IP address automatically. You can also use ipconfig /release to release the DHCP address from a network adapter.

If the IP address is invalid, communication might fail. If the subnet mask is incorrect, you might have problems communicating with local or remote hosts. If the default gateway is invalid, you will have problems communicating with remote hosts, but you can still communicate with local hosts. If the DNS server is incorrect or missing, the computer might not be able to resolve names and communication might fail.

If a computer is configured to receive an IP address from a DHCP server and one does not respond, the computer uses the Automatic Private IP Addressing, which generates an IP address in the form of 169.254.xxx.xxx and the subnet mask of 255.255.0.0. When you have an automatic private IP address, you can only communicate with computers on the same network/subnet that have an automatic private IP address. Therefore, you will most likely not be able to communicate with any host on the network without the proper IP address and subnet mask.

Testing Network Connectivity

Assuming that you have the correct IP configuration, you need to determine if you can communicate with the destination host. Windows 10 provides several tools to determine if you have network connectivity; if you don't have connectivity, Windows 10 helps you pinpoint where the failure is occurring.

An extremely valuable tool in troubleshooting is the ***ping command***. The ping command verifies IP-level connectivity to another TCP/IP computer by sending Internet Control Message Protocol (ICMP) Echo Request messages. The receipt of corresponding Echo Reply messages is displayed along with round-trip times. Ping is the primary TCP/IP command used to troubleshoot connectivity, reachability, and name resolution. Because it gives you the round-trip times, the ping command can also tell you if the link is slow between your host and the destination host.

To ping a host, you would execute ping followed by a host name or IP address. The ping command also supports the following parameters:

- **–t:** Specifies that ping will continue sending Echo Request messages to the destination until interrupted. To interrupt and display statistics, press Ctrl+Break. To interrupt and quit ping, press Ctrl+C.
- **–a:** Specifies that reverse name resolution is performed on the destination IP address. If this is successful, ping displays the corresponding host name.
- **–n Count:** Specifies the number of Echo Request messages sent. The default is 4.
- **–l Size:** Specifies the length, in bytes, of the data field in the Echo Request messages sent. The default is 32. The maximum size is 65,527.

A *Request Timed Out* response indicates that there is a known route to the destination computer, but one or more computers or routers along the path, including the source and destination, are not configured correctly. *Destination Host Unreachable* indicates that the system cannot find a route to the destination system and, therefore, does not know where to send the packet on the next hop.

Two other useful commands are the ***tracert command*** and ***pathping command***. The tracert command traces the route that a packet takes to a destination and displays the series of IP routers that are used in delivering packets to the destination. If the packets are unable to be delivered to the destination, the tracert command displays the last router that successfully forwarded the packet. The tracert command also uses the ICMP protocol.

Pathping traces a route through the network in a manner similar to tracert. However, pathping also provides more detailed statistics on the individual hops.

TAKE NOTE

Because ICMP packets can be used in Denial of Service (DoS) attacks, some routers and firewalls block ICMP packets. Therefore, when you try to ping a host with the ping, tracert, or pathping command, it might not respond even though the host is connected.

To isolate network connectivity problems, use the following troubleshooting process:

1. Verify host IP configuration.
2. Use the ping command to gather more information on the extent of the problem:
   - Ping the destination address.
   - Ping the loopback address (127.0.0.1).
   - Ping a local IP address.

- Ping a remote gateway.
- Ping a remote computer.

3. Identify each hop (router) between two systems using the tracert or pathping command.

To determine whether you have a network connectivity problem, you should ping the destination by name or by IP address. If the ping command shows you have network connectivity, your problem is most likely with the host requesting the services; or, the services on the destination could be down. It should be noted that if you ping by name, you should verify that the correct address was used.

If you appear not to have network connectivity to a server or service, you need to isolate where the connectivity problem occurs, starting with the host computer. Therefore, you should ping the loopback address and local IP address to determine whether your TCP/IP components are functioning. Next, if you ping a local IP address, your results demonstrate whether you can communicate on the local subnet that you are connected to. If you still have not found the problem, you can then ping the remote gateway (most likely your default gateway) to determine if you can communicate with the router. Next, pinging a remote computer determines if you can communicate through your default gateway to a remote subnet. Finally, use the tracert and pathping commands to determine exactly where the problem is.

Testing Name Resolution

Because we often use names instead of addresses, you might need to verify that you have the correct name resolution when specifying a name. In Windows, the most common tool is nslookup.

Nslookup.exe is a command-line administrative tool for testing and troubleshooting DNS name resolution. Entering *hostname* in nslookup provides a forward lookup of the host name to IP address. Entering *IP Address* in nslookup performs a reverse lookup of IP address to host name.

Entering nslookup puts you into an nslookup command environment that allows you to query specific servers using the server command and to query for specific resource records using the set type command.

If you found problems with the DNS, the ipconfig command can be used in certain situations:

- **ipconfig /flushdns:** Flushes and resets the contents of the DNS client resolver cache. During DNS troubleshooting, you can use this procedure to discard negative cache entries from the cache, as well as any other entries that have been added dynamically.

- **ipconfig /displaydns:** Displays the contents of the DNS client resolver cache, which includes both entries preloaded from the local hosts file and any recently obtained resource records for name queries resolved by the computer. The DNS Client service uses this information to resolve frequently queried names quickly, before querying its configured DNS servers.

- **ipconfig /registerdns:** Initiates manual dynamic registration for the DNS names and IP addresses that are configured at a computer. You can use this parameter to troubleshoot a failed DNS name registration or resolve a dynamic update problem between a client and the DNS server without rebooting the client computer. The DNS settings in the advanced properties of the TCP/IP protocol determine which names are registered in DNS.

If you used the nslookup command to test DNS resolution and found a problem with name resolution, you would fix the problem at the DNS server. Unfortunately, previous DNS results that your system processes, such as when you access a web page using a browser, are cached in your memory. Therefore, if you correct the problem, you might need to flush your DNS cache using the ipconfig /flushdns command so that it can query and obtain the corrected values.

TAKE NOTE

If you use host files or lmhosts files, you should check to see if any entries might be incorrect. Nslookup only tests DNS name resolution and does not check to see if a hosts file or lmhosts file is correct.

Viewing Port Usage

In some situations, you might not be able to test network connectivity with ping or similar utilities because ICMP packets are blocked by a firewall. In addition, even if a computer responds to ICMP packets, it doesn't tell you whether the computer is running the network service that you need to access. Therefore, you can use one of several tools to look at the client and server network connections and services.

The *netstat command* displays active TCP connections, ports on which the computer is listening, Ethernet statistics, the IP routing table, IPv4 statistics (for the IP, ICMP, TCP, and UDP protocols), and IPv6 statistics (for the IPv6, ICMPv6, TCP over IPv6, and UDP over IPv6 protocols). Used without parameters, netstat displays active TCP connections. See Figure 6-13.

Figure 6-13

Netstat command

```
C:\Users\jsmith>netstat

Active Connections

  Proto  Local Address          Foreign Address        State
  TCP    192.168.3.95:50884     msnbot-65-52-108-236:https  ESTABLISHED
  TCP    192.168.3.95:50926     msnbot-65-52-108-187:https  ESTABLISHED
^C
C:\Users\jsmith>netstat -a

Active Connections

  Proto  Local Address          Foreign Address        State
  TCP    0.0.0.0:80             Win10A:0               LISTENING
  TCP    0.0.0.0:135            Win10A:0               LISTENING
  TCP    0.0.0.0:445            Win10A:0               LISTENING
  TCP    0.0.0.0:49664          Win10A:0               LISTENING
  TCP    0.0.0.0:49665          Win10A:0               LISTENING
  TCP    0.0.0.0:49666          Win10A:0               LISTENING
  TCP    0.0.0.0:49667          Win10A:0               LISTENING
  TCP    0.0.0.0:49669          Win10A:0               LISTENING
  TCP    0.0.0.0:49687          Win10A:0               LISTENING
  TCP    0.0.0.0:49699          Win10A:0               LISTENING
  TCP    192.168.1.95:139       Win10A:0               LISTENING
  TCP    192.168.3.14:139       Win10A:0               LISTENING
  TCP    192.168.3.95:2090      Win10A:0               LISTENING
  TCP    192.168.3.95:50884     msnbot-65-52-108-236:https  ESTABLISHED
  TCP    192.168.3.95:50926     msnbot-65-52-108-187:https  ESTABLISHED
  TCP    192.168.3.95:51072     91.190.217.50:12350    ESTABLISHED
  TCP    192.168.3.95:51441     msnbot-65-52-108-76:https  ESTABLISHED
  TCP    192.168.3.95:51442     a23-5-232-93:http      ESTABLISHED
  TCP    192.168.3.95:51444     a184-51-102-51:http    ESTABLISHED
  TCP    192.168.3.95:51445     a184-51-102-51:http    ESTABLISHED
  TCP    192.168.3.95:51446     a184-51-102-51:http    ESTABLISHED
```

Netstat supports the following parameters:

- **–a:** Displays all active TCP connections and the TCP and UDP ports on which the computer is listening.
- **–e:** Displays Ethernet statistics, such as the number of bytes and packets sent and received. This parameter can be combined with –s.
- **–n:** Displays active TCP connections; however, addresses and port numbers are expressed numerically and no attempt is made to determine names.

- **–o:** Displays active TCP connections and includes the process ID (PID) for each connection. You can find the application based on the PID on the Processes tab in Windows Task Manager. This parameter can be combined with –a, –n, and –p.

- **–p** *Protocol*: Shows connections for the protocol specified by Protocol. In this case, the Protocol can be tcp, udp, tcpv6, or udpv6. If this parameter is used with –s to display statistics by protocol, Protocol can be tcp, udp, icmp, ip, tcpv6, udpv6, icmpv6, or ipv6.

- **–s:** Displays statistics by protocol. By default, statistics are shown for the TCP, UDP, ICMP, and IP protocols. If the IPv6 protocol for Windows XP is installed, statistics are shown for the TCP over IPv6, UDP over IPv6, ICMPv6, and IPv6 protocols. The –p parameter can be used to specify a set of protocols.

- **–r:** Displays the contents of the IP routing table. This is equivalent to the route print command.

- *Interval*: Redisplays the selected information every *x* seconds. Press Ctrl+C to stop the redisplay. If this parameter is omitted, netstat prints the selected information only once.

If you want a graphical tool to view port usage, you can use Resource Monitor's Network tab, specifically the TCP connections and Listening Ports section. See Figure 6-14.

Figure 6-14

Using Resource Monitor to view port usage

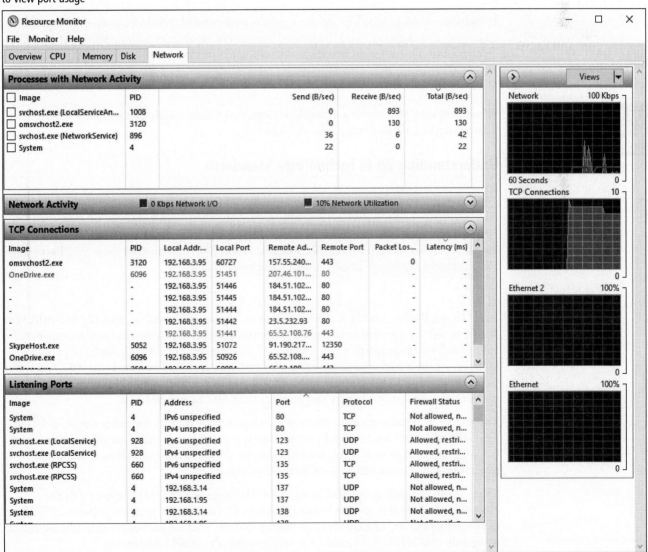

Telnet is a text-based communication program that allows you to connect to a remote server over a network to execute commands at a remote command prompt. Unfortunately, using the telnet command is frowned on in IT because telnet packets are not encrypted. Therefore, it is recommended that you use Secure Shell (SSH). However, you can also use the telnet command to test connectivity to a network service, such as checking a web server (port 80), checking a POP3 mail server (port 110), and checking an SMTP mail server (port 25).

```
telnet hostname port
```

To check port 25 on a mail server (Server01), you can type:

```
telnet server01 25
```

TAKE NOTE By default, the telnet client is not installed and will need to be installed with the Turn Windows features on or off option.

■ CONFIGURING WIRELESS NETWORKS AND CONNECTIONS

 THE BOTTOM LINE Introducing wireless networks and devices into your network involves having a strategy for addressing compatibility issues, addressing encryption capabilities for protecting data, and determining when to use ad hoc versus infrastructure modes.

CERTIFICATION READY
Configure Wi-Fi settings
Objective 2.1

When designing your wireless network strategy, you must consider compatibility issues between devices, wireless standards, and security.

Understanding Wi-Fi Technology Standards

When purchasing wireless network equipment, you need to be aware of issues regarding compatibility between devices. You will face an array of different types of wireless equipment, each built using one or more of the Wi-Fi technology standards. Wireless devices that are based on these specifications can be Wi-Fi certified to show they have been thoroughly tested for performance and compatibility.

802.11b was the first widely accepted wireless technology, followed by *802.11g* and *802.11n*. See Table 6-3. As a general rule, devices supporting the newer, faster standards are capable of falling back to slower speeds when necessary. Therefore, 802.11n is backward compatible with 802.11g, which is backward compatible with 802.11b. It should be noted that *802.11a* is not compatible with 802.11b because each use different frequencies and modulation techniques; however, some network adapters may support both 802.1a and 802.11b.

The 802.11 workgroup currently documents usage in three distinct frequency ranges, 2.4-GHz, 3.6-GHz, and 4.9/5.0-GHz bands. Each range is divided into a multitude of channels. Countries apply their own regulations to both the allowable channels, allowed users, and maximum power levels within these frequency ranges.

There are 14 channels designated in the 2.4-GHz range spaced 5 MHz apart (with the exception of a 12-MHz spacing before Channel 14). Because the protocol requires 25 MHz of channel separation, adjacent channels overlap and can interfere with each other. Consequently, using only channels 1, 6, 11, and 14 is recommended to avoid interference.

Table 6-3

Wi-Fi Technology Standards

STANDARD	DESCRIPTION
802.11b	Supports bandwidth up to 11 Mbps; uses the 2.5-GHz frequency; susceptible to interference with cordless phones and microwaves operating in the same frequency; WEP- and WPA-supported.
802.11a	Supports bandwidth up to 54 Mbps; uses the 5-GHz frequency; less interference with common household devices; higher frequency means shorter range compared with 802.11b and also less apt to penetrate walls; incompatible with 802.11b because they use different frequencies; WEP- and WPA-supported.
802.11g	Supports bandwidth up to 54 Mbps; uses the 2.5-GHz frequency; backward compatible with 802.11b; 802.11g was designed to use the best features of both 802.11b and 802.11a; WEP- and WPA-supported.
802.11i	Has improved encryption for networks using the 802.11a, 802.11b, and 802.11g standards; introduces new encryption key protocols: Temporal Key Integrity Protocol (TKIP) and Advanced Encryption Standard (AES).
802.11n	Supports bandwidth up to approximately 300 Mbps; uses 2.5- and 5-GHz frequencies; uses four spatial streams to simultaneously transfer data by using a channel width of 40 Hz designed to replace 802.11a, b, and g; backward compatible with 802.11g; supports Wi-Fi Protected Access version 2 (WPA v2), usually referred to as WPA2.
802.1X	Security standard for 802.11 networks that use RADIUS for authentication; provides key management; RADIUS provides centralized authentication, authorization, and accounting for remote connections.

Utilizing Wireless Security

Because wireless technology sends radio waves out into the open, anyone can capture data within the range of the antennas. Therefore, you need to implement encryption and other security measures to prevent data from being read over wireless technology.

The first widely used encryption algorithm used on wireless networks is ***Wired Equivalent Privacy (WEP)***. WEP is often inaccurately referred to as Wireless Encryption Protocol. With WEP, you encrypt data using 40-bit, 128-bit, 152-bit, or higher bit-length private key encryption. With WEP, all data is encrypted using a symmetric key derived from the WEP key or password before it is transmitted, and any computer that wants to read the data must be able to decrypt it using the key. Although WEP was intended to provide confidentiality comparable with that of a traditional wired network, WEP was easily cracked with readily available software within minutes. Therefore, it is recommended that you use WPA or WPA2.

Within a few months after the security weaknesses were identified with WEP, IEEE created ***Wi-Fi Protected Access (WPA)*** as an interim standard prior to the ratification of 802.11i followed by WPA2. WPA provides strong data encryption via Temporal Key Integrity Protocol (TKIP), while ***Wi-Fi Protected Access 2 (WPA2)*** provides enhanced data encryption via Advanced Encryption Standard (AES), which meets the Federal Information Standard (FIPS) 140-2 requirement of some government agencies. To help prevent someone from hacking the key, WPA and WPA2 rotate the keys and change the way keys are derived.

WPA devices can operate in the following modes:

- Personal mode
- Enterprise mode

Personal mode, designed for home and small office networks, provides authentication via a pre-shared key or password. Each wireless network device encrypts the network traffic using a 256-bit key. This key may be entered either as a string of 64 hexadecimal digits, or as a pass-phrase of 8 to 63 printable ASCII characters. The pre-shared encryption key is programmed into the access point and all wireless devices, which is used as a starting point to mathematically generate session keys. The session keys are then changed often and handled in the background.

Enterprise mode provides authentication using IEEE 802.1X and Extensible Authentication Protocol (EAP). 802.1X provides an authentication framework for wireless LANs, allowing a user to be authenticated by a central authority such as a RADIUS server (RADIUS is described in more depth later in this lesson). Because it uses EAP, the actual algorithm that is used to determine whether a user is authentic is left open so that multiple algorithms can be used and even added as new ones are developed. Enterprise mode uses two sets of keys: the session keys and group keys. The session keys are unique to each client associated between an access point and a wireless client. Group keys are shared among all clients connected to the same access point. Both sets of keys are generated dynamically and are rotated to help safeguard the integrity of keys over time. The encryption keys could be supplied through a certificate or smart card.

> **TAKE NOTE**
>
> The *Extensible Authentication Protocol (EAP)* is used in wireless networks to expand the number of authentication methods available. It supports one-time passwords, certificates, smart cards, and public key encryption. When users connect to an AP using EAP, their authentication request is forwarded to a *Remote Authentication Dial-In User Service (RADIUS) server*. When the RADIUS server receives the request from the AP, it searches its database for the name listed and the password. If the information is correct, the appropriate parameters (IP address, route information, protocol to use) are returned to the AP.

Connecting to a Wireless Network

Wireless devices can be connected in two ways, as shown in Figure 6-15. *Ad hoc* allows wireless clients to connect to each other without the use of a wireless access point (AP). *Infrastructure mode* has wireless clients connect to a wireless AP. The AP does not have to be connected to a wired network.

The Wi-Fi properties are very similar to the settings for any other network card, but let's take a closer look at what is different. The Wi-Fi properties can be found by opening Control Panel. Under Network and Internet, click View network status and tasks. Click Change adapter settings and then right-click the wireless adapter and choose Status, as shown in Figure 6-16.

Figure 6-16 shows that additional information is provided for a Wi-Fi connection, including the following:

- **SSID:** *Service Set Identifier (SSID)* is the name of the wireless local area network, which consists of a case-sensitive, 32-alphanumeric character string. All wireless clients must use the same SSID to communicate.
- **Speed:** This shows the connection speed for the wireless connection.
- **Signal Quality:** This is the current signal strength between the wireless client and the wireless AP. More bars mean a stronger signal.

By clicking the Details button, you can view the network connection details (address, DHCP-enabled, IPv4/IPv6 configuration information).

Figure 6-15

Connecting wireless devices
in an ad hoc network and in
infrastructure mode

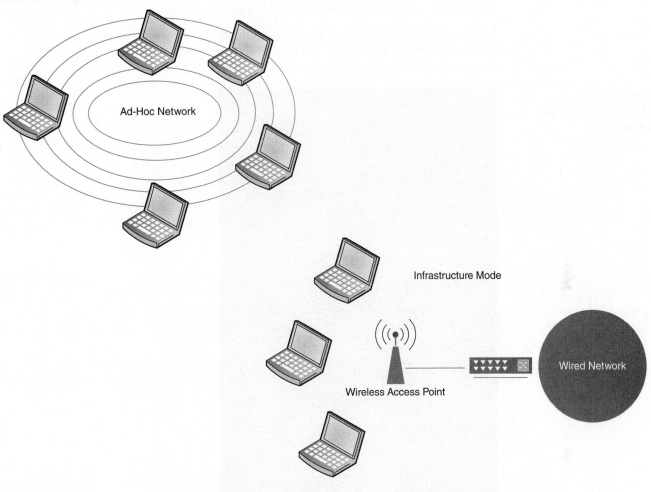

Figure 6-16

Reviewing Wi-Fi status

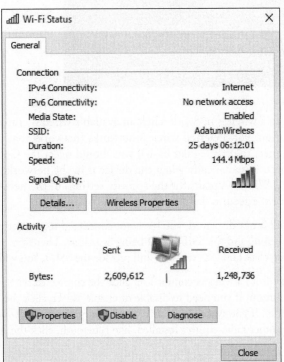

By clicking the Wireless Properties button, the Connection tab provides the name of the wireless local area network (SSID), network type (ad hoc vs. access point), and options for connecting to the wireless local area network (WLAN). The Security tab provides information regarding the security type used (WPA v2-personal, WPA-enterprise), the encryption type (TKIP, AES), and the network security key, if used.

To view available wireless connections, you can right-click the network status icon on the taskbar, as shown in Figure 6-17. If a wireless network broadcasts its name or SSID, the wireless network is automatically listed.

Figure 6-17

Viewing available wireless connections

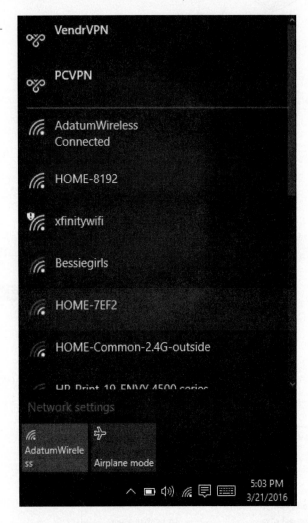

To connect to a wireless network, click an available wireless connection, and then click the Connect button. For preferred wireless networks (networks that you know and trust and that you connect to on a regular basis), you should select the Connect automatically option, which connects automatically when the device is in the network's range. Once you click or tap Connect, Windows scans for the security settings of the network. If required, you are then prompted for the security key.

If the network is not displayed, you have not connected to the network and stored the SSID and security key before, and the SSID is not being broadcast. Therefore, you can scroll down to the bottom of the list, click Hidden Network, and provide the SSID. You will then provide the security key.

To disconnect from a wireless connection, click the connected wireless connection, and click the Disconnect button. If you need to disable or enable Wi-Fi, click the Wi-Fi button (button next to Airplane mode). If you want to enable or disable airplane mode, which disables both the wireless card and any other radio emitter installed, like Bluetooth, click the Airplane mode button.

CONNECT TO A WIRELESS NETWORK

GET READY. To connect to a wireless network, perform the following steps.

1. Log on to a computer running Windows 10 with a wireless adapter.
2. Make sure the wireless adapter is on. Most mobile computers have a switch to enable or disable the wireless adapter.
3. Right-click the **Start** button and then click **Control Panel.**
4. When the Control Panel window opens, click **Network and Internet > Network and Sharing Center.**
5. When the Network and Sharing Center control panel opens, click **Change adapter settings.**
6. If the Wireless Network Connection is disabled, right-click the connection and select **Enable.**
7. Right-click the **Wireless Network Connection** and select **Properties.**
8. Right-click **Wireless Network Connection** and select **Connect/Disconnect.**
9. Click **Open Network and Sharing Center.**
10. Click **Manage wireless networks.**
11. Click the **Add** button.
12. When prompted how you want to add a network, click the **Manually create a network profile** option.
13. For the Network name, type **Adatum01** (or another name provided by your instructor). For the Security type, select WPA2-Personal. Type **Pa$$w0rd** for the security key.
14. Deselect the **Start this connection automatically** and select **Connect even if the network is not broadcasting.** Click **Next.**
15. Click the **Close** button.
16. Go back to the **Manage Wireless Networks.** You should notice the Adatum01 connection is there.
17. Go back to the **Network Connections,** right-click **Wireless Network Connection,** and then click **Connect/Disconnect.**
18. Click **Adatum01** and click **Connect.**
19. Click **Adatum01** and click **Disconnect.**

CONFIGURING WI-FI DIRECT

THE BOTTOM LINE

When a computer connects to a wireless network, it is most likely using IEEE 802.11 wireless standards. When you connect to a wireless network, you connect through an access point (infrastructure mode), or you can connect directly to another device (ad hoc mode). *Wi-Fi Direct* is a Microsoft implementation that uses ad hoc wireless networking that allows you to easily connect to another wireless device.

CERTIFICATION READY
Configure Wi-Fi Direct
Objective 2.1

Bluetooth is a wireless technology that was used to exchange data between two devices. It could be used to share pictures between two smartphones, or connect a wireless headset to a computer. Unfortunately, Bluetooth is limited to a short distance and has a slower speed compared with other wireless technologies.

Wi-Fi Direct can be used with a wide range of computers, components, and applications, including desktop computers, mobile computers, smartphones, music players, headphones, projectors, speakers, and printers.

Wi-Fi Direct is an application programming interface (API), for which software developers can create Wi-Fi Direct–enabled applications. To use Wi-Fi Direct with Windows 10, you would first create a pairing between two devices, similarly to what you would do with Bluetooth.

Once the devices are paired, the device you added appears on the Windows 10 computer in the Devices list on the PC Settings page. If appropriate, you can use the Play To function to push a media file to the device, or connect to it in other ways, depending on the application you are using.

■ CONFIGURING WINDOWS FIREWALL

THE BOTTOM LINE

Designing a strategy for protecting your network involves implementing multiple levels of defense. Although most companies have a firewall to protect their perimeter, they don't normally do a good job of protecting the individual hosts behind the firewall.

CERTIFICATION READY
Configure Windows
Firewall
Objective 2.1

After you determine your IP addressing schemes and how you want to configure your network from a logical/physical layout, it's time to determine how to secure it. This starts with looking at your network perimeter(s), which are the locations in your network in which your trusted network connects to another probably untrusted network. These gateways between networks enable you to implement security, control the types of traffic allowed to enter and exit your network, and reduce your overall network traffic. The most obvious perimeter is where your company's network connects to the Internet, but other perimeters might exist.

It's common for administrators to build network subnets to isolate and control traffic within their own private network so they can restrict traffic to a certain subnet and improve overall performance. It can also help isolate certain areas of the network that contain sensitive information. For example, you might create a subnet that contains just the finance department's systems due to the confidential nature of the information they work with.

The device used to segment a network is a *router*. Although routers can provide basic traffic management (inbound/outbound), their primary role is to forward traffic between networks. Companies that are serious about their network security add a commercial-level firewall at the perimeter that leads to the Internet. In most cases, that should be sufficient enough to protect your network, but what happens if something is compromised on that firewall or if misconfiguration allows it to be bypassed? What if mobile users connect behind the firewall and attempt to gain access to a server or computer they are not authorized to use? This is where a host-based firewall can help.

A *firewall* is a software program or piece of hardware that protects networks or individual computers by screening and controlling incoming and outgoing network traffic based on a set of rules. There are two basic types of firewalls (see Figure 6-18):

- *Network perimeter firewalls:* These firewalls are found on the boundary between an internal and external network. They can be hardware- or software-based, and provide several types of functionality, including managing and monitoring traffic through stateful connection analysis, providing Internet Protocol security (*IPsec*) authentication and encryption, and providing NAT.

Figure 6-18

Reviewing a network
firewall and host-based
firewall deployment

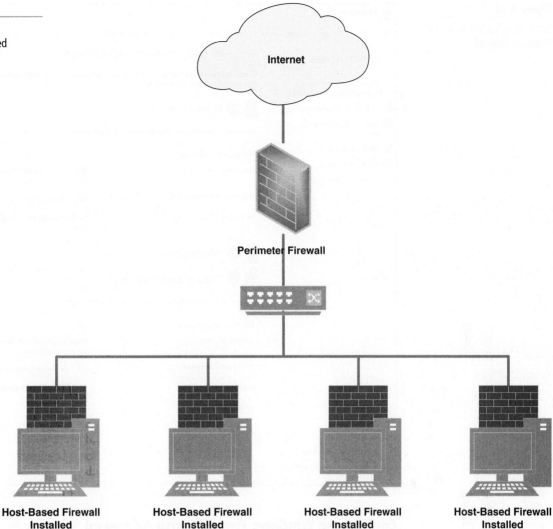

- *Host-based firewalls*: These firewalls run on individual computers (hosts) within the local network. They are designed to provide a second layer of defense, protect the computer from attacks and unauthorized access, and block specific types of traffic.

Because a network perimeter firewall monitors only traffic coming in and out of the network, it represents a single point of failure and does very little to protect against attacks that occur from within the private network. Without an additional layer of defense, using just a network perimeter firewall can put your entire network at risk. To create an additional level of protection, consider using a host-based firewall such as the Windows Firewall with Advanced Security (WFAS).

Windows Firewall is a host-based firewall that is included with Windows 10. Basic Windows Firewall operations are controlled from the Windows 10 Control Panel, as shown in Figure 6-19. You can view the firewall status, and enable or disable the Windows Firewall based on network locations.

In Control Panel, you can click the Allow apps to communicate through Windows Firewall option to easily control what applications can communicate through the firewall. Limiting what programs can access through the firewall stops unknown programs from communicating over the Internet or with other suspicious systems.

Figure 6-19

Controlling the Windows 10 Windows Firewall

Configuring Windows Firewall with Advanced Security

> *Windows Firewall with Advanced Security (WFAS)* combines a stateful host-based firewall with IPsec. It is designed to protect against attacks that originate from within your network or those that might bypass the network perimeter firewall(s). WFAS inspects both IPv4 and IPv6 packets that enter and leave your computer and then compares them against the criteria contained in the firewall's rules. If the packet matches a rule, the action configured in the rule is applied. If the packet does not match a rule, the firewall discards it and records an entry in its log files.

CERTIFICATION READY
Configure Windows Firewall with Advanced Security
Objective 2.1

WFAS is network location–aware, so it can determine the type of network you are connecting to. After it identifies the type of network, it applies the appropriate profile to provide protection against attacks that can originate from inside and outside of your network. The following WFAS profiles (see Figure 6-20) can be used to apply settings to your computer:

- A *domain profile* is used when your computer is connected to its corporate domain and can authenticate to the domain controller through one of its connections.
- A *private profile* is used when your computer is connected to a private network location (home or small office network) and is located behind a firewall and/or a device that performs NAT. If you are using this profile with a wireless network, you should implement encryption (WPA v2).

Figure 6-20

WFAS profiles

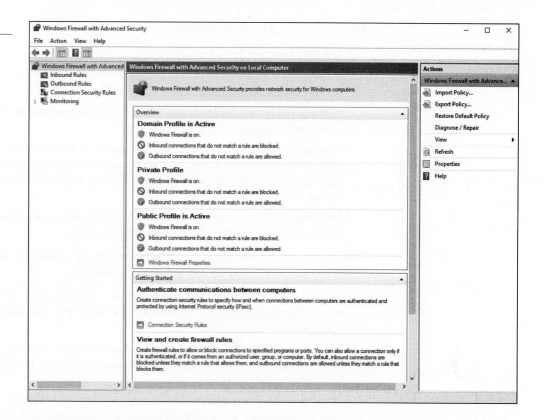

- A *public profile* is used when your computer is connected to a public network (for example, directly connected to the Internet). It is assigned to the computer when it is first connected to a new network; rules associated with this profile are the most restrictive.

You can click the Windows Firewall Properties link to see the range of settings available within each of the three profiles (see Figure 6-21).

Figure 6-21

Understanding WFAS profile property settings

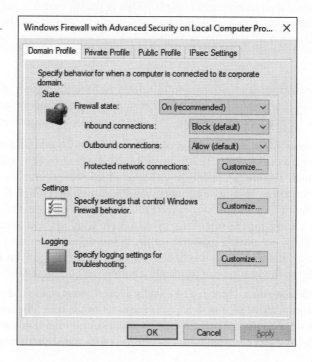

These settings include the following:

- **Firewall state:** Set to On or Off.
  - **Inbound connections:** Set to Block, Block all connections, or Allow.
  - **Outbound connections:** Set to Allow or Block.
  - **Protected network connections:** Select the connections/interfaces you want Windows Firewall to help protect.
- **Settings:** Display notifications when a program is blocked from receiving inbound connections; allow unicast response to multicast or broadcast network traffic; rule merging (allow rules created by local administrators to be merged with rules distributed via Group Policy).
- **Logging:** Set the location for storing firewall logs along with the size limit for the log file; log dropped packets; log successful connections.

IPsec settings can be configured to control how keys are exchanged, how your data is protected, and the authentication methods you want to use:

- **IPsec defaults:** These settings determine how your computer will establish a secure connection by identifying how the keys will be exchanged, how data will be protected, and the authentication method to use.
- **IPsec exemptions:** This setting enables you to exempt Internet Control Message Protocol (ICMP) to simplify the troubleshooting process; ICMP is designed to detect and report error conditions.
- **IPsec tunnel authorization:** This setting enables you to specify the users and computers that are authorized to establish IPsec tunnel connections with your computer.

Understanding Inbound Rules, Outbound Rules, and Connection Security Rules

WFAS enables you to configure three types of firewall rules (inbound, outbound, and connection security) that can be applied to one or more of the profiles (domain, private, public). These rules govern how the computer sends and/or receives traffic from users, computers, applications, and services. When a packet matches the rule's criteria, it allows the connection, explicitly blocks the connection, or allows it only if the connection is using IPsec to secure it.

When configuring inbound/outbound rules, you have the option of selecting criteria that include a program name, TCP/UDP port number, system service name, local and remote interfaces, interface types, users/groups, computers/computer groups, and protocols:

- *Inbound rules:* These rules explicitly allow or block inbound traffic that matches the criteria set in the rule. To set up an inbound rule, select the type (program, port, predefined, or custom), select the entity to which the rule applies (for example, program [all or path to specific .exe], port name/number), determine the action (allow, block, or allow if it is secure), select the profile it applies to (domain, private, public), and provide a name for the rule. When your system is set up, it is automatically configured to not allow unsolicited inbound traffic. If you decide to set up a service on your computer (a test website) and want others to connect to it, configure an inbound rule that allows traffic to the web service (typically running on TCP port 80).
- *Outbound rules:* These rules explicitly allow or deny outbound traffic that originates from the computer when it matches the criteria set in the rule. The setup for an outbound rule is identical to the options discussed in the inbound rule. Because outbound traffic is allowed by default, you create an outbound rule to block traffic that you do not want to send.

- *Connection security rules:* These rules secure the connection with both authentication (Kerberos, digital certificates, pre-shared keys) and encryption protocols. Connection security rules are used to determine how the traffic between the computer and others is secured. The process for creating a connection security rule involves setting the type of connection security you want to create (isolation, authentication exception, server-to-server, tunnel), selecting when you want authentication to occur on inbound/outbound connections (request but don't require it, require it for inbound but request for outbound, require for both), selecting the authentication method to use, selecting which profile to apply the rule to (domain, private, public), and then providing a name for the rule.

TAKE NOTE Connection security rules specify how and when authentication occurs, but they do not allow connections. You need to create an inbound or outbound rule to allow the connection.

When firewall rules conflict, they are applied in the following order (as soon as an incoming packet matches a rule, that rule is applied and processing stops):

1. **Authenticated bypass rules:** These are rules that allow a connection even if the existing firewall rules would block it. For example, you might be blocking a specific type of traffic but then want to allow a certain group of users and computers to bypass the block. These types of rules require that the authenticated computers utilize IPsec to prove their identity.
2. **Block connection:** Rules block matching inbound traffic.
3. **Allow connection:** Rules allow matching inbound traffic.
4. **Default profile behavior:** Block unsolicited inbound traffic; allow all outbound traffic.

 CREATE AN OUTBOUND RULE

GET READY. To create an outbound rule, perform the following steps.

TAKE NOTE Before performing the following steps, close Internet Explorer.

1. On LON-CL1, click the **Start** button. When the Start menu opens, type **Windows Advanced**. From the results, choose **Windows Firewall with Advanced Security**.
2. Right-click **Outbound Rules** and then click **New Rule.**
3. Select **Program** and then click **Next.**
4. Click **Browse** and then navigate to the location of your installation of Internet Explorer. This can usually be found at c:\%ProgramFiles%\Internet Explorer\iexplore.exe.
5. Click **iexplore.exe** and then click **Open.**
6. In the New Outbound Rule Wizard dialog box, click **Next.**
7. Select **Block the connection** and then click **Next.**
8. Select **Domain**, **Private**, and **Public**, and then click **Next.**
9. For the name of the profile, type **IE Restriction**; for the description, type **Restricts IE from connecting to the Internet.**
10. Click **Finish.**

    Do not close the Windows Firewall with Advanced Security dialog box.

11. Attempt to access the Internet using Internet Explorer. You should see the This page can't be displayed message.

12. Close the Internet Explorer window.

13. In the Windows Firewall with Advanced Security window, click the **Windows Firewall with Advanced Security** option in the left pane, click **Action**, and then choose **Export Policy**.

14. Navigate to a folder that you can access from your Windows 10 computer. In the File name field, type **IE Restriction** and then click **Save**.

    Make a note of where you stored this policy; you will use it in the next exercise.

15. When the Policy successfully exported message is displayed, click **OK**.

16. Return to the Windows Firewall with Advanced Security dialog box and click **Outbound Rules**.

17. Locate the two Internet Explorer restriction rules you created earlier, right-click them, and then choose **Delete**. Click **Yes** to confirm you want to delete the rules.

18. Attempt to access the Internet using Internet Explorer. You should be successful.

19. Close the Internet Explorer window and close the Windows Firewall with Advanced Security window.

 CREATE AN INBOUND RULE

GET READY. To create an inbound rule based on ports, perform the following steps.

1. On LON-CL1, click the **Start** button. When the Start menu opens, type **Windows Advanced**. From the results, choose **Windows Firewall with Advanced Security**.

2. Right-click **Inbound Rules** and then click **New Rule**.

3. On the Rule Type page, select the **Port** option, and click **Next**.

4. On the Protocol and Ports page, with TCP selected, select **Specific local ports**. Then type the following ports, and click **Next**:

   22,80,443

5. On the Action page, with the Allow the connection option already selected, click **Next**.

6. On the Profile page, click **Next**.

7. On the Name page, in the Name text box, type **Allow SSH, HTTP, and HTTPS**, and click **Finish**.

After you export the current firewall configuration from the Action menu in the Windows Firewall with Advanced Security window, you can then import it on another stand-alone system or copy it to a folder to use as a backup in case you make changes to the policy and need to return it to a known state. Policy files are exported as (*.wfw) files.

Configuring Connection Security Rules (IPsec)

IP security (IPsec) is a suite of protocols that provides a mechanism for data integrity, authentication, and privacy for the Internet Protocol by providing message authentication and/or encryption. It can be used to protect data sent between hosts on a network by creating a secure electronic tunnel between two hosts. It can also be used for remote access/VPN connections.

To ensure that data cannot be viewed or modified by unauthorized users, the source computer uses IPsec to encrypt the information by encapsulating each data packet in a new packet that contains the information to set up, maintain, and tear down a virtual tunnel. The data is then decrypted at the destination computer.

IPsec includes a couple of modes and a couple of protocols. The two modes include:

- *Transport mode*: Used to secure end-to-end communications such as between a client and a server.
- *Tunnel mode*: Used for server-to-server or server-to-gateway configurations by creating a virtual path that a packet takes from the source computer to the destination computer. When packets are sent along this path, the packets are encrypted.

The two IPsec protocols are:

- *Encapsulating Security Payload (ESP)*: Provides confidentiality (encryption), authentication (proves identity), integrity (verifies the packet has not been changed), and anti-replay (prevents packets from being reused to bypass security) for the IP payload only, not the entire packet. ESP operates directly on top of IP, using IP protocol number 50.
- *Authentication Header (AH)*: Provides authentication, integrity, and anti-replay for the entire packet (both the IP header and the data payload carried in the packet). Because the payload is not encrypted, it does not provide confidentiality. The data is readable but protected from modification. AH operates directly on top of IP, using IP protocol number 51.

ESP and AH can be combined to provide authentication, integrity, and anti-replay for the entire packet, and confidentiality for the payload.

The AH protocol is not compatible with Network Address Translation (NAT) because NAT devices need to change information in the packet headers. To allow IPsec-based traffic to pass through a NAT device, you must ensure that IPsec NAT-T is supported on your IPsec peer computers.

To configure IPsec between two hosts, you will configure connection security rules using the Windows Firewall with Advanced Security. The rules that you will create include:

1. Enable the protocol that you want to secure.
2. Create a Connection Security rule on the first host.
3. Create a Connection Security rule on the second host.
4. Test the rules and monitor the results.

 ENABLE THE ICMP TRAFFIC ON THE SENDING HOST

GET READY. To enable ICMP traffic on a computer running Windows 10, perform the following steps.

1. On LON-CL1, click the **Start** button, and in the Search box, type **Windows Firewall with Advanced Security**, and then press the **Enter** key.
2. Click **Inbound Rules**, right-click it, and then choose **New Rule**.
3. In the New Inbound Rule Wizard dialog box, on the Rule Type page, click **Custom**, as shown in Figure 6-22, and then click **Next**.
4. On the Program page, click **Next**.
5. On the Protocols and Ports page, in the Protocol type list, click **ICMPv4** and then click **Next**.

Figure 6-22

Opening the New Inbound
Rule Wizard

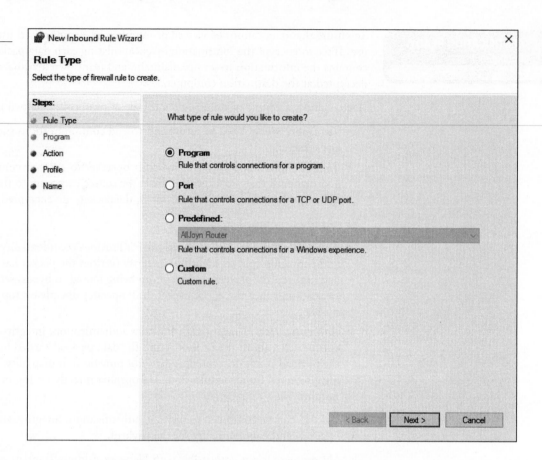

6. On the Scope page, click **Next**.

7. On the Action page, click **Allow the connection if it is secure** and then click **Next**.

8. On the Users page, click **Next**.

9. On the Computers page, click **Next**.

10. On the Profile page, click **Next**.

11. On the Name page, in the Name box, type **ICMPv4 Allowed** and then click **Finish**.

 CREATE A CONNECTION SECURITY RULE

GET READY. To create a connection security rule, perform the following steps.

1. On LON-CL1, in the Windows Firewall with Advanced Security console, click **Connection Security Rules**, right-click it, and then choose **New Rule**.

2. In the New Connection Security Rule Wizard, on the Rule Type page, click **Server-to-Server**, as shown in Figure 6-23, and then click **Next**.

3. On the Endpoints page, click **Next**.

4. On the Requirements page, click **Require authentication for inbound and outbound connections** and then click **Next**.

5. On the Authentication Method page, click **Advanced** and then click **Customize**.

6. In the Customize Advanced Authentication Methods dialog box, under First authentication, click **Add**.

7. In the Add First Authentication Method dialog box, click **Preshared Key**, type **secret**, and then click **OK**.

Figure 6-23

Opening the New Connection
Security Rule Wizard

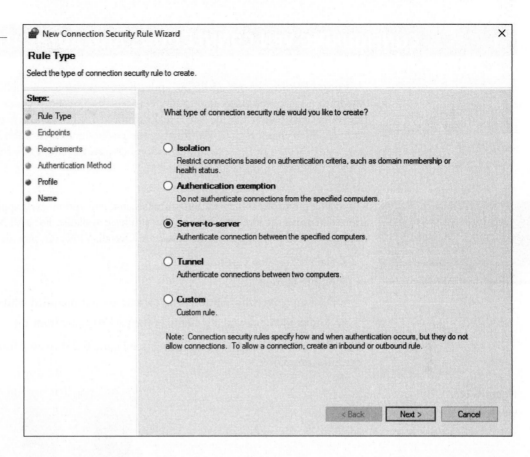

8. In the Customize Advanced Authentication Methods dialog box, click **OK**.
9. On the Authentication Method page, click **Next**.
10. On the Profile page, click **Next**.
11. On the Name page, in the Name box, type **Adatum-Computer-to-Computer** and then click **Finish**.
12. Repeat the steps on Win10B.

 TEST THE RULES AND MONITOR THE RESULTS

GET READY. To test the rules Contoso-Computer-to-Computer, perform the following steps.

1. On LON-CL1, right-click the **Start** button and choose **Command Prompt (Admin)**.
2. At the command prompt, type **ping 192.168.1.60** and then press the **Enter** key.
3. Switch to **Windows Firewall with Advanced Security**.
4. Expand **Monitoring**, expand **Security Associations**, and then click **Main Mode**.
5. In the right-pane, double-click the listed item.
6. View the information in Main Mode and then click **OK**.
7. Expand **Quick Mode**.
8. In the right-pane, double-click the listed item.
9. View the information in Quick Mode and then click **OK**.

CONFIGURING VPN CONNECTIONS AND AUTHENTICATION

THE BOTTOM LINE

A *Virtual Private Network (VPN)* is a private network that uses a public network (for example, the Internet) to connect remote sites and users. The VPN makes it appear to computers, on each end of the connection, as if they are actually connected to the same network. This point-to-point connection is emulated by encapsulating the packet in an IP header. The information in the header is used to route the information between the two VPN endpoints.

CERTIFICATION READY
Configure VPN, such as
app-triggered VPN, traffic
filters, and lockdown VPN
Objective 2.1

Tunneling protocols, authentication protocols, and encryption levels applied to the VPN connections determine the level of VPN security you have available. For a VPN to work, both the client and server need to utilize the same protocols. Overall, VPNs can provide the following capabilities:

- Data encryption (confidentiality)
- Authentication
- Data integrity, which ensures the packets are not modified while in transit
- Nonrepudiation, which guarantees the packets came from the source at a specific time

The VPN uses the concept of tunneling (see Figure 6-24) to establish and maintain a logical network connection.

Figure 6-24

VPN tunnel

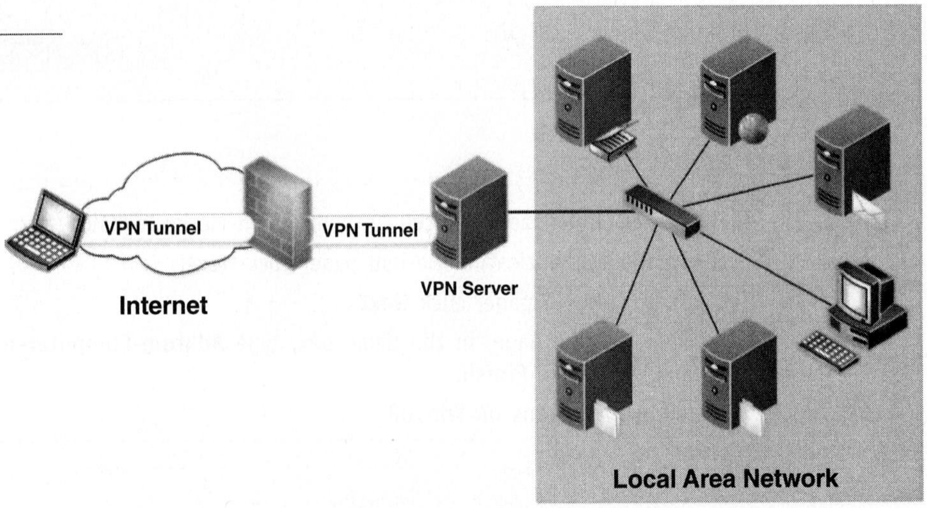

VPN Tunnel VPN Tunnel

Internet **VPN Server**

Local Area Network

Selecting Types of VPN Protocols

There are four types of VPN tunneling protocols that are available in Windows 10. They include Point-to-Point Tunneling Protocol (PPTP), Layer 2 Tunneling Protocol over IPsec (L2TP/IPsec), Secure Socket Tunneling Protocol (SSTP), and VPN Reconnect (or IKEv2).

Point-to-Point Tunneling Protocol (PPTP) has widespread support with nearly all versions of Windows. It uses the Microsoft Point-to-Point Encryption (MPPE) protocol with RC4 (128-bit key) to protect data that is in transit. Although not as secure as L2TP/IPsec (discussed later), it can provide a reasonably secure option for remote access and site-to-site VPNs when used in combination with an authentication protocol, such as MS-CHAPv2.

PPTP provides confidentiality, meaning that it prevents the data from being viewed, but it does not provide data integrity. In other words, it does not protect the packet from being intercepted and modified. PPTP does not implement any mechanisms that ensure the data is actually sent by the authorized person.

TAKE NOTE PPTP is typically used for remote access and site-to-site VPNs, works with IPv4, and uses Network Address Translation (NAT), which is supported via PPTP-enabled NAT routers. It uses PPP for user authentication and RC4 for data confidentiality.

Whereas PPTP supports authentication of the user only, *Layer 2 Tunneling Protocol over IPsec (L2TP/IPsec)* requires that the computers mutually authenticate themselves to each other. The computer-to-computer authentication takes place before the user is authenticated.

L2TP provides a support mechanism for pre-shared keys, digital certificates, or Kerberos for mutual authentication. Pre-shared keys are basically passwords and should only be used in test networks when you don't want to set up a public key infrastructure (PKI). Digital certificates, which are stored in a format that cannot be modified, offer a more secure option. They are issued by certificate authorities that you trust. Kerberos is the native authentication protocol for Windows Server 2003 and later and provides the easiest way to secure VPN connections in a domain-based environment. It provides mutual authentication, anti-replay, and nonrepudiation just like digital certificates.

Kerberos can only be used when both computers involved in the L2TP tunnel are in the same forest. L2TP uses IPsec to encrypt the Point-to-Point Protocol (PPP) packets. L2TP/IPsec provides data confidentiality and data integrity as well as proof that an authorized individual sent the message.

TAKE NOTE L2TP with IPsec is typically used for remote access and site-to-site VPNs, works over IPv4 and IPv6, and supports Network Address Translation. It uses IPsec with 3DES (168-bit key) and uses UDP ports (500, 1701, 5500). It uses IPsec for machine authentication followed by PPP for user authentication.

Secure Socket Tunneling Protocol (SSTP) improved upon the PPTP and L2TP/IPsec VPN tunneling protocols. It works by sending PPP or L2TP traffic through an SSL 3.0 channel.

The SSTP protocol uses SSL and TCP port 443 to relay traffic. By using TCP port 443, it will work in network environments where other VPN protocols might be blocked when traversing firewalls, Network Address Translation (NAT) devices, and web proxies. SSTP uses a 2048-bit certificate for authentication and implements stronger encryption, which makes it the most secure VPN protocol.

IKEv2 consists of the following protocols: IPsec Tunnel Mode, IKEv2, Encapsulating Security Payload (ESP), and MOBIKE. IKEv2 is used by IPsec for key negotiations, ESP for securing the packet transmissions, and MOBIKE (Mobility and Multi-homing Protocol) is used for switching tunnel endpoints. MOBIKE ensures that if there is a break in connectivity, the user can continue without restarting the connection.

TAKE NOTE SSTP is supported by Windows Vista SP1 and higher client operating systems, and Windows Server 2008 and higher server operating systems. It is designed for remote access VPNs; works over IPv4 and IPv6 networks; and traverses NAT, firewalls, and web proxies. It uses a generic port that is rarely blocked by firewalls. It uses PPP for user authentication and RC4/ AES for data confidentiality.

VPN Reconnect, also known as *Internet Key Exchange version 2 (IKEv2)*, is a feature introduced with Routing and Remote Access Services (RRAS) in Windows Server 2008 R2 and Windows 7. It is designed to provide users with consistent VPN connectivity and automatically reestablishes a VPN when users temporarily lose their Internet connection.

VPN Reconnect was designed for those remote workers who are sitting in the coffee shop, waiting at the airport for their next plane to arrive, trying to submit that last expense report from their hotel room, or working anywhere Internet connections are less than optimal.

It differs from other VPN protocols in that it will not drop the VPN tunnel that is associated with the session. Instead, it keeps the connection alive for 30 minutes by default after it's been dropped. This allows you to reconnect automatically without having to go through the process of selecting your VPN connection and reauthenticating yourself all over again.

TAKE NOTE

VPN Reconnect is designed for remote access VPNs. It works well over IPv4 and IPv6 networks and traverses NAT. It also supports user or machine authentication via IKEv2 and uses 3DES and AES for data confidentiality.

When selecting the appropriate VPN protocol to use, you must take into consideration operating systems, authentication requirements, and limitations. Therefore, you should consider the following:

- Operating systems that you will be using and their ability to traverse firewalls, NAT devices, and web proxies
- Authentication requirements (for computers as well as users)
- Implementations: Site-to-site VPN or a remote access VPN

In most situations, using VPN Reconnect (IKEv2) will provide you the best option for security and uninterrupted VPN connectivity. You can then use SSTP for your VPN solution as a fallback mechanism.

Selecting Authentication for VPN Connections

During a VPN connection, the user will have to be authenticated to prove who is logging on. Therefore, you will need to choose the most secure form of authentication that can be deployed to your remote users.

Authentication for VPN connections takes one of the following forms:

- User-level authentication by using Point-to-Point Protocol (PPP) authentication. User-level authentication is usually user name and password. With a VPN connection, if the VPN server authenticates, the VPN client attempts the connection using a PPP user-level authentication method and verifies that the VPN client has the appropriate authorization. If the method uses mutual authentication, the VPN client also authenticates the VPN server. By using mutual authentication, clients are ensured that the client does not communicate with a rogue server masquerading as a VPN server.
- Computer-level authentication that uses IKE to exchange either computer certificates or a pre-shared key. Microsoft recommends using computer-certificate authentication because it is a much stronger authentication method. Computer-level authentication is performed only for L2TP/IPsec connections.

When using VPNs, Windows 10 supports the following forms of authentication:

- *Password Authentication Protocol (PAP):* A basic authentication method that uses plaintext (unencrypted passwords). PAP is the least secure authentication and is not recommended.
- *Challenge Handshake Authentication Protocol (CHAP):* A challenge-response authentication that uses the industry standard MD5 hashing scheme to encrypt the response. CHAP was an industry standard for years and is still quite popular.
- *Microsoft CHAP version 2 (MS-CHAPv2):* A mature authentication method that provides two-way authentication (mutual authentication). MS-CHAPv2 provides stronger security than CHAP. Finally, MS-CHAPv2 is the only authentication protocol that Windows Server 2012 provides that allows you to change an expired password during the connection process.

- **Extensible Authentication Protocol (EAP-MS-CHAPv2):** A universal authentication framework that allows third-party vendors to develop custom authentication schemes, including retinal scans, voice recognition, fingerprint identifications, smart cards, Kerberos, and digital certificates. It also provides a mutual authentication method that supports password-based user or computer authentication.

It is always best to use EAP-MS-CHAPv2 or MS-CHAPv2 whenever possible.

Using Connection Manager (CM) and the Connection Manager Administration Kit (CMAK)

Connection Manager (CM) is a client network connection tool that helps administrators to simplify the management of their remote connections.

CM uses profiles that consist of settings that allow connections from the local computer to a remote network.

You use the **Connection Manager Administration Kit (CMAK)** to create and customize the profiles for CM and to distribute them to users. The profile, once completed, contains all the settings necessary for the user to connect, including the IP address of the VPN server.

CM supports different features in a profile depending upon the operating system that is running on the client computer. You must create a connection profile on a computer that uses the same architecture (32/64-bit) as the clients on which you will install the profile.

When running the CMAK Wizard, you will be asked to specify the operating system on which the Connection Manager profile will be run. Options include:

- Windows Vista or above
- Windows Server 2003, Windows XP, or Windows 2000

 INSTALL CMAK ON WINDOWS SERVER 2012 R2

GET READY. To install CMAK on Windows Server 2012 R2, perform the following steps.

1. Open **Server Manager**.
2. Click **Manage > Add Roles and Features**.
3. Click **Next**.
4. Click **Role-based or feature-based installation**.
5. Select a server from the server pool and then click **Next**.
6. Click **Next** to move past the Roles selection.
7. Click **RAS Connection Manager Administration Kit (CMAK)** and then click **Next**.
8. Confirm installation selections and then click **Install**.
9. Confirm the installation completes and then click **Close**.

 SET UP A SIMPLE VPN-ONLY PROFILE USING CMAK

GET READY. To set up a simple VPN-only Profile using CMAK, perform the following steps.

TAKE NOTE

This activity is designed to expose the features and options available when creating a Connection Manager profile using CMAK from Windows Server 2012 R2. As you walk through each step, be sure to read the explanation behind it to gain more insight into how CMAK could be used in your specific network environment.

1. Start Connection Manager by clicking **Server Manager > Tools > Connection Manager Administration Kit.**

2. After reading the Welcome message, click **Next.**

3. On the Select the Target Operating System page, click **Windows Vista or above** and then click **Next.**

4. On the Create or Modify a Connection Manager Profile page, click **New Profile** and then click **Next.**

5. On the Specify the Server Name and the File Name page, in the Service name text box and the File name text box, type **MyVPN** and then click **Next.**

6. On the Specify a Realm Name page, click **Do not add a realm name to the user name** and then click **Next.**

7. On the Merge Information from Other Profiles page, where you could merge information from an existing profile, click **Next.** If you had an additional profile, you could merge phone book information, access numbers, and VPN host address information.

8. On the Add Support for VPN Connections page, select **Phone book from this profile.** Then in the Always use the same VPN server text box, type **RemoteServer. adatum.com** and then click **Next.**

9. On the Create or Modify a VPN Entry page, click **Edit** to view the settings that can be configured for this VPN profile (see Figure 6-25).

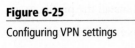

Figure 6-25

Configuring VPN settings

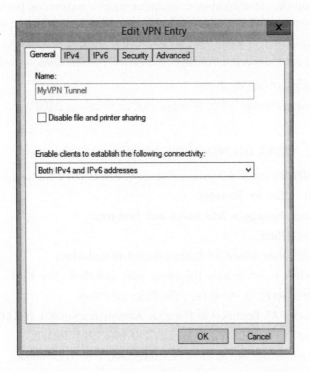

10. Click **OK** to close the Edit VPN Entry dialog box.

11. Back on the Create or Modify a VPN Entry page, click **Next.**

12. On the Add a Custom Phone Book page, clear the **Automatically download phone book updates** option and then click **Next.**

13. On the Configure Dial-Up Networking Entries page, click **Next.**

14. On the Specify Routing Table Updates page, make sure the **Do not change the routing tables** option is selected and then click **Next.**

15. On the Configure Proxy Settings for Internet Explorer page, make sure **Do not configure proxy setting** is selected and then click **Next.**

16. On the Add Custom Actions page, click **Next** to *not* add any custom actions.

17. On the Display a Custom Logon Bitmap page, click **Next** to display a default graphic or select one of your own.

18. On the Display a Custom Phone Book Bitmap page, click **Next** to display a default graphic as a custom phone book.

19. On the Display Custom Icons page, click **Next** to use default icons for the Connection Manager user interface.

20. On the Include a Custom Help File page, click **Next** to use the default help file.

21. On the Display Custom Support Information page, add any text you want to appear in the logon dialog box and then click **Next**. (For example, type **Contact Support at 800-123-1234**.)

22. On the Display a Custom License Agreement page, enter the path to a text file containing a custom license agreement and then click **Next**.

23. On the Install Additional Files with the Connection Manager Profile page, specify any additional files that the Connection Manager profile will require and then click **Next**.

24. On the Build the Connection Manager Profile and Its Installation Program page, select the **Advanced customization** option and then click **Next**.

25. On the Make Advanced Customizations page, set the values shown in Figure 6-26 and then click **Apply**. Click **Next**.

Figure 6-26

Performing advanced customization of the profile

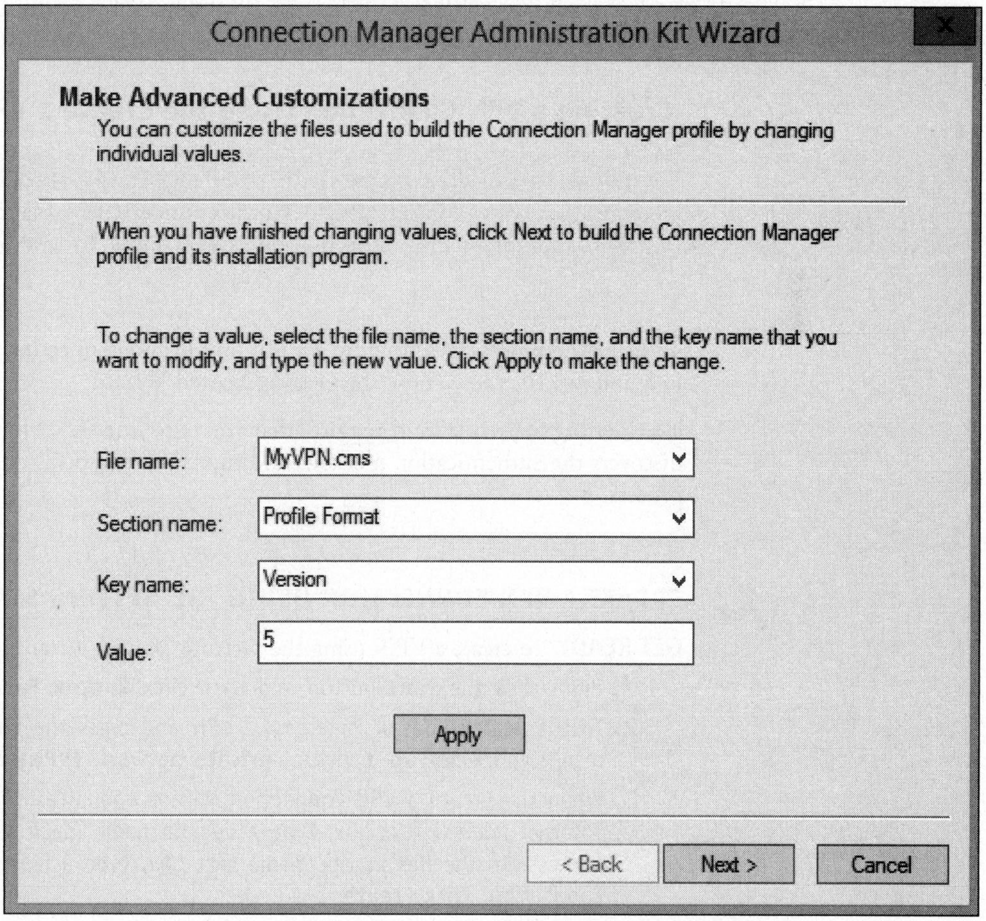

Connection Manager Administration Kit Wizard

Make Advanced Customizations

You can customize the files used to build the Connection Manager profile by changing individual values.

When you have finished changing values, click Next to build the Connection Manager profile and its installation program.

To change a value, select the file name, the section name, and the key name that you want to modify, and type the new value. Click Apply to make the change.

File name: MyVPN.cms

Section name: Profile Format

Key name: Version

Value: 5

Apply

< Back   Next >   Cancel

26. Make a note of the location where the profile will be saved. By default, this will be: c:\Program Files\CMAK\Profiles\Windows Vista and above\MyVPN\MyVPN.exe

27. Click **Finish**.

On the Add Support for VPN Connections page, you can specify the VPN server name or IP address. If you select the Allow the user to choose a VPN server before connecting, you can provide a text file that lists the VPN servers from which the user can choose. The following provides you with an example that can be created and modified within Notepad:

```
[Settings]
default=Adatum CorpHQ
UpdateURL=http://remoteusers.adatum.com/MyVPNfile.txt
Message=Select a server that is closest to your location.
[Adatum VPN Servers]
Adatum Computers CorpHQ=remoteusers.adatum.com
Adatum Computers Los Angeles=LA.remoteusers.adatum.com
Adatum Computers Austin=Austin.remoteusers.adatum.com
```

By using Phone Book Administrator, which is included with Connection Point Services (CPS), you can create a phone book file that contains a list of multiple access numbers that can be used to connect to a remote dial-up network. CPS consists of a Phone Book Service (PBS) and the Phone Book Administrator (PBA). PBS is an extension to the Internet Information Services extension. The PBA allows you to create and edit up to 100 unique phone books. Each phone book is a collection of Points of Presence (POPs) or dial-up entries. The PBA allows you to associate POPs with the network configurations you define in the Connection Manager profile.

Creating a VPN Connection Using the Create a VPN Connection Wizard

Windows 10 provides a simple Getting Started Wizard—also known as the Get Connected Wizard (GCW) and Create a VPN Connection Wizard—that helps make the setup and configuration of a VPN connection quick and simple for end users.

To make the process of setting up a VPN profile and connecting to a VPN much simpler in Windows 10, you can use the Getting Started Wizard.

The Getting Started Wizard requires that you enter the server information and then it auto-discovers the authentication methods and tunneling protocols during the initial connection process.

 CREATE A VPN CONNECTION USING THE GETTING STARTED WIZARD

GET READY. To create a VPN using the Getting Started Wizard, perform the following steps.

1. Right-click the **Start** button and then click **Control Panel.**
2. In the Search Control Panel, type **VPN** and press the **Enter** key. From the search results, click **Set up a virtual private network (VPN) connection.**
3. When the Create a VPN Connection Wizard opens (as shown in Figure 6-27), in the Internet address text box, type a domain name (such as **vpn.adatum.com**) or IP address. In the Destination name text box, type a label that will identify the VPN connection. Click **Create.**
4. Right-click the **network status** icon on the taskbar, and click **Open Network and Sharing Center.**
5. When the Network and Sharing Center opens, click **Change adapter settings.**
6. When the Network Connections window opens, right-click the **VPN connection** and click **Properties.**

Figure 6-27

Creating a VPN connection

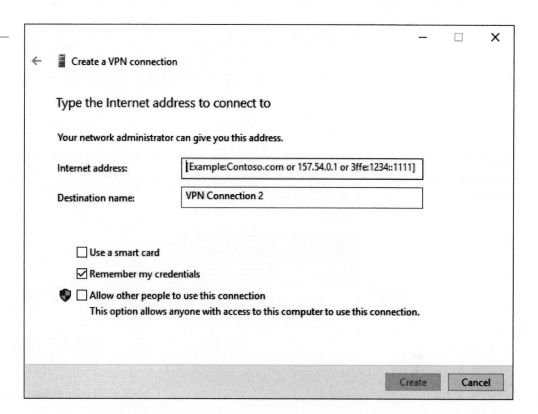

7. Click the **Security** tab, as shown in Figure 6-28. The Security tab allows you to specify the VPN protocol—Point-to-Point Tunneling Protocol (PPTP), Layer 2 Tunneling Protocol over IPsec (L2TP/IPsec), Secure Socket Tunneling Protocol (SSTP), and IKEv2—and the authentication method.

Figure 6-28

Configuring VPN security settings

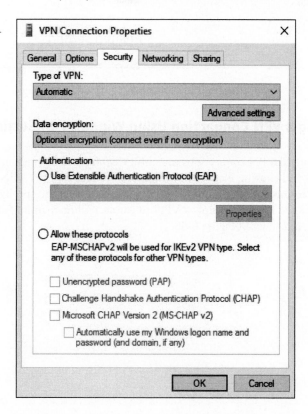

8. To close the VPN Connection Properties dialog box, click **OK**.

To connect to the remote network using the VPN connection, click the network status icon on the taskbar, and click the VPN connection that you just created. When the Settings\ Network & Internet window opens, click the VPN Connection (as shown in Figure 6-29) and click Connect. You will then be asked to specify a user name and password, and click OK.

Figure 6-29

Connecting to a VPN connection

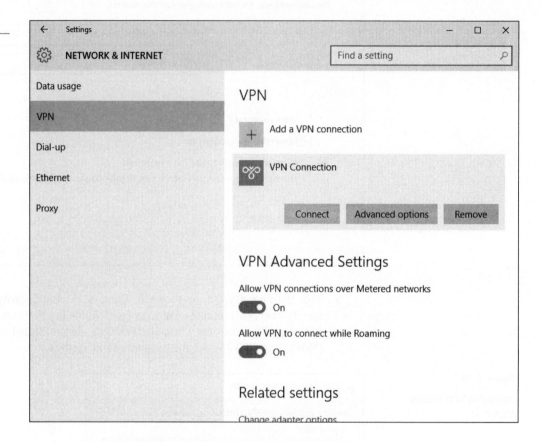

Creating a VPN Connection Using Windows 10 Settings

Windows 10 VPN connections can also be configured by opening the Windows 10 Settings and clicking Network & Internet > VPN. From the VPN page, you can add a VPN connection, connect to a current VPN connection, specify a VPN connection over metered networks, allow a VPN to connect while roaming, and select other advanced options, as shown in Figure 6-30.

Figure 6-30

Managing Connections
in Windows 10 Settings

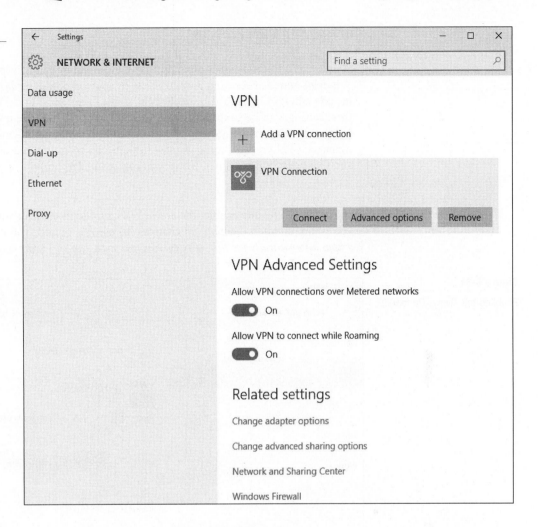

 CREATE A VPN CONNECTION USING WINDOWS 10 SETTINGS

GET READY. To create a VPN using the Windows 10 Settings, perform the following steps.

1. On Win10A, log on as **adatum\administrator** with the password of **Pa$$w0rd**.
2. Click the **Start** button and then click **Settings**.
3. When the Settings page opens, click **Network & Internet**. Click **VPN**.
4. Click **Add a VPN connection**.
5. On the Add a VPN Connection page, in the VPN provider, select **Windows (built-in)**.
6. In the Connection name text box, type **MyVPN2**.
7. In the Server name or address text box, type **vpn.adatum.com**.
8. In the VPN type drop-down menu, you can select the appropriate VPN protocol, such as **L2TP/IPsec with pre-shared key**.
9. In the pre-shared key text box, type **Pa$$w0rd**.
10. For the type of sign-in info option, User name and password is already selected. Click **Save**.

Configuring VPN Profiles

Windows 10 has additional capabilities that were not available in previous versions of Windows aimed at securing remote access to your corporate network. These features include Always On, App-triggered VPN, Traffic Filters, and LockDown VPN. Some of these settings can be configured with Mobile Device Management (MDM) software such as Microsoft Intune, or configuration software such as System Center Configuration Manager VPN Profiles. Some of these options can be configured using Windows Imaging and Configuration Designer, which was covered in Lesson 5.

The Always On feature enables the active VPN profile to connect automatically when the user logs on, or when the network changes. To use this option, you just have to select the *Let apps automatically use this VPN connection*, as shown in Figure 6-31.

Figure 6-31

Enabling the Always On feature

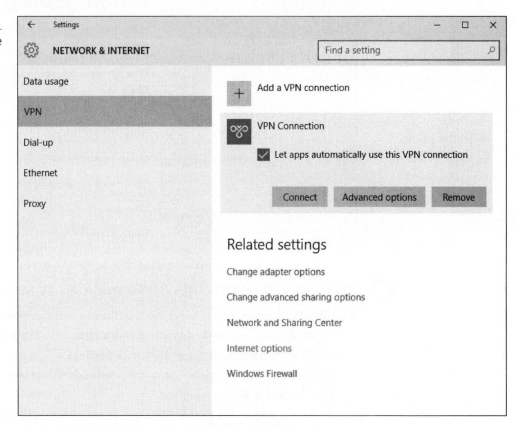

The App-triggered VPN connects automatically when a specified set of applications launch. The applications can be defined using the following:

- Package family name for Universal Windows Platform (UWP) apps
- File path for Classic Windows applications

For example, to start the VPN Connection *VPNConnection*, when the NotePad is opened, execute the following Windows PowerShell command:

```
Add-VpnConnectionTriggerApplication -ConnectionName "VPNConnection"
-ApplicationID
```

```
"C:\Windows\System32\WindowsPowerShell\v1.0\powershell.exe","C:\
Windows\Notepad.exe"
```

Traffic filters allow you to filter traffic through the client VPN based on app-based rules or traffic-based rules (based on ports, addresses, and protocol). For granular control, these rules can be linked with AND and OR components.

The LockDown option secures the corporate devices by configuring the following:

- The system attempts to keep the VPN connected at all times.
- The user cannot disconnect the VPN connection.
- The user cannot delete or modify the VPN profile.
- The VPN LockDown profile uses forced tunnel connection.
- If the VPN connection is not available, outbound network traffic is blocked.

Only one VPN LockDown profile is allowed on a device.

■ CONFIGURING DIRECTACCESS

THE BOTTOM LINE

DirectAccess is a new feature introduced with Windows 7 and Windows Server 2008 R2 that provides seamless intranet connectivity to DirectAccess client computers when they are connected to the Internet. Different from the traditional Virtual Private Network (VPN) connections, DirectAccess connections are automatically established and they provide always-on seamless connectivity.

CERTIFICATION READY
Configure DirectAccess
Objective 2.1

DirectAccess overcomes the limitations of VPNs by automatically establishing a bidirectional connection from client computers to the organization's network using IPsec and Internet Protocol version 6 (IPv6). For organizations that have not deployed IPv6, you can use transition mechanisms such as 6to4 and Teredo IPv6 transition technologies for connectivity across the IPv4 Internet and the Intra-Site Automatic Tunnel Addressing (ISATAP) IPv6 transition technology, so that DirectAccess clients can access IPv6-capable resources across your IPv4-only intranet. As a result, remote client computers are automatically connected to the organization's network so that they can be easily managed and kept up to date with critical updates and configuration changes.

Understanding the DirectAccess Connection Process

A DirectAccess connection to a target intranet resource is initiated when the DirectAccess client connects to the DirectAccess server through IPv6. IPsec is then negotiated between the client and server. Finally, the connection is established between the DirectAccess client and the target resource.

This general process can be broken down into the following specific steps:

1. The DirectAccess client computer running Windows 7, 8/8.1, or 10 Enterprise, Windows 7 Ultimate, or Windows 10 Education detects that it is connected to a network.
2. The DirectAccess client computer determines whether it is connected to the intranet. If the client is connected to the intranet, it does not use DirectAccess.
3. The DirectAccess client connects to the DirectAccess server by using IPv6 and IPsec.
4. If the client is not using IPv6, it tries to use 6to4 or Teredo tunneling to send IPv4-encapsulated IPv6 traffic.

5. If the client cannot reach the DirectAccess server using 6to4 or Teredo tunneling, the client tries to connect using the Internet Protocol over Secure Hypertext Transfer Protocol (IP-HTTPS) protocol. IP-HTTPS uses a Secure Sockets Layer (SSL) connection to encapsulate IPv6 traffic.

6. As part of establishing the IPsec session for the tunnel to reach the intranet DNS server and domain controller, the DirectAccess client and server authenticate each other using computer certificates for authentication.

7. If Network Access Protection (NAP) is enabled and configured for health validation, the Network Policy Server (NPS) determines whether the client is compliant with system health requirements. If it is compliant, the client receives a health certificate, which is submitted to the DirectAccess server for authentication.

8. When the user logs on, the DirectAccess client establishes a second IPsec tunnel to access the resources of the intranet. The DirectAccess client and server authenticate each other using a combination of computer and user credentials.

9. The DirectAccess server forwards traffic between the DirectAccess client and the intranet resources to which the user has been granted access.

For the clients to use DirectAccess, the clients must be joined to an Active Directory domain. In Windows 8/8.1 and 10, the *Network Connectivity Assistant (NCA)* determines if the client computer is connected to the corporate intranet or the Internet. It also provides tools to help users reconnect if a problem occurs, and it can provide diagnostics used by the help desk. When DirectAccess is installed and configured, GPOs are created that will configure the clients to use DirectAccess.

A DirectAccess client uses a Network Location Server (NLS) to determine its location. If a client computer can securely connect to a Network Location Server by using HTTPS, the client computer assumes it is on the intranet, and the DirectAccess policies are not enforced. If the Network Location Server cannot be contacted, the client assumes it is on the Internet.

The Network Location Server can be installed on the DirectAccess server with the Web Server role. The URL for the Network Location Server is distributed by using a Group Policy Object (GPO).

When DirectAccess is configured, a GPO configures the clients to use the DirectAccess server for DNS anytime they are not connected to the intranet. The *Name Resolution Policy Table (NRPT)* contains the settings used by the DNS client on the computer that determines what happens to DNS queries.

Running the DirectAccess Getting Started Wizard

To configure DirectAccess itself, you use the Remote Access Management Console. By using the Remote Access Management Console, you can configure DirectAccess using a visual step-by-step wizard or wizards.

The Remote Access Management Console includes two wizards. The Getting Started Wizard allows you to quickly configure DirectAccess with the default recommended settings.

 RUN THE DIRECTACCESS GETTING STARTED WIZARD

GET READY. To perform the quick configuration of DirectAccess, using the Getting Started Wizard, perform the following steps.

1. Start **Server Manager.**

2. Click **Tools > Remote Access Management.** The Remote Access Management Console opens (see Figure 6-32).

Figure 6-32

Opening the Remote Access
Management Console

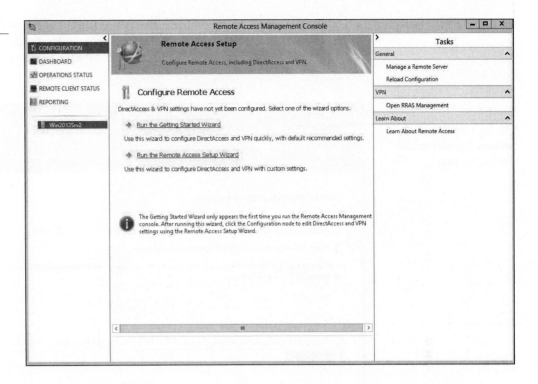

3. Click **Run the Getting Started Wizard** link.

4. When the Getting Started Wizard starts (see Figure 6-33), click **Deploy DirectAccess only**.

Figure 6-33

Starting the Getting Started
Wizard

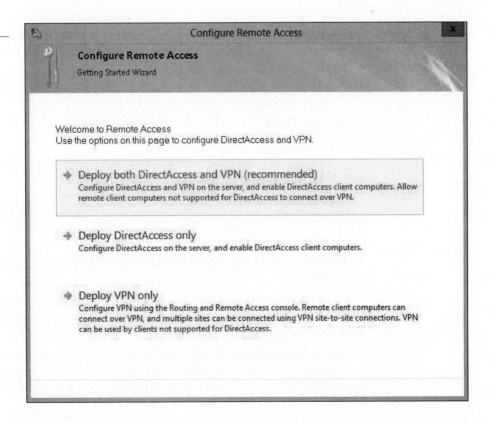

5. On the Configure DirectAccess and VPN Settings page (see Figure 6-34), select the appropriate topology—Edge, Behind an edge device (with two network adapters), or Behind an edge device (with a single network adapter).

Figure 6-34

Selecting a topology on the Configure DirectAccess and VPN Settings page

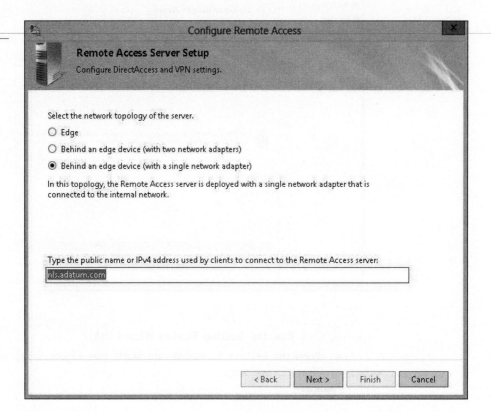

6. Specify the public name or IPv4 address that the clients will use to connect to the Remote Access server in the appropriate text box. Click **Next**.
7. The Configure Remote Access page should display a message that says the Remote Access settings will be applied. Click the **here** link to show the settings that have been modified.
8. Click **Finish**.

Running the Remote Access Setup Wizard

For more control, you can run the Remote Access Setup Wizard instead.

The Remote Access Setup Wizard breaks the installation into the following steps, as shown in Figure 6-35:

Step 1: Remote Clients: Allows you to specify which clients within your organization can use DirectAccess. You specify the computer groups that you want to include and specify if you want to include Windows 7 clients.

Step 2: Remote Access Server: Configures the network connections based on one or two network cards and which adapters are internal and which adapters are external. You can also specify the use of smart cards and specify the certificate authority (CA) to use for -DirectAccess to provide secure communications.

Figure 6-35

Using the Remote Access Setup Wizard

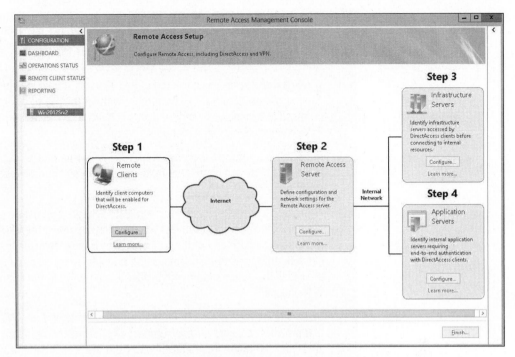

Step 3: Infrastructure Servers: Allows you to configure how the clients access the core infrastructure services such as Active Directory domain controllers and DNS servers. You also specify an internal web server that can provide location services for infrastructure components to your DirectAccess clients.

Step 4: Application Servers: Allows you to configure your end-to-end authentication and security for the DirectAccess components. It also allows you to provide secure connections with individual servers that you want to establish secure connections with.

SKILL SUMMARY

IN THIS LESSON YOU LEARNED:

- When accessing computers on a network, you typically communicate by using their host names. If you are accessing a website, you enter a friendly name such as www.microsoft .com. Every device that connects to your network or the Internet must have an Internet Protocol (IP) address. You also need a way to associate these names to their assigned IP address.

- Network settings can be configured either manually or automatically using DHCP. Using manual settings can introduce configuration issues that can affect communications. Using a centralized approach to IP address management requires you to have a solid understanding of DHCP.

- Windows 10 has advanced sharing settings that allow you to configure network sharing settings based on your network location.

- Although networks can be simple or complex, several tools are invaluable when troubleshooting network connectivity problems. No matter how complex the network is, you should always follow a troubleshooting methodology, which will help you quickly isolate and pinpoint the problem.

- Because wireless technology sends radio waves out into the open, anyone can capture data within the range of the antennas. Therefore, you need to implement encryption and other security measures to prevent data from being read over wireless technology.

- Wireless devices can be connected in two ways, as shown in Figure 6-15. Ad hoc allows wireless clients to connect to each other without the use of a wireless access point (AP). Infrastructure mode has wireless clients connect to a wireless AP. The AP does not have to be connected to a wired network.

- A firewall is a software program or piece of hardware that protects networks or individual computers by screening and controlling incoming and outgoing network traffic based on a set of rules.

- A Virtual Private Network (VPN) is a private network that uses a public network (for example, the Internet) to connect remote sites and users. The VPN makes it appear to computers, on each end of the connection, as if they are actually connected to the same network. This point-to-point connection is emulated by encapsulating the packet in an IP header. The information in the header is used to route the information between the two VPN endpoints.

- DirectAccess is a new feature introduced with Windows 7 and Windows Server 2008 R2 that provides seamless intranet connectivity to DirectAccess client computers when they are connected to the Internet. Different from the traditional Virtual Private Network (VPN) connections, DirectAccess connections are automatically established and they provide always-on seamless connectivity.

■ Knowledge Assessment

Multiple Choice

Select the correct answer for each of the following questions.

1. Which of the following are true regarding IPv4?
   a. 32-bit address
   b. 128-bit address
   c. Consists of a network ID and MAC address
   d. Consists of a host ID and MAC address

2. How many bits does a standard IPv6 unicast address use to represent the network ID?
   a. 32
   b. 64
   c. 128
   d. 10

3. Which of the following Windows PowerShell commands performs a DNS name query for www.contoso.com?
   a. `ping www.contoso.com`
   b. `dnsquery www.contoso.com`
   c. `resolve-DNSName -Name www.contoso.com`
   d. `resolve-DNSquery www.comcast.net`

4. Which of the following commands is used to test network connectivity between two hosts?
   a. ipconfig
   b. ping
   c. nslookup
   d. netstat

5. 802.11b uses a frequency of _____.
   a. 2.4 GHz
   b. 3.7 GHz
   c. 5 GHz
   d. 8 GHz

6. Which of the following forms of wireless security is easily cracked?
   a. WEP
   b. WPA
   c. WPA2
   d. IPsec

7. _____ provides an authentication framework for wireless LANs.
   a. WEP
   b. WPA
   c. 802.1n
   d. 802.1X

8. Which of the following modes should be used when connecting to a wireless access point that requires a pre-shared encryption key?
   a. Personal mode
   b. Enterprise mode
   c. Share mode
   d. Password mode

9. Which of the following rules specifies how and when authentication occurs?
   a. Public rule
   b. Inbound rule
   c. Connection security rule
   d. Outbound rule

10. Which of the following is true regarding WFAS rules? (Choose all that apply.)
    a. Outbound traffic is allowed by default.
    b. Unsolicited inbound traffic is not allowed.
    c. Solicited inbound traffic is allowed.
    d. Connection security rules require inbound/outbound rules to allow connections.

11. Which of the following Windows Firewall profiles should a user configure if she is at the airport?
    a. Domain
    b. Private
    c. Public
    d. Protected

12. If a user wants to use VPN Reconnect, which of the following VPN protocols should be used?
    a. PPTP
    b. L2TP
    c. IKEv2
    d. SSTP

13. An administrator wants to change a server running Windows Server 2016 into a VPN server. However, the networking team allows only HTTPS through the firewall. Which of the following VPN protocols should be used?
    a. PPTP
    b. L2TP
    c. IKEv2
    d. SSTP

14. Which of the following methods is the easiest way to set up a VPN client on a computer for a user who is not technical?
    a. Use PAP.
    b. Type up step-by-step instructions with screenshots to give to the user.
    c. Use a group policy to configure the settings.
    d. Use CMAK to create an executable to install.

15. With DirectAccess, which table is used to determine the behavior of the DNS clients when determining the address of internal resources?
    a. NAP
    b. NPS
    c. NRTP
    d. NCA

Best Answer

Choose the letter that corresponds to the best answer. More than one answer choice may achieve the goal. Select the BEST answer.

1. Which of the following TCP/IP settings should be configured to specify DNS suffixes to use other than resolving names through a parent domain?
   a. DNS suffix for this connection
   b. Append these DNS suffixes (in order)
   c. Append primary and connection-specific DNS suffixes
   d. DNS server address, in order of use

2. When communicating with a server on another subnet, which of the following settings is used to determine which direction it needs to go to get to its final destination?
   a. Subnet mask
   b. Default gateway
   c. DNS
   d. IP address

3. A user has a personal computer that she uses at her workplace. Which of the following network locations should she use?
   a. Home
   b. Work
   c. Public
   d. Domain

4. When connecting a Windows 10 computer to a wireless AP, which of the following Wi-Fi encryption protocols provides the highest level of security?
   a. WPA
   b. WEP
   c. WPA v2
   d. IPsec

5. A user is at work with a laptop that is running Windows 10. He brings up the list of available wireless networks, but the corporate network is not available. What should he do?
   a. Provide the SSID and security key.
   b. Turn on the wireless adapter.
   c. Turn off airplane mode.
   d. Turn on Network Discoverability.

6. Which of the following is the primary objective of a firewall?
   a. To permit traffic in and out for legitimate users, and to block the rest
   b. To authenticate and authorize users past the network perimeter
   c. To compare traffic information against a list of known valid traffic
   d. To protect a network by allowing certain types of network traffic in and out of the system

7. When creating a firewall exception, what is the difference between opening a port and allowing an application?
   a. Opening a port is permanent, and thus is less risky than allowing an application.
   b. Allowing an application opens the specified port only while the program is running, and thus is less risky.
   c. Both options are available in the Windows Firewall with Advanced Security console.
   d. There is no functional difference between opening a port and allowing an application.

8. A company has a main office and 12 branch offices. The users and computers are within a single domain. All servers are Windows Server 2016. The administrator must make sure that all data is encrypted by using end-to-end encryption. In addition, instead of using user names and passwords, he needs to use computer-level authentication. What should he do?
   a. Configure a PPTP connection and MS-CHAPv2.
   b. Configure L2TP with IPsec and EAP-TSL authentication.
   c. Configure L2TP with IPsec and MS-CHAPv2.
   d. Configure SSTP with IPsec and PAP.

Matching and Identification

1. Match the following terms with the related description or usage.
   _____ a. AAAA record
   _____ b. DNS server
   _____ c. LLMNR
   _____ d. Subnet mask
   _____ e. ANDing
   _____ f. Stateful

1. The process a computer uses to determine whether another computer is on the same network
2. Used to associate a computer name to an IP address; stores host-to-IP address mappings in a zone file
3. Used to determine the bits associated with the network ID and host ID
4. An IPv6 address (host name) mapping to its IP address
5. A fallback name resolution technique when DNS and WINS are not available
6. One of the ways you can configure a DHCP IPv6 server; provides IP address configuration to DHCP clients

2. Identify the Wi-Fi Technology standard (802.11a, 802.11b, 802.11g, 802.11i, 802.11n, and 802.1x).

Supports bandwidth up to 54 Mbps by using 5 Ghz

Supports bandwidth up to 54 Mbps by using 2.5 GHz

Uses RADIUS authentication

Can use 2.5- and 5-GHz frequencies and support up to 300 Mbps

Uses encryption for wireless protocols

Build a List

1. Specify the correct order of the steps that must be completed to create an outbound rule that blocks a program.

_____ Browse to the program's install location, select the program's executable, and then click Open.

_____ Open the Windows Firewall with Advanced Security console.

_____ Select the program to block and then click Next.

_____ Right-click Outbound Rules and then choose New Rules.

_____ Select Block the connection.

_____ Type a name and description for the rule and then click Finish.

_____ Select Domain, Private, and/or Public profile.

■ Business Case Scenarios

Scenario 6-1: Configuring a Network Location

As an administrator of the Contoso Corporation, you are responsible for configuring the users' mobile computers. You want to ensure that when a computer system accesses a public network—such as the local coffee shop, the airport, or the user's home network—other computers and devices cannot find your system. In addition, you want to disable file and printer sharing access. However, when in the office and the computers connect to the office using a VPN client, you want network discovery and file and printer sharing available. What should you do?

Scenario 6-2: Configuring a Wireless Connection

You are an administrator for the Contoso Corporation and you use a mobile computer for troubleshooting. You want it to automatically connect to wireless connections at the main office, the primary data center, and two large offices, which each have their own hidden wireless network. What should you do?

Scenario 6-3: Configuring Windows Firewall

As an administrator at the Contoso Corporation, you have had several reports that the computers of users who are traveling have been hacked and accessed without the users' knowledge. What can you do to ensure that the systems are secure and that would prevent these types of access while out of the office, but would also allow full access when at work?

Configuring Storage

70-698 EXAM OBJECTIVE

Objective 2.2 – Configure Storage. This objective may include but is not limited to: Configure disks, volumes, and file system options using Disk Management and Windows PowerShell; create and configure VHDs; configure removable devices; create and configure storage spaces; troubleshoot storage and removable devices issues

LESSON HEADING	EXAM OBJECTIVE
Configuring Disks, Volumes and File System Options	Configure disks, volumes, and file system options using Disk Management and Windows Powershell
Understanding Disk and Drive Types	
Using Disk Management to Configure Disks, Volumes, and File Systems	
Using Windows PowerShell to Configure Disks, Volumes, and File Systems	
Creating and Configuring VHDs	Create and configure VHDs
Supporting Storage Pools and Storage Spaces	
Creating Storage Pools	
Creating Storage Spaces	Create and configure storage spaces
Configuring Removable Storage Devices	Configure removable devices
Troubleshooting Storage and Removable Devices Issues	Troubleshoot storage and removable devices issues

KEY TERMS

- basic disks
- Disk Management
- dynamic disks
- Extended File Allocation Table (exFAT)
- file allocation table (FAT)
- FAT32
- file system
- mirrored volume
- New Technology File System (NTFS)
- parity
- partitions
- Serial Advanced Technology Attachment (SATA)
- simple (no resiliency)
- simple volume
- Small Computer System Interface (SCSI)
- spanned volume
- storage pool
- Storage Spaces
- striped volume
- three-way mirror
- two-way mirror
- Universal Serial Bus (USB)

■ CONFIGURING DISKS, VOLUMES, AND FILE SYSTEM OPTIONS

The Bottom Line

Although the average disk capacity of storage devices has increased dramatically over the years, there is one thing you can count on: users will always find a way to store enormous amounts of data on volumes they have access to. Therefore, you will need to know how to configure, manage, and support storage on the Windows clients.

CERTIFICATION READY
Configure disks, volumes, and file system options using Disk Management and Windows Powershell
Objective 2.2

User data typically includes multiple versions of their documents, copies of other users' documents, high-definition videos downloaded from the Internet, or just about anything else the user is not ready to delete. As users' appetites for more storage continue to increase, administrators find themselves purchasing and using a wide variety of drives with different capacities (1 TB, 2 TB, 4 TB, or larger) and different drive interfaces to fit their data storage needs. The type of interface you select depends a lot on the connections available with your motherboard and the performance you need from the drive. Examples of drive interfaces include:

- **Small Computer System Interface (SCSI):** A set of standards for interfaces designed to connect and transfer information between high-speed hardware devices and a motherboard. Devices are connected in a chain. Each device in the chain gets a SCSI ID and the last device in the chain must be terminated. SATA has replaced SCSI on most modern computers.

- **Serial Advanced Technology Attachment (SATA):** A serial interface that transfers data in bursts instead of parallel. It comes in three varieties: 1.5 Gbps (SATA-1.0), 3 Gbps (SATA-2.0), and 6 Gbps (SATA 3.0). These have maximum throughputs of 150 Mbps, 300 Mbps, and 600 Mbps. **External SATA (eSATA)** extends the SATA bus to external devices.

- **Universal Serial Bus (USB):** A serial interface that is used to connect keyboards, mice, printers, scanners, and removable media drives. Up to 127 peripherals can be connected to a single USB port. USB 2.0 has a maximum transfer rate of 480 Mbps, whereas USB 3.0, released in 2008, claims a theoretical maximum transmission speed of up to 5 Gbps.

A *file system* is the overall structure your computer uses to name, store, and organize files and folders on a hard disk or partition. The file system provides a map of the clusters (the basic units of logical storage on a hard disk) that a file has been stored in. When you install a hard disk in a computer, you must format it with a file system. Today, the primary file system choices for a computer that will run Windows are New Technology File System (NTFS), File Allocation Table (FAT), and FAT32. In Windows 10, you can use the Disk Management Microsoft Management Console (MMC) snap-in, which is available from the Computer Management console, to view the file systems in use on your computer.

When a disk or volume is added to Windows 10, you have to partition and format the drive. The three primary types of file systems for Windows are FAT, FAT32, and NTFS. *FAT32* and *File Allocation Table (FAT)* (which is seldom used today) were popular in earlier versions of Windows (such as Windows 95, Windows 98, Windows Millennium Edition, Windows NT, and Windows 2000). The limitations of FAT32 make it less desirable than NTFS:

- A FAT32 partition is limited to a maximum size of 32 gigabytes (GB).

- The maximum size of a file that can be stored on a FAT32 volume is 4 GB.

New Technology File System (NTFS) is the preferred file system that supports much larger hard disk and a higher level of reliability than FAT based file systems. In addition, NTFS offers better security through permissions and encryption.

TAKE NOTE

You can view all available disks or volumes that have been formatted with a file system in the Windows Computer folder in the Hard Disk Drives section.

Table 7-1 compares the attributes of FAT, FAT32, and NTFS.

Table 7-1

Comparing FAT, FAT32, and NTFS

FILE SYSTEM	MAXIMUM PARTITION SIZE	MAXIMUM FILE SIZE
FAT	2 GB	2 GB
FAT32	32 GB	4 GB
NTFS	256 TB*	Limited by the size of the volume on which it resides
exFAT	128 PB	Limited by the size of the volume on which it resides

*with 64 KB clusters

Another file system worth mentioning is the ***Extended File Allocation Table (exFAT)***, which is a Microsoft file system optimized for flash drives. It is typically used where NTFS file system is not ideal because of the data structure overhead. exFAT supports a larger volume than FAT or FAT32 supports. exFAT has been adopted by the SD Card Association as the default file system for SDXC cards larger than 32 GB.

Understanding Disk and Drive Types

Windows 10 supports two partition styles, master boot record (MBR) and GUID partition table (GPT); and two primary types of disks, basic and dynamic. In addition, the operating system supports simple, spanned, striped, and mirrored volumes. You use the Disk Management tool in the Computer Management snap-in to manage disks, partitions, and volumes.

In Windows 10, a physical hard drive can be designated as a basic disk or a dynamic disk. ***Basic disks*** contain only simple volumes. ***Dynamic disks*** can contain simple, spanned, striped, and mirrored volumes.

TAKE NOTE You cannot use Windows PowerShell to manage dynamic disks. The storage cmdlets will not recognize dynamic disks.

Traditionally, basic disks use partitions and logical drives. A ***partition*** is a defined storage space on a hard disk. To be usable, a hard disk needs to have at least one partition.

The MBR partition style has been around for quite a while and all Windows operating systems support MBR partitions. The MBR is stored at a consistent location on a physical disk, enabling a computer's BIOS to reference it. After the computer examines the MBR to determine the active partition, it then loads the operating system startup files from the active partition.

But as with most legacy technologies, MBR partitions have their limitations, including.

- MBR partitions are limited to four basic partitions and each partition is limited to 2 terabytes (TBs) in size.
- The four basic partitions can be either four primary partitions or three primary partitions with one extended partition, which can be further divided into multiple logical partitions.

- The MBR is a single point of failure. If it becomes corrupted or damaged, it could prevent the computer from starting.

A GPT partition style allows for more partitions and larger volume sizes. Features of GPT disks include:

- A disk initialized as a GPT partition style may contain up to 128 primary partitions.
- Each partition can be as large as 9.4 zetabytes (ZB). One zetabyte is equal to one billion terabytes.

TAKE NOTE
You can implement GPT disks on Windows Server 2008 and newer versions, such as Windows 10, Windows 8.1, Windows 8, Windows 7, and Windows Vista. You cannot use the GPT partition style on removable disks.

With dynamic disks, free space on a hard drive is divided into **volumes** instead of partitions. Dynamic disks are not limited by partition styles like basic disks are. You can configure dynamic disk volumes as simple, spanned, mirrored, or striped:

- *Simple volume*: Uses free space available on a single disk.
- *Spanned volume*: Extends a simple volume across multiple disks, up to a maximum of 32.
- *Mirrored volume*: Duplicates data from one disk to a second disk for redundancy and fault tolerance; if one disk fails, data can be accessed from the second disk. You cannot span a mirrored volume; a mirrored volume must reside on a single disk. Mirroring is also referred to as RAID-1.
- *Striped volume*: Stores data across two or more physical disks. Data on a striped volume is written evenly to each of the physical disks in the volume. You cannot mirror or span a striped volume. Striping is often referred to as RAID-0.

You can typically convert a basic disk to a dynamic disk without losing any data; however, you should back up all data before attempting the conversion just to be safe. You might need to convert a hard disk from dynamic to basic at some point.

Disks, volumes and file systems can be managed with the following Windows 10 tools:

- *Disk Management*: A GUI tool based on the MMC for managing disks and volumes locally and remotely. Disk Management is located in the Administrative Tools, and is part of the Computer Management console.
- **Windows PowerShell 5.0:** A scripting language/and command environment that accomplishes many of these tasks in Disk Management. You can execute these commands as stand-alone commands or as part of a script.
- **DiskPart:** A scriptable command-line tool that has similar functionality as Disk Management. You can create scripts to automate disk-related tasks, such as creating volumes or converting disks to dynamic. This tool can only be executed locally.

Using Disk Management to Configure Disks, Volumes, and File Systems

When you add a new hard drive to a computer, there are a few steps you need to take to introduce a new drive to the operating system. You need to initialize the disk and then choose a drive type and a partition style (for basic disks). You can perform all of these steps in the Disk Management tool, which is part of the Computer Management MMC snap-in.

To open Computer Management, click the Start button, type computer, and then select Computer Management from the resulting list. Alternately, you can right-click the Start button, and click Computer Management. After Computer Management is open, click the Disk Management node.

Figure 7-1 shows the tools in the Computer Management snap-in. The tool you use to work with disks is the Disk Management tool.

Figure 7-1

The Disk Management snap-in

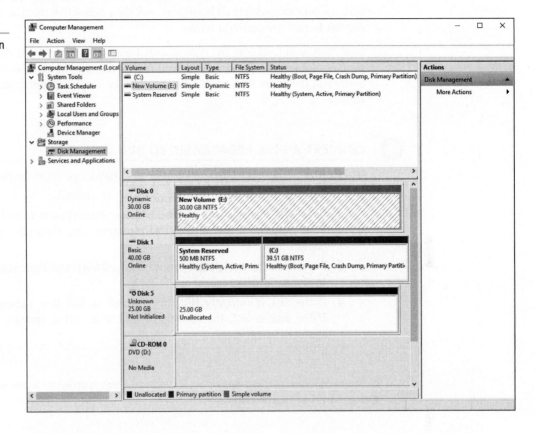

If you just installed a new hard disk and the disk is not initialized, right-click the disk, and click Initialize Disk. When the Initialize Disk window opens, you are prompted to select a partition style, as shown in Figure 7-2.

Figure 7-2

The Initialize Disk dialog box

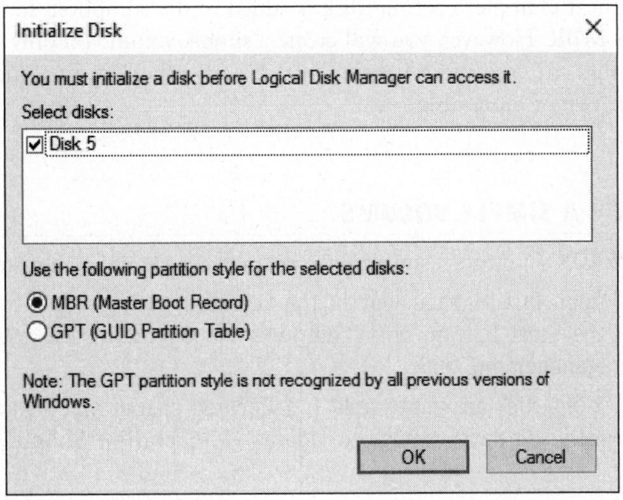

Initialize Disk   ✕

You must initialize a disk before Logical Disk Manager can access it.

Select disks:

☑ Disk 5

Use the following partition style for the selected disks:

⦿ MBR (Master Boot Record)
◯ GPT (GUID Partition Table)

Note: The GPT partition style is not recognized by all previous versions of Windows.

OK   Cancel

The first choice you need to make is to choose the partition style of the disk. Be sure you select the correct partition style because this is not something you can easily change later. The two partition styles are MBR and GPT.

You can change your partition style as long as you have not created any partitions. If you have created partitions that contain data and want to change the partition style, you need to back up your data, delete all partitions, and then right-click the disk number and choose to convert to the new partition style.

Next, you need to choose the type of disk: basic or dynamic. Basic disks contain only simple volumes. The partition style you choose dictates the number of partitions you can create and their sizes. Dynamic disks can contain simple, spanned, striped, and mirrored volumes.

 CONVERT A DISK FROM BASIC TO DYNAMIC

GET READY. To convert a disk from basic to dynamic, perform the following steps.

1. Back up all data on the disk you want to convert.
2. Open Disk Management in the Computer Management console. Right-click the **Start** button, click **Computer Management**, and then click the **Disk Management** node.
3. Right-click the basic disk you want to convert and then select **Convert to Dynamic Disk**.
4. If the disk is currently MBR, the Convert to GPT Disk option appears. If the disk is GPT, the Convert to MBR Disk option appears. Select the appropriate option.

After you convert the partition style, you can create partitions again and restore the data that you previously backed up.

TAKE NOTE

The conversion from basic to dynamic can occur automatically based on the type of volume you create. You'll see this in action in the step-by-step exercise named "Create a Spanned Volume."

In the next example, a second disk is added to the computer, so two disks have been initialized as MBR. However, you will create a simple volume on only one of the dynamic disks. Spanning, striping, and mirroring, which you will do in subsequent step-by-step exercises, involve two or more disks.

 CREATE A SIMPLE VOLUME

GET READY. To create a simple volume, perform the following steps.

1. Open Disk Management in the Computer Management console. Right-click the **Start** button, click **Computer Management**, and then click the **Disk Management** node.
2. Right-click an empty area (unallocated space) of a dynamic disk. The New Volume menu displays, similar to Figure 7-3. Click **New Simple Volume**.

Figure 7-3

The New Volume menu

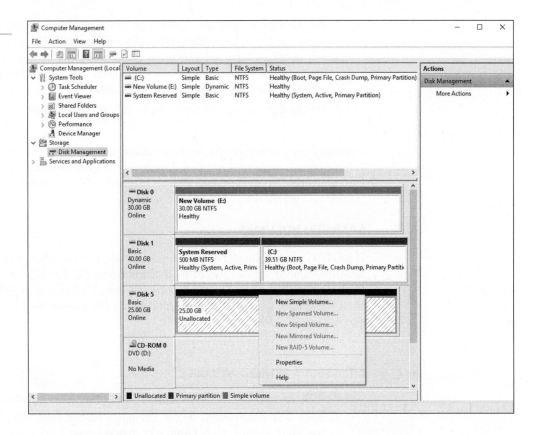

3. The New Simple Volume Wizard starts. Click **Next** on the welcome screen. Click Next to accept default volume size.

4. On the Assign Drive Letter or Path screen (as shown in Figure 7-4), assign a drive letter or path, click Next and then on the Format Partition screen, choose a file system such as FAT, FAT32, or NTFS.

Figure 7-4

Formatting a partition

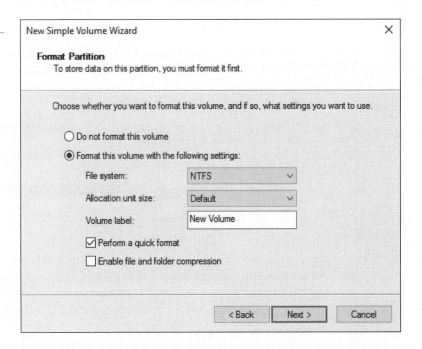

5. On the Format Partition screen, you can also choose an allocation unit size and a name for the volume label. (If you're not familiar with allocation unit sizes, accept the default.) There are two other options you can set: Perform a quick format (selected by default, which is a good idea) and Enable file and folder compression, which is not selected by default. Click **Next**.

6. On the Completing the New Simple Volume Wizard screen, click **Finish**.

You now have a new partition on the dynamic disk on which you can store data. All the other volume types—spanned, striped, and mirrored—require two or more disks. Therefore, if you have only one disk, the options to create spanned volumes, striped volumes, or mirrored volumes are grayed out and cannot be selected.

SPANNED VOLUMES

If you have an additional disk with unused space, you can create a ***spanned volume***. Spanned volumes include two or more disks (up to 32) that are represented in Windows Explorer as a single drive letter. They are sometimes referred to as ***fill and spill*** because all of the storage space on the first disk must be filled before data is stored on the second and subsequent disks.

 CREATE A SPANNED VOLUME

GET READY. To create a spanned volume, perform the following steps.

1. Open Disk Management in the Computer Management console. Right-click the **Start** button, click **Computer Management**, and then click the **Disk Management** node.

2. Right-click an empty area of a dynamic disk and then click **New Spanned Volume**.

3. Click **Next** on the Welcome to the New Spanned Volume Wizard screen.

4. Highlight the desired disk in the Available box, as shown in Figure 7-5. Click **Add**. (You can also double-click the available disk to add it to the selected box.)

Figure 7-5

The Select Disks page

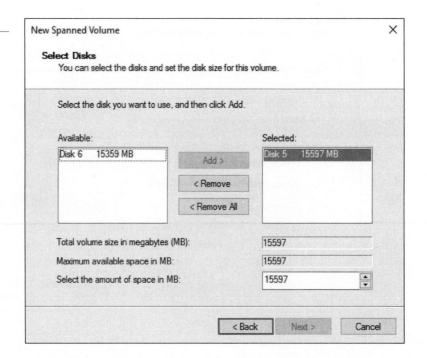

5. When you add disks to the Selected box, the Total volume size in megabytes (MB) box displays the combined sizes of all disks. When you highlight one of the disks in the Selected box, the Maximum available space in MB box and the Select the amount of space in MB box show what you have selected for that specific disk. You can select a different amount of space for each disk you add. You can continue to add as many disks as you would like included in your spanned volume. After you have selected the disks, click **Next**.

6. On the Assign Drive Letter or Path screen, select a drive letter and click **Next**.

7. The Format Volume screen is the same as creating a simple volume. Set your format volume options and click **Next**.

8. Click **Finish** on the Completing the New Spanned Volume Wizard page.

9. A warning message displays letting you know that to create a spanned volume, the basic disk will be converted to a dynamic disk. If you convert the disk to a dynamic disk, you will not be able to start installed operating systems from any volume on the disk. Click **Yes** to continue or **No** to cancel the operation.

Do not plan to use spanned volumes for fault tolerance. If one disk in the spanned volume fails, all data in the spanned volume is lost unless you have a backup.

STRIPED VOLUMES

Creating a *striped volume* is similar to creating a spanned volume in that almost all of the steps are the same. However, the way data is stored on a striped volume is different from a spanned volume. As with a spanned volume, striped volumes must contain at least 2 disks and can contain up to 32 disks. But when the data is stored, it is separated into 64 kilobyte (KB) chunks. The first 64 KB is stored on Disk 1 in the striped volume, the second 64 KB chunk is stored on Disk 2, and so on. Figure 7-6 shows a striped volume. The data is literally striped across multiple drives.

Figure 7-6

A striped volume

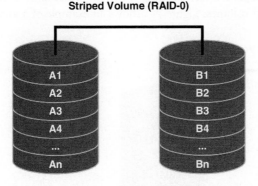

Striped Volume (RAID-0)

Accessing data on a striped volume is faster than accessing data on a spanned volume because a striped volume has multiple sets of read/write heads working simultaneously when reading and writing data. In this regard, spanned volumes are good for high capacity, whereas striped volumes are better for performance.

 CREATE A STRIPED VOLUME

GET READY. To create a striped volume, perform the following steps.

1. Open Disk Management in the Computer Management console. Right-click the **Start** button, click **Computer Management**, and then click the **Disk Management** node.

2. In Disk Management, right-click an empty disk and choose **New Striped Volume**. Click **Next** on the Welcome to the New Striped Volume Wizard screen.

3. Highlight the second disk from the Available box and then click **Add**.

   When you add disks to the Selected box, the Total volume size in megabytes (MB) box displays the combined sizes of all disks. This is where one of the big differences between spanned volumes and striped volumes takes place: on spanned volumes you could take different amounts of hard drive space from each disk— you cannot do this with striped volumes. Striped volumes must use the same amount of disk space from each disk you take to the striped volume. So after you add two or more disks to the Selected box, if you change the Select the amount of space in MB setting (regardless of which disk is highlighted in the Selected box), the size difference will be reflected on both (or all) disks that you added.

4. After you have selected the disks, click **Next**.

5. On the Assign Drive Letter or Path screen, select your drive letter and then click **Next**. The Format Volume screen appears. Set your format volume options and then click **Next**. Click **Finish**.

6. A warning appears that says that to create a striped volume, the basic disk will be converted to a dynamic disk. If you convert the disk to dynamic, you will not be able to start installed operating systems from any volume on the disk. Click **Yes** to continue or **No** to cancel.

Striped volumes do not offer fault tolerance. Just as with spanned volumes, if one disk in the striped volume fails, all data from the entire striped volume is lost. You will have to retrieve the data from a previous backup.

MIRRORED VOLUMES

Mirrored volumes require only two disks. You cannot mirror to a third or fourth disk. Mirrored volumes store an exact copy of data from the first member of the mirrored volume to the second member. Because the data is written across both drives, you do get fault tolerance with mirrored volumes. Figure 7-7 shows an example of a mirrored volume.

Figure 7-7

A mirrored volume

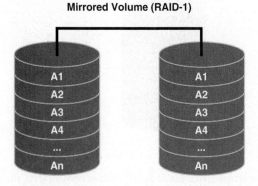

Mirrored Volume (RAID-1)

 CREATE A MIRRORED VOLUME

GET READY. To create a mirrored volume, perform the following steps.

1. Open Disk Management in the Computer Management console. Right-click the **Start** button, click **Computer Management**, and then click the **Disk Management** node.

2. In Disk Management, right-click an empty disk and then click **New Mirrored Volume**. Click **Next** on the Welcome to the New Mirrored Volume Wizard screen.

3. Highlight the second disk from the Available box. Mirrored volumes require the same amount of disk space from each disk. When you add a disk to the Selected box, the Total volume size in megabytes (MB) box displays the most available free space from the disk with the smallest amount. You can reduce the amount of space, but it will be reduced on both disks. This makes sense because you're creating an exact copy of data stored on the source disk, so you don't need the destination disk to have additional free space that you will never use. After you have selected the disks, click **Next**.

4. On the Assign Drive Letter or Path screen, select a drive letter and then click **Next**. The Format Volume screen is the same as the previous Format Volume screens. Set your format volume options and then click **Next**. Click **Finish**.

5. A warning message appears, informing you that the basic disk will be converted to a dynamic disk. If you convert the disk to a dynamic disk, you will not be able to start installed operating systems from any volume on the disk. Click **Yes**.

After you create a few different types of volumes, it's easy to figure out which volume is which—they're identified by a strip of color at the top of the volume, as follows:

- **Simple volumes:** Dark blue strips
- **Spanned volumes:** Purple strips
- **Striped volumes:** Aquamarine strips
- **Mirrored volumes:** Burgundy red strips

Using Windows PowerShell to Configure Disks, Volumes, and File Systems

Just as you can manage disks, volumes, and file systems with Disk Management, you can also use Windows PowerShell. Windows PowerShell allows for task automation and configuration management that consist of a command-line shell and associated scripting language.

In Windows PowerShell, administrative tasks are generally performed with cmdlets. However, when executing many of these commands to manage a system, you will have to run the Windows PowerShell cmdlets as an administrator.

USING WINDOWS POWERSHELL

You can perform Windows storage management with the following Windows PowerShell by using the following cmdlets:

- **Clear-Disk:** Removes all partition information and un-initializing the disk. As a result, all data is erased from the disk.
- **Format-Volume:** Formats an existing volume.
- **Get-Disk:** Displays available disks as seen by the operating system.
- **Get-Partition:** Displays all partitions on a disk.

- **Get-PartitionSupportedSize:** Displays a list of partitions on a disk.
- **Get-PhysicalDisk:** Displays a list all PhysicalDisk objects.
- **Get-ResiliencySetting:** Displays Windows-based resiliency settings (also known as storage layouts) for the specified storage subsystem.
- **Initialize-Disk:** Initializes a RAW disk for first time use, enabling the disk to be formatted and used to store data.
- **Mount-DiskImage:** Mounts a disk image (virtual hard disk or ISO), so that it appear as a normal disk.
- **New-Partition:** Creates a new partition on an existing Disk object.
- **New-Volume:** Creates a volume with the specified file system.
- **Remove-Partition:** Deletes the specified Partition object, and any underlying Volume objects.
- **Repair-Volume:** Attempts to repair a volume.
- **Resize-Partition:** Resizes a partition and the associated file system.
- **Set-Partition:** Sets attributes of a partition, such as active, read-only, and offline states.
- **Set-PhysicalDisk:** Sets attributes on a specific physical disk.
- **Set-ResiliencySetting:** Modifies the resiliency setting of a storage system.
- **Set-Volume:** Sets or changes the file system label of a volume.

When using Windows PowerShell to manage disks, you have to organize your commands just like you would if you were using Disk Management. To list all disks in the system, perform the following Windows PowerShell command:

```
Get-Disk
```

To initialize a disk to allow creation of a partition and volume, type the following Windows PowerShell command, where <DiskNumber> is the number of the disk to initialize:

```
Initialize-Disk <DiskNumber>
```

All disks are initialized as GPT by default unless otherwise specified.

To initialize a disk as MBR, use the –PartitionStyle parameter. For example, to initialize disk 1, execute the following Windows PowerShell command:

```
Initialize-Disk 1 -PartitionStyle MBR
```

To list all disks that are currently offline, type the following command:

```
Get-Disk | Where-Object IsOffline -Eq $True
```

To bring all offline disks online, execute the Windows PowerShell command:

```
Get-Disk | Where-Object IsOffline -Eq $True | Set-Disk -IsOffline $False
```

To list all partitions on all disks, type the following Windows PowerShell command:

```
Get-Partition
```

To create a new partition on a blank initialized disk, use the following command:

```
New-Partition -DiskNumber <DiskNumber>

-UseMaximumSize -AssignDriveLetter
```

To list all of the volumes that have been formatted with a file system, execute the following Windows PowerShell command:

```
Get-Volume
```

To format a volume with the NTFS file system, type the following, replacing <DriveLetter> with the letter of the drive you want to format:

```
Format-Volume -DriveLetter <DriveLetter>
```

To resize a volume to 3 GB, execute the following Windows PowerShell command:

```
Resize-Partition -DiskNumber 1 -PartitionNumber 1
-Size 3GB
```

To resize a volume to the maximum size, execute the following Windows PowerShell command:

```
Resize-Partition -DiskNumber 1 -PartitionNumber 1
-Size $size.SizeMax
```

To clear all of the partitions and volumes from a disk, perform the following Windows PowerShell command:

```
Clear-Disk 1 -RemoveData
```

If the specified disk contains an OEM partition, for system recovery, for example, you should also specify the –RemoveOEM switch when using the clear-disk cmdlet.

Creating and Configuring VHDs

Lesson 2 introduced VHDs when looking at various methods to install Windows and Lesson 4 discussed using virtual disks with Hyper-V virtual machines. In this section, you will find out how to manage VHDs using Disk Management.

CERTIFICATION READY
Create and configure VHDs.
Objective 2.2

With Disk Management, you can create a new .vhd/.vhdx file by using the available disk space on the computer and saving it to the location that you specify. If you have a .vhd/vhdx file, you can mount the drive to your system running Windows 10.

 CREATE A VHD

GET READY. To create a VHD using Disk Management, perform the following steps.

1. Open Disk Management in the Computer Management console. Right-click the **Start** button, click **Computer Management**, and then click the **Disk Management** node.
2. Right-click the **Disk Management** node, and click **Create VHD.**
3. When the Create and Attach Virtual Hard Disk dialog box opens (as shown in Figure 7-8), specify the location of the virtual hard drive, such as **C:\VDisk.vhdx.** Alternatively, you can use the **Browse** button to navigate to the folder and specify the file name.
4. In the Virtual hard disk size text, type **5**, and change **MB** to **GB**.
5. To create a .vhdx file, select **VHDX**.
6. With the Dynamically expanded (Recommended) option already selected, click **OK**. The disk will be created.
7. To initialize the disk, right-click the new disk and click **Initialize Disk**.
8. When the Initialize Disk dialog box opens, click **OK**.

Figure 7-8

Creating and attaching a virtual hard disk

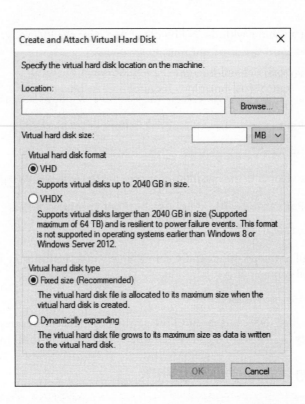

9. Right-click the new disk unallocated space, and click **New Simple Volume**.

10. When the New Simple Volume Wizard opens, on the Welcome page, click **Next**.

11. On the Specify Volume Size page, click **Next**.

12. On the Assign Drive Letter or Path page, click **Next**.

13. On the Format Partition page, for the Volume label, type **VDisk** and click **Next**.

14. When the wizard is complete, click **Finish**.

To attach a .vhd or .vhdx file, right-click the Disk Management node, and click Attach VHD. You then specify the location of the .vhd or .vhdx file, and click OK. To detach a .vhd or .vhdx file, right-click the virtual disk, and click Detach VHD.

➕ **MORE INFORMATION**

Detaching a .vhd or .vhdx file does not delete the file from the disk. If you want to free up the disk space the file is taking, you have to manually delete the file.

■ SUPPORTING STORAGE POOLS AND STORAGE SPACES

The Bottom Line

Storage Spaces is a feature in Windows 10 that allows you to combine multiple disks into a single logical volume that can be mirrored to protect against one or more drive failures.

CERTIFICATION READY
Create and configure storage spaces.
Objective 2.2

The Storage Spaces feature in Windows 10 allows you to combine several physical drives, which the operating system will see as one large drive. The drives can be any capacity and can consist of a variety of different drive interfaces, such as Small Computer System Interface (SCSI), Universal Serial Bus (USB), and Serial ATA (SATA).

When the drives are combined, Windows places them into a ***storage pool***. These storage pools can then be segmented into multiple Storage spaces, which are then formatted with a file system and can be used just like any other regular disk on your computer. New disks (internal/external) can be added to the storage pool as space requirements increase over time.

Although data can be stored on the drives, you cannot use Storage Spaces to host the Windows operating system files.

Storage Spaces offer two key benefits:

- By spreading data across multiple disks you achieve data resiliency, which can protect your data against hard disk failure.
- Volume sizes can be larger than the actual physical size of your drives in the storage pool. This is accomplished through a process called thin provisioning.

Creating Storage Pools

> Creating a storage pool allows you to combine multiple smaller drives that you might not otherwise be able to use by themselves into a larger single logical volume.

To create a storage pool on a Windows 10 client, you use the Manage Storage Spaces tool found in the Control Panel. The Wizard prompts you to select the disks that you want to use and then adds them to the storage pool. For example, if you have two physical disks with capacities of 200 GB and 300 GB, it creates a pool that has a total capacity of 500 GB (as shown in Figure 7-9).

Figure 7-9

Creating a storage pool with two disks

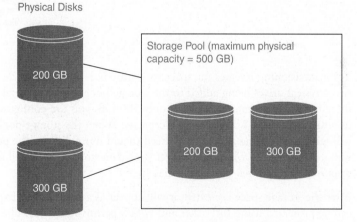

Creating Storage Spaces

> After selecting the drives to include in your storage pool, you are prompted to create the storage space. This involves entering a name, selecting a drive letter, identifying the type of resiliency you want to configure, and setting the maximum size that you want to assign to the storage space.

When creating storage spaces, there are four resiliency types to select from. Only three of them provide real fault-tolerance, as shown in the following list:

- ***Simple (no resiliency):*** Writes one copy of your data but doesn't protect against drive failures; requires at least one drive.

- *Two-way mirror:* Writes two copies of your data to protect against a single drive failure; requires at least two drives.
- *Three-way mirror:* Writes three copies of your data to protect against two simultaneous drive failures; requires at least five drives.
- *Parity:* Writes data with parity information to protect against single drive failures; requires at least three drives.

You also need to decide how much of the total storage pool capacity you want to use for your new storage space. By using a process called **thin provisioning** (see Figure 7-10), you can create a storage space that is larger than the available capacity of the storage pool. After setting the size, the Wizard will create the storage space based on the parameters you provided.

Figure 7-10

An example of thin provisioning

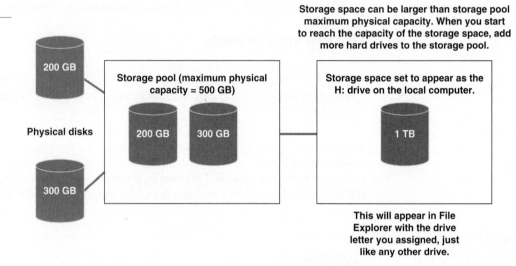

Thin provisioning reserves the space for future use. For example, in Figure 7-10, there are two physical drives being added to the storage pool to create a total capacity of 500 GB. Even though you have a total capacity of only 500 GB, you can configure the storage space that uses this pool to be 1 TB or greater capacity. When the storage pool approaches capacity, you will receive a warning and you will need to add more disks to the pool. This approach works well in situations in which you expect your data storage needs will grow, but you don't want to purchase additional disks immediately.

After the storage space is created, it will appear as a drive in File Explorer. The drive can be protected using BitLocker and NTFS permissions—just like any other drive in Windows 10.

 CREATE A STORAGE POOL AND A STORAGE SPACE IN WINDOWS 10

GET READY. To create a storage pool and storage space, perform the following steps.

1. Connect the drives you want to use to your computer.
2. On Win10A, log on with administrative credentials.
3. Click the **Start** button. From the Start page, type **Storage Spaces**. From the Results list, click **Storage Spaces**.
4. When the Manage Storage Spaces window opens (as shown in Figure 7-11), click **Create a new pool and storage space**.
5. Select the drive(s) you want to include in the new storage pool. (Warning: Any data on these drives will be deleted.)

Figure 7-11

Managing Storage Spaces

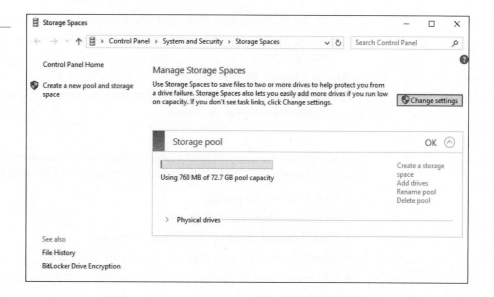

6. Click **Create pool**.

Once the pool is created, you will be taken automatically to the Create a storage space screen shown in Figure 7-12.

Figure 7-12

Creating a storage space

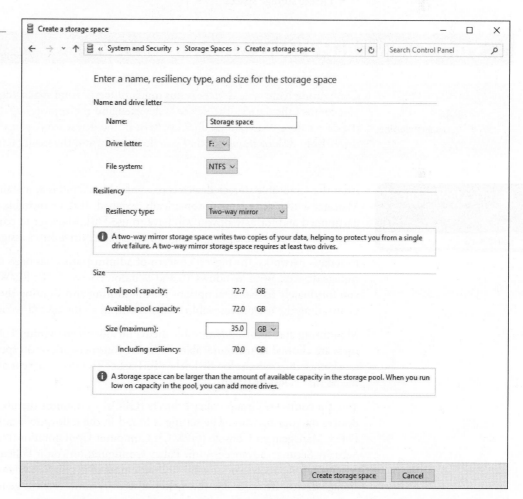

7. In the Name field, type a name for your storage space.

8. In the Drive letter field, click the down arrow and then choose a drive letter for the storage space.

9. In the Resiliency type field, click the down arrow and then choose the resiliency type.

10. In the Size (maximum) field, type the maximum size that you want for your storage space.

11. Click **Create storage space**.

12. Open File Explorer and confirm that the new storage space appears under the drive letter you assigned in Step 8.

After completing the setup of your storage space, you can continue to monitor and manage it from the Manage Storage Space tool. You can perform the following tasks:

- View your storage pool(s).
- View the storage spaces in the pools.
- View the physical drives included in the pool(s).
- Identify how much pool capacity is currently being used.
- Add more drives to the pool.
- Rename the pool.
- Change the size of storage spaces.
- View files stored in storage spaces.
- Delete storage spaces.

■ CONFIGURING REMOVABLE STORAGE DEVICES

The Bottom Line

Configuring removable devices is not much different from managing fixed disks. Basically, you connect the device. The device is detected and the appropriate driver is loaded from the driver store. If the driver does not exist in the driver store, you will have to install the driver from disk or from files that you download from the manufacturing website.

CERTIFICATION READY
Configure removable devices.
Objective 2.2

After the removable storage device is recognized by Windows, it should appear in the Disk Manager with a drive letter automatically assigned. If the removable storage device is not partitioned and formatted, you will have to use Disk Manager to partition and format the removable device. You can also assign or change the drive letter assigned to the partition.

In today's networks, the biggest concern of administrators has been the arrival of removable storage devices. With Windows 10 and Windows Server 2012 R2/Windows Server 2016, you fortunately have several options for monitoring and securing these types of devices. Controlling the use of removable media is critical to the overall security of your network.

Monitoring and securing removable media includes using Group Policy to control whether users are allowed to use removable media on your network or on specific computers as well as whether they can deploy BitLocker/BitLocker To Go to encrypt and protect removable media that is lost or stolen.

You can configure Group Policy Objects (GPOs) to monitor the use of removable storage devices on your network. The setting is found in the following location using the Group Policy Management Console (GPMC): Computer Configuration\Policies\Windows Settings\Security Settings\Advanced Audit Policy Configuration\Audit Policies. The Audit Removable Storage setting allows you to audit user attempts to access file system objects on a removable storage device. If you enable this policy, a security audit event is generated each time an account accesses the removable storage device.

You can also configure GPOs to prevent the use of removable media on your network for computers and/or users.

The settings is found in both Computer and User locations in the GPMC:

- Computer Configuration\Policies\Administrative Templates\System\Removable Storage Access: These settings are applied to the computer and every user who logs on to it.
- User Configuration\Policies\Administrative Templates\System\Removable Storage Access: These settings are applied to only users/groups that are included in an Active Directory container to which you link the GPO.

For example, to deny read access to removable hard drives or USB flash drives, enable the Removable Disks: Deny read access option.

On Windows 10 clients, you can configure similar settings using the Local Group Policy Editor (LGPE)—gpedit.msc. When enabled and applied, the Computer Configuration\ Policies\Administrative Templates\System\Device Installation\Device Installation Restrictions\ Prevent installation of removable devices setting (see Figure 7-13) prevents Windows from installing removable devices. A device is considered removable when the driver for the device to which it is connected indicates the device is removable. For example, a USB device is reported removable by the drivers for the USB hub to which it is connected.

Figure 7-13

Preventing the installation of removable devices using a local GPO

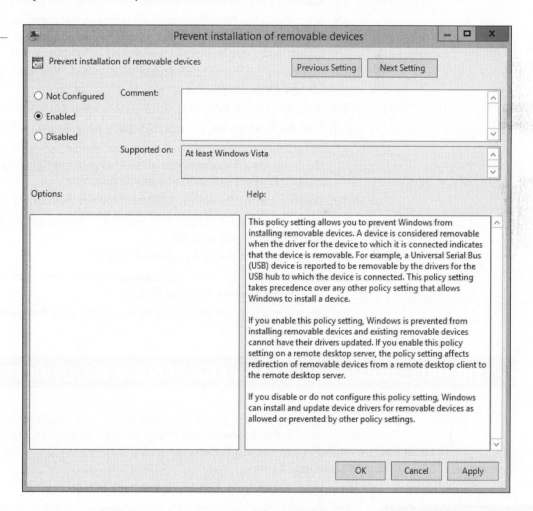

CONFIGURE REMOVABLE STORAGE ACCESS POLICIES

GET READY. To create a storage pool and storage space, perform the following steps.

1. Logon to the LON-DC1 as adatum\administrator with the password of **Pa$$w0rd**.
2. When Server Manager opens, open the **Tools** menu and click **Active Directory Users and Computers**.

3. When the Active Directory Users and Computers console opens, expand the **adatum.com** node.

4. Right-click the **adatum.com** node and select **New > Organizational Unit.**

5. When the New Object – Organizational Unit dialog box appears, in the Name text box, type **Restricted**.

6. To close the New Object Organizational Unit dialog box, click **OK.**

7. Close Active Directory Users and Computers.

8. Go back to **Server Manager**, open the Tools menu, and click **Group Policy Management.**

9. When the Group Policy Management console opens, expand the **Forest: adatum.com** node, expand the **Domains** node, expand the **adatum.com** node, and then expand the **Group Policy Objects** node.

10. Right-click **Group Policy Objects** and choose **New.**

11. When the New GPO window displays, in the Name text box, type **Removable Storage Restrictions**, and then click **OK.**

12. Right-click the Removable Storage Restrictions GPO and choose Edit.

13. When the Group Policy Management Editor window opens, under the User Configuration node, expand the **Policies** node, expand the **Administrative Templates**, expand the **System** node, and then click the **Removable Storage Access** node.

14. To stop writing to writable optical disk, in the right pane, double-click **CD and DVD: Deny Write access.**

15. When the CD and DVD: Deny write access dialog box opens, click the **Enabled** option.

16. Click **OK** to close the CD and DVD: Deny write access dialog box.

17. To prevent the installation of removable devices, navigate to and click the Computer Configuration\Policies\Administrative Templates\System\Device Installation\Device Installation Restrictions node.

18. Double-click the Prevent installation of removable devices setting.

19. When the Prevent installation of removable devices dialog box appears, select **Enabled** and click **OK.**

20. Close the Group Policy Management Editor.

21. Back on the Group Policy Management console, right-click the **Restricted** OU and choose **Link an Existing GPO.**

22. When the Select GPO dialog box opens, double-click **Removable Storage Restrictions.**

■ TROUBLESHOOTING STORAGE AND REMOVABLE DEVICES ISSUES

The Bottom Line

When troubleshooting any kind of storage device, you don't want to rush in and start doing things without thinking everything through. Remember, that if you rush into the troubleshooting and you perform the wrong task, you could erase all of the information on the storage device.

CERTIFICATION READY
Troubleshoot storage and removable devices issues.
Objective 2.2

When you are having a problem with storage devices, including removable storage devices, use the following basic troubleshooting methodology:

1. Ensure the device is connected properly and turned on.
2. Ensure the port or storage interface is enabled in the system's BIOS.
3. Ensure the device driver is installed.

4. Ensure that the storage device is initialized, partitioned, formatted and assigned a drive letter.

5. Check for malware.

6. Check for GPO settings that would disable removable storage devices.

When you connect a storage device to a system running Windows 10 and it does not come up, make sure that it is properly connected (data link and power connections). Most fixed disks should not be connected or disconnected while the system is running. Only drives that are marked as hot pluggable can be connected while the system is running. When the disks are connected and the system is running, you should look for lights indicating that the device is on. For mechanical drives, verify whether the platters are spinning by feeling or listening to the drive or picking it up and feeling the torque that is created by the spinning disks.

You should also try removing and reseating the device, as well as connecting the device on a different port or connector. To determine whether the device is the problem, you can connect the storage device to another system, or connect a known working device to your current system to see if it works. Also ensure the port or storage interface is enabled in the system's BIOS.

If your computer still does not recognize the device, see if the device is recognized by Disk Manager. If it is not recognized by Disk Manager, open Device Manager to see if the drive is recognized. If it is not, try to find and install the appropriate driver.

If the storage device (fixed or removable) is connected properly, open Disk Manager to see if the drive is initialized, partitioned, formatted, and assigned a drive letter. If you are sure that the drive already has data on it, try reconnecting the device. If the data still does not appear, try connecting the storage device to another system to see if the data is available.

If data doesn't appear when you connect the storage device to a new system, check for malware/viruses. If it is a removable disk, check for GPO settings that would disable removable storage devices.

SKILL SUMMARY

IN THIS LESSON YOU LEARNED:

- A file system is the overall structure your computer uses to name, store, and organize files and folders on a hard disk or partition. The file system provides a map of the clusters (the basic units of logical storage on a hard disk) that a file has been stored in. When you install a hard disk in a computer, you must format it with a file system.

- NTFS is the preferred file system that supports much larger hard disk and a higher level of reliability than FAT-based file systems. In addition, NTFS offers better security through permissions and encryption.

- Windows 10 supports two partition styles, MBR and GPT; and two primary types of disks, basic and dynamic. In addition, the operating system supports simple, spanned, striped, and mirrored volumes. Use the Disk Management tool in the Computer Management snap-in to manage disks, partitions, and volumes.

- With Disk Management, you can create a new .vhd/.vhdx file by using the available disk space on the computer and saving it to the location that you specify. If you have a .vhd/vhdx file, you can mount the drive to your system running Windows 10.

- Storage Spaces is a feature in Windows 10 that allows you to combine multiple disks into a single logical volume that can be mirrored to protect against one or more drive failures.

■ Knowledge Assessment

Multiple Choice

1. Which of the following drives can be added to a storage pool? (Choose all that apply.)
   a. SATA
   b. eSATA
   c. USB
   d. SCSI

2. When creating a storage space, which of the following resiliency settings requires at least five drives?
   a. Parity
   b. Three-way mirror
   c. Two-way mirror
   d. Simple

3. Which of the following processes reserves space for future use when working with storage spaces/storage pools?
   a. Partitions
   b. Thin provisioning
   c. SMB blocks
   d. Provisioned storage blocks

4. When creating a storage space, how many disks are needed when setting up parity for resiliency settings in a storage pool?
   a. 2
   b. 3
   c. 5
   d. 4

5. Which of the following tools prevents the installation of removable devices on a stand-alone Windows 10 computer?
   a. GPMC
   b. LGPE
   c. BitLocker Group Policy
   d. BitLocker To Go Group Policy

6. Which of the following statements are true of striped volumes? (Choose all that apply.)
   a. Striped volumes provide enhanced performance over simple volumes.
   b. Striped volumes provide greater fault tolerance than simple volumes.
   c. You can extend striped volumes after creation.
   d. If a single physical disk in the striped volume fails, all of the data in the entire volume is lost.

7. Which of the following are requirements for extending a volume on a dynamic disk? (Choose all that apply.)
   a. If you want to extend a simple volume, you can use only the available space on the same disk, if the volume is to remain simple.
   b. The volume must have a file system before you can extend a simple or spanned volume.
   c. You can extend a simple or spanned volume if you formatted it using the FAT or FAT32 file systems.
   d. You can extend a simple volume across additional disks if it is not a system volume or a boot volume.

8. Which of the following volume types supported by Windows 10 does *not* provide fault tolerance? (Choose all that apply)
   a. Striped
   b. Spanned
   c. Mirrored
   d. None of the above

9. Which of the following is the next step after creating a virtual hard disk (VHD)?
   a. Mounting it either through Server Manager or the Disk Management snap-in
   b. Initializing the disk and creating volumes on it, just as you would a physical disk
   c. Using the VHD (creation of the VHD file readies the disk for storage)
   d. Mounting the VHD file to a Hyper-V virtual machine

10. What is the maximum size of an NTFS volume with 64 kb clusters?
    a. 2 GB
    b. 32 GB
    c. 4 TB
    d. 256 TB
    e. 512 TB

Best Answer

Choose the letter that corresponds to the best answer. More than one answer choice may achieve the goal. Select the BEST answer.

1. When creating storage spaces, which of the following types of resiliency works best for protection against two drives failing simultaneously while setting up storage space?
   a. Three-way mirror
   b. Two-way mirror
   c. Parity
   d. Simple

2. Which of the following approaches is best to reserve at least 500 GB of space for a new storage space when there is only 100 GB of actual physical disk space?
   a. Wait until there is enough physical disk capacity to create the 500 GB storage space.
   b. Purchase new drives before creating the space.
   c. Use thin provisioning and create the larger space. Drives can be purchased later when needed.
   d. Configure one pool now and another when the drives are available.

3. Which of the following tools is the best solution for adding more drives to a storage pool and also renaming the pool?
   a. PowerShell
   b. Disk Manager
   c. Manage Storage Space
   d. Additional drives cannot be added to the pool without re-creating it.

Build a List

1. Specify the correct order of the steps necessary to creating a storage pool.
   _____Click Create pool.
   _____Log on with administrative credentials.
   _____Select the drive(s) you want to include in the new storage pool.
   _____Click Create a new pool and storage space.
   _____Connect the drives to your computer.
   _____Press the Windows logo key + r, type Storage Spaces, and then select it from the Results list.
   _____From the Results list, click Storage Spaces.

2. Specify the correct order of steps necessary to creating and mounting a VHD.

_____ Log on with administrative privileges and open Server Manager.

_____ Click Tools > Computer Management.

_____ Click Disk Management and then click Create VHD from the Action menu.

_____ Specify the Location path and name for the new VHD file and then specify the maximum size of the disk.

_____ Select the virtual hard disk format option (VHD or VHDX).

_____ Select one of the following VHD types (Fixed size or Dynamically expanding).

_____ Click OK for the system to create and attach the VHD file. The VHD appears as a disk in the Disk Management snap-in.

Business Case Scenarios

Scenario 7-1: Configuring a Storage Space/Storage Pool

You create a new storage pool for the following disks on your Windows 10 computer:

- **Serial ATA (SATA):** 1 TB
- **Serial Attached SCSI (SAS):** 1 TB

SATA and SAS are two different types of drives with different connectors/interfaces.

What is the maximum size you can allocate for your new storage space?

Scenario 7-2: Creating a Large Volume

You have a new desktop running Windows 10. However, you try to copy your file repository and find out that you do not have enough disk space. You have 400 GB of free disk space on your C drive and you have 3 smaller 500 GB drives. What can you do?

Configuring Data Access and Usage

70-698 EXAM OBJECTIVE

Objective 2.3 – Configure data access and usage. This objective may include but is not limited to: Configure file and printer sharing and HomeGroup connections; configure folder shares, public folders, and OneDrive; configure file system permissions; configure OneDrive usage; troubleshoot data access and usage.

Objective 3.2 – Monitoring Windows. This objective may include but is not limited to: Monitor and manage printers. * Additional Objective 3.2 topics are covered in Lesson 12.

Objective 3.4 – Configure authorization and authentication. This objective may include but is not limited to: Configure HomeGroup settings. * Additional Objective 3.4 topics are covered in Lesson 14 and Lesson 5.

LESSON HEADING	EXAM OBJECTIVE
Configuring File Sharing	Configure file sharing
	Configure folder shares
Configuring File System Permissions	Configure file system permissions
Understanding Effective NTFS Permissions	
Viewing Effective Permissions on a Resource	
Combining NTFS and Share Permissions	
Troubleshooting Data Access and Usage	Troubleshoot data access and usage
Understanding the Windows 10 File Structure	
Configuring Libraries	
Configuring Public Folders	Configure public folders
Configuring HomeGroup Connections	Configure HomeGroup connections
	Configure HomeGroup settings
Configuring OneDrive	Configure OneDrive
Accessing OneDrive for Business from a Browser	Configure OneDrive usage
Understanding OneDrive for Business Permissions	
Creating a File within OneDrive for Business	
Uploading Files to OneDrive	
Sharing a Document in OneDrive	
Accessing OneDrive from the OneDrive Desktop App for Windows	

Lesson Heading	Exam Objective
Configuring OneDrive Usage	
Configuring Printers	Configure printer sharing
Installing Printers	
Understanding Printer Properties	
Configuring Printer Sharing	
Monitoring and Managing Printers	Monitor and Manage Printers

KEY TERMS

advanced sharing	inherited permissions	OneDrive for Business
basic sharing	library	Pictures library
compression	local printer	print device
disk quotas	Music library	print job
Documents library	network printer	print spooler
effective permissions	NTFS permissions	printer
explicit permissions	OneDrive	Public folder
fetching	OneDrive desktop app for Windows	shared folder
Homegroup		Video library

■ CONFIGURING FILE SHARING

THE BOTTOM LINE

Most users are not going to log onto a server directly to access their data files. Instead, a drive or folder will be shared (known as a ***shared folder***), and they will access the data files over the network. To help protect against unauthorized drive or folder access, you should use share permissions along with NTFS permissions (assuming the shared folder is on an NTFS volume). When a user needs to access a network share, he or she will use the universal naming convention (UNC), which is \\servername\sharename.

CERTIFICATION READY
Configure file sharing
Objective 2.3

CERTIFICATION READY
Configure folder shares
Objective 2.3

Traditional Windows file sharing allows you to restrict access to specific shared files and folders, and choose which users have access. ***Basic sharing*** allows you to share a file or folder with a specific user and restrict the user to Read or Read/Write actions.

Advanced sharing offers the greatest amount of control; you can do the following:

- Share files, folders, or an entire drive
- Choose users or groups with which to share files and folders
- Limit the number of users who can use a file or folder at the same time, mainly for security purposes
- Set permissions on shared files and folders, such as allowing users Read, Change, or Full Control permissions
- Choose which files are available to users offline

TAKE NOTE   You'll learn about permissions later in this lesson.

CROSS-REFERENCE

For more information about the Advanced sharing settings, refer to Lesson 6.

To set up basic or advanced shares, you must make sure that file sharing and network discovery are turned on. You should also turn on password-protected sharing for security purposes. File sharing, network discovery, and password-protected sharing is enabled by default in the Network and Sharing Center, Advanced sharing settings page.

 SET UP A BASIC SHARE

GET READY. To set up a basic share for a specific user, perform the following steps.

1. In File Explorer, navigate to the file or folder you want to share.

2. Right-click the file or folder, select **Properties**, click the **Sharing** tab in the Properties dialog box, and then click the **Share** button to open the File Sharing dialog box (see Figure 8-1). You can also right-click the file or folder, click **Share with**, and then click **Specific people**.

Figure 8-1

Windows 10 basic sharing

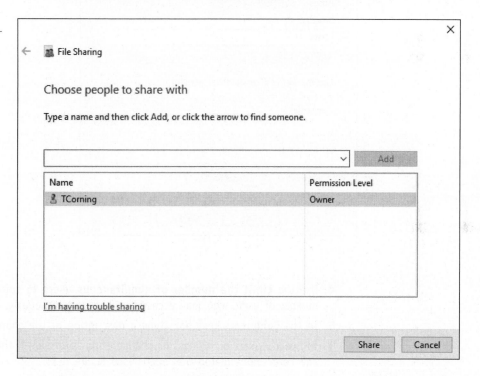

3. Click the arrow next to the text box, click a name from the list, and then click **Add**. Alternately, if you know the user name of the person you want to add, type it in the text box and click **Add**.

4. In the **Permission Level** column, click the down arrow for the new user and select **Read** or **Read/Write**. Read allows the user to open and view items but not make changes or delete them. Read/Write allows users to open, modify, and delete items. You can also click **Remove** to remove the user.

5. When you're finished, click **Share**. If you're prompted for an administrator password or confirmation, type the password or provide confirmation.

6. After you set up a basic share for a user, Windows lets you send a confirmation to that user via email, or you can copy and paste a link to the shared item and send it to the user via email or instant message, for example.

7. When you're finished, click **Done**.

SET UP AN ADVANCED SHARE

GET READY. To set up an advanced share, perform the following steps.

1. In File Explorer, navigate to the folder, or drive you want to share. This exercise assumes you are not working with Public folders.

2. Right-click the item to be shared, select **Properties**, click the **Sharing** tab in the Properties dialog box, and then click the **Advanced Sharing** button. If you're prompted for an administrator password or confirmation, type the password or provide confirmation.

3. In the Advanced Sharing dialog box, select the **Share this folder** check box (as shown in Figure 8-2).

Figure 8-2

The Advanced Sharing dialog box

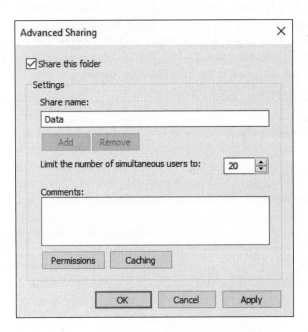

4. Use the **Limit the number of simultaneous users to** spin box to select the number of users who may access the item simultaneously.

5. In the **Comments** text box, type a description of the shared item (if desired).

6. To specify users or groups, or change permissions, click the **Permissions** button. The Permissions dialog box opens (see Figure 8-3).

7. Click **Add** to add a user or group. (You can also click **Remove** to remove a user or group from the share.) The Select Users or Groups dialog box displays.

8. Type a user or group name in the text box or click **Locations** to find a user or group to add. When you're finished, click **OK**.

9. In the Permissions dialog box, select a user or group, select the checkboxes for the permissions you want to assign, and then click **OK**.

10. When you're finished, click **OK** to close the Advanced Sharing dialog box.

Share permissions are set for folders when they are shared in workgroups and domain-based networks and are only associated with the folder. They determine the type of access that others will have to the folder when they connect to it over the network.

Figure 8-3

The Permissions dialog box

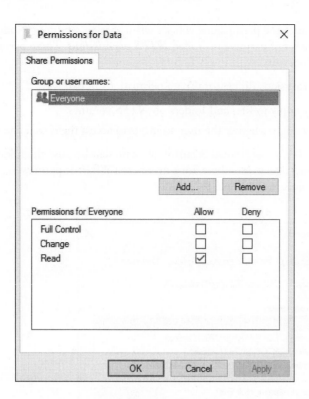

Share permissions only apply when you are accessing a shared folder via the UNC. If you log on locally and access the files directly without using the UNC, these permissions will not apply. Share permissions are not granular; therefore, the permission you assign to the share will automatically apply to the files and subfolders within the share itself.

In Windows 10, you will create and manage shares and share permissions from the folder properties Sharing tab. To see the permissions, click Advanced Sharing and click the Permissions button. Table 8-1 shows the available permissions.

Table 8-1

Understanding Share Permissions

PERMISSION	DESCRIPTION
Read	Enables user/group to view file and subfolder names, view data in files, and run programs
Change	Enables user/group to add files and subfolders to the shared folder, change data in files, delete subfolders and files, and change any permission associated with Read
Full Control	Enables user/group to change file permissions (NTFS only), take ownership of files (NTFS only), and perform tasks associated with Change/Read

Configuring File System Permissions

The NTFS file permission tool is powerful and enables you to control access to your files and folders whether they are accessed across the network or by someone logging onto the computer locally.

CERTIFICATION READY
Configure file system
permissions
Objective 2.3

In addition to the permissions you set when sharing a folder, Windows offers a more comprehensive set of permissions called ***NTFS permissions***. These permissions are available on volumes formatted with the NTFS file system.

NTFS permissions differ from share permissions in two ways.

- They apply to files and folders on NTFS volumes.
- They apply whether the user attempts to access them over the network or locally.

In Figure 8-4, an additional Security tab is present because the folder is located on an NTFS volume. As you can see, there are a number of different permissions available for selected users and groups (see Table 8-2).

Figure 8-4

Managing NTFS Permissions

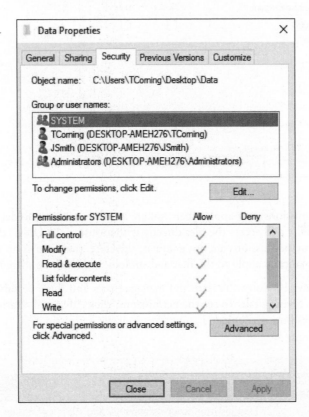

Groups or users that are granted Full Control permission on a folder can delete any files in that folder regardless of the permissions protecting the file. In addition, the permissions for the List folder contents are inherited by folders but not files, and it should only appear when you view folder permissions. In Windows 10, the Everyone group does not include the Anonymous Logon group by default, so permissions applied to the Everyone group do not affect the Anonymous Logon group.

Each of the standard permissions consists of a logical group of special permissions. The available special permissions are as follows:

- **Traverse folder/Execute file:** When it is applied to a folder, it allows or prevents a user or group to move through folders to reach other files or folders, even if the user has no permission for the parent folder. When applied to a file, it allows the user or group to run program files. By default, the Everyone group is granted the Bypass traverse checking user right, which is applied to folders only. Setting the Traverse folder permission on a folder does not automatically set the Execute file permission on all files within that folder.

Table 8-2

NTFS Permissions

PERMISSION	DESCRIPTION
Read	Folder: Enables user/group to read the contents of the folder.
	File: Enables user/group to read the contents of the file.
Read & Execute	Folder: Enables user/group to read the contents of the folder and execute programs in the folder.
	File: Enables user/group to read the contents of the file and execute the program.
Write	Folder: Enables user/group to create files and folders.
	File: Enables user/group to create a file.
Modify	Folder: Enables user/group to read and write permissions. User can delete files within the folder and view the contents of subfolders.
	File: Enables user/group to read and write permissions. User can modify the contents of the file.
List Folder Contents	Folder: Enables user/group to view a list of files in the selected folder; user is not allowed to read the contents of a file or execute a file.
	File: There is no equivalent permission for files.
Full Control	Folder: Enables user/group to add, change, move, and delete items. User can also add and remove permissions on the folder and its subfolders.
	File: Enables user/group to change, move, delete, and manage permissions. User can also add, change, and remove permissions on the file.

- **List folder/Read data:** When it is applied to a folder, it allows or prevents the user or group, to see a list of files and subfolders in the folder. When it is applied to a file, you can open and read the file.
- **Read attributes:** When it is applied to files and folders, it allows or prevents the viewing of file or folder attributes, such as read-only and hidden.
- **Read extended attributes:** When it is applied to files and folders, it allows or prevents the viewing of extended attributes of a file or folder. Extended attributes are defined by programs and may vary by program.
- **Create files/Write data:** When it is applied to a folder, it allows or prevents a user or group to create new files within the folders. When it applies to a file, it allows the user or group to add to or modify the file, including overwriting existing content.
- **Create folders/Append data:** When it is applied to a folder, it allows you to create subfolders within the folder. When it is applied to a file, allows the user or group to add data to the end of a file, but not to change, delete, or overwrite existing data.
- **Write attributes:** When applied to files or folders, it allows or prevents the changing the attributes of files or folders, such as read-only or hidden.
- **Write extended attributes:** When applied to files or folders, it allows or prevents the changing the extended attributes of a file or folder.

- **Delete subfolders and files:** When applied to files or folders, it allows the user or groups to delete subfolders and files.
- **Delete:** When applied to files and folders, it allows or prevents the deleting the file or folder.
- **Read permissions:** When applied to a file or folder, it allows or prevents you to view the permissions of the file or folder.
- **Change permissions:** When applied to a file or folder, it allows or prevents the user or group to change the permissions of a file or folder.
- **Take ownership:** When applied to a file or folder, it allows or prevents taking ownership of the file or folder. As an owner, you can change permissions regardless of permissions that you are explicated granted to the file or folder.

To simplify administration, you can use groups to grant permissions. By assigning NTFS permissions to a group, you are granting permissions to one or more people simultaneously, reducing the number of entries in each access list, as well as the amount of effort required to grant multiple people access to certain files or folders.

Understanding Effective NTFS Permissions

The folder/file structure on an NTFS drive can be complicated, with many folders and nested folders. In addition, because you can assign permissions to groups and at different levels on an NTFS volume, figuring out the effective permissions of a particular folder or file for a particular user can be tricky.

There are two types of permissions used in NTFS:

- *Explicit permissions*: Permissions granted directly to a file or folder.
- *Inherited permissions*: Permissions that are granted to a folder (parent object or container) that flow into child objects (subfolders or files inside the parent folder).

In a file system, a folder with subfolders is considered the parent folder. The subfolders are considered child folders. After you set permissions on a parent folder, new files and subfolders that are created in the folder inherit these permissions.

To stop permissions from being inherited, select the "Replace all existing inheritable permissions on all descendants with inheritable permissions from this object" check box in the Advanced Security Settings dialog box. You are then asked whether you are sure you want to proceed. You can also clear the "Allow inheritable permissions from parent to propagate to this object" check box. When you clear this check box, Windows responds with a Security dialog box. In the Security dialog box, when you click the Copy button, the explicit permission is copied from the parent folder to the subfolder or file. You can then change the subfolder's or file's explicit permissions. If you click the Remove button, you remove the inherited permission altogether.

By default, any objects within a folder inherit the permissions from that folder when they are created, as shown in Table 8-3. However, explicit permissions take precedence over inherited permissions, as shown in Table 8-4. So, if you grant different permissions at a lower level, the lower-level permissions take precedence.

For example, say you have a folder called Data. Within the Data folder, you have Folder1, and within Folder1, you have Folder2. If you grant Allow full control to a user account, the Allow full control permission will flow down to the subfolders and files within the Data folder.

Table 8-3

Inherited Permissions

OBJECT	NTFS PERMISSIONS
Data	Grant Allow full control (explicit)
Folder1	Allow full control (inherited)
Folder2	Allow full control (inherited)
File1	Allow full control (inherited)

In comparison, if you grant Allow full control on the Data folder to a user account and you grant Allow read permission to Folder1, the Allow read permission will overwrite the inherited permissions and will then flow down to Folder2 and File1.

Table 8-4

Explicit Permissions Overwrite Inherited Permissions

OBJECT	NTFS PERMISSIONS
Data	Grant Allow full control (explicit)
Folder1	Allow read (explicit)
Folder2	Allow read (inherited)
File1	Allow read (inherited)

If a user has access to a file, he or she can still gain access to the file even if he or she does not have access to the folder containing the file. Of course, because the user doesn't have access to the folder, the user cannot navigate or browse through the folder to get to the file. Therefore, the user will have to use the universal naming convention (UNC) or local path to open the file.

When you view permissions of a file or folder, they will appear in one of the following ways:

- **Checked:** Permissions are explicitly assigned.
- **Cleared (unchecked):** No permissions are assigned.
- **Shaded:** Permissions are granted through inheritance from a parent folder.

Besides granting the Allow permission, you can also grant the Deny permission. The Deny permission always overrides other permissions that have been granted, including when a user or group has been given Full control. For example, if a group is granted Read and Write permission and one person within the group is denied the Write permission, the user's effective rights is the Read permission.

When you combine applying Deny versus Allowed with explicit versus inherited permissions, the hierarchy of precedence of permission is as follows:

1. Explicit Deny
2. Explicit Allow
3. Inherited Deny
4. Inherited Allow

Because users can be members of several groups, it is possible for them to have several sets of explicit permissions for a particular folder or file. When this occurs, the permissions are combined to form the *effective permissions*, which are the actual permissions when logging in and accessing a file or folder. These consist of explicit permissions plus any inherited permissions.

When you calculate effective permissions, you must first calculate the explicit and inherited permissions for an individual or group and then combine them. When combining user and group permissions for NTFS security, the effective permission is the cumulative permission. The only exception is that Deny permissions always apply.

For example, you have a folder called Data. Within the Data folder, you have Folder1, and within Folder1, you have Folder2. If User 1 is a member of Group 1 and Group 2 and you assign the following:

- The Allow write permission to the Data folder to User 1
- The Allow read permission to Folder1 to Group 1
- The Allow modify permission to Folder2 to Group 2,

then User 1's effective permissions would be as shown in Table 8-5.

Table 8-5

Calculating effective permissions

OBJECT	USER 1 NTFS PERMISSIONS	GROUP 1 PERMISSIONS	GROUP 2 PERMISSIONS	EFFECTIVE PERMISSIONS
Data	Allow write (explicit)			Allow write
Folder1	Allow write (inherited)	Allow read (explicit)		Allow read and write
Folder2	Allow write (inherited)	Allow read (inherited)	Allow modify* (explicit)	Allow modify*
File1	Allow write (inherited)	Allow read (inherited)	Allow modify* (inherited)	Allow modify*

*The Modify permission includes the Read and write permissions.

As another example, say you have a folder called Data. Within the Data folder, you have Folder1, and within Folder1, you have Folder2. If User 1 is a member of Group 1 and Group 2 and you assign the following permissions:

- The Allow write permission to the Data folder to User 1
- The Allow read permission to Folder1 to Group 1
- The Deny modify permission to Folder2 to Group 2,

User 1's effective permissions would be as shown in Table 8-6.

The concept of inheritance is important to keep in mind when setting NTFS permissions. Remember the following:

- When users copy files and folders, the files and folders inherit the permissions of the destination folder.
- When users move files and folders within the same volume, they retain their permissions.
- When users move files and folders to a different volume, they inherit the permissions of the destination folder.

Effective permissions for an object, such as a folder, are permissions granted to a user or group based on the permissions granted through group membership and any permissions

Table 8-6

Effective Permissions Affected
by Deny Permissions

OBJECT	USER 1 NTFS PERMISSIONS	GROUP 1 PERMISSIONS	GROUP 2 PERMISSIONS	EFFECTIVE PERMISSIONS
Data	Allow write (explicit)			Allow write
Folder1	Allow write (inherited)	Allow read (explicit)		Allow read and write
Folder2	Allow write (inherited)	Allow read (inherited)	Deny modify (explicit)	Deny modify
File1	Allow write (inherited)	Allow read (inherited)	Deny modify (inherited)	Deny modify

inherited from the parent object. Windows does not include share permissions as part of the effective permissions.

NTFS permissions are cumulative. For example, if you give a user in the sales group Read permissions to a folder and its contents, and the user is also a member of the marketing group, which has been given the Write permission to the same folder, the user will have Read+Write permissions. In this type of situation, if you do not want the user to be able to write to the folder, you can use the Deny permission and select the specific user account. The Deny permission always overrides the Allow permission.

Viewing Effective Permissions on a Resource

In Windows 10, the Effective Access tab has been added to enable you to view the effective NTFS permissions for a user, group, or device account on a resource. To access this tab, right-click the file or folder, choose Properties, click the Security tab, and then click Advanced.

For example, let's say you create a folder called Data and then share the folder, allowing the Sales group full control. You also configure the NTFS permissions for JSmith, a member of the group, with the following settings: Read & Execute, List Folder Contents, and Read. What would Jsmith's effective permission be?

To determine JSmith's effective permissions, right-click the Data folder and choose Properties. Click the Security tab and then click Advanced. Once you are in the Advanced Security Settings for Data dialog box, click Select a user and then search for JSmith's account. Once you find his account, select it and then click View effective access to see the permissions he has for the folder.

As shown in Figure 8-5, even though JSmith has Full Control to the share due to his membership in the Sales group, NTFS permissions restrict him to only reading, listing folder contents, and executing files within the folder. He cannot create files, folders, or make any changes to the documents.

 REVIEW PERMISSIONS USING THE EFFECTIVE ACCESS TAB

GET READY. To view the effective permissions for the local Administrator account, log on to your computer with Administrative credentials and then perform the following steps.

1. To open File Explorer, click the **File Explorer** icon on the taskbar.
2. Click **Local Disk (C:)**.
3. Right-click the **Windows** folder and choose **Properties**.

4. Click the Security tab and then click Advanced.

5. Click the **Effective Access** tab.

6. Click **Select a user**.

7. In the Enter the object name to select field, type **Administrator** and then click **OK**.

8. Click **View effective access**.

9. Review the current permissions for the local Administrator account on C:\Windows and then click **OK**.

10. Click **OK** to accept your changes and to close the Windows Properties dialog box.

Figure 8-5

Viewing a user's effective permissions

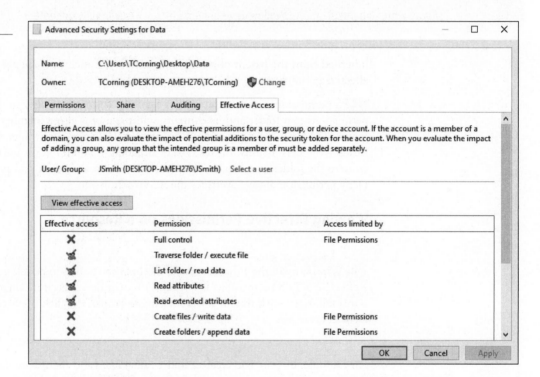

When planning your NTFS/Share permissions on storage spaces or any volumes in which files/folders are shared, the best approach is to set the Share permissions to provide Full Control to the appropriate user group and then use NTFS permissions to further lock down access to the resource. This process ensures that resources are secured regardless of how they are accessed (remotely or locally).

Combining NTFS and Share Permissions

It is very common to combine share and NTFS permissions when providing access to resources on NTFS volumes. When this happens, you must have a good understanding of the cumulative effects to ensure that your resources remain protected. Now that you have a better understanding of NTFS permissions and share permissions, you need to understand what happens when you combine the two permissions on the same resource.

For example, let's say you create and share a folder with the following settings:

- **Share permission (Share tab)**: Sales group, Read
- **NTFS permission (Security tab)**: Sales group, Full Control

When users connect to the share over the network, both the share and NTFS permissions combine, and the most restrictive set is applied. In the preceding example, the share permission of Read is more restrictive than the NTFS permission, so users can read the folder and its contents. If the same users were to log on locally to the computer in which this share is located, they would bypass the share permissions and their level of access would be based on the NTFS permission. In this example, they would have Full Control.

Troubleshooting Data Access and Usage

CERTIFICATION READY
Troubleshoot data access
and usage
Objective 2.3

Users tend to store everything and do not make much of an effort to delete old or unneeded files. Eventually, this can cause problems because you have to scramble to ensure that your users have enough disk space to store the necessary files. You also have to make sure the system keeps working properly without running of disk space.

USING STORAGE SENSE

Storage Sense is a built-in Windows 10 tool that allows you to get an overview of the types of files that are taking up space on the hard disks.

To open Storage Sense, open File Explorer, select This PC, and then on the Computer tab, click Open Settings. Click System > Storage and then click a volume to see how much space is being consumed. Storage Space shows you the size of the following categories of files (as shown in Figure 8-6):

- System & reserved
- Apps & games
- Documents
- Pictures
- Music
- Videos
- Mail
- OneDrive
- Desktop
- Maps
- Other users
- Temporary files
- Other

The categories are color-coded to make it easier to see how the space is divided.

If you click a category, you can see a list of those files and you can sort by name, size, or date, or you can click a button to open a specific folder with File Explorer. Then you can use File Explorer to sort by name, date modified, type, or size just by clicking the appropriate column title.

Figure 8-6

Viewing storage usage

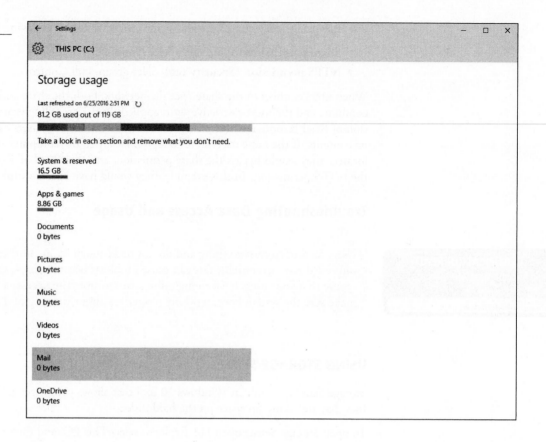

Using NTFS Folder and File Compression

Compression is the process of decreasing the size of files or folders without affecting the files' content. The purpose of compression is to decrease large files that would otherwise use a lot of storage space. Because files often include a lot of redundant, repeated data, compressing them replaces repeated data with pointers to the data. The pointers take up much less space than the repeated data, so the size of the file is reduced. If you are running out of disk space and you cannot add additional storage, you can use compression to increase disk space.

TAKE NOTE You cannot encrypt files or folders that are compressed and you cannot compress a file that is encrypted using EFS.

COMPRESS A FILE OR FOLDER

GET READY. To compress a file or folder, perform the following steps.

1. In File Explorer, right-click the file or folder you want to compress and then click **Properties**. The Properties dialog box opens.
2. On the **General** tab, click the **Advanced** button. The Advanced Attributes dialog box opens.
3. Select the **Compress contents to save disk space** check box and then click **OK**. Figure 8-7 shows the Compress contents to save disk space box selected on a compressed folder.

Figure 8-7

The Advanced Attributes dialog box

The compressed file or folder displays with two blue arrows pointing toward each other in Windows Explorer. To uncompress the file or folder, select it, return to the Advanced Attributes dialog box, and deselect the Compress contents to save disk space check box.

USING DISK QUOTAS

If you let users store their files and folders on the network, some users may take advantage of the network space. As an administrator, your goal is to provide storage space while minimizing the costs of adding more storage. *Disk quotas* enable you to maintain a balance between the two by limiting the amount of storage space you allocate to your users.

Disk quotas, a feature first introduced in Windows 2000, are available in Windows 10 and Windows Server 2016 editions. They enable you to set the amount of storage space available to each user. When enabled, the Disk Quota Manager monitors and tracks the files that are owned by a specific user. It then compares the amount of disk space being consumed by the user to the limit set by the administrator. When users reach their limit, the Disk Quota Manager notifies them and/or restricts them from adding more data to the disk.

The following things you should know about using disk quotas:

- Quotas can be configured only on NTFS volumes.
- Only files that users own apply to the amount of the space used by the user.
- Quotas must be enabled separately on each volume and are applied on a per-user basis.
- Quotas do not apply to administrators.
- Only domain administrators or local administrators can enable quotas.

Configuring disk quotas involves three steps:

1. Enable quotas on the volume.
2. Configure the quota settings.
3. Create quota entries for specific users.

To enable quota management, you can use Disk Management (diskmgmt.msc) or File Explorer to locate the volume on which you want to enable the feature. Right-click it and choose Properties. Click the Quota tab and then click the Show Quota Settings button, which displays the Enable quota management option. Figure 8-8 shows the Enable quota management option selected. From the Quota tab, you can also deny disk space to users who exceed their quota limit, set the amount of disk space available to users along with their warning levels, and log events. Logging identifies the user and what triggered the event (for example, a warning or an exceeded quota limit).

Figure 8-8

Reviewing disk quota settings

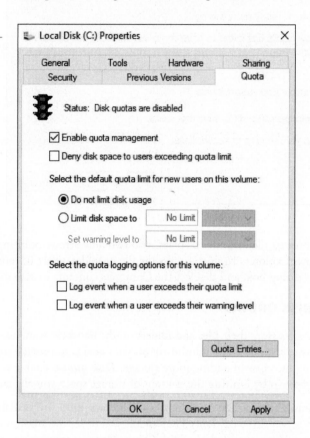

If you enable the Deny Disk Space to users exceeding quota limit option, users who reach the limits you set will be denied additional storage space on the volume. Users will receive an "insufficient disk space" error on their screens. If the check box is not selected, users are warned when they reach their limits, but not restricted from adding more data to the volume. By not restricting users initially, you can get a better picture of who is using the volume to store data and how much space they are actually using. This information can then be analyzed to determine effective quota policies.

When you configure quotas, you apply a default setting for all users and then click the Quota Entries button to configure exceptions for specific users/groups. In other words, when you create a quota entry for a user, the default setting no longer applies to that user. Because quotas are enabled on a per-volume basis, you may decide that you want to configure the exact same quota entries for another volume. To do this, click Quota Entries, choose the entries you want to use on the other volume, and then click Quota > Export. You can then enable quota management on the other volume and import the quota entries.

TAKE NOTE

When you enable disk quotas for a volume, they apply only to new users who have not placed data on the volume. If existing users already have files/folders on the volume, you have to add them as new quota entries.

When planning your quota strategy, consider grouping your users based on the amount of disk space you think they will require. For example, your marketing and graphic design staff typically needs more space than other groups. Set default limits that are not too restrictive for all users' accounts and then modify them for users who need more disk space. Consider growth requirements and increase as needed.

 ENABLE DISK QUOTAS ON WINDOWS 10

GET READY. To enable a disk quota, perform the following steps.

1. Right-click the **Start** button, select **Disk Management.**

2. When Disk Management opens, right-click the volume you want to enable quota management on and choose **Properties.**

3. Click the **Quota** tab and then click **Enable quota management.**

    Do not click the Deny disk space to users exceeding quota limit option. If you don't select this option, you can audit how the volume is being consumed without restricting access to users who exceed the quota limit.

4. Select **Limit disk space to** and type **300** in the field provided. Click the arrow to select **MB.**

5. For the Set warning level to setting, type **250** in the field provided. Click the arrow to select **MB.**

6. In the Select the quota logging options for this volume section, select both **Log event when a user exceeds their quota limit** and **Log event when a user exceeds their warning level.**

7. Click **OK.**

8. After reading the disk quota message, click **OK.**

9. Right-click the volume you enabled quota management on and choose **Properties.**

10. Click the **Quota** tab and then click **Quota Entries** to see whether any user accounts are currently reaching their limits.

11. On the top menu, click **Quota.** (The Export option can be used to export your quota settings to another NTFS volume; do not export at this time.)

12. Click **Quota > Close** to exit the Quota Entries screen.

13. Remove the check mark next to Enable quota management to return your system to its original setting. Click **OK** to close.

14. After reading the message indicating the volume will be rescanned, click **OK.**

You can also use Group Policy to manage disk quotas on selected computers at the site, domain, or organizational unit (OU) level. This policy can be found in the Computer Configuration\Administrative Templates\System\Disk Quotas section of a Group Policy. On Windows 10, these are the six disk quota settings you can use:

- **Enable disk quotas**: Turns on disk quota management on all NTFS volumes of the computer and users cannot turn it off.

- **Enforce disk quota limit**: Determines whether disk quota limits are enforced and prevents the user from changing the setting.

- **Specify default quota limit and warning level**: Specifies the default disk quota limit and warning level for all new users as soon as they write to the volume. It does not affect disk-quota limits for current users. The policy settings here determine how much disk space can be used by each user on each of the NTFS file system volumes on a computer. It also specifies a warning level.

- **Log event when quote limit is exceeded**: This setting determines whether the system records an event in the local Application log when users reach their disk quota limit.
- **Log event when quota warning level is exceeded**: This setting determines whether the system records an event in the Application log when users reach their disk quota warning limit.
- **Apply policy to removable media**: This policy extends the disk quota policies in this folder to NTFS file system volumes or other removable media.

■ UNDERSTANDING THE WINDOWS 10 FILE STRUCTURE

THE BOTTOM LINE

As you manage and support Windows 10, you need to understand the Windows file structure. Table 8-7 shows the folders most commonly referred to when supporting Windows 10. Windows is installed in the C:\Windows folder. Programs are installed in the C:\Program Files and C:\Program Files (x86) folders.

Table 8-7

Windows 10 Folders

FOLDER	DESCRIPTION
C:\Windows	Holds the Windows operating system.
C:\Windows\System32	Contains many of the Windows system programs.
C:\Windows\CSC	Stores offline files.
C:\Windows\Fonts	Is used to add fonts. You typically use an install program or use the Fonts applets in Control Panel.
C:\Windows\Logs	Stores a wide range of logs.
C:\Windows\Winsxs	Stores all versions of components, including DLLs, so that the system, upgrades, and rollbacks are more reliable. As you install more updates, the folder grows quite large.
C:\Windows\Syswow64	Contains 32-bit binary files required for compatibility on 64-bit Windows.
C:\Users	Contains individual folders for each user who has logged on to the computer. It stores the Desktop, Documents, Start Menu, and Favorites.
C:\Program Files	Contains programs that are not part of Windows. On a 64-bit version of Windows, it contains 64-bit programs. On an x86/32-bit Windows, it contains the 32-bit programs.
C:\Program Files (x86)	Loads x86/32-bit programs on a 64-bit version of Windows.
C:\ProgramData	Is used by applications to store data for standard users because it does not require elevated permissions.
C:\Windows\Temp	Stores temporary files.
System Volume Information	Stores information and restore points; is a system folder that is used by the System Restore tool.

■ CONFIGURING LIBRARIES

↓ THE BOTTOM LINE	Libraries were introduced in Windows 7. A library looks like an ordinary folder, but is a virtual folder that simply points to files and folders in different locations on a hard disk, network drive, or external drive.

In Windows 10, a *library* is a virtual folder that can display content from different locations (folders, for example) on your computer or an external drive. A library looks like an ordinary folder but simply points to files and folders that are located elsewhere. You access libraries in Windows Explorer, just like you do files and folders.

To show libraries in File Explorer, select the View tab, and then select Navigation pane > Show libraries. Windows 10 includes the following default libraries (see Figure 8-9):

- *Documents library*: Stores word-processing documents, spreadsheets, and similar files.
- *Music library*: Stores audio files, such as those you've downloaded from the Web, transferred from a portable device (music player), or ripped from a CD.
- *Pictures library*: Stores digital image files.
- *Video library*: Stores video files.

Figure 8-9

Default libraries in Windows 10

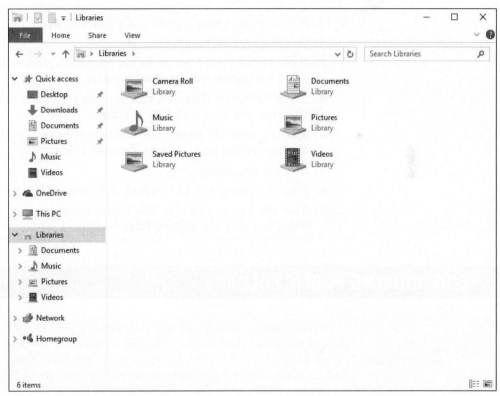

If multiple users share a Windows 10 system, each user will have his or her own separate libraries and folders, which are stored in the C:\Users*username* folder.

When creating a new library, you must include at least one folder within the library for organizational purposes. You can then copy, move, or save files to the folder in the library. You can add a location such as a folder on your C: drive, a second hard drive in your computer, or an external drive to an existing library.

ADD A FOLDER TO A LIBRARY

GET READY. To add a folder to a library, perform the following steps.

1. Click **Start > File Explorer**.
2. When File Explorer opens, locate and click the folder you want to include in a library. The folder cannot already be included in another library.
3. Right-click the folder, click **Include in library**, and then click a library (such as Documents, Music, Pictures, or Videos).

You can also include external drives in a library, as long as the folder is indexed for search or available offline. Make sure the external hard drive is connected to your computer and that your computer recognizes the device. You can't include content on removable media, such as a CD or DVD, in a library. Some USB flash drives devices don't work with libraries either.

To remove a folder, navigate to the library in the File Explorer navigation pane, right-click the folder you want to remove, and then click Remove location from library.

You can also create your own library.

 CREATE A LIBRARY

GET READY. To create a library, perform the following steps.

1. Click **Start > File Explorer**.
2. If the Libraries don't appear in the navigation pane, select the **View** tab and then select **Navigation pane > Show libraries**.
3. In the Navigation pane, left click the **Libraries** node to select it, right-click **Libraries**, and then click **New > Library**.
4. A Library node will appear with the default name New Library. Rename the Library to whatever you want, such as **Personal Library**.
5. Click the new library.
6. Since the Library was just created, it is empty. Click the **Include a folder** button.
7. When the Include Folder in New Library dialog box opens, navigate to the desired folder, and click the **Include folder** button.

CONFIGURING PUBLIC FOLDERS

THE BOTTOM LINE

The *Public folder* is an easy and convenient way to share files on your computer. You can share files in your Public folders with other people using the same computer and with people using other computers on your network. Any file or folder you put in a Public folder is automatically shared with the people who have access to your Public folders.

CERTIFICATION READY
Configure public folders
Objective 2.3

The folders that make up the Public library, are stored in the C:\Users\Public folder. The Public folders contains subfolders (Public Documents, Public Music, Public Pictures, Public Videos, and more) that help you get organized; however, those folders do not have any files in them until you or other people use your computer to add files to them.

By default, Public folder sharing is turned off, except when the system is part of a homegroup. To enable or disable public folders, open the Network and Sharing Center, and click Change advanced sharing settings, as shown in Lesson 6. When Public folder sharing is turned on, anyone on your computer or network can access these folders. When Public folder sharing is off, only people with a user account and password on your computer can access the public folders.

 CONFIGURE PUBLIC FOLDERS

GET READY. To create a library, perform the following steps.

1. Log on to **LON-CL1** as **adatum\administrator** with the password of **Pa$$w0rd**.
2. On the taskbar, right-click the **network status** icon and then click **Open Network and Sharing Center**.
3. When the Network and Sharing Center window opens, click **Change Advanced sharing settings**.
4. Under All Networks, select the **Turn on sharing so anyone with network access can read and write files to the Public folders** option.
5. Click **Save changes** and close Network and Sharing Center.

After you turn on Public folder sharing, local users can navigate to C:\Users\Public to open the public folders. If you want the Public folders to be available over the network, you can share the Public folder so that it can be easily accessed using a UNC.

■ CONFIGURING HOMEGROUP CONNECTIONS

When you are running Windows 10 within a domain, Windows servers and clients have several tools and mechanisms to share files and printers. Today, many households have multiple computers. A **homegroup** is a group of computers on a home network that can share files and printers. To protect your homegroup, you use a password. Similar to share permissions, other people cannot change the files that you share unless you give them permission to do so. Homegroups are relatively limited, when compared to folder sharing, because you can only share the contents of the libraries in the user's profile.

CERTIFICATION READY
Configure HomeGroup connections
Objective 2.3

CERTIFICATION READY
Configure HomeGroup settings
Objective 3.4

Homegroup is available with Windows 7, Windows 8/Windows 8.1 (including Windows RT 8.0/8.1), and Windows 10. Windows RT, Starter and Windows Home Basic editions can join a homegroup, but you cannot create a homegroup from them. For the system to use homegroups, the system cannot use a public network. If a system is part of a domain, you cannot create your own homegroup, but you can join one that is created by someone on your network.

If the system does not detect a homegroup, the Network and Sharing Center control panel contains a link that provides access to the Create a Homegroup Wizard.

 CREATE A HOMEGROUP

GET READY. Log on to Windows 10 using an account with Administrator privileges. Make sure that the system is configured to use the Private network location. Perform the following steps.

1. Right-click the **Start** button and click **Control Panel**.
2. In the search box, type, **Homegroup**. In the search results, click **HomeGroup**. The HomeGroup page opens as shown in Figure 8-10.

Figure 8-10

Opening the Control Panel
HomeGroup

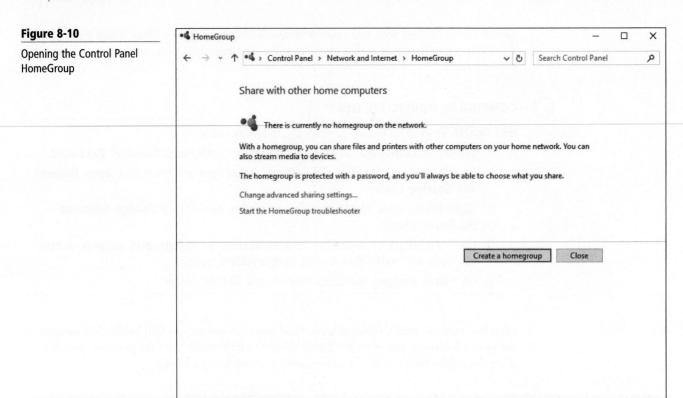

3. Click **Create a HomeGroup**.
4. When the Create a HomeGroup Wizard opens, click **Next**.
5. On the Share with other homegroup members page (as shown in Figure 8-11), select the libraries that you want to share and click **Next**.

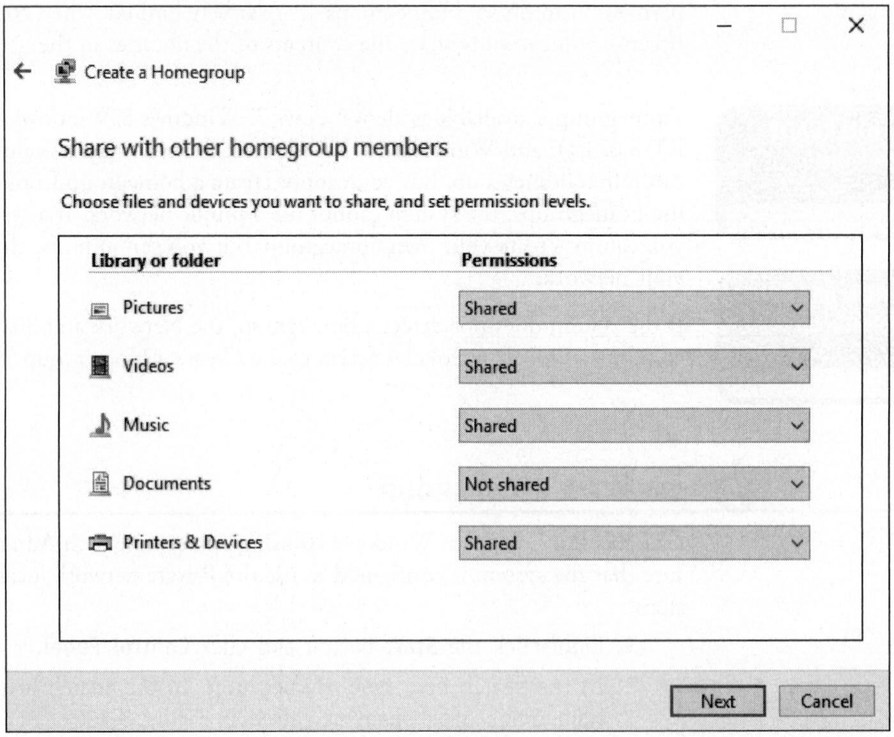

Figure 8-11

Sharing libraries and folders
with homegroup members

6. The wizard creates the homegroup and assigns it a password. Be sure to record this password and store it in a safe place.

7. Click **Finish**.

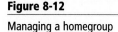 **JOIN A HOMEGROUP**

GET READY. Log on to Windows 10 using an account with Administrator privileges. Make sure that the system is configured to use the Private network location. To join an existing homegroup, perform the following steps:

1. Right-click the **Start** button and click **Control Panel.**

2. In the search box, type, **Homegroup.** In the search results, click **HomeGroup.**

3. When the HomeGroup page opens, Click **Join Now.**

4. When the Join a HomeGroup Wizard opens, click **Next.**

5. When the Share with other homegroup members page appears, select the libraries that you want to share and click **Next.**

6. When the Type the homegroup password page appears, in the Type the password text box, type the password supplied by the Create a HomeGroup Wizard, and then click **Next.**

7. When the You have joined the homegroup page appears, click **Finish.**

After you have created and joined a homegroup, you can manage the homegroup settings using the HomeGroup page, as shown in Figure 8-12. The Homegroup options include:

- **Share libraries and printers**: Select the libraries and printers you want to share in their entirety with your homegroup.

- **Share media with devices**: Use this setting to share media with all devices on your network. For example, you can share pictures with an electronic picture frame, or share

Figure 8-12

Managing a homegroup

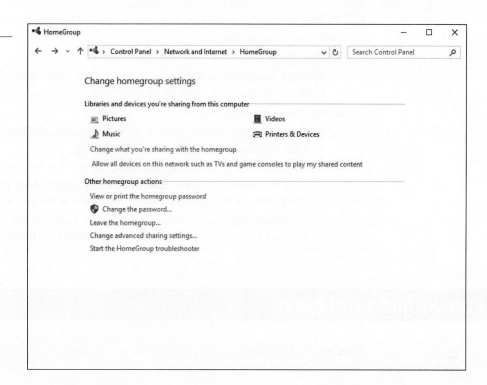

music with a network media player. Unfortunately, shared media is not secure. Anyone connected to your network can receive your shared media.

- **View or print the homegroup password**: View or print the password for your homegroup.
- **Change the password**: Change the password for your homegroup.
- **Leave the homegroup**: Leave your homegroup.
- **Change advanced sharing settings**: Change the settings for network discovery, file sharing, Public folder sharing, password-protected sharing, homegroup connections, and file sharing connections.
- **Start the HomeGroup troubleshooter**: Troubleshoot homegroup problems.

 REMOVE A COMPUTER FROM A HOMEGROUP

GET READY. To remove a computer from a homegroup, follow these steps on the computer you want to remove.

1. Right-click the **Start** button and click **Control Panel**.
2. In the search box, type **Homegroup**. In the search results, click **HomeGroup**.
3. Click **Leave the homegroup**.
4. Click **Leave the homegroup** and then click **Finish**.

To modify the default homegroup sharing configuration, you can select one of your shared libraries in File Explorer and click Share in the toolbar. Using the controls that appear in the ribbon, you can change other homegroup users' access to the library from Read to Read/Write. You can also limit access to specific homegroup users, or prevent anyone on the network from accessing that library.

 SPECIFY SHARED FILES AND FOLDERS IN A HOMEGROUP

GET READY. To specify shared files and folders in a homegroup, follow these steps on the computer you want to remove.

1. Click the Start button and click File Explorer.
2. Navigate to the file or folder (such as Desktop, Downloads, Documents, Pictures, Music, or Videos) you want to exclude from sharing, and then select it.
3. Do one of the following:
   a. To prevent the file or folder from being shared with anyone, in the toolbar, click the **Share** tab, and click **Stop sharing**.
   b. To share the file or folder with some people but not others, in the toolbar, click the **Share** tab, click **Specific people**, select each person you want to share with, and then click **Add**. Click **Share** when you are finished.
   c. To change the level of access to a file or folder, in the toolbar, click the Share tab and then select either **Homegroup (Read)** or **Homegroup (Read/Write)**.

■ CONFIGURING ONEDRIVE

THE BOTTOM LINE

OneDrive is a file hosting service that allows you to store and create files and folders and share them with other users and groups.

CERTIFICATION READY
Configure OneDrive
Objective 2.3

CERTIFICATION READY
Configure OneDrive
usage
Objective 2.3

OneDrive is a free (up to 1 GB), secure file-hosting service that enables your users to store, synch, and share files across devices using the cloud. Office 365 comes with 1 GB of OneDrive storage for each user. Additional storage can be purchased. You can also use it to synchronize files and folders that you select across multiple devices. If you forget to include a file within your synch folder, you can use OneDrive to connect to your remote computer, locate the file, and then upload it to your OneDrive space. This process is called *fetching*.

The public offering of OneDrive is intended for personal use and is easily comparable to Dropbox. You store files in in your OneDrive and access them from anywhere. **OneDrive for Business** is different from the public version of OneDrive because it is based on SharePoint. This allows team members to use it to store and work on documents with others. It can also help ensure that your users' business files are stored in a central location.

Accessing OneDrive from a Browser

You can access OneDrive from a browser using your Microsoft User Account from anywhere you have an Internet connection.

While OneDrive can be accessed from a browser at http://onedrive.live.com, OneDrive for Business is accessed from the Office 365 Admin Portal. After you are logged in to Office 365, you can click the OneDrive button to open the OneDrive for Business Console (see Figure 8-13), where you can upload, download, create, and share folders and files. If your computer is configured to support fetching, you can also connect to it remotely from the OneDrive for Business Console.

Figure 8-13

The OneDrive for Business Console

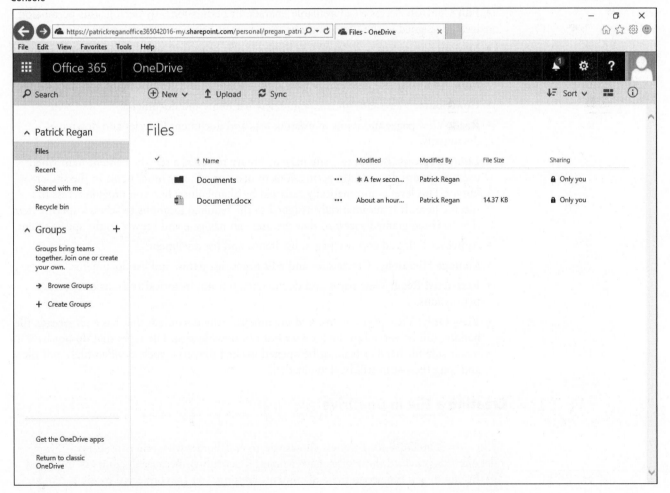

The following options are available:

- **Files**: Includes folders created on the OneDrive account. You can also see the number of files each folder contains by looking at the number located in the lower-right corner of each folder. Select any of these folders to open and display its contents.
- **Recent**: Includes a list of documents that have been recently created on the OneDrive account.
- **Recycle Bin**: Is a temporary holding area for deleted documents that can be restored.
- **Groups**: Displays a list of groups that include users with whom you frequently communicate and share documents. When you create a group, users receive emails asking them to join. After clicking the link, they are taken to the Groups page, on which they can communicate with other members via email and also view any files that have been shared to the group.

Understanding OneDrive for Business Permissions

Since OneDrive for Business is really an online SharePoint site, OneDrive for Business has the same permissions that you would find in Online SharePoint.

By design, all of the sites and site content in a collection inherit the permissions settings of the root, or top-level, site. If you assign unique permissions to sites, libraries, and items, those items no longer inherit permissions from their parent site.

The following are the SharePoint/OneDrive for Business default permissions:

- **Full Control:** Access to all available SharePoint permissions. By default, this permission level is assigned to the Owners group. You cannot delete or customize this permission.
- **Design:** Create lists and document libraries, edit pages and apply themes, borders, and style sheets on the site.
- **Edit:** Add, edit, and delete lists; view, add, update, and delete list items and documents.
- **Contribute:** View, add, update, and delete list items and documents.
- **Read:** View pages and items in existing lists and document libraries and download documents.
- **Limited Access:** Browse to a site page or library to access a specific content item when users or groups do not have permissions to open or edit any other items in the site or library. This level is automatically assigned by SharePoint when you provide access to a specific item. It is automatically assigned to the required locations to access a specific item that has been granted access so that the user can navigate and browse to the specific item.
- **Approve:** Edit and approve pages, list items, and list documents.
- **Manage Hierarchy:** Create sites and edit pages, list items, and list documents.
- **Restricted Read:** View pages and documents, but not historical versions or user permissions.
- **View Only:** View pages, items, and documents. Any document that has a server-side file handler can be viewed in the browser but not downloaded. File types that do not have a server-side file handler (cannot be opened in the browser)—such as video files, .pdf files, and .png files—can still be downloaded.

Creating a File in OneDrive

OneDrive/OneDrive for Business allows you to collaborate with others users on documents (provided those users have Microsoft accounts). Because documents are stored in the cloud, you can access these documents anytime you are connected to the Internet.

OneDrive/OneDrive for Business includes a light version of Microsoft Office apps (Word, Excel, PowerPoint, and OneNote), which allows you to create and edit documents directly from your browser.

CREATE A WORD DOCUMENT WITHIN ONEDRIVE FOR BUSINESS USING A WEB BROWSER

GET READY. To create a Word document in OneDrive using a web browser, log on to a Windows 10 computer with Internet access and perform the following steps.

1. Open **Internet Explorer**, open the **http://portal.office.com** page, and log on to Office 365.
2. Click **OneDrive**.
3. Click the **Documents** folder.
4. From the menu at the top of the page, click **New > Folder**.
5. Name the folder **Project Files** and then click the folder to open it.
6. From the menu at the top of the page, click **New > Word document**.
7. Type a few words in the document, as shown in Figure 8-14.

   As you type text, the Word document will be saved frequently.

Figure 8-14

Saving a Word Web document in OneDrive

8. To specify a file name, click **Document1** at the top of the window and then replace that name by typing **Project Scope**.
9. Click the **OneDrive** link (located at the upper-left corner, next to Word Online) to return to the main screen.

Uploading Files to OneDrive

In the previous activity, you learned how to create a file directly in OneDrive using the Word Web App. You can also upload files directly to OneDrive.

If you have existing files on your computer that you want to upload to OneDrive, you can use either of the following two options:

- From the OneDrive Dashboard, navigate to the folder in which you want to store the file. On the menu, click Upload. Browse to the file you want from your computer and then click Open.

- From the OneDrive app installed on your local computer, drag and drop the files you want to upload into the OneDrive folder. This automatically syncs with OneDrive. You can also configure OneDrive for the desktop to allow you to fetch files on your PC from other devices.

Sharing a Document in OneDrive

You can also share a document with others by sending it via email, posting it, or sending others a link to it.

When sharing documents, you have the following options:

- **Send e-mail**: Used to give individual users or groups permission to a file or folder. You can then remove permissions for a specific group or individual if necessary. When users receive the link via email and visit OneDrive, the file or folder will appear in their list of shared files. You do not have to know their Microsoft user account address. If they do not have one, they can create one for free after clicking the link.

- **Post to**: Used to share the link on Facebook, LinkedIn, or Twitter. Anyone who views the post on your network can forward the link. If you selected the option to allow recipients to edit the document, anyone the link is forwarded to can view and edit the file or folder.

- **Get a link**: Used to share the file with a larger number of recipients. For example, you could post the link on your blog or your website. You can also include this link in an email or instant message. When using this option, you can choose from the following types of links:

  - **View only**: Anyone who receives this link can see the files you share.
  - **View and edit**: Anyone with this link can see and edit the files you share.
  - **Public**: Anyone can search for and view your public files, even if you don't share a link, if you decide to make it public.

 SHARE A DOCUMENT VIA EMAIL

GET READY. To share the Word document you created in the previous exercise with others via email, perform the following steps.

1. From the main screen of OneDrive, click **Files > Documents > Project Files**.
2. Right-click the Word document you saved in the previous exercise (**Project Scope. docx**) and choose **Share.**
3. Type the email address of the person you want to share it with and, if necessary, type a message.
4. If you want the recipient to be able to edit the document, click the **Recipients can edit** option.
5. Click **Share** to send the email message.
6. Click **Close.**

Accessing OneDrive from the OneDrive Desktop App for Windows

> With the *OneDrive desktop app for Windows* installed on your local computer, you can automatically sync files and folders to the OneDrive cloud. You can then access your resources across multiple devices, such as computers and smartphones.

The OneDrive app is already built into Windows 10. When you install the app, a folder is created on your desktop automatically. Anything that you place into this folder is synced with OneDrive.com as well as with your other computers. You can access the folder from within File Explorer, drag new files into the folder, and choose the folders you want to sync on your computer.

TAKE NOTE

> While OneDrive and OneDrive for Business perform similar functionality, they are based on different technologies. However, by clicking the Microsoft OneDrive desktop app Account tab, you can add or define a personal (OneDrive) and/or business account (OneDrive for Business). Of course, while you can access both sets of files using the OneDrive desktop app, the two repositories are separate and you cannot access OneDrive from your OneDrive for Business account and vice versa.

 CONFIGURE THE ONEDRIVE DESKTOP APP

GET READY. To configure your OneDrive Desktop App running on Windows 10, perform the following steps.

1. From the Show hidden icons area, right-click the **OneDrive** icon, and click **Settings**.
2. When the Microsoft OneDrive dialog box opens, click the **Settings** tab.
3. If you don't want OneDrive to automatically load when you logon, deselect the **Start OneDrive automatically when I sign into to Windows** option.
4. Click the **Account** tab.
5. If you need to add a OneDrive account, you would click the Add a personal account button. To add a OneDrive for Business account, click **Add a business account**.
6. If you clicked the Add a business account, the Microsoft OneDrive window opens. Log on with your Office 365 account credentials (email address and password).
7. When the This is your OneDrive folder page is displayed, click **Next**.
8. In the page that asks if you want to sync files from your OneDrive, the Sync all files and folders in my OneDrive and Sync only these folders are already selected. Leave the defaults and then click **Next**.
9. When it says that your OneDrive is ready for you, click **Open my OneDrive folder**. A File Explorer window opens.
10. Back in the Microsoft OneDrive dialog box, click **OK**.

As part of the setup of OneDrive, the Let me use OneDrive to fetch any of my files on this PC option is enabled. This allows you to use OneDrive to fetch files from this PC. This process works when a file is in a folder outside of the OneDrive folder on your PC, or when the file is one that you did not configure to synch with OneDrive when you initially set it up. When a PC has been configured to allow fetching, you see it in your OneDrive Dashboard under PCs when you log on to http://onedrive.live.com.

FETCH A FILE USING ONEDRIVE

GET READY. To fetch a file using OneDrive, log on to a Windows 10 computer with Internet access and then perform the following steps.

1. Open **Internet Explorer**, go to **http://onedrive.live.com,** and then click **Sign In.**
2. Type your Microsoft User Account associated email address and Password.
3. In the left pane, click the remote PC from which you want to fetch files. Remote PCs will appear under the PCs section of the left pane.
4. If this is the first time you have attempted to connect to the PC, you will be presented with a security page. When the page appears, click **Sign in with a security code.**

    This option automatically sends a seven-digit code to the device you configured when setting up your Microsoft account. This could be your cell phone number or an email address you provided.

5. After you receive the code, type it into the field provided. The folders on your remote PC will appear in OneDrive.
6. Navigate to any folder and select a file that you want to upload. Notice that you have access to your entire PC. This includes all partitions as well as the DVD drive and any external drives attached to the computer.
7. Right-click the file and choose **Upload to OneDrive.**
8. When The selected item will be uploaded to: dialog box appears, double-click **Documents**, choose **ProjectFiles**, and then click **Upload.**
9. From the main screen of OneDrive, click **Files > Documents > Project Files** and then confirm the file you uploaded appears in the folder.

Configuring OneDrive Usage

> When using OneDrive for Business, you need to monitor OneDrive usage to see how much space you are using and to clean up space if you are getting close to your storage limit.

To view the total space used, click the settings (gear) button, and select Site settings. When the Site Settings page opens, under Site Collection Administration, click Storage Metrics. The storage metrics is displayed as shown in Figure 8-15. You can also download a script that will create OneDrive for Business Usage reports for all users.

 VIEW ONEDRIVE STORAGE METRICS

GET READY. To view OneDrive storage metrics, log on to a Windows 10 computer with Internet access and then perform the following steps.

1. Open **Internet Explorer**, open **portal.office.com** website, and login with your Office 365 credentials.
2. Click the **OneDrive** icon.
3. At the top of the page, click the **settings (gear)** button, and click **Site settings.**
4. Under Site Collection Administration, click **Storage Metrics.**

Figure 8-15

Viewing storage metrics

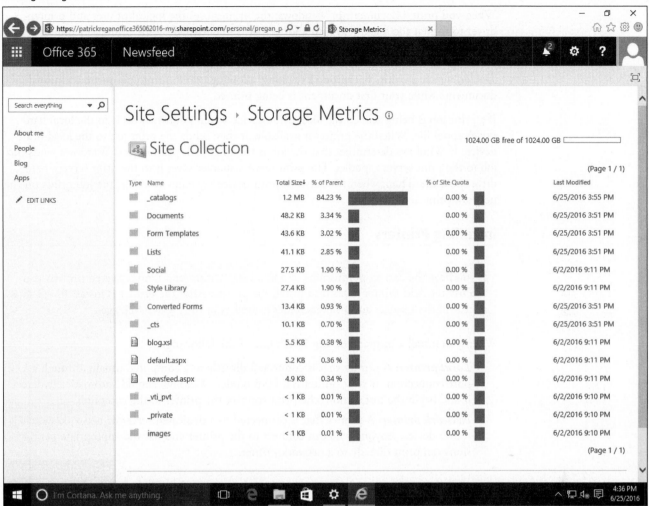

■ CONFIGURING PRINTERS

THE BOTTOM LINE

One basic network service is network printing, in which multiple users can share the same printer. This is a cost-effective solution when you have multiple employees in different locations

As an administrator, you can install two types of printers: local and network. Today, most local printers are connected using USB ports, although some legacy printers may use parallel or serial ports. Network printers can be shared local printers or printers that connect directly to a network with built-in network cards or expandable jet-direct cards.

When you install a physical printer, which Microsoft calls a ***print device***, you must first connect the printer and turn it on. Next, you need to create a logical printer (Microsoft refers to this as the ***printer***), which provides a software interface between the print device and the applications. When you create the printer, you also load a print driver that acts as a translator for Windows and the programs running on Windows so that they do not have to worry about the specifics of the printer's hardware and printer language.

When you print a document in Windows, the printer uses the logical printer and printer driver to format the document into a form that is understood by the printer, including rendering it into a printer language such as HP's Printer Control Language or Adobe's PostScript to create an enhanced metafile (EMF). The print job is then sent to the local spooler, which provides background printing, allowing you to print and queue additional documents while your first document is being printed.

If a print job is being sent to the local print device, it temporarily saves it to the local hard drive's spool file. When the printer is available, it then sends the print job to the local print device. If Windows determines that the job is for a network print device, Windows sends the job to the print server's spooler. The print server's spooler saves it to the print server's hard drive spool file. Then, when the network print device becomes available, the job prints on the network print device.

Installing Printers

If you have the correct permissions to add a local printer or a remote shared printer, you can use the Add Printer Wizard to install the printer. After the printer is installed, it will appear in the Devices and Printers folder as well as in the Device Manager.

When you install a printer, you can install one of the following:

- **Local printer**: A printer that is connected directly to a computer, usually through a USB port/connection. If your printer is a USB model, Windows should automatically detect it and begin the installation when you connect the printer to the computer.
- **Network printer**: A printer that is connected to a dedicated server or network/switch/router device. Anyone who can connect to the printer and has the appropriate permissions can print directly to a network printer.

 ADD A LOCAL PRINTER

GET READY. To add a local printer to a Windows 10 PC, perform the following steps.

1. Right-click the **Start** button and then click **Control Panel.**
2. Under Hardware and Sound, click **Devices and Printers.** The Devices and Printers folder opens, as shown in Figure 8-16.
3. To start the Add Printer Wizard, click **Add a printer.**
4. If a printer is not found, click the **The printer that I want' isn't listed** option.
5. On the find a printer by other options page, select **Add a local printer or network printer with manual settings** and click **Next.**
6. On the Choose a printer port, do one of the following and click **Next:**
   - In the Use an existing port option, specify the port, such as **LPT1 (Printer Port), COM1 (Serial port),** or **File (Print to File).**
   - Select **Create a new port,** and click **Next.**
7. On the Install the Printer Driver page, select the manufacturer and printer, as shown in Figure 8-17. If your printer is not listed, click the **Have Disk** button, so that you can navigate to drivers that you have downloaded or received with the printer. Click **Next.**

Figure 8-16

Managing Devices and Printers

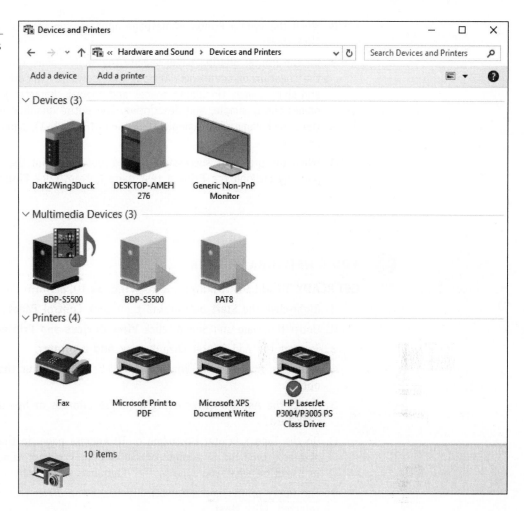

Figure 8-17

Specifying the manufacturer and printer

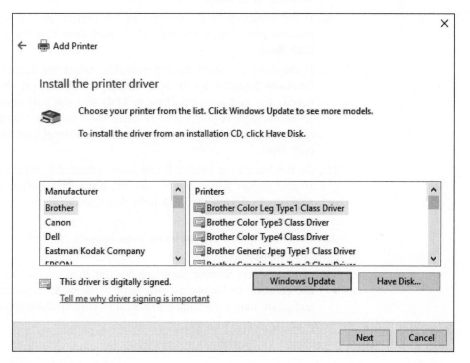

8. When the Type a Printer Name page appears, specify the name of the printer. Click **Next**.

9. On the Printer Sharing page, specify the share name. You can also specify the Location or Comments. Although Windows 10 supports long printer names and share names (including spaces and special characters), it is best to keep names short, simple, and descriptive. The entire qualified name, including the server name (for example, \\Server1\HP4100N-1), should be 32 characters or fewer.

10. When the printer is successfully added, you can print the standard Windows test page by clicking the **Print a test page** button. Click **Finish**.

 ADD A NETWORK PRINTER

GET READY. To add a network printer to Windows 10, perform the following steps.

1. Right-click the **Start** button and then click **Control Panel**.

2. Under Hardware and Sound, click **View Devices and Printers**.

3. To start the Add Printer Wizard, click **Add a printer**.

4. When the Add a Device Wizard opens, click the **Printer that I want isn't listed** option.

5. Select the **Add a Printer using a TCP/IP address or hostname** option and click Next.

6. On the Type a Printer Hostname or IP Address page, in the Hostname or IP address text box, type the IP address of the printer. The Port name will automatically fill in based on what you type in the Hostname or IP address text box.

7. The Query printer and automatically select the driver to use option is already selected. Click **Next**.

8. If the device could not connect to the printer, on the Additional port information required page, select the type of network card that the printer is connected to. Click **Next**.

9. If the correct network card is available, select the Custom option, to open the Configure Standard TCP/IP Port Monitor dialog box (as shown in Figure 8-18. Then specify the port protocol (**Raw** or **LPR**) and the port number. The default TCP/IP printer port is port 9100. To close the Configure Standard TCP/IP Port Monitor dialog box, click **OK**. Then back on the Additional port information required page, click **Next**.

10. On the Install the Printer Driver page, select the manufacturer and printer. If your printer is not listed, click the **Have Disk** button so you can navigate to drivers that you have downloaded or received with the printer. Click **Next**.

11. When the Type a Printer Name page appears, specify the name of the printer. Click **Next**.

12. On the Printer Sharing page, specify the share name. You can also specify the Location or Comments. Although Windows 10 supports long printer names and share names (including spaces and special characters), it is best to keep

Figure 8-18

Specifying TCP/IP Port Monitor settings

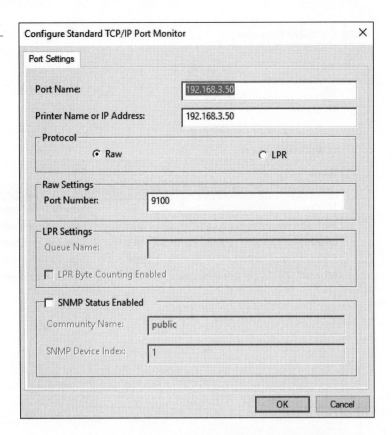

names short, simple, and descriptive. The entire qualified name, including the server name (for example, \\Server1\HP4100N-1), should be 32 characters or fewer.

13. When the printer is successfully added, you can print the standard Windows test page by clicking the **Print a test page** button. Click **Finish**.

When you install a printer, the printer that you just added will become the default printer. To make your printer the default printer, right-click the printer, and click Set as default printer.

Windows can provide a driver to the clients if the driver is loaded on the server. Because Windows 10 is available in 32-bit and 64-bit editions, many companies have a mix of 32-bit and 64-bit computers. If other Windows clients connect to the printer on your local computer, Windows can provide 32-bit and 64-bit print drivers to those clients.

 ADD ADDITIONAL PRINT DRIVERS

GET READY. To add additional print drivers in Windows 10, perform the following steps.

1. Right-click the **Start** button and then click **Control Panel.**
2. Under Hardware and Sound, click **View Devices and Printers**.
3. Click any printer, and click the **Print server properties** option.
4. When the Print Server Properties dialog box opens, select the **Drivers** tab, as shown in Figure 8-19.

Figure 8-19

Managing printer drivers

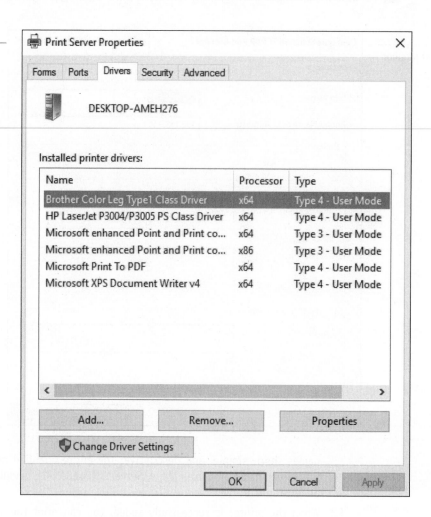

5. Click **Change Driver Settings**.
6. Click the **Add** button.
7. When the Welcome to the Add Printer Driver Wizard opens, click **Next**.
8. On the Processor Selection page, select the appropriate processor (x64 and/or x86), and then click **Next**.
9. On the Install the Printer Driver page, select the manufacturer and printer. If your printer is not listed, click the **Have Disk** button so you can navigate to drivers that you have downloaded or received with the printer. Click **Next**.
10. When the wizard is complete, click **Finish**.

TAKE NOTE   You can also use Group Policy to install and configure printers.

You can also install and configure printers from Windows 10 Settings, specifically Devices > Printers & scanners. If you don't want the default printer to be the last used printer, you can turn off the appropriate setting.

Understanding Printer Properties

With most printers, you have a wide range of options. Although these options vary from printer to printer, they are easily accessible by right-clicking the printer in the Devices and Printers folder and selecting Printer Properties.

When you open Printer Properties (Figure 8-20), you will find the following options:

- **General tab**: Allows you to configure the printer name, location, and comments and to print a test page. In addition, if you click the Printing Preferences button on the General tab, the default paper size, paper tray, print quality/resolution, pages per sheet, print order (such as front to back or back to front), and number of copies will display. The actual options that are available will vary depending on your printer.

- **Sharing tab**: Allows you to share a printer. You can also publish the printer in Active Directory if you chose the List in the directory option. Because a printer on a server can be used by other clients connected to the network, you can add additional drivers by clicking the Additional Drivers button. When sharing a printer, you are using TCP ports 139 and 445 and UDP ports 137 and 138.

Figure 8-20

Printer Properties

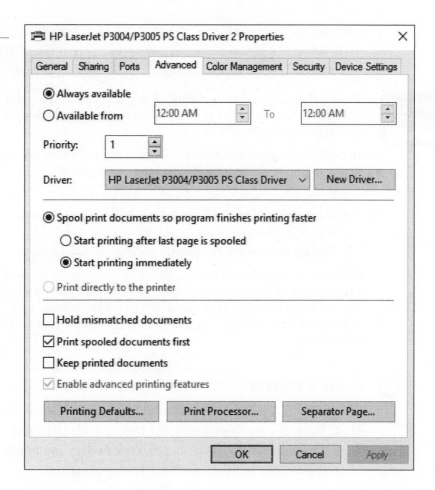

- **Ports tab**: Allows you to specify which port (physical or TCP/IP) the printer will use as well as create new TCP/IP ports.
- **Advanced tab**: Allows you to configure the driver to use with the printer, the priority of the printer, when the printer is available, and how print jobs are spooled.
- **Security tab**: Allows you to specify the permissions for the printer.
- **Device Settings tab**: Allows you to configure the trays, font substitution, and other hardware settings.

Some printers may have additional tabs such as Color Management.

If you right-click a printer, and select Printing preferences, you can specify the following default settings when you print a document:

- Orientation (Portrait or Landscape)
- The type of paper or paper tray
- Black & White or Color

You can click the Advanced button to specify other advanced default settings, such as number of copies, print quality, page order, watermark, and sleep time settings.

Configuring Printer Sharing

Printers are considered objects. Therefore, as with NTFS files and folders, you can assign permissions to a printer so that you can specify who can use the printer, who can manage the printer, and who can manage the print jobs.

When you open the printer properties dialog box, you can configure sharing using the Sharing tab. You can change the share name and specify whether you want to render the print jobs on the client computer or not.

To configure the print sharing permissions, click the Security tab, as shown in Figure 8-21. Windows 10 provides three levels of **printer permissions**:

- **Print**: Allows users to send documents to the printer.
- **Manage this printer**: Allows users to modify printer settings and configurations, including the ACL itself.
- **Manage documents**: Provides the ability to cancel, pause, resume, or restart a print job.

By default, the Print permission is assigned to the Everyone group. If you need to restrict who can print to the printer, you remove the Everyone group and add another group or user and assign the Allow print permission to the group or user. Of course, it is still recommended that you use groups instead of users. As with file permissions, you can also deny print permissions.

 SHARE A PRINTER

GET READY. To share a printer in Windows 10, perform the following steps.

1. Right-click the **Start** button and then click **Control Panel**.
2. Under Hardware and Sound, click **View Devices and Printers**.
3. Right-click the printer, and click **Printer properties**.
4. To share a printer, click the **Sharing** tab.

Figure 8-21

Printer permissions

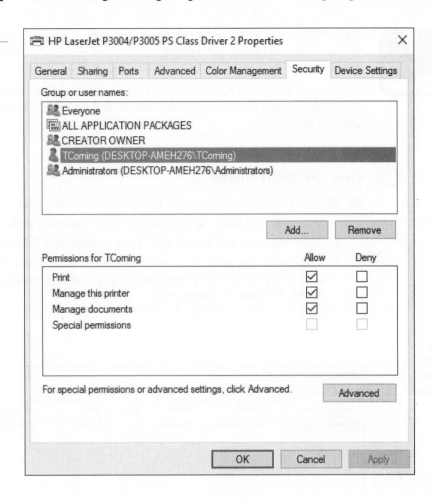

5. If you need to share the printer, select the **Share this printer** option, and in the Share name text box, specify the share name of the printer.

6. Click the **Security** tab.

7. To add a group or user, click the **Add** button.

8. When the Select Users, Computers, Service Accounts, or Groups dialog box opens, in the Enter the object names to select, type the name of the user or group. Click **OK.**

9. Back on the Security tab, select the user or group.

10. Specify the print permissions for the user or group and click **OK.**

Monitoring and Managing Printers

The *print spooler* is an executable file that manages the printing process, which includes retrieving the location of the correct print driver, loading the driver, creating the individual print jobs, and scheduling the print jobs for printing.

A ***print job*** is a file or set of files that have been sent to a printer. The printer then processes the file or files, and prints the document. The print job specifies which printer it is supposed to print to, the media size, the number of copies, and the priority.

On occasion, you might accidentally send a print job that you didn't mean to, or you might decide that it is not necessary to print a job. In that situation, you need to delete the print job from the print queue.

⊕ **VIEW THE PRINT QUEUE**

GET READY. To view the print queue, perform the following steps.

1. Right-click the **Start** button and then click **Control Panel.**

2. Under Hardware and Sound, click **View Devices and Printers.**

3. Double-click the printers for which you want to view the print jobs waiting to print or right-click the printer and click **See what's printing.** The document queue opens, as shown in Figure 8-22.

Figure 8-22

Viewing the print queue

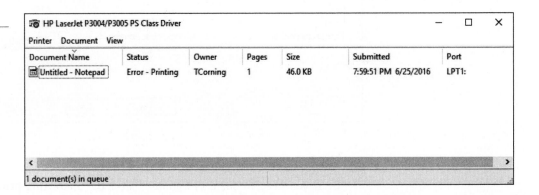

The print queue shows information about a document, such as print status, owner, and number of pages to be printed. To pause a document, open the print queue, right-click on the document you want to pause, and select Pause. If you want to stop printing the document, right-click on the document that you want to stop printing and select Cancel. If you want to cancel the printing of more than one document, hold down the Ctrl key, select each document, right-click, and then select Cancel.

By default, all users can pause, resume, restart, and cancel their own documents. To manage documents that are printed by other users, however, you must have the Allow manage documents permissions.

When the print device is available, the spooler retrieves the next print job and sends it to the print device. By default, the spool folder is located at C:\Windows\\System32\Spool\Printers. If you have a server that handles a large number of print jobs or several large print jobs, make sure the drive where the spool folder is has sufficient disk space.

⊕ CHANGE THE LOCATION OF THE SPOOL FOLDER

GET READY. To change the location of the spool folder in Windows 10, perform the following steps.

1. Right-click the **Start** button and then click **Control Panel.**
2. Under Hardware and Sound, click **View Devices and Printers.**
3. Click a printer and select the **Print server properties** button.
4. Click the **Advanced** tab.
5. Click the **Change Advanced Settings** button.
6. On the Advanced tab (shown in Figure 8-23), specify the new location and then click **OK.**

Figure 8-23

Configuring the location of the spool folder

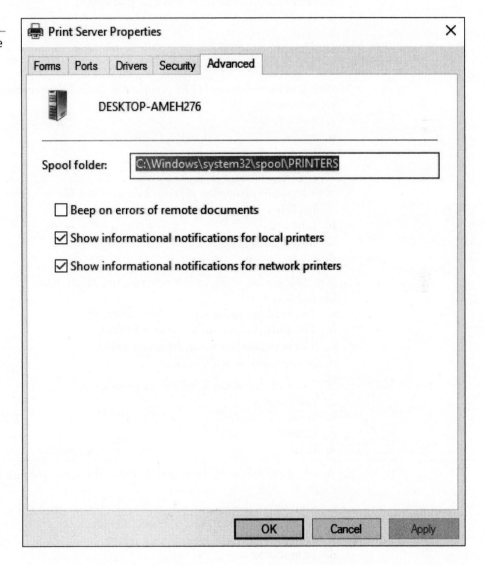

On occasion, the print spooler might freeze or become unresponsive. You can restart the print spooler by following these steps:

1. Open the Services console located in Administrative Tools.
2. Right-click Print Spooler and then click Restart.

You can also stop and start the service.

■ Knowledge Assessment

Multiple Choice

1. Which of the following share permissions on a FAT32 volume enable adding files and folders to a shared folder? (Choose all that apply.)
   a. Read
   b. Write
   c. Change
   d. Full Control

2. Which of the following NTFS permissions is needed to change attributes and permissions?
   a. Full Control
   b. Modify
   c. Read and Execute
   d. Write

3. Which type of permission is granted directly to a file or folder?
   a. Explicit
   b. Inherited
   c. Effective
   d. Share

4. If you copy a file or folder to a new volume, which of the following permissions will that file or folder have?
   a. The same permissions that it had before.
   b. The same permissions as the target folder.
   c. The same permissions as the source folder.
   d. No permissions at all.

5. Which of the following is *not* a share permission?
   a. Full Control
   b. Write
   c. Change
   d. Read

6. Which of the following terms best describes the actual physical hardware that prints data?
   a. Print server
   b. Printer
   c. Print device
   d. Print spooler

7. The logical printer that users can access in Windows is known as a _____.
   a. print device
   b. printer
   c. printer job
   d. printer spooler

8. Which of the following ports are used by TCP/IP printers?
   a. 443
   b. 23
   c. 9100
   d. 3000

9. To manage other people's print jobs, a user needs to be assigned which of the following permissions?
   a. Print
   b. Manage this printer
   c. Manage documents
   d. Full Control

10. Which of the following ports are used by shared printers?
    a. 80
    b. 139
    c. 143
    d. 443

11. Which of the following methods provides the easiest way to quickly share files and folders with other users on the network just by copying the files and folders?
    a. Advanced Sharing
    b. Quick share
    c. Public folders
    d. HomeGroup

12. A user has several folders on his computer that contain pictures that he accesses often. What can he do so that he can quickly access all of these pictures?
    a. Create a new homegroup.
    b. Make sure the files are available offline.
    c. Configure the folders so that they are indexed.
    d. Add the folders to the Pictures library.

13. In which of the following locations are the Public folders stored on a local machine?
    a. C:\Public
    b. C:\Users\Public
    c. C:\Windows\Public
    d. C:\HomeGroup\Public

14. Which of the following methods is used to prevent outside systems from accessing homegroups?
    a. Specify a homegroup password.
    b. Create a trust list.
    c. Configure private IP addresses.
    d. Add the system to a workgroup.

15. An administrator needs users to manage their own print jobs. What is the minimum printer permission needed for users to manage their own print jobs?
    a. Print
    b. Manage this printer
    c. Manage documents
    d. Full Control

Best Answer

Choose the letter that corresponds to the best answer. More than one answer choice may achieve the goal. Select the BEST answer.

1. A manager decided to implement cloud storage for his company so that users can access their files from anywhere. However, he needs to ensure that it is reliable and secure. Which of the following methods should be used?
    a. OneDrive
    b. OneDrive for Business
    c. On-Premise SharePoint
    d. Create a storage space

2. An administrator at a large corporation is responsible for Active Directory, Exchange, and File/Print servers. A user has a laptop running Windows 10 Professional. She is trying to create a homegroup so that her team can access her shared files easily. Which of the following is the most likely reason the user cannot create a homegroup?
    a. The location is set to Public.
    b. Windows 10 Professional does not allow users to create homegroups.
    c. Because the computer is part of the domain, she can only join a homegroup, not create a homegroup.
    d. Homegroups are disabled via a GPO.

3. Which of the following methods allows users on a home network to quickly and easily share files and printers?
    a. Enable Public folders.
    b. Create a universal shared folder.
    c. Use a shared USB device.
    d. Use homegroups.

4. A user's printer is connected to another user's computer running a 64-bit edition of Windows 10. What can be done so that 32-bit and 64-bit clients can use the printer?
    a. Create two printers on the client computer. One printer will contain the 32-bit driver and the other will contain the 64-bit driver.
    b. Create a translation job that converts 64-bit jobs to 32-bit jobs.
    c. Load both the 32-bit and 64-bit drivers for the printer on the client computer.
    d. It is not necessary to do anything. Windows automatically supports printing for 32-bit and 64-bit version clients.

Matching and Identification

1. Specify the correct order of the steps necessary to sharing a document from the Project Files folder using OneDrive.

    _____ Click Done.

    _____ Click Share to send the email message.

    _____ Type the email address.

    _____ Right-click the document and choose Sharing.

    _____ Click Files > Documents > Project Files.

    _____ Type your Microsoft user account and password.

    _____ Log on to a Windows 10 client computer and open your browser to http://onedrive.live.com.

2. Identify the minimum printer permission (Print, Manage this printer, Manage documents) needed to perform the specified task.

    Manage own print jobs

    Delete print jobs

    Manage this printer

    Print a document

    Manage this printer

Build a List

1. Specify the correct order of steps necessary to creating a homegroup on a system that is running Windows 10.

    _____ Open Control Panel and access the Homegroup page.

    _____ Select the libraries to share.

    _____ Record the secret password.

    _____ Click Create a HomeGroup.

    _____ Click Finish.

▪ Business Case Scenarios

Scenario 8-1: Configuring Permissions

You have set up a shared folder on a FAT32 volume that is set with the following permissions:

Share name: **MyDocs**

Share Permission: **Read**

Group: **Everyone**

After configuring the share, you notice that multiple people have added files to it. What is the problem and how should you address it?

Scenario 8-2: Managing Printers

You are an administrator for the Contoso Corporation and you administer several sites. These sites have a file server and several shared printers. You need to make sure that the manager at each site can delete print jobs that get stuck or have problems while allowing users to manage their own print jobs. Describe how to configure the printers for this scenario.

Scenario 8-3: Sharing Files at Home

You have a user who uses a laptop running Windows 10 Enterprise. When the user uses his work computer at home, the user needs to connect to his home computer running Windows 10 Pro to print documents, and to access some documents on his home computer. What can you do so that the user can securely access those documents and the printer easily?

Implementing Apps

70-698 EXAM OBJECTIVE

Objective 2.4 – Implement apps. This objective may include but is not limited to: Configure desktop apps; configure startup options; configure Windows features; configure Windows Store; implement Windows Store apps; implement Windows Store for Business; provision packages; create packages; use deployment tools; use the Windows Assessment and Deployment Kit (ADK)

LESSON HEADING	EXAM OBJECTIVE
Configuring Applications	
Configuring Desktop Apps	Configure desktop apps
Configuring Windows Features	Configure Windows features
Configuring Startup Options	Configure startup options
Managing Windows Store Apps	
Configuring the Windows Store	Configure Windows Store
Implementing Windows Store Apps	Implement Windows Store apps
Implementing Windows Store for Business	Implement Windows Store for Business
Using Deployment Tools to Deploy Applications	Use deployment tools
Installing Software with Group Policy	Use the Windows Assessment and Deployment Kit (ADK)
Sideloading and Deeplinking Apps	
Creating Provisioning Packages with ICD	Provision packages Create packages

KEY TERMS

app	Line of Business (LOB) apps	service
assign software to a computer	Microsoft account	sideloading
assign software to a user	Microsoft Software Installation (MSI) file	software program
Bring Your Own Device (BYOD) policies		Task Manager
	Program Compatibility Troubleshooter	Universal Windows Platform (UWP)
Certificate Authority (CA)		Windows Installer
deeplinking	provisioned apps	Windows Store
desktop apps	publish software to a user	Windows Store for Business

■ CONFIGURING APPLICATIONS

A *software program* (also known as *app*) is a sequence of instructions written to perform a specified task for a computer. Today, most of these programs are installed as desktop apps or Windows Store apps.

Desktop apps are traditional apps, such as Microsoft Office or Adobe Acrobat. The applications are installed using an .exe or .msi installer file, which is obtained from a DVD, over a network from a shared folder, or over the Internet from the vendors' websites.

Configuring Desktops Apps

One of the advantages of any modern operating systems is that you can run a wide range of applications. Because each application is unique, each program has its own settings. To determine the settings for a desktop application, you will have to refer to the documentation that is included with the desktop application.

CERTIFICATION READY
Configure desktop apps.
Objective 2.4

Since those applications are running in the Windows 10 desktop environment, there are centralized settings that you can configure each application. For example, you can specify which files are associated with an application, and you can configure how older applications interact with Windows 10.

CHANGING DEFAULT APPS

To start the program, you:

- Double-click an icon, which is usually a shortcut to the executable file
- Double-click a data file that is tied to or associated with the application

For example, when you install Microsoft Office, .doc and .docx files are associated with Microsoft Word. Therefore, anytime you double-click a .doc or .docx file on a system with Microsoft Office installed, Microsoft Word opens, which then opens the document.

 CHANGE THE DEFAULT APPS

GET READY. To change the default apps in Windows 10, perform the following steps.

1. Click the **Start** button and click **Settings**.
2. When Settings window opens, click **System**.
3. On the System page, click the **Default apps** vertical tab. To change the primary web browser from Microsoft Edge to Microsoft Internet Explorer, scroll down (as shown in Figure 9-1) and under Web browser, click **Microsoft Edge**, and then select **Internet Explorer**.
4. To reset the Microsoft recommended default apps, click the **Reset** button. After the applications have been reset, a checkmark appears next to the Reset button.
5. Click **Choose default apps by file type**.

Figure 9-1

Managing default apps

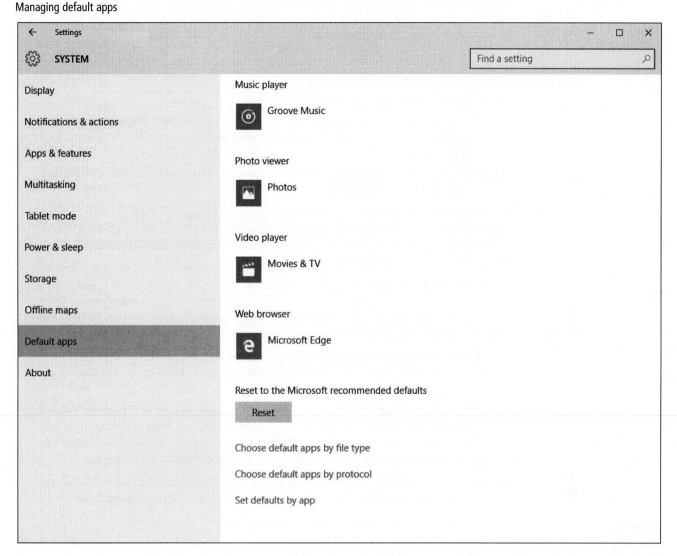

6. On the CHOOSE DEFAULT APPS BY FILE TYPE page, scroll down to .gif. The current program to open a .gif file is Photos. To change the default program for .gif files, click **Photo** and select **Paint.**

7. Close the Settings window.

DEALING WITH APPLICATION COMPATIBILITY PROBLEMS

Since Windows 10 follows the same architecture used in with Windows Vista, Windows 7, and Windows 8/8.1, most applications written for Windows Vista, Windows 7, and Windows 8/8.1 will run on Windows 10. There are a few applications that will not run. They are usually primarily security-class applications or applications that bypass the Windows application programming interface (API) to communicate with system hardware by performing low-level kernel calls. If an application does not run on Windows 10, even under the application Compatibility Mode, you can try to run the application under a Hyper-V virtual machine, a RemoteApp, or App-V.

Before you deploy Windows 10 in an organization, you must thoroughly test each application to make sure that it runs as expected. If it does not, you will then need to take additional steps to make the application run on Windows 10, or you will have to contact the vendor to get an upgraded version of the application.

Of course, as with any problem, when dealing with application compatibility issues, don't forget to follow basic troubleshooting:

1. Record any error messages that are displayed.

2. Use the Event Viewer to look for additional warnings or errors. If applications seem to be slow, you can use Task Manager and other performance monitoring tools, such as Performance Monitor.

3. Don't be afraid to perform research on the Internet and to check the vendor website or contact the vendor directly.

The ***Program Compatibility Troubleshooter*** is a wizard-based solution that users or administrators can use to automatically configure an executable file to use an appropriate Windows 10 compatibility mechanism. Thus, the troubleshooter is not a compatibility mechanism in itself; it is simply a method for applying other mechanisms.

To run the Program Compatibility Troubleshooter, right-click an executable file or a shortcut to an executable file and select Troubleshoot Compatibility from the context menu. When the troubleshooter launches, it attempts to determine what is preventing the program from running properly. The troubleshooter then gives you two options:

- **Try Recommended Settings:** Implements the compatibility settings that the troubleshooter has determined will resolve the problem and configures the executable to use those settings whenever you run it.

- **Troubleshoot Program:** Displays a What problems do you notice? page, shown in Figure 9-2, from which you can select the problems you have experienced. The troubleshooter then leads you through a series of pages that further identify the problem and configure the executable with specific compatibility settings.

To overcome compatibility issues, you can also manually configure the compatibility settings for an executable file. To access these settings, right-click the executable file,

Figure 9-2

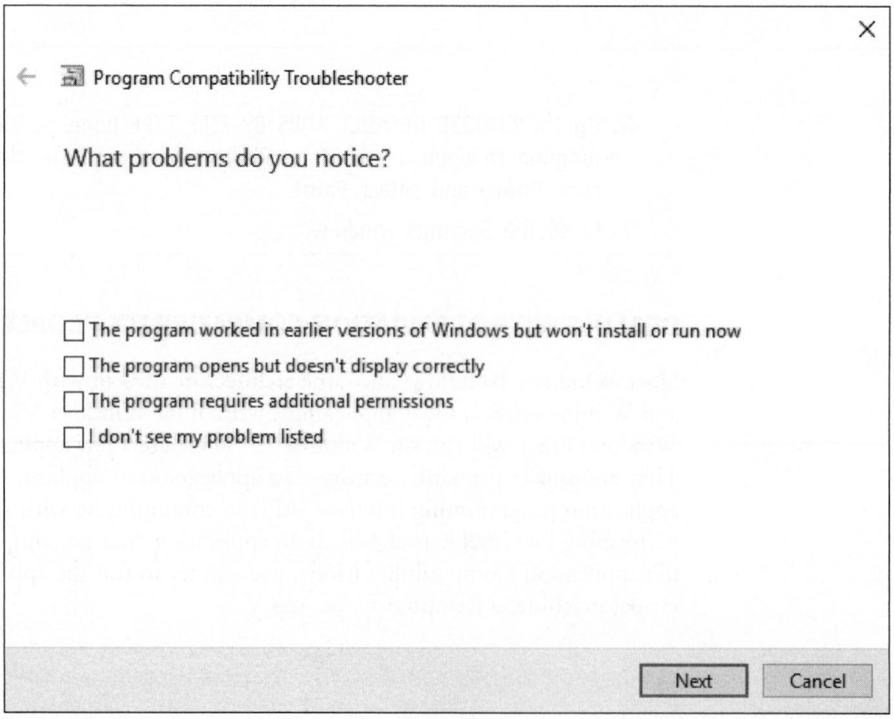

The What problems do you notice? page in the Program Compatibility Troubleshooter

click Properties, and click the Compatibility tab (as shown in Figure 9-3). You can then define the compatibility mode for the application, such as Windows 95, Windows XP (Service Pack 3), Windows 7, or Windows 8. You can also reduce the color mode, run the application in a 640 x 480 screen resolution, or run the program as an administrator.

Figure 9-3

Manually configure a program compatibility settings

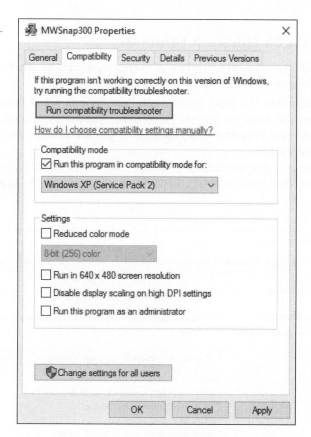

There are several other ways you can allow users to run the same application but with different versions. First, you can run Hyper-V on a client machine. Then you can create virtual machines that will run other versions of an application. You can also have users connect to remote desktop sessions, which include other versions of the application. You can also access RemoteApps, which are applications hosted on a server running remote desktop service, but appear as an application that is running locally.

Application Virtualization (App-V), which is part of the Microsoft Desktop Optimization Package (MDOP), is used to mitigate application-to-application incompatibilities or conflicts. To run virtual applications, you use the App-V 5.0 SP3 Sequencer, which converts an application into a virtual package. You then deploy the App-V 5 client, which runs the virtualized application on the computer. When you run the virtualized application on a local computer, the virtualized application runs in an isolated environment. Therefore, you can run different versions of the same application at the same time using App-V.

Configuring Windows Features

In Lesson 2, you learned how to install additional features that are included with Windows 10 via the Control Panel's Programs and Features. You can also use the Programs and Features to uninstall and change an installed program. Most Windows programs allow you to uninstall a program from your computer if you no longer use it or if you want to free up space on your hard disk.

In Windows 10, you can use the Control Panel's Programs and Features to uninstall programs or to change a program's configuration by adding or removing certain options. If the program you want to uninstall isn't listed, it might not have been certified for or registered with Windows. You should check the documentation for the software.

 UNINSTALL OR CHANGE A PROGRAM

GET READY. To uninstall a program or change a program in Windows 10, perform the following steps.

1. Right-click the **Start** button, and click **Programs and Features**. Alternatively, you can open the Control Panel and if you are in Category View, click **Programs** and click **Programs and Features**. If you are in Icon view, double-click **Programs and Features**.

2. Select a program such as Microsoft SQL Server 2012 Native Client (see Figure 9-4) and then click Uninstall. Click **No** to not uninstall the app.

Figure 9-4

Managing programs with
Programs and Features

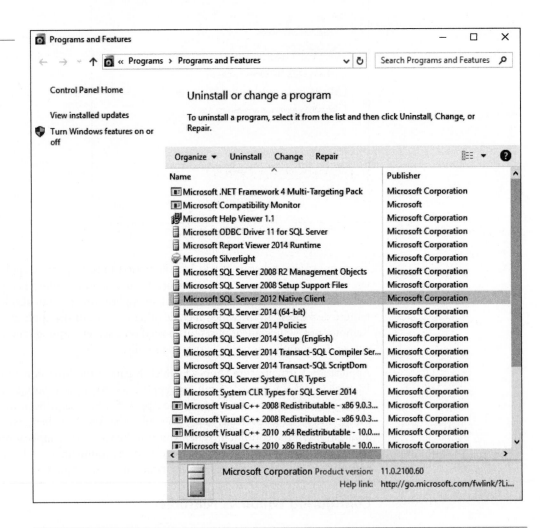

Some programs include the option to repair the program or to change the installed options, but many simply offer the option to uninstall the program. To change the program, click Change or Repair. If you are prompted for an administrator password or confirmation, type the password or provide confirmation.

Configuring Startup Options

Some programs start or have a component (program and service) that starts during the Windows boot process. Also, some of these programs allow the program to run faster, while others are required for the program to function properly. In some of these situations, you may not want these programs to start during boot up or continually consume resources at all times. Therefore, you need to know how to turn off or disable the startup programs.

Task Manager is one of the handiest programs you can use to take a quick glance at performance to see which programs are using the most system resources on your computer. You can see the status of running programs and programs that have stopped responding, and you can stop a program running in memory. For this lesson, you can also use Task Manager to manage your startup programs and services.

The Startup tab shows the programs that are configured to automatically start when you start Windows, as shown in Figure 9-5. You can disable the startup programs by right-clicking an item and clicking Disable. You can also access the properties of the program file for the application, and the location of the program file.

Figure 9-5

Managing startup programs

TO MANAGE STARTUP PROGRAMS

GET READY. To manage start up programs in Windows 10, perform the following steps.

1. Right-click the taskbar and click **Task Manager**.
2. When Task Manager opens, click More details.
3. To view the startup programs, click the Startup tab.
4. To disable a startup program, right-click the program, and click Disable.
5. Close the Task Manager.

A *service* is a program, routine, or process that performs a specific system function to support other programs or to provide a network service. A service runs in the system background without a user interface. Some examples include World Wide Publishing services, Server services, Workstation services, and Windows Event Log services.

The Task Manager Services tab displays all services on the computer that are running and not running. Similar to the Services console, you can start, stop, or restart services.

 MORE INFORMATION

For more information about Task Manager, see Lesson 12. For more information about services, see Lesson 15.

■ MANAGING WINDOWS STORE APPS

THE BOTTOM LINE

Windows Store apps is a class of applications for Microsoft Windows devices including PCs, tablets, phones, Xbox One, Microsoft Hololens, and Internet of Things and are typically distributed and updated through the Windows Store.

Universal Windows Platform (UWP) apps are a special type of Windows Store apps that can be installed on multiple hardware platforms, such as an Intel tablet that is running Windows 10 Pro, an Xbox One, or a Windows 10 Phone. The Windows Store apps differ from traditional applications in that they are designed to run in a single, full window display across multiple form factor devices (e.g., desktops, laptops, tablets). These devices can be touch-based or use a standard mouse and keyboard.

Configuring the Windows Store

The *Windows Store* provides a central location for you to purchase and download Windows apps that run on Windows 8 and later operating systems. The Windows store apps are special types of apps that work on computers that are running Windows 8 and newer. Windows Store apps do not run on Windows 7 or earlier versions of Windows. Windows Store apps tend to be smaller and faster than desktop apps.

CERTIFICATION READY
Configure Windows Store.
Objective 2.4

Windows 10 includes the Windows Store app, which can be accessed directly from the taskbar. In Windows 10, the Windows Store enables users to deploy both Windows Store apps and desktop apps. To browse the Windows Store, you do not have to sign in with a Microsoft account. However, if you want to download and install apps from the Windows Store, you do have to sign in with a Microsoft account.

A ***Microsoft account***, previously called Windows Live ID, is a unique account that is the combination of an email address and a password that you use to sign in to services like Outlook.com MSN.com, Hotmail.com, OneDrive, Windows Phone, or Xbox Live. When you set up a computer running Windows 10 for the first time, you have the option of creating a Microsoft account using an email address that you provide. The email address you use can come from any provider. After the account is set up, Microsoft will use it, along with your password, to help manage your settings across all of your PCs that run Windows 10. Microsoft accounts enable you to synchronize your desktop across multiple Windows 10 devices and provide a consistent experience when working with Windows Store apps. Purchased apps will be available from each device, feeds you add will be synced across all devices, and state information will be maintained, so you can start a game or read a book and pick it up later on another device. You can create a Microsoft account during the initial installation of the operating system or after the system is running.

When you open the Windows Store, you can click the Sign in icon (icon next to the Search text box). Also, if you click the Sign up button, you can also configure the following:

- **Downloads and updates:** Allows you to view the current downloads and allows you to check for updates for the Windows Store apps.
- **Settings:** Allows you to enable automatic updates, show products on the Live Tile, and stream-line purchases, and manage your devices that are connected to the Microsoft account. Figure 9-6 shows the Windows Store Settings page.

Figure 9-6

Managing Windows Store settings

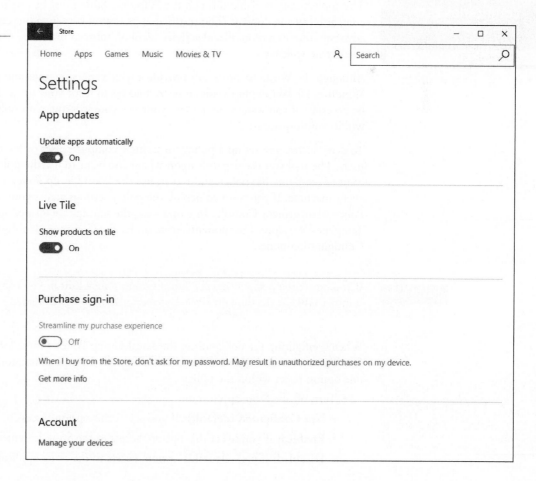

CONFIGURE THE WINDOWS STORE

GET READY. To configure the Windows Store, perform the following steps.

1. On the taskbar, click the **Windows Store** button.
2. To sign in to the Windows Store, click the **Sign In** button, and click **Sign In.**
3. When you are asked to choose an account, click **Microsoft account.**
4. Specify the proper credentials in the Email or phone dialog box and click **Sign in.**
5. Click the user icon, and click **Settings.**
6. To update apps automatically, ensure that the Update apps automatically is set to **On.**
7. To streamline your purchases so that you will not be asked for a password, ensure the Streamline my purchase experience is set to On.
8. To view your Downloads and updates, click the user icon again, and click Downloads and updates.

Implementing Windows Store Apps

Searching for a Windows Store app is quite easy. You just type what you are searching for (specific name or desired category), and Microsoft provides a list of available apps. Apps then install in the background. When the installation is done, the app appears in a tile on the Start page.

The applications available through the Windows Store must be certified by Microsoft for compatibility and content. The certified apps cannot contain adult content and cannot advocate discrimination, illegal activity, alcohol, tobacco products, drugs, weapons, profanity, or extreme violence.

Although the Windows Store can provide a wide variety of Apps and tools to enhance Windows 10, you might decide to restrict access to it for your users. This restriction might be necessary if you want to make sure your users are working with only authorized applications within your organization.

To deny access, you set up a policy for a single computer/user or for multiple computers and users. The tool you use depends upon where you want to use the policy. For example, if you want to configure the policy and test it, use the Local Group Policy Editor on a Windows 10 client machine. If you want to deploy the policy settings across your domain, use the Group Policy Management Console. In either case, the settings are located under the Administrative Templates\Windows Components\Store under the Computer Configuration and User Configuration nodes.

TAKE NOTE If you create the policy using the Local Group Policy Editor, you can export and import it into a GPO at the domain level. It does not have to be re-created.

When configuring the policy using the Local Group Policy Editor for a user (User Configuration\Administrative Templates\Windows Components\Store), there is only one option to set within the policy:

- Turn off the Store application:
  - **Not Configured (default):** If you select this option, access to the Store is allowed.
  - **Enabled:** If you select this option, access to the Store is denied.
  - **Disabled:** If you select this option, access to the Store application is allowed.

If you set the policy for a computer (Computer Configuration\Administrative Templates\ Windows Component\Store), the following options available:

- Turn off Automatic Download of updates:
  - **Not Configured (default):** Download of updates is allowed.
  - **Enabled:** Automatic downloads are turned off.
  - **Disabled:** Automatic downloads of updates are allowed.
- Allow Store to install apps on Windows To Go workspaces:
  - **Not Configured (default):** Access to the Store is not allowed.
  - **Enabled:** Access to the Store is allowed on the Windows To Go Workspace. Use this option only when the device is used with a single PC.
  - **Disabled:** Access to the Store is denied.
- Turn off the Store application:
  - **Not Configured (default):** If you select this option, access to the Store is allowed.
  - **Enabled:** If you select this option, access to the Store is denied.
  - **Disabled:** If you select this option, access to the Store application is allowed.

 RESTRICT ACCESS TO THE WINDOWS STORE USING A LOCAL GROUP POLICY

GET READY. Log into a Windows 10 computer with administrative credentials. In this activity, you will review the policy settings that control the Windows Store access for both computers and users by performing the following steps:

1. Click the **Start** button. Type **gpedit.msc** and press Enter. The Local Group Policy Editor opens.
2. Expand **Computer Configuration > Administrative Templates > Windows Components** and click **Store**.
3. Double-click the **Turn off the Store application** setting; the Turn off the Store application dialog opens. Click **Enabled**.
4. Attempt to access the Windows Store. Click the **Store** tile located on the Windows 10 startup screen. The message Windows Store isn't available on this PC appears.
5. Return to the group policy setting you enabled in Step 3 and click **Not Configured** to regain access to the Windows Store.

In some situations, you might have a computer in a public area (such as a library or kiosk) that needs to run just a single Windows app. In these situations, you can configure Windows 10 settings to restrict access to a single application.

When you assign access to a single Windows Store App, you restrict the application to a user account. When the user signs into the computer, that user can only access the assigned app.

 RESTRICT A USER ACCOUNT TO RUN A SINGLE WINDOWS STORE APP

GET READY. To restrict a user account to run a single Windows Store app, perform the following steps.

1. Click the **Start** button, and click **Settings**.
2. Click **Accounts** and then click **Family & other users**.
3. In the right pane, click **Set up assigned access**.

4. Click **Choose an account** and then select the account that you want to restrict.

5. Click **Choose an app** and then select the installed app to which you want to restrict the account.

6. Sign out of the computer to make the changes effective.

Implementing Windows Store for Business

To support larger organizations that have a need to control which apps are installed on the organization's computers, Microsoft developed the Windows Store for Business. The *Windows Store for Business* supports volume purchases of Windows apps, flexible distribution options, and the ability to reclaim or re-use licenses. You can also create a private store for your employees that includes apps from the Store as well as the organization's private apps.

Many organizations have policies in place that are designed to standardize the apps used on company-supplied computers. They do not want their users installing any applications they find, even if they are certified to work with Windows 10. *Bring Your Own Device (BYOD) policies* may also be in place that require you to control access to the Store. A BYOD policy defines the standards, restrictions, and procedures for end users who have authorized access to company data from their personal devices (tablet, laptop, smartphone). The policy also includes hardware and related software not approved, owned, or supplied by the company. In either case, as the administrator, you will need to make sure your strategy for accessing the Windows Store aligns with your company's policies.

In addition to determining your strategy for controlling access to Windows Apps and the Windows Store, you will need to consider the deployment of *Line of Business (LOB) apps*. LOB apps include apps that are critical to running the company business as well as apps that are unique to the company's main business. If you want to use the new Windows Apps format for your LOB apps, you can deploy them via the Windows Store or a process called sideloading. If you choose to deploy your LOB apps via the Windows Store, they must go through a certification process with Microsoft to ensure they are compatible with Windows 10 and meet the criteria for apps being deployed from the Store. The apps will also be available to the public, which may not be what you want. To bypass the Store requirements and make the apps available to your internal users only, consider sideloading them as part of your overall design strategy.

The steps to use the Windows Store for Business include:

1. Sign up for Windows Store for Business

2. Assign roles

3. Get apps and content

4. Distribute apps and content

 SIGN UP FOR WINDOWS STORE FOR BUSINESS

GET READY. To sign up for Windows Store for Business, perform the following steps.

1. Open Internet Explorer and open **https://www.microsoft.com/en-us/ business-store**.

2. Click the **SIGN UP NOW** link.

3. When the Sign up dialog box opens, in the Enter an email address, type the desired Microsoft Azure Active Directory (AD) account email address and click **Next**.

4. If the account is not a Microsoft Azure Active Directory (AD) account, you are prompted to create the Azure AD account by clicking **Sign up**.

5. On the Welcome page, enter the following information and click **Next**:

   Country: Specify the appropriate country

   First name: **<Your first name>**

   Last name: **<Your last name>**

   Business email address: Same email address that you used in Step 3.

   Business phone number: **<Your cell phone number>**

   Company name: **<Your Last Name> Corporation**

   Size of organization: **25–49 people**

6. On the Create your user ID page, enter the following information and click **Next**:

   Enter a username: **<FirstInitial><LastName>**

   Your company: **<Your Last Name>Corporation**

7. On the Prove. You're. Not. A. Robot. page, in the Phone number text box, type your cell phone number and click **Text me**.

8. In the enter your verification code text box, type the code that you received on your cell phone. Click **Create my account**.

9. Click **You're ready to go**.

10. When the Terms of Use are displayed, scroll down to the bottom. Select the I accept this agreement and certify that I have the authority to bind my organization to its terms and click **Accept**.

11. When the Welcome to the Windows Store for Business appears, click **OK**.

After you sign up for the Store for Business, you can assign roles to other employees in your organization. To add more people, click Settings > Permissions and then click Add people. You will be prompted to enter names or email addresses and to choose one of the following roles:

- **Admin:** Can configure account settings, acquire apps, distribute apps, and sign policies and catalogs
- **Purchaser:** Can acquire apps and distribute apps
- **Device Guard signer:** Can sign policies and catalogs

To manage your applications:

- To see your inventory, click Manage > Inventory, as shown in Figure 9-7.
- To add your own LOB apps, click Manage > New LOB apps.
- To show your order history, click Manage > Order history.

To distribute apps and content, you can use the following distribution options:

- After purchasing an app, you can send employees a link in an email message that they can use to install the app.
- Curate a private store for all employees. Add the app to the private store and have the users install the app when needed.

Figure 9-7

Manage inventory

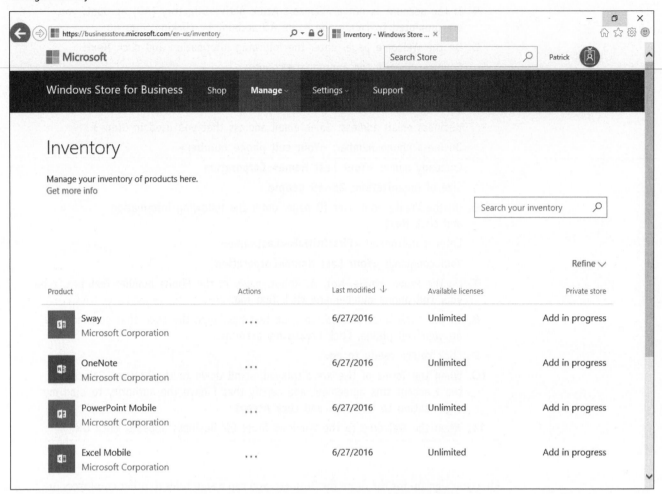

- Distribute the tool with a mobile device management (MDM) tool that can synchronize your Store for Business inventory and that is installed and configured in Azure Active Directory (AD).
- Organizations that use a Mobile Device Management (MDM) to manage apps can use a policy to show only the private store.

■ USING DEPLOYMENT TOOLS TO DEPLOY APPLICATIONS

THE BOTTOM LINE

Over the years, Microsoft has developed multiple methods to deploy applications. You can use tools that come with Windows domain controllers (Group Policy), you can implement tools with free tools such as Windows Assessment and Deployment Kit (ADK), or you can use more advanced technologies such as System Center Configuration Manager.

The simplest method of installing software is to manually install the application by downloading the installation files from the Internet, or inserting an installation disk into the drive to install the application. Unfortunately, if you have to install software on hundreds of machines, this can be a daunting task. Luckily, there are more automated methods.

Installing Software with Group Policy

If you need to install a program in Windows such as an antivirus software package or Microsoft Office that does not come with Windows 10, you often insert the disk, usually a CD or DVD, into the drive and the installation program will automatically start. Other programs are downloaded and installed over the Internet or over your organization's network. With some other programs, you may need to run a command, download and install using your browser, or double-click on an executable file such as file with an .exe or msi extension.

The *Windows Installer* is a software component used for the installation, maintenance, and removal of software on Windows. The installation information for software is stored in a *Microsoft Software Installation (MSI) file* in a database installation file that has an .msi filename extension. Besides performing installation, msi files can be used to self-heal damaged applications and to remove an application cleanly. Many of these applications can be automated and can be installed on multiple systems with Group Policy or System Center Configuration Manager, just to name a couple.

To deploy software with group policies, you need to take the following steps:

1. Create a distribution point on the publishing server.
2. Create a GPO to use to distribute the software package.
3. Assign or publish a package to a user or computer.

To create a distribution point on a server, you first create a shared network folder where you will put the Microsoft Windows Installer package and any related files that you need for the installation to succeed. Next, you set permissions on the share to allow access to the distribution package. Then copy or install the package to the distribution point. For most packages, you just copy the installation files to the shared folders. For other packages, such as Microsoft Office, you install the software to the distribution point (sometimes referred to as an administrative install), which allows for faster installations and customization. You need to contact the vendor or search the vendor's website to determine whether you should perform an administrative install.

Next, you should create a separate GPO to deploy the software. By using a separate GPO, you can disable the GPO or delete the GPO, and only the deployment of the software is affected.

When you deploy the installation via group policies, you can deploy the software to the user or the computer. Software that is installed for a user is not available for other users unless the software is also installed for the other users. When you install to a computer, the software is available to all users.

When you install to a user or computer, you can either assign software or publish software:

- *Assign software to a user*: The software is available on the user's Start menu when the user logs on. However, the installation does not occur unless the user clicks the application icon on the Start menu or a file that is associated with the application (for example, .docx then installs Microsoft Word) is opened.
- *Assign software to a computer*: The application is installed the next time that the computer starts.

- *Publish software to a user:* A program shortcut will be available in the Control Panel's Programs applet, or you can configure the application to be installed when a file that is associated with the application is opened.

An application cannot be published to a computer.

When configuring Group Policy to deploy applications, they must be mapped to UNC paths. If you use local paths, the deployment will fail. In addition, you need to be careful where you place the deployment servers and when the deployment will actually occur. Large applications can generate a lot of network traffic, which might affect local traffic and can greatly affect slower WAN links for remote sites.

When the software is installed using group policies, which uses the Windows Installer service, the service runs with elevated privileges. Therefore, no matter who is logged onto the system, the software will still be installed as long as the user has read access to the software distribution point.

When software is installed with group policies, the applications are resilient. If an application becomes corrupted, the installer will detect and reinstall or repair the application.

CREATE A NEW SOFTWARE INSTALLATION PACKAGE

GET READY. To create a new Windows Installer Package within a GPO on a domain controller running Windows Server 2012 R2, perform the following steps.

1. Log on to LON-DC1 as **adatum\administrator** with the password of **Pa$$w0rd**.
2. When Server Manager opens, open the **Tools** menu and click **Group Policy Management**.
3. Right-click the **Group Policy Objects** node and click **New**.
4. When the New GPO dialog box opens, in the Name textbox, type **SoftwareInstall** and click **OK**.
5. Right-click **the SoftwareInstall** GPO and click **Edit**.
6. When the Group Policy Management Editor opens, under the Computer Configuration or User Configuration node, open **\Policies\Software Settings**, as shown in Figure 9-8.

Figure 9-8

Opening the Software Installation node

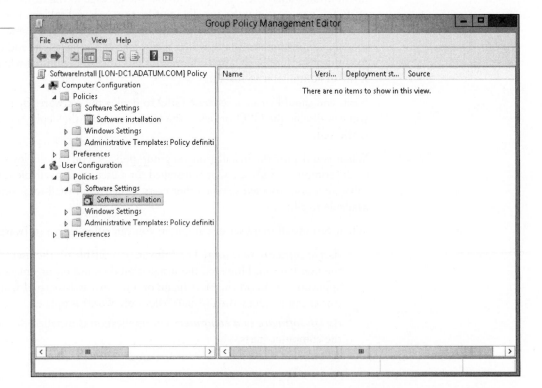

7. Right-click the **Software Installation** node, select **New**, and then click **Package**. The Open dialog box opens.

8. Navigate to the UNC path of the software distribution point for the Windows Installer packages (.msi file) and then click **Open.**

9. When the Deploy Software dialog box opens (shown in Figure 9-9), select one of the following:

   • **Published**

   • **Assigned**

   • **Advanced**

   The Advanced option is used to set properties for the Windows Installer package, including published or assigned options and modifications.

Figure 9-9

Selecting the deployment method

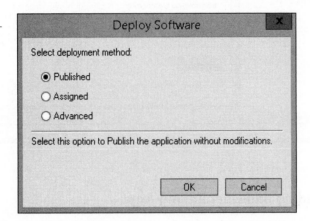

10. Click **OK.**

11. If you selected Published or Assigned, the Windows Installer package is added to the GPO. If you selected Advanced, the Properties dialog box for the Windows Installer package opens to allow you to set properties for the Windows Installer package, including deployment options and modifications. Make the necessary modifications and click **OK.**

12. Close the Group Policy Management Editor window.

If you selected the Advanced options when you created the installation package or if you right-click the package and select Properties, the Properties dialog box opens. You can further configure the package with the following tabs:

• **General:** Allows you to change the default name of the package and to specify a URL that points to a support Web page.

• **Deployment:** Allows you to change the Deployment Type, Deployment Options, and Installation User Interface Options (Basic or Maximum) (see Figure 9-10). The Advanced button contains additional deployment information, such as advanced deployment options and diagnostics information.

• **Upgrades:** Allows you to configure any upgrades that are applied to a package.

• **Categories:** Configures software categories in the Add/Remove Programs option of Control Panel.

• **Modifications:** Specifies the transform (.mst) files or patch (.msp) files that are to be applied to the package and order in which they will be applied.

• **Security:** Specifies who has permissions to install the software using this package.

Figure 9-10

Changing the deployment type
and deployment options

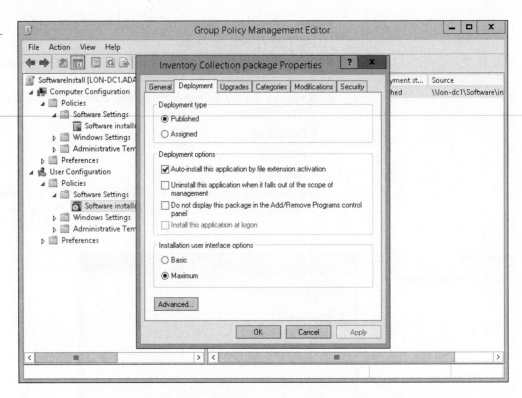

Sideloading and Deeplinking Apps

There are several ways in which you can install applications using Microsoft Intune. **Sideloading** is the process of installing Windows Store applications without using the Windows Store. **Deeplinking** identifies an application in the Windows Store by providing a link that will take the user directly to the app in the Windows Store.

In Lesson 3, you learned how to use the Deployment Image and Service Management (DISM) tool to capture an image and add packages to an image. DISM tool is also part of the Windows Assessment and Deployment Kit.

If you have access to the app installation files, you can sideload with Microsoft Intune. However, the application can only be deployed after the operating system is deployed. When you sideload an application, you can deploy an app to all Windows accounts on a device or to a specific Windows account on a device.

You can use Microsoft Intune only or integrate Microsoft Intune with System Center 2012 R2 or 2016 Configuration Manager. When using Configuration Manager, you have to install the Microsoft Intune connector. Before you can deploy or sideload your application to Microsoft Intune–managed devices, you need to upload the application into Microsoft Intune.

Besides using Microsoft Intune to sideload an app, you can sideload an app into online and offline images. If you have a Windows app that was created in-house and needs to be leveraged across your organization, you have two options:

- You can make it available from the Windows Store, which means the app has to adhere to certification policies and the processes used by all apps in the Windows Store. This is designed to ensure the app is compatible and meets the criteria of apps that are allowed to be deployed via the Windows Store.

- If you choose not to take that approach because you don't want the app available to the public but still want to take advantage of the portability and design of Windows apps, you can sideload the app using a tool such as DISM, PowerShell, or System Center Configuration Manager (SCCM).

To use sideloading, you need to make sure the following are in place with your computers:

- A Windows 10 Enterprise/Professional computer must be joined to an Active Directory domain.

- Group Policy must be set to Allow all trusted apps to install.

- The app must be signed by a ***Certificate Authority (CA)*** that is trusted by the targeted PCs on the network. A CA issues digital certificates that certify a person, organization, server, or computer is who it claims to be.

- A sideloading product activation key must be installed if the Windows 10 Enterprise/ Windows 10 Professional computer is not joined to a domain.

> **TAKE NOTE**
> You can sideload Windows apps only on Windows Server 2012 and above, Windows 8/8.1 Enterprise and above, and Windows 8/8.1 Professional and above devices that are joined to a domain.

The process for sideloading a Windows app is as follows:

1. Create a Windows Store app using Microsoft Visual Studio Express 2015 for Windows 10 or another similar tool. To do this, you need to have a developer's license.

2. Sign the app with a certificate that is chained to a trusted root certificate.

3. Confirm the computers that will be sideloaded are running Windows 10 Enterprise, they are joined to the domain, and the Allow all trusted apps to install Group Policy setting is enabled. If you need to sideload apps on Windows 10 Enterprise/Professional that are not joined to a domain, you need to install a sideloading product activation key. The key can be obtained from the Microsoft Volume Licensing Service Center (VLSC).

4. Sideload the app using the add-appxpackage "name of app" command if you want to make it available for the current user or use the DISM tool if you want to make it available for multiple users. DISM is a command-line tool that is used to service an online or offline Windows image. When Windows apps are installed via a Windows image, they are called ***provisioned apps***.

You can set Group Policy for a single Windows 10 computer by opening the Local Group Policy Editor and enabling the Allow all trusted apps to install setting, which is located in the following location:

```
Computer Configuration\Administrative Templates\Windows Components\
App Package Deployment
```

If you want to apply the policy to multiple computers, use the Group Policy Management Console (GPMC). The Allow all trusted apps to install Group Policy setting is located in the following location:

```
Computer Configuration\Policies\Administrative Templates\Windows
Components\App Package Deployment
```

It should be noted that the policy created using the Group Policy Management Console can also be applied to a single computer. The Local Group Policy is most commonly used in workgroup settings.

If you received an activation key from the VLSC, you can add it using the following commands from a command prompt window (cmd) while logged on as a local administrator. You will need to run this command from an elevated command prompt.

To add the key:

```
Slmgr /ipk <sideloading product key>
```

For example:

```
Slmgr /ipk ec67814b-30e6-4a50-bf7b-d55daf729d1e
```

To activate the key:

```
Slmgr /ato <sideloading product key>
```

After the computer is prepared, you can install the package on a per-user basis with the following Windows PowerShell command:

```
Add-appxpackage –Path c:\<directory>\<Winappv1.appx>
```

To update the package later, you can manually update the Windows app with the following command:

```
Add-appxpackage –Path \\<servername>\<share>\<Winappv2.appx>
```

> **➕ MORE INFORMATION**
>
> For more information on how to deploy images with Windows apps, visit TechNet.

Creating Provisioning Packages with ICD

In Lesson 5, you learned about using Windows Imaging and Configuration Designer (ICD) tool, which is part of the Windows Assessment and Deployment Kit (ADK), to configure an image or running system. However, you can also use ICD to deploy applications.

CERTIFICATION READY
Provision packages.
Objective 2.4

CERTIFICATION READY
Create packages.
Objective 2.4

*.appx and appxbundle files are file formats that are used to distribute and install apps on Windows 8.x and 10, and Windows Phone 8.1 and 10. Appx and appxbundle are the only installation methods allowed for Universal Windows Platform (UWP) apps. To deploy *.appx applications, you load the *.appx application using the ICD Deployment assets > Applications, as shown in Figure 9-11. While appx app targets a specific architecture, appxbundle supports multiple architectures.

Figure 9-11

Changing the deployment type
and deployment options

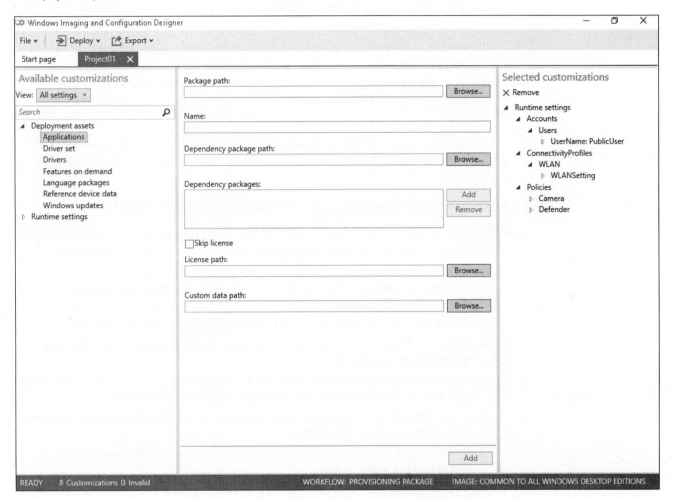

ACQUIRE OFFLINE WINDOW STORE APPS

GET READY. To acquire an offline Windows Store app, perform the following steps.

1. Open Internet Explorer and open the Windows Store for Business at **https://www .microsoft.com/en-us/business-store**.

2. Click the **SIGN IN** option and login with your Windows Store for Business account credentials.

3. Open the **Manage** menu and click **Account information**.

4. To see offline licenses apps in the Windows Store for Business, select the **Show offline licensed apps to people shopping in the store** option.

5. At the top of the page, click the **Search** icon and search for **PowerPoint**. From the search results, click **PowerPoint Mobile**.

6. For the Choose license type, select **Offline** and click the **Manage** button. If this is your first app download after creating an account, click the **Get the App** button, which will then take you to the Manage page.

7. Select the appropriate platform (Windows 10 desktop, Windows 10 HoloLens, Windows 10 phones, or Windows 10 Surface Hub). If you select Windows 10 desktops, specify the appropriate architecture (X86 or X64). For this exercise, select **Windows 10 desktop** and **X64**.

8. Click the **Download** button.

9. When you are asked to open or save the appx bundle, click the down arrow and click **Save As**.

10. When the Save As dialog box, navigate to the folder that you want to save the appx bundle and click Save.

In some instances, you will have to download an app license or a prerequisite package such as a framework package. Those packages will typically be available on the application page.

 CREATE A PROVISION PACKAGE FOR AN APPLICATION BUNDLE

GET READY. To create a provision package for an application bundle, perform the following steps.

1. Login to LON-CL1 as **adatum\administrator** with the password of **Pa$$w0rd**.

2. On LON-CL1, click **Start** and then click **All apps**. Scroll down the list, select and expand **Windows Kits**. Scroll down and then click **Windows Imaging and Configuration Designer**.

3. If you are asked to allow this app to make changes to your PC, click **Yes**.

4. When the Windows Imaging and Configuration Designer appears, click the **New provisioning package** icon.

5. When the New Project Wizard starts, on the Enter project details page, in the Name text box, in the Description text box, type **Project02**. Click **Next**.

6. In the New project dialog box, select **Common to all Windows desktop editions**, click **Next**, and then click **Finish**.

7. In Windows ICD, under Available customizations, expand **Deployment assets** and then click **Applications**.

8. In the Package path box, click **Browse**. Change the view to **Application Bundle (*.appxbundle)**, select the PowerPoint Mobile app bundle package (which was downloaded from the Microsoft Store earlier), and then click **Open**.

9. In the Name box, type **PowerPoint Preview**.

10. In the License path box, click **Browse**. Select the **PowerPoint Preview license file** and click **Open**.

11. Click **Add**. The app's name should appear in the Selected customizations pane.

12. Open the **Export** menu and click **Provisioning package**.

13. When the Build window opens, in the For the Owner drop-down list, change the value from OEM to **IT Admin** and then click **Next**.

14. On the Select security details for the provisioning package page, deselect the **Encrypt package** option and click **Next**.

15. On the Select where to save the provisioning package page, on the Select where to save the provisioning package text box, **type \\LON-DC1\Software\Project01 .ppkg**, and then click **Next**.

16. On the Build the provisioning package page, click **Build**.

17. When the package is built, click **Finish**.

You can then use the provisioning package to deploy the application.

SKILL SUMMARY

IN THIS LESSON YOU LEARNED:

- A software program (also known as app) is a sequence of instructions written to perform a specified task for a computer. Today, most of these programs are installed as a desktop app or a Windows Store apps.

- Since Windows 10 follows the same architecture used in with Windows Vista, Windows 7 and Windows 8/8.1, most applications written for Windows Vista, Windows 7, and Windows 8/8.1 will run on Windows 10. The few applications that do not run are usually primarily security-class applications or applications that bypass the Windows application programming interface (API) to communicate with system hardware by performing low-level kernel calls.

- Universal Windows Platform (UWP) apps are a special type of Windows Store apps that can be installed on multiple hardware platforms, such as an Intel tablet that is running Windows 10 Pro, an Xbox One, or a Windows Phone 10.

- The Windows Store provides a central location for you to purchase and download Windows apps that run on Windows 8 and later operating systems. The Windows store apps are special types of apps that works on computers that are running Windows 8 and newer.

- The Windows Store for Business supports volume purchases of Windows apps, flexible distribution options, and the ability to reclaim or re-use licenses. You can also create a private store for your employees that include apps from the Store as well as the organization's private apps.

- Over the years, Microsoft has developed multiple methods to deploy applications. You can use tools that come with Windows domain controllers (Group Policy), you can implement tools with free tools such as Windows Assessment and Deployment Kit (ADK), or you can use more advanced technologies such as System Center Configuration Manager.

■ Knowledge Assessment

Multiple Choice

1. Which of the following methods are available to deploy a Windows app that has been created within an organization and needs to be deployed to the users? (Choose all that apply.)
   a. Placing the app in the Windows Store
   b. Deploying the app using Group Policy
   c. Sideloading the app using Windows Intune
   d. Preloading the app using Windows To Go workspaces.

2. When preparing a computer to use a sideloaded app, which of the following commands activates a key?
   a. `Slmgr /ipk <sideloading product key>`
   b. `Slmgr /ato ec67814b-30e6-4a50-bf7b-d55daf729d1e /activate`
   c. `Slmgr /ipk <sideloading product key>`
   d. `Slmgr /<sideloading product key>`

3. You just created a runtime-analysis installation package, which is an executable file that needs to be installed on your client computers. Which of the following methods can be used to deploy the package to your users? (Choose all that apply.)
   a. Using Group Policy
   b. Using System Center Configuration Manager
   c. Storing the file on a network share
   d. Using removable media to distribute it to systems

4. An application will not run under Windows 10, even after running the Application Compatibility Wizard. Which of the following methods can be used so that the users can run the application? (Choose all that apply.)
   a. Using RemoteApp
   b. Using UE-V
   c. Using App-V
   d. Using Hyper-V

5. The OneDrive for Business application opens every time you start your program. You want to stop the program from automatically starting when you start your computer. Which of the following methods stops the program from starting automatically?
   a. Opening the Services console, and stop the OneDrive service
   b. Removing the Universal Windows Platform program
   c. Disabling the Microsoft account
   d. Using the Task Manager to disable the OneDrive startup program.

6. Which of the following is needed to download an application from the Windows Store?
   a. A domain account
   b. A local account
   c. A Microsoft account
   d. A hybrid account

7. Which type of software installation is used to add an icon to the user's Control Panel?
   a. Assign software to a user
   b. Assign software to a computer
   c. Publish software to a user
   d. Publish software to a computer

8. Which of the following applications can be deployed with Windows Imaging and Configuration Designer (ICD)?
   a. .msp
   b. .exe
   c. .appx
   d. .msi

9. You want configure your system to start the widget program when you double-click a .cml file. Which of the following should be performed?
   a. Reinstall the widget program.
   b. Run the Program Compatibility Troubleshooter.
   c. Open the Task Manager and configure the startup options.
   d. Configure a default app for the .cml files.

10. Which of the following provides a central location of Windows Apps that will run on Windows 8 and later operating systems?
    a. Certificate Authority
    b. iTunes
    c. Windows Store
    d. Google App Store

Best Answer

Choose the letter that corresponds to the best answer. More than one answer choice may achieve the goal. Select the BEST answer.

1. Which of the following can be used to give access your company apps needed by your Windows 10 Smartphones?
   a. Sideload the application
   b. Deeplink the application
   c. Load the application into the Windows Store
   d. Use the Windows Store for Business
   e. Configure the application to an appx application.

2. How can you prevent your users from accessing the Windows Store?
   a. Use a firewall to block access.
   b. Configure a GPO to turn off the Windows Store app.
   c. Use a DNS entry that points to another server.
   d. Delete the Windows store app from the taskbar.

Build a List

1. Specify the correct order of steps necessary for using Windows Store for Business?
   _____ Distribute apps and content
   _____ Assign Roles
   _____ Get apps and content
   _____ Signup for Windows Store Business

2. Specify the correct order of steps necessary for deploying software using a GPO? Not all steps will be used.
   _____ Create a GPO
   _____ Assign the deployment permission
   _____ Make the application files read-only
   _____ Package the installation program into an .msp file
   _____ Create a distribution point on a publishing server
   _____ Assign or publish a package to a user or computer

■ Business Case Scenarios

Scenario 9-1: Deploying Software to a Windows Phone

You need to deploy a software application to a Windows phone. Describe the best way to install this application.

Scenario 9-2: Deploying your LOB Applications

You need to deploy a new inventory programs to your users that are running Windows 10 on tablets, smartphones, and desktop computers. Describe how to deploy the application to everyone.

10 LESSON

Configuring Remote Management

70-698 EXAM OBJECTIVE

Objective 2.5 – Configure remote management. This objective may include but is not limited to: Choose the appropriate remote management tools; configure remote management settings; modify settings remotely by using the Microsoft Management Console (MMC) or Windows PowerShell; configure Remote Assistance, including Easy Connect; configure Remote Desktop; configure remote PowerShell.

Objective 3.5 – Configure Advanced Management tools. This objective may include but is not limited to: Configure and use the MMC * Additional Objective 3.5 topics are covered in Lesson 3 and Lesson 15.

LESSON HEADING	EXAM OBJECTIVE
Accessing a Computer Remotely	
Configuring Remote Desktop	Configure Remote Desktop
Configuring Remote Assistance	Configure Remote Assistance, including Easy Connect
Configuring Remote Management Settings	Configure remote management settings
	Modify settings remotely by using the Microsoft Management Console (MMC)
Using Microsoft Management Console to Manage Systems Remotely	Configure and use the MMC
Using Windows Remote Management	
Using WinRS.exe	
	Configure remote PowerShell
Using Remote Windows PowerShell	Modify settings remotely by using Windows PowerShell
Choosing the Appropriate Remote Management Tool	Choose the appropriate remote management tools

KEY TERMS

Computer Management

Microsoft Management Console (MMC)

PowerShell Remoting

Remote Assistance

Remote Desktop Connection (RDC)

Remote Desktop Protocol (RDP)

Remote Desktop Services (RDS)

snap-ins

Web Services for Management

Windows PowerShell

Windows Remote Management (WinRM)

WinRS.exe

■ ACCESSING A COMPUTER REMOTELY

↓
THE BOTTOM LINE

These days, there are large organizations that may be located throughout the country (or the world), have a mobile work force, and offer work-from-home capability. As an administrator, you need a way to access these systems remotely. Microsoft includes multiple tools within Windows that allow you to access clients and servers remotely.

These tools include the following:

- Remote Desktop Connections
- Remote Assistance
- Microsoft Management Console (MMC)
- Remote PowerShell

Configuring Remote Desktop

The **Remote Desktop Protocol (RDP)** is a proprietary protocol that was developed by Microsoft to connect to another computer over a network connection using the same graphical interface that you would use if you were sitting in front of the physical server. RDP uses TCP port 3389. Typically, you would access computers remotely using the **Remote Desktop Connection (RDC)**, which would allow you to connect to a Remote Desktop Session Host or to a Remote Application.

CERTIFICATION READY
Configure Remote Desktop.
Objective 2.5

Remote Desktop Services (RDS) allows users to access a remote computer just as if they were sitting in front of the computer. Within a Window, the user has a Start button, desktop, applications, and folders as well as access to local resources such as the user's local drive and mapped drives. Users could use the Remote Desktop Services to run applications that they can't run on their own machines. You could go one step further and use multiple servers to create an entire RDS infrastructure to provide a robust, resilient service for your users.

By default, Windows Server 2012 R2 and Windows Server 2016 can support up to two remote sessions at once, while Windows 10 only supports one remote connection. For servers, if you need additional users to access the server, you have to install a Remote Desktop Licensing server, and then add licenses based on either the number of devices that can connect to the RDS server or the number of concurrent users.

When planning for remote access, you must deliver a consistent experience to your users whether they connect over the local network or across low-bandwidth networks when working from remote locations. For users to be productive while working remotely, they must have access to their remote resources at all times. As part of your remote access design, review your current topology and ensure that you have redundancy built in not only to your devices (routers and switches), but also to your network links.

You need to ensure that the firewalls do not block access to the remote servers when access is needed. You typically would not make the remote access available through the RDP from the Internet unless the client is connected over a VPN tunnel or is using the Remote Desktop Services Gateway.

Although the RDP uses compression and caching mechanisms to limit the amount of traffic transmitted over network links, consider the different types of traffic that will traverse the network links. For example, if you are using virtualization for your operating systems and applications to support your remote users, expect to see large bursts of data when the operating system and applications are sent to the remote client. Make sure your core infrastructure is capable of providing the bandwidth needed by your users.

If you are concerned about protecting sensitive data sent between remote users and your servers, configure group policies to require the use of a specific security layer to secure communications during RDP connections. RDP connections can be configured to support 128-bit encryption (the maximum level of encryption supported by the client) or 52-bit encryption mechanisms. The option you choose for your design depends on the capabilities of your remote clients and the level of encryption needed to meet your specific data protection needs. In general, your design should use the strongest encryption supported by your remote clients.

RDP 10 is integrated with Windows Server 2016 and Windows 10. With RDP 10, you can deploy remote clients (laptops, desktops, and/or virtual machines hosted in a data center) as part of your remote access strategy.

To connect to a computer, you use the Remote Desktop Connections (mstsc.exe) program, which is found in the Windows Accessories folder. When the program opens (as shown in Figure 10-1), specify a server name or IP address, and click Connect.

Figure 10-1

Opening the Remote Desktop Connection program

CONNECT TO A REMOTE COMPUTER USING REMOTE DESKTOP CONNECTION

GET READY. To connect to a remote computer using Remote Desktop Connection, perform the following steps.

1. Log on to a Windows 10 computer.
2. Click the **Start** button and type **remote desktop**. From the search results, click **Remote Desktop Connection**.
3. In the Computer text box, type the computer name or IP address of the computer (such as Lon-DC1 or 192.168.1.68) and click the **Connect** button.
4. If you are prompted to confirm that you want to trust this remote connection, click the **Connect** button again.

On occasion, you might need to use the `mstsc.exe /admin` command connect to a server with the administrative session. This becomes particularly useful when the terminal server or Remote Desktop Services has exceeded the maximum number of allowed connections or when you get a black screen after you RDP to a system, assuming the system has not crashed.

When you open Remote Desktop Connection, click Show Options to display additional options (as shown in Figure 10-2). These options are arranged in the following tabs:

- **General:** Allows you to specify the remote computer and user name to connect to. At the bottom of the tab, you can save the current connection settings to an RDP file or open a saved RDP file.
- **Display:** Controls how the remote desktop appears on the client computer, including the size of the remote desktop in pixels (including the full screen option), use of all monitors for the remote session, and the number of colors.

- **Local Resources:** Allows you to control which client resources are available to the remote session.
- **Experience:** Specifies which display options are available for a remote connection. If you select LAN (10 Mbps or higher), all options are selected. However, if you select a faster option than what the network actually is, your remote session may be slow or have a choppy display.
- **Advanced:** Allows you to specify server authentication options and a Remote Desktop Gateway.

Figure 10-2

Remote Desktop options

On the Display tab (see Figure 10-3), you can specify the size of the remote desktop as it appears on the client computer. By default, the Remote Desktop size slider is set to Full Screen, which causes the client to occupy the client computer's entire display, using the computer's configured display resolution.

Figure 10-3

Remote Desktop Display tab

To avoid confusion when displaying multiple desktops on a system (the local desktop and one or more multiple remote desktops), the Display the connection bar when I use the full screen option is selected, which will display a title bar at the top of each remote desktop session.

In addition to the desktop size, you can use the Colors drop-down list to adjust the color depth of the RDC display. The settings available in this drop-down list depend on the capabilities of the video display adapter installed on the client computer.

One of the new features implemented in RDP 6.*x* is support for 32-bit color, which enables clients to run graphic-intensive applications, such as image editors, with a full color palette. However, the trade-off for this ability is the increased network bandwidth required to transmit the display information from the terminal server to the client.

For example, when you configure RDC to use 32-bit color, the client and the terminal server open a special RDP channel just for that color information. This enables the client to assign a lower priority to the extra color information so that it does not interfere with the basic functionality of the client. However, 32-bit color increases the overall bandwidth consumed by the connection substantially. As a general rule, you should set the Colors parameter to the High Color (16-bit) setting unless the client will be running terminal server applications that can benefit from the additional color information.

On the Local Resources tab, shown in Figure 10-4, you configure how the RDC client should reconcile the resources on the Remote Desktop server with those on the client computer. You can click the Settings button to specify whether audio playback is played on the local computer or the remote computer and whether remote audio recordings are recorded from the local computer.

Figure 10-4

Remote Desktop Local
Resources tab

To make the remote connection more flexible, Remote Desktop allows you to redirect many of the local resources, such as local printers and disk drives (including local mapped drives). When you log on to the remote computer, you can open a document on the remote computer and print the document to your local printer. In addition, you can open a document on your local hard drive on the remote computer.

By default, the Printers and Clipboard options are already selected. By redirecting the Clipboard, you can cut and paste to and from the remote computer. If you click the More button, you can specify ports, drives, and other supported Plug and Play (PnP) devices.

With Windows 10, you can select USB devices for redirection and swap them between the remote computer and the local computer. To redirect USB devices, you must enable the RemoteFX USB redirection feature in a Group Policy Object (GPO). Navigate to the Computer Configuration\Policies\Administrative Templates\Windows Components\Remote Desktop Services\Remote Desktop Connection Client\RemoteFX USB Device Redirection\ Allow RDP redirection of other supported RemoteFX USB devices from this computer, enable the policy, and specify whether you want to allow all users or only administrators to redirect devices. When RemoteFX USB Redirection is enabled, click the new Devices icon on the connection bar to choose which devices you want to redirect.

Configuring Remote Assistance

Remote Assistance is a Windows 10 feature that enables an administrator, trainer, or support person to connect to a remote user's computer, chat with the user, and either view all of the user's activities or take complete control of the system. Similar to Remote Desktop, it also uses TCP port 3389.

Remote Desktop is used to open a session with a computer, whereas Remote Assistance is used to view and interact with a user session remotely. It can be used by technical support people, administrators, and trainers to interact with the user without traveling to the user.

To ensure that a support person does not jump into a user session without proper authorization, you can send an invitation using one of the three methods:

- **Save this invitation as a file:** Use this option to save the invitation as a file that you can send to a user via an attachment, copy to a disk, or send over the network.
- **Use email to send an invitation:** Use this option to send the invitation to the sender through email. Of course, you cannot use this option if you do not have a configured email program, such as Microsoft Outlook.
- **Use Easy Connect:** If the local network uses the Peer Name Resolution Protocol (PNRP), which requires IPv6, you can use Easy Connect. The Windows 10 system will start listening for incoming connections without an invitation. Instead, you only need to share the unique password.

 CREATE AN INVITATION

GET READY. To create an invitation, perform the following steps.

1. Logon to a Windows 10 computer.
2. Right-click the **Start** button and click **Control Panel.**
3. When the Control Panel opens, click **System and Security**. In the System section, click **Launch remote assistance.**
4. When the Windows Remote Assistance dialog box opens (as shown in Figure 10-5), click **Invite someone you trust to help you.**
5. The *How do you want to invite your trusted helper?* page appears, as shown in Figure 10-6. Click **Save this invitation as a file.**
6. When the Save As dialog box opens, specify a name for the invitation file and the location of the folder in which the wizard should create the invitation and then click **Save.**
7. The Windows Remote Assistance window appears displaying the password you must supply to the support person.

Figure 10-5

The Windows Remote
Assistance Ask for or offer
help page

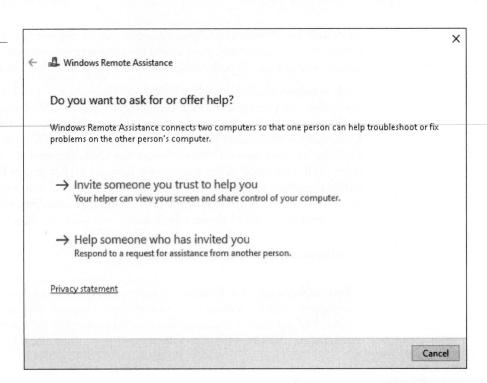

Figure 10-6

The Windows Remote
Assistance How do you
want to invite your trusted
helper? page

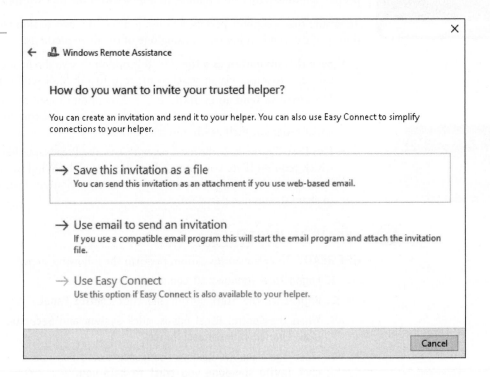

If the support person's system supports Remote Assistance, you just have to double-click the invitation. The support person is asked to enter the password. The user is then asked if the support person is allowed. When the user clicks Yes, the support person can see the session. Using the Windows Remote Assistance window, the support person and user can send messages back and forth, as shown in Figure 10-7. For the support person to take control, he or she has to click the Request control button.

Figure 10-7

Interacting with a user via Remote Assistance

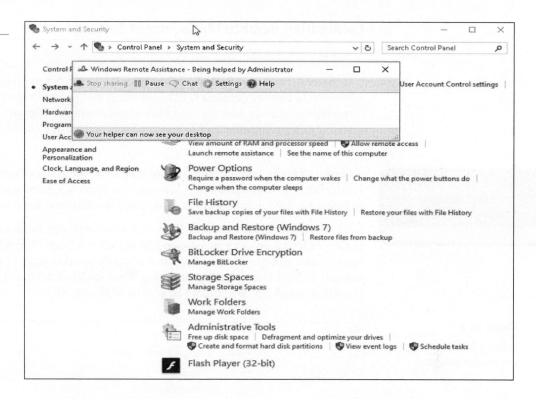

In the following exercise, you will use Remote Assistance Easy Connect. However, if you do not have Peer Name Resolution Protocol (PNRP) and IPv6, the Easy Connect options will be greyed out.

 USE EASY CONNECT

GET READY. To use Easy Connect to remotely connect to a computer, perform the following steps.

1. Logon to a Windows 10 computer that needs help.

2. Right-click the **Start** button and click **Control Panel**.

3. When the Control Panel opens, click **System and Security**. In the System section, click **Launch remote assistance**.

4. When the Windows Remote Assistance dialog box opens, click **Invite someone you trust to help you**.

5. The Windows Remote Assistance Wizard appears, displaying the How do you want to invite your trusted helper? page.

6. Click **Use Easy connect**. If you get a Can't connect to global peer-to-peer network error message, you probably do not have PNRP installed on your network.

7. When the Windows Remote Assistance window opens, record the unique password that you will provide to the user who is trying to help you.

8. Log on to the remote Windows 10 computer.

9. Right-click the **Start** button and click **Control Panel**.

10. When the Control Panel opens, click **System and Security**. In the System section, click **Launch remote assistance**.

11. When the Windows Remote Assistance dialog box opens, click **Help someone who has invited you**.

12. On the Windows Remote Assistance dialog box, click **Use Easy Connect**.

13. When the Remote Assistance dialog box opens, enter the Easy connect 12-character password and click **OK**.

Configuring Remote Management Settings

As mentioned in the previous two sections, the two methods to connect to a computer are Remote Desktop and Remote Assistance. However, before you can use Remote Desktop or Remote Assistance, you have to use the System Properties to enable these two technologies. In addition, you have to make sure the Windows Firewall (or whatever firewall you are using) will allow Remote Desktop and/or Remote Assistance traffic.

CERTIFICATION READY
Configure remote management settings.
Objective 2.5

To enable either or both of these technologies, open the System Properties (open Control Panel, click System and Security > Security, and then click Remote settings), as shown in Figure 10-8. By default, Remote Assistance is enabled and Remote Desktop is not.

Click the Advanced button in the Remote Assistance section to specify the maximum amount of time an invitation can remain open (the default is 6 hours) and whether the computer can be controlled remotely or not. You can also specify whether you can create invitations that can only be used from computers running Windows Vista or later, which will encrypt the IP address, which, in turn, cannot be read by Windows XP.

Figure 10-8

Enabling Remote Desktop and Remote Assistance

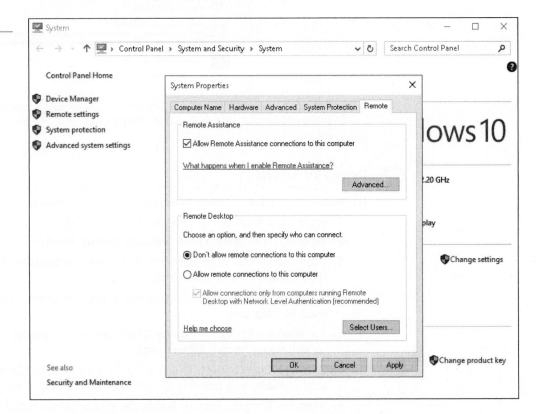

For Remote Desktop, the Allow connections only from computers running Remote Desktop with Network Level Authentication (recommended) option is used to require the user to be authenticated before the session is created, which helps protect the remote computer from malicious users and software. To use Network Level Authentication, the client computer must be using at least Remote Desktop Connection 6.0 and operating systems such as Windows XP with Service Pack 3, or Windows Vista and newer.

The Select Users button is used to specify which users can connect to the system using the RDP. These users are added to the local computer Remote Desktop Users group. The Administrators group already has access even though they are not listed in the Remote Desktop Users list.

CONFIGURE REMOTE MANAGEMENT SETTINGS

GET READY. To configure remote management settings, perform the following steps.

1. Logon to LON-CL1 as **adatum\administrator** with the password of **Pa$$w0rd**.

2. Right-click the **Start** button and click **System**.

3. When the Control Panel System window opens, click **Remote settings**.

4. When the System Properties dialog box opens, the Remote tab is already be selected. To enable Remote Assistance, make sure the **Allow Remote Assistance connection to this computer** option is selected.

5. In the Remote Assistance section, click the **Advanced** button.

6. When the Remote Assistance Settings dialog box opens, select the **Create invitations that can only be used from computers running Windows Vista or later** option to tighten security.

7. To close the Remote Assistance Settings dialog box, click **OK**.

8. In the Remote Desktop section, select the **Allow remote connection to this computer** option to enable remote connections.

9. Click the **Select Users** button.

10. When the Remote Desktop Users dialog box opens, click the **Add** button to add a user or group.

11. When the Select Users or Groups dialog box opens, in the Enter the object names to select text box, type the name of the user group and click **OK**.

12. To close the Remote Desktop Users dialog box, click **OK**.

13. To close the System Properties dialog box, click **OK**.

Using the Microsoft Management Console to Manage Systems Remotely

When assisting users with computer problems or maintaining systems, a support person often needs to check computer events, look at computer resource usage, or examine a disk's partition, among other tasks. You may use Microsoft Management Console (MMC) tools and utilities for this purpose.

CERTIFICATION READY
Modify settings remotely by using the Microsoft Management Console (MMC).
Objective 2.5

CERTIFICATION READY
Configure and use the MMC.
Objective 3.5

The *Microsoft Management Console (MMC)* is a collection of administrative tools called *snap-ins*. An MMC snap-in is a utility provided by Microsoft or a third party that's accessible through a common interface. Administrators use MMC tools for managing hardware, software, and network components on a computer. Administrative Tools is a popular collection of tools that use the MMC.

Computer Management, shown in Figure 10-9, is a popular snap-in that includes several tools such as Disk Management, which is used to configure hard disks and their partitions and Event Viewer, which allows you to view computer event information, such as program starting and stopping (including program crashes) and security problems. You can manage system performance and resources using Performance Monitor, which is under Performance > Monitoring Tools.

Some administrators and power users create custom MMCs that include only tools they use regularly—creating a toolkit of sorts.

Figure 10-9

The Computer Management
window

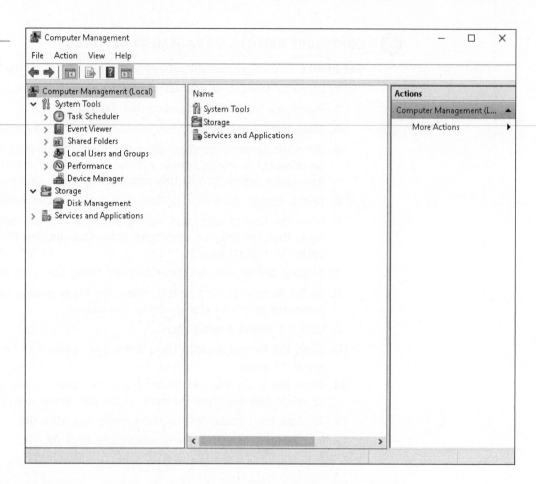

CREATE A CUSTOM MMC AND MODIFY SETTINGS REMOTELY

GET READY. To create a custom MMC and then modify settings remotely, perform
the following steps.

1. Right-click the Start button, and type **mmc** in the Run box. Click **Yes** to open
   the MMC Console.

2. In the MMC Console window, click **File > Add/Remove Snap-in**. The Add
   or Remove Snap-ins dialog box opens (as shown in Figure 10-10).

3. In the Available snap-ins list on the left, select a snap-in of your choice, such
   as **Computer Management.** In the middle of the dialog box, click the **Add** button.
   In the dialog box that appears, leave **Local computer** selected (unless the computer you want to manage is one other than the current computer).

4. Click **Finish.** The snap-in is added to the Selected snap-ins pane on the right.

5. You can then repeat step Repeat Steps 2 through 4 for each snap-in you want
   to include in the custom MMC.

6. When done adding snap-ins, click **OK.**

7. Click **File > Save As.** In the File name text box, type a name for the custom MMC
   and then click **Save.**

8. If you loaded the Computer Management MMC, expand System Tools > **Event
   Viewer** > Windows logs and click System.

9. View the logs on the remote computer.

10. Expand the Services and Applications node and click Services.

11. Right-click the Computer Browser service and click Restart.

12. Close the MMC console.

Figure 10-10

Selecting snap-ins
for a custom MMC

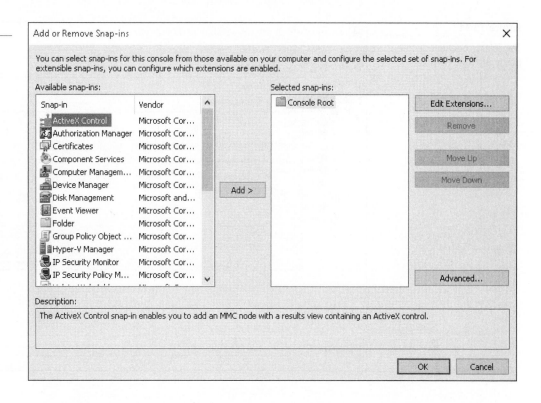

To avoid exposing a computer to malicious attacks, Microsoft recommends that you use MMC snap-ins when you are not logged on as Administrator.

Many of the snap-ins supplied with Windows 10 enable you to manage other Windows computers on the network as well. There are two ways to access a remote computer using a Microsoft Management Console (MMC) snap-in:

- Redirect an existing snap-in to another system
- Create a custom console with snap-ins directed to other systems

To connect to and manage another system using an MMC snap-in, you must launch the console with an account that has administrative credentials on the remote computer. You then click, then right-click the snap-in, and click Connect to another computer. The Select Computer dialog box shown in Figure 10-11 appears. If your credentials do not provide the proper permissions on the target computer, you will be able to load the snap-in, but you will not be able to read information from or modify settings on the target computer.

Not every snap-in has the ability to connect to a remote computer because some do not need it. For example, the Active Directory Domain Services consoles automatically locate a domain controller for the current domain and access the directory service from there. There is no need to specify a computer name. However, you will find Change Domain and Change Domain Controller commands in the Action menu in these consoles, which enable you to manage a different domain or select a specific domain controller in the present domain.

The other factor that can affect the ability of an MMC snap-in to connect to a remote computer is the existence of Windows Firewall rules that block the necessary network traffic between the computers. The traffic that an individual snap-in requires and whether the default Windows Firewall rules restrict it depends on the functions that the snap-in performs.

Connecting to a remote computer by redirecting an existing console is convenient for impromptu management tasks, but it is limited by the fact that you can only access one computer at a time. You also have to open the console and redirect it every time you want to access the remote system. A more permanent solution is to create a custom console with snap-ins that are already directed at other computers.

Figure 10-11

The Select Computer dialog box in an MMC console

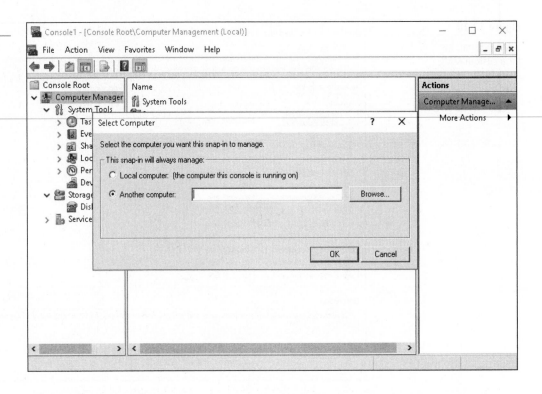

When you add a snap-in to a custom console, you select the computer you want to manage with that snap-in. You can also add multiple copies of the same snap-in to a custom console, with each one pointed at a different computer. This adds a whole new dimension to MMC's functionality. Not only can you create custom consoles containing a variety of tools, but you can also create consoles containing tools for a variety of computers. For example, you can create a single console containing multiple instances of the Event Viewer snap-in, with each one pointing to a different computer. This enables you to monitor the event logs for computers all over the network from a single console.

Using Windows Remote Management

Using Windows Remote Management, administrators can execute programs from the command line on remote computers without having to open a Remote Desktop session.

Windows Remote Management (WinRM) is a Windows 10 service that enables administrators to execute commands on remote computers using Windows PowerShell or the Windows Remote Shell (WinRS.exe) command-line program. However, Windows 10 does not start the service by default or configure the computer to allow remote management communications.

WinRM is responsible for routing the packets to the right location, while *Web Services for Management* structures the packets and requires a port to be made accessible via your firewall. To enable remote management for a target computer, you can do one of the following:

- Open a command prompt and execute the winrm quickconfig command
- Open Windows PowerShell on the computer, and then type Enable-PSRemoting.

The following tasks are performed when you run winrm quickconfig or Enable-PSRemoting:

- Start or restart (if already started) the WinRM service.
- Set the WinRM service startup type to automatic.
- Create a listener to accept requests on any IP address.

• Enable Windows Firewall inbound rule exceptions for WS-Management traffic (for http only). This inbound rule is listed as Windows Remote Management via WS-Management (TCP port 5985) in the inbound rules of your Windows Firewall.

CONFIGURE REMOTE MANAGEMENT WITH THE WINRM COMMAND

GET READY. Log on to Windows 10 using an account with administrative privileges and then perform the following steps.

1. Open a Command Prompt with Administrator privileges. If User Account Control dialog appears asking you to continue, click **Yes**.
2. Execute the following command:

   `winrm quickconfig`

   The command prompts you to start the WinRM service.
3. When it says that it will start the WinRM service and set the WinRM service to delayed auto start, type **y** and then press **Enter** to continue.
4. When you are asked to create a WinRM listener, enable the WinRM firewall exception, type **y**, and then press **Enter** to continue.
5. **Close** the Administrator: Command Prompt window.

> **TAKE NOTE**
>
> The WinRM.exe program will fail to configure the required firewall exception if the computer's network location is set to Public. The computer must use either the Private or Domain location settings for the remote management configuration process to succeed.

WinRM can be enabled for all computers within a domain via a Group Policy Object. To help keep the use of WinRM secure, you can enable the Computer Configuration\Policies\ Administrative Templates\Windows Components\Windows Remote Management (WinRM)\ WinRM Service\Allow remote server management through WinRM setting, and specify the IP Address ranges that the service will accept connections from.

Using WinRS.exe

After you have configured the Remote Management service, you can execute commands on other computers that have been similarly configured. To execute a command from the Windows 10 command prompt, you must use the *WinRS.exe* program.

To use WinRS.exe, you frame the command you want to execute on the remote computer as follows:

`winrs -r:computer [-u:user] [-p:password] command`

• **–r:*computer*:** Specifies the name of the computer on which you want to execute the command, using a NetBIOS name or a fully qualified domain name (FQDN)
• **-u:*user*:** Specifies the account on the remote computer that you want to use to execute the command
• **-p:*password*:** Specifies the password associated with the account specified in the –u parameter. If you do not specify a password on the command line, WinRS.exe prompts you for one before executing the command.
• ***command*:** Specifies the command (with arguments) that you want to execute on the remote computer.

Using Remote Windows PowerShell

Windows PowerShell is a command-line interface used mainly by IT professionals to run cmdlets (pronounced command-lets), complete background jobs (processes or programs that run in the background without a user interface), and run scripts to perform administrative tasks.

CERTIFICATION READY
Configure remote
PowerShell.
Objective 2.5

CERTIFICATION READY
Modify settings remotely
by using the Windows
PowerShell.
Objective 2.5

The Windows PowerShell environment is built on the .NET Framework, which allows administrators to use many more tools and commands than the MS-DOS command window environment. PowerShell and the MS-DOS command environment are compatible, however. For example, you can run Windows command-line programs in Windows PowerShell and also start Windows programs like Calculator and Notepad at the Windows PowerShell prompt.

Another feature of Windows PowerShell is remoting. Administrators can use cmdlets to access remote computers or use the Windows PowerShell Remoting service to run commands on remote computer or even many remote machines. Windows PowerShell Remoting can require substantial setup, which is not within the scope of this book.

RUN A CMDLET IN WINDOWS POWERSHELL

GET READY. To run a cmdlet in Windows PowerShell, perform the following steps.

1. Click the **Start** button and type **PowerShell**. From the results, click **Windows PowerShell**.

2. A commonly used command is ps (or get-process). The ps command lists the currently running processes and their details, such as the process ID, process name, and percentage of processor usage (CPU). Type **ps** and press **Enter**, as shown in Figure 10-12.

3. To get help with the ps command, type **get-help ps** and press **Enter**.

4. To view running services, type **get-service** and then press **Enter**. A list of services displays along with their status (Running or Stopped).

5. To exit the Window PowerShell window, type **exit** and then press **Enter**.

PowerShell Remoting is a server-client application that allows you to securely connect to a remote PowerShell host and run script interactively. It allows you to run commands on a remote system as though you were sitting physically at its console. PowerShell Remoting is built upon the Web Services for Management protocol and uses Windows Remote Management service to handle the authentication and communication elements.

There are two types of remoting:

- **One-to-one remoting:** Allows you to bring up the PowerShell prompt on a remote computer. The credentials you use are delegated to the remote computer. Any commands you run will run under those credentials.

- **One-to-many remoting:** Allows you to send one or more commands, in parallel, to multiple computers. Each of these computers runs the command, produces the results into an XML file, and then returns the results to your computer over the network. When the results are returned, they include the computer name.

Figure 10-12

Running the ps command
in Windows PowerShell

```
Administrator: Windows PowerShell                                    ─   □   ×
Windows PowerShell
Copyright (C) 2015 Microsoft Corporation. All rights reserved.

PS C:\Users\Administrator.ADATUM> ps

Handles  NPM(K)    PM(K)      WS(K) VM(M)   CPU(s)     Id ProcessName
-------  ------    -----      ----- -----   ------     -- -----------
    378      20    11812      23964 ...91     0.45   2600 ApplicationFrameHost
    111       8     1264       7088 ...04     0.05   1132 ChsIME
    111       8     1280       7100 ...04     0.06   3476 ChtIME
    127      12     4896      13512 ...47     0.06    448 conhost
    254      13     1156       3732 ...02     0.67    520 csrss
    297      15     1248       4576 ...12     2.34    616 csrss
    352      34    25892      48376 ...30     4.16    488 dwm
   1634      76    35972      40304 ...31    17.41   3376 explorer
    285      17     3572      21348 ...04     0.28   3332 HelpPane
      0       0        0          4     0        0      0 Idle
   1096      32     5164      17096 ...40     5.13    740 lsass
    226      13     2308      15044 ...55     0.08   4740 mobsync
    524      64   103772      91480 ...87    20.95   2392 MsMpEng
    262      13     6020       2840 ...14    24.86   3232 NisSrv
    366      23     5096       1436   128     2.06   4920 OneDrive
    663      38    77284      89980 ...10     3.59   4688 powershell
    366      23     8316      27628 ...95     0.92   3096 RuntimeBroker
   1185      85    37412      39308 ...84     4.42   4544 SearchIndexer
   1139      88    89300     140208 33226    10.19   4160 SearchUI
    284      11     3916       8804 ...86     2.09    732 services
    626      32    19440      55276   256     5.91   3068 ShellExperienceHost
    399      17     4468      21372 ...57     0.80    668 sihost
     49       3      344       1160 ...56     0.22    404 smss
    400      24     5608      15392 ...17     0.30   1796 spoolsv
    498      49    92832       4224   396     1.34   2656 sqlservr
    106       9     1416       7096    42     0.03   2672 sqlwriter
   1523      73    16220      39604 ...78    16.36    476 svchost
    929      53     9368      21052 ...56     4.36    496 svchost
    275      18     2992      10540 ...09     0.55    796 svchost
    599      22     6260      17548 ...21     1.92    836 svchost
    719      33    36756      51828 ...04    72.39    876 svchost
    537      17     3220       8064 ...89     3.47    896 svchost
    689      31    12924      20192 ...49     2.44   1108 svchost
    678      36     7212      20804 ...96     4.22   1116 svchost
    229      20     2204       8328 ...97     0.45   1252 svchost
    205      11     1616       8108 ...91     0.19   1696 svchost
    490      45    27816      35548 ...86    10.53   1740 svchost
    270      20     5020      18192 ...93     0.55   2072 svchost
    208      21     5200      16628 ...67     2.69   2288 svchost
    172      12     2080      12072 ...27     0.08   3988 svchost
   1120       0      128        572     4    15.06      4 System
    318      33     6672      16140 ...49     0.52   2152 taskhostw
    468      21     8980      22328    67     0.39   2868 vmms
```

 USE POWERSHELL (ONE TO ONE REMOTING)

GET READY. To connect to a target Windows 10 computer using PowerShell and use one-to-one remoting, perform the following steps.

To enable PSRemoting on a target computer:

1. Log in with administrative privileges to a computer running Windows 10

2. Click the **Start** button and type **PowerShell**. From the results, click **Windows PowerShell**.

3. From the Windows PowerShell window, type **Enable-PSRemoting** and then press Enter (see Figure 10-13).

4. Read the tasks that will be performed, type **A** and then press **Enter**.

Figure 10-13

Enabling PS Remoting

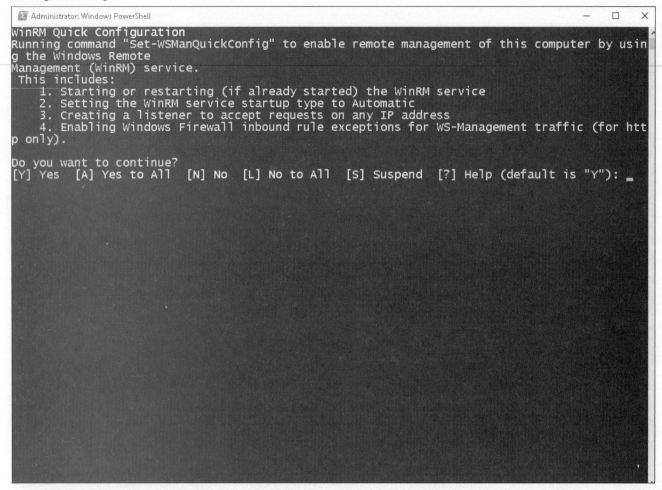

 GET READY. From the source Windows 10 computer, log in with administrative privileges to the domain and perform the following.

1. Press the **Windows logo key + r**, type **Powershell** in the Run box, and then click **OK.**

2. From the Windows PowerShell window, type the following and press Enter:

   enter-pssession –ComputerName <computername>

   Replace <computername> with your domain controller's name. Once connected, the PowerShell prompt should include the name of the computer you are currently connected to remotely.

3. Type **get-service** and press **Enter** to see the services running on the domain controller.

4. Type **get-process** and press Enter to see a list of all processes running on the domain controller.

5. Type **get-acl c:** and press Enter to see the access control list applied via NTFS for the c: drive.

6. Type **exit-pssession** and press Enter to exit PowerShell.

Choosing the Appropriate Remote Management Tool

As you have seen throughout this lesson, there are multiple tools that you can use to remotely control and configure computers. Each tool has it strength and weaknesses.

If you have a need to configure a computer remotely, such as a server, you would use Remote Desktop to provide a GUI interface, a MMC, or remote Windows PowerShell. PowerShell can be the most flexible because you can configure settings that may not be available in other tools, and it can be used in scripting. If you need to assist someone remotely, use Remote Assistance.

SKILL SUMMARY

IN THIS LESSON YOU LEARNED:

- With large organizations that may be located throughout the country (or the world), have a mobile work force, and offer work-from-home capability, you need to have a way to access systems remotely. Microsoft includes multiple tools within Windows to access clients and servers remotely.

- The Remote Desktop Protocol (RDP) is a proprietary protocol that was developed by Microsoft to connect to another computer over a network connection using the same graphical interface that you would use if you were setting in front of the physical server. RDP uses TCP port 3389. Typically, this would be done with Remote Desktop Connection (RDC), which would allow you to connect to a Remote Desktop Session Host or to a Remote Application.

- Remote Assistance is a Windows 10 feature that enables an administrator, trainer, or support person to connect to a remote user's computer, chat with the user, and either view all of the user's activities or take complete control of the system. Similar to Remote Desktop, it also uses TCP port 3389.

- The Microsoft Management Console (MMC) contains a collection of administrative tools called snap-ins. An MMC snap-in is a utility provided by Microsoft or a third party that's accessible through a common interface. Administrators use MMC tools for managing hardware, software, and network components on a computer.

- Windows PowerShell is a command-line interface used mainly by IT professionals to run cmdlets (pronounced command-lets), complete background jobs (processes or programs that run in the background without a user interface), and run scripts to perform administrative tasks.

■ Knowledge Assessment

Multiple Choice

1. Which of the following remote access solutions requires a user to be present at the remote site and allow the connection to be established?
   a. Remote Desktop
   b. Remote Assistance
   c. WinRM
   d. WinRS.exe

2. Which of the following are true statements regarding the capabilities of Remote Desktop connections? (Choose all that apply.)
   a. Allows you to operate the remote computer as if you were sitting at its console
   b. Requires a separate license for each connection
   c. Communicates with the host computer over RDP
   d. Requires that you have an account on the remote computer to access the system

3. Which of the following use Windows Remote Management to execute commands on remote computers? (Choose all that apply.)
   a. RDP
   b. WinRS.exe
   c. Windows PowerShell
   d. Remote Assistance

4. To receive remote help, the computer running Windows 10 can be configured to use remote assistance. Where can this setting be configured? (Choose all that apply.)
   a. Control Panel > System and Security > System > Remote settings >Remote tab
   b. Using the Group Policy Object Editor snap-in
   c. Control Panel > System > Remote settings >Remote tab
   d. Control Panel > System and Security > Remote settings >Remote tab

5. Which of the following can be used to initiate a Remote Assistance session? (Choose all that apply.)
   a. Create and send invitation via email
   b. Create and send invitation via file
   c. Accept an approve a remote assistance connection on the client computer
   d. Through Windows PowerShell.

6. Which of the following are true statements regarding the use of snap-ins? (Choose all that apply.)
   a. Not all snap-ins have the ability to connect to a remote computer
   b. The Windows Firewall can block a snap-in's functionality
   c. A single console can only manage one instance of each snap-in
   d. A single console can be created that contains multiple instances of the same snap-in (e.g., Event Viewer)

7. Remote Assistance can provide which of the following benefits to administrative personnel? (Choose all that apply.)
   a. Installing of software
   b. Observing a remote user's activities
   c. Assisting a remote user who has lost connectivity to the Internet
   d. Training end users on their local system

8. Remote Assistance provides which of the following protective features? (Choose all that apply.)
   a. Invitations
   b. Interactive connectivity
   c. Client-side control
   d. A valid user account on the client computer

9. Which of the following commands is used to start the Windows Remote Management service from a command prompt?
   a. winrm quickconfig
   b. winrm startconfig
   c. win quickconfig
   d. winrm quickconfig /start

10. Which of the following best describes how to execute a command on a remote computer?
    a. Using the winrs command
    b. Using the winremote command
    c. Using the RMWeb command
    d. Using the WSMan command

Best Answer

Choose the letter that corresponds to the best answer. More than one answer choice may achieve the goal. Select the BEST answer.

1. Which tool works best when passively observing and assisting a remote user as that user attempts to learn a new program while still providing interactive assistance when necessary?
   a. Remote Desktop
   b. Remote Assistance
   c. PowerShell
   d. WinRS.esxe

2. An administrator has configured a remote computer for one of the company's employees. She knows the IP address and the computer's name. Which option allows her to remotely assist the employee with the least amount of effort assuming the employee is currently sitting in front of his or her computer?
   a. Have the remote employee send an invitation via email.
   b. Have the remote employee send an invitation via chat.
   c. Have the remote employee call the administrator and then walk him or her through the setup of a Remote Assistance connection.
   d. Initiate a Remote Assistance connection to the remote employee's computer by specifying its name and IP address. Ask the remote employee to accept the connection.

3. A junior administrator would like the ability to take full control of a remote computer to perform a service pack upgrade. The computer is currently stored in a locked room in which she does not currently have the key. Which of the following options ensures she can access the computer with the least amount of effort?
   a. Find someone who has a key to the room and ask them to let her in.
   b. Use Remote Desktop to connect to the server and perform the service pack upgrade.
   c. Configure the computer for Remote Assistance and then send an invitation to her email address.
   d. Contact the help desk and submit a ticket to upgrade the computer at a later date and time.

4. There are 25 Windows 10 computers on the Windows domain. You want to configure them for Remote Management. Which of the following options is the most efficient way to accomplish this task?
   a. Visit each computer and run the winrm quickconfig command.
   b. Visit each computer and configure the Local Group Policy to start the Windows Remote Management service automatically.
   c. Use Remote Desktop to connect to each computer and run the winrm quickconfig command.
   d. Configure Windows Remote Management using Group Policy and apply it to the selected computers in the domain.

5. Which of the following best describes what happens if you attempt to connect to another computer using an MMC snap-in without the appropriate level of permissions on the target computer?
    a. The snap-in will not load.
    b. The snap-in will load but you will not be able to read information from or modify settings on the target computer.
    c. The snap-in will load but you will have to provide the appropriate credentials to be able to read information from the target computer.
    d. The snap-in will load with read permission only but you will not be able to make any modifications to the target computer.

Matching and Identification

1. Match the term or tool with its corresponding definition
    1. Remote Assistance
    2. WinRS.exe
    3. Remote Desktop
    4. Remote Desktop Protocol (RDP)
    5. Windows Remote Management
    6. Windows PowerShell
    7. Microsoft Management Console
    8. Invitation
    9. Invoke-Command
    10. TCP port number 3389

    A. Administrative feature that enables users to access computers from remote locations, with no interaction required at the remote computer.
    B. A service that enables administrators to execute commands on remote computers using Windows PowerShell or WinRS.exe.
    C. Used to execute a command from the Windows 10 command prompt.
    D. Used by Remote Assistance for all its network communications.
    E. Provides an interface for system administrators to configure and monitor the local and remote systems.
    F. Allows an expert/helper to chat and take control of a remote computer.
    G. Transmits screen information, keystrokes and mouse movements between two computers.
    H. Is a command-line shell and scripting language.
    I. The *icm* command is an alias for this cmdlet.
    J. Is sent by email, file, or chat to an Expert/Helper to get help.

Build a List

1. Specify the correct order of steps necessary to using PowerShell Remoting to connect and manage a remote server named Orion:
    _____ Start PowerShell on your computer
    _____ Perform any remote commands on Orion to complete the administration task
    _____ enter-pssession –ComputerName Orion
    _____ Run the enable-psremoting command to configure Orion to receive remote commands.
    _____ Enter exit-pssession to close the remote session

■ Business Case Scenarios

Scenario 10-1: Troubleshooting Remote Assistance

Joe is a new IT Director who is tasked with making sure his Windows 10 computer users can be assisted remotely. On his first day at the company, Joe was told that the Remote Assistance feature was not working for users after a new firewall was installed. What could be causing the problem and how should it be addressed?

Scenario 10-2: Using Remote Assistance to Help a User

You are an administrator at the Contoso Corporation. You have a 12-person help desk that supports about 10,000 users spread out over a 5-building campus. You don't have enough people to provide support staff visits to a user who is having problems. Describe the actions you can take to support your company users.

11 LESSON | Configuring Updates

70-698 EXAM OBJECTIVE

Objective 3.1 – Configure updates. This objective may include but is not limited to: Configure Windows Update options; implement Insider Preview, Current Branch (CB), Current Branch for Business (CBB), and Long-Term Servicing Branch (LTSB) scenarios; manage update history; roll back updates; update Windows Store apps.

LESSON HEADING	EXAM OBJECTIVE
Configuring and Managing Updates	
Configuring Windows Update Options	Configure Windows Update options
Managing Update History and Rolling Back Updates	Manage update history
	Roll back updates
Configuring Windows Update Policies	
Updating Windows Store Apps	Update Windows Store apps
Managing the Update Life Cycle	
Implementing Insider Preview	Implement Insider Preview scenario
Implementing Current Branch (CB), Current Branch for Business (CBB), and Long-Term Servicing Branch (LTSB) Scenarios	Implement Current Branch (CB), Current Branch for Business (CBB), and Long-Term Servicing Branch (LTSB) scenarios

KEY TERMS

critical update

cumulative patch

Current Branch for Business (CBB) servicing

Current Branch (CB) servicing

hotfix

Long-Term Servicing Branch (LTSB) servicing

out-of-band patches

Patch Tuesday

security update

service pack

Windows 10 Anniversary Update

Windows 10 Enterprise Long-Term Servicing Branch (LTSB)

Windows Insider program

Windows Update

■ CONFIGURING AND MANAGING UPDATES

THE BOTTOM LINE

Intruders and some viruses, worms, rootkits, spyware, and adware gain access to a system by exploiting security holes in Windows, Internet Explorer, Microsoft Office, or other software applications. Therefore, the first step you should take to protect yourself against malware is to keep your system up to date with the latest service packs, security patches, and other critical fixes.

Microsoft routinely releases security updates on the second Tuesday of each month, commonly known as *Patch Tuesday*. Although most updates are released on Patch Tuesday, there might be occasional patches (known as *out-of-band patches*) released at other times when the patches are deemed critical or time-sensitive.

Because computers are often used as production systems, you should test any updates to make sure they do not cause problems for you. Although Microsoft performs intensive testing, occasionally problems do occur, either as a bug or as a compatibility issue with third-party software. Therefore, always be sure you have a good backup of your system and data files before you install patches so that you have a back-out plan, if necessary.

Microsoft classifies updates as Important, Recommended, or Optional:

- **Important updates:** These updates offer significant benefits, such as improved security, privacy, and reliability. They should be installed as they become available and can be installed automatically with Windows Update.
- **Recommended updates:** These updates address noncritical problems or help enhance your computing experience. Although these updates do not address fundamental issues with your computer or Windows software, they can offer meaningful improvements.
- **Optional updates:** These updates include updates, drivers, or new software from Microsoft to enhance your computing experience. You need to install these manually.

Depending on the type of update, Windows Update can deliver the following:

- **Security updates:** A *security update* is a broadly released fix for a product-specific, security-related vulnerability. Security vulnerabilities are rated based on their severity, which is indicated in the Microsoft security bulletin as critical, important, moderate, or low.
- **Critical updates:** A *critical update* is a broadly released fix for a specific problem addressing a critical, non-security-related bug.
- **Service packs:** A *service pack* is a tested, cumulative set of hotfixes, security updates, critical updates, and updates, as well as additional fixes for problems found internally since the release of the product. Service packs might also contain a limited number of customer-requested design changes or features. After an operating system is released, many corporations consider the first service pack as the time when the operating system has matured enough to be used throughout the organization.

Not all updates can be retrieved through Windows Update. Sometimes, Microsoft might offer the fix for a specific problem in the form of a hotfix or cumulative patch that you can install. A *hotfix* is a single, cumulative package that includes one or more files that are used to address a problem in a software product, such as a software bug. Typically, hotfixes are made to address a specific customer situation, and they often have not gone through the same extensive testing as patches retrieved through Windows Update. A *cumulative patch* is multiple hotfixes combined into a single package.

Upgraded builds of Windows 10 will occasionally be made available, and will be identified by a version number based on year and month. The original version was 1507, because it was released in July of 2015. Microsoft's first major update was version 1511, which consisted of general bug fixes and improvements, streamlined activation, restored colored window title bars, integrated Skype, and improvements to the Edge browser. You can also use the Find My Device option under Settings > Update & security to use built-in tracking, so you can track your laptop or tablet—via GPS and location services—if you lose it.

In August of 2016, Microsoft will be releasing the ***Windows 10 Anniversary Update***. It will introduce a number of new features and enhancements over the previous November Update release. Microsoft Edge will get new extension support, biometric authentication support with Windows Hello, improvements to Cortana, and Windows Inking.

Configuring Windows Update Options

CERTIFICATION READY
Configure Windows
Update options
Objective 3.1

Windows Update provides your Windows 10 users with a way to keep their computers current by checking a designated server. The server provides software that patches security issues, installs updates that make Windows and your applications more stable, fixes issues with existing Windows programs, and provides new features. The server can be hosted by Microsoft or it can be set up and managed in your organization by running the Windows Server Update Services (WSUS) or System Center 2012 R2/2016 Configuration Manager.

When you first install Windows 10, you can choose how you want Windows Update to function. On a Windows 10 computer, you can open Settings and click Update & security to open the Windows Update page (see Figure 11-1).

Figure 11-1

The Windows Update page

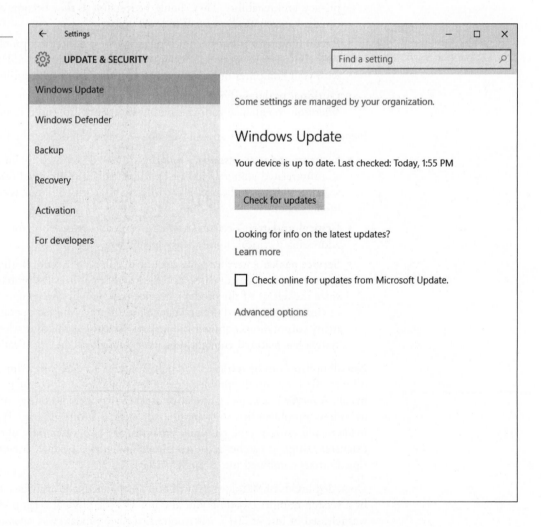

By clicking Advanced options, you can configure for Automatic Updates, give updates for other Microsoft products when Windows is updated, defer upgrades, and view update history (as shown in Figure 11-2).

Figure 11-2

The Windows Update Advanced Options page

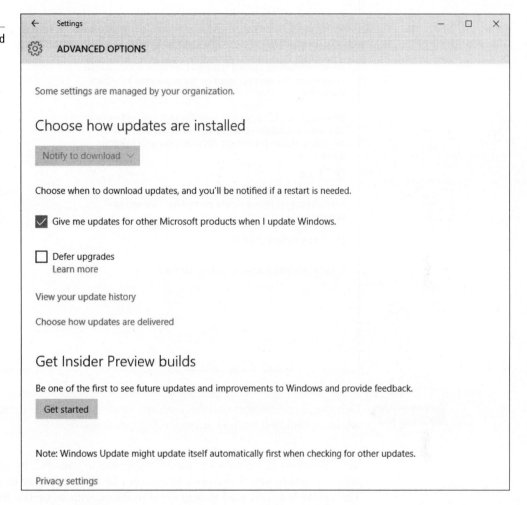

For corporations, you can also use Windows Server Update Services (WSUS) or System Center 2012 R2/2016 Configuration Manager to keep your systems updated. Smaller organizations might use WSUS or cloud-based services such as Microsoft Intune to keep systems up to date. The advantage of using one of these systems is that it allows you to test the patch, schedule the updates, and prioritize client updates. Once you determine a patch is safe, you can enable it for deployment.

If you click the Choose how updates are delivered option, the Updates from More Than One Place page displays (see Figure 11-3). Unless you are part of a corporation that is using WSUS or System Center 2012 R2/2016 Configuration Manager, you must use your Internet connection to retrieve updates from Microsoft. Starting with Windows 10, you can enable the Updates from more than one place option, which also allows you to get updates from other computers on the same network as your local computer and from computers on the Internet.

Under Advanced options, you can customize how updates are installed. By default, the Choose how updates are installed option is set to Automatic (recommended), which means Windows selects a time when you don't use your computer to install the updates and reboot the system. Most organizations would prefer the Notify to schedule restart option so that Windows does not reboot your computer when you least expect it.

Figure 11-3

The Updates from More Than
One Place page

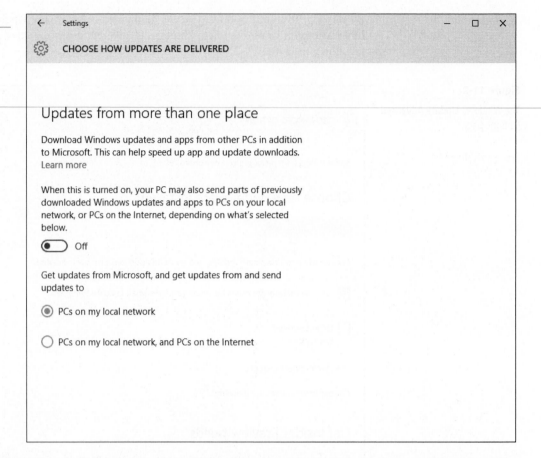

Deferring upgrades does not affect security updates, but it does prevent you from getting the latest Windows features as soon as they are available.

Some Windows 10 editions let you defer upgrades to your PC. By selecting the Defer upgrades option, new Windows features won't be downloaded or installed for several months. This option is usually used to help avoid problems with an update that might cause problems within your organization.

Managing Update History and Rolling Back Updates

You can view your update history by opening the Advanced Options and selecting View your update history. On the Installed Updates page, each update, including the KB article number, the version, and the date installed, is displayed. If you click *Successfully installed on <date>* for a specific update, it gives a short description of the update.

At the top of the View Your Update History page, you can click Uninstall updates to open the Control Panel Installed Updates page, as shown in Figure 11-4. To uninstall or roll back an update, right-click the desired update, and click Uninstall. You are then prompted to uninstall the update. When you click Yes, the update will be uninstalled.

Configuring Windows Update Policies

Normally, you do not need to create a domain GPO to support Configuration Manager software updates. However, if you use a GPO to perform a Configuration Manager client agent installation, you must also configure the Windows Update server update options for clients to use the active software update point.

Figure 11-4

The Control Panel Installed
Updates page

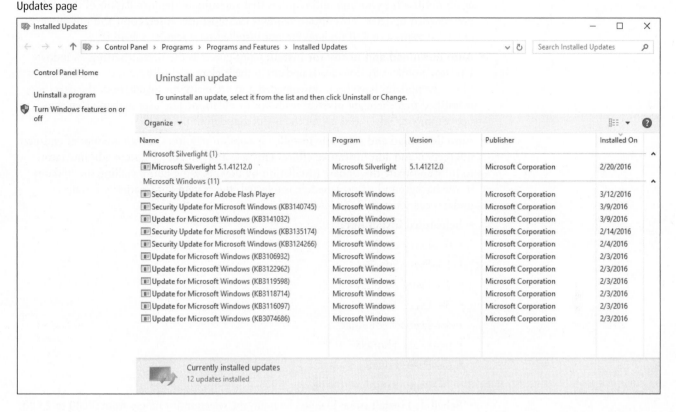

To view the configurable Windows Update policy settings, launch the Local Group Policy Editor or open a GPO in the Group Policy Management Editor and navigate to the Computer Configuration\Policies\Administrative Templates\Windows Components\Windows Update folder.

The Specify intranet Microsoft Update service location policy enables administrators to configure devices meeting the scope of the policy to receive updates from an intranet Windows System Update Services (WSUS) or System Center Configuration Manager (SCCM) server.

The following options are configurable within this policy setting:

- **Enabled:** When enabled, the device within the scope of the policy detects and downloads selected updates from the specified intranet WSUS or SCCM server. Additionally, the Set the intranet update service for detecting updates option and the Set the intranet statistics server option require the fully qualified domain name (FQDN) and the port of the WSUS or SCCM server issuing the updates.

- **Disabled:** When disabled, clients receive their updates from the Internet, not from an intranet server.

- **Not Configured:** When not configured, clients receive their updates from the Internet, not from an intranet server.

One of the required policies for systemwide control of Automatic Updates, the Configure Automatic Updates policy sets the method of downloading and installing Automatic Updates.

The following options are configurable within this policy setting:

- **Enabled:** When enabled, you must select one of the following additional options:
  - **Notify for download and notify for install:** This option requires user intervention to both download and install available updates. When updates are made available

for download, the end user is notified. The end user must then initiate the download of available updates. Once the updates have been downloaded, Windows Update again notifies the end user and requires that she initiate the installation of the recently downloaded updates. This option requires the most user interaction and might leave critical systems at risk if updates are not installed on a regular schedule.

- **Auto download and notify for install:** Configured as the default setting, Windows Update automatically downloads updates in the background without user intervention. Once the updates have been downloaded and are ready for installation, the user is notified that there are updates ready for installation. The user is then given the opportunity to select and install the queued updates.
- **Auto download and schedule install:** This option requires the least amount of end-user interaction and administrative effort. This selection enables a system administrator to fully automate the update installation by downloading and installing the updates in the background. If no schedule is selected, the system automatically installs updates every day at 3:00 A.M.
  - **Scheduled install day:**
    - 0—Every day
    - 1—Every Sunday
    - 2—Every Monday
    - 3—Every Tuesday
    - 4—Every Wednesday
    - 5—Every Thursday
    - 6—Every Friday
    - 7—Every Saturday
  - **Scheduled install time:** Defined by hour, the selection list ranges from 00:00 to 23:00.
- **Allow local admin to choose setting:** Local administrators to the system are allowed to choose their own download and installation settings; they are not allowed to disable Automatic Updates.
- **Disabled:** When disabled, all update downloads and installations require the end user to manually initiate the process.
- **Not Configured:** When not configured, the end user can configure Automatic Updates from within Control Panel.

If you set the Configure Automatic Updates setting to Disabled, the Windows Update Agent (WUA) does not automatically update itself from WSUS. It is generally recommended for you to set this setting to Disabled and distribute an updated Windows Update Agent using software distribution in Configuration Manager.

 CREATE A GPO TO ENABLE AUTOUPDATE FOR CLIENT COMPUTERS

GET READY. To create a GPO to enable AutoUpdate for client computers in an Active Directory domain, log on with administrative credentials, and then on your domain controller, perform the following steps.

> **TAKE NOTE** This can be performed on a Windows 10 client with Administrative Tools or at the domain controller for the domain using the Group Policy Management Console.

1. The Server Manager console opens automatically. If it does not open, on the taskbar, click the **Server Manager** icon.
2. Click **Tools > Group Policy Management**.

3. Right-click the **Group Policy Objects** folder and click **New**.

4. In the Name field, type **WSUS AutoUpdate** and then click **OK**.

5. Expand the **Group Policy Objects** folder, right-click **WSUS AutoUpdate**, and then click **Edit**.

6. Expand the **Computer Configuration > Policies > Administrative Templates > Windows Components > Windows Update**, and then select Configure Automatic Updates, as shown in Figure 11-5.

Figure 11-5

Configuring Automatic Updates using a GPO

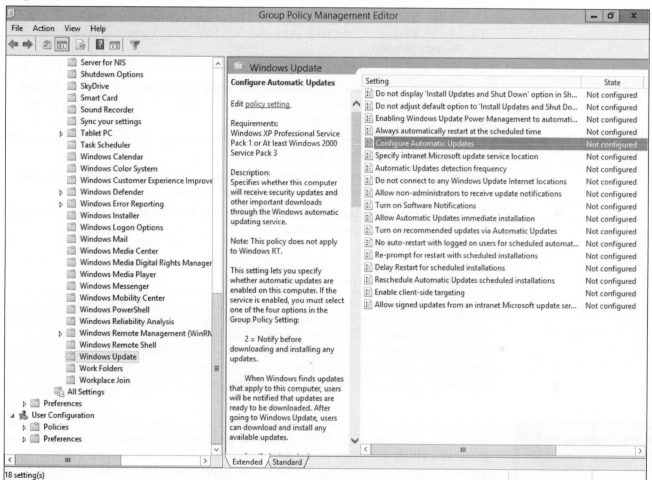

7. In the details pane, double-click **Configure Automatic Updates**.

8. Under Configure Automatic Updates, click **Enabled** and under Configure automatic updating, review the options.

9. Under Configure automatic updating, make sure **3 - Auto download and notify for install** is visible. Read the information in the help panel to understand how this setting works. Click **OK** when finished.

10. Double-click **Specify intranet Microsoft update service location**.

11. Under Specify intranet Microsoft update service location, click **Enabled** and then type the URL of the upstream WSUS server you set up earlier. For example, if your domain controller's name is AdatumDC, type **http://AdatumDC:8530** (8530 is the default port used by WSUS).

12. For the intranet statistics server, type the same information.

13. Click **OK**.

14. Close the **Group Policy Management Editor**.

15. Right-click the domain container (**adatum.com**) and choose **Link an existing GPO**.

16. Choose **WSUS AutoUpdate** and then click **OK**.

17. Close the Group Policy Management Console.

Perform these steps on a Windows 10 computer that is a member of the Active Directory domain.

18. On the Windows 10 machine, right-click the **Start** button and click **Command Prompt (Admin)**.

19. From the Command Prompt window, type **gpresult /r** and then press the **Enter** key. The WSUS AutoUpdate GPO should appear under the Computer Settings > Applied Group Policy Objects section of the report. If it does not, type **gpupdate /force** and then try **gpresult /r** again.

20. Type **wuauclt /detectnow** and then press the **Enter** key. This forces the Windows 10 computer to contact the WSUS server immediately.

21. Open the Update Service console on the domain controller running WSUS (**Server Manager > Tools > Windows Server Update Services**).

22. Expand the **Computers > All Computers** group. You can see the computer under the Unassigned Computers group.

Updating Windows Store Apps

For all intents and purposes, mobile devices (including smartphones and tablets) are computers that can run a wide range of applications. Because these devices usually contain personal and corporate information, these devices are also targets of intruders and malware. Therefore, you need to keep the operating system and the applications up to date so that security patches can be applied as they are released.

CERTIFICATION READY
Update Windows Store apps
Objective 3.1

Applications on smartphones and tablets are usually updated through stores such as Microsoft Store, Google Play, and iTunes. Fortunately, these stores offer mechanisms to notify you when updates are available and to automatically install these updates as they become available. For example, for Windows 10, the live tile, for the Store app, changes to indicate the number of app updates that are available; you can launch the Store app, click the updates link, select all the updates, and click Install. By default, Windows 10 has been automated, where these updates are automatically downloaded and installed as soon as they are available with no user interaction.

 MANAGE WINDOW STORE APPS UPDATES

GET READY. To manage Windows Store apps updates, perform the following steps.

1. Log on to a computer running Windows 10 with an Internet connection.

2. On the taskbar, click the **Microsoft Store** button.

3. When the Store window opens, if you are not logged on to the Microsoft Store, at the top of the page, click the **Sign in** icon and then click **Sign in**. Then log on with your Microsoft account.

4. At the top of the window, click the user icon, and click **Settings**.

5. The Update apps automatically option should already be set to On. If not, click the slider button to change it from Off to **On**.

6. Click the **Back** button (left arrow at top of the Store window).

7. Click the user icon and click **Downloads and updates**.

8. To check for updates, click the **Check for updates** button.

■ MANAGING THE UPDATE LIFE CYCLE

↓
THE BOTTOM LINE

Before Windows 10, a new version of Windows was released every few years. And with each new version that was released, it was usually a daunting task to upgrade or replace each machine with the new versions of Windows. You had to worry about hardware and software compatibility and a different user interface that might have affected the users' acceptance and usage.

Windows 10 is being released as a service, which means that Windows 10 will be receiving rolling feature additions, improvements, and updates. Anytime updates are released, you will have to make sure that the update will not affect system or application functionality. Therefore, you will have to thoroughly test the update before you deploy it to users within a company.

New features are even more problematic because they might change how Windows functions or interacts with other components. For many production systems, companies would rather have stable systems that don't change much so that they can focus on other tasks and projects.

Implementing Insider Preview

In the past, the *Windows Insider program* (which was previously accessible to developers only) allowed users to sign up for early builds of the Windows operating system. Today, the Windows Insider program has been expanded to include enterprise testers and advanced users so that Microsoft could get feedback before a new feature or update is released to the general public and a way to test upcoming Windows features before they are released to the general public.

CERTIFICATION READY
Implement Insider
Preview scenario
Objective 3.1

If you decide to use the Insider Preview, you need to keep in mind that you will often be receiving updates to Windows that might not be fully tested. There are risks that might actually take your system down and possibly corrupt data. So, you want to make sure that you only implement Insider Preview on test machines and make sure you have backups of all important data and programs.

 ENABLE INSIDER PREVIEW BUILD

GET READY. To enable the Insider Preview Build Updates, perform the following steps.

1. Log on to a computer running a genuine, activated copy of Windows 10 with an active Internet connection.

2. Click the **Start** button and then click **Settings**.

3. When the Settings window opens, click **Update & security**.

4. In the Windows update section, click **Advanced options**.

5. Scroll down to see the Get Insider builds section, and click the **Get started** button.

6. Sign in with a Microsoft account.

7. When you are warned that the prerelease software and services may not be fully tested, click **Next**.

8. On the Before You Confirm page, click **Confirm**.

9. On the One More Step to Go page, click **Restart now**.

Implementing Current Branch (CB), Current Branch for Business (CBB), and Long-Term Servicing Branch (LTSB) Scenarios

Enterprise companies are usually not willing to upgrade to the newest version of Windows, and most responsible corporations would deploy the monthly updates that Microsoft publishes every month. However, these corporations are not usually willing to deploy new or updated features because they can cause a wide range of problems. So rather than force the new and updated features to corporations, Microsoft has developed Windows 10 servicing options, which allow you to configure devices into one of three tiers based on how often you want these features deployed.

Table 11-1

The Windows 10 Servicing Options

The Windows 10 servicing options or scenarios are shown in Table 11-1.

Servicing Option	Availability of New or Upgraded Features	Minimum Length of Servicing Lifetime	Supported Editions
Current Branch (CB) servicing	Receives upgrades immediately after Microsoft makes them publicly available	Approximately 4 months	Home, Pro, Education, Enterprise, IoT Core, Windows 10 IoT Core Pro (IoT Core Pro)
Current Branch for Business (CBB) servicing	Defers receiving feature upgrades for 4 months after Microsoft makes them publicly available	Approximately 8 months	Pro, Education, Enterprise, IoT Core Pro
Long-Term Servicing Branch (LTSB)	Are available immediately after being published by Microsoft, but allows for long-term deployment of selected Windows 10 releases in low-change configuration (up to 10 years)	10 years	Enterprise LTSB

CERTIFICATION READY
Implement Current Branch (CB), Current Branch for Business (CBB), and Long-Term Servicing Branch (LTSB) scenarios.
Objective 3.1

For systems that are configured for the *Current Branch (CB) servicing*, you will deploy the new features within four months after they are publicly released. This gives a corporation four months to deploy the new or updated features.

The *Current Branch for Business (CBB) servicing* is a slower track, which gives you 4 months to test and evaluate the new or updated features, and then four months to test and deploy the new or updated feature. Unless you are controlling your updates with Windows Server Update Services (WSUS), System Center Configuration Manager (SCCM), or some similar technology, you can use the Defer upgrades option to move a computer into CBB servicing.

Windows 10 Enterprise Long-Term Servicing Branch (LTSB) is similar to Windows 10 Enterprise, but will be a stripped-down version. It does include Internet Explorer 11, and is compatible with Windows 32-bit version of Microsoft Office. It does not include Microsoft Edge, Windows Store Client, Cortana, Outlook Mail, Outlook Calendar, OneNote, Weather, News, Sports, Money, Photos, Camera, Music, and Clock. *Long-Term Servicing Branch (LTSB) servicing* is intended for scenarios during which changes to software running on devices is limited to only essential updates (vulnerabilities and other important issues). Only Windows 10 Enterprise LTSB supports LTSB.

SKILL SUMMARY

IN THIS LESSON YOU LEARNED:

- Intruders and some viruses, worms, rootkits, spyware, and adware gain access to a system by exploiting security holes in Windows, Internet Explorer, Microsoft Office, or other software applications. Therefore, the first step you should take to protect yourself against malware is to keep your system up to date with the latest service packs, security patches, and other critical fixes.

- Windows Update provides your Windows 10 users with a way to keep their computers current by checking a designated server. The server provides software that patches security issues, installs updates that make Windows and your applications more stable, fixes issues with existing Windows programs, and provides new features.

- For all intents and purposes, mobile devices (including smartphones and tablets) are computers that can run a wide range of applications. Because these devices usually contain personal and corporate information, these devices are also targets of intruders and malware. Therefore, you need to keep the operating system and the applications up to date so that security patches can be applied as they are released.

- The Windows Insider program has been expanded to include enterprise testers and advanced user so that Microsoft could get feedback before a new feature or update is released to the general public and a way to test upcoming Windows features before they are released to the general public.

- Microsoft has developed Windows 10 servicing options, which allow you to configure devices into one of three tiers based on how often you want these features deployed.

■ Knowledge Assessment

Multiple Choice

Select the correct answer for each of the following questions.

1. A family has three computers that have Windows 10 installed. In Windows 10, how can network traffic be minimized when downloading Windows updates?
   a. Enable file caching.
   b. Enable the WriteFile function.
   c. Enable the Get updates from more than one place option.
   d. Enable Internet Sharing.

2. An administrator has just added a new update to the WSUS server and she wants to test the update to the test group. Which of the following commands should she use so that she doesn't have to wait for the update to be deployed?
   a. `gpupdate /force`
   b. `wuauclt.exe /detectnow`
   c. `update /now`
   d. `wsusserver /startupdate`

3. Which of the following types of update is a tested, cumulative set of hotfixes, security updates, critical updates, and updates, as well as additional fixes for problems found internally?
   a. Security update
   b. Critical update
   c. Service pack
   d. Cumulative patch

4. Which of the following features should be selected so that machines can get updates from Windows Update or from another local computer running Windows 10 that already has the update?
   a. Download locally
   b. Automatic (recommended)
   c. Quick update
   d. Updates from more than one place

5. Which of the following tools is used to remove a Windows update?
   a. Windows Settings
   b. Windows Control Panel
   c. Windows GPO
   d. Windows WSUS

6. Which of the following should be used to update applications on a Windows phone?
   a. Launch the store app and click the Updates link.
   b. Use WSUS.
   c. Use Windows Update for Business.
   d. Open the Microsoft Update website.

7. Which of the following options should be used to get the newest and upcoming Windows updates?
   a. Schedule daily updates.
   b. Select the Accelerated option in Windows Update.
   c. Use the CB configuration.
   d. Sign up for the Insider Preview Build.

8. Which type of servicing offers the longest Windows build without additional features being added or significantly changed?
   a. LTSB
   b. CBB
   c. CB
   d. Insider Preview Build

Best Answer

Choose the letter that corresponds to the best answer. More than one answer choice may achieve the goal. Select the BEST answer.

1. Which of the following can be used to control updates that are being deployed to users?
   a. Use the Defer upgrades option.
   b. Use WSUS or System Center Configuration Manager.
   c. Disable Insider Preview.
   d. Install Windows 10 Enterprise LTSB.

■ Business Case Scenarios

Scenario 11-1: Distributing Windows Updates Across a Network

You support Richman Investments, a brokerage firm that employs 20 brokers. Each broker has his own client computer, and the firm has a server running Windows Server. All of the client computers are configured identically.

Over the past six months, some Windows updates have caused the computers to hang, leaving the brokers without computers to conduct business. How can you ensure that the Windows updates that install on client computers will not cause usability issues?

Scenario 11-2: Managing Manufacturing Computers

You have multiple manufacturing computers that control the machinery to several assembly lines. The software for the assembly line controls rarely changes. The assembly lines cannot go down because of problem Windows updates or new features. What do you recommend?

Monitoring Windows

70-698 EXAM OBJECTIVE

Objective 3.2 – Monitor Windows. This objective may include but is not limited to: Configure and analyze Event Viewer logs; configure event subscriptions; monitor performance using Task Manager; monitor performance using Resource Monitor; monitor performance using Performance Monitor and Data Collector Sets; monitor system resources; configure indexing options; manage client security by using Windows Defender; evaluate system stability using Reliability Monitor; troubleshoot performance issues. * Monitor and manage printers is covered in Lesson 8.

LESSON HEADING	EXAM OBJECTIVE
Configuring and Analyzing Event Viewer Logs	Configure and analyze Event Viewer logs
Understanding Logs and Events	
Filtering Events	
Adding a Task to an Event	
Configuring Event Subscriptions	Configure event subscriptions
Managing Performance	Troubleshoot performance issues
Monitoring Performance Using Task Manager	Monitor performance using Task Manager
Monitoring Performance Using Resource Monitor	Monitor performance using Resource Monitor
Monitoring Performance Using Performance Monitor	Monitor performance using Performance Monitor
Monitoring System Resources	Monitor system resources
Monitoring Performance Using Data Collector Sets	Monitor performance using Data Collector Sets
Configuring Performance Alerts	
Managing Client Security Using Windows Defender	Manage client security by using Windows Defender
Using the Home Tab	
Using the Update Tab	
Using the History Tab	
Using Windows Defender Settings	
Using Reliability Monitor	Evaluate system stability using Reliability Monitor
Configuring Indexing Options	Configure indexing options

bottleneck

Data Collector Sets (DCS)

event subscription

Event Viewer

Microsoft Active Protection Service (MAPS)

performance

performance alert

Performance Monitor

process

Reliability Monitor

Resource Monitor

Task Manager

Windows Defender

■ CONFIGURING AND ANALYZING EVENT VIEWER LOGS

THE BOTTOM LINE

One of the most useful troubleshooting tools is Event Viewer, which is essentially a log viewer. Whenever you have problems, you should look in Event Viewer to see any errors or warnings that might reveal what the problem is.

CERTIFICATION READY
Configure and analyze
Event Viewer logs
Objective 3.2

Event Viewer is an MMC snap-in that enables you to browse and manage event logs. It is included in the Computer Management console and is included in Administrative Tools as a stand-alone console. You can also execute the eventvwr.msc command.

Event Viewer enables you to perform the following tasks:

- View events from multiple event logs (see Figure 12-1).
- Save useful event filters as custom views that can be reused.

Figure 12-1

Event Viewer

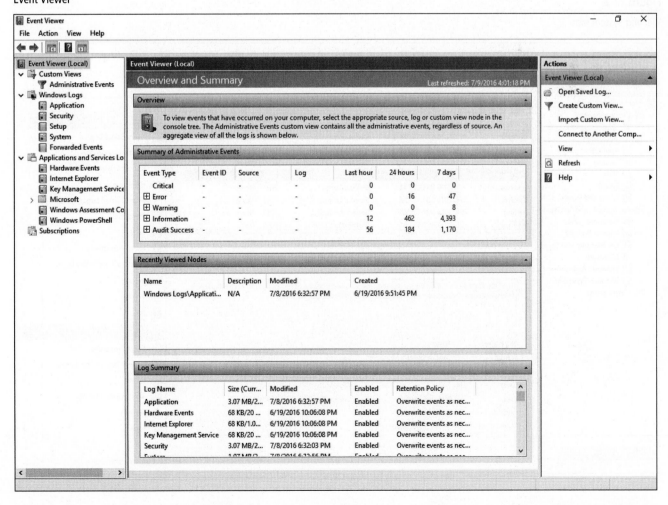

- Schedule a task to run in response to an event.
- Create and manage event subscriptions.

Understanding Logs and Events

> To get the best use of Windows logs, you need to understand how the logs are organized and how the events are categorized.

When you examine Event Viewer more closely, you will see the following items:

- **Custom Views:** Allows you to create custom views of events. By default, it includes Administrative Events, which collects Critical, Error, and Warnings from all logs on the server. However, you can create your own custom view by right-clicking Custom Views and selecting Create Custom View.
- **Windows Logs:** Includes logs that were available in previous versions of Windows. They include:
  - **Application:** Contains events logged by applications or programs.
  - **Security:** Contains events such as valid and invalid logon attempts and access to designated objects such as files and folders, printers, and Active Directory objects. By default, the Security log is empty until you enable auditing.
  - **Setup:** Contains events related to application setup.
  - **System** (see Figure 12-2): Contains events logged by Windows system components, including errors displayed by Windows during boot and errors with services.
  - **Forwarded Events**: Stores events collected from remote computers. To collect events from remote computers, you must create an event subscription. It should be noted

Figure 12-2

Viewing System logs

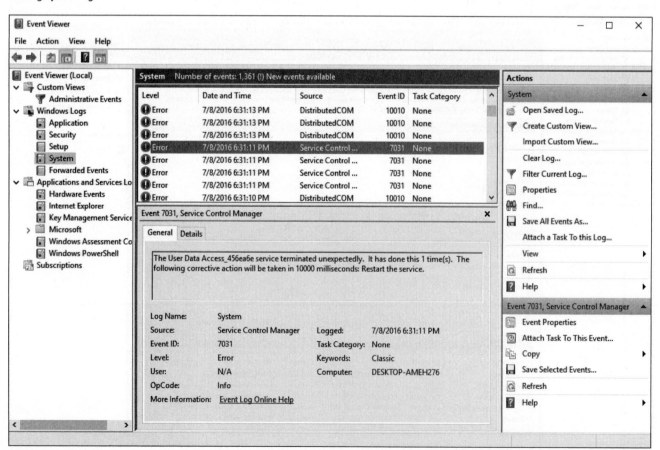

that Forwarded Events does not work with pre-Windows 7 and Windows Server 2008 operating systems.

- **Applications and Services Logs**: Displays a set of events related to an application or service. Some examples include DHCP, DNS, and Active Directory.

When you open an event, you will see the Log Name, Source, Event ID, Level, User (if applicable), Logged details (date and time), Computer, and other information. Table 12-1 shows the common fields displayed in the Event Viewer logs.

Table 12-1

Common Files Displayed in the Event Viewer Logs

PROPERTY NAME	DESCRIPTION
Source	The software that logged the event, which can be a program name (such as "SQL Server") or a component of the system or of a large program (such as a driver name)
Event ID	A number identifying the particular event type
Level	A classification of the event severity:
	Information: Indicates that a change in an application or component has occurred (such as an operation has successfully completed, a resource has been created, or a service has started)
	Warning: Indicates that an issue has occurred that can impact service or result in a more serious problem if action is not taken
	Error: Indicates that a problem has occurred that might impact functionality that is external to the application or component that triggered the event
	Critical: Indicates that a failure has occurred from which the application or component that triggered the event cannot automatically recover
	Success Audit: Indicates that the exercise of a user right was successful
	Failure Audit: Indicates that the exercise of a user right has failed

Filtering Events

When looking at the logs shown by Event Viewer, you can be overwhelmed by the number of events. Therefore, you need to know how to filter events so that you can focus on specific information.

When you open any of these logs, particularly the Application, Security, or System logs, they might display thousands of entries. Unfortunately, this means that it might take some time to find what you are looking for.

To begin with, you can sort Event Viewer by clicking the column header. For example, by clicking the Date and Time column header, you can sort the events by date and time. This comes in handy when you know that a problem started at a certain time and you want to view the events that were generated at that time.

To reduce the number of items that are displayed, you can use a filter to reduce the number of entries shown. To filter a log, click Action > Filter Current Log. When the Filter Current Log dialog box opens (see Figure 12-3), you can select when the event was logged, the Event level, Task category, Keywords, User, and Computer(s).

Figure 12-3

Filtering an event log

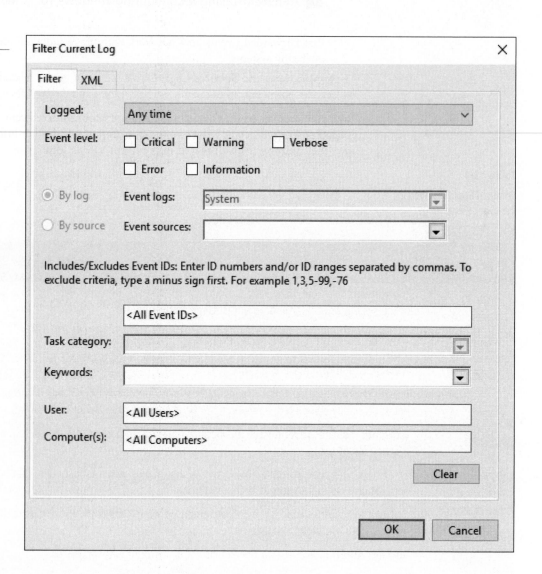

⊖ **VIEW AND MANAGE EVENTS**

GET READY. To view and manage events, perform the following steps.

1. Log on to LON-CL1 as **adatum\administrator** with the password of **Pa$$w0rd**.
2. Right-click the **Start** button and click **Event Viewer**.
3. Expand the **Windows Logs** and click **System**.
4. Right-click **System** and click **Filter Current Log**.
5. When the Filter Current Log dialog box opens, select **Critical**, **Warning**, and **Error**, and click **OK**.
6. After you view the listed events, right-click **System** and click **Filter Current Log**.
7. Deselect **Critical**, **Warning**, and **Error**.
8. In the <All Event IDs> text box, type **8015** and click **OK**.
9. Click the **Application** node. Double-click the first warning or error.
10. When the Event Properties dialog box opens, click **Close**.
11. Expand the **Applications and Services Logs**, expand **Microsoft**, expand **Windows**, expand **GroupPolicy**, and then click the **Operational** node.
12. Close Event Viewer.

Adding a Task to an Event

When certain events occur, there are times you will want to execute a task. With Event Viewer, you can attach a task to any event in Event Viewer.

When you associate a task to an event, you create a scheduled task that can be found in Task Scheduler. Therefore, whenever the specified event appears, the task will be executed. If you need to modify the task after it has been created, you can open Task Scheduler to modify the task.

 CREATE A BASIC TASK

GET READY. To create a basic task to an event, perform the following steps.

1. Right-click the **Start** button and click **Event Viewer**.
2. Right-click an event that you want to add a task to and choose **Attach 5, step 5, step 5 Task To This Event**.
3. When the Create Basic Task Wizard starts, click **Next**.
4. When the When a Specified Event Is Logged page opens, click **Next**.
5. On the Action page (see Figure 12-4), observe the following options:

   Start a program

   Send an e-mail

   Display a message

   Because *Send an e-mail* and *Display a message* are being deprecated (which means that you should not use these options unless you really need to and that they might not be available in the future), you should select **Start a program** and then click **Next**.

Figure 12-4

Choosing an action

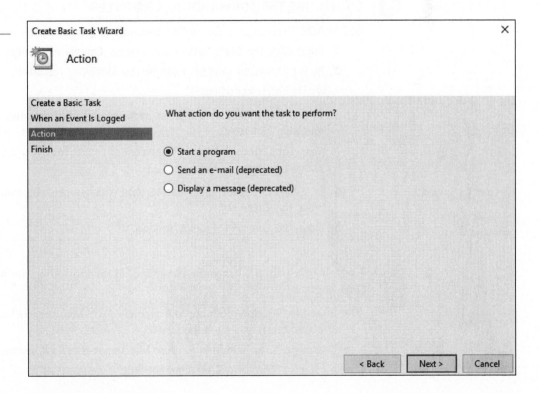

6. On the Start a Program page, in the Program/script text box, type the location and name of a program or script. If necessary, add any arguments and specify the directory to start in when the program or script is executed. Click **Next**.

7. On the Summary page, click **Finish**.

8. When an Event Viewer dialog box opens, click **OK**.

9. Close Event Viewer.

Configuring Event Subscriptions

Originally, Event Viewer allowed you to view events on a single computer. However, troubleshooting an issue might require you to examine a set of events stored in multiple logs on multiple computers. Therefore, Microsoft enhanced Event Viewer to capture events from multiple computers so that you can view the events using one console.

Today's Event Viewer can be used to collect copies of events from multiple remote computers and store them locally. To specify which events to collect, you create an *event subscription*. Among other details, the subscription specifies exactly which events will be collected and in which log they will be stored locally. Once a subscription is active and events are being collected, you can view and manipulate these forwarded events as you would any other locally stored events. Events are forwarded using Hypertext Transfer Protocol (HTTP) or Hypertext Transfer Protocol Secure (HTTPS).

To configure event subscriptions, perform the following steps:

1. Configure the forwarding computer.

2. Configure the collecting computer.

3. Create an event subscription.

 CONFIGURE THE FORWARDING COMPUTER

GET READY. To configure a forwarding computer to forward events, perform the following steps.

1. Right-click the **Start** button and choose **Command Prompt (Admin)**.

2. At the command prompt, execute the following command:

   Winrm quickconfig

3. To add the collecting computer name to the Administrators group, execute the following command:

   Net localgroup "Administrators" <collecting_computer_name>$@ <domain_name> /add

4. If a message appears, indicating that changes must be made, type **Y** and then press the **Enter** key.

5. Close the Command Prompt window.

Executing the winrm quickconfig command on the forwarding computer accomplishes the following:

- It sets the Windows Remote Management (WS-Management) service to Automatic (Delayed Start) and starts the service.

- It configures the Windows Remote Management HTTP listener.

- It creates a Windows Firewall exception.

CONFIGURE THE COLLECTING COMPUTER

GET READY. To configure a collecting computer to forward events, perform the following steps.

1. Right-click the **Start** button and choose **Command Prompt (Admin)**.

2. At the command prompt, execute the following command:

   `Wecutil qc`

3. Click **Y** and press the **Enter** key to change the service startup mode to Delay-Start. Close the Command Prompt window.

By executing the wecutil qc command, you configure the receiving computer to receive events. The last step is to then specify the events you want to send to the receiving computer.

 CREATE AN EVENT SUBSCRIPTION

GET READY. To create an event subscription on the collecting computer, perform the following steps.

1. Right-click the **Start** button and click **Event Viewer**.

2. Right-click **Subscriptions** and choose **Create Subscription**. The Subscription Properties dialog box opens, as shown in Figure 12-5.

Figure 12-5

Creating a subscription

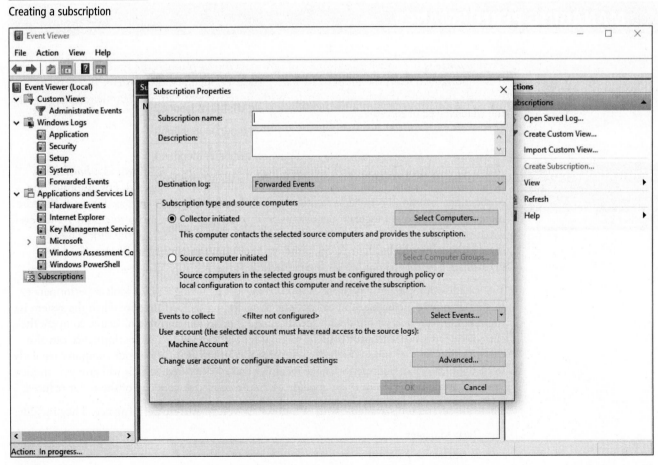

3. In the Subscription name text box, type the name for the subscription.

4. If necessary, in the Description text box, type a description.

5. In the Subscription type and source computers section, choose one of the following two options:

   • **Collector initiated:** The collecting computer polls the source computers to retrieve events. Then click the **Select Computers** button to select which computers to poll.

   • **Source computer initiated:** The forwarding computer contacts the collection computer. Then click the **Select Computer Groups** button to specify the forwarding computers.

6. Click **Select Events**. The Query Filter dialog box opens.

7. Specify the time range (by using the Logged drop-down box), event level (by selecting the appropriate check box), event logs (by using the Event Logs drop-down box), event sources (by using the Event sources drop-down box), keywords (by typing in the Keywords text box), or other parameters that specify which events you want forwarded.

8. Click **OK** to apply your settings and close the Query Filter dialog box.

9. Optionally, you can click the **Advanced** button to open the Advanced Subscription Settings dialog box and then configure the bandwidth used (Normal, Minimize Bandwidth, and Minimize Latency) and the protocol (HTTP or HTTPS). Click **OK** to close the Advanced Subscription Settings dialog box.

10. Close Event Viewer.

■ MANAGING PERFORMANCE

THE BOTTOM LINE

Performance is the overall effectiveness of how data moves through the system. Of course, it is important to select the proper hardware (processor, memory, disk system, and network) to satisfy the expected performance goals. Without the proper hardware, bottlenecks limit the effectiveness of software.

CERTIFICATION READY
Troubleshoot performance issues
Objective 3.2

When a component limits overall performance, that component is known as a *bottleneck*. When you relieve one bottleneck, another bottleneck might be triggered. For example, one of the most common bottlenecks is the amount of memory the system has. By increasing the memory, you can often increase the overall performance of a system (up to a point). However, when you add more RAM, then RAM needs to be fed more data from the disk. Therefore, the disk becomes the bottleneck. So, although the system might become faster, if your performance is still lacking, you will have to look for new bottlenecks.

You usually cannot identify performance problems just by taking a quick look at performance. Instead, you need a baseline. You can get one by analyzing the performance when the system is running normally and within design specifications. Then when a problem occurs, compare the current performance with your baseline to see what is different. Because performance can also change gradually over time, it is highly recommended that you baseline your computer regularly so that you can chart your performance measures and identify trends. This will give you an idea about when the server needs to be upgraded or replaced or the workload of the server reduced.

There are several tools available with Windows for you to analyze performance. They include:

• Task Manager

• Performance Monitor

• Resource Monitor

Monitoring Performance Using Task Manager

Task Manager gives you a quick glance at performance and provides information about programs and processes running on your computer. A *process* is an instance of a program that is being executed.

Task Manager is one of the handiest programs you can use to take a quick glance at performance to see which programs are using the most system resources on your computer. You can see the status of running programs and programs that have stopped responding, and you can stop a program running in memory.

To start Task Manager, right-click the empty space on the taskbar and click Task Manager (or you can open the Security menu by pressing the Ctrl+Alt+Del keys and choosing Start Task Manager). When Task Manager starts, it displays only the running applications (see Figure 12-6).

Figure 12-6

Using Task Manager

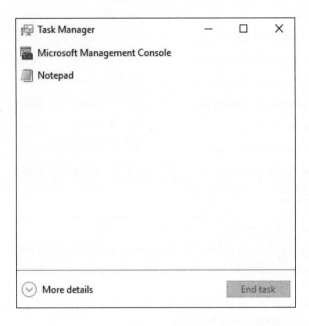

Click the More Details down-arrow to show all the available tabs (see Figure 12-7). When you first start Task Manager on a computer running Windows 10, seven tabs are opened for Task Manager:

- Processes
- Performance
- App history
- Startup
- Users
- Details
- Services

The Processes tab shows all processes running in memory and how much processing and memory each process uses. The processes will display applications (as designated by Apps), background processes, and Windows Processes. On the Processes tab, you can perform the following tasks:

- To see the processes that use the highest percentage of CPU utilization, click the CPU column header.

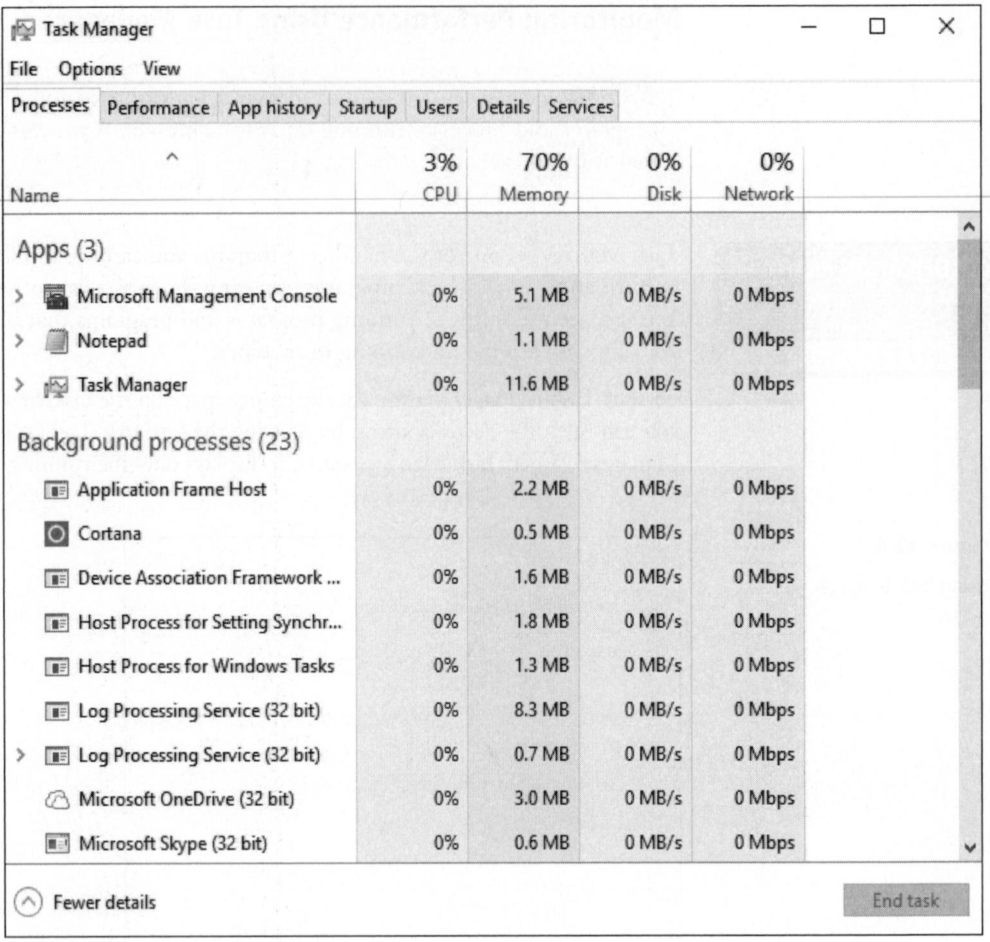
Task Manager
File Options View
Processes Performance App history Startup Users Details Services
Name
3% CPU
70% Memory
0% Disk
0% Network
Apps (3)
Microsoft Management Console 0% 5.1 MB 0 MB/s 0 Mbps
Notepad 0% 1.1 MB 0 MB/s 0 Mbps
Task Manager 0% 11.6 MB 0 MB/s 0 Mbps
Background processes (23)
Application Frame Host 0% 2.2 MB 0 MB/s 0 Mbps
Cortana 0% 0.5 MB 0 MB/s 0 Mbps
Device Association Framework ... 0% 1.6 MB 0 MB/s 0 Mbps
Host Process for Setting Synchr... 0% 1.8 MB 0 MB/s 0 Mbps
Host Process for Windows Tasks 0% 1.3 MB 0 MB/s 0 Mbps
Log Processing Service (32 bit) 0% 8.3 MB 0 MB/s 0 Mbps
Log Processing Service (32 bit) 0% 0.7 MB 0 MB/s 0 Mbps
Microsoft OneDrive (32 bit) 0% 3.0 MB 0 MB/s 0 Mbps
Microsoft Skype (32 bit) 0% 0.6 MB 0 MB/s 0 Mbps
Fewer details
End task

Figure 12-7

Viewing the Task Manager tabs

- To stop a process, right-click the process and select End task.
- To jump to the Details tab for a particular process, right-click the process and choose Go to details.
- If you want to see the executable that is running the processes, right-click the process and choose Open file location.

To add additional columns, right-click a column header, and select or deselect the desired column such as Process Identification (PID) or process name.

The Performance tab (as shown in Figure 12-8) displays the amount of CPU usage, physical Memory usage, and Ethernet throughput. For CPU usage, a high percentage indicates the programs or processes are requiring a lot of CPU resources, which can slow your computer. If the percentage seems frozen at or near 100%, a program might not be responding.

Click Memory to display how much of the paging file is being used (*In use* and *Available*), the amount of Committed and Cached memory, Paged pool, and Non-paged pool. It also shows you the total amount of RAM, the Speed of the RAM, and the number of Slots used for memory on the motherboard.

The App history tab displays how much resources (including CPU time and network) an application has been using over a period of time. The Startup tab was already discussed in Lesson 9. The Startup tab shows the programs that are configured to automatically start when you start Windows. You can disable the startup programs by right-clicking an item and clicking disable.

The Users tab displays the users who are currently logged on, the amount of CPU and memory usage that each user is using, and the processes the user is running. It also gives you the ability to disconnect them.

Figure 12-8

Viewing CPU usage

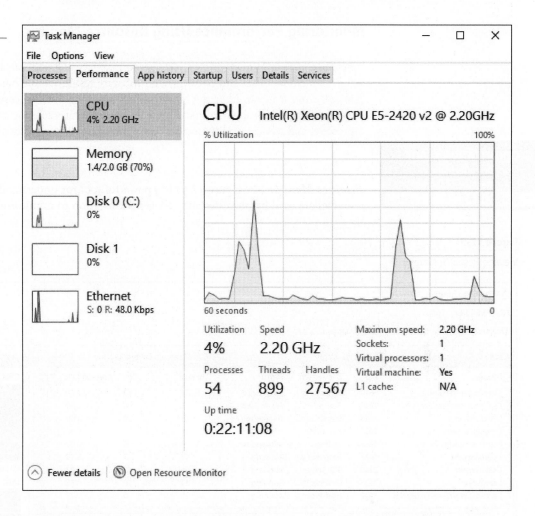

The Details tab displays a more detailed look at the processes running on the computer, including the Process Identification (PID). The PID is composed of unique numbers that identify a process while it is running. Similarly, you can stop the process and you can increase or decrease the process priority.

If you are an advanced user, you might want to view other advanced memory values on the Details tab. To do so, right-click the column heading and click Select Columns and then select or deselect values to be displayed or not displayed. While there are nearly 40 columns to display, some of the more useful values include the following:

- **Working set (memory):** Shows the amount of memory in the private working set plus the amount of memory the process is using that can be shared by other processes.
- **Peak working set (memory):** Shows the maximum amount of working set memory used by the process.
- **Working set delta (memory):** Shows the amount of change in working set memory used by the process.
- **Commit Size:** Shows the amount of virtual memory that is reserved for use by a process.
- **Paged pool:** Shows the amount of committed virtual memory for a process that can be written to another storage medium, such as the hard disk.
- **NP pool:** Shows the amount of committed virtual memory for a process that can't be written to another storage medium. (NP is an abbreviation for Non-Paged.)

The Services tab displays all services on the computer that are running and not running. Similar to the Services console, you can start, stop, or restart services.

Monitoring Performance Using Resource Monitor

Resource Monitor is a system tool that allows you to view information about the use of hardware (CPU, memory, disk, and network) and software resources (file handlers and modules) in real time. You can filter the results according to specific processes or services that you want to monitor. In addition, you can use Resource Monitor to start, stop, suspend, and resume processes and services, and to troubleshoot when an application does not respond as expected.

CERTIFICATION READY
Monitor performance
using Resource Monitor
Objective 3.2

Resource Monitor (see Figure 12-9) is a powerful tool for understanding how your system resources are used by processes and services. In addition to monitoring resource usage in

Figure 12-9

Viewing Resource Monitor

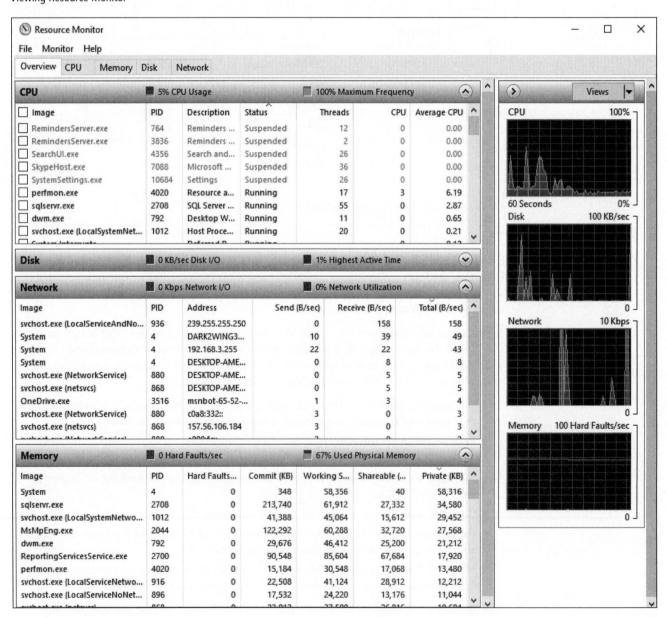

real time, Resource Monitor can help you analyze unresponsive processes, identify which applications are using files, and control processes and services. To start Resource Monitor, open Task Manager, click the Performance tab, and click Open Resource Monitor. You can also search for Resource Monitor from the Start page, or you can use a command prompt or Windows PowerShell to execute the resmon.exe command.

Resource Monitor includes five tabs:

- Overview
- CPU
- Memory
- Disk
- Network

The Overview tab displays basic system resource usage information; the other tabs display information about each specific resource. Each tab in Resource Monitor includes multiple tables that display detailed information about the resource featured on that respective tab.

The next four exercises cover common tasks for which you might use Resource Monitor. For example, if you want to determine the program (process) that is hogging the processor resources, you can use *Identify the highest current CPU usage*. If a file is locked and you cannot delete it because it is in use, you can use the *Identify the process that is using a file exercise* to see which process has the file open.

 ### IDENTIFY THE HIGHEST CURRENT CPU USAGE

GET READY. To identify a process that is using the highest current CPU usage, perform the following steps.

1. Click the **Start** button and type **Resource Monitor**. From the search results, click **Resource Monitor**.
2. Click the **CPU** tab.
3. In the Processes section, click **CPU** to sort processes by current CPU resource consumption.

 ### VIEW THE CPU USAGE OF A PROCESS

GET READY. To view the CPU usage for each process, perform the following steps.

1. Click the **Start** button and type **Resource Monitor**. From the search results, click **Resource Monitor**.
2. Click the **CPU** tab.
3. In the Processes section, in the Image column, select the check box next to the name of the service for which you want to see usage details. You can select multiple services. Selected services are moved to the top of the column.
4. Click the title bar of **Services** to expand the table. Review the data in Services to see the list of processes hosted by the selected services and to view their CPU usage.

IDENTIFY THE PROCESS THAT IS USING A FILE

GET READY. To identify the process that is using a file, perform the following steps.

1. Click the **Start** button and type **Resource Monitor**. From the search results, click **Resource Monitor**.
2. Click the **CPU** tab and then click the title bar of **Associated Handlers** to expand the table.
3. Click in the **Search Handlers** box, type the name of the file you want to search for, and then click **Search**.

 IDENTIFY THE NETWORK ADDRESS TO WHICH A PROCESS IS CONNECTED

GET READY. To identify the network address that a process is connected to, perform the following steps.

1. Click the **Start** button and type **Resource Monitor**. From the search results, click **Resource Monitor**.
2. Click the **Network** tab and then click the title bar of **TCP Connections** to expand the table.
3. Locate the process whose network connection you want to identify. If there are a large number of entries in the table, you can click **Image** to sort by executable file name.
4. Review the Remote Address column and the Remote Port column to see which network address and port the process is connected to.

Monitoring Performance Using Performance Monitor

Performance Monitor is an MMC snap-in that provides tools for analyzing system performance. It is included in the Computer Management console and it can be opened as a stand-alone console from Administrative Tools. It can also be started by executing the perfmon command. From a single console, you can monitor application and hardware performance in real time, specify which data you want to collect in logs, define thresholds for alerts and automatic actions, generate reports, and view past performance data in a variety of ways.

CERTIFICATION READY
Monitor performance using Performance Monitor
Objective 3.2

Performance Monitor (see Figure 12-10) provides a visual display of built-in Windows performance counters, either in real time or as a way to review historical data.

You can add performance counters to Performance Monitor by right-clicking the main pane and choosing Add Counters. Another way to add performance counters is to create and use custom Data Collector Sets. (Data Collector Sets are explained later in this lesson.) Figure 12-11 shows the Add Counters dialog box. You can create custom views that can be exported as Data Collector Sets for use with performance and logging features.

Figure 12-10

Viewing Performance Monitor

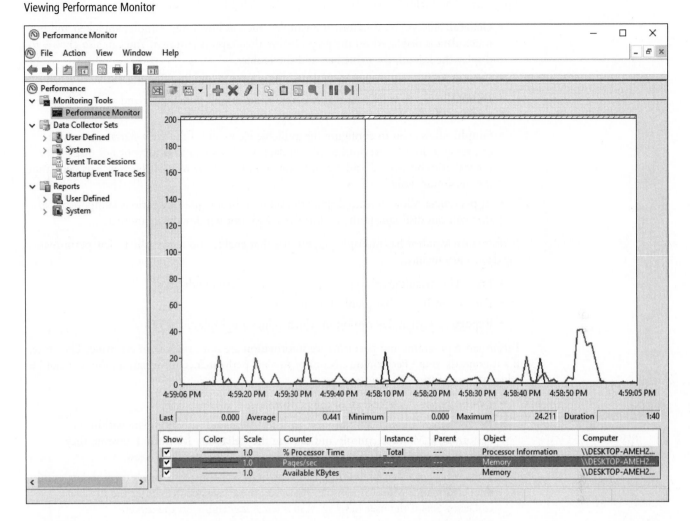

Figure 12-11

Adding counters
to Performance Monitor

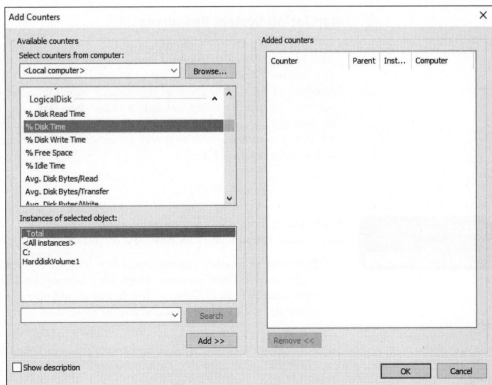

To control how and what is displayed, right-click Performance Monitor and choose Properties. The Performance Monitor Properties dialog box displays the following five tabs:

- **General:** Allows you to adjust the samples, such as how often samples are taken and how much data is displayed on the graph before the graph is redrawn. You can also choose to display the legend, the value bar, and the toolbar.
- **Source:** Allows you to display real-time data or to open a log file that you have saved.
- **Data:** Allows you to choose counters to appear as well as the color and scale of those counters.
- **Graph:** Allows you to configure the available views and if the view starts over or you can scroll to look at previous displayed data. It allows you to display or not display the vertical grid, horizontal grid, vertical scale numbers, time axis labels, as well as determine the maximum scale.
- **Appearance:** Allows you to display the color and fonts used by various components so that you can distinguish one Performance Monitor window from another.

Performance Monitor has multiple graph types that enable you to visually review performance log data. They include:

- **Line:** The default graph type; connects points of data with lines
- **Histogram Bar:** A bar graph showing data
- **Report:** A written description in which values are displayed as text

Performance programs and performance information are not available to everyone. Therefore, if a user needs to use Performance Monitor to view performance information, the user can be added to one of the following groups:

- *Administrators* can access all of the performance tools and data.
- *Performance Monitor Users* can view both real-time and historical data within the Performance Monitor console and can use the Reliability Monitor. However, they cannot create or modify Data Collector Sets or use the Resource View.
- The *Performance Log Users* group can view both real-time data and historical data within the Performance Monitor console. However, these users can create or modify Data Collector Sets if the user has *Log on as a batch user* rights on the server.

Monitoring System Resources

Task Manager, Resource Monitor, and Performance Monitor can be used to view the four primary systems that make up a computer. As previously mentioned, there are hundreds of counters available in Performance Monitor and as you add other services or applications, other counters are made available that allow you to monitor the performance of those applications. Although using all of these counters might take some heavy research, you should always start with some basic performance counters to get a glimpse of how your system is running.

CERTIFICATION READY
Monitor system resources
Objective 3.2

A computer is composed of four primary systems: a processor, memory, disk, and network. For the processor, memory, and disk performance, you should always start with these counters:

- Processor: %Processor Time measures how busy the processor is. Although the processor might jump to 100% processor usage, the processor should not be working at or above 80% capacity most of the time. If it is, you should upgrade the processor (using a faster processor or add additional processors) or move some of the services to other systems.

- A page fault occurs when a process attempts to access a virtual memory page that is not available in its working set in RAM. If the pages/sec is 1,000 or higher, you should increase the memory.
- Paging File: % Usage shows how much of the paging file is actually being used. If the paging file % usage is above 75%, you might need to increase memory or reduce the server's memory usage.
- Physical Disk: %Disk Time indicates how busy a disk is as measured by the percentage of time that disk was busy. If a disk is consistently approaching 100%, the disk is being overutilized.
- Physical Disk: %Avg. Disk Queue Length is the average number of read requests or write requests queued for the disk in question. A sustained average higher than 2 times the number of spindles (physical hard drives) indicates that the disk is being overutilized.

Monitoring Performance Using Data Collector Sets

> Rather than add individual performance counters each time you want to view the performance of a system, you can create *Data Collector Sets (DCS)* that allow you to organize a set of performance counters, event trace data, and system configuration data into a single object that can be reused as needed.

Windows Performance Monitor uses performance counters, event trace data, and configuration information, which can be combined into Data Collector Sets as follows:

- Performance counters are measurements of system state or activity. They can be included in the operating system or can be part of individual applications. Windows Performance Monitor requests the current value of performance counters at specified time intervals.
- Event trace data is collected from trace providers, which are components of the operating system or of individual applications that report actions or events. Output from multiple trace providers can be combined into a trace session.
- Configuration information is collected from key values in the Windows registry.

Windows Performance Monitor can record the value of a registry key at a specified time or interval as part of a file.

 CREATE AND USE A DATA COLLECTOR SET

GET READY. To create a DCS, perform the following steps.

1. Click the **Start** button and type **Performance Monitor**. Then from the results, click **Performance Monitor**.
2. In the left pane, expand **Data Collector Sets**.
3. Right-click the **User Defined** folder and choose **New > Data Collector Set**.
4. On the Create New Data Collector Set page, when you are prompted to create a new Data Collector Set, type a name in the Name text box. Ensure that the **Create from a template (Recommended)** option is selected and then click **Next**.
5. When you are prompted to choose a template (see Figure 12-12), click **System Performance** and then click **Next**.

Figure 12-12

Selecting a template

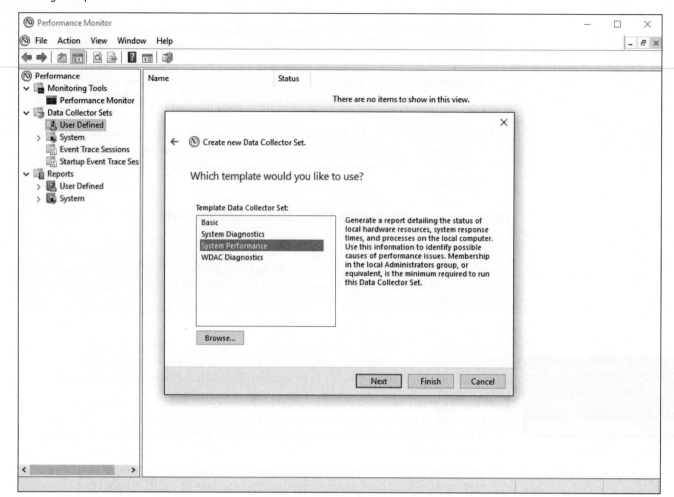

6. When you are prompted to choose where you would like the data to be saved, click **Next**. If you run Performance Monitor to collect data over an extended period, you should change the location to a nonsystem data drive.

7. When you are prompted to create the Data Collector Set, with the **Save and close** option selected, click **Finish**.

8. To start the Data Collector Set, right-click the DCS and choose **Start**.

9. Close Performance Monitor.

Configuring Performance Alerts

In Performance Monitor, a ***performance alert*** is a notification or task that is executed when a performance value is reached. Performance Monitor can also be used to start certain tasks when certain counters reach a particular value. For example, if the processor reaches 90%, you can have Performance Monitor run a command to stop a service or perform some other action in an effort to reduce burden on the processor.

When you configure performance alerts, you can perform almost any action that you want. You can send a network message or log events into the application event log. You can configure alerts to start applications and performance logs.

CREATE A PERFORMANCE ALERT

GET READY. To create a performance alert, perform the following steps.

1. Click the **Start** button and type **Performance Monitor**. Then from the results, click **Performance Monitor**.

2. In the left pane, expand **Data Collector Sets**.

3. Right-click the **User Defined** folder and then choose **New > Data Collector Set**.

4. On the Create New Data Collector Set page, when you are prompted to create a new Data Collector Set, type a name in the Name text box.

5. Select **Create manually (Advanced)** and then click **Next**.

6. Select **Performance Counter Alert** and then click **Next**.

7. When you are prompted to identify the performance counter you would like to monitor, click **Add** to open a dialog box, in which to select the desired counter. When you have added the counter, click **OK**.

8. The limit defines when a performance alert is triggered. For the *Alert when* option, select either **Above** or **Below** and then in the Limit box, type the value. Click **Next**.

9. When you are prompted to create the Data Collector Set, select **Open properties for this data collector set**. Click **Finish**.

10. When the Properties dialog box opens, click the **Task** tab.

11. In the Run this scheduled task when the data collector set stops text box, type the path of a script or command that you want to execute when the condition is met. If necessary, specify any task arguments in the Task Arguments text box.

12. To specify when the Data Collector Set will run, click the **Schedule** tab (see Figure 12-13).

13. Click **Add**. In the Folder Action dialog box, specify the Beginning date that the task will run, the Expiration date for the task, and the Launch time.

Figure 12-13

Viewing the Schedule tab

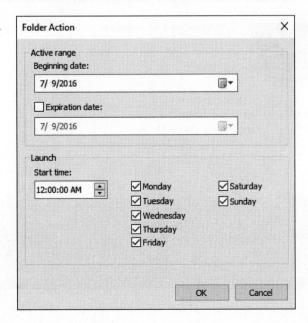

14. Click **OK** to apply your settings and then click **OK** again to close the Properties dialog box.

15. Close Performance Monitor.

■ MANAGING CLIENT SECURITY USING WINDOWS DEFENDER

THE BOTTOM LINE

Windows Defender is designed to protect your computer against viruses, spyware, and other types of malware. It protects against these threats by providing real-time protection in which it notifies you if malware attempts to install itself on your computer or when an application tries to change critical settings.

It can also be configured to scan your computer on a regular basis and remove or quarantine malware it finds.

TAKE NOTE Windows Defender automatically disables itself if you install another antivirus product.

CERTIFICATION READY
Manage client security by using Windows Defender
Objective 3.2

At the heart of Windows Defender are its definition files, which are downloaded from Windows Update. The definition files, which contain information about potential threats, are used by Windows Defender to notify you of potential threats to your system.

To access Windows Defender from the Windows 10 menu, click Start, type Windows Defender, and choose it from the Results. Figure 12-14 shows the Windows Defender Home tab.

Figure 12-14

Viewing the Windows Defender Home tab

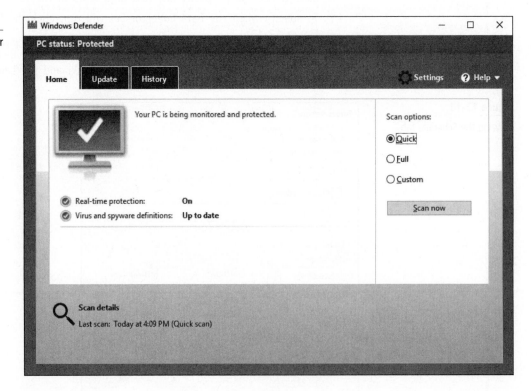

Using the Home Tab

The Home tab allows you to check the status of Windows Defender, including whether Windows Defender is up to date and whether Windows Defender is protecting your system. It also gives you the option to initiate a scan.

When looking at the Home tab, you should always look for a green message indicating *Your PC is being monitored and protected* and you should also make sure your system is up to date. Other components include:

- **Real-time protection:** Real-time protection uses signature detection methodology and heuristics to monitor and catch malware behavior. Signature detection uses a vendor's definition files to detect malicious programs. If the program contains code that matches the signature, the program most likely contains the virus. This works well when the threat has already been identified, but what happens in between the time the virus is released and the definition file is made available? That's where heuristics can help. It is used to monitor for suspicious activity by a program. Suspicious activity includes a program trying to copy itself into another program, a program trying to write to the disk directly, or a program trying to manipulate critical system files required by the operating system. These are indicators of possible malware activity that heuristics can detect.

- **Virus and spyware definitions:** When a new virus is discovered, Microsoft creates a new virus signature/definition update. Each definition file contains a piece of the actual virus code that is used to detect a specific virus or malware. During scans, the content on the computer is compared with information in the definition files. Because new viruses are created every day and existing viruses are modified regularly, it's important to keep your definitions updated.

- **Scan options (Quick, Full, and Custom):** A Quick scan checks the areas that malicious software, including viruses, spyware, and unwanted software, are most likely to infect. A Full scan checks all the files on your disk, including running programs. A Custom scan is designed to check only locations and files you specify.

- **Scan Details:** This area of the Home tab provides information on when the last scan was performed on the computer.

Using the Update Tab

The Update tab provides you with information about your virus and spyware definitions. It is important to keep these current to ensure your computer is protected at all times.

The Update tab provides information about when the definition files were created, the last time you updated them, and the current version numbers for the virus and spyware definitions. Windows Defender updates the definition files automatically, but you can manually check for updates by clicking *Update definitions* on this tab.

Using the History Tab

The History tab provides information about items that have been detected in the past and the actions that were taken with them.

The categories of items are as follows:

- **Quarantined Items:** These items were not allowed to run but were not removed from your computer.
- **Allowed Items:** These items were allowed to run on your computer.
- **All Detected Items:** These items provide a list of all items detected on your computer.

 REMOVE A QUARANTINED ITEM

GET READY. To remove an item that has been quarantined, perform the following steps.

1. Open **Windows Defender**.
2. Click the **History** tab.
3. Click **Quarantined Items**.
4. Click **View Details**.
5. Select the detected item and then read the description.
6. Click **Remove**.

Using Windows Defender Settings

If you click Windows Defender Settings, you will open the Windows 10 Settings Update & security > Windows Defender page, as shown in Figure 12-15. The Settings page is where you can fine-tune how Windows Defender works.

Figure 12-15

The Windows Defender Settings page

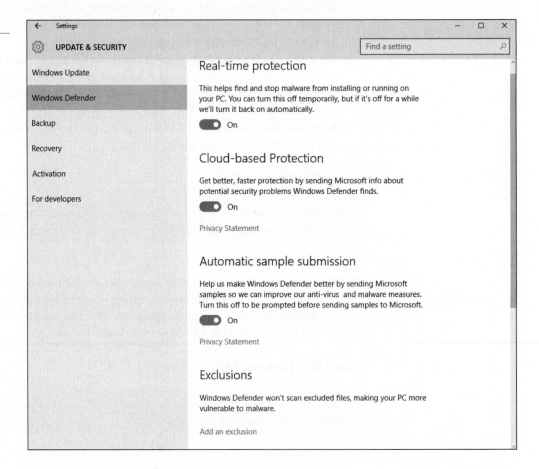

On the Settings page, you can:

- Enable or disable real-time protection.
- Select if you want to use cloud-based protection.
- Select the files and locations you want to exclude from the scanning process.
- Select the file types you want to exclude from the scan.
- Select the processes you want to exclude.
- Display the Windows 10 version information.
- Open Windows Defender.

Microsoft Active Protection Service (MAPS) is an online community that can help you decide how to respond to certain threat types, and it serves as a resource to help stop the spread of new viruses and malware. The information that you send helps Microsoft create new definition files. It can be enabled or disabled via the Windows Defender settings. When enabled, information is sent to Microsoft about where the software came from, the actions you took, and whether the actions you took were successful.

Windows Defender can also be configured via the Local Group Policy Editor or Group Policy Management Editor (AD domains). The following policies are located in the Computer Configuration\Administrative Templates\Windows Components\Windows Defender node:

- **Scan\Check for the latest virus and spyware definitions before a scheduled scan:** When enabled, Windows Defender checks for new signatures before running the scan.
- **Turn off Windows Defender:** This setting turns Windows Defender on or off.
- **Real-time Protection\Turn off Real-Time Monitoring:** This setting controls whether Windows Defender monitors your system in real time and alerts you if malware or potentially unwanted software attempts to install or run on the computer.
- **Threats\Specify threats upon which default action should not be taken when detected:** This setting determines whether Windows Defender automatically takes action on malware that it identifies.
- **MAPS\Join Microsoft MAPS:** This setting determines the type of membership you use with MAPS. Options include No Membership, Basic Membership, or Advanced Membership.

To keep your system more secure, you should schedule a Windows Defender scan.

 SCHEDULE A WINDOWS DEFENDER SCAN

GET READY. To schedule a Windows Defender scan, log on with administrative privileges and then perform the following steps.

1. Click the **Start** button and type **taskschd.msc**. From the results, click **Task Scheduler**.
2. In the left pane, expand **Task Scheduler Library > Microsoft > Windows > Windows Defender**.
3. Double-click **Windows Defender Scheduled Scan**.
4. When the Windows Defender Scheduled Scan Properties (Local Computer) dialog box opens (as shown in Figure 12-16), click the **Triggers** tab and then click **New**.
5. In the Begin the task field, choose **On a schedule**.

Figure 12-16

Scheduling a Windows
Defender scan

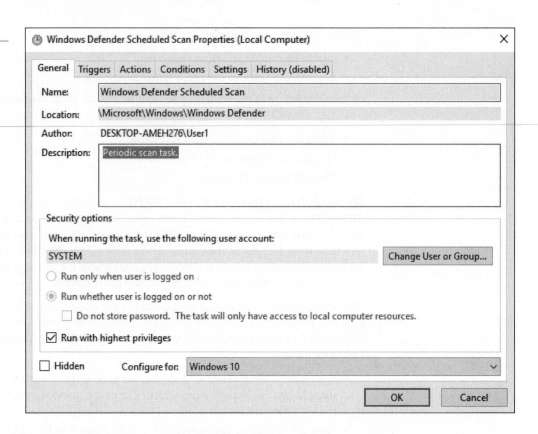

6. Under Settings, select **One time** and in the Start field, change the time to 5 minutes from your current time.

7. Make sure the **Enabled** check box is checked and then click **OK.**

8. To close the Windows Defender Scheduled Scan Properties (Local Computer) dialog box, click **OK.**

9. Open **Windows Defender** to see the status of the scan on the Home tab.

■ USING RELIABILITY MONITOR

THE BOTTOM LINE

Reliability Monitor is a Control Panel/Action Panel tool that measures hardware and software problems and other changes to your computer that could affect the reliability of the computer.

CERTIFICATION READY
Evaluate system stability
using Reliability Monitor
Objective 3.2

The *Reliability Monitor* provides a stability index that ranges from 1 (the least stable) to 10 (the most stable). You can use the index to help evaluate the reliability of your computer. Any change you make to your computer or problem that occurs on your computer affects the stability index.

To open the Reliability Monitor, execute the following command at a command prompt:

```
perfmon /rel
```

Or you can open it from Performance Monitor.

When the Reliability Monitor opens (see Figure 12-17), you can then:

- Click any event on the graph to view its details.
- Click Days or Weeks to view the stability index over a specific period of time.
- Click items in the Action column to view more information about each event.
- At the bottom of the page, click the View all problem reports link to view only the problems that have occurred on your computer. This view doesn't include the other computer events that show up in Reliability Monitor, such as events about software installation.

Figure 12-17

Viewing the Reliability Monitor information

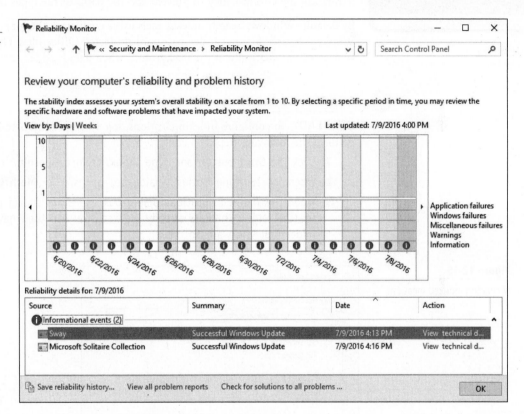

OPEN RELIABILITY MONITOR

GET READY. To open the Reliability Monitor, log on with administrative privileges and then perform the following steps.

1. Click the **Start** button, type **perfmon /rel**, and then press the **Enter** key.
2. When the Reliability Monitor window opens, click for any day that is not rated as a 10.
3. Click any red circle with a white X.
4. Click any blue circle with a white exclamation point.
5. If you have any events, click the **View technical detail** link.

■ CONFIGURING INDEXING OPTIONS

THE BOTTOM LINE

Windows can have hundreds or even thousands of data files spread through multiple folders or even drives. When you have this many files, you don't necessarily know where each file is and you might need to search for a specific file. To make your searches go smoothly and quickly, you need to have your data documents indexed. If the files are not indexed properly, it might take a long time to search for a file, and you might have trouble finding the file that you seek.

CERTIFICATION READY
Configure indexing options
Objective 3.2

Windows keeps one master index for each computer. Each user's data is identified by a unique user security identifier (SID), so users have access only to their own content. System administrators can use Group Policy to prevent specific paths or file types from being indexed.

By default, Windows Search indexes each user's email and Documents and Settings folders. Windows Search does not index password-protected Office files. The Windows Search index is updated automatically in the background when data is added, deleted, and modified.

 CONFIGURE INDEXING OPTIONS

GET READY. To configure indexing options, log on with administrative privileges and then perform the following steps.

1. Click the **Start** button and type **index**. From the results, click **Indexing Options**.
2. When the Indexing Options dialog box opens, click **Modify**.
3. When the Indexed Locations dialog box opens (as shown in Figure 12-18), you will see the folders that are already indexed. You can then navigate to and select any folder that you want to index.

Figure 12-18

Managing indexed locations

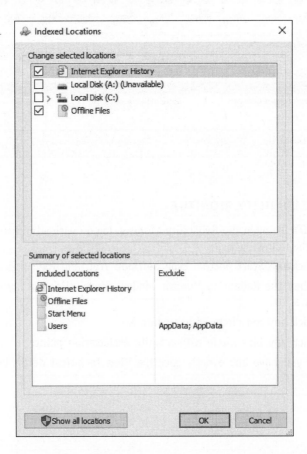

4. To close the Indexed Locations dialog box, click **OK**.

5. Click the **Advanced** button.

6. When the Advanced Options dialog box opens, if you are having problems with the index where you cannot find certain files that you know are indexed, you can click the **Rebuild** button.

7. If you need to change the location of the index files, in the New location, after service is restarted text box, you can type in a new path, and click the **Select new** button.

8. If you want to encrypt the index files, select the **Index encrypted files** option.

9. To close the Advanced Options dialog box, click **OK**.

10. To close the Indexing Options dialog box, click **Close**.

SKILL SUMMARY

IN THIS LESSON YOU LEARNED:

- Event Viewer is an MMC snap-in that enables you to browse and manage event logs. It is included in the Computer Management console and is included in Administrative Tools as a stand-alone console.

- Performance is the overall effectiveness of how data moves through the system. Of course, it is important to select the proper hardware (processor, memory, disk system, and network) to satisfy the expected performance goals. Without the proper hardware, bottlenecks limit the effectiveness of software. There are several tools available with Windows for you to analyze performance. They include Task Manager, Performance Monitor, and Resource Monitor.

- Task Manager gives you a quick glance at performance and provides information about programs and processes running on your computer. A process is an instance of a program that is being executed.

- Windows Defender is designed to protect your computer against viruses, spyware, and other types of malware. It protects against these threats by providing real-time protection in which it notifies you if malware attempts to install itself on your computer or when an application tries to change critical settings.

- Reliability Monitor is a Control Panel/Action Panel tool that measures hardware and software problems and other changes to your computer that could affect the reliability of the computer.

- To make your searches go smoothly and quickly, you need to have your data documents indexed. If the files are not indexed properly, it might take a long time to search for a file, and you might have trouble finding the file that you seek.

■ Knowledge Assessment

Multiple Choice

Select the correct answer for each of the following questions.

1. Which of the following is used to view the Windows logs?
   a. Performance Monitor
   b. Reliability Monitor
   c. System Viewer
   d. Event Viewer

2. When troubleshooting a problem and using Event Viewer, which of the following should be used to help focus on a reduced set of events?
   a. Permissions
   b. Rights
   c. Views
   d. Filters

3. Which of the following allows viewing events from multiple computers using Event Viewer?
   a. Subscriptions
   b. Web services
   c. Filters
   d. Remote Viewer

4. Which command is used to configure a collecting computer to receive an event subscription?
   a. `perfmon /rel`
   b. `wecutil qc`
   c. `winrm quickconfig`
   d. `winrm subscr`

5. Which program is used to stop a running process?
   a. Performance Monitor
   b. Reliability Monitor
   c. Task Manager
   d. Event Viewer

6. Which program is used to determine what process is using a file?
   a. Performance Monitor
   b. Reliability Monitor
   c. Task Manager
   d. Resource Monitor

7. Which of the following is used to group multiple performance counters so that they can be used over and over in Performance Monitor?
   a. Replay Monitor
   b. Event Viewer
   c. Data Collector Sets
   d. Task Manager

8. Which of the following features can protect a PC against malware?
   a. Windows Defender
   b. Windows Quicktime
   c. Windows File History
   d. Windows Antivirus

9. Which of the following scan options are available in Windows Defender? (Choose all that apply.)
   a. Quick
   b. Full
   c. Optional
   d. Custom

10. On which of the following tabs can the items Windows Defender quarantined be found?
   a. Home tab
   b. History tab
   c. Update tab
   d. Settings tab

Best Answer

Choose the letter that corresponds to the best answer. More than one answer choice may achieve the goal. Select the BEST answer.

1. An administrator has installed a new server (Server1), which is a file and print server. He has received several calls from users who are complaining of slow performance when opening files from the server. Which two tasks determine which application is using the most processing? (Choose two answers.)
   a. Open Event Viewer and review the Performance logs.
   b. Open Task Manager and view the Processes tab.
   c. Open Resource Monitor and use the Resource View to see the percentage of processor capacity used by each application.
   d. Open Performance Monitor and view the appropriate performance counter.

2. After creating a Data Collector Set, which of the following actions prevents the DCS from logging data when the server has less than 1 GB of available disk space?
   a. Modify the Data Manager settings of the DCS.
   b. Create a passive file screen.
   c. Modify the DCS Actions Properties.
   d. Modify the Disk Redirect option.

3. When forwarding events, which group on the forwarding computer should the collection computer name be added to?
   a. Performance Users
   b. Domain Admins
   c. Administrators
   d. System Logon

Matching and Identification

1. Match each Windows log to the appropriate description or usage.

    _____ 1. Application log

    _____ 2. Security log

    _____ 3. Setup log

    _____ 4. System log

    _____ 5. Forwarded events

    a. Shows boot errors

    b. Shows events collected from remote computers

    c. Shows events generated by applications

    d. Contains events related to the installation of applications

    e. Shows invalid logons and access to audited files

2. Identify the maximum value of the following performance counters.

    _____ % Processor Time

    _____ Pages/sec

    _____ Paging File:% Usage

    _____ % Avg. Disk Queue Length

Build a List

1. An administrator needs to configure WinStation2 to forward errors found in the System logs to WinStation1. Specify the correct order of steps necessary to configure WinStation1 and WinStation2. (Not all steps are necessary.)

    _____ Run `Winrm quickconfig` on WinStation1.

    _____ Run `Winrm quickconfig` on WinStation 2.

    _____ Create a subscription on WinStation1.

    _____ Create a subscription on WinStation2.

    _____ Run `wecutil qc` on WinStation1.

    _____ Run `wecutil qc` on WinStation2.

2. Specify the correct order of steps necessary to remove a quarantined item in Windows Defender.

    _____ Click Quarantined Items.

    _____ Open Windows Defender.

    _____ Select the detected item and read the description.

    _____ Click View Details.

    _____ Click the History tab.

    _____ Click Remove.

■ Business Case Scenarios

Scenario 12-1: Troubleshooting a Performance Problem

You manage several file servers. Several times during the day, the file server performance degrades significantly. Describe how to troubleshoot the problem.

Scenario 12-2: Monitoring the Event Viewer of Multiple Computers

You manage 40 essential servers that must run the best they can at all times. Describe the most efficient way to review key events on all 40 servers each day.

Configuring System and Data Recovery

70-698 EXAM OBJECTIVE

Objective 3.3 – Configure system and data recovery. This objective may include but is not limited to: Configure a recovery drive; configure a system restore; perform a refresh or recycle; configure restore points; restore previous versions of files and folders; configure File History; recover files from OneDrive; use Windows Backup and Restore; perform a backup and restore with WBAdmin; perform recovery operations using Windows Recovery. * Perform a driver rollback, resolve hardware and devices issues, and interpret data from Device Manager are covered in Lesson 3.

LESSON HEADING	EXAM OBJECTIVE
Configuring System Recovery	
Configuring a System Restore	Configure a system restore
	Configure restore points
Performing a PC Refresh or Reset	Perform a refresh or recycle
Configuring a Windows 10 File Recovery Drive	Configure a recovery drive
Restoring Previous Versions of Files and Folders with Windows Backup	Restore previous versions of files and folders
	Use Windows Backup and Restore
Performing a Backup and Restore with WBAdmin	Perform a backup and restore with WBAdmin
Configuring File History	Configure File History
Recovering Files from OneDrive	Recover files from OneDrive
Performing Recovery Operations Using Windows Recovery	Perform recovery operations using Windows Recovery

KEY TERMS

backup

File History

OneDrive Recycle Bin

PC refresh

PC reset

restore point

Safe mode

wbadmin.exe command

Windows 10 File Recovery drive

Windows 10 System Restore

Windows 7 File Recovery

Windows Recovery Environment (Windows RE or WinRE)

■ CONFIGURING SYSTEM RECOVERY

THE BOTTOM LINE

There is no good time for a system to fail. But when it does, you need to be ready. And the best way to be ready is to know what recovery options you have and what steps you should take before the problem occurs. However, the best method for system and data recovery is back up, back up, and then back up some more.

A *backup* or the process of backing up refers to duplicating data so that these duplications can be accessed in your efforts to restore the original after a data loss event. Backups can be used to restore entire systems following a disaster or to restore a small set of files that were accidentally deleted or corrupted.

When planning backups, you need to plan where backup files will be stored. If files are stored at various locations throughout your corporation—including users keeping their files on their local computers—it is very difficult to back up all of these files. Therefore, you will most likely need to use some form of technology that will store your files in a limited number of locations. For example, you can configure the user profiles for file redirection for the desktop and for My Documents so that files are stored on a file server.

Configuring a System Restore

Windows 10 System Restore is a recovery option for your computer that backs up your settings and registry, but does not back up your personal data.

CERTIFICATION READY
Configure a system restore
Objective 3.3

CERTIFICATION READY
Configure restore points
Objective 3.3

Windows 10 System Restore saves information about your drivers, registry settings, programs, and system files in the form of restore points for drives with system protection turned on. A *restore point* is a representation of the state of your computer's system files and settings.

You can then use the restore points to return these items to an earlier state without affecting your personal files. You should create restore points prior to performing any major system event, such as the installation of a program or a new device driver.

By default, Windows 10 automatically creates restore points every seven days if you have not created one during that time period. You can also create restore points manually any time you want.

 CONFIGURE A SYSTEM RESTORE

GET READY. To configure a System Restore, log on with local administrative privileges and then perform the following steps.

1. Click the **Start** button and type **System Restore**. From Results, click **Create a restore point**.

TAKE NOTE

You can also access System Restore via Control Panel > System and Security > System Protection.

2. Click the **C** drive, click **Configure**, and then make sure **Turn on system protection** is selected, as shown in Figure 13-1.
3. Drag the Max Usage slider to **10%**. This adjusts the disk space for system protection. When the space fills up, older restore points are deleted to make room for new ones.

Figure 13-1

Confirming system protection
is enabled

4. Click **Apply** and then click **OK**.

5. Click **Create** to create a new restore point.

6. In the Description text box, type text that describes the name of the restore point that you are creating.

7. Click **Create**.

8. When notified that the restore point was created successfully, click **Close**.

9. Click **OK** to accept your settings and to close the System Properties dialog box.

In most cases, you want to restore the most recent restore point, but you can choose from a list of restore points if you have more than one. The best approach is to use the restore point that was created just before you started experiencing problems with your computer.

In the exercise that follows, assume that the installation of an application was completed and your system is not functioning normally. To return your computer to a functioning state, use the restore point you just created.

 PERFORM A SYSTEM RESTORE USING A RESTORE POINT

GET READY. To perform a System Restore using a restore point, log on with local administrative privileges and then perform the following steps.

1. Click the **Start** button and type **System restore**. From Results, click **Create a restore point**.

2. Click **System Restore**.

3. Click **Next** to start the System Restore Wizard. A System Restore does not affect your documents, pictures, or other personal data. Recently installed programs and drivers may be uninstalled.

4. Select the desired restore point (see Figure 13-2) and then click **Scan for affected programs**. After the scan is complete, you will see any programs and drivers that will be deleted, as well as programs and drivers that might be restored.

Figure 13-2

Selecting a restore point

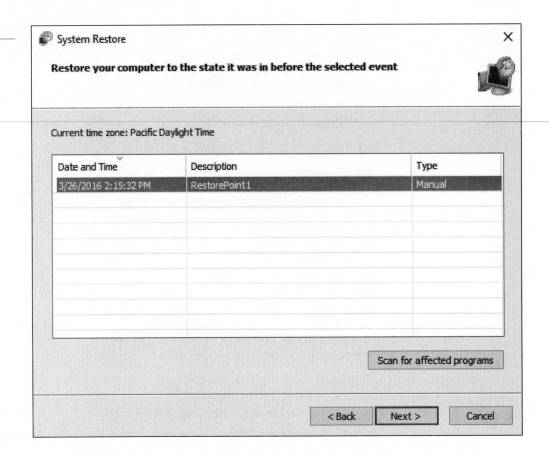

5. Click **Close** and then click **Next**.
6. Click **Finish**.
7. If you changed your Windows password, you should also create a password reset disk by clicking the **Start** button and then searching for **Create a password reset disk**.
8. Click **Yes** to begin the System Restore process. Windows restarts the computer, restores your files and settings, restores the registry, and removes temp files as part of the restore process.
9. After the restore process is complete, log back on to your system.

Performing a PC Refresh or Reset

Sometimes you might want to refresh, reset, or restore a PC to clean up the PC or to put the PC back to a new state. A *PC refresh* reinstalls Windows and keeps your personal files and settings. It also keeps the apps that came with your PC and any apps you may have installed from the Windows Store. A *PC reset* reinstalls Windows but deletes your files, settings, and apps, except for the apps that came with your PC. Restoring your PC is a way to undo recent system changes you've made.

CERTIFICATION READY
Perform a refresh
or recycle.
Objective 3.3

In most cases, when you start to refresh or reset your PC, it will finish on its own. However, if Windows needs missing files, you'll be prompted to insert recovery media, which is typically on a DVD or thumb drive.

→ **REFRESH YOUR PC**

GET READY. To perform a PC Refresh or PC Reset on a computer running Windows 10, log on with local administrative privileges and then perform the following steps.

1. Insert your Windows 10 installation media.
2. Click the **Start** button and click **Settings**.
3. Tap or click **Update and security** and then tap or click **Recovery**. Figure 13-3 shows the Recovery options.

Figure 13-3

Recovery options

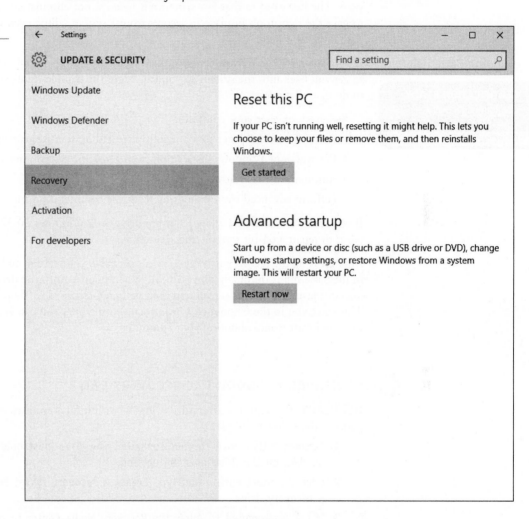

4. Under Reset this PC, click **Get started**.
5. When the Choose an Option page opens, click **Keep my files**. If you wanted to perform a PC Reset, you would click **Remove everything**.
6. On the Your Apps Will Be Removed page, click **Next**.
7. On the Ready to Reset This PC page, click **Reset**. The computer restarts.
8. On the Windows 10 logon screen, type your password to log on.

If your Windows 10 computer has traditional applications that were installed from a disc or from other websites, they are removed from your computer during a PC Refresh. Windows puts a link to a list of the removed applications on your desktop. If you click the link, you see a list of the applications removed. Clicking the application's name directs you to the manufacturer's website from which you can download and reinstall it.

Configuring a Windows 10 File Recovery Drive

If your system fails to boot and you do not have access to the installation media, you can create a recovery drive that includes a Windows 10 boot environment and troubleshooting tools to regain access to your computer.

With improvements in operating system design, system crashes have been reduced over the years. The key word in that last sentence is *reduced*, not eliminated; therefore, it's important to have the right tools in place to recover from a system failure even when you can't start your Windows 10 system.

A *Windows 10 File Recovery drive* can help by providing enough of a boot environment to get you back into the system so you can begin the troubleshooting process. It can be used to do the following:

- Refresh or reset your computer
- Restore your computer to a previously created System Restore point
- Recover your Windows installation from a specific system image file
- Automatically fix startup problems
- Perform advanced troubleshooting from the command prompt

If you create a Windows 10 File Recovery drive on a Windows 10 32-bit system, you cannot use it to repair a 64-bit system, and vice versa.

After creating the recovery drive, you need to enable your system to boot from a USB device in the basic input/output system (BIOS). When booting into the drive, you see the Windows logo displayed on a black screen and then you are prompted to choose your keyboard layout. This takes you to the Choose an Option screen on which you can access the troubleshooting tools and start troubleshooting your computer.

 CONFIGURE A WINDOWS 10 RECOVERY DRIVE

GET READY. To create a recovery drive, log on with local administrative privileges and then perform the following steps.

1. Connect a USB drive to your computer. The drive must hold at least 256 MB and all data on the drive must be deleted.
2. Click the **Start** button and type **Create a recovery drive**. From Results, click **Create a recovery drive**.
3. If you're prompted to Allow the Recovery Media Center to make changes to the computer, click **Yes**.
4. Click **Next**. Windows 10 searches and displays the available drives.
5. Click **Next** to use the drive you inserted.
6. After reviewing the Everything on the drive will be deleted message, click **Create**.
7. Click **Finish**.

RESTORING PREVIOUS VERSIONS OF FILES AND FOLDERS

Windows 7 File Recovery was designed to protect your computer in the event of a system failure by storing your data on another medium (hard drive, network folder, or CD/DVD). It can also back up a system image of your computer, including applications.

CERTIFICATION READY
Restore previous versions
of files and folders.
Objective 3.3

CERTIFICATION READY
Use Windows Backup
and Restore.
Objective 3.3

Windows 7 File Recovery, previously named Windows Backup and Restore, is available in Windows 10. Because this feature has been superseded in favor of the new File History feature (discussed later), Microsoft does not recommend using both at the same time. File History has been designed to check for an existing Windows Backup schedule. If one exists, it disables itself. To use the File History feature, delete your Windows Backup schedule if one has been enabled.

File History is designed to only back up your personal files. If you need to back up your applications and system files, consider using either PC Reset or PC Refresh, discussed earlier. If these tools do not meet your needs for managing your system and application files, the Windows 7 File Recovery tool can be used in Windows 10 as an alternative to a third-party backup program.

In the exercise that follows, you will learn how to use the Windows 7 File Recovery feature to make a full backup of your system, including a system image.

→ SCHEDULE A WINDOWS 10 BACKUP TO INCLUDE YOUR SYSTEM IMAGE

GET READY. To schedule a full Windows 10 backup to an external drive, log on with local administrative privileges and then perform the following steps.

1. Connect your external drive. This drive must have enough capacity to store your data files and a system image.
2. Right-click the **Start** button and click **Control Panel**.
3. In the Search Control Panel text box, type **File recovery**. From Results, click **Backup and Restore (Windows 7)**.
4. On the Backup and Restore (Windows 7) page, as shown in Figure 13-4, click **Set up backup**.

Figure 13-4

Opening the Control Panel Backup and Restore (Windows 7)

5. In the Select Where You Want to Save Your Backup screen, click your external drive, as shown in Figure 13-5.

Figure 13-5

Setting a location
for the backup

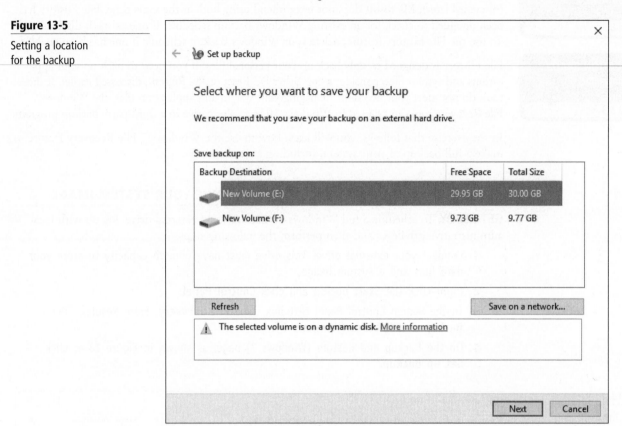

6. Click **Next**.
7. Select **Let Windows choose (recommended)** and click **Next**.

    Windows backs up data files saved in libraries, on the desktop, and in default Windows folders. It also creates a system image (only one per computer can be kept in the backup location), which can be used to restore your computer in case of failure.

    You can also select the Let me choose to select specific libraries and folders option and whether you want to include a system image as part of your backup.

8. Review the Backup Summary and then click **Change schedule**.
9. Select **Run backup on a schedule (recommended)** and click **OK** to accept the default settings.

    Your backup now runs every Sunday at 7:00 P.M.

10. Click the **Save settings and run backup** button.

You might need to create a system repair disk to restore a system image if you do not have your Windows 10 installation media. You can create this disk from within the Windows 7 File Recovery control panel by clicking Create a system image.

 RESTORE A FILE FROM A WINDOWS 10 BACKUP

GET READY. To schedule a full Windows 10 backup to an external drive, log on with local administrative privileges and then perform the following steps.

1. Connect your external drive that contains the backed-up files.
2. On Win10A, using Windows 7 File Recovery, under the Restore section, click the **Restore my files** button.

Figure 13-6

Restoring files

3. In the Restore Files window (see Figure 13-6), click **Browse for folders**.

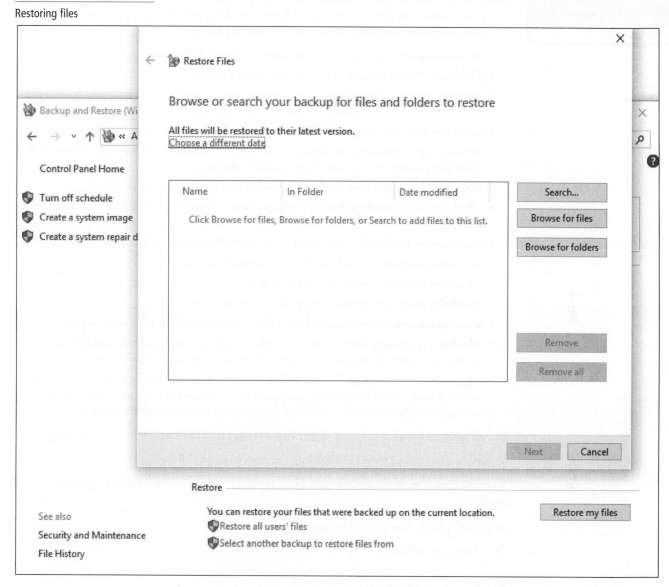

4. In the Browse the backup for folders or drives dialog box, click **Administrator's backup** and then click **Add folder**.

5. Back on the Browse or Search Your Backup for Files and Folders to Restore page, click **Next**.

6. When you are prompted to identify where you want to restore the files, the In the original location option is already selected. Click **Restore**.

7. In the Copy file dialog box, click to select the **Do this for all conflicts** option and then click **Copy and Replace**.

8. Click **Finish**.

9. Close Windows 7 File Recovery.

Performing a Backup and Restore with WBAdmin

The ***wbadmin.exe command*** enables you to back up and restore your operating system, volumes, files, folders, and applications from a command prompt. Since these commands can be executed at the command prompt, you can also create batch files/scripts that perform backups.

CERTIFICATION READY
Perform a backup and
restore with WBAdmin.
Objective 3.3

To configure a regularly scheduled backup, you must be a member of the Administrators group. To perform all other wbadmin tasks, you must be a member of the Backup Operators or the Administrators group, or you must have been delegated the appropriate permissions. You must run webadmin from an elevated command prompt.

- **wbadmin enable backup:** Configures and enables a daily backup schedule.
- **wbadmin disable backup:** Disables your daily backups.
- **wbadmin start backup:** Runs a one-time backup. If used with no parameters, uses the settings from the daily backup schedule.
- **wbadmin stop job:** Stops the currently running backup or recovery operation.
- **wbadmin get versions:** Lists details of backups recoverable from the local computer or, if another location is specified, from another computer.
- **wbadmin get items:** Lists the items included in a specific backup.
- **wbadmin start recovery:** Runs a recovery of the volumes, applications, files, or folders specified.
- **wbadmin get status:** Shows the status of the currently running backup or recovery operation.
- **wbadmin get disks:** Lists disks that are currently online.
- **wbadmin start systemstaterecovery:** Runs a system state recovery.
- **wbadmin start systemstatebackup:** Runs a system state backup.
- **wbadmin delete systemstatebackup:** Deletes one or more system state backups.
- **wbadmin restore catalog:** Recovers a backup catalog from a specified storage location in the case where the backup catalog on the local computer has been corrupted.
- **wbadmin delete catalog:** Deletes the backup catalog on the local computer. Use this subcommand only if the backup catalog on this computer is corrupted and you have no backups stored at another location that you can use to restore the catalog.

For example, to create a system state backup and save it to volume F, type the following:

```
wbadmin start systemstatebackup -backupTarget:F
```

To create a backup of the G drive and H\Data folder and save it to volume F, type the following:

```
wbadmin start backup -backupTarget:f:
-include:g:,h:\Data
```

Configuring File History

File History provides options for backing up and recovering access to your personal files in case of a system problem.

CERTIFICATION READY
Configure File History.
Objective 3.3

Folder Redirection and Roaming User Profiles, discussed in earlier lessons, are excellent ways to maintain your data if your system fails. These features store your user files and settings in a shared folder on a company server that is backed up as part of your organization's data-recovery strategies.

In the following section, you will learn about an additional option that is available for protecting your data: File History.

UNDERSTANDING FILE HISTORY

File History is a feature in Windows 10 that is designed to keep your personal files safe. It enables users who are not administrators to select an external drive or a folder on the network, and it automatically backs up and restores their personal files.

In Windows 10, File History simplifies the process of protecting your personal files. It eliminates the need to use a more complicated backup process included with previous releases of the operating system and introduces a process that is automatic and transparent to the user. It is disabled by default, so you need to enable it to take advantage of its features.

File History scans for changes to your personal files. When a change is detected, the file is moved to the external location you specify, so you can recover previous versions of files if necessary. To optimize performance, File History consults the NTFS change journal to determine whether a file has changed instead of scanning, opening, and reading directories on the volume. By default, File History backs up everything in your libraries, desktop, and favorites. The libraries contain items such as My Documents, My Music, My Pictures, and Public document folders. File History does not back up your system and application files.

File History does not require administrative privileges to set up and run. The user can decide when to turn it on and off, select the external drive to use, and restore files without having to contact an administrator. Although File History does not back up your files to the cloud as OneDrive does, it can be used to back up the OneDrive folder if you are using the OneDrive desktop app for Windows.

The following exercise describes how to turn on File History, which automatically begins scanning and copying all your files to an external USB drive.

 ENABLE AND CONFIGURE FILE HISTORY

GET READY. To enable File History, log on with a domain user account and then perform the following steps.

1. Connect an external drive.
2. Right-click the **Start** button and select Control Panel. Type **File History** in Search Control Panel text box. From Results, choose **File History**.
3. Click **Turn on** (see Figure 13-7).

   This option creates a folder named FileHistory on the drive selected and automatically begins copying your files to the drive.

Figure 13-7

Turning on File History

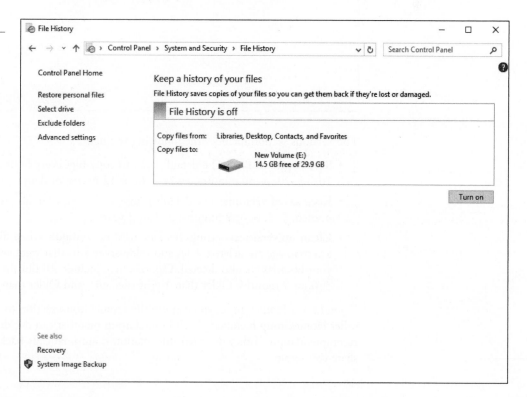

4. Close the File History dialog box.

5. Right-click your desktop and choose **New > Text Document**.

6. Type **FileHistoryTest** for the name and press the **Enter** key. This file is used in the exercise that follows.

The File History dialog box also includes the following two settings:

- **Exclude folders:** If you don't want to save copies of specific folders or libraries, you can specify them here.

- **Advanced settings:** You can identify the folders to exclude, the frequency for which they are backed up, and the amount of cache space you want to set aside for them.

When you click the Advanced settings link, the Advanced Settings dialog displays (see Figure 13-8).

Figure 13-8

Configuring advanced settings

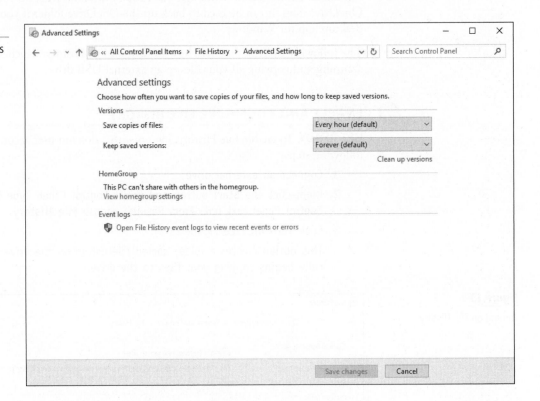

The Versions section includes the following settings:

- **Save copies of files:** The default is set to copy files every hour. Options include every 10, 15, 20, or 30 minutes; every 3, 6, or 12 hours; or daily.

- **Keep saved versions:** The default is forever, but you can also set it to keep until space is needed; 1, 3, 6, or 9 months; or 1 or 2 years.

- **Clean up versions:** Settings here are used to configure when files and folders older than a certain age are deleted. Files and folders/versions that were excluded or removed from your libraries are also deleted. Options here include All but the latest one; Older than 1, 3, 6, or 9 months; Older than 1 year (default); and Older than 2 years.

If you have a HomeGroup, you can use the HomeGroup section to recommend the drive to other HomeGroup members. Each HomeGroup member can decide whether to accept the recommendation. If they do, their information is automatically backed up to the network share you set up.

USING FILE HISTORY TO RESTORE FILES

You can restore files through a familiar File Explorer interface after File History has copied all files to an external location.

As you create and delete files over time, File History keeps track of each version. If you accidentally delete a file that you need, the recovery process is very simple. File History provides a new recovery interface that enables you to browse through a virtual view of your files, select the file you want, and quickly get you back to work.

When restoring files, you can browse your personal libraries, files, and folders; search for a file using keywords, file names, and dates; and preview versions of the files.

RESTORE A FILE USING FILE HISTORY

GET READY. To restore a file using File History, log on with the same domain account you enabled File History with in the previous exercise and perform the following steps.

1. Delete the **FileHistoryTest** document you created in the previous exercise.

   You will now use File History to restore it.

2. Right-click the **Start** button and select Control Panel. Type **File History** in Search Control Panel text box. From Results, choose **File History** .

3. From the left pane, click **Restore personal files** (see Figure 13-9).

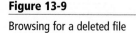
Figure 13-9

Browsing for a deleted file

4. Double-click the **Desktop** icon.
5. Double-click the **FileHistoryTest** document.

   You can now view its contents. If there are multiple versions of the same file, use the left and right buttons to see each version before choosing to restore.

6. Click the **Restore to original location** button, which is the round, green button (see Figure 13-10).

Figure 13-10

Clicking the Restore to Original Location button

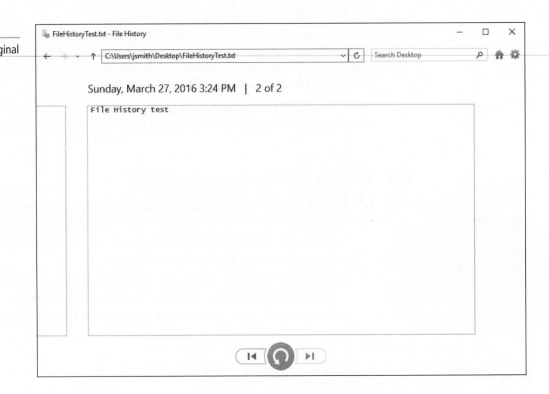

7. Confirm that the FileHistoryTest.txt document has been restored and then close the Desktop dialog box.

Recovering Files from OneDrive

As you recall from Lesson 12, OneDrive is a file hosting service that allows you to store and create files and folders and share them with other users and groups. Similar to deleting local files in Windows 10, if you accidentally delete a file, you have 30 days to recover it from the *OneDrive Recycle Bin*, a temporary storage place of deleted items.

CERTIFICATION READY
Recover files from OneDrive.
Objective 3.3

By default, OneDrive stores your deleted files for at least 3 days and a maximum of 30 days. Unless you exceed 10% of your storage to deleted files, the deleted files will be held for 30 days. However, if you exceed 10% of your total OneDrive storage, the duration of the file will be reduced. Once the file is deleted from OneDrive, the file will be deleted from all drives that are synced with OneDrive.

TAKE NOTE Deleted files do not count toward your OneDrive storage limit.

To restore a deleted file, you just have to go to the OneDrive website (https://onedrive.live .com) and click Recycle bin in the left pane. To restore all items, click Restore all items (as shown in Figure 13-11). To restore or permanently delete individual items, click their check boxes to select them and click Restore. To permanently delete all items, click Delete.

Figure 13-11

Accessing the OneDrive
Recycle Bin

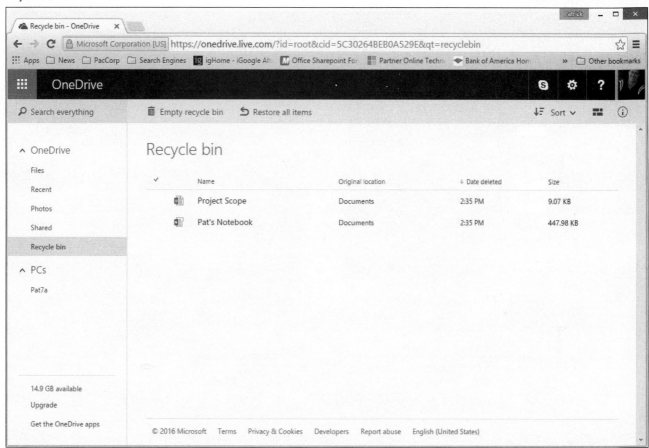

■ PERFORMING RECOVERY OPERATIONS USING WINDOWS RECOVERY

THE BOTTOM LINE

The ***Windows Recovery Environment (Windows RE or WinRE)*** can be used to repair common causes of unbootable operating systems. It is based on the Windows Preinstallation Environment (Windows PE).

CERTIFICATION READY
Perform recovery operations using Windows Recovery.
Objective 3.3

To access WinRE, boot the computer with the Windows 10 installation disk. When the Windows setup program starts, click Next and then click the Repair your computer option. Alternatively, if you are logged into Windows, you can run the Shutdown /r /o command. To reset your PC or access advanced options, click Troubleshoot. If you click Advanced options, you can see the following options, as shown in Figure 13-12:

Figure 13-12

Accessing Advanced options

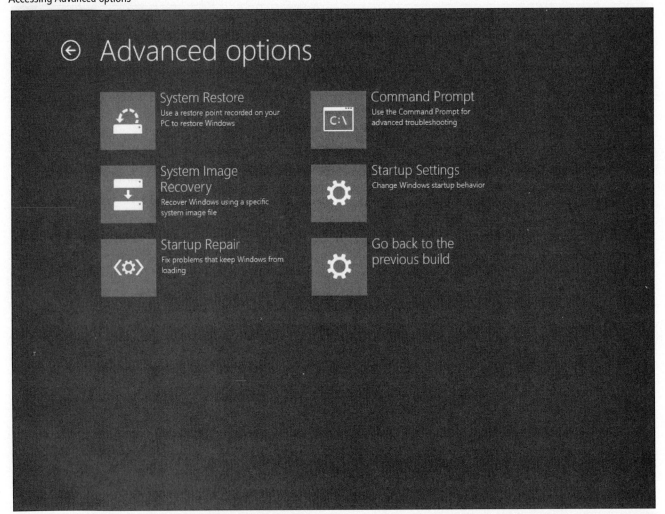

- **System Restore:** Restores your system to a chosen restore point.
- **System Image Recovery:** Recovers Windows using a system image file that you created with the recimg.exe command.
- **Startup Repair:** Reboots into a specific Windows Recovery Environment program known as Start Repair and runs a diagnosis and repair routine that seeks to make your PC bootable again.
- **Command Prompt:** Allows you to access the Command prompt while in Safe mode.
- **Startup Settings:** Reboots Windows and lets you choose which advanced boot option you want to boot into (see Figure 13-13). The Startup Settings are as follows:

Figure 13-13

Accessing Startup sessions

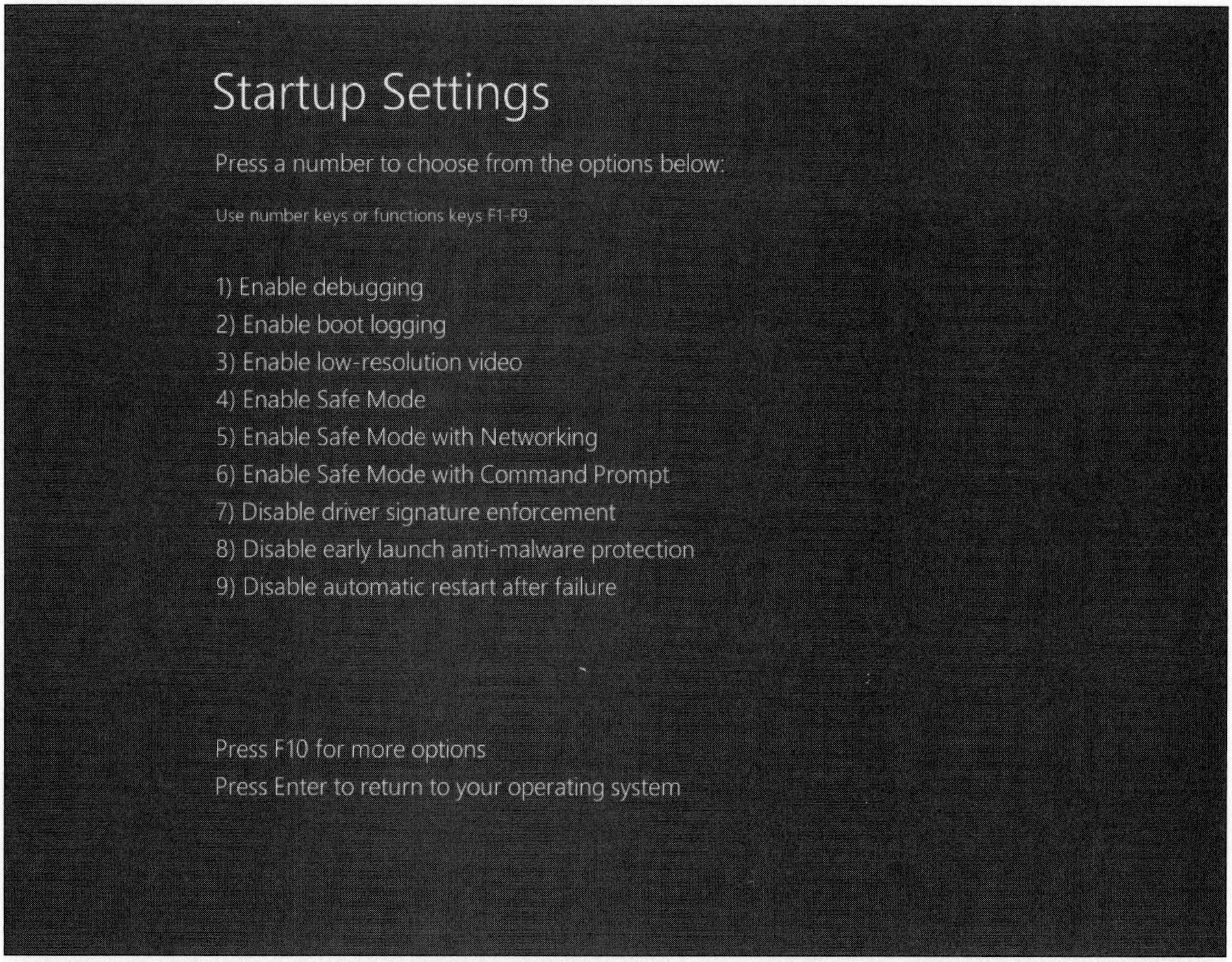

Startup Settings

Press a number to choose from the options below:

Use number keys or functions keys F1-F9

1) Enable debugging
2) Enable boot logging
3) Enable low-resolution video
4) Enable Safe Mode
5) Enable Safe Mode with Networking
6) Enable Safe Mode with Command Prompt
7) Disable driver signature enforcement
8) Disable early launch anti-malware protection
9) Disable automatic restart after failure

Press F10 for more options
Press Enter to return to your operating system

- **Enable debugging:** Starts Windows in an advanced troubleshooting mode intended for IT professionals and system administrators.
- **Enable boot logging:** Creates a file, ntbtlog.txt, that lists all the drivers that are installed during startup and that might be useful for advanced troubleshooting.
- **Enable low-resolution video:** Starts Windows using your current video driver and using low resolution (640 x 480) and refresh rate settings. You can use this mode to reset your display settings.
- **Enable Safe Mode:** Starts Windows with a minimal set of drivers and services. If you make a change to the system and Windows no longer boots, you can try Safe mode.
- **Enable Safe Mode with Networking:** Starts Windows in Safe mode and includes the network drivers and services needed to access the Internet or other computers on your network.
- **Enable Safe Mode with Command Prompt:** Starts Windows in Safe mode with a command prompt window instead of the usual Windows interface.
- **Disable driver signature enforcement:** Allows drivers containing improper signatures to be loaded.
- **Disable early launch anti-malware protection:** If you are having problems that are caused by your anti-virus program, you can stop the early launch anti-malware protection, which allows you to update your virus definitions and perform further scans.

- **Disable automatic restart on system failure:** Prevents Windows from automatically restarting if an error causes Windows to fail. Choose this option only if Windows is stuck in a loop where Windows fails, attempts to restart, and fails again repeatedly.

Safe mode is useful for troubleshooting problems with programs and drivers that might not start correctly or that might prevent Windows from starting correctly. If a problem doesn't reappear when you start in Safe mode, you can eliminate the default settings and basic device drivers as possible causes. If a recently installed program, device, or driver prevents Windows from running correctly, you can start your computer in Safe mode (see Figure 13-14) and then remove the program that's causing the problem.

Figure 13-14

Windows 10 Safe mode

While in Safe mode, you use the Control Panel to access the Device Manager, Event Viewer, System Information, command prompt, or Registry Editor.

Devices and drivers that start in Safe mode:

- Floppy disk drives (internal and USB)
- Internal CD-ROM drives (ATA, SCSI)

- External CD-ROM drives (USB)
- Internal DVD-ROM drives (ATA, SCSI)
- External DVD-ROM drives (USB)
- Internal hard disk drives (ATA, SATA, SCSI)
- External hard disk drives (USB)
- Keyboards (USB, PS/2, serial)
- Mice (USB, PS/2, serial)
- VGA video cards (PCI, AGP)

Windows services that start in Safe mode:

- Windows event log
- Plug and Play
- Remote procedure call (RPC)
- Cryptographic Services
- Windows Management Instrumentation (WMI)

Devices and services that start in Safe mode with networking:

- Network adapters (wired Ethernet and wireless 802.11x)
- Dynamic Host Configuration Protocol (DHCP)
- DNS
- Network connections
- TCP/IP-NetBIOS Helper
- Windows Firewall

SKILL SUMMARY

IN THIS LESSON YOU LEARNED:

- A backup or the process of backing up refers to duplicating data so that these duplications can be accessed in your efforts to restore the original after a data loss event. Backups can be used to restore entire systems following a disaster or to restore a small set of files that were accidentally deleted or corrupted.

- Windows 10 System Restore saves information about your drivers, registry settings, programs, and system files in the form of restore points for drives with system protection turned on. A restore point is a representation of the state of your computer's system files and settings.

- A Windows 10 File Recovery drive can help by providing enough of a boot environment to get you back into the system so you can begin the troubleshooting process. It can be used to refresh or reset your computer, restore your computer to a previously created System Restore point, recover your Windows installation from a specific system image file, automatically fix startup problems, and perform advanced troubleshooting from the command prompt.

- Windows 7 File Recovery was designed to protect your computer in the event of a system failure by storing your data on another medium (hard drive, network folder, or CD/DVD). It can also back up a system image of your computer, including applications.

390 | Lesson 13

- File History is a feature in Windows 10 that is designed to keep your personal files safe. It enables users who are not administrators to select an external drive or a folder on the network, and it automatically backs up and restores their personal files.

- The Windows Recovery Environment (Windows RE or WinRE) can be used to repair common causes of unbootable operating systems. It is based on the Windows Preinstallation Environment (Windows PE).

■ Knowledge Assessment

Multiple Choice

1. Which of the following is the best method of data recovery?
   a. Running scandisk
   b. Performing Windows updates
   c. Using an antivirus package
   d. Using backups

2. How frequently does Windows 10 automatically create restore points?
   a. Every 4 days
   b. Every 5 days
   c. Every 30 days
   d. Every 7 days

3. Which of the following Windows 10 features is used to create a restore point?
   a. System Restore
   b. PC Refresh
   c. PC Reset
   d. System Point Restore

4. Which of the following time frames best represents the point at which a restore point should be created?
   a. Daily
   b. Weekly
   c. After performing a major system event
   d. Prior to performing a major system event

5. Which of the following options will put a PC back to a new state and will reinstall Windows, but delete files, settings, and apps, except those apps that came with the PC?
   a. Reset
   b. Refresh
   c. PC Cleanup
   d. Windows Undo

6. Which of the following does File History not back up? (Choose all that apply.)
   a. System files
   b. Documents
   c. Application files
   d. Registry settings

7. Which mode starts Windows with a minimal set of drivers and services?
   a. Safe mode
   b. Last Known Good Configuration
   c. Full mode
   d. Standard mode

8. Which of the following programs restores files through a familiar File Explorer interface?
   a. OneDrive
   b. File Explorer History
   c. File History
   d. Windows 10 Backup and Restore

9. Which of the following allows users to schedule a weekly backup to a secondary disk?
   a. Using Windows 7 File Recovery
   b. Using File History
   c. Scheduling a system restore point
   d. Creating a Windows 10 File Recovery drive

10. By default, how many days is a file deleted with OneDrive kept in the Recycle Bin?
   a. 10 days
   b. 15 days
   c. 30 days
   d. 45 days

Best Answer

Choose the letter that corresponds to the best answer. More than one answer choice may achieve the goal. Select the BEST answer.

1. Which of the following approaches is considered most effective to decommission an older computer before donating it to charity?
   a. Initiate a PC Reset.
   b. Initiate a PC Refresh.
   c. Purchase a third-party disk wipe tool.
   d. Move all the data off of the hard drive and reinstall Windows manually.

2. Which of the following best describes the time when a manual restore point should be created?
   a. After completing the installation of a new application
   b. One day before performing an installation of a new application
   c. Two days before performing an installation of a new application
   d. Let Windows 10 perform an automatic restore point on its regularly scheduled interval

3. Which of the following tools best represents the preferred method to back up important documents so that a previous version can be found and restored quickly?
   a. OneDrive
   b. OneDrive for Business
   c. File History
   d. Windows 7 Backup and Restore

Build a List

1. Specify the correct order of steps necessary to creating a system restore point.

_____ Click Apply and then click OK.

_____ Click Create to create a new restore point.

_____ Click Create.

_____ Drag the slider to set the maximum disk space you want to use.

_____ Type a description for the restore point.

_____ Press the Windows logo key + w and then type System Restore.

_____ Click Create a Restore Point from the results.

_____ Click Configure and make sure the Turn on system protection option is enabled.

_____ Log on with local administrative privileges.

2. Specify the correct order of steps necessary to enabling File History on Windows 10.

_____ From Results, choose File History.

_____ Log on with local administrative privileges.

_____ Click Turn On.

_____ Press the Windows logo key + w and then type File History.

_____ Connect an external drive.

■ Business Case Scenarios

Scenario 13-1: Restoring Files

Support staff members have been complaining about the amount of time they are spending restoring selected users' files on their Windows 10 PCs. The users are pretty technically savvy and can perform the tasks themselves, but you don't want to give them administrative privileges on their PCs. Describe your recommended solution.

Scenario 13-2: Recovering Files

You use a laptop and tablet that sync with your OneDrive repository. You were working late one night, and you decided to do a little cleanup of your files. A few days later, you realized that you deleted a couple of reports that were in your sync folder for OneDrive. Describe how to recover those files.

Configuring Authorization and Authentication

70-698 EXAM OBJECTIVE

Objective 3.4 – Configure authorization and authentication. This objective may include but is not limited to: Configure Microsoft Passport; configure picture passwords and biometrics; configure workgroups; configure domain settings; configure Credential Manager; configure local accounts; configure Microsoft accounts; configure Device Registration; configure Windows Hello; configure Device Guard; configure Credential Guard; configure Device Health Attestation.* Configure HomeGroup settings is covered in Lesson 8 and configure UAC behavior is covered in Lesson 5.

LESSON HEADING	EXAM OBJECTIVE
Supporting Authentication and Authorization	
Supporting Multi-Factor Authentication	
Supporting Passwords, PINS, and Picture Passwords	Configure picture passwords
Supporting Digital Certificates and Smart Cards	
Configuring Biometrics, Windows Hello, and Microsoft Passport	Configure Microsoft Passport
	Configure biometrics
	Configure Windows Hello
Configuring Local Accounts, Domain Accounts, and Microsoft Accounts	Configure workgroups
	Configure domain settings
	Configure local accounts
	Configure Microsoft accounts
Authenticating Computers and Users	
Understanding Kerberos and NTLM Authentication	
Understanding Access Tokens and Credential Caching	
Configuring Credential Manager	Configure Credential Manager
Configuring Domain Settings with Account Policies	Configure domain settings
Configuring Device Registration	Configure Device Registration
Configuring Device Guard and Credential Guard	Configure Device Guard
	Configure Credential Guard
Configuring Device Health Attestation	Configure Device Health Attestation

KEY TERMS

access token	Device Registration	Password Settings Object (PSO)
Account Lockout Policy	Device Registration Service (DRS)	personal identification number (PIN)
account policies	digital certificate	
authentication	domain	picture password
authentication factor	Early Launch Antimalware (ELAM)	public key infrastructure (PKI)
authorization		Secure Boot
biometrics	fine-grained password policies	Security Accounts Manager (SAM)
BitLocker	Global Catalog	smart card
Bring Your Own Device (BYOD)	integrity	Trusted Platform Module (TPM) chip
certificate authority (CA)	Kerberos v5	
certificate chain	Key Distribution Center (KDC)	two-factor authentication
computer account	Local Security Authority (LSA)	user account
confidentiality	Microsoft Passport	vaults
credential caching	multi-factor authentication	virtual secure mode (VSM)
Credential Guard	nonrepudiation	virtual smart cards (VSCs)
Credential Manager	NTLM	Windows Hello
Device Guard	password	workgroup
Device Health Attestation (DHA)	Password Policy	X.509 version3

■ SUPPORTING AUTHENTICATION AND AUTHORIZATION

THE BOTTOM LINE

Today's network administrators are faced with securing network resources that are being accessed by employees both inside and outside of the organization. Having a well-designed authentication and authorization strategy is the key to ensuring resource availability and integrity.

Network administrators are often faced with the task of securing network resources that are being accessed by employees from both inside and outside of the company. When designing a strategy to secure these resources, you need to keep in mind these key pillars of information security:

- *Authentication*: Authentication represents the way that security principals (users, computers, and processes) prove their identity before they are allowed to connect to your network. In the past, authentication was handled through the use of passwords. Today, additional authentication tools, including digital certificates, smart cards, picture passwords, and biometrics, are used.

- *Authorization*: After security principals prove their identity, authorization determines what they can do. This is determined through the use of Access Control Lists (ACLs) that are attached to each resource.

- *Confidentiality*: This process is about preventing people from reading information they are not authorized to read. Confidentiality is handled through the use of encryption technologies.

- *Integrity*: This is the ability to guarantee that the information has not been arbitrarily changed from the time it was sent from the original source and received by the other party.
- *Nonrepudiation*: This is a method used to provide proof that a security principal (user, computer, or process) is the source of data, an action, or a communication. This is usually provided through the use of public key/private key technologies.

Each of these pillars of security should become part of your overall security design. This lesson focuses on two of them specifically: authentication and authorization.

Supporting Multi-Factor Authentication

Authentication is the process of verifying you are who you say you are. Two-factor authentication involves proving your identity using at least two authentication factors.

Authentication is the process of verifying that security principals (users, computers, or processes) are who they say they are. To prove their identity, security principals can use one or more authentication factors, which are basically pieces of information.

For example, you could use something you know (a password or PIN); something you have (a smart card); or something that is unique to you (a biometric), such as your fingerprint or an iris scan. These three pieces of information are called *authentication factors* (see Figure 14-1). When only one of these pieces of information is used (e.g., a password), it's called one-factor authentication. *Two-factor authentication* requires the use of two of the three authentication factors. Windows 10 supports the following methods of authentication: passwords, picture passwords, digital certificates, smart cards, and biometrics. *Multi-factor authentication* is an authentication method that uses two or more authentication factors.

Figure 14-1

Authentication factors

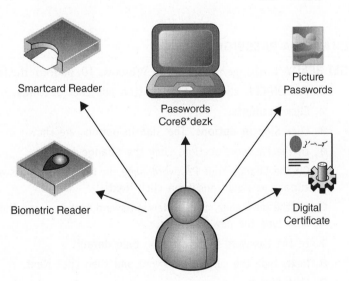

A user can authenticate via one or more of the following methods:

- **By using what he or she knows:** For instance, by supplying a password or personal identification number (PIN)

- **By using what he or she owns or possesses:** For example, by providing a passport, smart card, or ID card
- **By proving what he or she is:** For instance, by supplying biometric factors based on fingerprints, retinal scans, voice input, and so forth

Supporting Passwords, PINs, and Picture Passwords

Windows 10 supports multiple methods of authentication. The most common forms of authentication are based on what a user knows, such as passwords and PINs. However, with the popularity of smartphones, picture passwords are becoming common.

A *password* is a word or string of characters used for user authentication. Traditional passwords have been used for years to authenticate users. Although they are the most common method, they are also the weakest. Users will typically choose a very simple password, write it down, and store it in a very insecure place. There are also several different ways for someone to discover your password and assume your identity. Through brute force attacks, social engineering, and eavesdropping, even strong passwords can be compromised.

You can strengthen passwords by instituting the use of strong passwords in your organization and use Group Policy to enforce those policies. A strong password has the following characteristics:

- Contains at least eight characters
- Uses at least one character from the following: upper- and lowercase letters, punctuation marks, numbers
- Does not include your logon name, your real name, or your company name
- Does not include a complete word that can be found in the dictionary
- Should not be the same password that you have used in the past or used on other website accounts

 CHANGE A PASSWORD

GET READY. To change a password in Windows 10, perform the following steps.

1. On LON-CL1, click the **Start** button and click **Settings**.
2. Click **Accounts**.
3. Click **Sign-in options**. The Sign-in options are shown in Figure 14-2.
4. In the Password section, click the **Change** button.
5. On the Change Your Password page, in the Current password text box, type the current password and then click **Next**.
6. On the next page, in the New password text box and the Reenter password text box, type the new password.
7. In the Password hint text box, type **default**.
8. Next, type the current password and then click **Next**.
9. Click **Finish**.

When users are having problems logging on, check to see if their Caps Lock key on the keyboard is on. If the user still cannot log on, the administrator will have to check the following:

- If the user is allowed to log on during the specified time
- If the user can log on to the specific computer

Figure 14-2

Managing Windows 10 sign-in options

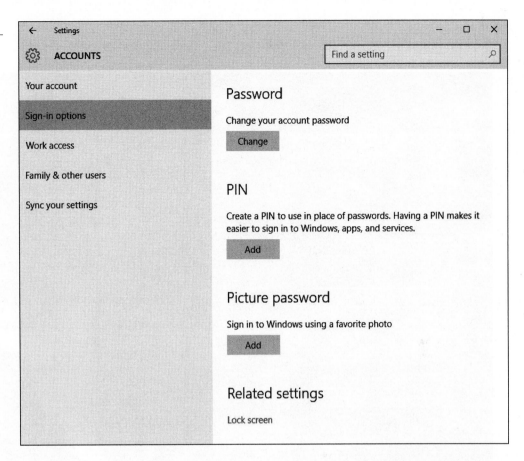

- If the account is disabled
- If the account is locked

A *personal identification number (PIN)* is a short numeric password used to authenticate a user to a system. A PIN is just about always used with an ATM or bank card, but can also be used as an alarm code, to unlock a smartphone, or to open a door.

CREATE A PIN

GET READY. To create a PIN in Windows 10, perform the following steps.

1. Click the **Start** button and click **Settings**.
2. Click **Accounts**.
3. Click **Sign-in options**.
4. In the PIN section, click the **Add** button.
5. On the First, Verify Your Account Password page, in the text box, type the current password and then click **OK.**
6. On the Set Up a PIN page, in the New PIN and Confirm PIN text boxes, type the PIN and then click **OK.**

CERTIFICATION READY
Configure picture passwords
Objective 3.4

A *picture password* (see Figure 14-3) consists of two components: a picture and a gesture that you draw on it. You can pick the image from a default set included with the Windows 10 installation or select your own. After the picture is selected, you can then place your gestures.

Figure 14-3

Showing a picture used in
a picture password

A picture password is limited to three gestures (circles, straight lines, and taps). Because the combination of the three is infinite, a picture password offers more security than a traditional password. When you sign in, the gestures you use are compared with those that you created when the password was set. If they are correct, you are authenticated. If they are wrong (for example, if you use a circle instead of a line), authentication fails.

 CREATE A PICTURE PASSWORD

GET READY. To create a picture password, perform the following steps.

1. On LON-CL1, click the **Start** button and click **Settings**.
2. Click **Accounts**.
3. Click **Sign-in options**.
4. In the Picture password section, click the **Add** button.
5. On the Create a Picture Password page, in the text box, type the current password and then click **OK**.
6. On the Welcome to Picture Password page, click **Choose Picture**.
7. When the Open dialog box opens, navigate to the picture you want to use, click the picture, and then click **Open**.

8. Click **Use this Picture**.

9. Draw three gestures on your picture. You can use any combination of circles, straight lines, and taps. Be sure to remember the order in which you use the gestures.

10. Repeat the same three gestures to confirm.

11. Click **Finish**.

12. Sign out with the user account.

13. Choose the user account to log on with.

14. Repeat the gestures you used when setting up the picture password.

When Microsoft releases the Windows 10 Anniversary Edition, the Credentials and User Account Control dialog boxes will be updated with a new look. In addition, when you enter credentials, you will be able to choose Windows Hello, a PIN, a certificate, or a password.

Supporting Digital Certificates and Smart Cards

Another form of authentication is based on what a user owns or processes. Some examples are a digital certificate and smart cards.

A ***digital certificate*** is a collection of data that binds an identity to a key pair. In addition to authentication, these certificates can be used for authorization, nonrepudiation, and other types of security control.

A digital certificate contains a name that indicates who or what owns the certificate: a public key, the name of the ***certificate authority (CA)*** that issued it, and the digital signature of the CA that issued it. A CA is the computer that creates and manages the distribution and revocation of certificates.

The most common digital certificate is the ***X.509 version 3***. The X.509 version 3 standard specifies the format for the public key certificate, certificate revocation lists, attribute certificates, and a certificate path validation algorithm (see Figure 14-4).

Figure 14-4

Viewing a digital certificate

The X.509 digital certificate includes the following fields:

- **Version:** The version of the certificate format, such as version 3.
- **Certificate Serial Number:** The unique serial number that is assigned by the issuing CA. Based on the serial number, the CA maintains an audit history for each certificate so that certificates can be traced, including when the certificate has been revoked.
- **Certificate Algorithm Identifier:** The public key cryptography and message digest algorithms that are used by the issuing CA to digitally sign the certificate.
- **Issuer:** The name of the issuing CA.
- **Validity Period including the valid-from and valid-to dates:** The certificate's start and expiration dates.
- **Subject:** The person, entity, or owner identified in the certificate.
- **Subject Public-Key Information:** The public key and a list of the public key cryptography algorithms.
- **Key-usage:** The purpose of the public key, such as encipherment, signature, certificate signing, and so on.
- **Certification Authority's digital signature:** The CA's digital signature that is used to verify it came from the issuer.

There are only so many root CA certificates that are assigned to commercial third-party organizations. Therefore, when you acquire a digital certificate from a third-party organization, you might need to use a certificate chain to obtain the root CA certificate so that it can be trusted. In addition, you might need to install an intermediate digital certificate that links the assigned digital certificate to a trusted root CA certificate. The *certificate chain*, also known as the certification path, is a list of certificates used to authenticate an entity. It begins with the certificate of the entity and ends with the root CA certificate.

The third tab of a certificate is the certification path, as shown in Figure 14-5. The path starts with the Subject certificate and proceeds through a number of intermediate certificates up to a trusted root certificate, typically issued by a trusted CA.

Figure 14-5

Viewing a certification path

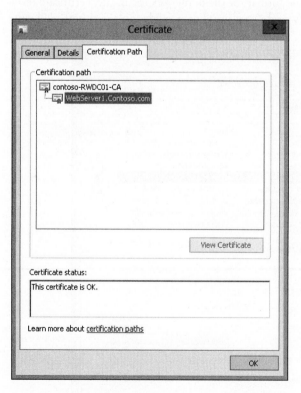

On a local computer running Windows, the certificates are stored in a certificate store. Using the Certificates MMC snap-in, you can display the certificate store for a user, a computer, or a service according to the purpose for which the certificates were issued or by using their logical storage categories. Certificates are then organized into the following folders:

- **Personal:** Certificates associated with public keys to which you have access. These are the certificates that have been issued to the user, the computer, or the service that you are viewing.

- **Trusted Root Certification Authorities:** Implicitly trusted CAs, including all of the certificates in the third-party root CA's store, plus root certificates from your organization and Microsoft.

- **Enterprise Trust:** A container for certificate trust lists, including self-signed root certificates from other organizations.

- **Intermediate Certification Authorities:** Certificates issued to subordinate CAs.

- **Trusted People:** Certificates issued to people or end entities that are explicitly trusted. Most often, these are self-signed certificates or certificates explicitly trusted in an application such as Microsoft Outlook.

- **Other People:** Certificates issued to people or end entities that are implicitly trusted. These certificates must be part of a trusted certification hierarchy. Most often, these are cached certificates for services such as Encrypting File System, where certificates are used for creating authorization for decrypting an encrypted file.

- **Trusted Publishers:** Certificates from CAs that are trusted by Software Restriction policies.

- **Third-Party Root Certification Authorities:** Trusted root certificates from CAs other than Microsoft and your organization.

- **Certificate Enrollment Requests:** Pending or rejected certificate requests.

- **Active Directory User Object:** Certificates associated with your user object and published in Active Directory.

Windows can also publish certificates to Active Directory. Publishing a certificate in Active Directory enables all users or computers with adequate permissions to retrieve the certificate as needed.

 ACCESS A CERTIFICATE STORE

GET READY. To access a certificate store, perform the following steps.

1. On LON-CL1, click the **Start** button, type **mmc.exe**, and then press the **Enter** key.

2. When the console opens, click **File > Add/Remove snap-in**.

3. When the Add or Remove Snap-ins dialog box opens, double-click **Certificates**.

4. In the Certificates snap-in dialog box, click one of the following:

   My user account

   Service account

   Computer account

5. If you select My user account, click **Finish**. If you select Computer account, click **Next**, choose **Local computer**, and then click **Finish**. If you select Service account, click **Local computer**, click **Next**, click a service account to manage, and then click **Finish**.

6. In the Add or Remove Snap-ins dialog box, click **OK**. Under Trusted Root Certification Authorities, select Certificates. The certificate store opens (see Figure 14-6).

Figure 14-6

Viewing a certificate store

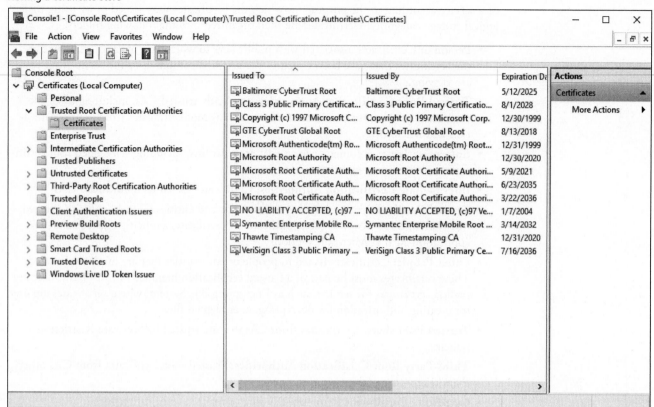

Digital certificates can be imported and exported via electronic files. Four common formats are as follows:

- **Personal Information Exchange (PKCS #12):** The Personal Information Exchange format (PFX, also called PKCS #12) supports secure storage of certificates, private keys, and all certificates in a certification path. The PKCS #12 format is the only file format that can be used to export a certificate and its private key. It usually has a .pfx or .p12 file name extension.

- **Cryptographic Message Syntax Standard (PKCS #7):** The PKCS #7 format supports storage of certificates and all certificates in a certification path. It usually has a .p7b or .p7c file name extension.

- **DER-encoded binary X.509:** The Distinguished Encoding Rules (DER) format supports storage of a single certificate. This format does not support storage of the private key or certification path. It usually has a .cer, .crt, or .der file name extension.

- **Base64-encoded X.509:** The Base64 format supports storage of a single certificate. This format does not support storage of the private key or certification path.

Smart cards, used with a smart card reader attached to a computer, contain an embedded processor that is used to communicate with the host computer and the card reader. They can be used to authenticate users, ensure data integrity when signing documents, and provide confidentiality when you need encryption. In order to authenticate, users insert their card into a reader connected to their computer and then enter their PIN. The smart card holds the users' logon information, private key, digital certificate, and other private information.

To deploy smart cards, you need a ***public key infrastructure (PKI)***, which includes digital certificates, CAs, and other components that are used to create, distribute, validate, and revoke certificates. Smart cards can be credit card–sized devices or a token style (USB device). Information stored on the cards cannot be extracted from the device, all communication with the card is encrypted to protect against malicious software intercepting it, and brute force attempts to hack the PIN will result in the card being blocked until an administrator can unlock it. Because both the smart card and a PIN are required, it is much less likely that someone will be able to steal both.

Windows 8 introduced *virtual smart cards (VSCs)*, which make additional hardware (smart card readers and smart cards) unnecessary. These cards emulate the functionality of regular smart cards but require a *Trusted Platform Module (TPM) chip* to protect the private keys. The TPM is used to encrypt the information, which is then stored on the computer's hard drive. If the user will need to access multiple computers using the VSC, one will have to be created and issued to the user for each system.

Configuring Biometrics, Windows Hello, and Microsoft Passport

Biometrics takes advantage of the uniqueness of every individual. By using a person's fingerprint, face, voice, or retina, biometrics offers advantages over other methods. For example, the user has to physically be present at the point of identification, does not need to remember passwords or a PIN, and does not have to carry smart cards that can be lost or stolen. Instead of using biometrics to replace other methods, consider using them as an additional layer of security.

CERTIFICATION READY
Configure Microsoft Passport
Objective 3.4

CERTIFICATION READY
Configure biometrics
Objective 3.4

CERTIFICATION READY
Configure Windows Hello
Objective 3.4

Before users can access a computer or a network resource, they will most likely log on to prove they are who they say they are and to see whether they have the required rights and permissions to access the network resources. Logging on is the process through which you are recognized by a computer system or network so that you can begin a session.

In the past, administrators had to struggle with managing third-party software and hardware to support biometrics. With each vendor providing different drivers, software, and management tools, it became very labor-intensive to support. Fortunately, Microsoft introduced native support for biometric technologies through its Windows Biometric Framework (WBF). WBF enables users to manage device settings for biometric devices through Control Panel, provides support for managing device drivers, and manages Group Policy settings that can be used to enable, disable, or limit use of biometric data for a local computer or domain. A fingerprint reader is the most commonly used biometric device in corporate networks. These devices can be purchased separately or can be built in to new laptops. The reader captures an image of your fingerprint and then saves it to the computer. The process is called enrolling. When you log on, the reader scans your fingerprint and compares it with the one on file.

Windows Hello is a Windows 10 biometric authentication system that uses a user's face, iris, or fingerprint to unlock devices. To use Windows Hello, you need specialized hardware, including a fingerprint reader, illuminated infrared (IR) sensor, or other biometric sensors. Hello will not work with an ordinary webcam, but it will work with an existing fingerprint sensor.

SET UP WINDOWS HELLO FACIAL RECOGNITION

GET READY. To set up Windows Hello facial recognition on a computer running Windows 10, perform the following steps.

1. On LON-CL1, click the **Start** button and click **Settings**.
2. Click **Accounts**.
3. Click **Sign-in options**.
4. Under Windows Hello, select the **infrared IR camera** option. If you do not have a Windows Hello section, you do not have compatible hardware.

5. On the Welcome to Windows Hello page, click the **Get Started** button.

6. Set up a PIN code if prompted to do so.

7. To scan your face, for best results, hold your face six to eight inches away from the front of the camera.

8. Click **Finish** to complete scanning or click **Improve Recognition** to continue scanning.

 SET UP WINDOWS HELLO FINGERPRINT READER

GET READY. To set up a Windows Hello fingerprint reader on a computer running Windows 10, perform the following steps.

1. On LON-CL1, click the **Start** button and click **Settings**.

2. Click **Accounts**.

3. Click **Sign-in options**.

4. Under Windows Hello, select the **Fingerprint** option and click **Set up**. If you do not have a Windows Hello section, you do not have compatible hardware.

5. On the Welcome to Windows Hello page, click the **Get Started** button.

6. Repeatedly place your preferred finger on the fingerprint ID sensor on your type cover. The system will tell you when setup is complete. You do have the option of setting up multiple fingers to be read by the scanner.

7. Click **Finish** to complete scanning.

Microsoft Passport is a two-factor authentication that consists of an enrolled device (such as a smartphone) and a Windows Hello (biometric) or PIN. The two factors are an encrypted key stored on the device combined with Windows Hello or a PIN. Microsoft Passport lets users authenticate to a Microsoft account, an Active Directory account, a Microsoft Azure Active Directory (AD) account, or a non-Microsoft service that supports Fast ID Online (FIDO) authentication.

> **TAKE NOTE**
>
> Don't confuse Microsoft Passport used with Windows 10 with the Microsoft Account, which was previously known as Microsoft Passport. The Microsoft Account, which will be discussed later in the Supporting Local Accounts, Domain Accounts, and Microsoft Accounts section, is a Single Sign-On web server developed and provided by Microsoft that allows users to log on to websites, devices, and applications using one account. It is also known as .NET Passport, Microsoft Passport Network, and Windows Live ID.

To implement Microsoft Passport, you need to have one of the following:

- Microsoft account
- Azure Active Directory
- Windows Server 2016 Active Directory

To implement Microsoft Passport using a Microsoft account, you would perform the following steps:

1. Log on with a Microsoft account on a computer running Windows 10.

2. Configure a PIN or Windows Hello.

After performing the initial two-step verification during Microsoft Passport enrollment, a Microsoft Passport is set up on the user's device and the user gets a gesture, which can be Windows Hello or a PIN.

To implement Microsoft Password in your organization, you need to create a Group Policy that will implement Microsoft Passport on devices running Windows 10. The GPO settings are located at:

Computer Configuration > Policies > Administrative Templates > Windows Components > Microsoft Passport for Work

■ CONFIGURING LOCAL ACCOUNTS, DOMAIN ACCOUNTS, AND MICROSOFT ACCOUNTS

THE BOTTOM LINE

User accounts allow employees to participate on the network and to gain access to the resources that are made available. Understanding which account to use and its limitations in regard to user experience, access to Windows apps, and password management will be important considerations when supporting the users and systems that require authentication.

CERTIFICATION READY
Configure workgroups
Objective 3.4

Computers and devices on a peer-to-peer network can be organized into logical subgroups called *workgroups*. In a workgroup, each computer has its own local security database so that it can track its own user and group account information. The user information is not shared with other workgroup computers.

CERTIFICATION READY
Configure domain settings
Objective 3.4

A *domain* is a collection of user and computer accounts that are grouped together to enable centralized management and to apply security. The user and computer accounts are stored in an Active Directory database that is stored on domain controllers. The advantages of using a domain is that one user can log on to multiple computers and access resources using the single account.

CERTIFICATION READY
Configure local accounts
Objective 3.4

During the next exercise, you will add a computer to the domain. Then, in the following exercise, you will remove the computer from the domain, which adds the computer to a workgroup that you define.

 ADD A COMPUTER TO THE DOMAIN

GET READY. To add a computer running Windows 10 to the domain, perform the following steps.

CERTIFICATION READY
Configure Microsoft accounts
Objective 3.4

1. On a computer that is running Windows 10, log on as a local administrator.
2. Right-click the **Start** button and click **System**.
3. When the Control Panel System page opens, in the Computer name, domain, and workgroup settings option, click the **Change settings** option.
4. When the System Properties dialog box opens, the Computer Name tab is already selected. Click the **Change** button.
5. When the Computer Name/Domain Changes dialog box opens, select the **Domain** option. Then type in the name of the domain, such as **Adatum.com**, and click **OK**.
6. When the windows Security dialog box opens, log on as **administrator** with the password of **Pa$$w0rd**, and click **OK**.
7. When you receive a welcome to the domain message, click **OK**.
8. When you are prompted to restart your computer to apply these changes, click **OK**.
9. Back at the System Properties dialog box, click **Close**.
10. When you are prompted to restart your computer to apply these changes, click **Restart Now**.

REMOVE A COMPUTER FROM THE DOMAIN

GET READY. To remove a computer from the domain, perform the following steps.

1. Log on to a computer that is part of domain as an administrative user.

2. Right-click the **Start** button and click **System**.

3. When the Control Panel System page opens, in the Computer name, domain, and workgroup settings option, click the **Change settings** option.

4. When the System Properties dialog box opens, the Computer Name tab is already selected. Click the **Change** button.

5. When the Computer Name/Domain Changes dialog box opens, select the **Workgroup name** option. Then type a name for the workgroup name, such as **WG**, and click **OK**.

6. When you are warned that you are leaving a domain, and you will need to know the password of the local administrator account, click **OK**.

7. When a Welcome to the workgroup message opens, click **OK**.

8. When you are prompted to restart your computer, click **OK**.

9. Back on the System Properties dialog box, click **Close**.

10. When you are prompted to restart your computer to apply these changes, click the **Restart Now** button.

Each type of user account provides a different level of control over the computers in your network. Matching the right type of account to each user will ensure you provide sufficient privileges to your users without giving them access to areas or resources that might compromise your network's security.

When working with Windows 10, there are three types of accounts:

- Local user accounts are created on individual computers that are members of a workgroup to provide access to resources on that computer.

- Domain-based accounts, also called Active Directory accounts, are stored as objects on a domain controller and provide access to resources on multiple systems.

- Microsoft user accounts enable you to synchronize your desktop across multiple Windows 10 devices.

Workgroup computers must be on the same network segment and will maintain their own local security database to store user accounts. This database, also called the *Security Accounts Manager (SAM)*, contains user accounts and their associated passwords. When you enter your user name and password on a Windows computer, a process called the *Local Security Authority (LSA)* queries the SAM database to determine whether an account with the user name and password you used exists. If it does, you will be granted access to the system. If you then need access to another computer in the workgroup, you must have a separate account stored in that computer's SAM. In addition to verifying users who log on, LSA also handles any password changes and enforces overall security policy on the system.

As you can imagine, as the number of computers increases, maintaining accounts for each user on multiple machines can become very labor-intensive. If an account is present on the other computer, users will not have to enter their user name and password again to connect and use the resource; it will be handled automatically in the background. If they attempt to access a resource on another computer and do not have an account, they will be prompted to enter a user name and password before connecting and using the resource. The user name and password must be stored in the computer's local SAM to gain access to its resources. Workgroups are very simple to design and don't require a Windows server to implement. On the other hand, they are designed for small groups of computers and provide very limited scalability.

Local user accounts allow a user to log on directly to a computer running Windows 10 for which the local account is created on. However, if a remote computer has a local account with the same user name and password, the user can access resources on the remote computer.

Local user accounts can be managed using the Windows 10 Settings or using Computer Management console.

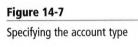 **CREATE A WINDOWS 10 LOCAL ACCOUNT USING SETTINGS**

GET READY. To create a Windows 10 local account using settings on a computer that is part of a domain, perform the following steps.

1. On LON-CL1, click the **Start** button and click **Settings**.
2. Click **Accounts**.
3. Click **Other Users**.
4. Click the **+ Add someone else to this PC** button.
5. On the How Will This Person Sign In? page, at the bottom of the page, click **I don't have the person's sign-in information**.
6. On the Let's Create Your Account page, at the bottom of the page, click the **Add a user without a Microsoft account**.
7. On the Create an Account for This PC page, in the Who's going to use this PC? text box, type the name of the local user, such as **User1**.
8. In the Enter password and Re-enter password text boxes, type the password, such as **Pa$$w0rd**.
9. In the Password hint text box, type **default**.
10. To make the user an administrator, click the new account and click **Change account type**.
11. When the Change account type dialog box opens, for the Account type, select **Administrator**, as shown in Figure 14-7.
12. Click **OK**.

Figure 14-7

Specifying the account type

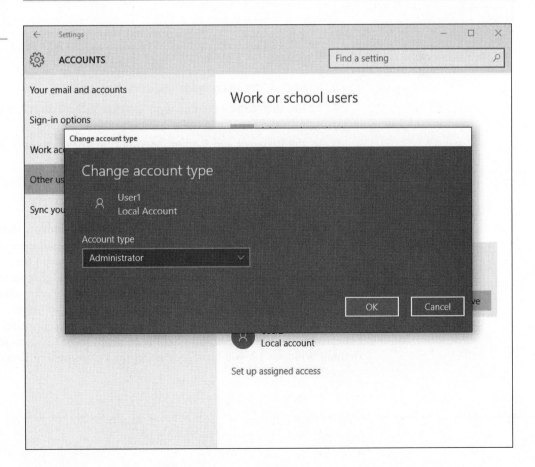

CREATE A WINDOWS 10 LOCAL ACCOUNT USING COMPUTER MANAGEMENT

GET READY. To create a Windows 10 local account using Computer Management, perform the following steps.

1. On LON-CL1, right-click the **Start** button and select **Computer Management**.

Figure 14-8

2. When the Computer Management console opens, expand **Local Users and Groups** and click **Users**, as shown in Figure 14-8.

Managing users with the Computer Management

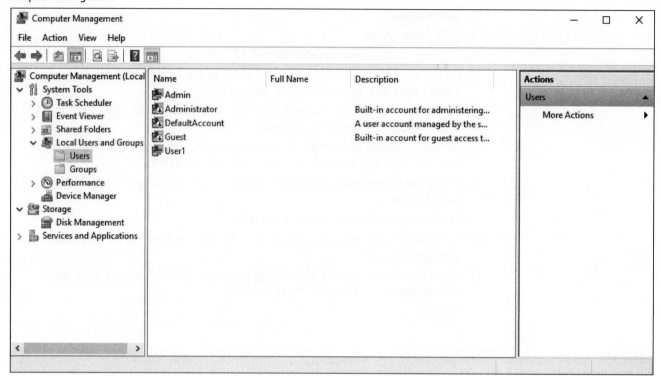

3. Right-click the **Users** node and click **New User**.
4. In the User name text box, type a name such as **User2**. In the Full name text box, type **User 2**.
5. In the Password and Confirm password text boxes, type a password such as **Pa$$w0rd**.
6. Click the **Create** button.

When users log on to a computer that is a member of a domain, they are not being authenticated by the computers on which they are working. Instead, their credentials (user name/password) are sent to a special computer that manages Active Directory. Active Directory is a database along with a collection of supporting components that are installed on one or more computers in the domain. These computers, called domain controllers, maintain a copy of the Active Directory that stores user accounts in the form of objects. These objects are then replicated between domain controllers. When using a domain model, you have to create only a single user account for each user to provide access to all resources in the domain. When running Windows 10, you must have either the Professional or Enterprise edition to join a domain.

It is possible that a company will have more than one domain as part of its Active Directory implementation. Multiple domains are connected to create trees, and multiple trees can be connected to create a forest. When you implement multiple domains, a feature named the *Global Catalog* is used to find users, computers, and resources throughout the other domains.

To create and manage domain users and groups, you will use the Active Directory Users and Computers console or the Active Directory Administrative Center. These tools are available on a domain controller or on a Windows 10 machine with the administrative tools installed.

➔ CREATE A DOMAIN USER ACCOUNT

GET READY. To create a domain user account on a domain controller, perform the following steps.

1. Log on to LON-DC1 as **adatum\administrator** with the password of **Pa$$w0rd**.
2. When Server Manager opens, open the **Tools** menu and click **Active Directory Users and Computers**.
3. Right-click the **Users** OU and click **New > User**. The New Object – User dialog box opens, as shown in Figure 14-9.

Figure 14-9

Creating a new domain Active Directory account

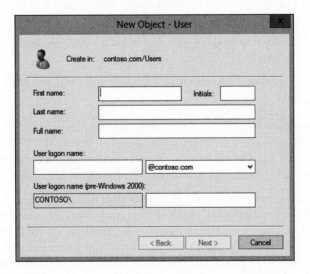

4. In the First name text box, type **John** and in the Last name text box, type **Smith**. In the Full name text box, type **John Smith**.
5. In the User logon name text box, type **JSmith** and click **Next**.
6. In the Password and Confirm password text boxes, type a password such as **Pa$$w0rd**. Click **Next**.
7. Click **Finish**.

A Microsoft user account is required in order to provide users with the ability to download apps from the Windows Store, synchronize their settings between Windows 10 computers and mobile devices, and run Windows 10 apps such as Mail, People, OneDrive, and Messaging. Although you can browse the Windows Store with a local user account, you cannot download Windows apps. If your strategy is to continue to use traditional applications (installed from DVDs or websites) and only download Microsoft updates, a local account would suffice.

A Microsoft account will be any account that uses outlook.com, hotmail.com, msn.com, live .com, or passport.com. However, you can also use an existing email address. To use an existing email address, you need to sign up for an account.

If your strategy includes setting up multiple Windows 10 computers on a network without Active Directory, Microsoft user accounts can reduce the administration overhead that is necessary when implementing local user accounts. Using local user accounts requires that you create the same account on each computer the user needs to access resources. Any changes the user makes to personalize her desktop will not follow her to other Windows 10 computers or devices. Using a Microsoft user account allows the user to access any of the Windows 10 computers and devices while maintaining a consistent desktop experience across each computer. On each computer or device, she can access her Windows Store apps, browse her favorites, review her history, and use many other settings stored in the cloud.

Implementing Microsoft user accounts can also simplify the process of recovering lost passwords. When you lose the password to a local user account, you must have access to the local administrator account to reset it, you must have created a password-reset disk beforehand, or you must use a third-party software program. When you use Microsoft user accounts, you can recover from a lost password by using a previously assigned hint or by resetting your password from the Microsoft website.

If you are considering working with Microsoft accounts in combination with domain-based accounts, there are two options:

- Sign in with your Microsoft user account when you need to run a Windows app.
- Connect your domain account to your Microsoft user account.

If you choose the first option, each time a user logs on with his domain account and then attempts to open a Windows app (Mail, People, OneDrive, or Messaging), he must enter his Microsoft user account credentials. This can become very time consuming because the process is repeated each time he opens another Windows app.

The second option is to connect your Microsoft user accounts to your domain accounts. For enterprise environments, Group Policy can be used to control whether users can link their Microsoft user accounts to their domain accounts as well as what can and cannot be synchronized. If linking your domain credentials to your Microsoft user account fits your authentication strategy, keep in mind that the domain credentials will not be uploaded to the cloud and are never synchronized with other computers.

 ADD A MICROSOFT ACCOUNT TO YOUR DOMAIN ACCOUNT

GET READY. To add a Microsoft account to your domain account, perform the following steps.

1. On LON-CL1, click the **Start** button and click **Settings**.
2. Click **Accounts**.
3. On the Your Account page, click the **Add a Microsoft account** option.
4. When the Add Your Microsoft Account page opens, in the Email or phone text box, type your Microsoft account email address.
5. In the Password text box, type the password for the Microsoft account email address.

■ AUTHENTICATING COMPUTERS AND USERS

↓
THE BOTTOM LINE

When designing an authentication strategy, you can choose between a workgroup and a domain. Workgroups provide a distributed authentication mechanism, whereas domains provide a central authentication mechanism that can support scalability.

A *user account* is used by Windows to determine what changes you can make on the computer, to determine which files and folders you can have access to, and to track personal preferences such as your choice of desktop wallpaper, color schemes, drive mappings, and/or screen savers. There are standard accounts used to perform daily tasks on the computer that are limited in what they can do as well as administrative accounts that provide full control over the computer.

Before users can access a network and its available resources, they must be authenticated. This involves entering a user name and password that was configured by the network's administrator as part of the initial setup of the user accounts. Once entered, the computer verifies the credentials against its database and determines whether or not to provide the user with access to its resources. These resources can be located on the local computer, distributed across the network, and/or be located somewhere out on the Internet.

Like user accounts, Windows *computer accounts* provide a means for authenticating and auditing the computer's access to a Windows network and its access to domain resources. Each Windows computer to which you want to grant access to resources must have a unique computer account. It can also be used for auditing purposes specifying which system was used when something was accessed.

Much like user accounts, computer accounts are assigned passwords when the computer is added to the domain and are automatically maintained between the computer and the domain controllers. Unfortunately, from time to time, a computer account can become untrusted where the security identifier (SID) or password is different from those stored in Active Directory. This is done when:

- You deploy a computer from an image of another computer and you do not use the sysprep tool to reset the SID.
- The computer account is corrupted.
- The computer is not connected to the domain network for long periods of time.

Unfortunately, you cannot reset the password. Instead, the best thing to do is to rejoin the computer to the domain. You can also use the Netdom command-line tool, which is included with Windows Server 2012 R2 and Windows Server 2016.

Understanding Kerberos and NTLM Authentication

When a user logs on to a computer, the user logs on using Kerberos or the NTLM protocol. Kerberos is the preferred method because it is more secure, but it is not always available in all situations.

When authenticating and using resources in a domain, you will use *Kerberos v5*. Kerberos v5 is a protocol that defines how clients interact with a network authentication service. Figure 14-10 provides a simplified explanation of what happens between a user/computer, a domain controller (running the *Key Distribution Center*, or *KDC*), and a file server containing the resource the user wants to access. The Key Distribution Center is the network authentication service that supplies ticket-granting tickets (TGTs) used by the Kerberos v5 protocol.

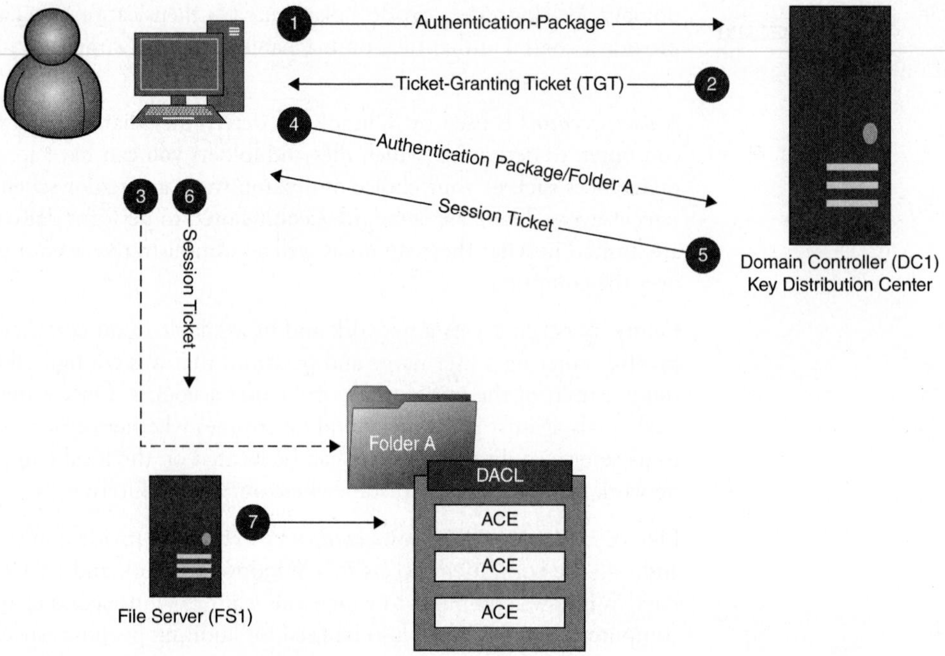

Figure 14-10

The Kerberos authentication process

As shown in Figure 14-10:

1. When a user logs on to a computer in a domain with the domain account, the LSA takes the information and creates an authentication package. This package is sent by the user's computer to the Key Distribution Center (KDC), which is a service running on a domain controller.

2. The KDC validates the authentication package and sends a ticket-granting ticket (TGT) to the user. The TGT contains information about the user's computer as well as a list of security identifiers (SIDs) for the user account and any group accounts the user belongs to.

3. When the user attempts to access a resource (e.g., a folder or file) on a file server named FS1, she will need a session ticket.

4. To get the session ticket, the client will create another authentication package and send it back to the KDC along with a request for that resource.

5. The KDC validates the authentication package and sends the user a session ticket.

6. The session ticket is then used to authenticate to FS1. FS1 decrypts the ticket and validates it.

7. FS1 then compares the ticket with a Discretionary Access Control List (DACL) that is attached to the resource. The DACL consists of one or more access control entries (ACEs). Each ACE contains a SID for a user account or group and the permissions applied to it for the resource. If the ACE contains one or more SIDs that match those in the user's ticket, the user is granted the permissions provided for that SID.

If a user is having problems logging on to the domain, you should check the Caps Lock key. You should also check the DNS setting for the client to make sure it can find Active Directory resources and you should make sure that the time is correct on the client.

NTLM is a family of authentication protocols first introduced with Windows NT. It is based on a challenge/response mechanism used to authenticate users and computers. Although Kerberos v5 is the preferred authentication protocol for Active Directory–based environments, NTLM is used for systems running Windows NT 4.0 and earlier and for computers that are a member of a workgroup. It is also used when authenticating to a server that belongs to a different Active Directory forest.

Understanding Access Tokens and Credential Caching

When a user is authenticated, the Local Security Authority (LSA) creates a primary access token for the user. An *access token* contains a security identifier (SID) for the user, all of the SIDs for the groups to which the user belongs, and the user's privileges. As the user accesses resources, a user does not have to keep entering his password. Instead, Windows submits the access token on behalf of the user.

If you add a user to a group after the user's access token has been issued, or if you modify privileges assigned to the user account, the user must log off and then log on again in order to obtain the updated access token.

Each time a user logs on to Windows, Windows securely caches the user's domain credentials by storing a hash of the password in the system registry (HKEY_LOCAL_MACHINE\ Security\Cache). By caching the user's domain credentials (*credential caching*), the user can log on when the domain controller is not available. When logging on to the domain, the cache credentials only provide the user with access to local resources; the credentials must be checked when accessing remote resources as well as to verify that the user has access.

If you do not want the credentials to be cached, you can disable the credential caching by using a GPO setting—Computer Configuration\Policies\Windows Settings\Security Settings\ Local Policies\Security Options\Interactive logon: number of previous logons to cache (in case the domain controller is not available). A value of 0 disables logon caching.

Configuring Credential Manager

Credential Manager allows you to store credentials (such as user names and passwords) that you use to log on to websites or other computers on a network. By storing your credentials, Windows can automatically log you on to websites or other computers. Credentials are saved in special folders on your computer called *vaults*.

CERTIFICATION READY
Configure Credential
Manager
Objective 3.4

Windows and programs (such as web browsers) can securely provide the credentials in the vaults to other computers and websites. Windows automatically adds credentials used to connect to shared folders to the Credential Manager. However, you can manually add a user name and password.

 ADD A WINDOWS CREDENTIAL USING CREDENTIAL MANAGER

GET READY. To add a Windows credential using Credential Manager, perform the following steps.

1. On LON-DC1, open **Control Panel** and click **User Accounts**.
2. Click **Credential Manager > Windows Credentials** (see Figure 14-11).
3. Click **Add a Windows credential**.

Figure 14-11

Managing Windows
Credentials with Credential
Manager

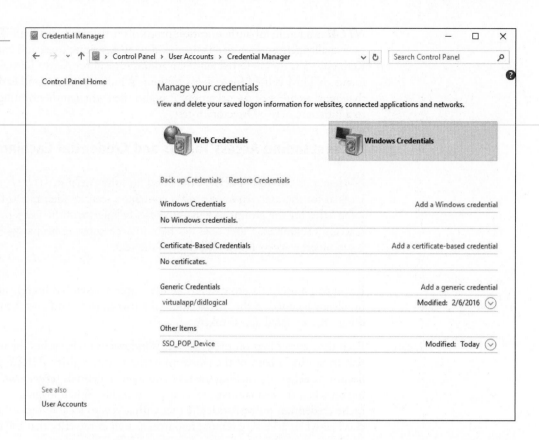

4. In the Internet or network address text box, type the name of the computer on the network that you want to access. This can be the NetBIOS name (for example, **server1**) or the DNS name (for example, **server1.adatum.com**).

5. In the User name text box and the Password text box, type the user name and password that you use for that computer or website and then click **OK**.

You might need to change the Windows credentials or perhaps you no longer want to store the credentials. In these situations, click the credentials that you want to manage and then click Edit or Remove.

■ CONFIGURING DOMAIN SETTINGS WITH ACCOUNT POLICIES

THE BOTTOM LINE

Group Policy is one of the most powerful features of Active Directory that controls the working environment for user accounts and computer accounts. Group Policy provides the centralized management and configuration of operating systems, applications, and users' settings in an Active Directory environment. For example, you can use group policies to specify how often a user has to change her password, to specify what the background image is on a person's computer, or to specify if spell checking is required before sending an email.

CERTIFICATION READY
Configure domain
settings
Objective 3.4

Account policies (see Figure 14-12) are domain-level policies that define the security-related attributes assigned to user objects. Account policies contain three subsets:

- *Password Policy:* Determines settings for passwords, such as enforcement and lifetimes.
- **Account Lockout Policy:** Determines the circumstances and length of time that an account is locked out of the system.

- **Kerberos Policy:** Determines Kerberos-related settings, such as ticket lifetimes and enforcement. Kerberos Policy settings do not exist in local computer policies.

Windows systems also include local policies, which have most of the settings that you will find in a group policy.

Figure 14-12

Managing Account Policies
Password Policy

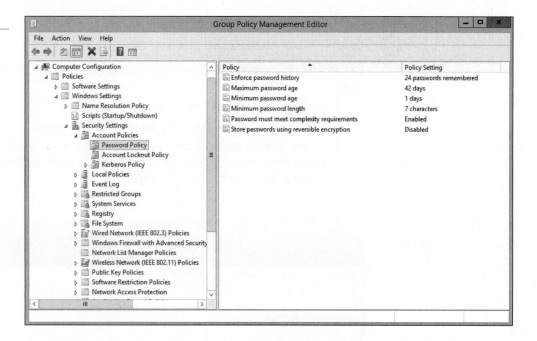

Group Policy can be used to control passwords, including how often a user changes a password, how long the password is, and whether the password is a complex password. To help manage passwords, you can configure settings in the Computer Configuration\Windows Settings\Security Settings\Account Policies\Password Policy node of a group policy. The settings are:

- **Minimum Password Length:** The minimum number of characters that a user's password must contain. You can set a value between 1 and 14 characters. To specify that no password is required, set the value to 0.

- **Passwords must meet complexity requirements:** If enabled, passwords must be at least six characters long, cannot use parts of the user's name, and must be a combination of at least three of the following four characteristics: uppercase, lowercase, digits, and nonalphanumeric characters.

- **Maximum Password Age:** The time before a password expires.

- **Enforce Password History:** The number of different passwords that users must have before they can reuse a password.

- **Minimum Password Age:** The time before users can change their passwords. This prevents users from changing their passwords numerous times, effectively surpassing the Enforce Password History setting in their efforts to reset their passwords to their original passwords.

If you need to use different password policies for different groups of users, you can use fine-grained password policies, which are applied to user objects or global security groups. *Fine-grained password policies* allow you to specify multiple password policies within a single domain so that you can apply different restrictions for password and account lockout policies to different sets of users in a domain. To use a fine-grained password policy, your domain functional level must be at least Windows Server 2008. To enable fine-grained password policies, you first create a *Password Settings Object (PSO)*. A PSO gives you granular control of password and account settings.

You then configure the same settings that you configure for the password and account lockout policies. You can create and apply PSOs in the Windows Server 2012 R2 environment by using the Active Directory Administrative Center (ADAC) or Windows PowerShell.

CREATE AND CONFIGURE THE PASSWORD SETTINGS CONTAINER

GET READY. To create and configure the Password Settings Container, perform the following steps.

1. On LON-DC1, open **Server Manager**.
2. Click **Tools > Active Directory Administrative Center**. The ADAC appears.
3. In the ADAC pane, click the arrow next to the domain and then click the **System** folder. Scroll down and double-click **Password Settings Container**. The Password Settings Container is shown in Figure 14-13.

Figure 14-13

Opening the Password Settings Container

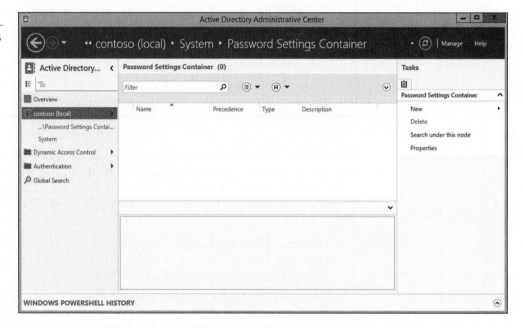

4. In the Tasks pane, click **New > Password Settings**. The Create Password Settings window opens (see Figure 14-14).
5. In the Name text box, type a name for the Password Settings Container.
6. In the Precedence text box, type a precedence number.

   Passwords with a lower precedence number overwrite Password Settings Containers that have higher precedence numbers.

7. Complete or edit the appropriate fields for the settings that you want to use.
8. Under Directly Applies To, click **Add**. In the Select Users or Groups dialog box, specify the name of the user or group that you want the Password Settings Container to affect and then click **OK**.
9. Click **OK** to submit the creation of the PSO.
10. Close the ADAC.

Figure 14-14

Creating a new Password
Settings Container

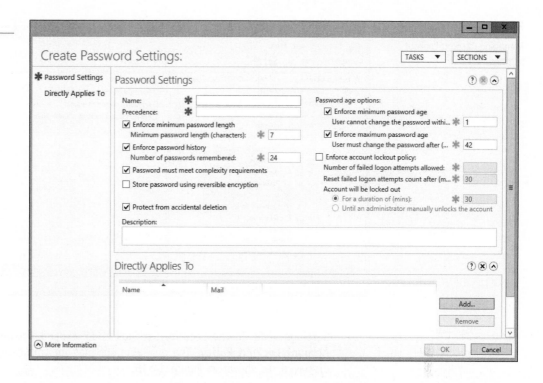

An ***Account Lockout Policy*** specifies the number of unsuccessful logon attempts that, if made within a predefined amount of time, might indicate that an unauthorized person is trying to access a computer or the network. An Account Lockout Policy can be set to lock the account in question after a specified number of invalid attempts. Additionally, the policy specifies the duration that the account remains locked.

The three policy settings used for account lockout are as follows:

- **Account lockout duration:** How long (in minutes) a locked-out account remains locked out (range is 1 to 99,999 minutes)
- **Account lockout threshold:** How many failed logons it takes until the account becomes locked out (range is 1 to 999 logon attempts)
- **Reset account lockout counter after:** How long (in minutes) it takes after a failed logon attempt before the counter tracking failed logons is reset to zero (range is 1 to 99,999 minutes)

If you set the account lockout duration to 0, the account stays locked until an administrator unlocks it. If the account lockout threshold is set to 0, the account will never be locked out no matter how many failed logons occur.

 CONFIGURE AN ACCOUNT LOCKOUT POLICY

GET READY. To configure a domain-wide account lockout policy, perform the following steps.

1. On LON-DC1, using Server Manager, click **Tools > Group Policy Management**.
2. Expand **Forest: contoso.com**, expand **Domains**, expand **contoso.com**, and then click **Group Policy Objects**.
3. Right-click the **Default Domain Policy** and choose **Edit**. A Group Policy Management Editor window for this policy is displayed.
4. In the left window pane, expand the **Computer Configuration** node, expand the **Policies** node, expand the **Windows Settings** node, and then expand the **Security**

Figure 14-15

Managing Account Lockout settings

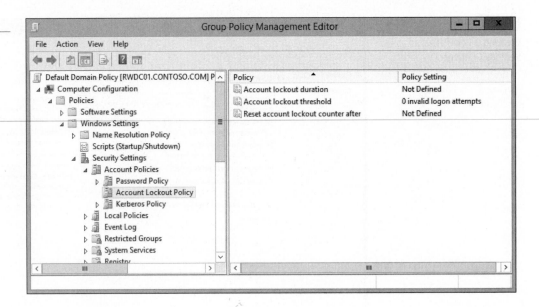

Figure 14-15

Managing Account Lockout settings

Settings node. In the Security Settings node, expand **Account Policies** and select **Account Lockout Policy**. The available settings for this category of the GPO are displayed, as shown in Figure 14-15.

5. In the right window pane, double-click the **Account lockout duration** policy setting to view the Properties dialog box.

6. Select the **Define This Policy Setting** check box.

Note the default setting of 30 minutes for account lockout duration. If you want to change the account lockout duration, you can do so here.

7. Click **OK** to accept the specified lockout duration. The Suggested Value Changes dialog box—which indicates other related settings and their defaults—is displayed.

8. Click **OK** to automatically enable these other settings or click **Cancel** to go back to the Account Lockout Duration Properties dialog box.

9. Click **OK** to accept the additional setting defaults.

10. Complete any additional changes, as necessary, to the other individual Account Lockout Policy settings.

11. Close the Group Policy Management Editor window for this policy.

■ CONFIGURING DEVICE REGISTRATION

THE BOTTOM LINE

Over the last several years, smartphones and tablets have become powerful devices that offer the convenience of mobile technology. Therefore, it is common for users to use multiple computers and devices to access email and other business-related applications services. In addition, many organizations implement *Bring Your Own Device (BYOD)* policies, which help administrators manage users who use their personal devices to access organizational resources. *Device Registration*, previously called Workplace Join, allows users to join their devices to the organization's network without joining the device to the Active Directory domain. You can then manage access based on a wide range of attributes.

When you join a device using Device Registration, ***Device Registration Service (DRS)*** registers a non-domain-joined device in Active Directory and installs a certificate on the device. By joining the device, Device Registration provides a secure Single Sign-On mechanism while controlling which resources can be accessed by the device.

When the user joins the devices using Device Registration technology, the device becomes a known device. To use Device Registration, you must have Windows Server 2012 R2 or Windows Server 2016 with the AD FS role service installed. In addition, the client must be using the Windows 8.1 or Windows 10 client operating systems or iOS-based devices (such as an iPad).

The certificate is used to represent device identity when accessing the organization's resources. When accessing resources on the organization, the SSO allows the user to be prompted for his domain credentials only once during the lifetime of the SSO session. However, an administrator can specify resources that enforce a password prompt or reauthentication.

To support Device Registration, you need to install and configure Active Directory Federation Services (AD FS) and the new Device Registration Service. To configure the Device Registration Service, execute the following Windows PowerShell commands:

```
Initialize-ADDeviceRegistration
```

```
Enable-AdfsDeviceRegistration
```

Then open the AD FS Management console, navigate to Authentication Policies, click Edit Global Primary Authentication, click to select the Enable Device Authentication, and then click OK. Lastly, the client must trust the SSL certificate that is used for the federation server and must be able to validate certificate revocation information for the certificate.

 JOIN A DEVICE

GET READY. To join a device in Windows 10, perform the following steps.

1. On LON-CL1, click the **Start** button and click **Settings**.
2. Click **Accounts**.
3. On the Accounts page, click **Work access**.
4. On the Work Access page, click **+ Connect**.
5. In the Enter your UserID to get workplace access or turn on device management dialog box, type the user name (such as **JSmith@contoso.com**) and then click **Join**.
6. When prompted for credentials, type the user name and associated password and then click **OK**. You should now see the message *This device has joined your workplace network*.

■ CONFIGURING DEVICE GUARD AND CREDENTIAL GUARD

THE BOTTOM LINE

Over the years, malware has changed dramatically and has become quite sophisticated. Microsoft developed Device Guard and Credential Guard that complement each other in protecting the system against malware.

Device Guard is a group of key features that hardens a computer system against malware by only running trusted applications, preventing malicious code from running. *Credential Guard* isolates and hardens key system and user security information (LSA credentials). However, both of these technologies are only available through Windows 10 Enterprise.

Device Guard and Credential Guard use Windows 10 *virtual secure mode (VSM)* that, in turn, uses the processor's virtualization to protect the PC, including data and credential tokens on the system's disks. By using hardware virtualization, Windows 10 will be divided into multiple containers. Windows will run in one container, and the security tokens from Active Directory that lets you access your organization's resources will run in another container. Each of these would be isolated from the other. Therefore, if Windows is compromised by malware such as a rootkit, the tokens are still protected and isolated in their own encrypted container.

To use VSM, you need the following:

- UEFI running in Native Mode (not Compatibility/CSM/Legacy mode)
- 64-bit version of Windows 10 Enterprise
- 64-bit processor that supports second level address translation (SLAT) and Virtualization Extensions (such as Intel VT or AMD V)

A Trusted Platform Module (TPM) is recommended.

You will then be able to install Hyper-V and Isolated User Mode using the following procedures.

INSTALL HYPER-V AND ISOLATED USER MODE ON WINDOWS 10

GET READY. To install Hyper-V and Isolated User Mode on Windows 10, perform the following steps.

1. On LON-CL1, right-click the **Start** button and click **Programs and Features**.
2. Click the **Turn Windows features on or off** option.
3. When the Windows Features dialog box opens, select **Isolated User Mode** and **Hyper-V Platform**, and click **OK**.

You will then enable Device Guard and Credential Guard with Group Policy. To enable Device Guard and Credential Guard, you would open a GPO, and navigate to Computer Configuration\Administrative Templates\System\Device Guard\Turn On Virtualization Based Security (as shown in Figure 14-16), and enable the option. To enable Device Guard, select the Enable Virtualization Based Protection of Code Integrity option. To enable Credential Guard option, select the Enable Credential Guard option.

ENABLE DEVICE GUARD AND CREDENTIAL GUARD

GET READY. To enable Device Guard and Credential Guard on Windows 10, perform the following steps.

1. On LON-CL1, log on as **adatum\administrator** with the password of **Pa$$WOrd**.
2. Click the **Start** button, type **gpedit.msc**, and press the **Enter** key.
3. When the Group Policy Management Editor opens, navigate to the **Computer Configuration\Administrative Templates\System\Device Guard** node. Then double-click the **Turn On Virtualization Based Security**.
4. When the Turn on Virtualization Based Security dialog box opens, select the **Enabled** option.

Figure 14-16

Enabling Device Guard
and Credential Guard

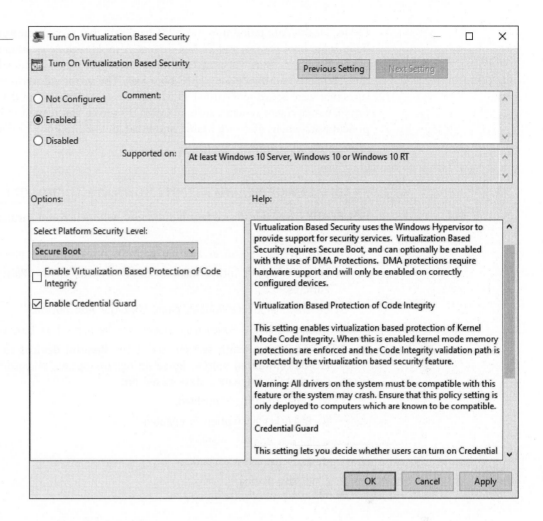

5. To enable Device Guard, select the **Enable Virtualization Based Protection of Code Integrity** option.

6. To enable Credential Guard option, select the **Enable Credential Guard** option.

7. To close the Turn on Virtualization Based Security dialog box, click **OK**.

■ CONFIGURING DEVICE HEALTH ATTESTATION

THE BOTTOM LINE

With Windows 10 and Windows Server 2016, you can enable *Device Health Attestation (DHA)* that can access device security health and verify that the device is using Secure Boot, BitLocker, or Early Launch Antimalware (ELAM). Device Health Attestation is aimed at malware that starts on a system before Windows defenses and antimalware load, which allow the malware to remain hidden.

CERTIFICATION READY
Configure Device Health
Attestation
Objective 3.4

Secure Boot is a security standard that makes sure that your PC boots only software that is trusted by the PC manufacturer. *BitLocker* is technology that can encrypt a volume, which is meant to protect the content if a system is stolen. *Early Launch Antimalware (ELAM)* is security technology that evaluates non-Microsoft Windows boot time device/application drivers for malicious code.

Device Health Attestation uses the TPM hardware that records measurements of the bootloader, boot drivers, and ELAM drivers. After Health Attestation is enabled on a workstation, the client will contact a health attestation server and send the server the signed measurements and the device's TMP boot logs. The server will verify and analyze the measures that were issued to a trusted TPM, and create a statement of device health. Then in the future, management systems, such as an MDM server, can request that an enrolled device present a statement of device health, and it can be used to grant or deny access based on the system's security health.

 ENABLE DEVICE HEALTH ATTESTATION WITH MICROSOFT INTUNE

GET READY. To enable device health attestation with Microsoft Intune, perform the following steps.

1. On LON-CL1, log on as **adatum\administrator** with the password of **Pa$$WOrd**.
2. In the Microsoft Intune administration console, choose **Policy > Compliance Policies**.
3. On the Compliance Policies page, click the **Add** button.
4. When the Create Policy page opens, in the name text box, type **Health Check**.
5. In the Device Health section, select the **Require devices to be reported as health is not configured** option. By selecting this option, Microsoft Intune will consider the overall compliance state based on:
   a. Code integrity is enabled.
   b. BitLocker encryption is enabled.
   c. Secure Boot is enabled.
   d. Early Launch Antimalware driver is loaded.
5. Click **Save Policy**.

SKILL SUMMARY

IN THIS LESSON YOU LEARNED:

- Authentication represents the way that security principals (users, computers, and processes) prove their identity before they are allowed to connect to your network. In the past, authentication was handled through the use of passwords. Today, additional authentication tools, including digital certificates, smart cards, picture passwords, and biometrics, are used.

- A user can authenticate via one or more of the following methods: by using what he or she knows, by using what he or she owns or possesses, and by proving who he or she is.

- Biometrics takes advantage of the uniqueness of every individual. By using a person's fingerprint, face, voice, or retina, biometrics offers advantages over other methods.

- When a user logs on to a computer, the user logs on using Kerberos or the NTLM protocol. Kerberos is the preferred method because it is more secure, but it is not always available in all situations.

- Credential Manager allows you to store credentials (such as user names and passwords) that you use to log on to websites or other computers on a network. By storing your credentials, Windows can automatically log you on to websites or other computers. Credentials are saved in special folders on your computer called vaults.

- Device Registration, previously called Workplace Join, allows users to join their devices to the organization's network without joining the device to the Active Directory domain. You can then manage access based on a wide range of attributes.

- Device Guard and Credential Guard use Windows 10 virtual secure mode (VSM) that uses the processor's virtualization to protect the PC, including data and credential tokens on the system's disks.

▪ Knowledge Assessment

Multiple Choice

Select the correct answer for each of the following questions.

1. Which of the following terms best describes the manner in which security principals prove their identity?
   a. Authorization
   b. Confidentiality
   c. Authentication
   d. Integrity

2. Which of the following are considered authentication factors? (Choose all that apply.)
   a. Wi-Fi Protected Access
   b. Biometrics
   c. Picture passwords
   d. Smart cards

3. Which of the following gestures are supported by picture passwords? (Choose all that apply.)
   a. Straight lines
   b. Circles
   c. Taps
   d. Angles

4. Which of the following authentication protocols is based on a challenge/response mechanism?
   a. NTLM
   b. Kerberos
   c. TLS/SLS
   d. File Replication Service

5. Which of the following characteristics describe the characteristics of a workgroup? (Choose all that apply.)
   a. All computers are located on same network segment.
   b. It has centralized management of user accounts.
   c. It is scalable.
   d. It uses the SAM database.

6. Which of the following authentication protocols is used in Windows Active Directory domains?
   a. Kerberos
   b. TGT
   c. KDC
   d. TLS/SSL

7. Which of the following components is used to create virtual smart cards?
   a. SSL certificate
   b. Smart card reader
   c. Trusted Platform Module
   d. Picture authentication

8. Which of the following certificate types is used with virtual smart cards?
   a. Smart card logon
   b. Basic EFS
   c. Workstation authentication
   d. User

9. Which of the following tools is used to remember user names and passwords when accessing a website?
   a. Local security policy
   b. HomeGroup control panel
   c. Access token generator
   d. Credential Manager

10. Which of the following mechanisms is used to secure HomeGroups?
   a. A pin
   b. A password
   c. A digital certificate
   d. Windows Hello

Best Answer

Choose the letter that corresponds to the best answer. More than one answer choice may achieve the goal. Select the BEST answer.

1. Suppose there are 10 computers on a network that are configured to share a few printers and a single document folder. The company is not expected to add more computers or users over the next year. There is also no IT staff to support the network. Which of the following models is the best fit for this network?
   a. Domain model
   b. Workgroup model
   c. Ad hoc model
   d. Infrastructure model

2. Which of the following authentication factors offers the most security?
   a. Passwords
   b. Picture passwords
   c. Smart cards
   d. Smart cards with a PIN

3. Which of the following authentication types is the least secure?
   a. Passwords (20 characters, mixed with upper- and lowercase letters, numbers, and symbols)
   b. Smart cards
   c. Smart cards with a PIN
   d. VSCs

4. Which of the following authentication protocols is best designed to support today's Active Directory–based networks?
   a. NTLMv2
   b. NTLMv1
   c. Kerberosv1
   d. Kerberosv5

5. Which of the following is used to verify the trustworthiness of a computer within a domain? (Choose two answers.)
   a. Computer SID
   b. Computer certificate
   c. User password
   d. Computer password

Matching and Identification

1. Match the following terms with the related description or usage.

_____ **a)** Authentication

_____ **b)** SAM

_____ **c)** Two-factor authentication

_____ **d)** Device Registration

_____ **e)** Authorization

_____ **f)** Workgroup

_____ **g)** Domain

_____ **h)** TGT

_____ **i)** Digital certificate

_____ **j)** Virtual secure mode

1. Contains user accounts and their associated passwords in a workgroup model

2. Determines what a security principal can do after being authenticated

3. Requires the use of two of the three authentication factors

4. Provides centralized account management

5. Is a collection of computers that interact with each other without any centralized authority

6. Contains information about the user's computer, a list of SIDs for the user account, and any group account memberships

7. Represents the way that security principals prove their identity

8. Allows users to join their devices to the organization's network without joining the device to the Active Directory domain

9. Authentication that is based on what you have

10. Used by Device Guard and Credential Guard

Build a List

1. Specify the correct order of steps necessary to using Kerberos for authentication.

_____ An authentication package is created and sent to the KDC.

_____ The user attempts to access a resource and needs a session ticket.

_____ The KDC validates the authentication package and sends the user a session ticket.

_____ The KDC validates the authentication package and sends the user a TGT.

_____ The client creates an authentication package (to get a session ticket) and sends it to the KDC along with a request for the resource.

_____ A session ticket is used to authenticate to the file server that contains the resource the user wants.

_____ The file server compares the ticket with a DACL.

2. Specify the correct order of steps necessary to creating a picture password.

_____ Choose Picture.

_____ Click Create a picture password.

_____ Draw three gestures.

_____ Confirm the gestures.

_____ Log on using the picture password.

■ Business Case Scenarios

Scenario 14-1: Allowing Personal Smartphones on the Corporate Network

You are an administrator for your company's Active Directory domain. Your manager has decided to allow users to use their own smartphones and tablets to access email and work documents. Explain what must be configured for users to use their own personal devices?

Scenario 14-2: Securing Your Computers

You are an administrator for the Contoso Corporation, which has about 1,200 computers, mostly running Windows 10. Over the past year, you have managed several instances of malware appearing on the computers of key personnel, leading to a compromise of some key systems. You want to ensure that this does not happen again. Explain how to make sure that users' credentials and other key parts of Windows are not compromised by rootkits or other forms of malware.

Configuring Advanced Management Tools

LESSON **15**

70-698 EXAM OBJECTIVE

Objective 3.5 – Configure advanced management tools. This objective may include but is not limited to: Configure services; configure Task Scheduler; configure automation of management tasks using Windows PowerShell. * Configure Device Manager is covered in Lesson 3. Configure and use the MMC is covered in Lesson 10.

LESSON HEADING	EXAM OBJECTIVE
Configuring Advanced Management Tools	
Configuring Services	Configure services
Using the System Configuration Utility (MSConfig.exe)	
Configuring Task Scheduler	Configure Task Scheduler
Configuring Automation of Management Tasks Using Windows PowerShell	Configure Automation of management tasks using Windows PowerShell

KEY TERMS

action	**services**	**Task Scheduler**
Another account	**Services console**	**trigger**
Local Service account	**System Configuration utility (msconfig.exe)**	**Windows PowerShell Integrated Scripting Environment (ISE)**
Local System account		
Network Service account		

■ CONFIGURING ADVANCED MANAGEMENT TOOLS

THE BOTTOM LINE

Throughout the book, you have used Advanced Management Tools, which are usually found in Administrative tools. The Administrative tools are based on the Microsoft Management Console (MMC), including the Computer Management console, as discussed in Lesson 10. However, as an administrator, you will need to learn how to manage services and scheduled tasks.

Remember that if there are MMC tools that you use over and over again, you can create your own management console. Therefore, if you constantly need to manage local system certificates and services, you can create your own console that will have those two snap-ins. If there are commands that you constantly have to type in, it is best to create a script that will contain those commands.

Configuring Services

> *Services* are programs that run in the background on a Windows system to provide a function or a network application, or help the operating system run other programs. The services are managed using the *Services console*, which can be opened by executing services.msc. The services can also be managed using Computer Management.

CERTIFICATION READY
Configure services
Objective 3.5

Windows uses services to handle requests for print spooling, file indexing, task scheduling, the Windows Firewall, and much more. Services run in the background, essentially helping the operating system work with other programs. For example, the server service allows the system to provide file and print sharing over the network, while the workstation service allows you to access file and print shares.

Although services do not usually have user interfaces, you can manage services through the Microsoft Management Console (MMC) Services snap-in shown in Figure 15-1. You can also manage services from the Task Manager and the System Configuration program (msconfig.exe). To use the Services snap-in and configure services, you must be a member of the Account Operators group, the Domain Admins group, or the Enterprise Admins group, or you must have received the appropriate authority.

Figure 15-1

The Services console in Windows 10

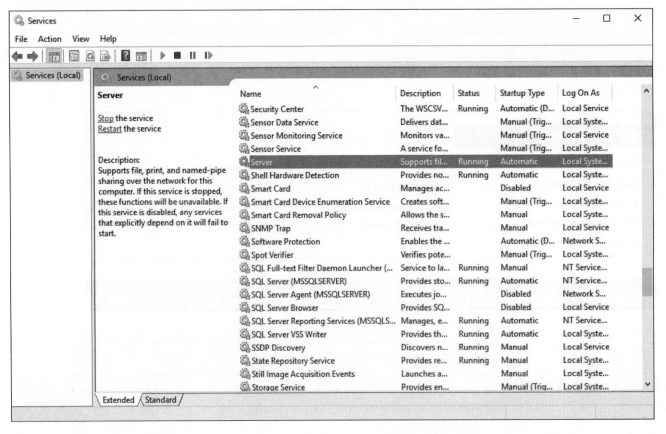

A Windows 10 system can have more than 100 services running at any one time. Each computer can have different services running, depending on the version of Windows in use, the computer manufacturer, and the applications installed; however, Windows 10 generally uses many of the same services across its editions.

The Extended and Standard tabs (at the bottom of the Services console) both display all of the services in the system; however, the Extended tab provides descriptive information for a selected service in the space to the left of the details pane. Sometimes a link is displayed for you to get more information about a particular service.

The Services console enables you to:

- View all services and their status
- Add, start, stop, or disable services
- Select user accounts that might run the service (for security purposes)
- Define how a service recovers from failures
- View a list of service, program, and driver dependencies

To use any of these options, double-click the service to open its Properties dialog box.

The General tab in the service's Properties dialog box (see Figure 15-2) provides options for setting a service's startup type:

- **Automatic (Delayed Start):** The service starts approximately two minutes after the system has completed starting the operating system.
- **Automatic:** The service starts as the operating system starts.
- **Manual:** The service must be started manually, by a user, a dependent service, or a program.
- **Disabled:** The service is disabled and will not start.

Figure 15-2

The General tab

You can also start, stop, pause, or resume a service using the buttons in the Service status section. For example, let's say a printer has several duplicate (unnecessary) print jobs and the queue is not responding. You've restarted the printer a few times but that didn't work. To fix the problem, just restart the Print Spooler service in the Services console to clear the print queues.

The Log On tab (see Figure 15-3) allows you to specify the user account the service can use, which might be different from the logged-on user or the default computer account. Your options are:

- *Local System account*: This account has extensive privilege on the local computer, but it does not have a password nor a profile of its own. When it tries to access a remote computer, it will present the computer's credentials (computername$).
- *Local Service account*: Click This account and then type NT AUTHORITY\LocalService. This account is a built-in account. (It's already created in the operating system.) It can run services in the background but has limited access to resources and objects, which helps protect the system if individual services are compromised. No password is required.
- *Network Service account*: Click This account and then type NT AUTHORITY\NetworkService. This account is similar to the Local Service account but is geared towards networking services. Like the Local Service account, the Network Service account can run services in the background but it helps protect the computer from compromise.
- *Another account*: Click This account, click Browse, browse for a different user account, select it, and then click OK. Type the password for the user account you selected and then click OK.

Figure 15-3

The Log On tab

The Recovery tab lets you choose recovery actions the computer will take if a service fails. For example, if a service fails, the computer might first try restarting the service. If that doesn't work, you can instruct the computer to restart the service again or you can restart the computer to clear memory and refresh connections.

The Dependencies tab shows you which services depend on other services to run. A dependent service starts after the service upon which it depends starts. Stopping a service also stops any other service that depends on it. There are no options available on this tab—it's informational only. However, before you stop or disable a service on the General tab, you should view the information on the Dependences tab to know which other services might be affected by your change.

CONFIGURE A SERVICE

GET READY. To configure a service in the Services console, perform the following steps.

1. Click **Start,** and type **services.msc.** From the results, click **Services.**
2. When the Services console opens, in the details pane, double-click the service that you want to configure, such as **Print Spooler.** The service's Properties dialog box displays.

3. On the General tab, click the **Startup type** drop-down list. Select **Automatic (Delayed Start)**, **Automatic**, **Manual**, or **Disabled**.

4. Click the **Log On** tab. To specify the user account that the service can use to log on, perform one of the following steps.

   - To use the Local System account, click **Local System** account.

   - To use the Local Service account, click **This account** and then type **NT AUTHORITY\ LocalService**.

   - To use the Network Service account, click **This account** and then type **NT AUTHORITY\NetworkService**.

   - To specify another account, click **This account**, click the **Browse** button, and then specify a user account in the Select User dialog box that displays.

   Click **OK** to save your changes and close the dialog box.

5. To specify another account, type the password for the user account in the Password text box and the Confirm password text box and then click **OK**. You do not have to type a password if you selected the Local Service account or Network Service account.

Using the System Configuration Utility (MSConfig.exe)

The *System Configuration utility (msconfig.exe)* lets you enable or disable startup services, set boot options (such as booting into Safe Mode), access tools like Action Center and Event Viewer, and more. You'll use this utility mainly to troubleshoot startup problems with Windows.

To open System Configuration, click Start, and type msconfig. From the results, click System Configuration. The System Configuration dialog box displays, showing the General tab (see Figure 15-4). Normal startup is selected by default (unless you've previously changed startup settings). A normal startup runs all device drivers and services. Other options include the following:

- **Diagnostic startup:** Runs basic devices and services only; equivalent to starting the computer in Safe Mode.

- **Selective startup:** Starts the system with some or all system services and startup items disabled.

Figure 15-4

The General tab

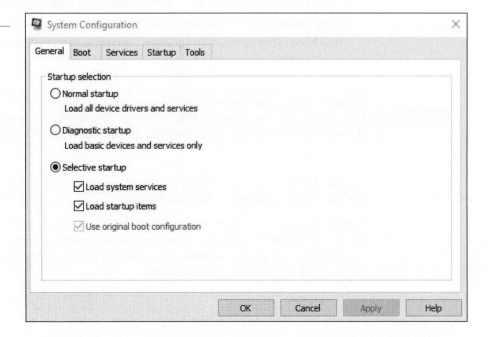

The options on the Boot tab (see Figure 15-5) enable you to adjust boot options, usually for diagnostic purposes. The Boot tab options match the options in the Advanced boot configuration menu that displays when you press F8 at startup (discussed in Lesson 13). To boot the system into Safe Mode, select the Safe boot check box. When you do this, the Minimal option is selected by default. The other safe boot options are:

- **Alternate shell:** Boots to the command prompt without network support.
- **Active Directory repair:** Boots to the Windows GUI and runs critical system services and Active Directory.
- **Network:** Boots into Safe Mode with network services enabled.

Figure 15-5

The Boot tab

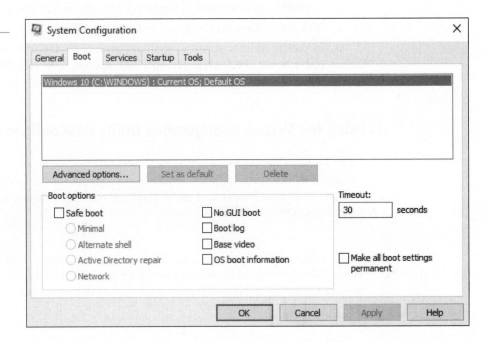

The options in the right column are as follows:

- **No GUI boot:** Disables the Windows Welcome screen.
- **Boot log:** Creates a boot log of startup activity in a file named ntbtlog.txt.
- **Base video:** Starts the Windows graphical user interface using standard VGA drivers.
- **OS boot information:** Displays driver names as drivers are installed during the startup process.

TAKE NOTE

To make the boot options permanent, select the Make all boot settings permanent check box, click Apply, and then click **OK**. Administrators often do this on test computers that they use to test new programs and updates before rolling them out to ordinary users.

You use the Services tab to enable or disable Microsoft and third-party services. These are the same services that display in the Services console covered earlier in this lesson.

Startup was meant to manage startup applications, but in Windows 10, the startup applications are managed from Task Manager. The Tools tab lists many programs you can start for reporting and diagnostic purposes. Some of the tools are Change UAC Settings, Event Viewer, Performance Monitor, and Task Manager.

Configuring Task Scheduler

> Many, but not all, Windows utilities have their own scheduling feature. For those utilities that you want to automate, you can use Task Scheduler. You can also use Task Scheduler to open programs on specific days and times, or at Windows startup.

Task Scheduler enables you to schedule and automate a variety of actions, such as starting programs, displaying messages, and even sending e-mails. You create a scheduled task by specifying a *trigger*, which is an event that causes a task to run, and an *action*, which is the action taken when the task runs.

The main Task Scheduler window is shown in Figure 15-6. The left pane lists the Task Scheduler Library, which contains several built-in tasks by Microsoft and other vendors.

Figure 15-6

The main Task Scheduler window with the built-in libraries expanded

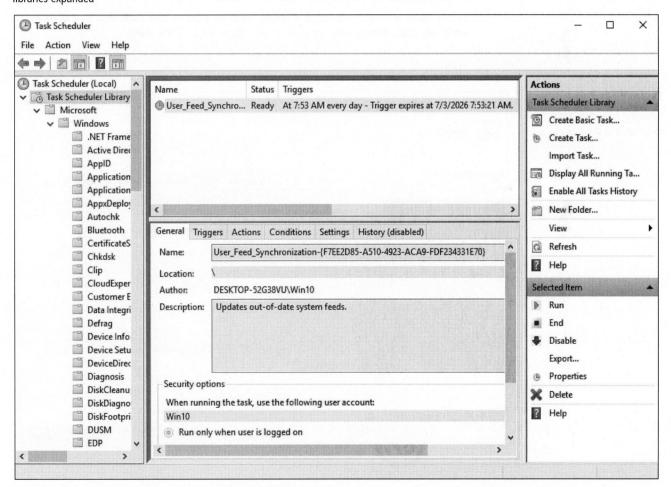

The middle pane has three panes. The Overview pane gives you an overview of Task Scheduler, the Task Status pane displays a summary of tasks that started in a certain time period (for example, within the last 24 hours), and the Active Tasks pane displays scheduled tasks. The information displayed in the middle pane can vary greatly from computer to computer.

To schedule tasks for all users on your computer, you must be logged on as the Administrator. If you're logged on as a Standard user, you can schedule tasks only for your user account.

 CREATE A TASK USING THE CREATE BASIC TASK WIZARD

GET READY. To create a task using the Create Basic Task Wizard, perform the following steps.

1. Click the **Start** button and type **Task Scheduler**. From the results, click **Task Scheduler**.

2. In the Actions pane on the right, click **Create Basic Task**.

3. When the Create Basic Task Wizard starts, in the Name text box, type a descriptive name of the task and click **Next**.

4. On the Task Trigger page, select the frequency the task should occur or an event that triggers the task, such as Daily, Weekly, Monthly, One time, when the computer starts, or when I log on. For our example, because this task will run weekly, select the **Weekly** option and then click **Next**.

5. In the Weekly screen, select a starting date as well as the time and day of the week the task should run, as shown in Figure 15-7. Click **Next**.

Figure 15-7

Selecting frequency and recurrence of the task

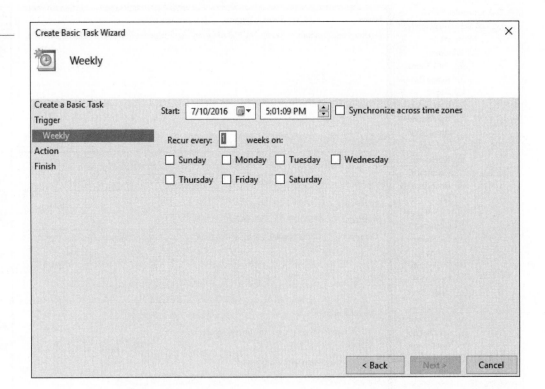

6. On the Action screen, select **Start a program** and click **Next**.

7. In the Start a Program window that displays, click **Browse** to find the Disk Cleanup program. The window shown in Figure 15-8 displays.

8. Click **Disk Cleanup** and then click **Open.** (If the window in Figure 15-8 does not display, navigate to the Disk Cleanup executable file in C:\Windows\system32\ cleanmgr.exe, click **cleanmgr.exe** and then click **Open.**) When the Start a Program screen displays again, which now indicates the path to the Disk Cleanup program executable, click **Next.**

Figure 15-8

Selecting the program to run

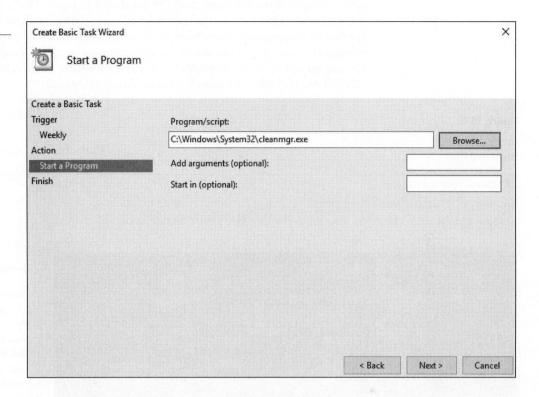

9. The Summary screen summarizes the task, indicating when it will run. If everything is correct, click **Finish.** If you need to make any changes, click the **Back** button, make the appropriate changes, and then click **Finish.**

After the task has been scheduled, you can double-click the task to open the task properties. The General tab will allow you to specify what account that task runs under and if the user has to be logged in or not. The Conditions tab can be used to specify conditions that the task will run under, such as if the task can run under AC or battery power, or if a network connection is required. The Settings tab will specify when to stop the task if the tasks runs too long.

Configuring Automation of Management Tasks Using Windows PowerShell

Lesson 10 introduced PowerShell, which is a powerful tool used to manage and configure Windows. Windows 10 includes the ***Windows PowerShell Integrated Scripting Environment (ISE)*** that helps you create Windows PowerShell scripts. If you need the scripts to be executed on a regular basis, you can execute the scripts using Task Scheduler.

CERTIFICATION READY
Configure Automation of
management tasks using
Windows PowerShell
Objective 3.5

ISE provides command-completion functionality, and enables you to see all available commands and the parameters that you can use with those commands. While you can use a text editor to create a PowerShell script, the Windows PowerShell ISE makes it easier, since you can view cmdlet parameters, which helps you create syntactically correct Windows PowerShell commands.

After you open Windows PowerShell ISE (as shown in Figure 15-9), you can use the File menu to create a new script, open saved scripts, save scripts, and run scripts. Windows PowerShell ISE provides color-coded cmdlets to assist with troubleshooting, and provides debugging tools that you can use to debug simple and complex Windows PowerShell scripts. You can use the Windows PowerShell ISE to view available cmdlets by module (such as DNSClient, Defender, WindowsSearch, or WindowsUpdate).

Figure 15-9

Opening Windows
PowerShell ISE

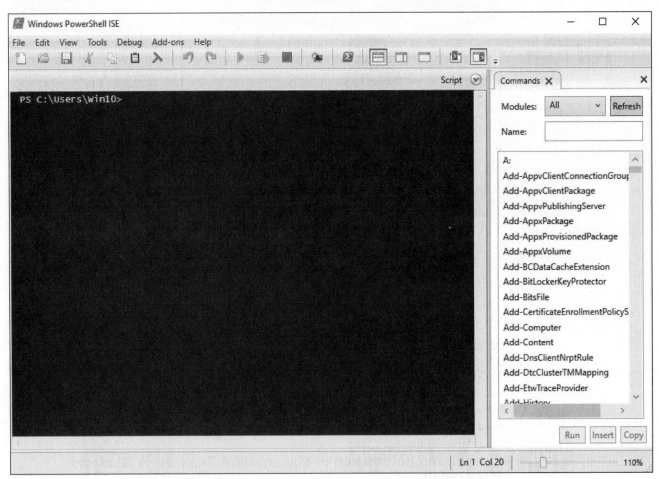

If you need help running a script, such as sending an email to a group of users, use the following command:

```
Send-MailMessage -SmtpServer smtp.adatum.com -From administrator@adatum
.com -To managers@adatum.com --BodyAsHtml "hello world"
```

You can start typing Send-. You will see a list of commands that begin with Send-. Click Send-MailMessage to get the syntax of the command, as shown in Figure 15-10.

Figure 15-10

Using Windows PowerShell ISE to get help on PowerShell Cmdlets

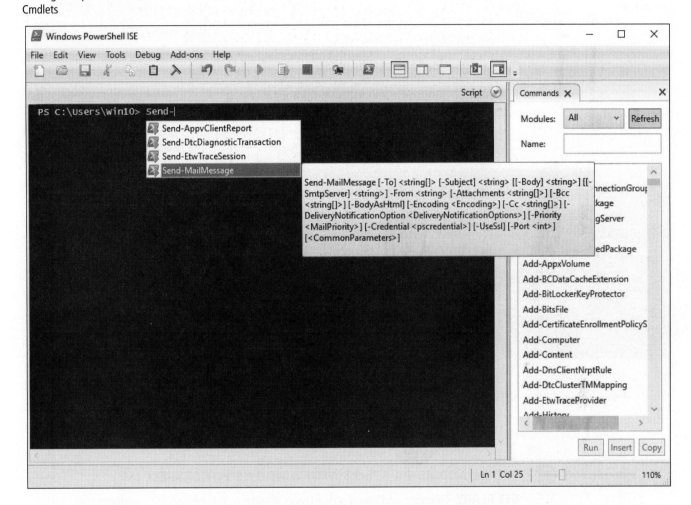

To create a script using the Windows PowerShell ISE, open the View menu and select Show Script Pane. Alternatively, you can click the down arrow next to script at the top of the main pane, type your commands (as shown in Figure 15-11), and then save the script with a .ps1 filename extension. You can execute the script to test it anytime by clicking the Execute button (right green arrow button). After the script has been thoroughly tested, you can then use Task Scheduler to automatically execute the script.

Figure 15-11

Creating a script with Windows
PowerShell ISE

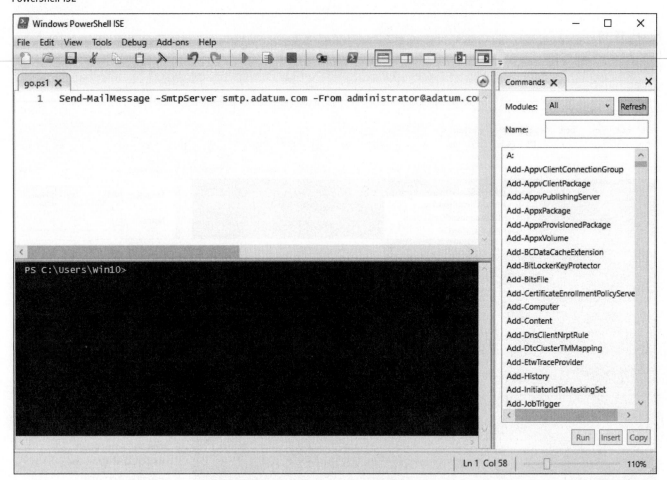

 CREATE AND RUN A SCRIPT WITH WINDOWS POWERSHELL ISE

GET READY. To create and run a script using Windows PowerShell ISE, perform the
following steps.

1. Click the **Start** button and type **powershell**. From the results, click **Windows
   PowerShell ISE.**
2. When the Windows PowerShell ISE window opens, open the **File** menu and
   click **New.**
3. In the Untitled1.ps1 tab box, type the following lines:

   ```
   Get-WmiObject –Class win32_OperatingSystem –ComputerName
   localhost

   Select-Object –Property CSName,LastBootUpTime
   ```

4. On the Windows PowerShell ISE toolbar, click the **Save** button.
5. In the File name text box, type **Script1.ps1** and click the **Save** button.
6. On the Windows PowerShell ISE toolbar, click the **Run Script** button (green arrow).

SKILL SUMMARY

IN THIS LESSON, YOU LEARNED:

- Services are programs that run in the background on a Windows system to provide a function, network application, or help the operating system run other programs. The services are managed using the Services console, which can be opened by executing services. msc. The services can also be managed using Computer Management.

- The System Configuration utility (msconfig.exe) lets you enable or disable startup services, set boot options such as booting into Safe Mode, access tools like Action Center and Event Viewer, and more. You'll use this utility mainly to troubleshoot startup problems with Windows.

- Task Scheduler enables you to schedule and automate a variety of actions, such as starting programs, displaying messages, and even sending e-mails. You create a scheduled task by specifying a trigger, which is an event that causes a task to run, and an action, which is the action taken when the task runs.

- Windows 10 includes the Windows PowerShell Integrated Scripting Environment (ISE) that helps you create Windows PowerShell scripts. If you need the scripts to be executed on a regular basis, you can execute the scripts using Task Scheduler.

■ Knowledge Assessment

Multiple Choice

1. Which of the following commands could be used to open the Services console?
   a. Services.exe
   b. Services.msc
   c. Services.ps1
   d. Services.mmc

2. In which of the following locations can you find the services snap-in?
   a. Computer Management
   b. Server Manager
   c. Add/Remove Programs
   d. System Configuraiton

3. Which of the following accounts allows full access to the system, while accessing other systems on the network?
   a. Local Admin account
   b. Local Service account
   c. Network Service account
   d. Local System account

4. When the Local System account tries to access another system on the network, which of the following credentials does it use?
   a. The local administrator
   b. The Administrators group
   c. Computername$
   d. The service account that you define

5. Which of the following programs allows you to specify what services start during boot up and can force the system to go into Safe mode?
   a. Services console
   b. Server Manager
   c. Task Manager
   d. System Configuration Utility

6. Which of the following items in Task Scheduler causes a task to run?
   a. An action
   b. A trigger
   c. An account parameter
   d. A startup parameter

Best Answer

Choose the letter that corresponds to the best answer. More than one answer choice may achieve the goal. Select the BEST answer.

1. You manage a program that requires several services. However, service1 has to start before service2. What should you do?
   a. Set Service 1 as Manual and set Service 2 as automatic
   b. Set Service 1 as Automatic and set Service 2 as Automatic (Delayed Start)
   c. Set Service 1 as Automatic (Delayed Start), and set Service 2 as Automatic
   d. Set Service 1 as Automatic, and set Service 2 as Manual

2. In Windows 10, which of the following is the best utility to create relatively complex management tasks with Windows PowerShell scripts?
   a. Notepad
   b. Windows PowerShell Integrated Script Environment
   c. Notepad++
   d. WordPad

Matching and Identification

1. Identify the type of account (Local System, Local Service, Network Service, or Another account) used to run a service.
   a) Uses computer's credentials when accessing remote resources
   b) Has full access to system, but cannot access remote systems
   c) Can be a specific user account that you create
   d) Can be used to run services in the background while helping protect the computer from being compromised

Build a List

1. Specify the correct order of steps necessary to creating a basic task in Task Scheduler.
   _____ Click Finish.
   _____ Specify task name and description
   _____ Open Task Scheduler.
   _____ Specify the task trigger
   _____ Click Create Basic Task
   _____ Specify the action.

Business Case Scenarios

Scenario 15-1: Managing your Widget System

You are an administrator at the Contoso Corporation. Equipment maintenance is performed a couple times a day; therefore, you need to close the Widget program and stop the three widget services. You also need to delete the temporary files used by the program. Explain how to simplify the startup and shutdown of the required components during the maintenance periods.

Appendix A
Exam 70-698: Installing and Configuring Windows 10

Objective Number	Exam Objective	Lesson
1.0	**Implement Windows**	
1.1	*Prepare for Installation Requirements*	
1.1.1	Determine hardware requirements and compatibility	1
1.1.2	Choose between an upgrade and a clean installation	1
1.1.3	Determine appropriate editions according to device type	1
1.1.4	Determine requirements for particular features, such as Hyper-V, Cortana, Miracast, Virtual Smart Cards, and Secure Boot	1
1.1.5	Determine and create appropriate installation media	1
1.2	*Installing Windows*	
1.2.1	Perform clean installations	2
1.2.2	Upgrade using Windows Update	2
1.2.3	Upgrade using installation media	2
1.2.4	Configure native boot scenarios	2
1.2.5	Migrate from previous versions of Windows	2
1.2.6	Install to virtual hard disk (VHD)	2
1.2.7	Boot from VHD	2
1.2.8	Install on bootable USB	1, 2
1.2.9	Install additional Windows features	2
1.2.10	Configure Windows for additional regional and language support	2
1.3	*Configuring Devices and Device Drivers*	
1.3.1	Install, update, disable, and roll back drivers	3
1.3.2	Resolve driver issues	3
1.3.3	Configure driver settings, including signed and unsigned drivers	3
1.3.4	Manage driver packages	3
1.3.5	Download and import driver packages	3
1.3.6	Use the Deployment Image and Service Management (DISM) tool to add packages	3

Objective Number	Exam Objective	Lesson
1.4	*Performing Post-Installation Configuration*	
1.4.1	Configure and customize start menu, desktop, taskbar, and notification settings, according to device type	4
1.4.2	Configure accessibility options	4
1.4.3	Configure Cortana	4
1.4.4	Configure Microsoft Edge	4
1.4.5	Configure Internet Explorer	4
1.4.6	Configure Hyper-V	4
1.4.7	Configure power settings	4
1.5	*Implementing Windows in an Enterprise Environment*	
1.5.1	Provision with the Windows Imaging and Configuration Designer (ICD) tool	5
1.5.2	Implement Active Directory–based activation	5
1.5.3	Implement volume activation using a Key Management Service (KMS)	5
1.5.4	Query and configure activation states using the command line	5
1.5.5	Configure Active Directory, including Group Policies	5
1.5.6	Configure and optimize user account control (UAC)	5
2.0	**Configure and Support Core Services**	
2.1	*Configure Networking*	
2.1.1	Configure and support IPv4 and IPv6 network settings	6
2.1.2	Configure name resolution	6
2.1.3	Connect to a network	6
2.1.4	Configure network locations	6
2.1.5	Configure Windows Firewall	6
2.1.6	Configure Windows Firewall with Advanced Security	6
2.1.7	Configure network discovery	6
2.1.8	Configure Wi-Fi settings	6
2.1.9	Configure Wi-Fi Direct	6
2.1.10	Troubleshoot network issues	6
2.1.11	Configure VPN, such as app-triggered VPN, traffic filters, and lockdown VPN	6
2.1.12	Configure IPsec	6
2.1.13	Configure Direct Access	6
2.2	*Configure Storage*	
2.2.1	Configure disks, volumes, and file system options using Disk Management and Windows PowerShell	7
2.2.2	Create and configure VHDs	7

(Continued)

OBJECTIVE NUMBER	EXAM OBJECTIVE	LESSON
2.2.3	Configure removable devices	7
2.2.4	Create and configure storage spaces	7
2.2.5	Troubleshoot storage and removable devices issues	7
2.3	*Configure Data Access and Usage*	
2.3.1	Configure file and printer sharing and HomeGroup connections	8
2.3.2	Configure folder shares, public folders, and OneDrive	8
2.3.3	Configure file system permissions	8
2.3.4	Configure OneDrive usage	8
2.3.5	Troubleshoot data access and usage	8
2.4	*Implement Apps*	
2.4.1	Configure desktop apps	9
2.4.2	Configure startup options	9
2.4.3	Configure Windows features	9
2.4.4	Configure Windows Store	9
2.4.5	Implement Windows Store apps	9
2.4.6	Implement Windows Store for Business	9
2.4.7	Provision packages	9
2.4.8	Create packages	9
2.4.9	Use deployment tools	9
2.4.10	Use the Windows Assessment and Deployment Kit (ADK)	9
2.5	*Configure Remote Management*	
2.5.1	Choose the appropriate remote management tools	10
2.5.2	Configure remote management settings	10
2.5.3	Modify settings remotely by using the Microsoft Management Console (MMC) or Windows PowerShell	10
2.5.4	Configure Remote Assistance, including Easy Connect	10
2.5.5	Configure Remote Desktop	10
2.5.6	Configure remote PowerShell	10
3.0	**Manage and Maintain Windows**	
3.1	*Configure Updates*	
3.1.1	Configure Windows Update options	11
3.1.2	Implement Insider Preview, Current Branch (CB), Current Branch for Business (CBB), and Long Term Servicing Branch (LTSB) scenarios	11
3.1.3	Manage update history	11
3.1.4	Roll back updates	11
3.1.5	Update Windows Store apps	11

Objective Number	Exam Objective	Lesson°
3.2	*Monitor Windows*	
3.2.1	Configure and analyze Event Viewer logs	12
3.2.2	Configure event subscriptions	12
3.2.3	Monitor performance using Task Manager	12
3.2.4	Monitor performance using Resource Monitor	12
3.2.5	Monitor performance using Performance Monitor and Data Collector Sets	12
3.2.6	Monitor system resources	12
3.2.7	Monitor and manage printers	8
3.2.8	Configure indexing options	12
3.2.9	Manage client security by using Windows Defender	12
3.2.10	Evaluate system stability using Reliability Monitor	12
3.2.11	Troubleshoot performance issues	12
3.3	*Configure System and Data Recovery*	
3.3.1	Configure a recovery drive	13
3.3.2	Configure a system restore	13
3.3.3	Perform a refresh or recycle	13
3.3.4	Perform a driver rollback	3
3.3.5	Configure restore points	13
3.3.6	Resolve hardware and device issues	3
3.3.7	Interpret data from Device Manager	3
3.3.8	Restore previous versions of files and folders	13
3.3.9	Configure File History	13
3.3.10	Recover files from OneDrive	13
3.3.11	Use Windows Backup and Restore	13
3.3.12	Perform a backup and restore with WBAdmin	13
3.3.13	Perform recovery operations using Windows Recovery	13
3.4	*Configure Authorization and Authentication*	
3.4.1	Configure Microsoft Passport	14
3.4.2	Configure picture passwords and biometrics	14
3.4.3	Configure workgroups	14
3.4.4	Configure domain settings	14
3.4.5	Configure HomeGroup settings	8
3.4.6	Configure Credential Manager	14
3.4.7	Configure local accounts	14

(Continued)

Objective Number	Exam Objective	Lesson
3.4.8	Configure Microsoft accounts	14
3.4.9	Configure Device Registration	14
3.4.10	Configure Windows Hello	14
3.4.11	Configure Device Guard	14
3.4.12	Configure Credential Guard	14
3.4.13	Configure Device Health Attestation	14
3.4.14	Configure UAC behavior	5
3.5	*Configure Advanced Management Tools*	
3.5.1	Configure Services	15
3.5.2	Configure Device Manager	3
3.5.3	Configure and use the MMC	10
3.5.4	Configure Task Scheduler	15
3.5.5	Configure automation of management tasks using Windows PowerShell	15

Index

Note: Page numbers followed by 'f' and 't' indicates figure and table respectively.